Morgantown: Fitness   1885693648

Handbook of Research in Applied Sport and Exercise Psychology: International Perspectives

Handbook of Research in Applied Sport and Exercise Psychology: International Perspectives

DIETER HACKFORT, PhD
ASPIRE Academy for Sports Excellence

JOAN L. DUDA, PhD
University of Birmingham

RONNIE LIDOR, PhD
The Wingate Institute

EDITORS

Fitness Information Technology

A Division of the International Center for Performance Excellence
262 Coliseum, WVU-PE
P.O. Box 6116
Morgantown, WV 26506-6116

Library of Congress Card Catalog Number: 2001012345

ISBN: 1885693648

Production Editor: Matt Brann
Cover Design: 40 West Studios
Typesetter: 40 West Studios
Copyeditor: Anita Stanley
Proofreader: Matt Brann
Indexer: Susan Case
Printed by: Sheridan Books

10 9 8 7 6 5 4 3 2 1

Fitness Information Technology
A Division of the International Center for Performance Excellence
West Virginia University
262 Coliseum, WVU-PE
PO Box 6116
Morgantown, WV 26506-6116
800.477.4348 (toll free)
304.293.6888 (phone)
304.293.6658 (fax)
Email: icpe@mail.wvu.edu
Website: www.fitinfotech.com

Table of Contents

Foreword

One of the most important missions of the International Society of Sport Psychology (ISSP) is to disseminate knowledge to advance the research and practices within our domain. Further, a prominent issue in sport psychology is the need to develop practice procedures that are accountable and trustful. Theory and research-based practices are procedures that must be applied routinely when psychological services are provided to athletes and exercise participants. As the general area of applied sport and exercise psychology continues to evolve and rapidly become a universally accepted sport science, the demand for credible research based on grounded theory has dramatically increased. Anecdotal evidence of the effectiveness of applied sport and exercise psychological interventions and techniques is no longer sufficient to justify the efficacy of the field.

Within the past few years, qualitative as well as quantitative research methodologies have been employed to investigate and justify frequently advocated applied psychological techniques. The editors of this handbook, and the authors of the 26 chapters composing this handbook, provide an excellent framework for knowledge-founded practices of psychological services to targeted samples within the sport and exercise domains.

The chapters in this handbook represent science-related practice perspectives from different continents and cultures. Practices that stem from different cultural roots and philosophies widen our horizons and enrich our knowledge. In today's era of globalization, it is common to realize how East and West complement each other in the practice of medicine. Similarly, it is common to see how ancient practices from the Far East are integrated within the psychological interventions of the West. This handbook is an additional contribution to the efforts ISSP invests in presenting unique practice approaches to be implemented and integrated in psychological services to people worldwide.

The multifaceted domain of the practice of sport and exercise psychology stems from the need to provide services to people of varying needs, not only athletes. Every person is entitled to live comfortably and happily by fulfilling his or her desires and motivations. Knowledge-based practices must therefore consider the knowledge foundation in the various disciplines related to sport and exercise; the recent advancements in the medical, behavioral, social, and methodological domains; and the cultural and social values and norms within which the practices are provided. This handbook consists of contributions aimed at disseminating these aspects to the community of practitioners, who strive to establish better psychological services to people who need them for improving their quality of life.

The contributing authors in this handbook are practitioners and scientists of considerable professional experience. The contributions center around three main areas: (a) techniques of psychological skill training; (b) social/educational perspectives; and (c) educational programs and ethical issues in applied sport and exercise psychology. Some of the contributions are theory-driven while others are practice-driven. Modern science perceives basic science and practical knowledge as complementing rather than segregated and distinguished areas. Basic research findings are the most practical tools for practitioners, and practitioners' experiences are the tools for generating research questions. Thus, the readers of this handbook should view the contributions within a holistic view where practices and scientific knowledge can be integrated into a unique and holistic approach.

Although this book will be responsive to many professional interests and needs, its primary purpose is to inform those individuals who work frequently in the applied areas. The authors have attempted to share their expertise, insights, and wisdom with those still gaining experience in the field. As ISSP current and past presidents, we welcome initiatives such as this, and hope that the ISSP mission continues to be accomplished through contributions such as this one.

Dr. Keith Henschen
ISSP President
2001-2005

Dr. Gershon Tenenbaum
ISSP President
1997-2001

Preface

Sport and exercise psychology—broadly defined as concerned with the psychological aspects of elite sport, recreational sport, health-related exercise, physical education, and further physical activity—has grown tremendously since its beginnings in the late 19th and early 20th centuries. The formation of national and international societies, like the International Society of Sport Psychology (ISSP) in 1965, and departments of sport science and kinesiology in universities around the world (as well as psychology departments embracing sport psychology as a sub-discipline), has contributed to this development. The corresponding explosion in sport and exercise-related research output over the last two decades in particular has made it necessary to continuously reflect on the state of the art. More than a decade ago, Singer, Murphy, and Tennant (1993) published the first *Handbook on Research in Sport Psychology*. This ambitious text was dedicated to a comprehensive review of theoretical perspectives and basic research findings in the field. Due to the rapid increase in the number and sophistication of research endeavors, a second edition (*Handbook of Sport Psychology*) was published in 2001 (Singer, Hausenblas, & Janelle, 2001). Again, the emphasis in this most impressive and wide-ranging edited text was on describing contemporary knowledge with respect to basic research and theoretical advancements in sport and exercise psychology. Paralleling the case in the first edition, the contributors represented leading scholars in the field from around the globe.

As the practice of sport psychology has also exhibited substantial growth during the past 20-plus years and has always held appeal to those involved in the "real world" of sport and physical activity, the mission of the present volume was to present diverse *applied* issues and different areas of *applied* research in sport psychology. More specifically, the purpose of this text was to bring together contributions from international authors, allowing a critical analysis evaluation of programs, techniques, and intervention methods that are available for sport/exercise psychology consultants in their applied work across various types and competitive levels of sport (including elite sport, recreational sport, adventure sport, and health-oriented physical activities). In essence, a major goal of the present book is to have an impact on the current knowledge of and reinforce effects to engage in an "evidence-based applied sport/exercise psychology."

In the case of those chapters reviewing applied work, the authors were asked to summarize the evidence, stemming from empirical sport and/or exercise-related applied and basic research (including single-subject and case studies), which legitimizes (or perhaps questions) the application of the programs, techniques, and interventions described. The authors were also requested to comment on the role of theory in the development and evaluation of the programs, techniques, and interventions targeted. Proposed new and innovative directions in applied work within these specific areas of sport and exercise psychology practice were called for as well. This edited volume also includes chapters focused on fundamental matters relating to effective and ethical practice (e.g., reflections on standards in/for the application of intervention methods; efforts around the world to ensure competency in applied practice).

Most would agree that a central question to ask of applied sport and exercise psychology is whether our applied programs and intervention efforts are effective. Regarding this effectiveness (or lack of), we also want to know: For Whom? When? Where? and What seem to be the processes involved? In terms of tackling such queries, an underlying concern is the interplay between theory and the intervention strategy evoked and then subsequently examined. From the standpoint of accountability and the future development and reputation of the field, interventions in sport and exercise psychology should be ethically delivered, critically evaluated, and demonstrated to be efficacious and expedient. They should have a conceptual basis and also further our theoretical understanding of behavior, cognitions, and affective responses in the sport milieu. It is the hope of the editors that the information presented in this text will hold some significance for moving the field further along in meeting these aspirations.

The Handbook of Research in Applied Sport and Exercise Psychology: International Perspectives represents the fruits of scientists/practitioners from Asia, Australia, Europe, and North America. Incorporating this international perspective posed logistical challenges to having the *Handbook* become reality in an abbreviated time frame, but we believe it has added to the excitement about and potential of the practice issues and applied directions addressed. Indeed, the authors whose writing is included here are actively engaged in shaping the nature and scope of applied research in sport and exercise psychology as manifested in many countries around the world.

The formation of an edited text is a team effort necessitating the willingness to be involved and ensuing concerted contribution of many individuals. We would like to express our deepest appreciation to all those who assisted us in this effort. Firstly, we give our heartfelt thanks to the ISSP Managing Council for providing the genesis to this project and support throughout the preparation of this book. We also extend our gratitude to all the colleagues who contributed chapters to this book. Their expertise, experience, and enthusiasm were key factors in the realization of this *Handbook*. Finally, we would like to thank Andrew Ostrow, the director, and Matthew Brann, the production editor, from Fitness Information Technology (FIT) for their cooperation and assistance at every stage of the preparation and publishing process. Their continued encouragement, valuable advice, and patience were paramount to the organization of the book and its progress along the road to publication.

References

Singer, R. N., Hausenblas, H. A., & Janelle, C. M. (Eds.) (2001). *Handbook of sport psychology.* New York: John Wiley.
Singer, R. N., Murphey, M., & Tennant, L. K. (Eds.) (1993). *Handbook of research on sport psychology.* New York: Macmillan Publishing Company.

Section I
Psychological Training

Introduction

This section refers to the classical concept and methods of psychological training. It comprises three contributions, which provide theoretical, empirical, and practical insights for the differentiation and specific application of the various forms of psychological training. An overview is offered from former understandings of mental training up to recent proposals of and experiences with modifications, variations, and designs for special applications.

The purpose of the first chapter is to outline a theoretical framework that is needed for a sufficient understanding of the functional meaning and systematic application of the various forms of mental training, mental practice, mental rehearsal, imagery, visualization, etc. Dieter Hackfort and Jörn Munzert argue from an action-theory perspective and describe a framework for a systematic approach to the scope and modes of mental simulation. Via functional analyses, they discuss individual differences that have to be considered in the application of mental simulation.

In the second chapter, Keith Henschen, based on his long-time experiences as a sport psychology consultant, offers his "personal philosophy" and theoretical basis of skill-oriented mental practice and reports on strategies of application. The given evidences are based on qualitative studies and are discussed with respect to various issues of concern.

The third chapter, authored by Nichola Callow and Lew Hardy, focuses on imagery. The authors critically analyze the research literature pertaining to factors that may contribute to the effectiveness of imagery interventions. There is still a lack of knowledge for ensuring a best practice in the delivery of imagery interventions and the authors not only highlight what is known and what is not known at present, but also what might be known with regard to optimizing future imagery interventions.

It is demonstrated in the chapters of this section that research studies and experiences with the application and praxis of psychological training contribute greatly to improve our understanding and differential usage of the methods. However, the awareness of the reader is also guided toward the complex interplay of personal, environmental, and task factors in psychological training interventions.

Courtesy of MediaFocus International

1.1

Mental Simulation

DIETER HACKFORT AND JÖRN MUNZERT

Introduction

Sport psychologists are properly concerned with mental processes, whether they are working in research or application settings. However, the scope of meaning of the phrase "mental processes" differs from language to language. Most English-speaking colleagues consider "mental processes" to be synonymous with "psyche" or "psychic" ("psychological" indicates a scientific or disciplinary perspective), whereas German-speaking colleagues refer to specific cognitive processes (e.g., thinking, imagination, attention, concentration). Cognitive processes are one side of the coin, but affective processes are the other side. Cognitive and affective processes always occur in combination, sometimes the cognitive processes dominating the affective processes and sometimes the other way around. There is a dialectic relation between these fundamental psychological dimensions. In addition to mental processes, emotional processes are also present, comprised of feelings, moods, and differential emotions. From an action theory perspective, cognitive and affective processes are the fundamental psychic action regulation subsystems, and these processes are working in the mental and emotional psychological domain. They are closely connected with biological and social processes as is illustrated in Figure 1. The focus here is on actions, which are a special class of behavior—intentional, organized, and purposive behavior (Nitsch & Hackfort, 1981; Nitsch, 2000)—but we refer especially to the *interplay* of cognitions and emotions.

With regard to the longstanding and ongoing debate on which comes first, cognition or emotion (thinking or feeling; Zajonc, 1980; "primacy of cognition"; Lazarus, 1984), it is our understanding that the two processes are interrelated and inextricable intertwined. In both the evolution of the species and in the individual, the emotional system dominated the mental (cognitive) system at first. With regard to the genesis of action regulation, feelings come faster than cognitions, but the development of both the species (phylogenesis) and the individual (ontogenesis) includes a stronger and better ability to organize behavior that is intentional, goal-directed, and

Figure 1: Action Regulation System

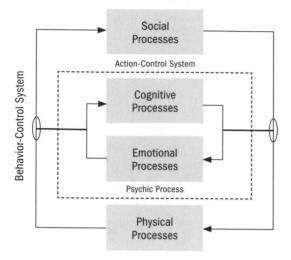

purposive behavior, which is to say actions (Nitsch, 2000; for a more general argumentation see Vygotskij & Luria, 1993). The process of acting is regulated by affective and cognitive processes, because we need energy and activation: valence-based orientation (the stimulation brought up by feelings and emotions) and rationality-based decisions (the intentions based on cognitive processes). We need a holistic impression signalized by feelings and emotions as it is not possible to analyze a situation completely and to calculate everything (e.g., the costs and benefits or threats and challenges with regard to all elements included in the situation by cognitive processes)—we would never be able to take action in time. The interplay of effective and cognitive processes enables us to. (Hackfort, 1986).

This chapter contains three parts. First, we provide an outline of our theoretical point of view, which we characterize as an action-theory perspective. Next, we describe the scope and modes of mental simulation. Finally, we look into individual differences in mental simulation, including methodological issues.

An Action Theory Understanding of Mental Simulation

Simulation can refer to the action of a person: as when an athlete models a desired behavior, for instance. Such a model may be live or on videotape. *Simulation* can also refer to the environment: The performance context is simulated by manipulating

the cognitive and emotional climate of the practice session. Recently, simulations are occurring through the development and application of a new medium known as *virtual reality* but this is not examined here. We refer to mental simulation as a concept realized by using various mental techniques.

Mental simulation refers to a situation and the action the subject has to organize and realize in that situation.

> Mental simulation is the imitative representation of some event or series of events... It may involve the replay of events that have already happened... It may involve the cognitive construction of hypothetical scenarios... It can involve fantasies... [I]t can involve mixtures of real and hypothetical events... Mental simulation can be useful for envisioning the future because it addresses the two fundamental tasks of self-regulation and coping, namely the management of affect or emotional states and the ability to plan and solve problems (Taylor, Pham, Rivkin, & Armor, 1998, p. 430).

Thus, mental simulation includes mental techniques or cognitive strategies (for a differentiation of psychological method and skill that is also of interest in this context, see Tremayne & Newbery in this volume) are well-known and often-used in sports. With regard to the improvement on the acquisition and performance of motor skills, the focus the regulation of psychomotor processes (processing). This is the case when talking about mental practice and imagery (see Callow & Hardy in this volume). With regard to techniques focusing on the regulation of psychovegetative processes, the focus is on activation, relaxation, or mobilization (tuning). This is emphasized in strategies of mental preparation, psyching-up or psyching-down techniques.

Imagery is a special type of mental simulation based on the visual representation of the movement action from either an internal or an external perspective to optimize the preconditions of external realization. Other types of mental practice are based on either proprioceptive or auditory channels of information. Imaginations (memory imaginations, fantasy imaginations, and hallucinatory imaginations have to be distinguished; cf. Raspotnig, 1996, p. 17) are the basis for various mental simulations and in general they refer to everything that is perceived in the various modes of the five senses without an external stimulus (cf. Weerth, 1992, p. 36). That is, imaginations are internally produced (remembered) and present (internal representations), grounded in preliminary experiences (episodic memory: memory for events that happened in a certain point in time and at a certain place; cf. Engelkamp, 1994), and thus, are specific with regard to the sense: modality specific. "Imagery" refers to picture-like visual imaginations. With regard to the structural and functional relation between perception and imagination (cf. Neisser, 1967; Kosslyn, 1980; Bischof, 1987), it is evident that picture-like imaginations are based on visual perceptions (analog representation; cf. Wessels, 1994). Movement imaginations are grounded on kinesthetic perceptions. Thus, the "visuo-motoric training" as a modality of mental practice can be regarded as a kinesthetic simulation. "Verbo-motoric training" (see below) is another modality-specific training based on verbal information. Already Paivio (1969) argued that words and pictures provide different kinds of information and that each one is connected with special information processing and memory systems. Engelkamp (1994) explained in detail the different memory systems and the different functions of visual and verbal information for these systems and information processing. As a consequence we have to consider modality-specific simulations. Furthermore, this is relevant with regard to emotions as verbal representations are (more) abstract and do not have a close link to emotions, whereas visual imaginations are less abstract and do have a (closer) link to emotions, especially if there is a (high) identification (as it is the case with the internal perspective) and thus there are associations are coming up in the active person. This is not or less the case if the imagination is based on the observer (external) perspective, which leads (more) to dissociation.

The goals and intentions of the various types of imagery, mental training, mental practice, and mental rehearsal differ: (a) the focus is on developing and fostering of skills; it is skill oriented to improve the proficiency of physical performance (see Rushall & Lippmann, 1998), and (b) the focus is on the preparation of performance in competition (situation oriented to improve coping by anticipation of the circumstances of performance).

> Sport psychology, and psychology in general, would benefit from determining what forms of mental practice are appropriate for particular purposes and activities. Specification of how each model is used would allow even further gain. Appropriate distinctions would allow guidelines to be developed that could benefit research and minimize inappropriate use in applied settings. (Rushall & Lippmann, 1998, p. 58)

It is assumed that "mental practice" influences the knowledge about and the concept of a movement or process of acting, that it improves the cognitive regulation and control of this process. What we are calling processing ("process regulation") refers to the regulation of the psychomotor course of an action. To know what is to be done, how it is to be done, and when it is to be done: In other words, to learn the entire process and to practice it internally by thinking and then externally by overt behavior leads to routines, which stabilize performance outcome.

"Mental preparation" is used when talking about the control of the inner state, techniques to manipulate the psychic situation before competition, the mental attitude toward competition, etc. We are talking about tuning ("basis regulation"), it refers to the regulation of the psychophysiological processes—the psychophysiological arousal—which are fundamental for being active and to be prepared for optimal processing. Tuning is of special importance in stress situations, when experiencing nervousness, anxiety, etc.

Tuning and processing are fundamental processes in action regulation. They are constitutive for the realization of an action. The unit "action" is subdivided into three phases, namely the anticipation phase, the realization phase, and the interpretation phase (cf. Nitsch & Hackfort, 1981; Nitsch, 2000). This is illustrated in Figure 2. We will refer to it in more detail in the following paragraphs.

Figure 2: The Structure and Process of an Action

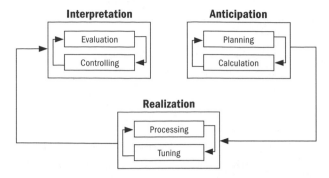

Interpretation — Evaluation, Controlling
Anticipation — Planning, Calculation
Realization — Processing, Tuning

action regulation system; Figure 1), but there are links to other systems illustrated in Figure 4.

Figure 3: The Action Situation Model

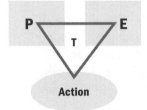

P   E
T
Action

Whereas Callow and Hardy (in this volume) develop their contribution on the basis of an analysis of available empirical studies in the field of imagery, the basis for this contribution is a theoretical approach, the action-theory perspective. From this point of view imagery and mental training have to be considered different concepts that refer to different practices. Imagery and mental rehearsal can be regarded as elements (strategies, subconcepts) of mental simulation. The scope of various strategies and partial concepts of mental simulation is structured by using the "person-environment-task" constellation (action situation) (cf. Munzert & Hackfort, 1999) and the phases and regulation processes of an action. This will be outlined in the following paragraphs.

Human action is not based on single movements or specific motor skills, but on the dynamic interplay of person and environment with regard to a specific task. In this sense we argue that intentionally organized and purposeful motor behavior (motor actions) is *behavior-in-situation*. This situation is defined by the components of person, environment, and task. These fundamental ideas are discussed in the works of Newell (1986) in the U.S. and Heuer (1991) in Germany.

The basic relationship is the person-environment relationship as explained by Kurt Lewin (1936). This relationship is fundamental for humans and for organism in general and for all behavior of living subjects. When this relation is specified by a task, goal-directed behavior as a special class of behavior has to be organized. We are talking about actions with regard to the unit of this special class of behavior and acting is the process of realizing this behavior. Figure 3 illustrates this understanding.

Human actions are organized, and the process of acting is regulated by psychic processes (see above:

The general intention underlying every action is to optimize the person-environment relationship, or one's *situation,* to maintain a favorable situation or to obtain a better fit between person and environment. In this sense, motor behavior is a functional element in the process of problem solving, as it was formulated by Bernstein (1967) and Luria (1970) out of the cultural historic school (one type of action theory). Similarly, Pribram (1971) argued that the determinants of problem solution and movement are encoded in the motor cortex, not the particular movement involved in the performance. This idea is integrated in the concept outlined in "Plans and the Structure of Behavior" by Miller, Galanter, and Pribram (1960), a further type of the action-psychology concept as it is outlined here.

Motor behavior is intentionally organized according to a person's subjective interpretation of a given person-environment-task constellation. However, this does not mean that actions are completely conscious. The assumption of intentionality has some important implications. At first, intentionality necessarily implies some kind of internal representation of the person-environment-task constellation. We (Hackfort, Munzert, & Seiler, 2000) have described how to analyze these interrelations within a script-concept. Again, this does not mean a representation of the movement but a representation of problem space. Secondly, we have to describe how intentions (ideas) find their path from the center to the periphery. It is our understanding that self-instructions build an important link between intentions and external behavior. For example, Weiss and Klint (1987) and Carroll and Bandura (1990) have demonstrated that verbalizations will support observational learning through the lifespan.

To use mental strategies and practices (the scope of mental simulation) effectively, it is necessary to go into detail, to consider functional relations as they are emphasized by the action-theory approach, and to refer to different modes.

Figure 4: Interrelations of Systems in the Organizations of Actions

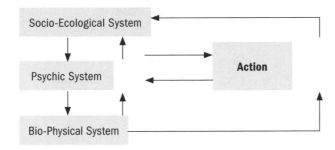

The Scope and Modes of Mental Simulation, Inner Speech, and Learning

The opposite of procedural knowledge, declarative knowledge is conscious and can be expressed verbally. Procedural knowledge is typically unconscious and therefore difficult to access verbally. Thus, to explain a procedure to someone, procedural knowledge must be translated into declarative knowledge. It is possible to argue that this form of communication also serves as a tool for the transformation of intentions into acts. Some of the general problems (the translation of procedural into declarative knowledge and the transformation of intentions into acts, for instance; general problems of transformation) can be discussed by using a model that was introduced by Annett (1996).

The model represents two channels—one for human actions and one for verbal instructions. Descending pathways represent simple imitation. That is, imitation of acts and imitation of verbal inputs. The two channels are linked at the representational level by the so-called "action-language bridge" so that verbal instructions can be transformed into acts and perceived actions can be expressed verbally. Bridging the gap between the two channels results in deeper processing of information and better memory

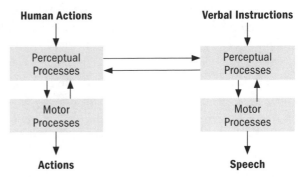

Figure 5: The ALI-Model by Annett (1996)

Reprinted with permission from Elsevier.

storage. For example, verbal pre-training or verbal training improves observational training and motor performance, and active gestures improve memory of verbal phrases as demonstrated by Engelkamp (1998) and by Helstrup (1986).

But how can this "action-language bridge" be established? Vygotski and Luria (1993) argued that speech as a form of communication becomes a means of organizing a person's behavior, and that the function that was previously divided between two people becomes an internal function of human behavior. Developmental experiments typically consisted of three series of tasks. In the first series, subjects were told to perform, silently, a movement in accordance with a verbal instruction. In the second series, they executed the same task in accordance with speech responses. Then the first series was usually repeated. The improvement in performance measures relative to the baseline are interpreted as consequences of external or internal speech. Later this concept was generalized and popularized by Meichenbaum (1974). He developed self-instruction methods, which reflected the order of developmental stages:

- External instruction
- Self-instruction aloud
- Fading of overt self-instruction
- Inner speech

In summary, the following functions of speech can be distinguished: At the first level, functions to communicate and to regulate action. For the last one, we distinguish motivational and directive functions.

The directive function of speech should be emphasized, as it seems to be neglected most of the time. Even the Russian founders of the cultural-historical approach analyzed aspects of the directive function using different experimental tasks. They separated semantic from impulsive aspects of inner speech. The impulsive aspect is often used in rhythmic movements when the semantic content of a self-instruction can be neglected. On the other hand, the special content of self-instructions can be used to select appropriate movements, to overcome conflicting sensations, and to inhibit inappropriate movements. Along with developmental studies, Lurias' (1967) neuropsychological studies added further knowledge about these processes.

Imagery and Thinking

Mental simulation can be executed by imagery in two modes—a *replay* mode or a *pre-play* mode. Replay is an inner (mental) repetition of actions, situations, and events. This can be done to store successful actions or situations in the memory for further actions. On the other hand, failures can be analyzed to identify problems and explore alternatives for future improvements. This replay can be for the sake of instrumental as well as emotional aspects of the experience (see Pennebaker, 1988). Pre-play is the inner construction or anticipation of a hypothetical or expected scenario. It can help people to formulate successful actions and avoid situations and actions that probably won't be successful.

Mental simulation in this mode can include pure fantasies or a mixture of fantasies and real experiences. If critical or inappropriate moments are detected in a replay, these elements can be substituted by appropriate ones in a pre-play to heighten the probability of success. Mental simulation in this mode is effective when it refers to if-then situations and when the probability of certain consequences of actions is heightened. This includes calculation and planning, as they are characteristic of anticipation (anticipation phase of action; see Figure 2), as well as controlling and attributions as they are characteristic for interpretations (interpretation phase of action; see Figure 2). In this way, imagery and thinking lead to higher flexibility in the organization of actions in achievement situations. When a person becomes aware of the causes and effects of certain behaviors, he or she has a heightened self-consciousness and action security.

- It happens that effective processes are amplified and emotions are induced so that emotion control can also be simulated. Such simulations and strategies have been used for a long time in systematic desensitization programs.

- Mental simulation is combined with certain instructions such as the "stop-think-get control-act" instruction, a well-known strategy in diving. With such instructions, a cognitive control strategy is established that refers to special moments in a situation or action process. Mental simulation focuses on selected checkpoints ("stop-think"), helps to get control by using additional techniques (e.g., progressive muscle relaxation, respiration techniques), and enables goal-directed behavior ("act").

Figure 6: The Scope of Mental Simulation

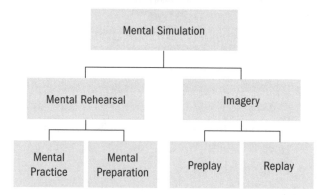

Mental Training and Mental Rehearsal

Various authors refer to different processes, methods, and objectives when discussing the concept of mental training. The need to standardize terminology becomes apparent upon consideration of the confusion that grew out of the variety of terms and each term's extension. Three main interpretations have to be distinguished:

1. Training of mental processes

With this interpretation, the object of mental training is improving mental (psychic) functioning, which is possible with regard to three fundamental psychic processes:

- a. *Cognitive processes* (e.g., by attentional control training, training of concentration techniques)

- b. *Affective processes* (e.g., by emotion control strategies or anxiety control training)

- c. *Motivational processes* (e.g., by goal-setting strategies, techniques to control volition)

It should be recognized that the term "mental training" in this interpretation refers to the objective of a special (mental) training.

2. Mental practice

This interpretation is connected with the idea to support the learning process (acquisition) or to improve the execution of motor skills (performance). It should be noted that the term "mental practice" refers to a method. Mental practice can be realized by emphasizing one of three different orientations:

- a. *Visual-oriented mental practice—imagery is the prototype for this form.*

- b. *Verbal-oriented mental practice—self-talk with the strategies of self-argumentation, self-instructions, and self-suggestions, which have different meaning in influencing psychic processes (see below), are the characteristic forms.*

- c. Kinaesthetic-oriented mental practice—focusing on self-movement feelings.

3. Mental preparation

This interpretation is based in the idea of improving attitude, motivation, mood, etc., as the athlete moves toward competition and sees the problem as one of "tuning for performance. It should be noted that the term "mental preparation" refers to an objective and this objective is realized by three different strategies:

- a. *Simulation of the situation. This situation-oriented strategy focuses on the environment and is characterized as "inner theater."*

- b. *Control of the psychophysiological activation. This arousal-oriented strategy focuses on the person and is characterized as "psyching up" and "psyching down." We are talking about "psychoregulation."*

- c. *Simulation of the action. This skill- or movement-oriented strategy focuses on the task at hand and can be regarded as a psychic warming up. It is close to the form described in 2a.*

Thus, mental simulation can be realized either by mental practice when the imagination of the movement execution aims to improve the psychomotor control, or by mental preparation when the imagination of the environmental circumstances aims to stabilize the psychosocial control (competitive attitude), and further on by psychoregulation (psyching) when the imagination refers to psychic states (mood, feeling) to optimize the psychovegetative control. Whereas mental practice serves to develop or actualize task-specific competencies (competence related), mental preparation serves to cope with situational demands that are connected with the value system of the person (valence related). Being aware of these two different relations should lead to a better understanding, analysis, and design of mental rehearsal.

A Special View of Mental Simulation

In the action-theoretical context, it is possible to differentiate mental simulation as a form of *situational anticipation*. A description of the phenomena of anticipation could, for instance, include a person imagining himself or herself entering the shot put ring, putting the shot with a particular technique and "seeing" the flight of the shot. One would call up characteristics of the action from memory, which could then be further differentiated into its modality-specific parts. Central to mental simulation are questions concerning the relationship of visual and kinesthetic images. However, acoustic imagination (for instance, the "edge grip" in skiing) can play an important role. These single aspects are part of a clear and complete situation anticipation. Again, the situation concept is theoretically broken down into characteristics of the person, the task, and the environment. With regard to the imaging of a task performance, this includes the performing person as part of the situation. It is not possible to image an ongoing action without an actor. The task, that is the mastering of the task, refers to the internal representation of the movement. This is the special objective of mental practice, but for a sufficient understanding of mental simulation, this is too narrow as only one part of the situation is accentuated, that is the progression of the movement. The third aspect of the situation concept refers to the environmental conditions. Once again, it is not possible to generate a mental simulation of an action without imaging environmental circumstances or effects, like imaging the ground in skiing or the flight of a shuttlecock in badminton.

Because of the specificity of the tasks, special instructions and varied individual conditions can either emphasize or neglect certain aspects of situation anticipation. This may concern, for instance, the reality of the imagined actor: The grade of the reality of the imagined can vary from a vague to a concrete image of a particular person. It is possible to further differentiate whether one imagines oneself or another person. In the early learning phases, mental practice is used in the framework of model learning; in later learning phases, where the optimization of task performance is concerned, the important learning effect is based on self-participation and the actualization of one's own problem solving-activity.

In the outlined theoretical framework, the above-mentioned psyching aspect of mental simulation (emotional, motivational with regard to performance preparation) has a special link to action-regulation processes. Two processes are differentiated in the realization phase of an action-tuning and processing. Whereas *processing* refers to the psychomotor functioning responsible to realize goal-directed movements, *tuning* refers to the activational preconditions necessary for optimal functioning (e.g., to induce or amplify arousal in order to activate full power and energy-psyching up—or to reduce arousal in order to overcome excitation and nervousness-psyching down). The later processes (*psyching,* which refers to *tuning*) have a special functional meaning and should be distinguished from the skill-oriented aspect and psychomotor processes emphasized in mental practice.

Furthermore, mental rehearsal can be differentiated from movement imagery, which often occurs in the framework of action planning, where an athlete anticipates and "plays through" the action in the imagination. This is done to prepare for and support the subsequent action, and not necessarily to achieve a learning effect with regard to improving skills. As already mentioned above, this form of mental simulation, "mental preparation," refers to the preparation for competition and should be considered a special strategy.

This action-theory-based understanding of the concept "mental simulation" makes it clear why certain forms of mental rehearsal or imagery are favored, and why specific questions—for instance, whether expected or actual aspects and values of the task performance should be considered and imagined—are discussed. However, it should not be forgotten that skill-orientation, activation-orientation, etc., are analytic conceptual differentiations. It is not possible to exclude the effects of mental practice on motivational processes when using this form.

Furthermore, it is fundamentally true that inner speech and mental rehearsal are linked together closely. Both refer to the situational concept and help to bridge the gap between declarative and procedural knowledge. Referring to both of these processes when designing mental simulation is important in applied sport psychology.

Mental Simulation and Individual Differences

Evidence suggests that mental rehearsal and imagery are not as effective as one would expect from theoretical considerations (see also the chapter by Callow & Hardy in this volume). There are two major methodological and practical reasons for this discrepancy:

1. In most studies, additional effects of mental rehearsal or imagery have to be considered, which is even more difficult when naïve, uninstructed visualization strategies are used in control groups (cf. Hall, Rodgers, & Barr, 1990; Mahoney, Gabriel, & Perkins, 1987).

2. In groups with mental training as well as in groups using naïve visualization strategies, people have varying dispositions for imagery of their own movements.

With regard to studies on imagery, up to 10% of the subjects report that they are not capable of picturing something in their mind's eye (Richardson, 1969). But even for people who are capable of mental imagery, the distinctness and the amount of details in the images vary strongly. Another problem is errors in the imagery process (e.g., "freezing" during imagery, skipping or continuous repetition of sequences, involuntary addition of errors, or leaps to other imagery contents). These problems, but also vivid and controlled movement imagery, are based on individual competencies that can be labeled "imagery abilities." These abilities are assumed to be modifiable to a certain extent; moreover, they are domain-specific in the sense that experience in a certain domain determines the individual competence level. Therefore, we will talk of "imagery competencies" instead of "abilities."

As a first step, one can distinguish between different components of the imagery competencies by looking at the corresponding sense modalities. In the case of movement imagery, these modalities are spatial-pictorial (visual) and kinesthetic imagery. Auditory perception and imagery processes are often ignored, unjustly, as it is demonstrated by rowing studies (Lippens, 1993). An advantage of this sense and imagery modality is that essential temporal features of the movement sequence are represented.

Apart from the modality distinction, additional characteristics can be derived from reports on imagery content and form. These can be used to differentiate individual preferences, especially in visual imagery. The following distinctions are of primary importance:

1. **Preferred sense modality**

   The first question is whether there is a bias towards a specific sense modality in the movement imagery process. In general, imagery can be multimodal. At a minimum, the use of different imagery modalities and the subject's attention focus can be reported.

2. **Vividness of imagery**

   This aspect concerns the amount of detail in and the intensity of the imagery process. One difference between perception and imagery is that imagery is less strong and rich in detail compared to perception. But different instances of imagery can also be distinguished according to these criteria (a case of extremely vivid imagery are hallucinations). In addition, the vividness of the movement imagery depends on the subjective involvement of the person: Does the subject imagine him- or herself or another person during movement execution?

3. **Perspective of visual imagery**

   We distinguish between inner and outer perspective in spatial-pictorial imagery. The question of whether attention is directed to muscle sensations is not part of the inner perspective but concerns the preferred sense modality. Whether the (visual) inner perspective is associated with stronger kinaesthetic sensations and stronger ideomotoric phenomena is a question that needs to be addressed in further research.

4. **Control of imagery**

   The two extremes of this dimension are the intentional generation of images on the one hand and the passive, unintentional emergence of images on the other. This involves a formal-temporal aspect—whether the subject is able to generate a certain image right at this point in time—and a content aspect—whether, in fact, it is the intended image.

5. Modifiability of imagery

It is possible to distinguish between the extent to which a person is able to modify a currently entertained image and the ability to include new aspects into the image—aspects that are not directly derived from experience. In this sense, imagery can be classified as "reproductive" or as "creative/productive," respectively. The necessity to perform one or the other of these imagery modes certainly depends on the kind of sport.

6. Temporal sequence of imagery

This relates to the evaluation of smoothness, speed, and rhythm of the imagined movement sequence (cf. Decety, Jeannerod, & Prablanc, 1989; Munzert, 2002, 2003).

These distinctions between different characteristics of imagery competencies demonstrate that the differentiation between good and bad visualizers ("imagers") captures only a small part of the individual differences. High imagery competencies are generally characterized by high vividness and temporal accuracy of the imagery. In most cases, the control is high as well. The important question is whether there is a linear relation to performance. Possibly, there is an optimal level of imagery vividness that is less accurate than an imagery with a maximum of details. These questions have not been addressed sufficiently in research in this domain. But in modeling research, there is evidence that the presentation of abstract contours (like in pictographs) can be more effective than the presentation of real movements or line drawings (cf. Daugs, Blischke, Olivier, & Marschall, 1989, pp. 149-156). This suggests that there are critical structural characteristics of a movement. Therefore, certain kinds of instructions in mental simulation are successful in emphasizing the essential features of the movement sequence. When these "crucial points" are presented to subjects in pictographs, they cause involuntary movements (cf. Ennenbach, 1989). This can be seen as an instructional means to support mental simulation.

The distinction between good and bad "imagers" is based on the phenomenal description of the imagery process. But there is also neurophysiological evidence for different processes in subjects with high vs. low imagery competencies (cf. Rösler, Heil, Pauls, Bajric, & Hennighausen, 1994). This evidence is derived from experiments that recorded slow brain potentials during imagery. In general, the difficulty of the imagery task is correlated with the strength and task duration of the neurons' potentials. Subjects with low imagery competencies show stronger potentials in the left hemisphere. A possible interpretation is that these subjects require a higher cognitive effort during the task. Such findings are strong hints to refer in more detail to the interrelations of systems in the organization of actions as it was outlined above in Figure 5.

A precondition to detecting and measuring individual differences in imagery competencies is the development of appropriate instruments. The purpose of the final part of this contribution is to discuss the state of the art of methodology in this domain.

Measuring Individual Imagery Competencies

The most commonly used test for the measurement of general imagery abilities is the Betts Test. It is usually administered in a short version (cf. Richardson, 1969). The test comprises self-evaluation of imagery vividness in different sense modalities. It asks subjects to imagine everyday actions. A second widely-used test is the "Vividness of Visual Imagery Questionnaire" (VVIQ) by Marks (for an overview, see Marks, 1989). The items are confined to the visual imagery modality. The most well-known test for the measurement of imagery control is the "Gordon Test of Visual Imagery Control" ("Gordon Test"; cf. Richardson, 1969). In this test, subjects have to evaluate their ability to manipulate visual imagery processes. Analyses of its test criteria show satisfactory reliability. And, though the assumed independence of vividness and control of imagery could not be confirmed, the two dimensions are strongly related (cf. White, Sheehan, & Ashton, 1977).

The "Vividness of Movement Imagery Questionnaire" (VMIQ) is a parallel form of the VVIQ specialized for movement imagery (cf. Isaac, Marks, & Russell, 1986). Subjects have to imagine everyday actions like "kicking a ball into the air" or "running up the stairs." They have to evaluate these actions according to their vividness. For each item, people have to imagine themselves, as well as another person, in this situation. The scores in the movement-specific version (VMIQ) are highly correlated with the scores in the general version (VVIQ). Since the correlation is higher than the retest stability, the two tests cannot measure distinct dimensions.

The most widely used test for evaluating movement imagery abilities is the "Movement Imagery Questionnaire" (MIQ; Hall, Pongrac, & Buckolz, 1985). During the test, subjects have to execute precisely defined movements, and after that, they have to imagine the same movements. The ease of generating the image (visual dimension) and generating the feeling of movement (kinesthetic dimension) have to be judged. In contrast to the VMIQ, the generation of the image is evaluated, not the vividness. In cases where the subjects are, in fact, able to follow the instructions, it seems more likely that imagery control is tested instead of vividness. The two subscales of the test correlate with r = .58. This implies that two independent factors are measured. The relationship to general imagery tests has not been investigated yet. In the meantime, a revised and abridged version has been published, the MIQ-R (Hall & Martin, 1997).

Is the confidence in the use of imagery tests justified? A frequently discussed problem is that most tests use self-evaluation. Two common arguments are (1) that most of the tests use self-evaluation, which is connected with a number of well known problems and (2) that the tests are too general to study (cf. McKelvie, 1993). Whether the movement-specific imagery tests solve these problems has to be investigated in further research. The trouble with these tests is that only everyday actions but no sport-related items were included. Another argument is that certain logical item analyses are missing (Kihlstrom, Glisky, Peterson, Harvey, & Rose, 1991); in particular, analyses of imagery instructions and item selection. A third problem that concerns general as well as

movement-specific imagery tests is the low item difficulty. The test is not able to differentiate adequately between different individuals. It is rarely the case that images are labeled as "vague" or "very vague"; this would only be possible or valid if there existed a well known standard or the possibility to compare one's own impression with that of other persons.

Which inferences and practical tips can be derived from these methodological problems? The concept of the self-evaluation scales is based upon the assumption that the scales are more directly and intimately related to the notion of imagery than so-called "objective" tests (Hall, Pongrac, & Buckolz, 1985). If one wants to use these advantages, one has to assess the internal evaluation standards (McKelvie, 1993) and the phenomenally salient processes in greater detail. Therefore, the data from self-evaluation scales have to be corroborated by questionnaire data. In this way, more specific results on the individual dispositions for movement imagery can be obtained.

Criteria for the Validity of Questionnaire Data on Movement Imagery

Communication situations have to be assessed with respect to their congruence. In a *congruent situation,* the two interview participants assign the same meaning to their verbal signals, and they understand each other or, at least, realize when they do not. Moreover, different aspects of the interview behavior in general and the verbal behavior in particular show how the interviewee performs in the situation. Do we have congruent situations most of the time? Is there evidence that the interviewee does, in fact, refer to her images? In this case, the type of interview used can be considered an appropriate method for the subject matter. In the case of incongruent situations, the method has to be improved.

The following aspects are indicative of a congruent situation; that is, the interviewee does actually refer to the interview topic. These criteria are neither necessary nor sufficient, but they can be used for the interview analysis (see Munzert, Dültgen, & Möllmann, 2000):

- The interviewee takes his or her time for the image generation. He first imagines the situation extensively and then reports when the imagery has ended. (The imager defocuses his/her gaze, some of them close their eyes. The signal for the end of the imagery can be a nod or a short remark.)

- The interviewee realizes where and when an image becomes blurred; he or she can distinguish between different levels of accuracy. (For example, he or she is unable to see certain body parts or the opponent's court side.)

- The interviewee can verbalize difficulties with the imagery task. (For example, the shift to another perspective does not succeed.)

- The interviewee explicitly refers to the process as "imagery." He or she is aware of the fact that imagery is a way to represent reality. (During the imagery process, the question may arise whether the image of his or her movements corresponds to an outer perspective or not.)

- Without being asked, certain aspects of the interviewee's imagery change from instance to instance. (This can be the specific course of a rally, but also the arrangement of a scene or the occurrence of certain sensations.)

- The interviewee is able to appreciate when his or her statements are contradictory. (Contradictory reports may arise when the imagery mode, like perspective, has changed without being reported.)

- If necessary, the interviewee reconfirms the task. (He or she tries to get a more specific task description; sometimes he or she asks for details that have been left out deliberately.)

- The interviewee describes details he or she has not been explicitly asked for. (For example, he or she reports about other people or certain sensations that have not been addressed yet.)

- The interviewee has difficulty verbalizing impressions; he or she mentions that the report captures only part of the image.

(He or she begins, for example, reports with the caveat that he or she is not able to report on "it" accurately.)

- The interviewee notices effects of the imagery on current mood. (He or she is in an aroused state that continues after the end of the imagery.)

At the same time, one has to be aware of indications that a report does not refer to a current image. Some of the following statements suggest an incongruent situation, in contrast to the statements listed above.

- The interviewee does not take his or her time to perform the imagery (i.e., he or she immediately starts with the report). (In this case, a good indicator is when he or she reports and imagines at the same time.)

- The interviewee reports that the image always has the same amount of detail, although he or she is not able to describe any of them precisely.

- The interviewee gives short answers without adding any details.

- The interviewee uses terms like "perhaps" or "possibly."

- The interviewee uses explicit descriptions as well as general statements.

- The interviewee reports normative aspects as a part of his or her statements. He or she changes the report modality from the factual to the obligatory mode (instead of "I play. . ." he or she uses "I have to play . . .").

These cues can be helpful for assessing the validity of the verbal reports. It is not only a question of social desirability of the subjects' reports but a question of the familiarity with imaging procedures and the need to verbalize specific aspects of the images. Following these guidelines a combination of verbal reports and questionnaires may be helpful to assess imagery competencies in individuals.

Conclusion

When we refer to the domain and objective of the training, we are talking about strength training, technique training, and endurance training. Thus, we should only use mental training in the scientific discussion when we refer to the objective of improving mental processes by the simulation of cognitive processes (perceptual training, concentration training, etc.) or affective processes (anger-control training, anxiety-control training, etc.). When using mental skills like imagery to improve the acquisition and performance of movement actions, it is necessary to consider the modality (e.g., visual or verbal imagination), with regard to the objective of the simulation and the individual person/athlete and his/her predispositions. To organize optimal mental simulation, we have to refer to the action situation and incorporate the components of the situation (the person, the environment, and the task). The scope of mental simulation includes mental rehearsal. This is either oriented toward *processing,* to control the psychomotor processes (mental practice), or toward *tuning,* to control the psycho-physiological arousal (mental preparation).

These differentiations from an action-theory perspective may be helpful for further research to develop mental simulation strategies, for evaluation studies on its effectiveness, *and* for an appropriate understanding to design suitable interventions.

References

Annett, J. (1996). On knowing how to do things: A theory of motor imagery. *Cognitive Brain Research, 3,* 65-69.

Bernstein, N.A. (1967). *The co-ordination and regulation of movement.* Oxford: Pergamon Press.

Bischof, K. (1987). *Individuelle Unterschiede beim visuellen Vorstellen (Individual differences in visual imagery).* Bern: Lang.

Carroll, W.R., & Bandura, A. (1990). Representational guidance of action production in observational learning: A causal analysis. *Journal of Motor Behavior, 22,* 85-97.

Daugs, R., Blischke, K., Olivier, N., & Marschall, F. (1989). *Beiträge zum visuomotorischen Lernen (Issues in perceptual-motor learning).* Schorndorf: Hofmann.

Decety, J., Jeannerod, M., & Prablanc, C. (1989). The timing of mentally represented actions. *Behavioural Brain Research, 34,* 35-42.

Engelkamp, J. (1994). Episodisches Gedächtnis: Von Speichern zu Prozessen und Information (Episodic memory: From storage to processes and information). *Psychologische Rundschau, 45,* 195-210.

Engelkamp, J. (1998). *Memory for actions.* Hove: Psychology Press.

Ennenbach, W. (1989). *Bild und Mitbewegung.* Köln: bps-Verlag.

Hackfort, D. (1986). *Theorie und Analyse sportbezogener Ängstlichkeit (Theory and analysis of sport-related trait anxiety).* Schorndorf: Hofmann.

Hackfort, D., Munzert, J., & Seiler, R. (2000). *Handeln im Sport als handlungspsychologisches Modell (Acting in sports as an action-psychology model).* Heidelberg: Asanger.

Hall, C. R., & Martin, K. E. (1997). Measuring movement imagery abilities: a revision of the Movement Imagery Questionnaire. *Journal of Mental Imagery, 21,* 143-154.

Hall, C.R., Pongrac, J., & Buckolz, E. (1985). The measurement of imagery ability. *Human Movement Science, 4,* 107-118.

Hall, C.R., Rodgers, W.M., & Barr, K.A. (1990). The use of imagery by athletes in selected sports. *The Sport Psychologist, 4,* 1-10.

Helstrup, T. (1986). Separate memory laws for recall of performed acts? *Scandinavian Journal of Psychology, 27,* 1-29.

Heuer, H. (1991). A note on limitations and strategies in movement production. In R. Daugs, H. Mechling, K. Blischke, & N. Olivier (Eds.), *Sportmotorisches Lernen und Techniktraining, Vol. 1* (pp. 117-131). Schorndorf: Hofmann.

Isaac, A., Marks, D.F., & Russell, D.G. (1986). An instrument for assessing imagery of movement: The Vividness of Movement Imagery Questionnaire (VMIQ). *Journal of Mental Imagery, 10*(4), 23-30.

Kihlstom, J.F., Glisky, M.L., Peterson, M.A., Harvey, E.M., & Rose, P.M. (1991). Vividness and control of mental imagery: A psychometric analysis. *Journal of Mental Imagery, 15* (3/4), 133-142.

Kosslyn, S. M. (1980). Image and mind. Cambridge: Harvard University Press.

Lazarus, R.S. (1984). On the primacy of cognition. *Amercian Psychologist, 39,* 124-129.

Lewin, K. (1936). *Principles of topological psychology.* New York: McGraw-Hill.

Lippens, V. (1993). Wenn alles läuft! Zur Modifikation der Subjektiven Theorien von Rennruderern in Training und Wettkampf (In the case everything runs well! Modification of subjective theories of rowers in training and competition). In V. Lippens (Ed.), *Forschungsproblem: Subjektive Theorien. Zur Innensicht in Lern- und Optimierungsprozessen.* Köln: Sport und Buch Strauß.

Luria, A.R. (1967). The regulative function of speech in its development and dissolution. In K. Salzinger, & R. Salzinger (Eds.), *Research in verbal behavior and some neurophysiological implications* (pp. 405-422). New York: Academic Press.

Luria, A.R. (1970). *Die hoeheren kortikalen Funktionen des Menschen und ihre Stoerungen bei oertlichen Hirnstoerungen [Higher cortical functions of man and their disturbances following local brain lesions].* Berlin: Deutscher Verlag der Wissenschaften.

Mahoney, M.J., Gabriel, T.J., & Perkins, T.S. (1987). Psychological skills and exceptional athletic performance. *The Sport Psychologist, 1,* 181-199.

Marks, D.F. (1989). Bibliography of research utilizing the Vividness of Visual Imagery Questionnaire. *Perceptual and Motor Skills, 69,* 707-718.

McKelvie, S.J. (1993). Vividness of visual imagery for faces: as a predictor for facial recognition memory performance: A revised review. *Perceptual and Motor Skills, 76,* 1083-1088.

Meichenbaum, D. (1974). Self-instructional strategy training: A cognitive prothesis for the aged. *Human Development, 17,* 273-280.

Miller, G.A., Galanter, E., & Pribram, K.H. (1960). *Plans and the structure of behavior.* New York: Holt, Rinehart & Winston.

Munzert, J. (2002). Temporal accuracy of mentally simulated transport movements. *Perceptual and Motor Skills, 94,* 307-318.

Munzert, J. (2003). Timing accuracy in actual and mental walking tasks. (unpublished paper)

Munzert, J., Dültgen, K., & Möllmann, H. (2000). Individuelle Merkmale von Bewegungsvorstellungen. Eine explorative Untersuchung im Badminton (Individual characteristics of movement imagery. An explorative study in badminton). *Psychologie und Sport, 7,* 15-25.

Munzert, J., & Hackfort, D. (1999). Individual preconditions for mental training. *International Journal of Sport Psychology, 30,* 41-62.

Neissser, U. (1976). *Cognition and reality.* San Francisco: Freeman.

Newell, K.M. (1986). Constraints on the development of coordination. In M.G. Wade, & H.T.A. Whiting (Eds.), *Motor skill acquisition in children: Aspects of coordination and control* (pp. 341-361). Amsterdam: Martinus Nijhoff.

Nitsch, J.R. (2000). Handlungstheoretische Grundlagen der Sportpsychologie (Action theory fundamentals for sport psychology). In H. Gabler, J.R. Nitsch, & R. Singer (Eds.), Einführung in die Sportpsychologie, Teil 1 (Introduction to sport psychology, Part 1, pp. 43-164). Schorndorf: Hofmann.

Nitsch, J.R., & Hackfort, D. (1981). Stress in Schule und Hochschule – eine handlungspsychologische Funktionsanalyse (Stess in school and university – an action psychology functional analysis). In J.R. Nitsch (Ed.), *Stress* (pp. 263-311). Bern: Huber.

Paivio, A. (1969). Mental Imagery in associative learning and memory. *Psychological Review, 76,* 241-263.

Pennebaker, J.W. (1988). Confiding traumatic experiences and health. In S. Fisher, & J. Reason (Eds.), *Handbook of life stress, cognition and health* (pp. 671-684). New York: Wiley.

Pribram, K.H. (1971). *Languages of the brain. Experimental paradoxes and principles in neuropsychology.* Englewood Cliffs, NJ: Prentice-Hall.

Raspotnig, M. A. (1996). *Visuelle Vorstellungen (Imagery) und Gefühlsmanagement.* Frankfurt/M: Lang.

Richardson, A. (1969). *Mental imagery.* Routledge & Kegan Paul.

Rösler, F., Heil, M., Pauls, A.C., Bajric, J., & von Hennighausen, E. (1994). Individual differences in spatial cognition: Evidence from slow event-related brain potentials. In M. Amelang & D. Bartussek (Eds.), *Fortschritte der Differentiellen Psychologie und Psychologischen Diagnostik (Advances in differential psychology and psychological diagnostics;* pp. 115-129). Göttingen: Hogrefe.

Rushall, B.S., & Lippmann, L.G. (1998). The role of imagery in physical performance. *International Journal of Sport Psychology, 29,* 57-72.

Taylor S.E., Pham, L.B., Rivkin, I.D., & Armor, D.A. (1998). Harnessing the imagination: Mental simulation, self-regulation, and coping. *American Psychologist, 53,* 429-439.

Vygotsky, L.S., & Luria, A.R. (1993). *Studies on the history of behavior: Ape, primitive, and child.* Hillsdale, NJ: Erlbaum.

Weiss, M.R., & Klint, K.A. (1987). "Show and tell" in the gymnasium: An investigation of developmental differences in modeling and verbal rehearsal of motor skills. *Research Quarterly for Exercise and Sport, 58,* 234-241.

Weerth, R. (1992). *NLP & Imagination: Grundannahmen, Methoden, Möglichkeiten und Grenzen (NLP & imagination: Fundamental assumptions, procedures, possibilities, and limits).* Paderborn: Junfermann.

Wessels, M.G. (1994). *Kognitive Psychologie (Cognitive psychology).* München: Reinhardt.

White, K., Sheehan, P.W., & Ashton, R. (1977). Imagery assessment: A survey of self-report measures. *Journal of Mental Imagery, 1,* 145-170.

Zajonc, R.B. (1980). Feeling and thinking. Preferences need no inferences. *American Psychologist, 35,* 151-175.

Courtesy of Gary Lake/WVSports.com

1.2

Mental Practice— Skill Oriented

KEITH HENSCHEN

Introduction

As the field of applied sport psychology has evolved during the last 30 years to what we know it to be today, a constant source of controversy has been the efficacy of mental practice. Professionals who consider themselves 'applied sport psychologists' or 'applied sport psychology consultants' teach their clients a number of skill interventions that are purported to enhance the mental and emotional aspects of performance. As one who has utilized a variety of interventions to teach mental skills, it is my purpose in this chapter to discuss the following: (a) personal philosophy; (b) theoretical basis of skill-oriented mental practice; (c) strategies of application; (d) empirical support for mental practice interventions; and (e) issues of concern. All, or at least most, of the information presented in this chapter is based on qualitative research.

Personal Philosophy

After years of reading other professional philosophies and trial and error ventures, every sport psychology professional slowly amasses enough experience to formulate their own personal philosophy, which governs their actions/behaviors. Initially, our philosophy is often a mirror of our mentor's because they exert considerable influence over our efforts. In fact, our admiration for them as people and their successes as professionals can be the impetus to pursue a career in the same discipline. We attempt to pattern our approaches and thinking patterns after them because there is security in knowing that success can be achieved by following the same path. What we fail to comprehend is that their success is not only what they do or how they do it; but rather, it is an interaction between their techniques and themselves—their unique personalities. No two of us are exactly alike because our perceptions, experiences, and subsequent beliefs have been forged from different compositions. Mimicking our mentor's successes is a natural first approach, but only a "baby step." The next phase of our career is usually one of trial and error. We cognitively are voracious in our quest to find our identities and unique approaches. In other words, we attempt to meld what we think we know and apply this knowledge in a manner that is comfortable to us. This is a dangerous time in our careers because we are like a ship without a rudder. In our quest for stability, we float rather aimlessly as we try to locate the philosophy that can be properly embraced as "ours." We are working to develop a philosophy in which we feel confident, secure, and comfortable, and one that we totally trust.

The third phase of establishing our philosophy is the most productive. We are now ready to actually 'spread our wings' and work within the boundaries that are effective, pleasing to us, and meet our personal needs. It is this personal philosophy that evolves or shapes the art of the possessor. Of course, no two artists are exactly the same. Following is my personal philosophy that I use to govern my consulting practices.

Whole Person Development. Mental skills training, to me, has its foundation in the philosophy of contributing to the development of the entire person. As a sport psychology consultant, I am not interested in only the athletic portion of the person; rather, I desire to see improvement in all facets of an athlete's makeup. He/she should emerge from our relationship with many skills that can be incorporated into all parts of life, instead of being limited just to the athletic portion of the self. At the conclusion of mental skills training, the athlete (performer) should be able to deal more effectively in all aspects of life (i.e., sports, social situations, occupational demands, and relationships). Athletes are not special people; rather they are people with special physical talents. My objective is to affect them as people first and as performers second.

Theory

Even though by reputation I am probably recognized as a total applied oriented sport psychology practitioner, I feel that that is a misconception. Everything that I do in applying mental skills training and counseling with performers is steeped in rich theory. Theory is and must be the foundation of all we do and/or profess. Graduate education has a foundation of theory, which is knowledge; but then we must also provide application of this theory, which is the essence of wisdom. See, I have already waxed theoretical. Seriously, theory is essential, but it is only the first step in establishing a sound applied practice. Theories or conceptual frameworks that have provided guidelines and standards for my style are: instructional counseling, learning theory with an Adlerian bent, and self-theory. The reader should note that all of these theories are ways of working with people. When we are teaching mental skills, the other half of the relationship is another person. Recognize this fact and you have taken the initial 'baby step' to understanding that if the teaching is successful, then both parties must be serviced.

Instructional Counseling. "Instructional counseling is intended to provide counselors and counselor-educators with a conceptual framework within which it is possible to relate counseling practice relevant theory in a direct manner." (Martin & Hiebert, 1985, p xi). Maybe from a theoretical point of view the term "instructional counseling" looks like a contradiction, but I view it as a description of a pragmatic strategy.

Actually, this instructional framework is compatible with approaches to counseling that view the athlete's job in the counseling as learning—learning various attitudes, emotional reactions, cognitions, behaviors, and skills. So this theoretical approach is basically an educational process. The challenge to the counselor is to assist the athlete to learn the desired performance enhancement or mental skills. The instructional counseling process contains five essential components:

1. General objectives—toward which learning is directed.

2. Preassessment—determining the athlete's current capabilities and characteristics (i.e., what are their present mental skills).

3. Outcomes—specific desires for personal learning that are suggested by the preassessment data.

4. Instructional activities—the actual interventions and the subsequent exercises to perfect the requisite skills.

5. Evaluation-changes in behaviors and attitudes due to the interventions.

When athletes who work with sport psychologists are viewed primarily as learners, it then becomes appropriate to describe counseling (applied sport psychology) as an instructional process and to view the sport psychologist as an instructor (Martin & Hiebert, 1985). As instructors, sport psychology consultants engage in careful evaluations of athletes' learning to determine if the counseling has been effective. Instructional counseling is a conceptual framework which allows for a client-centered instructional learning system.

Learning Theory with an Adlerian Approach. Although Adler (1870-1937) is commonly considered one of the greatest Freudians, most of his theoretical positions contradict the classical psychoanalytic tenets. Adler advocated for the importance of the individual and his/her interaction with their environment (Hansen, Stevic, & Warner, 1972). The name Adler gave to his school of thought was "Individual Psychology." Basically, this theory posits that the interaction of heredity, the environment, and the individual were the determiners of behavior. Adler felt that it was not events that determined behavior, but rather the cause of behavior depended upon the individual's perceptions of the events. Adler also felt strongly that all people have a "life goal" that directs their behavior. He also placed great emphasis on the social context of human behavior (Hansen et al., 1972). Adlerian thinking has had a significant impact on the field of counseling, and on my thoughts and concepts concerning how to deal with individual athletes. My mental practice teaching and my counseling approach have both been influenced by Adler's theory of therapy (Adler, 1930). I attempt to change an individual's perceptions about themselves and their environment by teaching them new and effective mental skills. Both Alfred Adler and Carl Rogers would probably view my combining their theories as strange, but I have learned from both their perspectives and have applied parts of their theories into my personal philosophy. As there are different elements in my strategies and basic holistic approach, I refer to theories in which the essential elements are discussed—here the problems or phenomena are of predominant importance and the fit of concepts is less important.

The behavioral approach to counseling makes the assumption that the athletes' problems are actually problems in learning. With this in mind, the sport psychology consultant is a counselor first, but is also a special kind of learning specialist. This approach to sport psychology counseling is just not a bag of tricks, but is a system of working with the whole person based on learning theory. Part of this theoretical approach is the idea that all behavior is formed through a learning process. The individual manifests certain patterns of behavior because it has brought him/her reinforcement and satisfaction. Changing this behavior necessitates recognizing the established patterns and then using learning theory to modify them (Bandura, 1969). Mental skill training is just adding to the whole person development through appropriate learning theory.

Self-Theory. This theoretical approach is associated with many great psychologists (i.e., Rollo May, Abraham Maslow, Karen Horney, Erich Fromm, and Carl Rogers), but in this chapter I want to concentrate on the perspective from Carl Rogers. Rogers, in one way or another, influenced most of the practicing psychologists of the twentieth century (Hansen, Rossberg, & Cramer, 1994). He developed a system of nondirective counseling that has resonated with my training and personal characteristics. Rogers believed that individuals have within themselves the capacity for self-understanding, for altering their self-concept, and their self-directed behavior, and that "these resources can be tapped only if a definable climate of facilitative psychological attitudes can be provided" (Rogers, 1980. p.49). This nondirective approach to intervention eventually evolved into a theory of personality that is called self-theory. Some of the key concepts of this theory are that people are motivated and socialized, and can determine their own destiny. Roger asserted that "the individual has the capacity to guide, regulate, and control himself providing . . . that certain definable conditions exist" (Rogers, 1959, p. 221). The sport psychologist, through interaction with the athlete, provides the environment that allows self-actualization to emerge from within the person. For this type of client-centered self-theory to be successful, Rogers also proposed six conditions that must occur:

1. Two persons must be in psychological contact.

2. The athlete must at least have a feeling of vulnerability and/or anxiety. The athlete must be in a state of incongruence.

3. The sport psychology consultant (counselor) must be genuine in the relationship.

4. The consultant must exhibit unconditional positive regard for the athlete.

5. The consultant must experience an empathic understanding of the athlete, especially the athlete's internal frame of reference.

6. The athlete must perceive that genuineness and empathy are the actual feelings of the consultant (Hansen et. al., 1994).

Rogers contributed greatly to the basic understanding of effective counseling. He was a leader of humanistic psychology and the field of applied sport psychology can benefit enormously by adopting some of his theoretical positions. From this information concerning theory, I trust that you (the reader) have become cognizant that the theories I embrace may not be the same as those of others in the applied area. They work for me.

Strategies and Techniques

Based upon a review of a number of how-to books outlining various mental practice strategies that have become popular during the last two decades, it appears that the actual areas emphasized are commonly agreed upon; the difference occurs in the style of application by the mental training consultant (Gallway, 1974; Henschen & Straub, 1995; Orlick, 1986). This chapter represents a particular approach to mental training and the rationale that supports this approach. I will attempt to detail the interventions I normally employ, as well as the steps I follow in the mental training process. An effort will be made to present the steps in the art of reinforcing performance enhancement strategies and to possibly reduce the ambiguities frequently associated with mental training. My basic philosophy underlining

this approach is to assure that I (the sport psychology consultant) become unnecessary in the life of the athlete as quickly as possible. Therefore, it is imperative that the athlete fully comprehends the principles of mental training and is able to apply them at their discretion. I view mental practice as the mastering of a number of mental skills, however, prior to teaching these skills I must know a little about the athlete I am teaching.

Counselor—Athlete Relationship

Eschelle is an 11-year-old gymnast whose mother says needs some sport psychology. Actually, both Eschelle and her mother asked if I would work with her. During our initial interview (Eschelle, mother, father, and coach), Eschelle seems a little fearful, tentative, and anxious concerning seeing a 'shrink.' After introductions, I ask Eschelle, "What do you think I do?" She kind of grunts and shrugs her shoulders, indicating she is not really sure what I do. I explain to her that there is nothing clinical that I will be doing and that I am not a psychologist or a psychiatrist. I will be primarily trying to identify her psychological strengths and areas that may need some improvement. I will not be psychoanalyzing her; hopefully, I will teach her some new techniques that will help her become a better gymnast. I explain to her that I have worked with Olympic and All-American gymnasts, and that she will be learning the same skills as they did. I ask her to explain what kind of skills she thinks will help her. I instruct her to tell me how she feels in practice and competition.

At the end of our first meeting, I ask Eschelle to go home and think about whether she feels comfortable working with me. I explain to her what we will be doing, the schedule of our meetings, and that she will have 'homework' every night, if she plans to work with me. I ask her to discuss with her parents if she would like to work with me. If she decides not to, that is fine. It should be her decision; but if she decides to, I expect her to commit to what we are doing.

This initial interview is designed to build rapport with the performer. I want the athlete to get to know me and to determine if my style is acceptable to them. I would say that approximately 98% of the time, I receive a call indicating that the athlete would like to start their mental training enhancement. The athlete-counselor relationship is crucial if mental practice training is to be successful. It normally takes me 4-6 months (meeting every other week) for the athlete to become competent in their use of mental skills.

Psychometrics. I realize that few applied sport psychology practitioners use psychometrics in their practice, but I find them invaluable. Assessment is a tool in my toolbox that adds immensely to building rapport with the athlete. Plus, reliable psychometric data provides a most effective way of speeding up the process of comprehending individual differences. Simple tests such as the State-Trait Anxiety Inventory (STAI) (Spielberger, Gorsuch, & Lushene, 1970), the short form of the Test of Attention and Interpersonal Styles (TAIS) (Nideffer, 1989), and the Competitive Styles Profile (CSP) (Ogilvie & Greene, 1994) are examples of the tests I use. The tests used depend upon the reason the athlete is seeing me. There are different tests for different problems. One of the most significant values that emanate from a psychometric review are the beginnings of a bridge of trust. The feedback validation session (discussion of the testing results) provides an excellent opportunity for the athlete to measure the consultant's ethical positions, non-judgment posture, competency, and the extent to which the athlete is valued as a person as well as an athlete. Most importantly, the athlete realizes that I really do know something about them and I care about their growth and development. Few other counseling experiences offer the setting that enables the athlete to make his/her own evaluation as to the trustworthiness of the sport psychology consultant. The feedback session provides a counselor-athlete interaction that lays the foundation for the overall mental practice effectiveness.

Mental Practice Techniques. The psychometric results and the interviewing process provide me with sufficient information to develop a mental practice program unique to the individual athlete with whom I am working. My mental practice strategies are founded on teaching the "Cardinal Skills" of mental practice. These skills are relaxation, concentration, imagery, self-talk, and a pre-competitive mental routine. A few other interventions that are frequently employed are confidence training, fear reduction, and hypnosis. You will probably notice that goal setting is absent from my list of mental practice skills. I will explain the reasons for this later in the chapter.

As was explained earlier in this article, it is not that I do anything different than any other sports psychologist, but how I do what I do is the real difference. My art is my success and in the remainder of this chapter I will attempt to give it justice.

Mental practice techniques should be taught in a particular sequence to be most effective. Relaxation is the foundational skill. Being relaxed is a precursor to concentration. Relaxation and concentration are necessary for effective imagery techniques, and imagery mastery is necessary for effective self-talk. These four skills then become integral components of a precompetition mental routine. Sequence = RELAXATION, CONCENTRATION, IMAGERY, SELF-TALK, PRE-COMPETITION MENTAL ROUTINE.

A. Relaxation

Jeremy is a college basketball player who is able to shoot foul shots at 90+ percent in practice and in early parts of a game. But as the end of the game approaches and pressure mounts in close games, he becomes anxious and misses most all of his free throws. He knows he becomes anxious and tense, but does not know what to do about these feelings. When he came to me for assistance, I spent a good deal of time assuring him that he had the ability to feel relaxed if he would just learn what relaxation actually felt like. We first began with simple diaphragm-based breathing exercises, then spent a couple of weeks practicing progressive relaxation, and then a couple more weeks using autogenic training. Within one month, Jeremy was feeling relaxed when shooting all of his free throws. He just needed to train his body to retain the appropriate relaxed feeling.

Performance of any type is a complex process. For any performer to be truly proficient there are a number of physical control skills which must be mastered. This involves the preparation of the mind and the body by establishing the ideal activation level. To accomplish this feat, relaxation training has become one of the most widely used mental practice techniques. Traditionally, relaxation has been used for reducing excessive levels of anxiety and stress that have negative effects on performance. Even though relaxation training frequently lowers precompetition apprehension and performance anxiety, it also contains at least one other crucial benefit—it trains the mind to communicate effectively with the feelings of the body. The mind and body listen to each other's signals (Henschen & Straub, 1995).

Physical relaxation is based on the principle that tension and relaxation are opposites and can not occur simultaneously in the body. As an athlete learns from the skill of relaxation, it becomes possible to monitor desirable levels of tension or relaxation in all the muscle groups of the body. This entails becoming aware of how activation and/or tension feel on many different levels. Initially, these levels will be difficult for the performer to distinguish; but as they are practiced they become easier and easier to recognize. Eventually, the performer will learn to create the level to perform optimally in any situation and at various levels of pressure.

Relaxation training is not new to the world of performance. A relaxation method called Qi Gong was introduced in China more than 4,000 years ago. The essence of this technique was deep breathing exercises. Other cultures in various parts of the world have developed and advocated additional relaxation techniques such as yoga, meditation, and hypnosis. Contemporarily, many professionals working in the field of applied sport psychology utilize relaxation as the *foundational* psychological skill (Benson & Proctor, 1984).

Normally, I use three types of relaxation techniques when working with athletes—-breathing awareness, progressive relaxation, and autogenic training. Breathing awareness is learning to breathe deeply through the stomach (diaphragm) instead of the chest. This type of breathing is also important when mastering autogenic training. Once the athlete has mastered breathing awareness, I then have them move on to progressive relaxation.

Progressive relaxation is a "muscle to mind"' method where the objective is to contrast relaxation and tension as opposites. This is achieved by tensing and then relaxing the same muscle group. Following is an exercise in progressive relaxation. While it is easy to learn, I frequently put the instructions on a cassette tape so the athlete can follow the method on their own. That allows them to be more passively involved and thus more relaxed.

1. Lie down on your back in a comfortable position, with your arms at your sides, and your legs straight and slightly apart. Close your eyes and begin to focus on your breathing. As in breathing awareness, do not attempt to control the speed of your breathing, just let it happen. With every exhalation you will feel your tension reducing and your body becoming more relaxed to get totally comfortable. If at any time you feel you need to move to get more comfortable, do so.

2. Beginning with your feet, tighten all the muscles in both feet as tight as you can without hurting yourself. Hold this tightness as I count to 10 and then I will instruct you to release the tension. Try to feel the difference between being tight and being relaxed. Remember to tighten only one muscle group at a time. The rest of your body should be totally relaxed. Next, move to your calves and tighten them as I count to 10 and then release. Again feel the difference. Next, tighten your quadriceps for a count of 10 and release for 20-30 seconds. Feel the difference. Now go to your hamstrings and buttocks and tighten and release. Finally, tighten (10 seconds) and then release every muscle in your lower body for a count of 10 while the upper body is totally relaxed.

3. Do the same thing with your stomach and then move to the lower back. Next, clench your hands and forearms then release. Now do the same with the upper arms. Next tighten and release your chest muscles. Finally, tighten all the muscles

of your upper body (lower back, stomach, hands and forearms, upper arms and chest). Remember to tighten for 10 seconds and release, feeling the tension leave each area as you relax.

4. Next move to your neck muscles, then to your facial muscles. The facial tensing should be fun because I instruct them to make their face like a prune.

5. Next is tensing and releasing every muscle of the body at the same time. Make your body like a "bar of iron."

6. Now you should scan your muscle groups from head to toe for those areas that may still be a little tense and repeat the tightening and relaxing there (Jacobson, 1930).

I ask the athletes to practice this exercise every night (for about two weeks) just before going to sleep. It takes about 10-15 minutes a night.

Autogenic training is a "mind to muscle" relaxation technique that involves repeating a series of formulas to oneself while controlling one's diaphramic breathing. The autogenic formulas include:

Comfortably warm

Comfortably heavy

Heart beat calm and regular

Breathing, it breathes me

Solar plexus comfortably warm

Forehead pleasantly cold

Each of these formulas is practiced twice a day for the duration of one week. Under this schedule, the total autogenic training exercises will take six weeks to complete. Each formula is repeated silently by the athlete to each appendage seven times during each session. The athlete should exhale every time they repeat the formula, therefore the breathing becomes rhythmic. Following is a sample exercise.

Repetition	Formula
1	Right arm comfortably warm
2	Right arm comfortably warm
3	Right arm comfortably warm
4	Right arm comfortably warm
5	Right arm comfortably warm
6	Right arm comfortably warm
7	Right arm comfortably warm
1	Left arm comfortably warm
2	Left arm comfortably warm
3	Left arm comfortably warm
4	Left arm comfortably warm
5	Left arm comfortably warm
6	Left arm comfortably warm
7	Left arm comfortably warm
1	Both arms comfortably warm
2	Both arms comfortably warm
3	Both arms comfortably warm
4	Both arms comfortably warm
5	Both arms comfortably warm
6	Both arms comfortably warm
7	Both arms comfortably warm
1-7	Right leg comfortably warm
1-7	Left leg comfortably warm
1-7	Both legs comfortably warm
1-7	Arms and legs comfortably warm (Krenz, 1983).

This entire sequence should be repeated one more time during the session. At the end of each week, you should change the formula.

The reason I give each athlete two different types of relaxation exercises is because some will like one technique while others may prefer another. Each athlete is unique and will respond differently to the various methods. If only one technique is presented, then a certain percentage of performers will not respond adequately; if a variety of techniques are presented, then the performer can select the one that is most suitable to him/her. Table 1 presents a number of empirical studies concerning the efficacy of relaxation.

B. Concentration

Jake is a young quarterback of an American football team at a prominent university. He has a lot of trouble reading defenses and is making a number of mistakes because he is focusing on the wrong things during competition. He seems to be distracted by all the events going on at the same time. When he came to me for concentration training, he was determined to learn the skills for appropriate attentional styles during pressure situations. Jake was an avid learner when presented with the various concentration exercises. After about two months of concentration training he was able to master all of the attentional styles and focus appropriately on the relevant cues instead of the distractions, but he still was having trouble reading defenses quickly. To improve his quickness and efficiency for this task, I devised a strange exercise. I had the coaching staff take still photographs of about 20 different defenses and place them on a video. Initially, we set the video to show the defense for a 2-second duration and then I would ask Jake to identify the defense. Then, we lowered the time to 1.5 seconds of exposure. He soon became proficient at identifying the defenses at this speed. Finally, he was given only 1 second to determine the defenses and he was able to do this with great accuracy. Jake has enjoyed a fine career in the National Football League (NFL) for the past decade and is known for his accurate decision making ability.

Talk to performers of any ability about their mental approach to their performances and immediately the terms "focus," "attention," or "concentration" will be verbalized. All athletes recognize very quickly that without appropriate "concentration" their performances are erratic, inconsistent, and generally error laden. After an athlete learns how to relax, it is the time to teach a number of concentration skills. Whatever this phenomenon entails, it is obvious that good performers have it and less good performers need it (Cox, 1998).

The interesting thing about concentration is that there are five attentional styles that need to be mastered because each sport, and each event or position in that sport, require specific attentional styles to perform adequately. For example, a center forward in soccer will need different attentional skills than a goalie. A gymnast will need some of the concentration skills that does an archer, but not all of them and vice versa. In other words, the skills of concentration are many and very specific to the situation.

Concentration can be defined as the ability of the performer to focus on the appropriate cues in a given situation and to control his/her responses to these cues for the execution of a particular skill by itself or within a complex situation (Nideffer, 1985). Also, it should be recognized that the desired concentration in sport situations is almost always a passive concentration. Intensifying efforts to concentrate often results in an inappropriate attentional style. Concentration training should emphasize all the attentional styles so that they occur automatically as the situation demands. Listed below are the many types or styles of concentration that all performers should master.

A. Broad External—allows you to be aware of everything that is going on around you, a total awareness.

B. Narrow Internal—A narrow focus on an internal object or task.

C. Narrow External—A narrow focus on an external object or task.

D. Broad Internal—Directing your attention internally to analyze, think about, and deal with a lot of information.

E. Shifting—The ability to move from one type of attentional style to another very quickly (Nideffer, 1989).

It is not sufficient for a coach or even an athlete to tell themselves to "just concentrate." Since concentration is a multifaceted skill, I attempt to provide training (exercises) to help performers improve in this area. Following are a number of exercises that I have utilized over the years to train literally hundreds of elite-level and world-class performers.

1. **The grid concentration exercise (narrow external) and (shifting).** This is an enjoyable exercise that can be administered to an entire group. Make copies of the grid so that all members have one. When you distribute the grid, make sure that it is face down so that no one sees the numbers. Have the athletes break into pairs. The directions are for one member of the pair to turn over the page and cross out as many numbers as possible, in consecutive order, starting with 00, 01, 02, ---. They are to continue crossing out numbers for one minute. While one person is

84	27	51	78	59	52	13	85	61	55
28	60	92	04	90	97	31	57	29	33
32	96	65	39	80	77	49	86	18	70
76	87	71	95	98	81	01	46	88	00
48	82	89	47	35	17	10	42	34	62
44	67	93	11	07	43	72	94	69	56
53	79	05	22	54	74	58	14	91	02
06	68	99	75	26	15	41	66	40	20
50	09	64	08	38	30	36	45	83	24
03	73	21	23	16	37	25	19	12	63

crossing out numbers, the other member of the pair is doing everything possible to distract the person who is crossing out the numbers. They can talk, whistle, or shout in an attempt to be a distraction. The only stipulation is that they cannot touch the other person. After one minute, tally the score, and then reverse the roles. It is interesting to note that 1st graders frequently reach the number of 25, while adults can only get into the middle teens. The reason being that children can become more absorbed in what they are doing.

2. **Listening to outside sounds (broad external).** Have the athlete lie down with his/her eyes closed and just concentrate on the sounds that are occurring around them (3 minutes).

3. **Monitoring the sounds of your body (broad internal).** Have the athlete lie on their back with eyes closed and fingers in their ears. They then focus on all the sounds of their body—growling of stomach, breathing, heartbeat (2 minutes).

4. **Flowing thoughts (narrow internal).** While resting comfortably with their eyes closed, have the athletes pay particular attention to the thoughts that their minds bring to the surface. This is to be done in a non-judgmental and passive attitude. Passively recognize the thoughts and allow them to come into and leave the mind at their own pace (2 minutes).

5. **Pick a problem (narrow internal).** Pick an issue that has been bothering you and ask your mind to give you as many solutions as it can. As the mind presents each solution, place it into a bubble and allow it to slowly float away. Quietly wait for the next solution to appear. This is also accomplished in a nonjudgmental fashion (5 minutes).

6. **Study an object (narrow external).** Take any small object that can easily be manipulated in your hand (coin, paper clip, ring, etc.) and focus intently on this object. If the mind becomes bored and begins to wander, refocus on the object. Each time you perform this exercise change the object (5 minutes).

7. **Listen to own heartbeat (narrow internal).** Close your eyes while in a comfortable position and listen to your heartbeat. Attempt to hear nothing but your own heart beating (3 minutes).

8. **Blank mind (narrow internal).** Try to think of nothing. No thoughts, think only of blackness. Attempt to control your mind so that it cannot feed you any thoughts (1 minute).

9. Shifting exercise. This is a three-week exercise for 10 minutes each time. For the first week the athlete needs to find an interesting book to read which has no pictures. The athlete should read in a quiet place and focus on comprehension of the material. The second week, they should read the book and listen to the radio at the same time. Again, they do this for 10 minutes and tell someone what they have read and what has been playing on the radio. During the third week, they read the book, listen to the radio, and watch television simultaneously for 10 minutes. This is a fun exercise, and it forces the athlete to learn to shift quickly from one thing to another.

These concentration exercises are ones that I have used effectively for more than 30 years with all types of athletes. These exercises should be practiced daily for about two weeks to receive the full effects. When I work with performers I have always required them to do at least 10 minutes of the previous exercises everyday as their sport psychology "homework." How can you master these skills if you don't practice them?

The skills of concentration are probably the most crucial of all the mental practice skills to actual performance. Concentration, arousal, anxiety, and self-confidence are intricately interwoven with each of these variables greatly influencing the others. Athletes must be proficient in all the attentional styles so that they can become automatic in their deployment. No one can give you concentration skills, you must earn them yourself. This occurs only after many hours of dedicated practice (Henschen & Straub, 1995). Table 1 lists a number of studies involving concentration/attentional styles.

As anxiety increases, concentration ability goes out the window

As arousal levels increase, the ability to focus narrows

Athletes with high levels of confidence are able to handle more arousal without losing focus

C. Imagery

Ray is a young, competent, and aspiring teenage golfer. He has won two high school state championships and a number of amateur tournaments. He realizes that if his game is going to continue to improve, it will be the mental aspects that will require attention. One area that needs particular attention is Ray's tendency to think of what could go wrong in pressure situations. Ray revealed that his negative thoughts sometimes affect his shot making precision.

As I started to work with Ray, I initially attempted to determine what style of imagery he used. He was more visual than kinesthetic. After practicing his visual ability through a variety of exercises, Ray was able to execute the shots that were called for according to the situation. Not only did Ray's shot improve, due to the imagery training, but his confidence appeared to increase, also.

It is my opinion that after an athlete masters the skills of relaxation and concentration, it becomes easier for him or her to perfect their imaging abilities. "Because imagery allows a focus on important visual cues and physical skills as they unfold in the moment, it functions like a language for action" (Heil, 1995, p. 183). Often imagery is used synonymously with visualization but this is incorrect. Visualization is only one form of imagery. Most athletes are visual and/or kinesthetic imagers. Other types of performers frequently use other sensory perceptual modalities for their imagery (auditory, olfactory, cutaneous, etc.). Visual and kinesthetic images are a key to effective mental rehearsal (Murphy, 1990; Murphy, 1995).

Imagery offers a number of possibilities. Guided imagery can be used to enhance physical training and competition, to cope with pain, or to aid with injury rehabilitation. The effectiveness of imagery training depends upon a number of individual differences: creating an "inner theater," following a progressive learning sequence, and generalizing from mental skill to performance skill (Heil, 1995). Following are a few exercises I have used to train the mental practice skill of imagery:

1. Guided imagery. You are in the middle of a forest and it is the dead of winter. You are in a log cabin with a fire in the fireplace. The fire provides the only light in the cabin. As you sit in the cabin you feel the warmth of the fire, hear the crackle and pops as the logs burn, and you smell the burning wood. You decide to take a short walk outside. You put on your boots, heavy parka, hat with earmuffs, and gloves. When you open the door you feel the bitter cold on your face, and as you walk in the snow you hear it crackle and crunch. The moon is shining brightly and there is an eerie blue atmosphere. You enjoy the smell of the pine trees. After a little while, you return to the cabin and enjoy the warmth of being inside. You remove your hat, gloves, parka, and boots and then lay down on a bear skin rug right in front of the fireplace. You become very relaxed as you feel the warmth of the fire and the softness of the bear skin rug.

2. Sport specific exercise. A golfer is standing on the tee. Water borders both sides of the fairway and there is a large sand trap about 200 yards in the middle of the fairway. I ask the golfer to select a spot in the fairway and visually and kinesthetically hit the ball to that spot. This process includes the following skills:

> observe the situation
>
> make your strategy
>
> see the shot
>
> feel the shot
>
> trust your body

3. Happiness room. Get yourself in a comfortable and relaxed position and close your eyes. Picture yourself at the bottom of a set of stairs (about 15 steps). At the top of these stairs is a big door. Climb the stairs and when you get to the top, open the door. When you open the door, you will see a large room with nothing in it. For the next 90 seconds, I will remain silent as you decorate this room. This is your happiness room. You can put anything you want in this room. But whatever you place in it must give you pleasure—it must make you feel good. Money is no object. There is no other room like this in the world and it is all yours. Go ahead and decorate your happiness room (wait for 90 seconds). Now keep your eyes closed and try to follow my directions. I want you to go to your bed or chair and face one of the walls in the happiness room. On this wall, place the newest type of big screen television. It is about 5'X5' and is an inch thick and hangs on the wall. Now take your remote control and turn on the TV and watch yourself perform. I want you to perform perfectly and to feel how good it is to see yourself perform. Now turn off your TV, walk to the door and turn around and feel how good your happiness room is to you. Walk down the stairs and when you get to the bottom open your eyes. The athlete is asked to go to their happiness room frequently and redecorate it at their leisure. They can use the TV to watch themselves practice difficult skills.

The use of imagery as a mental training technique allows performers to draw on their imagination to envision the possibilities of performance. The athlete who learns effective imagery skills acquires a valuable life skill which has a wide variety of applications.

D. Self-talk

During the 2000 Summer Olympic Games, I was one of the sport psychology consultants employed by the United States track and field team. As a team we left the United States about six weeks prior to the actual Olympic competition in order for the team to train and compete in Australia. Early in our trip, two sprinters (400 meters) asked if I could help them get over the pain they were experiencing at about the 300 meter distance. This pain caused them to think only of their discomfort and interfered with the rhythm of their running (they tightened up during the last 100 meters). I asked each of them to come back the next day with two positive cue words that aroused them. At the 300 distance in each race, they were instructed to repeat their cue words over and over until they finished the race. At first they were a little skeptical, but agreed to try this exercise. The first time they tried the exercise it worked, and each time their times got better. At the actual games, one received a silver medal in the 400, and both earned a gold medal in the 4X400 relay.

All of us talk to ourselves. Some of us even get a few answers now and then through the dialogue that exists in our minds. Self-talk is actually the mental activity commonly known as thinking or cognition. We actually "talk to ourselves in our head," using emotional tones as well as words. The tone of this dialogue can affect our behaviors, emotions, and even our physical states (Reardon, 1995). Negative self-talk that is habitual frequently leads to the frustration, anxiety, and depression commonly felt about training and competition.

You would think that our self-talk would be an easy thing to change and/or control, but that is far from the truth. We are surrounded by negativity and it is easy to accept this form of feedback or reinforcement. Negative thinking is also often reinforced by coaching styles that emphasize mistakes/errors. Once this pattern of self-talk is ingrained, it is very difficult to deter. Successful athletes, on the other hand, learn to manage their thinking and guide it in a positive direction to help maximize their performances. The following exercises aid in developing the positive self-talk perspective:

1. Positive cue or trigger words repeated over and over in the mind while competing. Have the athlete select a few of these that have special and powerful meanings to them individually. The mind can only focus on one thing at a time. If it is being positive, then it can not be negative at the same time (the inverse is equally as true).

2. Focus on what you want to accomplish. Talk and think about the objective in the short term. For example, as the golfer stands on the tee, he/she should think and focus on a chosen spot on the fairway and ignore the traps, out of bounds, water, etc.

3. Stay in the present. Become immersed or absorbed in what is happening at the present time instead of thinking of the past or the end result (future).

4. Differentiate between practice self-talk and competition self-talk. Many athletes fail to differentiate between self-talk that is helpful in improving skill and the ability to perform well, and the variety of self-talk that is essential when actually in the act of performing or competing. "Practice self-talk" is characterized by questioning, introspection, and searching for ways to change. Competitive self-talk is in the present and is characterized by strong affirmative statements. Confident competitive self-talk produces a sense of control and reduces doubt or uncertainty (Reardon, 1995 p. 207).

5. Have two athletes face each other. One athlete spreads his/her arms to the sides. The other places their hands on the wrists of the first one. The first one is instructed to think first of a negative thought—something that makes them feel sad and depressed. When they have this thought in their head, they are to nod their head. The second one then attempts to pull their hands and arms down. The first one

is instructed to resist this lowering of their arms. The positions are reversed so both partners have the opportunity to think negatively. The second part of the exercise is to think a very positive and arousing thought and again attempt to pull the arms down. Reverse the positions. Inevitably the person will be stronger when thinking positive and uplifting thoughts.

Self-talk is such a crucial mental practice skill because it dictates the likelihood of successful or unsuccessful results (performance). How we think and talk to ourselves in our minds dictates the directions our body will follow. The mind controls the body. One interesting fact is that the body will follow the subject of the thought, not exactly what is said or thought. When a basketball player is at the free throw line and thinks "don't miss," actually they just instructed their body to miss the shot. When a golfer says to themselves "don't hit it into the water," the body actually hears water and attempts to hit in that direction. The body is a servomechanism of the mind, and self-talk is the messenger. Table 1 lists a number of studies concerning self-talk.

E. Pre-competition Performance Routines

After learning the mental practice skills of relaxation, concentration, imagery, and self-talk, the athlete should be able to utilize these skills in a variety of ways. Not only should these skills be used on a daily basis to perfect their physical skills, but they should also be incorporated into the competitive realm. A mental pre-competitive routine is putting all of the mental skills into a sport routine that will enhance the probability of a good physical performance. A mental routine is characterized by:

Being short (1-3 minutes)

Unique to each athlete

A combination of a number of mental
    practice skills

Places the mind in a condition where it is ready to allow the body to perform

A pre-competitive mental routine is a simple technique which is quite effective in quelling the anxious mind in preparation for optimal performance.

Table 1 Studies of the Mental Skills

Relaxation
A. Crocker & Graham (1995)
B. Greenspan & Feltz (1989)
C. Hall & Hardy (1991)
D. Jiang (1991)
E. Lanning & Hisanaga (1989)
F. Muangnapol & Morris (1999)
G. Solberg, Berglund, Engen, Ekberg, & Loeb (1996)
Concentration
A. Kerle & Hawkins (1982)
B. Moran (1993)
C. Starkes & Allard (1983)
Imagery
A. Feltz & Landers (1983)
B. Feltz, Landers, & Becker (1988)
C. Hall, Rodgers, and Barr (1990)
D. Hird, Landers, Thomas, & Horan (1991)
E. Mahoney, Gabriel, & Perkins (1987)
F. Moritz, Hall, Martin, & Valoez (1996)
G. Weinberg, Seabourne, & Jackson (1981)
Self-Talk
A. Ming & Martins (1996)
B. Rushall, Hall, Roux, Sasseville, & Rushall (1998)
C. Rushall & Shewchuk (1989)

F. Other Mental Practice Skills

There are other mental practice skills that have been important in my working with performers—fear mitigation, confidence enhancement, and hypnosis. These interventions are not considered foundational mental skills, but are nevertheless a frequent necessity. Each of these would require an entire chapter to fully do them justice and many other textbooks have covered these topics adequately. I would like to discuss each of these in a superficial manner, not to presenting strategies or techniques, but rather emphasizing their importance.

Fear mitigation. Although anxiety can be regarded as meaningful from a functional perspective (Hackfort & Schwenkmezger, 1993), fear is a special emotion as manifested in elite sports. Fear is one of the greatest debilitating emotions the human animal possesses. It affects almost all performers in one situation or another, yet this phenomenon is rarely adequately addressed in the sport psychology literature. Much of what I do as a sport psychology consultant is to take away or lessen the fears of athletes. There are a number of recent contributions to strategies and techniques for lessening fear as reported in various chapters of this handbook, but my main strategy is to educate the individual concerning fear, in general, and then the specific fears affecting them (fear of success, fear of failure, rational, irrational, etc.). Once the athlete understands their fears, overcoming the fear becomes easier. Fear activates defense mechanisms. It can be employed from a positive or negative perspective, and understanding its ramifications is the first step to controlling it. Fear always has an object and when the object is identified it can be treated. I am amazed that our discipline has not researched more in the area of fear because it is so prevalent in the arena of performance.

Confidence enhancement. Confidence is another topic that is immensely crucial in performance. All textbooks cover this area and most provide excellent strategies and techniques to enhance this emotion. The only thought I have concerning confidence that might be different is that it is a state and not a trait. Humans are confident in specific skills, contexts, situations, and at certain times. There is really no such thing as a confident person. As an applied sport psychology consultant, I need to be cognizant of the areas where my clients are confident, and also where they are not. The mental skills we teach are an effort to provide a level of control to the athlete so that they can become more confident in many more situations.

Hypnosis. I rarely use this technique, but it can be very effective with some athletes. Hypnosis is an altered state of consciousness that can be used clinically as well as in some applied circumstances. It can produce negative consequences under the guidance of an untrained individual. Suffice it to say that training is key to utilizing this technique.

One final intervention that I *do not* use in my practice that may be surprising is *goal setting.* I believe goal setting is the single greatest fraud ever perpetuated by our discipline. A great amount of information has been presented on this topic, but invariably no author explains that this is a practice strategy that should not be used during performance (Cox, 1998; Gould, 1992; Henschen & Straub, 1995; Orlick, 1986). If an athlete is thinking of their goals during competition, then their minds are inappropriately attending that topic. Goals are an analytical function and during competition our minds should be devoid of analytical processing. Almost all performers have experienced numerous peak performances. During a peak performance, the mind is entertaining very few thoughts and is surely not thinking of goals—just the opposite. If an athlete starts to analyze during peak performance, the state is broken and the performance immediately deteriorates. In my mind, goal setting interferes with what mental skills are actually attempting to accomplish—quelling the active mind.

There are only two ways to become a great performer:

A. Cut off your head

B. Become so mentally effective that you do not interfere with yourself at the wrong time

Goal setting does not contribute to either of the above scenarios. It detracts from rather than enhances their accomplishment.

Summary

In this chapter, I have attempted to provide my thoughts concerning the meaning of theory in my practice with special reference to mental practice. My personal philosophy was presented which is from a whole person development perspective with contributions from instructional counseling, learning theory with Adlerian leanings, and self-theory. The main portion of the chapter discussed the strategies and techniques that I use when working with athletes. All of this information is based on qualitative research. These practices include the counselor-athlete relationship, psychometrics, and the teaching of a variety of mental skills techniques (relaxation, concentration, imagery, self-talk, pre-competition mental routines, fear mitigation, confidence training, and hypnosis). Exercises that I use to teach each of the mental skills are also presented. To substantiate why I do many of the things presented, I have also discussed my philosophy concerning all of these interventions. In addition, I have attempted to explain my rationale for not including goal setting in mental practice skills. The techniques I use may not be appropriate for everyone reading this chapter because you are unique. You must determine what works effectively for you. Good luck!

References

Adler, A. (1930). Individual Psychology. In Murchison, C. (Ed.). *Psychologies of 1930.* Worchester, MA: Clark University Press.

Bandura, A. (1969). *Principles of Behavior Modification.* New York: Holt, Reinhart and Winston.

Benson, H. & Proctor, W. (1984). *Beyond the Relaxation Response.* New York: Berkley.

Cox, R. H. (1998). Sport Psychology: *Concepts and Applications.* (4th ed.). Boston: WCB/McGraw Hill.

Crocker, P. R. D., & Graham, T. R. (1995). Coping by competitive athletes with performance stress: Gender differences and relationships with affect. *The Sport Psychologist, 9,* 325-338.

Feltz, D. L., & Landers, D. M. (1983). The effects of mental practice on motor skill learning and performance: A meta-analysis. *Journal of Sport Psychology, 5,* 25-57.

Feltz, D. L., Landers, DlM., & Becker, B. J. (1988). A revised meta-analysis of the mental practice literature on motor skill learning. In D. Drukman & J. Swets (Eds.). *Enhancing Human Performance: Issues, Theories and Techniques.* Washington, D.C.: National Academy Press. pp. 1-65.

Gallway, T. (1974). *The Inner Game of Tennis.* New York: Random House.

Gould, D. (1992). Goal setting for peak performance. In J. M. Williams (Ed.). *Applied Sport Psychology: Personal Growth for Peak Performance.* (2nd ed.). Palo Alto, CA: Mayfield, pp. 158-169.

Greenspan, M. J., & Feltz, D. L. (1989). Psychological interventions with athletes in competitive situations: A review. *The Sport Psychologist, 3,* 219-236.

Griffiths, T. J., Steele, D. H., Vaccaro, P., & Karpman, M. B. (1981). The effects of relaxation techniques on anxiety and underwater performance. *International Journal of Sport Psychology, 12,* 176-182.

Hackfort, D. & Schwenkmezger, P. (1993). Anxiety. In R. N. Singer, M. Murphy, & L. K. Tennant (Eds.) *Handbook of Research on Sport Psychology.* New York: Macmillan, pp. 328-364.

Hall, C. R., Rodgers, W. M., & Barr, K. A. (1990). The use of imagery by athletes in selected sports. *The Sport Psychologist, 4,* 1-10.

Hall, E. G., & Hardy, C. J. (1991). Ready, aim, fire - Relaxation strategies for enhancing pistol marksmanship. *Perceptual and Motor Skills, 72,* 775-786.

Hansen, J. C., Rossberg, R. H., & Cramer, S. H. (1994). *Counseling Theory and Process.* Boston, MA: Houghton Mifflin.

Hansen, J. C., Stevic, R. R., & Warner, R. W. (1972). *Counseling: Theory and Process.* Boston, MA: Allyn and Bacon, Inc.

Heil, J. (1995). Imagery. In K. P. Henschen and W. F. Straub (Eds.). *Sport Psychology: An Analysis of Athlete Behavior.* Lonymeadow, MA: Monument Publications. pp. 183-191.

Henschen, K. P., & Straub, W. F. (1995). *Sport Psychology: An Analysis of Athlete Behavior.* (3rd ed.). Lonymeadow, MA: Monument Publications.

Hird, J. S., Landers, D. M., Thomas, J. R., Horan, J. J. (1991).

Physical practice is superior to mental practice in enhancing cognitive and motor task performance. *Journal of Sport & Exercice Psychology, 8,* 281-293.

Jacobsen, E. (1930). *Progressive Relaxation.* Chicago: University of Chicago Press.

Jiang, Z. (1991). The effects of Qi Gong training on post-workout anxiety, mood state, and heart rate recovery of high school swimmers. An unpublished doctoral dissertation. University of Utah, 1991.

Keele, S. W., & Hawkins, H. L. (1982). Explorations of individual differences relevant to high level skill. *Journal of Motor Behavior, 14,* 3-23.

Krenz, E. W. (1983). *Modified Autogenic Training.* Salt Lake City, UT: I.I.P. Associates.

Lanning, L., & Hesanaga, T. (1983). A study of the relationship between the reduction of competitive anxiety and an increase in athletic performance. *International Journal of Sport Psychology, 14,* 219-227.

Mahoney, M., Gabriel, T., & Perkins, A. (1998). Psychological skills and exceptional athletic performance. *The Sport Psychologist, 1,* 181-199.

Martin, J., Hiebert, B. A. (1985). *Instructional Counseling—A Method for Counselors.* Pittsburgh, PA: University of Pittsburgh Press.

Ming, S., & Martins, G. L. (1996). Single-subject evaluation of a self-talk package for improving figure skating performance. *The Sport Psychologist, 10,* 227-238.

Moran, A. (1993). Conceptual and methodological issues in the measurement of Mental imagery skills in athletes. *Journal of Sport Behavior, 16,* 156-170.

Moritz, S. E., Hall, C. R., Martin, K. A., & Valoez, E. (1996). What are confident athletes imaging? An examination of image content. *The Sport Psychologist, 10,* 171-179.

Muangnapoe, P., & Morris, T. (1997). Thc effects of meditation and relaxation on perceived uncertainty and perceived importance. Proceedings for IX World Congress of Sport Psychology. Israel. 510-512.

Murphy, S. (1990). Models of imagery in sport psychology: A review. *Journal of Mental Imagery, 14,* pp 153-173.

Murphy, S. M. (Ed.). (1995). *Sport Psychology Interventions.* Champaign, IL: Human Kinetics.

Nideffer, R. M. (1985). *Athlete's Guide to Mental Training.* Champaign, IL: Human Kinetics.

Nideffer, R. M. (1989). *Attention Control Training for Sport.* Los Gatos, CA: Enhanced Performance Services.

Ogilvie, B. & Greene, D. (1994). *Competitive Styles Manual.* Los Gatos, CA: Pro Mind Institute.

Orlick, T. (1986). *Psyching for Sport: Mental Training for Athletes.* Champaign, IL: Leisure Press.

Reardon, J. P. (1995). Handling the self talk of athletes. In K. P. Henschen and W. F. Straub (Eds.). *Sport Psychology: An Analysis of Athlete Behavior.* Lonymeadow, MA: Monument Publications. pp. 203-211.

Rogers, C. R. (1959). A theory of therapy, personality, and interpersonal relationships as developed in the client-centered framework. In S. Koch (Ed.). *Psychology: A Study of Science.* (Vol. 3). New York: McGraw-Hill.

Rogers, C. R. (1980). *A Way of Being.* Boston, MA: Allyn and Bacon.

Rushall, B. S., & Shewchuk, M. L. (1989). Effects of thought content instructions on swimming performance. *Journal of Sports Medicine and Physical Fitness, 29,* 326-335.

Rushall, B. S., Hall, M., Roux, L., Sasseville, J. I., & Rushall, A. S. (1988). Effects of three types of thought content instructions in skiing performance. *The Sport Psychologist, 2,* 283-297.

Solberg, E. E., Berglund, K., Engen, O., Ekberg, O., & Loeb, M. (1996). The effect of meditation on shooting performance. *British Journal of Sports Medicine, 30,* 342-346.

Spielberger, C. D., Gorsuch, R. L., & Lushene, R. E. (1970). *Manual for the State—Trait Anxiety Inventory.* Palo Alto, CA: Consulting Psychological Press.

Starkes, J. L., & Allard, F. (1983). Perception in volleyball: The effects of competitive stress. *Journal of Sport Psychology, 5,* 189-196.

Weinberg, R., Seabourne, T., & Jackson, A. (1981). Effects of visuo-motor behavior rehearsal, relaxation, and imagery on karate performance. *Journal of Sport Psychology, 3,* 228-238.

Courtesy of U.S. Army

1.3

A Critical Analysis of Applied Imagery Research

NICHOLA CALLOW AND LEW HARDY

What Is Imagery?

Imagery has been defined as "an experience that mimics real experience. We can be aware of "seeing" an image, feeling movements as an image, or experiencing an image of smell, tastes, or sounds without actually experiencing the real thing... It differs from dreams in that we are awake and conscious when we form an image" (White & Hardy, 1998, p. 389).

This definition highlights the fact that imagery is a sensory experience in which the real world can be represented using combinations of different sensory modalities. According to Short, Bruggeman, Engel, Marback, Wang, Willadsen, and Short. (2002), imagery is one of the most popular techniques used in psychological skills training within sport. Indeed, athletes report its use for a wide variety of functions including the rehearsal of skills and/or enhancing confidence (e.g., Martin, Moritz, & Hall, 1999). Due to its prevalent use, and the importance placed on imagery by elite performers (Greenleaf, Gould, & Dieffenbach, 2001), it is vital that imagery interventions are delivered in such a way as to maximize their effectiveness. However, researchers (e.g., Hardy, 1997; Holmes & Collins, 2002) have proposed that some of the applied recommendations offered for imagery interventions are based on questionable theoretical and empirical foundations. Thus, in this chapter, we attempt to critically analyze the research literature pertaining to factors that may contribute to the effectiveness of imagery interventions. More specifically, we have two purposes: 1) to highlight what is known, what might be known, and what is not known, with regard to effective imagery interventions; and 2) to propose future research questions, which, if examined, would provide useful information regarding the delivery of imagery interventions.

Effectiveness of Imagery Interventions

Numerous studies have explored the efficacy of imagery, focusing mainly on its effects on the acquisition and performance of motor skills (see Driskell,

Copper, & Moran, 1994; Feltz & Landers, 1983; Jones & Stuth, 1997 for reviews). However, very few studies have actually explored the effects of imagery intervention training programs on performance (cf. Martin et al., 1999). Indeed, an on line literature search from 1980 to November 12, 2001, (using PsychINFO, Sport Discus and Social Sciences Citation Index [SSCI]) identified only seven intervention studies that employed imagery exclusively as the independent variable, with performance as the dependent variable.

Comparison of these seven studies reveals equivocal findings for the effectiveness of the interventions examined. To summarize briefly, Mumford and Hall (1985) examined the effect of an intervention consisting of four one-hour imagery sessions on ice-skating performance. No significant differences were found on post-performance tests between the imagery groups and the control group. Similarly, Rogers, Hall, and Buckolz (1991) explored the effects of a 12-week imagery intervention on ice-skating performance and found no significant differences between the imagery, verbal strategy, and control groups on performance measures. Burhans, Richman, and Bergey (1988) assessed the effects of a 12-week imagery intervention on long distance running speed. The only significant result found was at four weeks, where running speeds in the imagery (skills) group were found to be superior relative to the control group. However, no significant differences were evident between the imagery skills, imagery results, combined imagery skills/results, and control groups at the end of the 12 week period. Conversely, when Blair, Hall, and Leyshon (1993) conducted a six-week imagery training program, a significant increase was found between the control and imagery group in response time for a soccer task, but not for performance accuracy of the same task. Isaac (1985) examined the effect of three six-week training periods on trampoline skill. Significant effects for performance were found for the imagery group in comparison to the control group. Using a multiple baseline design, Shambrook and Bull (1996) found a significant increase in basketball performance for only one participant out of four. In the first study of Hardy and Callow (1999) the effect of an imagery intervention involving six one-hour imagery sessions on a kata performance was explored. Results suggested that external visual imagery was significantly more effective than internal visual imagery, but both visual perspectives were significantly more effective than stretching.

The highlighted studies clearly reveal equivocal findings, although the reasons for these equivocal findings are not obvious. In order to identify these reasons, the wider imagery research literature needs to be examined. Scrutiny of this literature indicates that, despite a wealth of information in the area of imagery (cf. Hall, 2001), the imagery research base fails to take mediating variables into account (cf., Murphy, 1990); its research design is often flawed (cf., Goginsky & Collins, 1996); it lacks empirically tested theories (cf., Hardy, Jones, & Gould, 1996); and the functions of imagery have not been clearly differentiated (cf., Rushall & Lipman, 1998). These four factors have led to equivocal research findings (cf., Moran, 1993; Wollman, 1986) and misinterpretations of research literature (cf., Hardy, 1997). We will now examine these four factors in greater depth.

Moderators/Mediators of Imagery Effectiveness

To clarify the results of imagery research, Feltz and Landers (1983), Hinshaw (1991), and Driskell et al., (1994) conducted meta-analyses of the research literature. These researchers found effect sizes of .48, .68, and .26, respectively, indicating that imagery can have a small to large effect on performance. The relative difference in these effect sizes can be attributed to the different criteria that were used to code imagery studies for inclusion into the meta-analyses. Driskell et al. state that any interpretations based on the results of Feltz and Landers (1983) needs to be viewed with caution because they included mental practice studies that examined independent variables other than imagery such as psyching-up strategies (e.g., Shelton & Mahoney, 1987). Further to this, the results of Hinshaw's analysis should also be viewed with caution because of the small number of studies included in the meta-analysis. Despite the differences in effect sizes from these meta-analyses, the received view is that imagery enhances the acquisition and performance of motor skills (e.g., Hardy, 1997; Vealey, 1994). It has also been proposed that task type and athlete expertise may moderate the effectiveness of imagery (e.g., Suinn, 1984), and that imagery perspective, imagery ability, and confidence may mediate the effect of imagery on behavior (e.g., Murphy & Jowdy, 1992; Paivio, 1985). Before exploring these variables in more detail, an examination of the conceptual difference between moderating and mediating variables is required. Examination of this conceptual difference establishes that imagery perspective and imagery ability are moderating *not* mediating variables. The following explanation attempts to clarify this issue. For a more detailed examination of the moderator/mediator differentiation refer to Barron and Kenny (1986) and Markland (2000).

A moderating variable alters the effect of an independent variable on a dependent variable with the ensuing pattern of effects being indicative of a factorial interaction. For example, Hardy (1997) suggests that task type may moderate the effect of visual imagery perspectives on performance. Specifically, Hardy proposes that, for tasks requiring form of movement, the use of external visual imagery will produce greater performance gains in comparison to the use of internal visual imagery. In contrast, with tasks that rely heavily on perceptual information, Hardy proposes that the use of internal visual imagery will produce greater performance gains in comparison to the use of external visual imagery.

Conversely, a mediating variable is a mechanism or process through which an independent variable exerts its effect upon a dependent variable. For example, an imagery intervention may improve task performance by increasing the participant's confidence with the task. With this example, confidence is the mediator; it does not change the effect of the independent variable (imagery), rather it is a possible mechanism through which imagery enhances performance.

It is important that the correct conceptual differentiation between moderating and mediating variables occurs within imagery research. This is because experimental designs and statistical analyses should be chosen depending on the type of variable being examined. In the broader sense, using an appropriate design and statistical analysis with a moderating or mediating variable means that causal pathways can be established. With this differentiation in mind, it can be seen that Murphy and Jowdy (1992) should have termed imagery perspective and imagery ability as moderating, not mediating, variables.

Moderating Factors

Imagery perspective

The findings of previous research investigating the effects of different imagery perspectives on motor performance and learning have been somewhat equivocal. For example, Mahoney and Avener (1977) reported that gymnasts who were successful in qualifying for the U.S. Olympic team used internal imagery more than gymnasts who were unsuccessful. However, Meyers, Cooke, Cullen, and Liles (1979) found no significant differences in imagery perspectives between more and less successful racquetball players. Furthermore, Ungerleider and Golding (1991) found that successful U.S. track and field Seoul Olympic trialists used external imagery more than internal imagery, and had stronger physical sensations accompanying their imagery than their unsuccessful colleagues. Despite these conflicting results, many applied consultants recommend using the internal perspective (e.g., Hale, 1998; Weinberg, 1988); or starting with the internal perspective and then progressing onto the external perspective (Miller, 1997). However, recent research brings this advice into question, and provides possible explanations for the equivocal research findings in the area.

One possible explanation for some of these findings is that researchers have confounded internal visual imagery with kinesthetic imagery in the definitions that they have provided for athletes (Hardy, 1997; White & Hardy, 1995). Mahoney and Avener (1977) described internal imagery as "requiring an approximation of the real life phenomenology such that the person actually imagines being inside his/her body and experiencing those sensations which might be expected in the actual situation." Similarly, Mahoney and Avener (1977) appeared to assess gymnasts' use of internal imagery by asking them whether they experienced what the image would feel like in their muscles. As White and Hardy (1995) have indicated, such a question clearly assesses the kinesthetic, rather than the internal visual, component of the performer's image.

Task type

A second possible explanation for some reported result differences is that certain types of imagery are more effective for some tasks than others. Meyers et al. (1979) and Highlen and Bennett (1979) examined the imagery use of participants in racquetball and wrestling, both sports that rely heavily on open skills. However, Mahoney and Avener (1977) examined imagery use in gymnastics, a sport which relies almost exclusively on closed skills. Furthermore, Highlen and Bennett (1979) argued that it may be easier to use imagery in closed skills because performers can image without the external distraction of an opponent. Consequently, the absence of imagery differences reported by Meyers et al. (1979) and Highlen and Bennett (1979), could be due to task differences.

Imagery perspective and task type

Using a pseudo-laboratory study, White and Hardy (1995) explored the effect of imagery perspectives on different tasks. For a task that required form of movement for its successful execution, these researchers found external visual imagery (EVI) to be superior to internal visual imagery (IVI) in both task acquisition and retention trials. However, with a task that relied heavily on perceptual information, participants who used IVI made significantly fewer mistakes on a transfer trial than participants who used EVI; but participants who used EVI performed significantly faster than participants using IVI on both the acquisition and transfer trials. White and Hardy (1995) suggested that this speed-accuracy trade off might have been due to EVI enhancing the competitive drive of the participants. To further examine the imagery perspectives/task issue Hardy and Callow (1999) conducted three field studies. Taken together the results of the three studies provide confirmation that EVI enhances form of movement. They also provide some interesting findings in relation to imagery and the expertise of an athlete that will be discussed in the next section. What is not known is whether, within a field setting, IVI produces superior performance gains for tasks that rely heavily on perceptual information. Future research should examine this question.

Expertise of the athlete

Hardy and Callow's (1999) first study explored the effects of EVI and IVI on the acquisition and retention of a new karate kata; experienced karateists were used as the participants. Kinaesthetic imagery was not manipulated. The results indicated that EVI had superior effects to IVI. Furthermore, the analysis of a post-experimental questionnaire revealed that there were no significant differences in the use of kinesthetic imagery between imagery groups.

The second study explored the effects of visual imagery perspectives and kinesthetic imagery (Kin) on the acquisition and retention of a simple gymnastics floor routine. Relatively unskilled (adult) gymnasts were used as the participants. The results showed a main effect for visual imagery during the acquisition phase with EVI having the superior effect. Additionally, a significant interaction in the retention phase was revealed. However, despite the fact that the group using EVI plus Kin performed better than the group using IVI and Kin, Tukey tests failed to find any significant differences between the groups. Results from a post-experimental questionnaire revealed that participants who received Kin had significantly greater confidence in their ability to perform the task with good form than those participants who did not receive Kin.

The third study examined the effects of visual imagery perspectives and Kin on the performance of four rock-climbing problems. Experienced rock climbers were used as participants. The results indicated that EVI was superior to IVI and Kin was superior to no Kin. Taken together, the results of the three studies offer strong support for the notion that EVI is superior to IVI for the acquisition and performance of this type of task, and, that once performers have acquired a degree of expertise, Kin can contribute an additional beneficial effect on performance. Numerous applied research questions emerge from this area. For example, will the combination of IVI and Kin imagery produce superior performances for experienced performers with tasks that require heavily on perceptual information? At what level of expertise will Kin produce beneficial effects? Would directing a beginner towards the kinesthetic component of performance help them to develop and utilize Kin?

Confidence as a mediating variable and as a dependent variable

Paivio (1985) proposed that imagery might exert its influence upon behavior via both a cognitive and motivational function. Despite researchers proposing the mediating effect of confidence (e.g., Hall, Buckolz, & Fishburne, 1992; Holmes & Collins, 2001) the present authors are not aware of any direct examination of the question: "Does confidence mediate the imagery/performance relationship?" Instead "motivational" imagery research has focused on two different directions. These include: 1) mastery/goal-orientated imagery as the independent variable imagery (i.e., performers imaging themselves being confident); and 2) confidence as the dependent variable.

Moritz, Hall, Martin, and Vadocz (1996) found that high *state* sport-confident athletes used more mastery imagery and arousal imagery (imagining the excitement associated with competing) than their less *state* sport-confident counterparts. Similarly, Abma, Fry, Yuhua, and Relyea (2002) found that high *trait* confident track and field athletes used more mastery and arousal imagery than their less *trait* confident associates. It must be noted that the two previously mentioned studies are correlational in nature, thus causal interpretations can not be determined (Heyman, 1982). That is, it cannot be established if having high self-confidence causes performers to use Motivational General-Mastery imagery, or using Motivational General-Mastery imagery causes an increase in confidence, or, alternatively, some other variable causes both. However, the following four studies provide some evidence on the causal direction of the motivational imagery/confidence relationship.

Martin and Hall (1995) examined the effect of performance plus outcome imagery or performance imagery on intrinsic motivation and self-efficacy. Participants in the performance imagery group spent significantly more time practicing in comparison to the performance plus outcome imagery group or the control group, but there was no difference in self-efficacy between the groups. In contrast, using a multiple-baseline across participants design, Callow, Hardy, and Hall (2001) found significant effects for imagery on state sport confidence. Specifically, using a multiple-baseline across participants design,

the effects of a Motivational General-Mastery imagery intervention on the sport confidence of four high level junior badminton players was examined. Results of visual inspection and Binomial tests[1] suggested significant increases in sport confidence for Participants 1 and 2, a significant decrease in sport confidence for Participant 3, and a delayed increase in sport confidence for Participant 4. These results provide initial confirmation that motivational imagery can enhance confidence.

A recent nomothetic study examined the effects of imagery type (mastery imagery or imaging skills) and imagery direction (facilitative or debilitative) on self-efficacy and golf putting performance (Short et al., 2002). Partial support was provided for the notion that mastery imagery enhances self-efficacy. Specifically, for females, a mastery imagery group had higher self-efficacy ratings than both the control group and cognitive specific group (i.e., imaging skills). Whereas, for males, the cognitive specific group had higher self-efficacy than the mastery and the control group.

An interesting observation is made when examining the imagery scripts employed in the Short et al. (2002) study. As the extract below highlights, it can be seen that kinesthetic imagery was incorporated into the mastery imagery script. "Concentrate on how your body is feeling: your body feels strong, you can feel the strength and energy surge with every breath you take. When people look at you, they see a confident golfer." (p. 56). Thus, it could have been the kinesthetic imagery that enhanced confidence, rather than the mastery or cognitive content. Indeed, recent research suggests that kinesthetic imagery enhances confidence. Specifically, Callow and Waters (in press) conducted a multiple-baseline design to examine the effects of kinesthetic imagery on the sport confidence of three professional flat-race horse jockeys. The data were analyzed using ITSACORR (Crosbie, 1993). ITSACORR is a statistical method for analyzing serially-dependent single-subject data that overcomes the problems associated with binomial tests. A significant increase in sport confidence was revealed for two participants, and a non-significant increase in sport confidence was revealed for the third participant.

[1] Refer to Callow and Waters (in press) for a criticism of the use of the Binomial test with serially dependant single-subject data.

Taken together, the previous four studies suggest that imagery type (e.g., mastery imagery) and imagery modality (e.g., visual/kinesthetic) can positively affect confidence. However, a number of interesting applied questions remain. Specifically, future research should examine the nature of the following possible interactions of gender and imagery type upon self-confidence, and imagery modality and imagery type. For example, does imagery modality moderate the mastery imagery/confidence relationship in high-level performers?

More Moderating Variables

Imagery research has been criticized because of the variation in methodological parameters within imagery studies. Differences in imagery instructions, distribution of imagery, and duration of imagery practice have been identified as the possible causes of inconsistent findings within imagery research (cf. Goginsky & Collins, 1996; Moran, 1993). Failure to produce systematically designed studies, based on previous findings, leads to a difficulty in assembling facts and interpreting the correct parameters required for an effective imagery intervention. We do not propose that methodological variation per se should be reduced, as variety is required to answer questions. However, we propose that researchers should acknowledge and be mindful of how methodological parameters can moderate the effectiveness of imagery, so that these moderating factors can be ruled out as confounding variables. With regard to the current imagery research literature, specific conclusions can be drawn with regard to imagery and the moderating effect of relaxation prior to imagery, imagery ability, and the timing of imagery, on performance.

Imagery practice conditions
Driskell et al's 1994 meta-analysis demonstrated a small effect size for imagery on performance. In an attempt to examine the imagery practice conditions that produce the most positive effects on performance Driskell et al. (1994) focused on the following three conditions of imagery: the number of trials or sessions of imagery, the total duration of imagery practice, and the retention interval between imagery and performance. No significant relationship was found between the number of practice trials and the magnitude of the imagery effect ($r = .019$, $z = 0.214$, $p > .10$). However, a significant negative relationship was found between the duration of imagery and the magnitude of effect ($r = -.185$, $p = .03$). Driskel et al. report that a mean effect size of .261 may be attained with a length of practice of approx 20.8 min, but after this length of time the beneficial effects are reduced. A significant negative relationship between the length of the retention interval and the magnitude of the imagery-performance effect ($r = -.216$, $z = 2.453$, $p < .01$) was also found. Of interest is the fact that the initial effects of imagery are reduced to approximately one-half of their initial magnitude if the retention period is extended from immediately after imagery practice to 14 days, with the decay accelerating after four days. Although the results from the meta-analysis provide evidence for the most effective imagery practice conditions, a quasi-experimental design examining whether these imagery practice conditions do, in fact, lead to optimal acquisition and retention effects would be particularly pertinent.

Relaxation
Applied texts (e.g., Suinn, 1980; Syer & Connolly, 1998) often advocate relaxation prior to the use of imagery. Results from Hinshaw's (1991) meta-analysis have been used to support this view (e.g., Suinn, 1997). However, although Hinshaw did calculate the effect size of studies involving imagery with relaxation ($r = .84$) and the effect size of studies involving imagery without relaxation (.65), due to the unequal number of studies in these two groups, statistical comparison of the effect sizes was not conducted. Hinshaw herself contends that the relaxation results are merely exploratory, and, due to the lack of a reported statistical difference, any interpretation of the findings should be viewed with caution.

White (1996) and Holmes and Collins (2001) note that, although relaxing prior to imagery may have cognitive benefits (e.g., clearing the mind of distractions), the somatic influence of relaxation may conflict with the desired somatic state for performance. For example, a center in rugby union, imaging a rugby tackle, may not want to be somatically relaxed prior to the image because a certain level of physiological arousal is required to perform a task of this nature (cf. Parfitt, Jones, & Hardy, 1990). Indeed,

Gray, Haring, and Banks (1984) contend that relaxation prior to imagery may have a negative effect on performance because a "reduced" somatic state may inhibit the possible transfer effects of the imagery to physical performance.

Imagery ability

Imagery ability has been suggested to possess two principal characteristics; vividness and controllability (e.g., Start & Richardson, 1964). Vividness relates to the participant's self-report of clarity and reality in the image, and controllability to the control that the participant has over the image. Within the sport domain, the use of subjective tests to measure imagery ability is a common practice, with the two most popular tests being the Vividness of Movement Questionnaire (VMIQ; Isaac, Marks, & Russell, 1986) and the Movement of Imagery Questionnaire (MIQ; Hall & Pongrac, 1983). Only a few studies have investigated the effect of imagery ability on performance. Isaac (1985) examined the effect of three six-week training periods on trampoline skill. Irrespective of skill level, higher ability imagers improved significantly more than low ability imagers. Based on MIQ scores, Goss, Hall, Buckolz and Fishburne (1986) and Hall, Buckolz, and Fishburne (1989) classified participants in terms of imagery ability. The former study revealed that imagery ability was significantly related to the acquisition and retention of movement patterns. The latter study revealed no significant differences in high and low imagers for the recall of movement patterns; however, higher imagery ability participants were more accurate in their reproduction of movement patterns. These three studies support Mark's (1977) suggestion that, irrespective of skill level, when using imagery, the variable of importance (when learning new tasks) is imagery ability. However, an important question remains unanswered, at what imagery ability level do particular imagery interventions become most effective?

Timing of imagery

To ease the transfer from imagery to real life, it is generally recommended that imagery be performed in real time, at the speed at which athletes actually perform the actions (e.g., Bull, Albinson, & Shambrook, 1996; Nideffer, 1985). However, the theoretical foundation and empirical evidence that substantiates this advice is limited. To bridge this gap, Boschker, Bakker, and Rietberg (2000) examined the effect of imaging at different speeds on subsequent actual performance. Participants who imaged at a slow speed showed a reduction in speed during the retention test (relative to the baseline test), whereas participants who imaged at a fast speed showed an increase in speed during the retention test. The effect was greater for the slow group. Thus, if temporal patterning is important for performance of the task, the advocacy of imagery in real time seems justified. However, further examination reveals that this issue may be more complex. Firstly, if slow motion imagery produces slower performance in transfer, then this might be a useful strategy for skills that are sometimes rushed under stressful conditions, for example, a golf swing. Secondly, certain applied texts (e.g., Taylor, 1993) advise that athletes should use slow motion imagery to examine technique and correct problems. Indeed, this method has been used successfully by one of the present authors to help an international windsurfer identify where and how a technique should be refined. Recently, Calmels and Fournier (2001) noted that elite gymnasts imaged difficult elements of a routine slower than the easier elements, and post-experimental discussion with the gymnasts confirmed that they perceived the difficult elements to be difficult. These researchers interpreted their results to be in line with a finding of White and Hardy (1998) namely, that elite gymnasts used imagery to improve self-confidence "if there was a degree of uncertainty about the performance outcome, such as when a move was perceived to be difficult" (p. 400). As the gymnasts were elite, they did not need to slow the whole routine down to learn it. Rather, they appeared to slow certain elements down so that they could see themselves successfully performing the task. If the gymnasts were able to see themselves successfully perform the task, then this performance accomplishment information might enhance their confidence (cf. Bandura, 1997; Callow et al., 2001). Consequently, the use of slow motion imagery may relate to the function that it is to play. We will return to the issue of the function of an image in the next section. As Hardy et al. (1996) suggest, it is clear that more needs to be known about the appropriateness of using different speeds of imagery for different purposes. Indeed, many questions remain unanswered, for example, does slow motion imagery aid confidence/performance for specific tasks? Does slow motion imagery aid the performance of specific tasks in "stressful" conditions?

Other Factors That Might be Important for Imagery Effectiveness

From the preceding critique it is apparent that there are moderating and mediating factors that may influence the effectiveness of imagery. Research also indicates that there are other factors that might be important for imagery effectiveness; namely, the outcomes of images, the content of imagery scripts, the concurrent use of actual physical practice, the use of simulated physical practice, the use of videos, and the nature of imagery instructions. These factors will now be explored.

Outcome of imagery

Nearly all imagery studies published to date have focused on the participant imaging some form of success, be it memorizing a movement or learning a skill successfully. Indeed, athletes are frequently advised to only image positive outcomes (e.g., Murphy & Jowdy, 1992). This advice is based on research suggesting that poorer performance is associated with negative (or debilitative) images (e.g., Powell, 1973; Short et al., 2002; Woolfolk, Parrish, & Murphy, 1985). However, anecdotal evidence indicates that athletes do use negative imagery. For example, prior to the 1996 Badminton World Championships Peter Rasmussen imagined himself losing, so that he could become comfortable with the concept of losing, and gain an understanding that it was his expectations were important (Eaton, 1997). Rasmussen went on to win the final against Sun Jun. Negative imagery is often used within the clinical literature in systemic desensitization. Specifically, imagery is used to recreate anxiety-provoking situations, and the client then learns to relax in response to these scenes. Positive effects on behavior have been demonstrated with this method (e.g., Jones & River, 1997). In the present authors' opinion, it might not be the direction of the imagery that is important (i.e., positive or negative imagery) rather it might be the function and meaning of the image that are important.

The function of an image relates to the purpose that an image may have for a performer. For example, a footballer might image taking a penalty kick in football for the function of improving her technical proficiency (cognitive function) or for the function of psyching herself up (motivational function). The meaning of an image relates to the interpretation placed on the image. The footballer may image taking a penalty kick for the function of improving skill, but the image may be interpreted as being a challenge or a threat. Hale and Whitehouse (1998) found that if the situation participants were imagining was manipulated to be a pressure situation, they had less confidence in successfully achieving the task than those who had the same situation manipulated to be a challenge. Although researchers have generally defined imagery function by the imagery content (i.e., the type of imagery), with cognitive types of imagery being related to cognitive functions and motivational types of imagery being related to motivational functions, and recent research alludes to the notion that athletes' type and function of imagery are generally congruent (Short, Monsma, & Short, 2004), the research by Hale and Whitehouse (1998) demonstrates that cognitive imagery can be interpreted in such away as to have both a cognitive and motivational function. Thus the following question needs to be examined in relation to the different types of imagery. Does the meaning of an image moderate the imagery type/imagery function relationship?

Scripts

One of the most common ways to elicit an image in an athlete is through the use of imagery scripts. For example, the athlete has a script of a situation read to them and they then try and image the scene (for example scripts see Syer & Connolly, 1996). Based on Lang's (1977) bio-informational theory of emotional imagery, researchers have proposed that specific types of propositions should be included within imagery scripts. Lang proposes that an emotional image contains two fundamental classes of statements: stimulus propositions and response propositions. Stimulus propositions describe the content of the scenario to be imagined, for example, the physical details of a situation. Response propositions contain assertions about behavior, for example, verbal responses, somatic and visceral responses. Researchers have demonstrated that images that contain response propositions are likely to produce more vivid images (Lang, Kozak, Miller, Levin, & McLean, 1980) and to elicit more physical responses (EMG activity) than images that contain only stimulus propositions (Bakker, Boschker, & Chung, 1996). Implicit within this, is that greater physical responses have more beneficial effects on performance because the muscles are more prepared for efficient response (cf., Slade, Landers, & Martin, 2002). Clearly, future research is warranted to explore this proposal.

With reference to writing scripts, we concur with the advice of Collins and Hale (1997) that the terminology used in imagery scripts should reflect that used by athletes. In particular, it is proposed that response propositions should fit the movements, so that the athlete can identify with the image. Further to this, Holmes and Collins (2001) make an interesting point with regard to the fact that verbal and written imagery scripts direct conscious attention to task relevant cues, and that "athletes rarely report comprehensive conscious, verbal reports of good performances in visuomotor terms" (p. 68). Three issues arise from this statement. First, we agree that athletes sometimes have difficulty in verbally reporting good performances, but this is because of the difficulty in verbally *accessing* the automatic procedural knowledge used to produce high level performance (e.g., Anderson, 1993). Secondly, the majority of imagery research has explored the effect of imagery on learning. Therefore, if *learning* is the function of the image, then directing athletes towards task relevant cues through an imagery script makes sense from a cognitive learning perspective (cf. Magill, 2001). Third, if the function of the imagery is to maintain or produce good performance, then the use of task relevant verbal cues may cause the athlete to lapse into conscious control (of both imagery and task), and this could disrupt the automatized task (Keele, 1973; Langer & Imber, 1979). Indeed, Qualls (1982) found that the nature of imagery instruction has an impact on the response pattern generated. Further, Qualls suggested that spontaneously generated images, rather than those produced by prescriptive explicit instruction may be even more effective because the explicit instructions may stop spontaneity. The use of holistic process-oriented scripts (written in conjunction with the athlete) may overcome the problem of prescriptive scripts, as the holistic scripts can be written in such away that allows the athlete to generate their own holistic image (see Hardy et al., 1996 for a similar argument relating to goal-setting). Examples of holistic scripts do already exist (e.g., Hale, 1998, p. 43). However, the following question remains, does the use of "task relevant" scripts cause a performer to "lapse" into conscious control?

Use of actual and simulated physical activity

Research has shown that actual physical activity plus imagery is more effective than imagery alone (e.g., Feltz & Landers, 1983; Kohl, Ellis, & Roenker, 1992). However, from a research perspective the addition of physical performance changes the focus of research from the effects of imagery on performance to the relationship between imagery and practice as they relate to performance. From an applied perspective this combined use seems to be appropriate, but in many situations actual physical practice is not possible. In this situation, the use of simulated physical practice and imagery would be advised because it is proposed that this method aids in the perfection of the imagery (Orlick, 1990, p. 71-72). Gould and Damarjian (1996, p. 39) take this a step further, and state that the use of sporting equipment and replication of physical movements increases the vividness of the imagery by enabling performers to more easily recall the sensations associated with their performance. To the best of our knowledge there is no published empirical literature within the sport domain to support this. However, mainstream psychology researchers have provided evidence to suggest that physical actions do in fact facilitate imagery. For example, Schwartz and Holton, (2000) found that pulling a string from a spool facilitated participants' mental rotation of an object sitting on the spool in comparison to the no action group. The researchers proposed that mental models of tools help people imagine how one movement causes a second movement within a physical situation and that learned knowledge may mediate the effect of action on imagery. Indeed, the use of physical simulation and sports equipment, while imaging, has been advised by one of the present authors when working with elite slalom kayakers. Competing slalom kayakers are given a map of the course that they are to race, they are able to see the course, and watch demonstrators going down the course, but they are not allowed to "get on the water" to practice the course. In this situation, the kayakers were advised to walk down the riverbank, paddle in hand, imaging and physically simulating the movements that they were going to take with the paddle in order to follow the best line down the course. Following the results of Schwartz and Holton (2000), if a kayaker uses the paddle (the tool) to physically simulate the movements that he will conduct while paddling the course, this may facilitate the imagery of the movement of his kayak, as paddle movement is a major factor in determining kayak movement. Indeed, the simulation technique proved particularly popular and successful with the kayakers. Clearly, future research examining the effectiveness of "in vivo" imagery (i.e., conducting imagery in the sport situation) is warranted.

Use of videos and imagery instructions

Gould and Damarjian (1996, p. 39) recommended that athletes support their imagery with the use of video taped recordings of themselves performing. Holmes and Collins (2001) suggested that the use of videos might help in the generation of the content of the imagery by making it as multisensory as possible. However, there is little empirical evidence to support this claim. Nevertheless, the examination of research relating to the technique of combining imagery and relaxation, that is, visuomotor behavior rehearsal (VMBR: Suinn, 1972), can help in drawing inferences with regard to the use of videos. For example, Hall and Erffmeyer (1983) examined the effect of VMBR plus video-taped modeling on basketball free throw performance in highly skilled performers. A significant effect was found for free throw performance for the VMBR plus video-taped modeling group, in comparison to the VMBR alone group. Interestingly, all participants in the VMBR plus video-taped modeling group reported kinesthetic sensations associated with their imagery. Similarly, Gray (1990) found a significant increase in novice racquetball players' forehand shot, but not backhand shot, in a VMBR plus video-taped modeling group in comparison to the VMBR group. Because imagery and relaxation were combined in these studies, any interpretations relating to imagery per se should be viewed with caution because it cannot be established if the video modeling was interacting with the relaxation, imag-

ery, a combination of both or simply having a separate main effect. Clearly, more research is needed in the area, especially as the study by Hall and Erffmeyer (1983) seems to support the contention that video-taped modeling should be used with imagery because it may increase the kinesthetic sensations associated with imagery.

Other research within the modeling literature relating to the "picture" that a performer sees may have implications for improving imagery. For example, Maile (cited in Franks & Maile, 1991) used self-modeling to train a nationally ranked power lifter. Maile produced edited videotapes to make it appear that the performer was lifting more weight than they had actually had done previously. Performance gains were significant using this technique, even though the athlete was aware of the editing. Orlick (1986) has reported that performers often have difficulty imaging themselves achieving something they have not yet actually done. Thus, if a video could be edited so the performer was actually carrying out the tasks that they could not do, and they were to view this prior to imagery, it may aid them with their imagery. Research conducted by Yamamoto and Inomata (1982) relates to the importance for performers to be able to "complete" their images for tasks that they are learning. Specifically, these researchers presented part verses whole demonstrations of swimming skills to participants prior to having them create an image of the skill. A non-significant decrease in swimming speed was found for the whole demonstration group. Yamamoto and Inomata (1982) argued that the novice performer could not create the whole image from the part presentation, and as a consequence the image was incomplete and less effective. The decrease in swimming speed demonstrates that this *may* be a fruitful area for future research. In particular, if video footage is being used to help to create an image of a situation, how much video information does a novice require to recreate an accurate image?

Surburg (1968) examined the effects of different delivery methods of imagery instruction on imagery and the forehand tennis drive. It was found that those who received audio instruction had greater performance benefits and more controllable images in comparison to those who had visual and audio-visual imagery instruction. Through post-hoc interpretations the researchers suggest that the audio imagery instructions gave the participants the opportunity to receive and interpret the information prior to their creating their own actual visual image, whereas because the visual groups did not have to create their images (because they were supplied with an actual visual image), they had lower controllability of the image. There could be other explanations for the results. For example, the audio instructions might have caused contextual interference when trying to create the visual image. This contextual interference could, perhaps, have increased the controllability of the imagery, and the transfer of the effects to the task (cf. Schmidt, 1982). More recently, Smith and Holmes (2004) examined the effect of different imagery intervention delivery methods on golf-putting performance in experienced golfers. A significant positive performance effect was found for the videotaped imagery intervention and the audiotaped imagery intervention in comparison to the placebo-control intervention; however, there was no significant difference between the written imagery script intervention and the placebo-control intervention. Based on the notion of functional equivalence (Jeannerod, 1999) the researchers proposed that, in comparison to the written imagery script intervention and placebo-control group, the videotaped and audiotaped "imagery" stimulated more of the neural pathways involved in the execution of the task, and, as a consequence of this "extra" stimulation, the imagery was more beneficial in strengthening the neural pathways, which in turn produced the positive performance effects. At a theoretical level this proposal is plausible. However, as the authors contend, in order to establish the mechanism(s) by which the performance effects are gained, future research needs to examine the vividness and controllablity of the imagery experienced, and the brain activity during the different delivery methods. Another finding of interest from the study relates to the fact that the written imagery script intervention participants reported problems with timing during their imagery of the task, and that the script interfered with the control of the image. Perhaps the scripts were disrupting the automaticity of timing; this finding and its interpretation provides further support for the importance of examining the use of holistic verses task-relevant scripts by experienced performers.

Theoretical Underpinnings

Psychoneuromuscular theory and the Symbolic Learning theory

Traditionally, two predominant theories have been used within the sports domain to explain how imagery might exert its effects upon performance, Psychoneuromuscular theory and Symbolic Learning theory. The Psychoneuromuscular theory (Jacobson, 1930) proposes that the muscles involved in the skill being imaged become slightly innervated, and, that these innervations provide kinesthetic feedback that strengthens existing motor programs. Jacobson (1930) demonstrated that low-level innervations do occur in the muscle that is being imaged. However, some researchers suggest that the muscular response is indicative of a more general arousal (e.g., Shaw, 1938) and that muscle activity during actual and imaginary practice is not, in fact, similar (Slade et al., 2002). Furthermore, it has yet to be demonstrated that there is a relationship between muscle activity during imagery and subsequent performance. The lack of controlled research supporting this theory has led many researchers to question the parsimony of the theory to explain the processes involved in imagery associated improvements in motor performance (e.g., Hecker & Kaczor, 1988; Murphy & Jowdy, 1992).

Symbolic Learning theory proposes that imagery allows the performer to cognitively prepare for and plan performance (e.g., Minas, 1980; Wrisberg & Ragsdale, 1979) and that imagery therefore exerts its effect at a higher level of control. Two specific predictions of the theory have been tested. Firstly, that the efficacy of imagery is dependent on the extent of the cognitive element of the task. There has been some support for this contention in the research literature (Minas, 1978). However, other studies have found large imagery effects for motor tasks with few symbolic elements (e.g., Woolfolk, Parrish, & Murphy, 1985). Secondly, the Symbolic Learning theory predicts that imagery effects will occur in the early stages of learning rather than later stages of learning because cognitive cues are more frequently utilized in the early stages (Fitts, 1962). This prediction has received little support in the research literature as imagery effects have been found in both the early and later stages of learning (Corbin, 1967; Wrisberg

& Ragsdale, 1979). The theory leaves many questions unanswered; for example, the theory does not explain how performance is enhanced in experienced athletes. Indeed, Murphy and Jowdy (1992) contend that the theory is too simplistic and does not provide a rigorous explanation of where beneficial effects actually occur.

Without a set of guiding principles provided by a rigorously tested theory, imagery research has lacked progressive direction. Consequently, the research area has failed to develop a systematic and heuristic profile, making it difficult to assemble a knowledge base that can then be used to substantiate, refute, or refine the predictions of the theory. The magnitude of this problem has been further exasperated by the large number of potential effects that imagery can have, making it difficult to develop an all encompassing theory to explain the many potential effects that imagery might produce.

However, alternative theories have recently been used to explain the effects of imagery. Three of these are: Ahsen's triple code model for imagery and psychophysiology (1984); Lang's bio-informational theory of emotional imagery (1977; 1979; 1984); and Bandura's self-efficacy theory (1977; 1986; 1997). The adoption and integration of specific tenants from these theories has provided the foundation for two useful models for the applied context. These are Martin et al.'s (1999) Applied Model of Mental Imagery Use and Holmes and Collin's (2001) PETTLEP model. These three theories and two applied models will be examined in more detail in the following subsections.

Ahsen's Triple Code Model (1984)

Ahsen's triple code model (1984) deals specifically with interconnections between the image (I), the psychophysiological response (S) and the meaning of the image (M). The I, S, and M factors may combine in various orders (e.g., ISM; IMS; SIM); each order serves various operations. The most natural and useful order of the triple code model is the ISM (Ahsen, 1984); that is, the evocation of a visual image (or another sensory image) is followed by a somatic response, and then by a meaning. The image serves as the central mode from which a somatic response is produced, and a significance or meaning is imparted. The model overcomes the failure of Paivio's (1971) dual code theory to acknowledge the significance of the somatic response that can be associated with the imagery, and the general failure of imagery researchers to recognize the importance of the meaning of images to performers.

Despite the intuitive appeal of the model, it does not explain the underlying processes and mechanisms of how and why imagery may alter behavior. Furthermore, the ISM model is based on clinical examples rather than empirically tested research. In addition, it is the authors' opinion, that Ahsen's model was superseded by Lang's bio-informational theory (1977) when Lang's theory was developed and then subsequently modified (1984) to include the meaning of an image.

Lang's Bio-informational Processing Theory

In 1977, Lang proposed his bio-informational theory of emotional imagery; in 1984 the theory was modified to provide a more general framework for understanding affective behavior. The 1984 theory assumes an image to be a functionally organized, finite set of propositions (statements) stored by the brain. To this end, an image can contain three main types of propositions: stimulus propositions, response propositions, and meaning propositions. Stimulus propositions are statements that describe the content of the image; response propositions describe the imager's overt and covert response to the image; and meaning propositions are analytical in nature and interpret the meaning of the image to the imager. Response propositions are hypothesized to be double coded in that their deep structure is linked to the motor command system that generates efferent output. The complete set of propositions is organized into an associative network, and the associated motor program contains instructions for how the imager is to respond.

Lang (1979) has demonstrated that imagery is accompanied by an efferent outflow, which is EMG activity. Further, more vivid images produce a greater magnitude of physiological response, and greater changes in accompanying behavior (Lang, Melamed, & Hart, 1970). Thus, modifying or creating a vivid image will result in changing the overt behavior of the imager and visa versa. Lang's theory provides a possible explanation of how and why imagery may work. This explanation requires empirical verification in the field of sport psychology; however, recent research evidence with regard to stimulus and response propositions has produced tentative support for Lang's theory in a sport setting. Bakker et al. (1996) found that participants who had received a response proposition imagery script had greater EMG activity during the imagery of a biceps curl, than participants who had received a stimulus imagery script, suggesting that Lang's model is applicable to emotionally neutral movement imagery.

Bandura's Self-Efficacy theory (1977)

Bandura's self-efficacy theory (1977; 1986; 1997) could be used to explain the motivational effects of imagery. Bandura (1997) states that four sources of information can serve to increase an individual's self-efficacy; that is, enactive mastery, vicarious experience, verbal persuasion, and emotional and affective state. Techniques that provide the performcr with mastery or vicarious experience such as video feedback and modeling (watching someone else successfully perform a skill) have been shown to increase self-efficacy in sport settings (Feltz, 1982; Gould & Weiss, 1981; McAuley, 1985). Since imagery can provide both mastery and vicarious information (depending upon the degree of identification with the image), imagery has been suggested as a strategy to enhance the self-efficacy of sports performers because imagery could serve to increase efficacy expectations via these two sources of information (Callow et al., 2001; Callow & Waters, in press)

An Applied Model of Mental Imagery

Martin et al.'s (1999) Applied Model centers on the type of imagery used by athletes (as defined by Hall et al., 1998). The model is based upon four imagery related variables; namely, the sport situation, the type of imagery used, imagery ability, and outcomes associated with imagery use. In addition, the model reflects the notion that different images are associated with different cognitive, affective, and behavioral reactions and that images may have different functions for athletes.

Martin et al.'s (1999) model predicts 15 specific and testable hypotheses that relate to sport situation, type of imagery used, and the predicted effects/outcomes. The authors acknowledged that variables such as skill level and sport type may moderate the type of imagery to be used in different situations.

The model provides a foundation from which a systematic research profile can be developed. For example, recent research by Callow and Hardy (2001) has indicated that in a team sport, mastery imagery and imagery relating to strategies of the game significantly predicted confidence in moderately skilled performers; whereas in higher standard performers, goal achievement oriented imagery was the only significant predictor in confidence. These findings have specific applied implications, which will be discussed in the next section.

The PETTLEP model

The PETTLEP model (Holmes & Collins, 2001) is based on the notion that imagery, motor preparation, and motor performance have central (e.g., Schnitzler, Salenius, Salmelin, Jousmaki, & Hari, 1997), peripheral (e.g., Decety, Jeannerod, Germain, & PastÊne, 1991), and behavioral (Farah, 1985) commonality, and that the degree of functional equivalence between imagery and actual performance will influence the effectiveness of the imagery. To clarify, if functional equivalence, in terms of brain innervation during actual performance and imagery is closely matched, then the imagery will be more effective. The PETTLEP model highlights seven elements that should be taken into account to optimize this process; namely, Physical, Environment, Task, Timing, Learning, Emotion, and Perspective. Although the model provides a useful checklist of factors that should be considered when delivering imagery interventions, two important criticisms become apparent when its conceptual foundation is examined.

Firstly, Holmes and Collins (2001) do not mention that the degree of coincidence between the neural structures involved in motor imagery and motor generation remains controversial, with some experimental data questioning this equivalence (e.g., Deiber, Ibanez, Honda, Sadato, Raman, & Hallett, 1998). Additionally, Farah (1989) cites neurological evidence in which brain lesions selectively disrupted mental imagery without disrupting other types of cognitive or motor processes. Furthermore, certain researchers (e.g., Kosslyn, 1988; Shepard & Copper, 1982) contend that specific imagery processes, such as imagery generation (that is the creation of the image) and imagery transformation (that is the manipulation of an image) are not activated by actual events.

We concur with Holmes and Collins that imagery may work by strengthening the memory trace of the imagined action, but there may be other mechanisms unique to imagery that account for some of it effects. For example, Richardson (1980, p. 43) proposes that because of its generation and transformational qualities, imagery allows for an elaborate form of rehearsal that facilitates retention. Further to this, it must be remembered that imagery can be generated by systems other than the motor system, for example from reasoning or memory itself (cf. Grant & Schmuckler, 1996). Images arising from reasoning (e.g., imaging a new strategy of play) could perhaps be bound by the intelligence and creativity of the athlete to create and transform the image, and as a consequence individual differences must be taken into account.

The second point relates to the fact that Holmes and Collins' (2001) suggestions are based on the notion of functional equivalence, but they then use Lang's (1984) bi-informational theory to explain how functional equivalence may work. However, Lang proposes that imagery is an amodal phenomenon that can be expressed in an abstract representation (namely, as propositions) which is not specific to any modality or language (Eysenck & Keane, 1990). This is in direct contrast to the functional equivalence approach, which is based on an information processing paradigm. Although we are keen for applied practitioners to consider specific tenets of this model in their work, and for researchers to test these tenets, we would advise that the two points raised here be kept in mind.

Applied Implications

It is outside the scope of this chapter to provide detailed recommendations on how to consult effectively with an athlete. However, the consultancy model that an applied practitioner adopts will have a bearing not only on the structure of the interventions they deliver, but also the effectiveness of their work (e.g., Hardy & Parfitt, 1994; Orlick & Partington, 1988). If the recommendations detailed below are to be effective, then practitioners should be mindful of the consultancy model that they adopt with athletes.

Imagery perspectives

In view of the research critiqued in this chapter, the following applied recommendations are made with regard to the ideal visual imagery perspective to suggest to athletes. The first recommendation is that the requirement of the task to be imaged must be taken into account. Based on the findings of White and Hardy (1995), and Hardy and Callow (1999), external visual imagery should be prescribed for tasks that require form of movement, because this form of imagery seems to have superior learning and performance effects. For tasks that rely heavily on perceptual information White and Hardy (1995) seem to suggest that internal visual imagery should be prescribed.

Kinaesthetic imagery

The results on which to base recommendations with regard to kinesthetic imagery are less clear cut. However, a further explanation can allow for greater clarification. Theoretical reasoning (e.g., Fitz & Posner, 1967; Whiting & den Brinker, 1981) and results presented in Hardy and Callow (1999) seem to indicate that, when performers are experienced at a form based task, kinesthetic imagery can produce additional performance benefits. The implication for this is that when a performer is perfecting a form based skill, kinesthetic imagery should be prescribed to help the performer with the precise detail of the skill, including information such as the force, effort, and spatial sensations of the movement. Thus, performers should be directed towards how a movement feels so that they can use this information to develop vivid kinesthetic images and thus create an image of achievement (Whiting & den Brinker, 1981).

Empirical research has yet to examine if, with tasks that require perceptual information, the use of kinesthetic imagery produces additional performance gains over and above those produced through the use of internal visual imagery. However, it makes intuitive sense that, for a task of this nature, kinesthetic imagery would provide useful additional information that would aid performance. Thus, for tasks that rely heavily on perceptual information and with performers who have experience of a task, the authors would tentatively recommend the use of kinesthetic imagery.

Although cognitive theorists do contend that kinesthetic cues are used in the later stages of learning, some researchers (e.g., Phillips, 1941; Phillips & Summers, 1954) have found kinesthetic cues to be related to early, but not later, stages of learning. Furthermore, Graydon and Townsend (1984) found that participants who were asked to maximize attention to the feel of a move produced better performances, when learning a trampoline forward summersault, a task which requires form of movement, than those who were given visuo-spatial information. However, the reverse was true for learning a badminton serve, a task which is performed in accordance with an external reference point. Thus, it seems that kinesthetic cues can be used even in the early stages of learning depending on the type of task. However, coaches may have to direct the performer's attention towards their kinesthetic sensations so that vivid kinesthetic images can be developed; this may be particularly important with junior performers. This is because, as Zaporozehets (1961) suggests, children are usually more concerned with the end results of their actions, than with the means by which they achieve them.

Kinaesthetic imagery and videos

Further support for directing the performer's attention towards their own sensations can be found from a study by Callow and Hardy (2004). Specifically, when participants were the agent of the image (i.e., they were in their image) there was a significant relationship between external visual imagery and kinesthetic imagery. However, when somebody else was the agent of the image, the relationship between external visual imagery and kinesthetic imagery was not significant. As sport psychology consultants suggest that performers should use video analysis to enhance their images (e.g., Smith & Holmes, 2004; Orlick, 1986), then, in view of the Callow and Hardy (2004) findings, if the performer observing the video is not the performer on the video, then the observer should be directed to pay attention to how the move would feel for them, and given advice on how to translate themselves into the image so that they can fully develop their kinesthetic images.

One possible way to help the performer translate themselves into their images would be through the use of edited videos. This is where the performer is edited to be the object of the video performing the task that they are trying to image. The performer then watches the video prior to imaging the task. For non-form tasks where the use of internal visual imagery may be appropriate, depending on the logistics imposed by the sport, a head-mounted camera could, perhaps, be used to gain video footage from an internal visual perspective.

Imagery perspective preference

The recommendations relating to imagery perspectives must be viewed with caution because the findings on which they are based do not take into account imagery perspective preference. For example, some performers may have a strong preference for kinesthetic imagery and may not be able to image from an external visual perspective, thus affecting the potential that the external visual perspective may have. Coaches and applied sport psychology practitioners would be well-advised to measure the imagery ability and imagery perspective preference of performers prior to administering any imagery intervention, as the performers may need some specific imagery training to improve a particular perspective if they are going to get the maximum benefits from the imagery intervention. Ensuring that performers can image from both visual perspectives would enable them to switch between imagery perspectives. Switching between perspectives may be required for certain skills. For example, a double straight-back somersault in gymnastics has an obvious requirement for form while taking off and rotating, but adjustments to perceptual information about environmental changes might be the dominant factor in landing (Lee, Young, & Rewt, 1992). Similar arguments can be made for sports of an "open" nature. For example, in canoe slalom, (where performers have to maneuver their canoe through a series of "gates" positioned along a stretch of fast moving water) requirements for form are needed when maneuvering around and through a gate, whereas adjustments to perceptual information about the environment are required when moving from gate to gate (cf. Shipley, 2001). Thus, it may be necessary to use both external visual imagery and internal visual imagery in relation to gain maximum performance benefits.

Imagery ability

It is clear that we do not yet know the level at what imagery ability specific imagery interventions become effective. However, Callow et al. (2001) used a score of at least a mean of 16 for both the visual and kinesthetic scales of the MIQ-R (Hall & Martin, 1997). This meant that each participant was scoring an average of at least "not easy nor hard" for the task they imagined on the MIQ-R. It makes intuitive sense that an athlete who scores at least this value will be able to image, and as a consequence, imagery has the potential to be effective. Indeed, imagery effects were produced in the Callow et al. study. Similarly, the same criterion for imagery ability was employed by Short et al., (2002) and Callow and Waters (in press), and the imagery interventions in these studies revealed significant results on certain dependent variables.

Clearly, because research suggests that imagery is more effective when athletes have higher imagery ability (e.g., Isaac, 1985), if imagery has been identified as the psychological skill to be employed to aid performance or deal with a problem, then the first step in working with the athlete is to assess their imagery ability. If initial evaluation indicates that athletes have "low" imagery ability, then we recommend that they are given imagery exercises to improve their imagery ability before imagery is used for the intended purpose. We would recommend using general imagery exercises of activities about which performers may be familiar (e.g., Hardy & Fazey, 1990), and then progressing onto exercises that can be adapted to a sports situation (e.g. Hale, 1998) and/or sport specific imagery programs where appropriate (e.g. Hogg, 1995).

Imagery practice conditions

When educating athletes in the use of imagery, the research literature seems to suggest that durations of 20 minutes bring about the best returns, and that the amount of practice does not have an influence on the effect of imagery (Driskel et al., 1994). However, Driskel et al.'s (1994) meta-analysis revealed that the effect of imagery decays as the time from its use increases, this suggests that imagery needs to be practiced regularly to maintain its effect. Orlick (1990) suggests that non-elite athletes are advised to practice for five minutes every day, and reports that

Olympic athletes use imagery for more than 15 minutes per day. However, athletes that we have worked with, especially those under age 18, struggle to conduct the imagery every day. Thus, as the decay effects for imagery start to accelerate after four days, scheduled practice at least every four days would seem appropriate as a minimum requirement to maintain the effects of the imagery.

Although the research literature suggests that imagery should be conducted in real time, two applied implications are worthy of comment here. The first implication we alluded to earlier in the chapter. That is, imaging in slow time can, in some situations, aid performance. Secondly, research has shown that when force is involved in the task, there is a dissociation between actual and imaged tasks in terms of time. For example, Decety, Jeannerod, and Prablanc (1989) found that blindfolded subjects who walked various distances, with a 25kg weight in their rucksack, significantly increased their imagined walking duration by 30% for all target distances in comparison to their actual walking time. Thus, if force is important to the task, practitioners need to carefully monitor the real effect that imagery is having so that it is actually mimicking, as closely as possible, the actual task.

The meaning of an image

Clearly there are individual differences in imagery ability. However, for interventions to be effective, individual differences that go beyond imagery ability should be taken into account. In particular, the research literature seems to imply that careful consideration should be given to the meaning that an image has for an individual. As a consequence the authors advise that practitioners write imagery scripts with the performer so that the appropriate stimulus, response, and meaning propositions can be incorporated into the script. If the function of the image is learning, then task relevant cues should be used. However, if the function of the image is to get a performer into a heightened somatic state, because this is their optimal performance state, then the script should be written as such, and as a consequence relaxation should not be employed before the imagery. These recommendations highlight the care that needs to be taken when delivering imagery through the medium of a workshop with large numbers of athletes, where it may be difficult to assess if the imagery proposed actually has the appropriate meaning and function for an athlete.

Moritz et al. (1996) and Callow and Hardy (2001) indicate that confidence and imagery use are linked. Indeed, Callow et al. (2001) found that mastery imagery had a motivational function by facilitating confidence. Additionally, Callow et al. found provisional evidence to suggest that mastery imagery helped to stabilize sport confidence. Indeed, it was proposed that the mastery imagery helped to develop "resilience" (Bandura, 1997, p. 80) in confidence. This resilience may protect against disconfirming experiences that an athlete may encounter, and thus stabilize the performer's confidence. These results provide a possible answer to the following question recently posed by Gould, Guinan, Greenleaf, Medbery, and Peterson (1999) "What can be done to sturdy one's confidence, particularly in an environment that is different from all other competitions and occurs only once every four years?" (p. 391). This question was posed because Gould et al. (1999) found that the confidence levels of some athletes competing at the Olympic Games were atypically "fragile" and more easily shaken. The results from Callow et al. suggest a strategy to develop the performer's resilience with respect to self-confidence. In addition, imagery provides a way to recreate aspects of the Olympic experience as often as the performer desires. A common strategy to help athletes prepare for major competition is through "what if" scenarios (e.g., Miller, 1997). This is where athletes identify possible problems that they may encounter prior to and during the event. They then work out solutions to deal with and overcome these problems. The impact of this strategy could, perhaps, be enhanced by the athlete actually imaging him or herself mastering these identified problems. Olympians could then provide themselves with a way of developing resilience in their confidence when faced with disconfirming experiences. Care needs to be taken with these recommendations for two reasons. Firstly, future research is needed to confirm that mastery imagery can develop the resilience of a performer's self-confidence. Secondly, the participants in Callow et al.'s study were high level performers, not Olympians, thus the findings may not generalize to Olympic athletes (cf. Murphy & Jowdy, 1992).

Future Directions

Recommendations for improving research design for intervention studies

Imagery research has been criticized due to the use of flawed research design (e.g., Goginsky & Collins, 1996, Hall, 2001; Murphy & Jowdy, 1992; Wollman, 1986). The main criticisms have centered on: inadequate methodological control leading to intervening and confounding variables influencing the dependent variable (cf. Goginsky & Collins, 1996); inadequate and inappropriate use of control groups (cf. Wollman, 1986); a lack of the use of manipulation checks to confirm what the participants are actually imaging (Murphy & Jowdy, 1992); and the lack of use of single-subject design research (Wollman, 1986). Additionally, in the past few years there has been an increase in the publication of descriptive and correlational research designs (e.g., Abma et al., 2002; Callow & Hardy 2001; Moritz et al., 1996). Although these studies provide relevant information with regard to use of different types of imagery, they do not answer important applied questions such as what is the most useful type of imagery to use? Or, why is a particular type of imagery the most useful to use? Causal studies that enable any mediating and moderating variables to be established are fundamental if researchers and practitioners are to learn what makes imagery interventions effective. These causal studies must control for intervening and confounding variables such as imagery ability, task type, skill level, sex, and delivery of the imagery. For example, are imagery scripts administered? If so, how are the imagery scripts delivered and what is the content of the imagery scripts? We also stress that manipulation checks must be employed to establish if athletes are engaging in the imagery, how often they are conducting the imagery (frequency), and if they are adhering to the imagery intervention. The answers to these types of questions can be obtained through self-report diaries or post-experimental questionnaires.

The nature of control groups for use in imagery research is a difficult issue. If a control group is not employed how does a researcher know if the effects gained were not due to some intervening variable such as physical practice? However, what does the researcher have the control condition do? If, for example, the control group is given a task of counting backwards instead of practicing the imagery, how does a researcher know that this task will not interfere with performance on the dependent variable(s)? This interference could then lead to confounded results for the control group. Interestingly, in Driskel et al.'s (1994) meta-analysis, the effect of imagery on performance for 39 hypothesis tests using no-contact control groups (i.e., control groups that did not conduct an activity for the condition) was $r = .327$ $d = .693$ and significant $z = 12.337, p < .001$, whereas the effect of imagery on performance for the 20 hypothesis tests using contact control groups (i.e., control groups that did have an activity to conduct for the condition) was smaller in magnitude $r = .122$, $d = .246$ and non-significant ($z = 1.053, p > .10$). As the effect size was smaller for the contact as oppose to the non-contact control groups (in comparison to imagery) this could indicate that interference, perhaps, did not occur with the contact control groups. (If interference was occurring, then it would be expected that the effect size would be larger for the contact groups as opposed to the non-contact groups.) These results could be interpreted as meaning that the use of contact control groups would be appropriate. Having said this, because the difference in effect sizes between the no-contact control groups and the contact control groups was not significant ($z = 1.173$, $p > .10$), the authors would propose that the use of no-contact control groups is not superior to the use of contact control groups and visa versa. However, there is another important issue with regard to control groups. Psychology research per se has been criticized because it often uses students as its participant population and the effects found with students may not generalize to high level or elite performers (cf. Greenspan & Feltz, 1989). But when using high level or elite performers as participants, the practice of withholding a potentially beneficial intervention for the control group is ethically questionable. Yet, with a single-subject multiple-baseline design a control group is not needed. Specifically, the multiple-baseline design introduces the intervention to different baselines (e.g., behaviors or participants) at different points in time. If the baselines of all participants change when the intervention is introduced, then the effects can be attributed to the intervention. The present authors recommend the use of this design in conjunction with the statistical analysis ITSACORR

(Crosbie, 1993). ITSACORR represents a method for statistically analyzing single-subject data without the violation of statistical assumptions (cf. Callow & Waters, in press). We also contend, however, that single-subject designs are not a substitute for well-designed nomothetic studies.

Concluding Comments and Research Questions

The authors hope that this chapter has provided an overview of what is known, what might be known, and what is not known about effective imagery interventions. Through our critical analysis of the imagery research literature, we have developed the following applied research questions. Information gleaned from the empirical examination of these questions would provide useful information to enable sport psychologists and coaches to make imagery intervention more effective for athletes.

1. Does the combination of IVI and Kin imagery produce superior performances for experienced performers with tasks that require heavily on perceptual information?

2. Does imagery perspective preference moderate the effectiveness of visual imagery on specific tasks?

3. Does having a high imagery ability mean that performers can switch between external visual and internal visual imagery perspectives?

4. In tasks that rely on both form of movement and perception, does the use of switching visual imagery perspectives produce greater performance effects than the use of just external visual imagery or just internal visual imagery?

5. At what level of expertise does kinesthetic imagery produce beneficial effects?

6. Would directing a beginner towards the kinesthetic component of performance help them to develop and utilize kinesthetic imagery?

7. Does confidence mediate the imagery-performance relationship?

8. Does imagery modality moderate the mastery imagery-confidence relationship in high level performers?

9. Does mastery imagery increase the resilience of confidence in sport performers?

10. Which imagery practice conditions lead to optimal acquisition and retention effects?

11. Does relaxation prior to imaging a task that requires high physiological arousal inhibit the possible transfer effects of the imagery to physical performance?

12. Does slow motion imagery aid confidence or performance for specific tasks?

13. Does slow motion imagery aid performance for specific tasks in "stressful" conditions?

14. Does the use of imagery scripts with task relevant cues cause high-level performers to "lapse" into conscious control?

15. Does "in-vivo" imagery aid imagery vividness and performance?

16. Does the use of videotapes prior to imagery increase physiological sensations and consequently the vividness of the associated imagery?

17. Does the meaning of an image moderate the imagery type-imagery function relationship?

18. Does the function and meaning of an imagery effect performance over and above any effects caused by the direction of the imagery (i.e., whether the image is positive or negative).

19. If video footage is being used to help to create an image of a situation, how much information, from the video, does a novice required to recreate an accurate image?

References

Abma, C. L., Fry, M. D., Yuhua, L., & Relyea, G. (2002). Differences in imagery content and imagery ability between high and low confident track and field athletes. *Journal of Applied Sport Psychology, 14*, 67-75.

Ahsen, A. (1984). ISM: The triple code model for imagery and psychophysiology. *Journal of Mental Imagery, 8*, 15-42.

Anderson, J. R. (1993). *Rules of the mind.* Hilsdale, NJ: Erlbaum.

Bakker, F. C., Boschker, M. S. J., & Chung, T. (1996). Changes in muscular activity while imagining weight lifting using stimulus and response propositions. *Journal of Sport and Exercise Psychology, 18*, 313-324.

Bandura, A. (1977). Self-efficacy: Towards a unifying theory of behavioural change. *Psychological Review, 84*, 191-215.

Bandura, A. (1986). *Social foundations of thought and action: A social cognitive theory.* Englewood Cliffs, NJ: Prentice Hall.

Bandura, A. (1997). *Self-efficacy: The exercise of control.* New York: Freeman & Company.

Barron, R. M., & Kenny, D. A. (1986). The moderator-mediator variable distinction in social psychological research: Conceptual, strategic, and statistical considerations. *Journal of Personality and Social Psychology, 51*, 1173-1182.

Blair, A., Hall, C., & Leyshon, G. (1993). Imagery effects on the performance of skilled and novice soccer players. *Journal of Sports Science, 11*, 95-101.

Boschker, M. S. J., Bakker, F.C., & Rietberg, M. B. (2000). Retroactive interference effects of mentally imagined movement speed. *Journal of Sports Sciences, 18*, 593-603.

Bull, S. J., Albinson, J. G. & Shambrook, C. J., (1996). *The mental game plan: Getting psyched for sport.* Eastbourne, UK: Sports Dynamics.

Burhans, R. S., Richman, C.L., & Bergey, D. B., (1988). Mental imagery training effects on running speed performance. *International Journal of Sport Psychology, 19*, 26-37

Callow, N., & Hardy, L. (2001). Types of Imagery associated with sport confidence in netball players of varying skill levels. *Journal of Applied Sport Psychology, 13*, 1-17.

Callow, N., Hardy, L., & Hall, C. (2001). The effects of a Motivational General-Mastery imagery intervention on the sport confidence of four high-level badminton players. *Research Quarterly for Exercise and Sport, 72*, 389-400.

Callow, N., & Hardy, L. (2004). The relationship between kinesthetic imagery and different visual imagery perspectives. *Journal of Sports Sciences, 22*, 167-177.

Callow, N., & Waters, A. (in press). The effect of kinesthetic imagery on sport confidence. *Psychology of Sport and Exercise.*

Calmels, C., & Fournier, J. F. (2001). Duration of physical and mental execution of gymnastic routines. *The Sport Psychologist, 15*, 142-150.

Collins, D., & Hale, B. (1997). Getting closer. . . but still no cigar! Comment. *Journal of Sport & Exercise Psychology, 19*, 207-212.

Corbin, C. B. (1967). Effects of mental practice on skill development after controlled practice. *Research Quarterly, 38*, 534-538.

Crosbie, J. (1993). Interrupted time-series analysis with brief single-subject data. *Journal of Consulting and Clinical Psychology, 6*, 966-974.

Decety, J., Jeannerod, M., Germain, M., & PastËne, J. (1991). Vegetative response during imagined movement is proportional to mental effort. *Behavioral Brain Research, 42*, 1-5.

Decety, J., Jeannerod, M., & Prablanc, C. (1989). The timing of mentally represented actions. *Behavioural Brain Research, 34*, 35-42.

Deiber, M. P., Ibanez, V., Honda, M., Sadato, N., Raman, R., & Hallett, M. (1998). Cerebral processes related to visuomotor imagery and generation of simple finer movements studies with positron emission tomography. *Neuroimage, 7*, 73-85.

Driskell, J. E., Copper, C., & Moran, A. (1994). Does mental practice enhance performance? *Journal of Applied Psychology, 79*, 481-491.

Eaton, R. (1997). It's all in the mind. *World Badminton, 25*, 6-9.

Eysenck, M. W., & Keane, M. T. (1990). *Cognitive Psychology: A Students Handbook*, Lawrence Erlbaum, Hove, England.

Farah, M. J. (1985). Psychological evidence for a shared representational medium for mental images and precepts. *Journal of Experimental Psychology: General, 114*, 91-103.

Farah, M. J. (1989). The neural basis of mental imagery. *Trends in Neurosciences, 12*, 395-399.

Feltz, D. L. (1982). Path analysis of the causal elements in Bandura's theory of self-efficacy and an anxiety-based model of avoidance behavior. *Journal of Personality and Social Psychology, 42*, 764-781.

Feltz, D. L., & Landers, D. M. (1983). The effects of mental practice on motor skill learning and performance: A meta-analysis. *Journal of Sport Psychology, 5*, 25-57.

Fitts, P. M. (1962). Skill training. In R. Glaser (Ed.), *Training research and education* (pp. 177-199). Pittsburgh: University of Pittsburgh Press.

Fitts, P. M., & Posner, M. I. (1967). *Human performance.* Belmont, CA: Brooks/Cole.

Franks, I. M., & Maile, L. J. (1991). The use of video in sport skill acquisition. In P. W. Dowrick (Ed.), *Practical guide to using video in the behavioural sciences* (pp. 231-243). New York: Wiley.

Goginsky, A. M., & Collins, D. (1996). Research design and mental practice. *Journal of Sports Sciences, 14*, 381-392.

Goss, S., Hall, C., Buckolz, E., & Fishburne, G. (1986). Imagery ability and the acquisition and retention of movements. *Memory and Cognition, 14*, 469-477.

Gould, D. & Damarjian, N. (1996). Imagery Training for Peak Performance. In J.L. Van Raalte & B. W. Brewer (Eds.), *Exploring sport and exercise psychology* (pp. 25-50). Washington, DC: American Psychological Association.

Gould, D., Guinan, D., Greenleaf, C., Medbery, R., & Peterson, K. (1999). Factors affecting Olympic performance: Perceptions of athletes and coaches from more and less successful teams. *The Sport Psychologist, 13*, 371-394.

Gould, D. R., & Weiss, M. R. (1981). The effects of model similarity and model self-talk on self-efficacy and muscular endurance. *Journal of Sport Psychology, 3*, 17-29.

Grant, S. C., & Schmuckler, M. A. (1996). Alternative origins of motor images. *Behavioral and Brain sciences, 19*, 759-760.

Gray, J. J., Haring, M. J., & Banks, M. N. (1984). Mental rehearsal for sport performance: Exploring the relaxation-imagery paradigm. *Journal of Sport Behavior, 7*, 68-78.

Gray, S. W. (1990). Effect of visuomotor rehearsal with videotaped modeling on racquetball performance of beginning players. *Perceptual and Motor Skills, 70*, 379-385.

Graydon, J. K., & Townsend, J. (1984). Proprioceptive and visual feedback in the learning of two gross motor skills. *International Journal of Sport Psychology, 15*, 227-235.

Greenleaf, C., Gould, D., & Dieffenbach, K. (2001). Factors influencing Olympic performance: Interviews with Atlantic and Nagano Olympians. *Journal of Applied Sport Psychology, 13*, 154-184.

Greenspan, M. J., & Feltz, D. L. (1989). Psychological interventions with athletes in competitive situations: A review. *The Sport Psychologist, 3*, 219-236.

Hale, B. D. (1998). *Imagery training a guide for sports people.* Leeds, UK: National Coaching Foundation,

Hale, B. D., & Whitehouse, A. (1998). The effects of imagery-manipulated appraisal on intensity and direction of competitive anxiety. *The Sport Psychologist, 12*, 40-51.

Hall, C.R. (2001). Imagery. In R.N. Singer, H.A. Hausenblas, & C.M. Janelle (Eds.), *Handbook of Sport Psychology* (2nd ed., pp. 529-549). New York: John Wiley & Sons, Inc.

Hall, C. R., Buckolz, E., & Fishburne, G. J. (1989). Searching for a relationship between imagery ability and memory of movements. *Journal of Human Movement Studies, 17*, 89-100.

Hall, C. R., Buckolz, E., & Fishburne, G. J. (1992). Imagery and the acquisition of motor skills. *Canadian Journal of Sports Science, 17*, 19-27.

Hall, C. R., Mack, D., Paivio, A., & Hausenblas, H. A. (1998). Imagery use by athletes: Development of the Sport Imagery Questionnaire. *International Journal of Sport Psychology, 29*, 73-89.

Hall, C. R., & Martin, K. A. (1997). Measuring movement imagery abilities: A revision of the movement imagery questionnaire. *Journal of Mental Imagery, 21*, 143-154.

Hall, C. R., & Pongrac, J. (1983). *Movement Imagery Questionnaire.* London, ON: University of Western Ontario.

Hall, E. G., & Erffmeyer, E. S. (1983). The effect of visuo-motor behavior rehearsal with videotaped modeling on free throw accuracy of intercollegiate female basketball players. *Journal of Sport Psychology, 5*, 343-346.

Hardy, L. (1997). The Coleman Roberts Griffith address: Three myths about applied consultancy work. *Journal of Applied Sport Psychology, 9*, 277-294.

Hardy, L., & Callow, N. (1999). Efficacy of external and internal visual imagery perspectives for the enhancement of performance on tasks in which form is important. *Journal of Sport & Exercise Psychology, 21*, 95-112.

Hardy, L., & Fazey, J. (1990). *Mental rehearsal.* Leeds, UK: National Coaching Foundation.

Hardy, L., Jones, J. G., & Gould, D. (1996). *Understanding psychological preparation for sport: Theory and practice of elite performers.* Chichester, UK: Wiley.

Hardy, L., & Parfitt, P. (1994). The development of a model for the provision of psychological support to a national squad. *The Sport Psychologist, 8*, 126-142.

Hecker, J. E., & Kaczor, L. M. (1988). Application of imagery to sport psychology: Some preliminary findings. *Journal of Sport and Exercise Psychology, 10*, 363-373.

Heyman, S. R. (1982). Comparison of successful and unsuccessful competitors: A reconsideration of methodological questions and data. *Journal of Sport Psychology, 4*, 295-300.

Highlen, P. S., & Bennett, B. B. (1979). Psychological characteristics of successful and nonsuccessful elite wrestlers: An exploratory study. *Journal of Sport Psychology, 1*, 123-137.

Hinshaw, K. E. (1991). The effects of mental practice on motor skill performance: Critical evaluation and meta-analysis. *Imagination, Cognition and Personality, 11*, 205-212.

Holmes, P., & Collins, D. (2001). The PETTLEP approach to motor imagery: A functional equivalence model for sport psychologists. *Journal of Applied Sport Psychology, 13*, 60-83.

Holmes, P., & Collins, D. (2002). Functional equivalence solutions for problems with motor imagery. In I. Cockerill (Ed.), *Solutions in sport psychology* (pp. 120-140). UK: Thomson.

Hogg, J. M. (1995). *Mental skills for competitive swimmers.* Alberta, USA: Sport Excel Publishing Inc.

Isaac, A. R. (1985). *Imagery differences and mental practice.* In D. F. Marks & D. G. Russell (Eds.). Imagery 1. (pp. 14-18) Dunedin, NZ: Human Performance Associates.

Isaac, A. R., Marks, D. F., & Russell, D. G. (1986). An instrument for assessing imagery of movement. The Vividness of Movement Imagery Questionnaire. *Journal Of Mental Imagery, 10*, 23-30.

Jacobson, E. (1930). Electrical measures of neuromuscular states during mental activities. *American Journal of Physiology, 95*, 703-712.

Jeannerod, M. (1999). To act or not to act: Perspectives on the representation of actions. *The Quarterly Journal of Experimental Psychology, 52*, 1-29.

Jones, L., & River, E. M. (1997). Current uses of imagery in cognitive and behavioural therapies. *Innovations in clinical practice: A source book, 15*, (pp. 423-439) Sarasota, FL, US: Professional Resource Press/Professional Resource Exchange, Inc.

Jones, L., & Stuth, G. (1997). The uses of mental imagery in athletics: An overview. *Applied & Preventive Psychology, 6*, 101-115.

Keele, S. W. (1973). *Attention and human performance.* Pacific Palisades, CA: Goodyear.

Kohl, R.M., Ellis, S. D., & Roenker, D. L. (1992). Alternating actual and imagery practice: Preliminary theoretical considerations. *Research Quarterly for Exercise and Sport, 63*, 162-170.

Kosslyn, S. M. (1988). Aspects of cognitive neuroscience of mental imagery. *Science, 240*, 1621-1626.

Lang, P. J. (1977). Imagery in therapy: An information processing analysis of fear. *Behavior therapy, 8*, 862-886.

Lang, P. J. (1979). A bio-informational theory of emotional imagery. *Psychophysiology, 17*, 495-512.

Lang, P. J. (1984). Cognitions in emotion: Concept and action. In C. E. Izard, J. Kagan, & R. B. Zajonc (Eds.), *Emotions, Cognition, & Behavior* (pp. 192-226). New York: University of Cambridge.

Lang, P. J., Kozak, M., Miller, G. A., Levin, D. N., & Mclean, A. (1980). Emotional imagery: Conceptual structure and pattern of somato-viseral response. *Psychophysiology, 17*, 179-192.

Lang, P. J., Melamed, B. G. & Hart, J. D. (1970). A psychophysiological analysis of fear modification using an automated desensitization procedure. *Journal of Abnormal Psychology, 76*, 220-234.

Langer, E.J., & Imber, L.G. (1979). When practice makes imperfect: Debilitating effects of overlearning. *Journal of Personality and Social Psychology, 37*, 2014-2024.

Lee, D. N., Young, D. S., & Rewt, D. (1992). How do somersaulters land on their feet? *Journal of Experimental Psychology, 18*, 1195-1202.

Magill, R. A. (2001). *Motor learning: Concepts and applications* (6th ed.). Boston, Mass: McGraw-Hill.

Mahoney, M. J., & Avener, M. (1977). Psychology of the elite athlete: An exploratory study. *Cognitive Therapy and Research, 2*, 135-141.

Markland, D. (2000). Mediating and moderating variables: A conceptual clarification. *Journal of Sport Sciences, 18*, 373-374.

Marks, D. F., (1977). Imagery and consciousness: A theoretical review from an individual differences perspective. *Journal of Mental Imagery, 1*, 275-290.

Martin, K. A., & Hall, C. R. (1995). Using mental imagery to enhance intrinsic motivation. *Journal of Sport Exercice Psychology, 17*, 54-69.

Martin, K. A., Moritz, S. E., & Hall, C. R. (1999). Imagery use in sport: A literature review and Applied Model. *The Sport Psychologist, 13*, 245-268.

McAuley, E. (1985). Modeling and self-efficacy: A test of Bandura's model. *Journal of Sport Psychology, 7*, 283-295.

Meyers, A. W., Cooke, C. J., Cullen, J., & Liles, L. (1979). Psychological aspects of athletic competitors: A replication across sports. *Cognitive Therapy and Research, 3*, 361-366.

Miller, B. (1997). *Gold minds: The psychology of winning in sport.* Wiltshire, UK: The Crowood Press Ltd.

Minas, S. C. (1978). Mental practice of a complex perceptual-motor skill. *Journal of Human Movement Studies, 4*, 102-107.

Minas, S. C. (1980). Mental practice of a complex perceptual-motor skill. *Journal of Human Studies, 4*, 102-107.

Moran, A. (1993). Conceptual and methodological issues in the measurement of mental skills in athletes. *Journal of Sport Behavior, 16*, 156-170.

Moritz, S. E., Hall, C. R. Martin, K. A., & Vadocz, E. (1996). What are confident athletes imagining? An examination of image content. *The Sport Psychologist, 10*, 171-179.

Mumford, P., & Hall, C. (1985). The effects of internal and external imagery on performing figures in figure skating. *Canadian Journal of Applied Sport Sciences, 10*, 171-177.

Murphy, S. M. (1990). Models of imagery in sport psychology: A review. *Journal of Mental Imagery, 14*, 153-172.

Murphy, S. M., & Jowdy, D. P. (1992). Imagery and mental practice. In T. S. Horn (Ed.), *Advances in sport psychology* (pp. 221-250). Champaign, IL: Human Kinetics.

Nideffer, R. M. (1985). *Athlete's guide to mental training.* Champaign, IL: Human Kinetics.

Orlick, T. (1986). *Psyching for sport: Mental training for athletes.* Champaign, IL: Human Kinetics.

Orlick, T. (1990). *In pursuit of excellence.* (2 ed.). Champaign, IL: Human Kinetics.

Orlick, T., & Partington, J. (1988). Mental links to excellence. *The Sport Psychologist, 2*, 105-130.

Paivio, A. (1971). *Imagery and Verbal Processes* New York: Holt, Rinehart & Winston.

Paivio, A. (1985). Cognitive and motivational functions of imagery in human performance. *Canadian Journal of Applied Sports Sciences, 10*, 22-28.

Parfitt, C. G., Jones, J. G., & Hardy, L. (1993). Multidimensional anxiety and performance. In J.G. Jones and L. Hardy (Eds.), *Stress and performance* (pp. 43-80). Wiley: Chichester.

Powell, G. E. (1973). Negative and positive mental practice in motor skill acquisition. *Perceptual and motor skills, 37,* 312.

Phillips, B. E. (1941). The relation between certain phases in kinesthetic and performance during the early stages of acquiring two perceptuo-motor skills. *Research Quarterly, 12,* 571-586.

Phillips, M., & Summers, D. (1954). Relation of kinesthetic perception to motor learning. *Research Quarterly, 25,* 456-469.

Qualls, P. J. (1982). The physiological measurement of imagery: An overview. *Imagination, Cognition & Personality, 2,* 89-101.

Richardson, J.T.E. (1980). *Mental imagery and human memory.* New York: St. Martin's Press.

Rodgers, W. M., Hall, C. R., & Buckolz, E. (1991). The effect of an imagery training program on imagery ability, imagery use, and figure skating performance. *Journal of Applied Sport Psychology, 3,* 109-125.

Rushall, B. S., & Lipman, L. G. (1998). The role of imagery in physical performance. *International Journal of Sport Psychology, 29,* 57-72

Schmidt, R.A. (1982). *Motor control and learning: A behavioural emphasis.* Champaign, Illinois: Human Kinetics Publishers.

Schnitzler, A., Salenius, S., Salmelin, R., Jousmaki, V., & Hari, R. (1997). Involvement of primary motor cortex in motor imagery: A neuromagnetic study. *Neuroimage, 6,* 201-208.

Schwartz, D. L. & Holton, D. L. (2000). Tool use and the effect of action on the imagination *Journal of Experimental Psychology: Learning, Memory, & Cognition, 26,* 1655-1665.

Shambrook, C. & Bull, S. (1996). The use of single-case research design to investigate the efficacy of imagery training. *Journal of Applied Sport Psychology, 8,* 27-43.

Shaw, W. A. (1938). The distribution of muscular action potentials during imaging. *Psychological Record, 2,* 195-216.

Shelton, T. O., & Mahoney, M. J. (1978). The content and effect of "psyching-up" strategies in weightlifters. *Cognitive Therapy and Research, 2,* 275-284.

Shephard, R. N., & Cooper, L. A., (1982). *Mental images and their transformations.* Cambridge, MA: MIT Press.

Shipley, S. (2001). *Every crushing stroke: The book of performance kayaking.* Atlanta: Crab Apple.

Short, S. E., Bruggeman, J. M., Engel, S. G., Marback, T. L., Wang, L. J., Willadsen, A. & Short, M. W. (2002). The effect of imagery function and imagery direction on self-efficacy and performance on a golf-putting task. *The Sport Psychologist, 16,* 48-67.

Short, S. E., Monsma, E. V., & Short, M. W. (2004). Is what you see really what you get? Athletes' perceptions of imagery's functions. *The Sport Psychologist, 18,* 341-349.

Slade, J. M., Landers, D. M., & Martin, P. E. (2002). Muscular activity during real and imagined movements: A test of inflow explanations. *Journal of Sport & Exercise Psychology, 24,* 151-167.

Smith, D., & Holmes, D. (2004). The effect of imagery modality on golf putting performance. *Journal of Sport & Exercise Psychology, 26,* 385-395.

Start, K. B., & Richardson, A. (1964). Imagery and mental practice. *British Journal of Educational Psychology, 34,* 280-206.

Suinn, R.M. (1972). Behavior rehearsal training for ski racers. *Behavior Therapy, 3,* 519-520.

Suinn, R. M. (1980). *Psychology in sport: Methods and applications.* Minneapolis: Burgess.

Suinn, R. M. (1984). Imagery and sports. In W. F. Straub, & J. M. Williams (Eds.), *Cognitive sport psychology* (pp. 253- 271). New York: Sport Science Associates.

Suinn R. M. (1997). Mental practice in sport psychology: Where have we been, where do we go? *Clinical psychology: Science and practice, 4,* 189-207.

Surburg, P. R. (1968). Audio, visual, and audio-visual instruction with mental practice in developing the forehand tennis drive. *Research Quarterly, 39,* 728-734.

Syer, J., & Connolly, C. (1998). *Sporting body, sporting mind: An athlete's guide to mental training.* London: Simon & Schuster.

Taylor, J. (1993). *The mental edge for alpine ski racing.* Aurora, Colorado: Minuteman Press.

Ungerleider, S., & Golding, J. M. (1991). Mental practice among Olympic athletes. *Perceptual and Motor Skills, 72,* 1007-1017.

Vealey, R. S. (1994). Current status and prominent issues in sport psychology interventions. *Medicine and Science in Sports and Exercise, 26,* 495-502.

Weinberg, R. S. (1988). *The Mental Advantage: Developing your psychological skills in tennis.* Human Kinetics, Champaign, IL.

White, A. (1996). *Imagery and sport performance.* Unpublished doctoral dissertation, University of Wales, Bangor, UK.

White, A., & Hardy, L. (1995). Use of different imagery perspectives on the learning and performance of different motor skills. *British Journal of Psychology, 86,* 169-180.

White, A., & Hardy, L. (1998). An in-depth analysis of the uses of imagery by high level slalom canoeists and artistic gymnasts. *The Sport Psychologist, 12,* 387-403.

Whiting, H. T. A., & den Brinker, B. P. (1981). Image of the act. In J. P. Das, R. Mulcahy & A. E. Wall (Eds), *Learning Difficulties.* (pp. 217-235). New York: Plenum.

Wollman, N. (1986). Research on imagery and motor performance: Three methodological suggestions. *The Sport Psychologist, 8,* 135-138.

Woolfolk, R., Parrish, W., & Murphy, S. M. (1985). The effects of positive and negative imagery on motor skill performance. *Cognitive Therapy and Research, 9,* 335-341.

Wrisberg, C. A., & Ragsdale, M. R. (1979). Cognitive demand and practice level: Factors in the mental practice of motor skills. *Journal of Human Movement Studies, 5,* 201-208.

Yamamoto, K., & Inomata, K. (1982). Effect of mental rehearsal with part and whole demonstration models on acquisition of backstroke swimming skills. *Perceptual & Motor Skills, 3,* 1067-1070.

Zaporozehets, A. V. (1961). The origin and development of conscious control of movements in man. In N. O'Connor (Ed.), *Recent Soviet Psychology.* (pp. 104-124). Oxford: Pergamon Press.

Section II
Psychological Skill Training

Introduction

The objective of this section, which is comprised of four chapters, is to discuss various aspects of psychological skill training in sport. Each chapter focuses on a different aspect of psychological skill training: concentration and focusing attention, decision making, mental training, and learning strategies. An effort has been made in each chapter to discuss research findings emerging from applied investigations in which beginners as well as advanced performers were involved.

In the first chapter, Aidan Moran discusses training attention and concentration skills in athletes. The chapter explains the meaning of and the relationship between the terms *attention* and *concentration*, and summarizes some key principles of effective concentration. The nature and efficacy of the various techniques that purport to enhance attentional skills in athletes are reviewed. In addition, the chapter raises some practical issues that need to be considered before attentional training is conducted with athletes.

The second chapter, by Gershon Tenenbaum and Ronnie Lidor, elaborates on research that was conducted in both sport and nonsport environments, and explains how the mechanisms which determine the quality of decision making in sport are acquired and modified through practice and development of expertise. The chapter examines the contribution of cognitive strategies such as attentional control, preperformance routines, and simulation training to the enhancement of decision making in sport. The authors argue that selected cognitive strategies can aid athletes in facilitating certain aspects of decision making.

In the third chapter of this section, Patsy Tremayne and Glenn Newbery elaborate on the use of psychological skills training for children. They review the experimental studies of psychological skills training that involved children and adolescents, as well as the anecdotal reports on the guidelines for the development of such training programs. A synopsis of the principles of intrinsic motivation theory and its implications to children is provided, taking into account the children's cognitive and motor developmental stages. The authors also provide some recommendations for psychological skills training for children.

In the fourth chapter, Ronnie Lidor and Robert Singer focus on the implementation of various learning strategies in motor skill acquisition. They examine the trends observed in strategy research conducted during the past two decades in the motor domain under laboratory and field conditions. They also discuss knowledge based on strategy research that can be useful for practitioners. Finally, future studies are proposed that may increase the ecological validity of task-pertinent strategies.

Each of the four chapters in this section not only presents empirical evidence emerging from laboratory and field inquiries on the effectiveness of psychological skill training in sport, but also provides practical advice on how this training should be conducted. The body of knowledge presented in this section can be implemented by coaches, instructors, and sport consultants who work with both beginning and skilled athletes.

Courtesy of Robin Cresswell/U.S. Air Force

2.1

Training Attention and Concentration Skills in Athletes

AIDAN MORAN

Golfer Darren Clarke, after shooting a record-equaling score of 60 in the 1999 European Open championship in Kildare, Ireland (July 31, 1999): "I was in my own little world, focusing on every shot. I wasn't thinking what score I was on or anything... But today was probably as good as I have ever played" (cited in Otway, 1999, p. 13).

Former world champion snooker player, Stephen Hendry, on his narrow defeat (18-17) by Peter Ebdon in the 2002 World Snooker Championship in Sheffield, England (May 6, 2002): "The one thing you want in the last frame is a chance and I had three but I bottled it... My concentration went in the last frame. I don't know why" (cited in Everton, 2002, p. 25).

Introduction

Most athletes, coaches, and psychologists agree that attentional processes like *concentration*, or the ability to focus on the task at hand while ignoring distractions (Schmid & Peper, 1998), are vital determinants of athletic success. For example, the golfer Darren Clarke reported that his best-ever performance in achieving a total of 60 in a competitive round coincided with an effort to concentrate on one shot at a time, thereby suppressing a tendency to count his score. By contrast, the snooker star Stephen Hendry learned that attentional lapses can be costly when he lost the deciding frame of the 2002 World Championship final due to a concentration error. In view of such examples, it is not surprising that a large sample of athletes (*n*=335) in a recent survey by Durand-Bush, Salmela, and Green-Demers (2001) identified *focusing* skills as being crucial to their success in sport. Echoing these sentiments, Abernethy (2001) proclaimed that "it is difficult to imagine that there can be anything more important to the learning and performance of sport skills than paying attention" (p. 53). Despite such testimonials to the value of focusing skills, many conceptual and methodological issues remain unresolved in this field. For example, what are the relationships between *attention* and *concentration*? What psychological principles govern an optimal focus in athletes? Can the ability to concentrate effectively be trained in sport performers? If so, what exercise and techniques work best for this purpose? These questions will be addressed in the present chapter.

This chapter is organized into five parts as follows. To begin with, it explains the meaning of, and the relationship between, the terms *attention* and *concentration* in psychology. Next, the chapter summarizes some key principles of effective concentration derived from studies of the correlates of a *focused* state of mind in athletes. The third part of the chapter reviews the nature and efficacy of the various techniques that purport to enhance attentional skills in athletes. Then, the fourth part of the chapter raises some practical issues that need to be considered before attentional training is conducted with athletes. Finally, the chapter sketches some new directions in the field.

Part 1: Attention and Concentration in Psychology

According to Solso (1998), the term *attention* refers to "the concentration of mental effort on sensory or mental events" (p. 130). This term is one of the most popular and useful constructs in contemporary psychology. Not only has it been studied extensively by cognitive researchers (e.g., Matlin, 2005; Pashler, 1998) but it is also commonly encountered in athletes' everyday sporting discourse. Thus, terms like *concentration* and *focus* are ubiquitous in postmatch interviews with top-class athletes. For example, the Spanish tennis star, Alex Corretja attributed his defeat by Gustavo Kuerten in the final of the 2001 French Open championship to the fact that "once I lost the third set, I lost my focus, I lost my game..." (cited in Ramsay, 2001, p. 13).

Unfortunately, despite its popularity among researchers and athletes alike, the term *attention*

is potentially confusing. For example, some sport psychologists such as Cox (1998) regard it as being synonymous with *concentration*, although the latter term refers more accurately to the *conscious experience* of paying attention (Moran, 1996). In addition, Gauron (1984) claimed that "all of us suffer from divided attention" (p. 43; italics mine), a remark that suggests the ability to *divide* one's attention is an affliction rather than an asset. Perhaps more seriously, cognitive and sport psychologists differ significantly in their metaphorical understanding of attention. Specifically, whereas cognitive researchers regard this construct as a *spotlight* or as a *resource* (explained below), sport psychologists consider it to be a *skill* that can be improved by appropriate instruction and practice. In view of these conceptual issues, it is important to be clear about the precise meaning of the terms *attention* and *concentration* in the present chapter.

Within cognitive sport psychology, attention is a multidimensional construct with at least three different meanings (Moran, 1996; 2004). First, it can refer to a person's ability to concentrate or to exert deliberate mental effort as when, for example, a basketball player attempts to listen carefully to instructions delivered by his or her coach during an interval in the match. Second, attention may denote a skill in selective perception, the capacity to zoom in on task-relevant information while ignoring potential distractions. Thus, a goalkeeper in soccer who is trying to catch or punch an incoming corner kick must focus only on the flight of the ball while disregarding the jostling and movement of other players in the penalty area. Finally, the term *attention* may designate a form of mental time-sharing, whereby an athlete has learned through extensive practice to perform two or more concurrent actions equally well. For example, a skilful soccer defender can kill the ball with a single touch and simultaneously scan the immediate vicinity on the pitch for a teammate to whom to pass it. In summary, the term *attention* refers to at least three different cognitive processes: *concentration* or *effortful awareness, selectivity of perception*, and the *ability to co-ordinate two or more actions at the same time*.

Interestingly, these latter two meanings of the term—namely, the concepts of *selective* and *divided* attention—are encapsulated by influential metaphors in this field. More precisely, the spotlight metaphor of attention (see review by Fernandez-Duque & Johnson, 1999) suggests that it resembles a selective mental light-beam that can illuminate a given target located either in the external world or in the subjective domain of one's own thoughts and feelings. Curiously, however, it is only in recent years that sport psychologists have begun to explore empirically the vital question of which precise cues athletes should direct their mental spotlight at during a competition (see Mallett & Hanrahan, 1997; Singer, 2000). We shall return to this issue briefly later in the chapter. Next, the fact that attention can be divided successfully between concurrent actions has led some theorists (e.g., Kahneman, 1973) to conceptualize it as a resource or *pool of mental energy* that can be allocated to competing task demands depending on various principles (e.g., the more a task is practiced, the less conscious attentional resources it requires and so, the more mental energy is available to regulate other concurrent activities). In summary, concentration is one aspect of attention, which itself is best regarded as a multidimensional construct that links together consciousness, perception, and action.

Before concluding this section, it is important to examine briefly the question of whether or not attention may be regarded as a skill. To do so, we need to examine what *skill* means. According to Annett (1991), a skill is an aspect of behavior that is goal-directed, knowledge-based, and acquired through training and practice rather than through innate factors. Using this definition, attentional processes may be regarded as skill-based because they help people to overcome psychological problems such as how to translate plans or intentions into effective task-relevant actions.

Having explained the meaning of the terms *attention* and *concentration*, let us now consider what is known about the role of the latter cognitive process in producing a focused state of mind in athletes. This analysis is important because many attentional skills training programs in applied sport psychology (e.g., see Schmid & Peper, 1998) appear to be based more on intuition than on explicit theoretical principles.

Part 2: Research on a Focused State of Mind in Athletes: Principles of Effective Concentration

The claim that concentration skills play a vital role in determining optimal performance in sport can be supported by two types of evidence: by research on peak performance experiences and/or flow states and by studies of the relationship between attentional strategies and athletic performance. Let us consider each of these sources of evidence briefly.

First, the centrality of attentional factors to peak performance can be gauged from the fact that Jackson, Thomas, Marsh, and Smethurst (2001) defined *flow* as a "state of concentration so focused that it amounts to absolute absorption in an activity" (p. 130). Similarly, Jackson and Csikszentimihalyi (1999) concluded that concentration is "a critical component and one of the characteristics of optimal experience mentioned most often" (p. 25). More generally, peak performance research indicates that athletes tend to do their best when they are totally focused on the task at hand (Jackson, 1995). In this state of mind, the athlete is "cleared of irrelevant thoughts, the body is cleared of irrelevant tensions, and the focus is centered only on what is important at that moment" (Orlick, 1990, p. 18). The second line of research on attentional factors in optimal performance comes from studies that explore the effects of various attentional strategies on athletic performance. To illustrate, it is widely believed that the use of associative concentration techniques (in which athletes are trained to pay attention explicitly to bodily signals such as heart beat, respiratory signals, and muscular sensations) is linked significantly with faster performance in running (Masters & Ogles, 1998) and swimming (Couture, Jerome, & Tihanyi, 1999). Similar findings have been reported by Scott, Scott, Bedic, and Dowd (1999), who found that the greatest gains in rowers' performance on an ergometer occurred when they used associative attentional techniques. Further evidence on the value of attentional skills came from Mallett and Hanrahan (1997), who discovered that sprinters who had been trained to use race plans that involved deliberately focusing on task-relevant cues ran faster than those without such plans.

Based on findings from these two research traditions and drawing on more general reviews of the relationship between attention and athletic performance (Abernethy, 2001; Moran, 1996; 2004), at least five theoretical principles of effective concentration in sport may be identified (see Figure 1 below).

Figure 1: Concentration Principles

1. Concenetration as mental effort—Spotlight metaphor

2. One can focus on only one thought at a time.

3. Athletes are *focused* when they concentrate on actions that are specific, relevant, and under their own control.

4. Athletes lose concentration when they focus on irrelevant or out-of-control factors.

5. Anxiety disrupts concentration by including negative self-evaluation and *hypervigilance.*

To begin with, a focused state of mind does not occur by chance but appears to require intentionality and deliberate effort on the part of the athlete. For example, consider the importance that the sprinter Michael Johnson (9-times world gold medalist) attached to achieving a proper mental set before running competitively: "I have learned to cut out all the unnecessary thoughts... on the track. I simply concentrate. I concentrate on the tangible—on the track, on the race, on the blocks, on the things I have to do. The crowd fades away and the other athletes disappear and now it's just me and this one lane" (cited in Miller, 1997, p. 64). In a similar vein, Oliver Kahn, the German international and Bayern Munich goalkeeper, remarked that "if you don't prepare yourself mentally it's impossible to maintain consistently high standards" (cited in Brodkin, 2001, p. 34).

Second, although skilled athletes may be adept at dividing their attention between two or more concurrent actions, they can focus consciously on only one thought at a time. This one-thought principle emerges from research that highlights the fragility and limited span of the central executive (an hypothetical component of working memory which regulates the amount of attentional resources available for current conscious processing; see Logie, 1999).

Third, research on the phenomenology of peak performance indicates that athletes' minds are focused optimally when there is no difference between what they are thinking about and what they are doing. Put differently, sport performers tend to concentrate most effectively when they direct their mental beam (recall earlier reference to the spotlight metaphor of attention) at actions that are specific, relevant and, above all, under their own control.

Fourth, and by implication, research shows that athletes tend to *lose* their concentration when they pay attention to events and experiences that are in the future, out of their control, or otherwise irrelevant to the task at hand (Moran, 1996).

The final principle of effective concentration acknowledges the potentially disruptive effects of emotions such as anxiety. Specifically, anxiety impairs athletes' concentration system in several distinctive ways (Moran, Byrne, & McGlade, 2002). For example, it *floods* their limited working memory resources with worries. In addition, anxiety tends to restrict the beam of their mental spotlight and to shift its focus onto self-referential stimuli. Thus, Janelle, Singer, and Williams (1999) found that anxious drivers who participated in a motor-racing simulation were more likely to attend to irrelevant cues than non-anxious counterparts. Anxiety also influences the direction of athletes' attentional focus by encouraging them to dwell on real or imagined personal weaknesses (self-focused attention) and on potential threats in the environment (thereby inducing a state of hypervigilance; see also Janelle, 2002). In short, anxiety affects the content, direction, and width of athletes' concentration beam.

To summarize, at least five attentional principles may be formulated concerning either the maintenance or loss of an optimal focus for athletes in competitive situations. These empirical principles serve to guide us in determining the best methods to use in attempting to train attention and concentration skills in athletes.

Part 3: Concentration Training Exercises and Techniques

Applied sport psychology is replete with techniques that are alleged to improve concentration skills in athletes (e.g., see Schmid & Peper, 1998). But do these methods have a coherent theoretical rationale and are they valid empirically? The purpose of this section of the chapter is to answer these questions.

In general, concentration skills programs consist of two types of psychological activities: Concentration training exercises and concentration techniques. The difference between these two components is that whereas the former activities (e.g., visual search tasks like the concentration grid; see Dalloway, 1993) are typically recommended for use in athletes' training sessions, the latter (see Figure 2 below) are designed for employment mainly in competitive situations.

Figure 2: Concentration Techniques

1. Specifying performance goals—actions that are under one's own control.

2. Using routines

3. Using *trigger* words

4. Mental practice

5. Simulation training

Unfortunately, most of the concentration exercises reviewed by Moran (1996) are flawed fundamentally due to a combination of inadequate theoretical rationale and a scarcity of empirical validation evidence. For example, consider the ubiquitous concentration grid. Sadly, no references were cited to support the claim that this exercise has been used "extensively in Eastern Europe as a pre-competition screening device" (Weinberg & Gould, 2003, p. 375) or that top athletes could obtain scores "in the upper 20s and even into the 30s" (ibid.) out of a possible total of 99 on it. Despite the dubious status of this grid as an attention enhancement procedure, however, Schmid & Peper (1998) recommend it uncritically as a "training exercise for practicing focusing ability" (p. 324). This recommendation highlights an unfor-tunate disjunction between theory and practice in applied sport psychology. In summary, it seems that there are no valid scientific grounds at present for using such exercises as watching a pendulum (Weinberg, 1988), watching a clock face (Albinson & Bull, 1988), or simply focusing on a sport object (Burke, 1992) in an effort to train concentration skills in athletes. But what about the second component of attentional interventions—namely, the five practical concentration techniques listed in Figure 2?

Figure 2 presents five concentration techniques that are widely recommended by sport psychologists for the purpose of concentration skills training (see Moran, 1996; 2000). These techniques include (i) specifying performance goals, (ii) using pre-performance routines, (iii) using trigger words, (iv) engaging in mental practice or visualization, and (v) simulation training.

(i) Specifying Performance Goals

Goals are targets or objectives that people strive to achieve. Without them, the motivational energy of athletes would be futile. For example, imagine sitting in a car that is being driven around in circles in a parking lot. Although energy is undoubtedly being consumed by this activity, one is not actually traveling anywhere. In the same way, athletes need a goal or a signpost to enable them to harness their attentional energy effectively. And so, goal-setting has been recommended as a useful technique for improving concentration, as long as it provides appropriate signposts or targets at which to shine one's attentional spotlight.

However, not all goals are equally effective in enhancing concentration. In particular, *result goals* (e.g., the outcome of a match) may be distracting as they encourage the performer to speculate about the future rather than to deal with the task at hand. Based on this logic, coaches and sport psychologists recommend that sport performers should concentrate as much as possible on achieving *performance goals*—tasks that are under their control and can be performed immediately. For example, a tennis player may try to improve his or her concentration on court simply by focusing solely on such performance goals as seeking 100% accuracy on his or her first serve or in endeavoring to attack any mid-court ball that s/he receives. In summary, performance goals are believed to improve concentration skills because they encourage the performer to focus on task-relevant and controllable actions (see Part 2 of this chapter).

Does research support the theory that performance goals improve concentration skills? One source of evidence on this question comes from research on the correlates of *best* and *worst* athletic performances. Thus, Jackson and Roberts (1992) discovered that collegiate athletes tended to give their worst performances when they were preoccupied by result goals. Conversely, their best displays coincided with a concern for performance or process goals. In a similar vein, Kingston and Hardy (1997) discovered that golfers who focused on process goals improved both their performance and their concentration. Supporting this finding, Burton, Weinberg, Yukelson, and Weigand (1998) examined the goal-setting practices of over 500 athletes and discovered that those who had set performance- or process-related targets claimed to have benefited more than did those who had set outcome or product goals for themselves. In summary, there are reasonable theoretical and empirical grounds for believing that specifying performance goals for oneself is a valid concentration technique.

(ii) Using Routines

It is well-known that most top-class athletes display characteristic sequences of preparatory actions before they perform key skills. For example, basketball free-throwers tend to engage in repetitive behavioral sequences before shooting, tennis players usually bounce the ball a set number of times before serving, and golfers typically take the same number of practice swings before they tee-off. These preferred action sequences and repetitive behaviors are called *pre-performance routines* and are widely practiced by sport performers prior to the execution of *self-paced skills* (i.e., actions that are typically performed with a stationary ball and which can be executed without interference from other people). According to Harle and Vickers (2001), they are designed "to improve concentration and performance." But what exactly do they involve? And how effective are they?

At least three types of routines are evident among athletes. First, *pre-event routines* are preferred sequences of actions to which sport performers like to adhere prior to competitive matches. Among these actions are what to do the night before the competitive event, on the morning of the match, and in the final hours before the game. The second type of routine concerns *pre-performance thoughts and actions*, as in the case of the basketball player, tennis server, and golfer mentioned previously. Finally, *post-mistake routines* are action sequences that purport to help performers to let go of mistakes and to continue with the task at hand. These routines may help to *re-focus* the minds of athletes after they have made mistakes (Syer, 1989). For example, a tennis player may shadow the correct movement of a stroke (such as a volley) that led to an unforced error, even though the ball may be lying at the bottom of the net. Of these three types of routines, the pre-performance ones offer the most plausible concentration aids.

To begin with, these routines may enhance concentration because they are intended to encourage athletes to develop an appropriate mental set for skill execution simply by helping them to focus on task-relevant information. For example, many soccer goalkeepers follow pre-kick routines to help them to block out the jeering directed at them by the supporters of the opposing team. Second, routines are believed to facilitate attentional processes by ensuring that athletes concentrate as much as possible on the here and now rather than on what happened in the past or on what may occur in the future. Finally, the use of routines may prevent expert sport performers from devoting excessive attention to the mechanics of their well-learned skills, a habit that can unravel automaticity (see Beilock & Carr, 2001; Beilock, Carr, MacMahon & Starkes, 2002). In other words, pre-performance routines may be valuable attentionally because they help to suppress inappropriate conscious control in pressure situations (Jackson, 2001). But does the systematic use of routines actually strengthen athletes' concentration skills?

Interestingly, there is growing research evidence, especially from case-studies, that routines can improve athletes' concentration and performance. For example, Crews and Boutcher (1986) compared the performances of two groups of golfers: those who had been given an eight-week training program of swing practice only and those who had participated in a practice-plus-routine program for the same duration. Results revealed that the more proficient golfers benefited more from using routines than did the less skilled players.

However, recent research suggests that the routines of expert athletes may be more variable than had been anticipated. Thus, Jackson and Baker (2001) conducted a case-study of the pre-strike routine used by the prolific former Welsh international rugby kicker, Neil Jenkins. On the one hand, they found that, as expected, he reported using a variety of concentration techniques (such as thought-stopping and mental imagery) as key components of his pre-kick routine. But on the other hand, they discovered that contrary to theoretical predictions, Jenkins varied the timing of his pre-kick behavior as a function of the difficulty of the kick he faced. More recently, Shaw (2002) described a case-study in which he evaluated the use of a pre-shot routine in a professional golfer. Although using only subjective interview data, Shaw reported that the golfer "was emphatic that the new routine had made him more focused for each shot and therefore less distracted by irrelevancies" (p. 117).

One problem with the use of routines, however, is that they may lead to superstitious behavior. If so, how can sport psychologists help athletes to distinguish between routines and superstitions? Two possible answers are apparent. The first concerns the issue of perceived control. Whereas a superstition arises from a fatalistic belief that one cannot change one's method of preparation lest it bring bad luck, the use of a routine can be shortened if necessary. By contrast, superstitious rituals tend to lengthen as more and more behavioral links are added to the imaginary causal chain between action and consequence. A second way of distinguishing between routines and superstitions concerns the technical role of each step in the repetitive sequence. Thus, whereas each part of a routine should be justifiable on logical grounds, the components of a ritual may seem irrational. Unfortunately, despite such apparently clear distinctions, the boundaries between routines and superstitions are often blurred in athletes' minds.

(iii) Using Trigger Words as Concentration Cues

Most sports performers talk to themselves silently as they train or compete. The content of this covert *self-talk* may involve praise (e.g., "Well done! That's good"), criticism ("You stupid fool—you've made another mistake") or instruction ("Keep your head steady"). In other words, self-talk may be positive, negative, or neutral. But how does self-talk affect athletic performance? More importantly for present purposes, what is its status as a concentration technique?

In general, research suggests that positive self-talk is associated with enhanced performance in such sports as skiing, golf, and swimming (see review by Van Raalte, Cornelius, Brewer & Hatton, 2000). Conversely, as one might expect intuitively, critical self-statements are associated with *worst ever* performances in such sports as bowling, field hockey, and darts (ibid.). Interestingly, the use of instructional self-talk in the form of *cue words* has been shown to enhance the learning and performance of skills in tennis (Ziegler, 1987) and figure-skating (Ming & Martin, 1996). More recently, a survey of the nature and uses of self-talk in athletes was conducted by Hardy, Gammage, & Hall (2001). One of the findings reported in this study was that athletes used it not only for skill-learning but also for *mastery* reasons, for the purpose of staying focused (p. 315).

Can self-talk improve concentration skills? Unfortunately, no published studies designed to address this question could be located. However, there are theoretical grounds for believing that positive and instructional self-statements could enhance attentional skills by encouraging athletes to remain calm and by reminding about what precisely to focus on in a given situation. Therefore, many applied sport psychologists recommend that athletes can benefit from the use of instructional self-talk comprising concise and vivid verbal cues (or trigger words) that should elicit an appropriate attentional focus for a particular type of skill execution. For example, in soccer, a cue-phrase like *get tight* may be used by coaches to remind players to shadow their opponents as closely as possible.

In general, applied sport psychologists recommend that effective trigger words should have four main characteristics (Schmid & Peper, 1998). First, they must be phrased to enable players to focus on positive (i.e., what to do) rather than negative (i.e., what to avoid) targets. Second, they should emphasize what needs to be done in the present situation rather than some in the future. Third, they should target the process of the skill instead of its outcome. Finally, it may be helpful for trigger words to be written down on cards and made visible to the player while she or he is training.

(iv)   Mental Practice

The term *mental practice*, or *visualization*, refers to the systematic use of mental imagery in order to rehearse physical actions. It involves *seeing* and *feeling* a skill in one's imagination before actually executing it (Moran, 2002).

Research on the imagery processes of athletes indicates that they tend to *visualize* for both motivational and cognitive purposes. Although the former category is rather ill defined, it includes the imagination of performance goals (see above) and lowered arousal levels. For example, Richard Faulds, Britain's 2000 Olympic gold-medallist in trap-shooting, used imagery to reduce performance anxiety: "The image is the ice-man. You walk like an ice-man and think like an ice-man" (cited in Nichols, 2000, p. 7).

Cognitively, athletes use imagery for learning skills and improving concentration. In the first case, mental rehearsal involves a sequence of relaxing physically, closing one's eyes, and trying to see and feel oneself repeatedly performing a specific skill (e.g., a tennis serve) successfully in one's imagination. This use of imagery, called *mental practice* (MP), is facilitated by a specially designed *script* that describes the skill to be learned in vivid, multisensory detail. Interestingly, reviews of controlled experimental studies using MP show that it has a small but reliable effect on skill-learning (see Driskell, Copper & Moran, 1994). Specifically, people assigned to a mental practice condition when learning a simple motor skill tend to improve significantly more than those who are assigned to a control condition, but not as much as those who have physically practiced the skill in question.

Another cognitive application of imagery is as a concentration technique (Moran, 1996). In this case, many athletes prepare for an event by visualizing intended actions while practicing in simulated competitive conditions. To illustrate, consider how Mike Atherton, the former England cricket captain, prepared mentally for a test match with Australia: "What I find really good for me is to spend a few soli-

tary moments out on the pitch either the day before or on the morning of the match which is when I do the visualization stuff—what's going to come, who's going to bowl, how they are going to bowl... so that nothing can come as a surprise... the visualization is vital" (cited in Selvey, 1998, p. 2). Clearly, a key function of imagery here is to automate one's responses to different possible competitive scenarios.

In summary, although mental imagery is known to improve athletic performance, its status as a concentration technique is uncertain. It may work, however, by helping athletes to code symbolically the sequence of movements to be learned and performed in a sport situation. In short, visualization may give athletes a mental blueprint of what is required. Incidentally, some helpful practical guidelines on the use of imagery in sport are provided by Hale (1998).

(v)   Simulation Training

The concept of *simulation training* (Orlick, 1990), also known as *adversity training* (Loehr, 1986), *dress rehearsal* (Schmid & Peper, 1998), *simulated practice*, (Hodge & McKenzie, 1999) and *distraction training* (Maynard, 1998), proposes that sport performers may become inoculated against the adverse effects of distractions by practicing in their presence during training sessions.

Anecdotal testimonials to the value of this hypothesis are plentiful in sport, both in individual events and in team games. To illustrate, Earl Woods, the father and early coach of Tiger Woods, used adversity training on him when he was a young boy. Specifically, he claimed that "all the strategies and tactics of distraction I'd learned I threw at that kid and he would just grit his teeth and play... and if anyone tries pulling a trick on him these days he just smiles and says 'my dad used to do that years ago'" (cited in Evening Herald, 2001, p. 61). With regard to adversity training for teams, Javier Aguirre, the coach of the Mexican national soccer team, instructed his players to practice penalty-taking after every friendly match in the year leading up to the 2002 World Cup in an effort to prepare for possible penalty-shootouts in the forthcoming competition. As he explained: "[T]here will always be noise and that is the best way to practice" (cited in Smith, 2002, p. S3). Simulation training in other team sports has been noted by Singer, Cauragh, Tennant, Murphey, Chen, and

Lidor (1991), who observed that in American football, coaches often "simulate opposing team fans and stadium loud noises during practice to acquaint their players with the potential distracting situations in the subsequent competitive game" (p. 101).

Figure 3: Simulation Training (Based on Sellars, 1996)

Distraction	Simulation / Sport
Crowd noise	Playing pre-recorded audiotapes of crowd noise during training sessions in hockey to familiarize players with expected distractions in an away venue.
Gamesmanship/intimidation	Arranging for teammates to simulate opponents' gamesmanship in basketball (e.g., insulting players) during practice matches.
Fatigue	Alternating normal training sessions in athletics with short bouts of high-intensity exercise in an effort to simulate fatigue effects.
Unfavorable refereeing decisions	Designing modified game-situations in tennis (e.g., where at least one unfair call is made in every game) to inoculate players against biased umpiring decisions.
Pressure	Simulating pressure situations in soccer (e.g., arranging for 10 players to compete against 11 in order to prepare for situations where a player has been sent off)

In Figure 3, some examples are offered to illustrate the use of simulation training in various sports.

Unfortunately, despite its intuitive appeal, simulation training has received little or no empirical scrutiny as a concentration technique. Nevertheless, some support for its theoretical underpinnings may be found in cognitive psychology. For example, research on the *encoding specificity* principle of learning shows that people's recall of information is facilitated by conditions that resemble those in which the original encoding occurred (Matlin, 2005). Extrapolating from this principle, the simulation of competitive situations in practice should lead to positive transfer effects in the competition itself.

In addition, adversity training can be justified on the grounds that it counteracts the tendency for novel or unexpected factors to distract sports performers in competition. Simulating these factors in training will reduce their subsequent attention-capturing qualities. Taken together, therefore, some theoretical grounds justify the claim that simulation training is a potentially valuable concentration strategy in team sports.

Part 4: Practical Issues to Be Considered Before Applying an Attentional Skills Intervention

This chapter mentioned earlier that sport psychologists have conducted relatively little research on the question of what athletes should focus on in competitive situations. Let us now re-consider this problem and specify some related issues involving the optimal usage of attention-enhancement techniques with athletes (see Simons, 1999).

First, applied sport psychologists should make sure to establish the precise nature of the concentration demands of the skill in which improved performance is required. For example, is this skill self paced or externally paced? Does it require precise, untimed motor movements (e.g., volleying in tennis) or does it depend more on timing and physical strength (e.g., tackling in rugby)? The views of an expert coach on the temporal constraints surrounding key skills should be sought before designing or implementing an attentional skills training program for a given athlete. Second, does the sport performer know precisely which cues he or she should concentrate on when attempting to perform the skill? This question is often neglected by applied sport psychologists in their enthusiasm to provide practical assistance to athletes. Thus, Simons (1999) recommends that instead of exhorting players to watch the ball, coaches and sport psychology consultants should ask such questions as "What way was the ball spinning as it came to you?" or "Did you guess correctly where the ball would land?" The value of such questioning is that it promotes discovery learning in the performers and encourages them to look for task-relevant advance cues in training situations. Third, it is essential to find out what distractions an athlete typically experiences before recommending a package of concentration techniques. After all, how can we train a player to focus effectively if we do not know why his or her mind tends to wander in the first place (see Moran, 1996)? Finally, it is vital for the coach or sport psychologist to evaluate the degree to which any motivational issues affect the attentional problem under investigation. To explain: Deficiencies in attention are sometimes attributable to a lack of interest on the part of the performer rather than to any lack of cognitive capacity.

Part 5: New Directions in Research on Concentration Skills Training

At least five potentially significant new directions may be identified for research in the field of concentration skills training.

To begin with, as mentioned earlier, it is extremely important to find out why athletes lose their concentration in competitive situations. Until recently, however, relatively little was known about the *internal* (or self-generated) distractions experienced by sport performers (see review by Moran, 1996). With the advent of new theoretical models (e.g., Wegner's theory of ironic processes, 1994; Janelle, 1999) and questionnaires designed to measure athletes' susceptibility to cognitive interference (Hatzigeorgiadis & Biddle, 2000), it should be possible to gain a comprehensive understanding of how athletes' own thoughts, feelings, and emotions affect their attentional processes.

A second fruitful avenue for further research on concentration in sport concerns the task of exploring *meta-attentional* processes in athletes—their theories about how their own concentration systems work. This topic is fascinating because most sports performers have developed, from their own competitive experience, various informal models of the way in which their minds operate. Indeed, the entire enterprise of attentional skills training in applied sport psychology could be viewed as an exercise in meta-attentional training: giving athletes insight into, and control over, their own concentration processes. As yet, however, we know very little about the nature, accuracy, or malleability of athletes' meta-cognitive models. Therefore, a number of interesting questions arise. For example, do sport performers' mental mod-

els become more sophisticated with increasing athletic expertise? If so, how and why does this occur? Research is needed to address such questions. Interestingly, Jackson and Baker (2001) discovered a discrepancy between belief and reality with regard to the consistency of rugby place-kicker Neil Jenkins' pre-kick routines. Briefly, these authors showed that the concentration time component of Jenkins' routine was longer for more difficult kicks than for easier ones.

Third, sport psychologists should explore the relationship between the structure of various athletic activities and their attentional demands. For example, do untimed games such as golf place different demands on the concentration system of performers than those imposed by timed activities (e.g., soccer)? If so, what theoretical mechanisms could account for such differences? Until such research is undertaken, psychologists will not be able to tailor generic attentional training programs to sport-specific situations.

Fourth, if we assume that attention is a skill, then it should be measurable. But what is the best way to assess attentional skills? This question was examined by Abernethy, Summers, and Ford (1998), who reviewed three types of attentional tests: behavioral measures (i.e., *dual-task* tests that assess people's skill in dividing their attention effectively between concurrent actions), psychophysiological indices (see also Hatfield & Hillman, 2001), and cognitive/self-report scales (e.g., the Test of Attentional and Interpersonal Style, TAIS; Nideffer, 1976). After these authors had reviewed available empirical evidence, they concluded that all three of these types of measures should be combined by researchers in order to assess adequately the multidimensional construct of attention in sport. Unfortunately, the tendency in this field is to select measures of attention more for reasons of face validity and brevity rather than on grounds of construct validity.

Finally, there has been a paucity of evaluative research on the efficacy of attentional skills techniques (especially when used in combination) and packaged training programs in sport psychology. Interestingly, Ziegler (1995) used a single-case design to demonstrate that two male collegiate soccer players could be trained to shift their attention as required by the demands of various sport-specific tasks. Unfortunately, research suggests that generalized visual skills training programs are not effective in enhancing soccer performance (Starkes, Helsen, & Jack, 2001; Williams, 2001), yet another fact that questions the validity of using visual search tasks like the *concentration grid* (Schmid & Peper, 1998) as concentration training tools.

Summary

Concentration, or the ability to focus mental effort on what is most important in any situation while ignoring distractions, is widely regarded as a vital determinant of athletic success. This principle was illustrated both by anecdotal examples (from the experiences of world-class athletes like Darren Clarke and Stephen Hendry) and by objective research evidence (namely, a survey of athletes' views about the relative importance of various mental skills). Nevertheless, at least three issues remain unresolved in this field. First, what psychological principles govern either the attainment or loss of an optimal focus in sport performers? Second, and more practically, can concentration skills be trained in athletes? Finally, if so, how valid and effective are the various techniques that applied sport psychologists recommend for improving attentional skills? The purpose of this chapter was to provide empirically based answers to these and other relevant questions.

In the first section of the chapter, we analyzed the meaning of and relationship between the terms *attention* and *concentration* in psychology. Briefly, we explained that attention is a multidimensional construct with at least three different meanings: *concentration* or *effortful awareness, selective perceptual ability,* and the *capacity to perform two or more actions simultaneously.* In the next section, we specified various principles of effective concentration that may be derived from research on the correlates of a focused state of mind in athletes. For example, athletes tend to do their best when they focus on actions that are specific, relevant, and under their control. This key principle undergirds most useful attentional training strategies in applied sport psychology. The third section of the chapter contains a review of the nature and efficacy of the various exercises and techniques that are alleged to enhance concentration skills in athletes. Included here were such popular methods as *specifying performance goals* and the *use of pre-performance routines,* and we explored some practical issues that need to be considered before attentional training programs can be used optimally with athletes. Finally, we identified some potentially fruitful new directions for research on attentional skills training in athletes.

References

Abernethy, B. (2001). Attention. In R. N. Singer, H. A. Hausenblas, & C. M. Janelle (Eds.), *Handbook of sport psychology* (2nd ed., pp. 53-85). New York: John Wiley.

Abernethy, B., Summers, J. J., & Ford, S. (1998). Issues in the measurement of attention. In J. L. Duda (Ed.), *Advances in sport and exercise psychology measurement* (pp. 173-193). Morgantown, WV: Fitness Information Technology.

Albinson, J. G., & Bull, S. J. (1988). *A mental game plan.* Eastbourne, UK: Spodyn.

Annett, J. (1991). Skill acquisition. In J. E. Morrison (Ed.), *Training for performance: Principles of applied human learning* (pp. 13-51). Chichester: Wiley.

Beilock, S. L., & Carr, T. H. (2001). On the fragility of skilled performance: What governs choking under pressure? *Journal of Experimental Psychology: General, 130,* 701-725.

Beilock, S. L., Carr, T. H., MacMahon, C., & Starkes, J. L. (2002). When paying attention becomes counterproductive: Impact of divided versus skill-focused attention on novice and experienced performers of sensorimotor skills. *Journal of Experimental Psychology: Applied, 8,* 6-16.

Brodkin, J. (2001). Pumped up for the mind games. *The Guardian,* 14 September, p. 34 (Sport).

Burke, K. L. (1992). Concentration. *Sport Psychology Training Bulletin, 4,* 1-8.

Burton, D., Weinberg, R. S., Yukeslon, D., & Weigand, D. (1998). The goal effectiveness paradox: Examining the goal practices of collegiate athletes. *The Sport Psychologist, 12,* 404-418.

Crews, D. J., & Boutcher, S. H. (1986). Effects of structured preshot behaviours on beginning golf performance. *Perceptual and Motor Skills, 62,* 291-294.

Couture, R. T., Jerome, W., & Tihanyi, J. (1999). Can associative and dissociative strategies affect the swimming performance of recreational swimmers? *The Sport Psychologist, 13,* 334-343.

Cox, R. H. (1998). Sport psychology: *Concepts and applications* (4th ed.). Boston, MA: WCB McGraw-Hill.

Dalloway, M. (1993). *Concentration: Focus your mind, power your game.* Phoenix: AZ: Optimal Performance Institute.

Driskell, J.E., Copper, C., & Moran, A (1994). Does mental practice enhance performance? *Journal of Applied Psychology, 79,* 481-492.

Durand-Bush, N., Salmela, J. H., & Green-Demers, I. (2001). The Ottawa Mental Skills Assessment Tool (OMSAT-3*). *The Sport Psychologist, 15,* 1-19.

Everton, C. (2002, May 8). Ebdon's regime pays off. *The Irish Times,* p. 25.

Fernandez-Duque, D., & Johnson, M. L. (1999). Attention metaphors: How metaphors guide the cognitive psychology of attention. *Cognitive Science, 23,* 83-116.

Gauron, E. (1984). *Mental training for peak performance.* Lansing, NY: Sport Science Associates.

Hale, B. (1998). *Imagery training: A guide for sports coaches and performers.* Headingley, Leeds: The National Coaching Foundation.

Hardy, J., Gammage, K., & Hall, C. (2001). A descriptive study of athletes self-talk. *The Sport Psychologist, 15,* 306-318.

Harle, S. K., & Vickers, J. N. (2001). Training quiet eye improves accuracy in the basketball free throw. *The Sport Psychologist, 15,* 289-305.

Hatfield., B. D., & Hillman, C. H. (2001). The psychophysiology of sport: A mechanistic understanding of the psychology of superior performance. In R. N. Singer, H. A. Hausenblas, & C. M. Janelle (Eds.), *Handbook of Sport Psychology* (2nd ed., pp. 362-388). New York: John Wiley.

Hatzigeorgiadis, A., & Biddle, S. J. H. (2000). Assessing cognitive interference in sport: Development of the Thought Occurrence Questionnaire for Sport. *Anxiety, Stress, and Coping, 13,* 65-86.

Hodge, K., & McKenzie, A. (1999). *Thinking rugby.* Auckland, New Zealand: Reed Publishing.

Jackson, R. C. (2001). The preshot routine: A prerequisite for successful performance? In P. R. Thomas (Ed.), *Optimising performance in golf* (pp. 279-288). Brisbane: Australian Academic Press

Jackson, R. C., & Baker, J. S. (2001). Routines, rituals, and rugby: Case study of a world class goal kicker. *The Sport Psychologist, 15,* 48-65.

Jackson, S. A. (1995). Factors influencing the occurrence of flow state in elite athletes. *Journal of Applied Sport Psychology, 7,* 138-166.

Jackson, S. A., & Roberts, G. C. (1992). Positive performance states of athletes: Toward a conceptual understanding of peak performance. *The Sport Psychologist, 6,* 156-171.

Jackson, S. A., & Csikszentmihalyi, M. (1999). *Flow in sports.* Champaign, Illinois: Human Kinetics.

Jackson, S. A., Thomas, P. R., Marsh, H. W., & Smethurst, C. J. (2001). Relationships between flow, self-concept, psychological skills and performance. *Journal of Applied Sport Psychology, 13,* 129-153.

Janelle, C. M. (1999). Ironic mental processes in sport: Implications for sport psychologists. *The Sport Psychologist, 13,* 201-220.

Janelle, C. M. (2002). Anxiety, arousal and visual attention: A mechanistic account of performance variability. *Journal of Sports Sciences, 20,* 237-251.

Janelle, C. M., Singer, R. N., & Williams, A. M. (1999). External distractions and attentional narrowing: Visual search evidence. *Journal of Sport and Exercise Psychology, 21,* 70-91.

Kahneman, D. (1973). *Attention and effort.* New York: Prentice Hall.

Kingston, K. M., & Hardy, L. (1997). Effects of different types of goals on processes that support performance. *The Sport Psychologist, 11,* 277-293.

Loehr, J. E. (1986). *Mental toughness training for sports: Achieving athletic excellence.* New York: The Stephen Greene Press.

Logie, R. H. (1999). Working memory. *The Psychologist, 12,* 174-178.

Mallett, C. J., & Hanrahan, S. J. (1997). Race modelling: An effective cognitive strategy for the 100m sprinter? *The Sport Psychologist, 11,* 72-85.

Masters, K. S., & Ogles, B. M. (1998). Associative and dissociative cognitive strategies in exercise and running: 20 years later, what do we know? *The Sport Psychologist, 12,* 253-270.

Matlin, M. W. (2005). *Cognition.* Hoboken, New Jersey: John Wiley.

Maynard, I. (1998). *Improving concentration.* Headingley, Leeds: The National Coaching Foundation.

Miller, B. (1997). *Gold minds: The psychology of winning in sport.* Marlborough, Wiltshire: The Crowood Press.

Ming, S., & Martin, G. L. (1996). Single-subject evaluation of a self-talk package for improving figure-skating performance. *The Sport Psychologist, 10,* 227-238.

Moran, A. P. (1996). *The psychology of concentration in sport performers: A cognitive analysis.* Hove, East Sussex: Psychology Press/Taylor & Francis.

Moran, A. (2000). Improving sporting abilities: Training concentration skills. In J. Hartley & A. Branthwaite (Eds.), *The applied psychologist* (2nd ed, pp. 92-110). Buckingham: Open University Press.

Moran, A. (2002). Playing in your mind's eye, *The Psychologist, 15,* 414-415.

Moran, A. (2004). *Sport and exercise psychology: A critical introduction.* London: Psychology Press/Routledge.

Moran, A., Byrne, A., & McGlade, N. (2002). The effects of anxiety and strategic planning on visual search behaviour. *Journal of Sports Sciences, 20,* 225-236.

Nichols, P. (2000, September 21). Ice-man Faulds keeps his cool. *The Guardian,* p. 7.

Nideffer, R. M. (1976). The Test of Attentional and Interpersonal Style. *Journal of Personality and Social Psychology, 34,* 394-404.

One Tiger that will never crouch. (2001, April 9). *Evening Herald,* p. 61.

Orlick, T. (1990). *In pursuit of excellence.* Champaign, Illinois: Leisure Press.

Otway, G. (1999, August 1). Clarke enjoys a special K day. *The Sunday Times,* p. 13 (Sport).

Pashler, H. (Ed.). (1998). *Attention.* Hove, East Sussex: Psychology Press.

Ramsay, A. (2001, June 11). Victorious Kuerten rises to challenge. *Irish Independent,* p. 13 (Sport).

Schmid, A., & Peper, E. (1998). Strategies for training concentration. In J. M. Williams (Ed.). *Applied sport psychology: Personal growth to peak performance* (3rd ed., pp. 316-328). Mountain View, California: Mayfield.

Scott, L. M., Scott, D., Bedic, S., & Dowd, J. (1999). The effects of associative and dissociative strategies on rowing ergometer performance. *The Sport Psychologist, 13,* 57-68.

Sellars, C. (1996). *Mental skills: An introduction for sports coaches.* Headingley, Leeds: National Coaching Foundation.

Selvey, M. (1998, November 20). Getting up for the Ashes. *The Guardian,* p. 2 (Sport).

Shaw, D. (2002). Confidence and the pre-shot routine in golf: A case study. In I. Cockerill (Ed.), *Solutions in sport psychology* (pp. 108-119). London: Thomson.

Simons, J. (1999). Concentration. In M. A. Thompson, R. A. Vernacchia, & W. E. Moore (Eds.), *Case studies in applied sport psychology: An educational approach* (pp. 89-114). Dubuque, Iowa: Kendall/Hunt.

Singer, R. N. (2000). Performance and human factors: Considerations about cognition and attention for self-paced and externally-paced events. *Ergonomics, 43*, 1661-1680.

Singer, R. N., Cauraugh, J. H., Tennant, L. K., Murphey, M., Chen, D., & Lidor, R. (1991). Attention and distractors: Considerations for enhancing sport performance. *International Journal of Sport Psychology, 22*, 95-114.

Smith, M. (2002, February 15). Practice makes perfect. *The Daily Telegraph*, p. S3.

Solso, R. (1998). *Cognitive psychology* (5th edition). Boston: Allyn & Bacon.

Starkes, J. L., Helsen, W., & Jack, R. (2001). Expert performance in sport and dance. In R. N. Singer, H. A. Hausenblas, & C. M. Janelle (Eds.), *Handbook of sport psychology* (2nd ed., pp. 174-201). New York: John Wiley.

Syer, J. (1989). *Team spirit*. London: Simon & Schuster.

Van Raalte, J. L., Cornelius, A. E., Brewer, B. W., & Hatten, S. J. (2000). The antecedents and consequences of self-talk in competitive tennis. *The Sport Psychologist, 22*, 345-356.

Weinberg, R. S. (1988). *The mental ADvantage: Developing your psychological skills in tennis*. Champaign, Illinois: Human Kinetics.

Weinberg, R. S., & Gould, D. (2003). *Foundations of sport and exercise psychology* (3rd ed). Champaign, Illinois: Human Kinetics.

Wegner, D. M. (1994). Ironic processes of mental control. *Psychological Review, 101*, 34-52.

Whitaker, D. (1999). *The spirit of teams*. Marlborough, Wiltshire: The Crowood Press.

Williams, M. (2001, May 28-June 1). Perceptual expertise in sport: Some myths and realities. In A. Papaioannou, M. Goudas, & Y. Theodorakis (Eds.), *Programme and Proceedings of 10th World Congress* (Vol. 1, pp. 206-211), Skiathos, Athens: International Society of Sport Psychology.

Ziegler, S. G. (1987). Effects of stimulus cueing on the acquisition of groundstrokes by beginning tennis players. *Journal of Applied Behaviour Analysis, 20*, 405-411.

Ziegler, S. G. (1995). The effects of attentional shift training on the execution of soccer skills: A preliminary investigation. *Journal of Applied Behavioural Analysis, 27*, 545-552.

Courtesy of iStockphoto Inc.

2.2

Research on Decision-Making and the Use of Cognitive Stratgies in Sport Settings

GERSHON TENENBAUM AND RONNIE LIDOR

Introduction

Most studies and conceptual frameworks related to decision-making (DM) and performance stem from the cognitive approach, Bernstein's *dynamic systems,* and the Gibsonian *ecological psychology* approach, which coined the terms *direct perception* and *perception-action coupling.* Others used *action theory* (Seiler, 2000) to account for the quality of DM and motor performance. DM in sport, mainly in open and dynamic environments, depends to a large extent on several cognitive mechanisms, which operate serially or in parallel as a function of the skill level and experience of the performer, the features of the task, and the constraints posed on the system by external or internal sources. The sequence of these mechanisms operates faster, more efficiently, and with less effort as practice and knowledge base accumulate. The main components, which constitute

the DM mechanism, are presented in Figure 1.

The schema depicted in Figure 1 illustrates that several decisions should be made prior to action execution. The first decision is choosing a visual strategy for fast and efficient visualization of the playing environment. The environment usually contains cues that are more and less relevant, some of which are hidden and have a *predictive* nature. The task is then selected and uses the most relevant cues for the moment for further elaboration. Next, based on the visualized information and made when time permits, one should decide what actions or events are expected and the probability with which they are likely to occur. The third decision results from deeper elaborations between the information fed forward to the central nervous system (CNS), if needed, and the neural network, which stores the experiences learned in similar situations and constitutes the declarative-and-procedural knowledge base

Figure 1: Sequence of Perceptual-Cognitive Stages Associated and Leading to Decision Making and Decision Modification

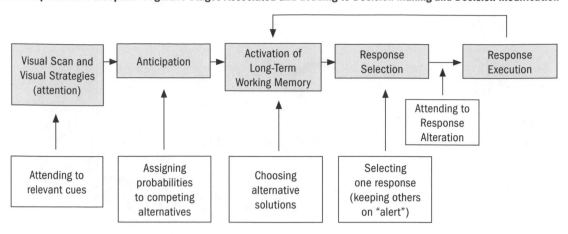

(long-term memory). The final decision is to choose which, and when, to execute a selected response, and at the same time being alert to potential decision alterations as the dynamic environment necessitates. With deliberate practice and competitive experience, these mechanisms operate as one unit, and the process becomes more efficient, effortless, and automatic, with shifts from automatic to intentional modes when required.

This chapter elaborates on research that was conducted in sport and nonsport environments, which together explain how the mechanisms, which determine the quality of DM, are acquired and modified through practice and development of expertise. In addition, the chapter examines the efficacy of cognitive strategies such as attentional control, pre-performance routines, and simulation training to the enhancement of DM in sport. Attention was given to strategies that can be applied by athletes and coaches during their practical work (e.g., practices, competitions, and games). The assumption is that selected cognitive strategies that are introduced to the athletes on a regular basis can assist them in improving some aspects of DM. A three-phase scheme was used to introduce these selected strategies.

The chapter consists of two interrelated points. The first part presents a conceptual framework for studying DM in sport and outlines the mechanisms involved in the DM process. The second part, oriented more toward applied concepts, introduces the use of a variety of cognitive strategies that affect the DM process.

Conceptual Framework

Response selection is directed by cognitive processes and mental operations (Estes, 1982). The effectiveness of these processes can be gauged by the richness and the variety of perceptions processed at a given time (Fisher, 1984), that is, by the system's capacity to encode (store and represent) and access (retrieve) information relevant to the task being performed. Because unique characteristics and requirements vary from task to task, it is assumed that the nature and integration of perceptual-cognitive components required for decision-making and action execution are also unique.

If one accepts the assumption that during an ongoing activity the athlete observes the environment and allocates attention, anticipates upcoming events, processes the information via long-term working memory mechanisms (relying on stored representations, which were acquired through learning and experience), and makes decisions and alterations, then these serial stages should operate (i.e., be organized) differently under temporal constraints of varying duration and structural complexity.

The events in open environments can be perceived as happening sequentially. A sequence, typical to the sport environment, was studied by applying the "mental chronometry" approach (Posner, Nissen, & Odgen, 1978). Such an approach introduces a *warning signal* in the form of cues that draw attention following an *imperative signal*, which imposes response-selection and execution. In sport, the events that consistently occur and alter are the *warning stimuli*, and the move that evokes an action on the part of the athlete is the *imperative stimulus*. This approach considers anticipation of upcoming events as a process that precedes response-selection and execution. Attention processes, both internal (attending to body and inner messages) and external (environmental cues received by senses), are assumed to underlie and determine the quality of decision-making. There are, however, covert processes (i.e., brain evoked potentials and electric and biochemical activities), not fully clear today, which take place during activation of the visual, anticipatory, and DM processes. However, a systematic study, which follows the chronometric conceptualization of events, is of major importance in the study of accessing expert DM in sport.

Decision-Making Related to Visual Attention

In a recent publication, Cave and Bichot (1999) argued that the research in visual attention was driven by the spotlight metaphor (Posner, Snyder, & Davidson, 1980). They extended the concept by addressing several questions related to the nature of visual attention such as "location versus objects-based selection, whether attention moves in analog fashion (i.e., passing over intermediate locations and taking longer for shifts that involve longer distances), the size and shape of the selected region, and, at a more basic level, whether attention works by facilitation targets or inhibiting distracters, and whether multiple and contiguous regions of space can be selected simultaneously" (p. 204).

Selection by location of objects in space is a simple mechanism in which the raw environmental input is organized spatially. Early cuing experiments (Eriksen & Hoffman, 1974; Posner et al., 1978; Posner et al., 1980) and late cuing experiments in sport (Ripoll, 1988; Tenenbaum, Stewart, & Sheath, 1999) have shown that reaction time is faster to cued (i.e., primed, anticipated) location than to unusual ones. However, the cuing effect was found to depend on the time lag between the cuing stimulus (i.e., "warning stimulus") and the "imperative stimulus" (Posner et al., 1978) and distance (see summary in Cave & Bichot, 1999). Reaction times (RTs) increased steadily with a longer time lag between the cued and imperative stimuli until two seconds, and with the distance

between the expected and actual target location. Downing and Pinker (1985) argue that RT increases with distance as a function of the "critical distance," rather than the actual distance between the two stimuli. It was also argued that more visual cortex is devoted to processing the center visual field, and therefore distance effects were larger when the two points were near the center of the visual field than when the two points were in the periphery. Furthermore, the distance effects were uniformly fast once the cue and the target were in the same field and uniformly slower when in different fields, and this was true whether tested left versus right or top versus bottom (Hughes & Zimba, 1985, 1987). In contrast, Rizzolatti, Riggio, Dascola, and Umilta (1987) found that there is an additional cost when cue and target were on opposite sides of either the horizontal or the vertical midline, and this was not due to cortical magnification but rather programming eye movements.

Visual attention was also found to operate differently in detection and discrimination tasks. Downing (1988) showed that attention increases perceptual sensitivity (Handy, Kingstone, & Mangun, 1996; Hawkins et al., 1990). Indeed, the experiments, which were conducted in the laboratory with blank screens and lack of distracters, were not mere representations of the attentional allocation and resources of attention in open-skill sport, where the environment is dynamic and intentionally altered within the rules and the given space. However, the findings suggest that *visual selection* plays an important role in visual processing. The *special location* facilitates *visual selection processing*, which is vital for making further decisions about the action. One should keep in mind that in classical experimentation the response time and accuracy depend on a predetermined plan, while in open-skill sports response-selection, though dependent on visual information (i.e., the location of players and ball in space), is flexible and may alter as a function of other environmental cues and prior experiences (i.e., knowledge base).

Visual selection consists of passing information from one region of the visual field to a higher level processing while moving the eyes to the other field. The visual system is organized by location, albeit retinal location, and location dominates many features in the organization, while this is dominated by time (Navon, 1978). "Eye movements constitute a selection mechanism that is based on location, and because we move our eyes all the time... attention selection within a fixation is done in the same way. ... Assuming that selection is based on location and that time and effort are required to shift attention from one location to another, then tasks involving multiple stimuli should be easier when the stimuli are at or near the same location" (Cave & Bichot, 1999, p. 206). Based on experimental findings, Cave and Bichot concluded that two objects can be processed quicker when they are closer to each other and once a visual object is selected, other objects near the selected object are attended to some degree (i.e., benefit), and objects far from the first object are at a disadvantage (i.e., cost). Furthermore, distracters near the target were found to interfere with naming the target, whereas targets far from the target were not. These interferences disappeared when the target location was cued at least 150 msec in advance. It was argued that interference occurred at the response stage; the interference was greater when the nearby distracters were associated with different responses (Eriksen & Eriksen, 1974; Eriksen & Hoffman, 1973). Studies that incorporated brain activity during visual selection indicated that probe stimuli at a target location were associated with enlarged P1 and N1 components relative to those elicited by probes at a distracter location (Luck, Fan, & Hillyard, 1993), similarly to results obtained in studies where targets were cued (Mangun & Hillyard, 1995).

The other question associated with location is the attention cost associated with different distances that attention travels. To also account for object-based location, it is assumed that the distance affects the way visual objects are organized by grouping, and attention is applied to representations of object groups. Grouping by coherent motion and grouping by color had a stronger effect than did spatial proximity (Driver & Baylis, 1989). Taking all into account, Cave and Bichot (1999) ask, "[A]t what level is it actually determined what information should be selected? Second, at what level is the selection actually accomplished? The decision about what to select may be made using high-level, conceptual representations, but these decisions may drive mechanisms that separate selected from unselected information by operating on raw, spatially organized input at a lower level. In other words, although decisions about what to select may be made on the basis of many different factors, including perceptual grouping by features such as color and motion, the selection may still be accomplished with one or more spotlights" (p. 209).

The main findings related to grouping were that visual stimuli are likely to be selected together if they are located near each other to form a perceptual cluster (Prinzmetal & Millis-Wright, 1984). Arranging elements by a cluster affects conjunction search but not feature search, and subjects tend to examine the entire group at once so that processing moves from one group to another serially (Treisman, 1982) and that two features were more likely to combine into an illusory conjunction if they were part of the same cluster despite the distance between them. Performance improves when the features in the display show a perceptual object (Treisman, Kahneman, & Burkell, 1983). In summary, "there is solid evidence for location and distance effects on visual selection; on the other hand, there is solid evidence for effects of grouping and object organization. There could easily be multiple mechanisms for visual selection operating independently on location-based and object-based representations (Vecera, 1997). However it may still be possible to explain all the results described here with single mechanism... spatial selection that is driven in part by visual organization of the objects in the visual field" (Cave & Bichot, 1999, p. 210). The question remains, however, how can one distinguish between early selection by location and late selection by perceptual grouping? The two-stage mechanism suggested by Cave and Bichot assumes that the selection by location, as a first mechanism, is powerful enough to allow the second stage to be operationalized. The first stage is executed in parallel and is simple. However, this is not yet conclusive, as there is still a possibility that both space-based and object-based mechanisms exist, and they operated independently under different environmental conditions.

The dynamic open-sport environment requires attention to be allocated to various locations and objects at the same time. The location of objects in the special space are known and anticipated as experience increase. In addition, the quality of the decision is not always judged against the quickness of the response-selection, but rather the accuracy and appropriateness of the selected response. In Figure 2, player A may gaze toward the right, middle, or left of the visual space; locate the defense (opponent) players (Δ), and the offense players (○) first; locate the *free* offense player (●), based on *grouping mechanism*; and finally, make the decision to pass the ball to this location. Locating the *free player* in the visual space for DM constitutes an advantage and is a key factor acquired through many years of practice and game experience. Whether selection is done by location and then by grouping and whether selection operates serially or in parallel are not clear yet. It is assumed that in the early age of motor skill development, the two-stage approach is evident, but with time, experience, and deliberate practice, locating and grouping operate in parallel and even under automatic modes, unless the visual system shifts from target control mode (i.e., visual systems moves serially from one target in the display to another target) to context control mode (i.e., visual system is fixated to one spot in space and captures its main target in a chunking fashion) and vice-versa, depending on the game situation.

Figure 2: Selection of a Target with a Visual Field

L selection by location
G selection by perceptual grouping

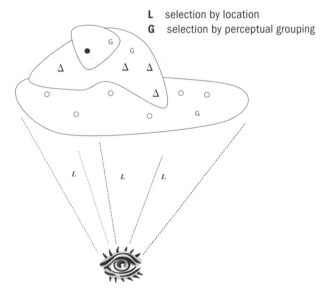

To capture the visual environmental space, the eyes and sometimes also the head must shift across the visual field. This is essential for response-selection. Shulman, Remington, and McLean (1979) used a specific paradigm to show that the attentional spotlight passes the near-fixation location on the way to far-fixation location, and expected location

facilitates (i.e., decreases RT) while unexpected location inhibits (i.e., increases RT) processing. However, the expected pattern of RT depends on the spread of attention over the area scanned (Yantis, 1988). Chestain (1992a, b) argues against an attention spotlight, which passes over intermediate locations. Cave and Bichot (1999) summarize the state of the art as follows: "[E]vidence to date appears to suggest that attention reserves are allocated to the new location as they are simultaneously deallocated at the old location, without passing over regions in between. Given current understanding of the physiology of visual attention (Motter, 1994; Shall, Hanes, Thompson, & King, 1995), an attention shift could plausibly be implemented in the brain by decreasing the activity in the pool of neurons with receptive fields covering the location previously selected while increasing the activity in the pool of neurons with receptive fields covering the new location to be attended" (p. 212).

The study of visual attention in sport was somewhat different from that in classical experimentation. Visual attention was studied through recording the number of eye-fixations and duration on particular stimuli in the visual field. Expert athletes had fewer fixations per longer duration than novice athletes (Abernethy & Russell, 1987; Ripoll, 1979). The novice athletes seem therefore to use a *target control* strategy, in which spotlight beam passes through the entire display, relevant and irrelevant alike. The experts seem to operate a *context control* strategy, which consists of eye fixation to a single location, from which it is possible to capture the events among the visual fixation point. Along with skill development, visual attention shifts from one location to another location by chunking the essential stimuli in the visual field and processing them into a meaningful and integrated image, which, with long-term memory elaboration, elicits a motor response. This response is not always evaluated by how fast it is executed (i.e., RT), but rather by its appropriateness to lead to an advantage over the opponent. Indeed, fast information processing may be of an advantage under some circumstances, but of a disadvantage once the selected response was not the correct one or was anticipated by the opponent.

Additional concerns related to visual attention raised up by Cave and Bichot (1999), which are of importance in sport, are the size of the selected attention area, the flexibility of adjusting that size, and once an area was selected, the attention directed to all the stimuli within this region. It is not just the attention spotlight that is directed towards the present stimuli in the sporting field, but also the expected location of the upcoming stimuli, which make information processing efficient. The earlier stimuli are anticipated in the sequence of information processing, the higher the probability that interference will be eliminated. It can be assumed that the larger the area within which events are expected to occur, the lower the probable sensitivity. This is more true for novices, who find it hard to attend and concentrate on a large array of stimuli, and less true for experts, who skillfully attend to the most relevant stimuli within this array (Tenenbaum & Bar-Eli, 1993, 1995).

At this stage, Cave and Bichot (1999) argue, it is not possible to point out which attention mechanism guides the different stages of processing of the size of the stimuli. Experiments by LaBerge (1983) have shown that attention can be spread over a narrow or over a large area, and there does not appear to be any tradeoff. In another study (Egeth, 1977), responses were slower when attention was spread over a large area. These results, though equivocal, do not indicate whether the spread of attention is related to the appropriateness of the response-selection. In experiments where few distracters were cued, these cued distracters interfered with the identification of the target, and this resulted in RT increase. Indeed the more locations that are cued, the harder is the discrimination task (Eriksen & St James, 1986). The question remains whether expert athletes benefit or pay the cost when more than one source of information is presented to them in the field. It is argued that through deliberate practice and experience, the more skilled the athlete, the more efficiently he or she processes more sources of relevant information for DM and the more efficient the processing and response-selection under such conditions—contrary to findings reported in the Cave and Bichot (1999) article. The inefficiency of processing information in a wide area of stimuli is characteristic of the novice and inexperienced athletes. The more efficient elaboration between working memory and long-term memory (Ericsson & Kintsch, 1995) by experts is evidence of this claim.

Another possibility is that a spotlight does not have strictly defined regions, and stimuli outside the target can be noticed, though not as efficiently. "Facilitation could be strong in the center of the selected region and drop off gradually with distance. Such an attention gradient could cover a large area. Because it is not as crucial to have the most important visual object always in the center of the spotlight, this facilitory spotlight might move more slowly when it changes position. A spotlight that was merely a facilitator could still play an important role in filtering out distracters, but additional selection mechanisms could be required at later stages of processing" (Cave & Bichot, 1999, p.213). The findings of Ripoll (1988) and Abernethy and Russell (1987) suggest that, as experience is accumulated, the number of eye fixations in a dynamic environment decreases and their duration increases to allow relevant and irrelevant information (distracters) to be accessed and processed for response selection.

The research on attention allocation (Downing, 1988; Downing & Pinker, 1985; Henderson & MacQuistan, 1993) indicates that attention is uniformly distributed within the targeted area, and then falls off gradually from the edge of that region. This claim is also supported by studies, which included brain evoked response potential (ERP) measures or P1 and N1 (Mangun & Hillyard, 1995). This observation, however, may be true for naive subjects or novice athletes, but not for experts who underwent extensive hours of deliberate practice and competition. One may expect that in those athletes, distracters are well attended and facilitation does not decrease as much as would be expected when far from a visual fixation point. It is further claimed that if a stimulus is anticipated to arrive from "out of the region of the fixation area," an additional region is facilitated and further adjustment in the visual field occurs to efficiently capture, process, and select a response required for that particular situation. It is equally logical to assume that experts' decisions in such situations may also be facilitated by anticipatory processes, which rely on inner neural processes (i.e., intuition), which strongly rely on knowledge structure (i.e., expertise). Thus, allocation of visual attention may be used to facilitate response-selection by feeding forward the relevant information to higher-level processing centers, but may also be used to facilitate anticipatory mechanisms. Such a strategy, which consists of expert knowledge base, minimizes the inhibition processes caused by environmental distracters in experts. However, a limited knowledge base gives rise to distracters, which slow down the response-selection (i.e., inhibition) as a consequence of drawing similar attention to relevant and irrelevant cues in the visual field. In novices, the anticipatory mechanisms are also limited or nonexistent. As Cave and Bichot argue, "further experiments are necessary to find the conditions that determine whether attention appears as a focused facilitation, a ring of facilitations, focused inhibition, or some other complex spatial pattern. If there are multiple selection mechanisms operating at different processing levels to control different types of interference and overload (Luck, Hillyard, Mouloua, & Hawkins, 1996), then we might expect the spatial pattern of attentional effects to vary considerably, depending on which mechanism is triggered by the demands of the current task" (p. 218). One might add that these issues should be studied in sport by taking into account skill-level and task-specific constraints.

Processing Information and Response-Selection

The visual system through its attention strategies, mainly target, series-type, and context modes, enables the performer to anticipate upcoming events with some certainty and prepare the system for response selection. The final selection of a response depends on how the information fed forward to the CNS is processed. In other words, the elaboration on this information through the use of long-term working memory (LTWM) enables the performer to anticipate the upcoming events, and prepare a response that will be the most appropriate for the particular situation. The research on anticipatory capabilities and LTWM is reviewed briefly.

Anticipatory Capability

Response selection depends to a large extent on anticipatory capability, and the variation among different caliber athletes is accounted for by these differences (Abernethy, 1987a). Repeated exposure to similar situations results in the development of mental representations in the brain neural network

that facilitate anticipatory capabilities (Keele, 1982). Research on athletes participating in fast ball games indicated that, under extremely short temporal conditions, expert athletes could predict the final ball location more accurately than novice athletes (Abernethy, 1987b). It was also revealed that shorter viewing times, fewer eye fixations, and longer visual durations accounted for the superior anticipatory final ball accuracy predictions of the expert players (see Tenenbaum & Bar-Eli, 1993, 1995 for extensive review).

However, a recent study by Tenenbaum, Sar-El, and Bar-Eli (2000) indicated that experts' advantages in accurately predicting final ball locations occurred only in about 50% of tennis strokes, and these were mainly under the shortest temporal visual exposures. Furthermore, experts were found to concentrate on several cues simultaneously at every stage of their opponent's actions rather than on one cue, a typical strategy used by novice and young players. Thus, response selection may be determined by additional mechanisms that elaborate on the information fed forward by the visual system to the CNS for further processing. In this respect, the knowledge structure takes a crucial role.

Another study by Tenenbaum, Levy-Kolker, Sade, Lieberman, and Lidor (1994), also indicated that intermediate players do not differ from expert players in anticipating the final ball location. However, the differences in anticipatory decision self-confidence at the time of ball-racket contact and beyond was significantly more pronounced in the expert tennis players. Not only is self-efficacy related to DM and may play an important role in the execution phase of the response, but it also may play an important role in the response quality and the awareness for change or adjustment, if necessary.

Working Memory-Long-Term Memory Linkage and Knowledge Structure

Traditional short-term memory experiments pointed out the limitations in storage capacity. Recall information was limited (Miller, 1956) and retained for few seconds in the absence of rehearsal (Peterson & Peterson, 1959). Later, Baddeley and Hitch (1974) viewed short-term memory as a limited system of cognitive resources that could be allocated either to storage or to processing. Working memory was considered a constraining factor on cognitive performance in that only small amounts of information could be temporarily stored while other information was being processed (Baddeley, 1986). These findings however failed to account for expert memory, which seemed to rely on different mechanisms, and therefore required an alternative theoretical conceptualization.

Early work on chess experts' memory by DeGroot (1965) and Chase and Simon (1973) has stimulated a vast research in other sport disciplines (Allard & Burnett, 1985; Allard, Graham, & Paarsalu, 1980; Allard & Starkes, 1980; Bard, Fleury, Carriere, & Halle, 1980; Borgeaud & Abernethy, 1987; Starkes & Allard, 1983; Starkes & Deakin, 1984; Tenenbaum, Levy-Kolker, Bar-Eli, & Weinberg, 1994). Recall, reconstruction, and recognition paradigms were used to examine athletes' memory for structural-meaningful situation and unstructured-transitional-randomized situations. The results indicated that expert athletes can memorize many bits of information after a relatively short visual glance on the structured meaningful situations presented to them. This, however, was not the case with nonstructured and randomized bits of information. The chunking hypothesis suggested by Chase and Simon was the main argument to account for this expert memory superiority. It elegantly accounted for the extended memory by reducing the degrees of freedom that the limited memory capacity had to deal with, and at the same time found a compromise with the traditional view of limited STM.

Several studies' findings have departed from the traditional chunking hypothesis predictions. Sloboda (1976) with musicians; Smyth and Pendleton (1994) with professional dancers; and Starkes, Caicco, Boutilier, and Sevsek (1990) with modern jazz dancers reported that these participants showed superiority over nonexperts in recalling domain-specific information that was not familiar and organized. Thus, recall advantage also occurred when it was not expected to occur. One may argue that music and dance are domains in which experience and expertise impose logical sequences on any combination and variation of music or movement elements; therefore, the nonstructured or unfamiliar information turned out to be familiar once it was presented. In any case, these findings called for the development of an alternative conceptualization of expert memory. Ericsson and Kintsch (1995) have suggested that with domain-specific practice, individuals can utilize long-term memory (LTM) as a means of extending short-term working memory. The LTM contribution occurs through the creation of a domain-specific retrieval structure that can be used to enhance storage and maintainance of items in a more accessible and less interference-prone state. They termed it long-term working memory (LTWM).

LTWM is a knowledge structure base concept. It assumes that after extended practice sessions athletes establish associations between previously presented situations via combinations of chunks and appropriate actions that are stored in LTM. During competition, experts more than novices use the situational cues to retrieve the associated action and bypass a complex DM process. Thus, skill-level develops through the acquisition and accumulation of knowledge patterns in a specific domain. The knowledge stored in LTM enables retrieval of memory traces, which are task-specific in an efficient and rapid rate. In memory tasks, the response is based on retrieval of identical information shown to the athletes prior to examination. In decision-making tasks, the same memory traces enable the actor to use the feed-forward information in order to retrieve a decision that is passed on to the motor system. It also enables experts to keep alternative responses in alert. The LTWM theory claims that experts encode information very fast into a form that can be readily stored and is readily retrieved from LTM. What is stored in short-term working memory is a retrieval cue that, once activated, allows the experts to retrieve and unpack the retrieval structure that has been stored. Accordingly, experts rapidly store domain-specific material in LTM and are able to rapidly retrieve it. Thus, working memory can be extended by acquiring domain-specific memory skills that ensure fast storage of information in LTM in such a way that this information can be easily and reliably retrieved (Ericsson & Kintsch, 1995). In this case, when the visual system through its attentional routes feed forward to LTM only "relevant and chunked" information, an optimal response can be selected faster from richer (Abernethy, Neal, & Koning, 1994) and activated LTM. During elaborations on relevant selected information, response-selection becomes more efficient as expertise level increases.

According to Ericsson and Kintsch, three conditions appear to be required for LTWM to be utilized: (1) subjects must have an extensive knowledge base and be able to store the information presented to them very rapidly to LTM, (2) the activity must be very familiar to allow future demands for retrieval of relevant information, and (3) subjects must associate the encoded information with appropriate retrieval cues. LTWM is mediated by a retrieval sequence, which is acquired and stored in LTM. Skilled performers are able to use their knowledge to rapidly encode information in appropriate manners and to set up cues that support rapid and efficient retrieval.

The studies of Sloboda (1976) with musicians, Smyth and Pendleton (1994) with professional dancers, and Starkes et al. (1990) with jazz dancers support the LTWM conceptualization. A recent study by Tenenbaum, Tehan, Stewart, and Christensen (1999) lends more support to the LTWM theory. The researchers examined the effect of age and expertise level on memory for elements' sequence in gymnastics, when some elements were omitted during the second trial after first exposure to new routines. As expected both expertise and experience had major effects on retrieving the 'missing elements' from LTM through the use of LTWM. DM in dynamic environments benefits when information is complete and the knowledge structure permits fast elaborations through cues, which serve as a retrieval route for response selection. In this respect, LTWM should not be limited only to expert memory accountability, but also to superior DM.

Deliberate Practice and Decision Making

The effect of practice on skill acquisition is undisputable and presented in many textbooks and articles. However, the effect of *deliberate practice*, a term and a concept coined by Ericsson, Krampe, and Tesch-Romer (1993), on skill development and DM received much attention only recently. It is not our intention to review the literature, which pertains to the effect of deliberate practice on DM. It is a concept that deserves a review for itself. We introduce it briefly to illustrate an additional view about DM and its development.

Experience, the opportunity to practice, and the instructions given to athletes by coaches during practice were the main determinants of instructional quality. Indeed, simple practice and repetition of memory tasks improved recall capabilities (Ericsson et al., 1993). However, deliberate practice entails deliberate effort to improve performance beyond its current level. It involves solving problems and finding better strategies. It consists of inventing new methods directed to enhance performance, so that each method will be effective for accumulated knowledge and skills (Ericsson, 2000). Deliberate practice, according to Ericsson et al. (1993), rests on the assumption that expert performance is acquired gradually and this development depends on the premise to isolate sequences of simple training that can be mastered sequentially. Furthermore, deliberate practice requires full concentration and incorporates the desire to reach top-level performance despite failures and errors. Repeated failures, though not enjoyable, are used for further improvements.

Bloom (1985) investigated expert performers in a variety of domains and reported that, in all cases, the number of hours and the systematic use of feedback and encouragement were the most important components for talent development. To extend the current knowledge to innovative and creative levels in a specific domain, deliberate practice is an undisputable requirement (Ericsson, 1998, 1999). The link between deliberate practice and performance was found in a variety of domains such as chess (Charness, Krampe, & Mayr, 1996), music (Krampe & Ericsson, 1996; Lehmann & Ericsson, 1996; Sloboda, 1996), and sport (Helsen, Starkes, & Hodges, 1998; Hodges & Starkes, 1996; Schneider, 1993; Starkes et al., 1996).

Cognitive Strategies and Decision-Making

An additional aspect within the cognitive approach to DM and expertise is the conscious use of strategies, which enable the athlete to make the most functional decisions within time and space. The term *cognitive strategies*, which is used in this chapter, refers to the behaviors and thoughts that a performer activates during performance in an attempt to influence information-processing and, in turn, the level of achievement in the activity (Lidor, 1999; Singer,

2001). A *cognitive strategy* is an optimal organization of cognitive processes designed to achieve a goal or a task (Logan & Zbrodoff, 1982). The term describes an intellectual capability that enables individuals to control the way that they think in problem-solving situations. These strategies increase athletes' awareness of the important role that thoughts play in determining cognitive behaviors such as mental readiness, focusing attention, and feedback provision (Hodges & Franks, 2000; Singer, 2001).

The research on linking the use of coping strategies with DM is extremely limited, and thus, several of the arguments made here need further scientific evidence. Cognitive strategies, however, have been widely linked to performance in the learning of sport and motor skills (Schmidt & Lee, 2005; Singer, Hausenblas, & Janelle, 2001). Both laboratory and applied studies have shown that participants who were taught cognitive strategies such as attentional control, visualization, imagery, learning strategies, and self-regulation incorporating biofeedback, gained higher proficiency than participants using strategy guidance (e.g., Lidor, Arnon, & Bornstein, 1999; Wulf & Toole, 1998; White & Hardy, 1998). Cognitive strategies assisted individuals in improving their skills both at the initial phases and at advanced learning phases (Singer, 2001). By implementing a cognitive strategy, individuals were able to stay focused on the task and target, control their thought processes while executing the task, have confidence in their ability to excel, and be able to provide themselves with feedback information (e.g., Singer, Lidor, & Cauraugh, 1994; Wrisberg & Anshel, 1989).

The purpose of using cognitive techniques in individual and team sports is to provide athletes with applied and usable tools that can assist them in effectively coping with interfering cues resulting from a nonoptimal anxiety state. Emotions, such as anxiety, and fears related to performance failure and self-value (Hardy, Mullen, & Jones, 1996; Jones & Hanton, 1996) are some of the common psychological barriers confronting athletes. Under stressful conditions resources are limited (Masters, 1992; Moran, 1996) and the probability of error increases (Abernethy, 2001). Efficient control over emotions and interfering thoughts, through self-regulatory monitoring, reduces the chance of errors (Hardy, Jones, & Gould, 1996; Moran, 1996).

Williams and Grant (1999), and Starkes, Helsen, and Jack (2001) provided extensive reviews on the effect of generalized visual training and sport-specific perceptual training programs on sport performance and DM in sport. In general, they claimed that visual functions can be enhanced through appropriate instruction and be transferred and implemented in real-game situations.

In this section selected cognitive strategies are presented in a three-phase scheme, as shown in Figure 3. The scheme consists of the time sequence from the preparation to the post-performance phase. Although some of the strategies (e.g., attentional control) can be used during several time periods, they are introduced in the model when they are most likely to occur in real-life situations. Accordingly the cognitive strategies are classified into three categories: (a) strategies that are typically implemented before the event (e.g., practices, workouts, etc.), namely *pre-performance strategies*, (b) strategies that are used by athletes during the actual performance (e.g., a game, a competition), namely *during-performance strategies,* and (c) strategies that are commonly used after the completion of the performance (e.g., after a game or a competition), namely *post-performance strategies.*

Pre-performance Strategies

Pre-performance strategies are used by athletes prior to the real event. The three categories of pre-performance cognitive strategies are mental preparation, simulation training, and pre-performance routines.

Mental Preparation

Several mental preparation techniques such as imagery, visualization, relaxation, self-talk, goal-setting, and group dynamics (Gill, 2000; Hardy, Jones, & Gould, 1996) are in the mainstream. The primary goal of using them is to help athletes to optimize their cognitive and mental operations during practice and competition. Athletes who used them efficiently are prone to making fewer errors or choosing better options for action execution.

Empirical evidence that supports the efficacy of each mental preparation technique on motor and physical performance and its direct effect on DM is unavailable. Imagery, for example, was reported to be a useful mental technique for facilitating

Figure 3: Strategies to Improve Decision-Making Processes

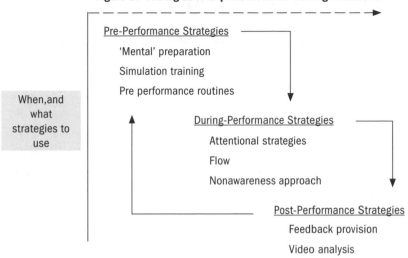

performance in sport (Hall, 2001), and therefore, one may assume that visualization of performance routines prevents possible errors in the real events through the enhancement of cognitive operations. The direct link between the mental technique practiced by the athlete and the decision made by him or her during the event, however, remains unclear.

Simulation Training

The purpose of simulation training is to mimic certain features of the real-world task or environment (Schmidt & Wrisberg, 2004; Williams & Grant, 1999). More specifically, simulation training mimics the actual performance conditions to a certain extent and prepares the individual for the task to be performed. Simulation training is frequently used in education, industry, military settings, and sport. The implication of this technique when used in sport is that by simulating sport-specific situations in practice, athletes learn to optimally transfer these experiences to the real event (Moran, 2003; Schmidt & Wrisberg, 2004).

Unfortunately, support for the use of simulation principles in sport practices has emerged mainly from anecdotal evidence. Coaches and players are in favor of simulations in sport, though empirical support is scarce. Schmidt and Wrisberg (2000) recommended that simulation training be used in sport settings; however, to ensure a transfer, a fair amount of time should be spent on the practice of simulation using task-specific technologies.

Pre-performance Routines

Pre-performance routine is referred to as the systematic mental practice of motor, emotion, and cognitive behaviors before the execution of self-paced tasks (Lidor & Singer, 2000, 2003; Moran, 1996). Self-paced tasks, unlike open-skills tasks, take place in a relatively stable and predictable environment where there is adequate time to prepare for the action to be executed (Lidor & Singer, 2003; Singer, 2001). Examples of self-paced events are the free throw in basketball, the serve in tennis, and the putting in golf. In these events, the environment is stable and anticipated, and a task-specific mental routine can be performed. Lidor and Singer (2003) argued that pre-performance routines can also be implemented in semi-stable and almost-predictable settings, such as the 11-meter penalty kick in soccer, and the 7-meter penalty throw in team-handball. In these events one cannot predict with certainty the goalkeeper's response, but an action can be planned and rehearsed prior to its execution.

Applied research on the effectiveness of pre-performance routines in closed skills tasks has indicated that performers who were encouraged to use a mental systematic routine before the execution of self-paced actions, such as the free throw in basketball, achieved better results than those who were not provided with routine guidance (Cohn, 1990). Furthermore, mental imagery and arousal adjustment (Wrisberg & Anshel, 1989), relaxation (Lamirand & Rainey, 1994), and visuo-motor behavioral rehearsal (VMBR; Hall & Erffmeyer, 1983) were found to enhance accuracy and consistency in such tasks. In addition, a mental routine helps performers to focus attention during action execution, which is likely linked to the DM process (Moran, 1996).

During-Performance Strategies

During-performance strategies can be viewed as an integral part of the DM process undertaken by the performer during the event. The use of cognitive strategies assist performers in focusing attention on essential environmental and internal cues and avoidance of distractions. The three main during-performance strategies are attention, flow, and non-awareness approach.

Attention Strategies

In sport events, such as ball game activities, the task requires the performer to draw attention to several cues simultaniously. Irrelevant sources of information need to be unattended to by the performer to increase the benefit and decrease the cost of the DM process. Singer et al. (1991), Wulf, Hob, and Prinz (1998), and Wulf and Toole (1998) studied the effectiveness of attention techniques on laboratory tasks. External instructions guided participants in directing attention to the effects of their movements and in being focused on one specific area of the apparatus, such as the center of the target. Internal guidance asked participants to pay attention to their own body movements, to feel their movements, and to pay attention to small details related to the act and the body. The findings indicated that external attention focus strategy has a greater impact on learning and performing self-paced tasks than internal attention focus. Increasing the awareness to one's own cues and states tend to hinder performance (see also Singer, Lidor, & Cauraugh, 1993).

Though these studies utilized closed-skill tasks, the performance of open skills can also be enhanced by using external attention strategy. Drawing attention to internal cues distracts the elaboration between working and long-term meomory mechanisms, by introducing information irrelevant to the DM process. As more degrees of freedom are added, the information processing is more complex, and a selection process is required to achieve a desired DM. Thus, external attention strategy utilizing context visual control is of utmost benefit for DM (Singer, 2001; Wulf et al., 1998).

Flow

According to Jackson and Csikszentmihalyi (1999), flow "is a state of consciousness where one becomes totally absorbed in what one is doing, to the exclusion of all other thoughts and emotions... [and] is a harmonious experience where mind and body are working together" (p. 5). When performers attain a high level of proficiency, it appears that they are not always aware of the details of their actions.

A major observation that emerged from studies on flow (see Jackson et al., 1998, 2001) was that skill-level is associated with the experience of flow. Skilled athletes who exhibit higher control over their mental and emotion states feel more autotelic experiences, time flow, and automaticity than less skilled athletes who are concerned with their performance and anxiety-level (Jackson et al., 1998, 2001). Jackson et al. claim that more research is needed to empirically examine the relationship between flow and performance in sport mainly under real-life conditions. Csikszentmihalyi (1990) has pointed out that flow is not an easy state to attain and getting into flow involves a certain level of psychological skills. Little empirical support for the effectiveness of flow in sport settings exists. Moreover, the strategies that should be used for establishing a flow state are unclear.

A Nonawareness Approach

This mental approach is considered a specific case of flow. According to Csikszentmihalyi (1997), the mastery of any skill, whether a routine daily task or a highly-refined talent, depends on the ability to perform it as if subconsciously, effectively meeting the challenge of the situation with minimal effort. Consistent with these observations, a nonawareness strategy to learning and performing motor skills was established in motor learning (e.g., Lidor, 1999; Lidor, Tennant, & Singer, 1996; Singer, Lidor, & Cauraugh, 1994). The nonawareness strategy requires performers to (1) preplan their actions, (2) focus attention on one cue that is most relevant to the performance, and (3) perform the task without conscious attention. Laboratory and field studies (e.g., Lidor et al., 1996; Singer et al., 1993, 1994) indicated that when learners were instructed to apply nonawareness guidelines in performing skills, accuracy and consistency were enhanced compared with awareness and no-instruction conditions.

The nonawareness strategy provides performers with some cognitive assistance on how to preplan their actions, focus attention, and process information during the performance. Although the goal of the strategy is not to directly improve the decisions made by the performer during action execution, it can affect some aspects of DM, such as the preplan act, the attention mode of the performer, and the ability to block irrelevant distractors during performing, all of which enable smooth information processing (see Figure 1).

Post-Performance Strategies

Post-performance strategies are used by athletes and coaches after the completion of the sport event. These strategies consist of careful retrospective analysis of the processes the athlete experienced while making decisions and executing actions. Post-performance strategies are directed toward enhancing future similar encounters. Two commonly used post-performance strategies in sport settings are feedback provision and video analysis (Schmidt & Wrisberg, 2004).

Feedback Provision

Feedback is one of the most efficient instructional techniques used to enhance academic and motor skills (Magill, 2001; Proctor & Dutta, 1995). Feedback types such as knowledge of performance (KP), knowledge of results (KR), and intrinsic feedback (e.g., Proctor & Dutta, 1995) were extensively studied. The effectiveness of these feedback types was evident and documented (see Magill, 2001 for review). The main concerns that still exist are at what points in the learning process learners should be exposed to feedback information, how many times feedback should be provided within a learning process, and how to enhance intrinsic feedback among novice learners.

Although the contribution of the feedback provision to the DM processes was not investigated directly, one may exert that it is essential in the development of expert performance through enhancing DM quality via long-term working memory (Ericsson & Kintsch, 1995) and knowledge structure (French & McPherson, 1999).

Video Analysis

Video analysis is a specific case of providing KP (Schmidt & Lee, 2005). It is designated as a separate entity because of its wide use in enhancing athletes' DM in sport events. Unfortunately, limited numbers of empirical studies examined the effect of video analysis to performance enhancement (Magill, 2001; Williams & Grant, 1999). However, in a few recent studies, one on tennis (Hebert, Landin, & Menickelli, 1998) and one on swimming (Starek & McCullagh, 1999), it was evident that video analyses during training resulted in a higher level of proficiency. The popularity and effect of video analysis on motor performance (Franks & McGarry, 1996; Hebert et al., 1998; Hughes, 1996) leaves little doubt as to its effect on DM in sport. Integrating simulation training and video analysis into a learning routine may result in task-specific DM enhancement.

Summary

Decision-making is a complex concept that deserves attention from scientists and practitioners alike. The chapter summarized the research on DM and emphasized the major role that visual attention plays in affecting anticipatory capability, which is crucial to the quality of DM primarily in open-skill tasks. DM depends also on deliberate practice and the development of experise level. It consists mainly of the interaction and collaboration between working memory and knowledge structure. These two determine the nature of information processing, and consequently, decision-making and action execution.

The links among coping strategies, self-regulatory mechanisms, and decision-making in sport are missing. The chapter introduced research findings, which link the use of mental strategies prior to, during, and after competitive events to the performance of motor skills. However, the nature of its effect on DM is unknown. When studied, such information may indicate which components' coping strategies and self-regulatory mechanisms directly and indirectly affect, and what are the nature and size of the effects. When clarified, both deliberate practice and performance will benefit and be enhanced.

References

Abernethy, B. (1987a). Anticipation in sport: A review. *Physical Education Review, 10,* 5-16.

Abernethy, B. (1987b). Selective attention in fast ball sports: II. Expert-novice differences. *Australian Journal of Science and Medicine in Sport, 19,* 7-16.

Abernethy, B. (2001). Attention. In R. N. Singer, H. A. Hausenblas, & C. M. Janelle (Eds.), *Handbook of sport psychology* (2nd ed.; pp. 53-85). New York: Wiley.

Abernethy, B., Neal, R. J., & Koning, P. (1994). Visual-perceptual and cognitive differences between experts, intermediate, and novice snooker players. *Applied Cognitive Psychology, 8,* 185-211.

Abernethy, B., & Russell, D. G. (1987). Expert-novice differences in an applied selective attention task. *Journal of Sport and Exercise Psychology, 9,* 326-345.

Allard, F., & Burnett, N. (1985). Skill in sport. *Canadian Journal of Sport Psychology, 39,* 294-312.

Allard, F., Graham, S., & Paarsalu, M. E. (1980). Perception in sport: Basketball. *Journal of Sport Psychology, 2,* 14-21.

Allard, F., & Starkes, J. L. (1980). Perception in sport: Volleyball. *Journal of Sport Psychology, 2,* 22-23.

Baddeley, A. D. (1986). *Working memory.* Oxford: Oxford University Press.

Baddeley, A. D., & Hitch, G. (1974). Working memory. In K. W. Spence & J. T. Spence (Eds.), *The psychology of learning and motivaiton* (Vol. 8). New York: Academic Press.

Bard, C., Fleury, M., Carriere, L., & Halle, M. (1980). Analysis of gymnastics judges' visual search. *Research Quarterly for Exercise and Sport, 51,* 267-273.

Bloom, B. S. (1985). *Developing talent in young people.* New York: Ballantine Books.

Borgeaud, P., & Abernethy, B. (1987). Skilled perception in volleyball defense. *Journal of Sport Psychology, 9,* 400-406.

Cave, K. R., & Bichot, N. P. (1999). Visuospatial attention: Beyond a spotlight model. *Psychonomic Bulletin and Review, 6*(2), 204-223.

Charness, N., Krampe, R. Th., & Mayr, U. (1996). The role of practice and coaching in entrepreneurial skill domain: An international comparison of life-span chess skill acquisition. In K. A. Ericsson (Ed.), *The road to excellence: The acquisition of expert performance in the arts and sciences, sports, and games* (pp. 51-80). Mahwah, NJ: Erlbaum.

Chase, W. G., & Simon, H. A. (1973). Perception in chess. *Cognitive Psychology, 4,* 55-81.

Chestain, G. (1992a). Analog versus discrete shifts of attention across the visual field. *Psychological Research, 54,* 175-181.

Chestain, G. (1992b). Time-course of sensitivity changes as attention shifts to an unpredictable location. *Journal of General Psychology, 119,* 105-111.

Cohn, P. J. (1990). Preperformance routines in sport: Theoretical support and practical implications. *The Sport Psychologist, 4,* 301-312.

Csikszentmihalyi, M. (1990). *Flow: The psychology of optimal experience.* New York: Harper and Row.

Csikszentmihalyi, M. (1997). *Finding flow: The psychology of engagement with everyday life.* New York: Harper Collins.

DeGroot, A. D. (1965). *Thought and choice in chess.* The Hague: Mouton.

Downing, C. J. (1988). Expectancy and visual-spatial attention: Effects of perceptual quality. *Journal of Experimental Psychology: Human Perception and Performance, 14,* 188-202.

Downing, C. J., & Pinker, S. (1985). The spatial structure of visual attention. In M. I. Posner & O. S. M. Marin (Eds.), *Attention and performance XI: Mechanisms of attention* (pp. 171-187). Hillsdale, NJ: Erlbaum.

Driver, J., & Baylis, G. C. (1989). Movement of visual attention: The spotlight metaphor breaks down. *Journal of Experimental Psychology: Human Perception and Performance, 15,* 448-456.

Egeth, H. (1977). Attention and preattention. In G. H. Bower (Ed.), *The psychology of learning and motivation* (Vol. 11, pp. 277-320). New York: Academic Press.

Ericsson, K. A. (1998). The scientific study of expert level of performance: General implications for optimal learning and creativity. *High Ability Studies, 9,* 75-100.

Ericsson, K. A. (1999). Creative expertise as superior reproducible performance: Innovative and flexible aspects of expert performance. *Psychological Inquiry, 10,* 329-333.

Ericsson, K. A. (2000). *Superior decision making as an integral quality of expert performance: Insights into the mediating mechanisms and the acquisition through deliberate practice.* Keynote address at the 5th international conference on naturalistic decision making. Tammsvik, Sweden, May 26-28.

Ericsson, K. A., & Kintsch, W. (1995). Long-term working memory. *Psychological Review, 102,* 211-245.

Ericsson, K.A., Krampe, R.T., & Tesch-Romer, C. (1993). The role of deliberate practice in the acquisition of expert performance. *Psychological Review, 100,* 363-406.

Eriksen, B. A., & Eriksen, C. W. (1974). Effects of noise letters upon the identification of a target letter in a nonsearch task. *Perception and Psychophysics, 16,* 143-149.

Eriksen, C. W., & Hoffman, J. E. (1973). The extent of processing of noise elements during selective encoding from visual displays. *Perception and Psychophysics, 14,* 155-160.

Eriksen, C. W., & Hoffman, J. E. (1974). Selective attention: Noise suppression or signal enhancement? *Bulletin of Psychonomic Society, 4,* 587-589.

Eriksen, C. W., & St James, J. D. (1986). Visual attention within and around the field of focal attention: A zoom lens model. *Perception and Psychophysics, 40,* 225-240.

Estes, W. K. (1982). Learning, memory and intelligence. In R. J. Sternberg (Ed.), *Handbook of human intelligence* (pp. 170-224). New York: Cambridge University Press.

Fisher, A. C. (1984). Sport intelligence. In W. F. Straub & J. M. Williams (Eds.), *Cognitive sport psychology* (pp. 42-50). Lansing, NY: Sport Science.

Franks, I. M., & McGarry, T. (1996). The science of match analysis. In T. Reilly (Ed.), *Science and soccer* (pp. 363-375). London: E and FN SPON.

French, K. E., & McPherson, S. l. (1999). Adaptation in response selection processes used during sport competition with increasing age and expertise. *International Jornal of Sport Psychology, 30,* 173-193.

Gill, D. (2000). *Psychological dynamics of sport and exercise* (2nd ed.). Champaign, IL: Human Kinetics.

Hall, C. R. (2001). Imagery in sport and exercise. In R. N. Singer, H. A. Hausenblas, & C. M. Janelle (Eds.), *Handbook of sport psychology* (2nd ed., pp. 529-549). New York: Wiley.

Hall, E. G., & Erffmeyer, E. S. (1983). The effect of visuo-motor behavior rehearsal with videotaped modeling on free throw accuracy of intercollegiate female basketball players. *Journal of Sport Psychology, 5*, 343-346.

Handy, T. C., Kingstone, A., & Mangun, G. R. (1996). Spatial distribution of visual attention: Perceptual sensitivity and response latency. *Perception and Psychophysics, 58*, 613-627.

Hardy, L., Jones, G., & Gould, D. (1996). *Understanding psychological preparation for sport: Theory and practice of elite performers.* Chichester: Wiley.

Hardy, L., Mullen, R., & Jones, G. (1996). Knowledge and conscious control of motor actions under stress. *British Journal of Psychology, 87*, 621-636.

Hawkins, H. L., Hillyard, S. A., Luck, S. J., Mouloua, M., Downing, C. J., & Woodward, D. P. (1990). Visual attention modulates signal detectability. *Journal of Experimental Psychology: Human Perception and Performance, 16*, 802-811.

Hebert, E., Landin, D., & Menickelli, J. (1998). Videotape feedback: What learners see and how they use it. *Journal of Sport Pedagogy, 4*, 12-28.

Helsen, W. F., Starkes, J. L., & Hodges, N. L. (1998). Team sport and the theory of deliberate practice. *Journal of Sport and Exercise Pschology, 20*, 12-34.

Henderson, J. M., & MacQuistan, A. D. (1993). The spatial distribution of attention following an exogenous cue. *Perception and Psychophysics, 53*, 221-230.

Hodges, N.J., & Franks, I.M. (2000). Attention focusing instructions and coordination bias: Implications for learning a novel bimanual task. *Human Movement Science, 19*, 843-867.

Hodges, N. J., & Starkes, J. L. (1996). Wrestling with the nature of expertise: A sport specific test of Ericsson, Krampe, and Tesch-Romer's (1993) theory of "deliberate practice." *International Journal of Sport Psychology, 27*, 400-424.

Hughes, M. (1996). Notational analysis. In T. Reilly (Ed.), *Science and soccer* (pp. 343-361). London: E and FN SPON.

Hughes, H. C., & Zimba, L. D. (1985). Spatial maps of directed visual attention. *Journal of Experimental Psychology: Human Perception and Performance, 11*, 409-430.

Hughes, H. C., & Zimba, L. D. (1987). Natural Boundaries for the spatial spread of directed visual attention. *Neuropsychologia, 25*, 5-18.

Jackson, S. A., & Csikszentmihalyi, M. (1999). *Flow in sports: The keys to optimal experiences and performances.* Champaign, IL: Human Kinetics.

Jackson, S. A., Kimiecik, J. C., Ford, S., & Marsh, H. W. (1998). Psychological correlates of flow in sport. *Journal of Sport and Exercise Psychology, 20*, 358-378.

Jackson, S. A., Thomas, P. R., Marsh, H. W., & Smethurst, C. J. (2001). Relationships between flow, self-concept, psychological skills, and performance. *Journal of Applied Sport Psychology, 13*, 129-153.

Jones, G., & Hanton, S. (1996). Interpretation of competitive anxiety symptoms and goal attainment expectations. *Journal of Sport and Exercise Psychology, 18*, 144-157.

Keele, S. W. (1982). Component analysis and conceptions of skill. In A. S. Kelso (Ed.), *Human motor behavior: An introduction* (pp. 29-61). Hillsdale, NJ: Erlbaum.

Krampe, R. Th., & Ericsson, K. A. (1996). Maintaining excellence: Deliberate practice and elite performance in young and older pianists. *Journal of Experimental Psychology: General, 125*, 331-359.

LaBerge, D. (1983). Spatial extent of attention to letters and words. *Journal of Experimental Psychology: Human Perception and Performance, 9*, 371-379.

Lamirand, M., & Rainey, D. (1994). Mental imagery, relaxation, and accuracy of basketball foul shooting. *Perceptual and Motor Skills, 78*, 1229-1230.

Lehmann, A. C., & Ericsson, K. A. (1996). Music performance without preparation: Structure and acquisition of expert sight-reading. *Psychomusicology, 15*, 1-29.

Lidor, R. (1999). Learning strategies and the enhancement of self-paced motor tasks: Theoretical and practical implications. In R. Lidor & M. Bar-Eli (Eds.), *Sport psychology: Linking theory and practice* (pp. 109-132). Morgantown, WV: Fitness Information Technology.

Lidor, R., Arnon, M., & Bornstein, A. (1999). The effectiveness of a learning (cognitive) strategy on free-throw performance in basketball. *Applied Research in Coaching and Athletics, 14*, 59-72.

Lidor, R., & Singer, R. N. (2000). Teaching preperformance routines to beginners. *Journal of Physical Education, Recreation, and Dance, 7*, 34-36, 52.

Lidor, R., & Singer, R. N. (2003). Preperformance routines in self-paced tasks: Developmental and educational considerations. In R. Lidor & K. Henschen (Eds.), *The psychology of team sports* (pp. 69-98). Morgantown, WV: Fitness Information Technology.

Lidor, R., Tennant, K. L., & Singer, R. N. (1996). The generalizability effect of three learning strategies across motor task performances. *International Journal of Sport Psychology, 27*, 22-36.

Logan, G.D., & Zbrodoff, N.J. (1982). Constraints on strategy construction in a speeded discrimination task. *Journal of Experimental Psychology: Human Perception and Performance, 8*, 502-520.

Luck, S. J., Fan, S., & Hillyard, S. A. (1993). Attention-related modulation of sensory-evoked brain activity in a visual search task. *Journal of Cognitive Neuroscience, 5*, 188-195.

Luck, S. J., Hillyard, S. A., Mouloua, M., & Hawkins, H. L. (1996). Mechanisms of visual-spatial attention: Resource allocation or uncertainty reduction? *Journal of Experimental Psychology: Human Perception and Performance, 58*, 977-991.

Magill, R. A. (2001). Augmented feedback in motor skill acquisition. In R. N. Singer, H. A. Hausenblas, & C. M. Janelle (Eds.), *Handbook of sport psychology* (2nd ed., pp. 86-114). New York: Wiley.

Mangun, G. R., & Hillyard, S. A. (1995). Mechanisms and models of selective attention. In M. D. Rugg & M. G. H. Coles (Eds.), *Electro-physiology of mind: Event-related brain potentials and cognition* (pp. 41-85). Oxford: Oxford University Press.

Masters, R. S. W. (1992). Knowledge, "knerves" and know-how: The role of explicit versus implicit knowledge in the breakdown of complex motor skill under pressure. *British Journal of Psychology, 83*, 343-358.

Miller, G. A. (1956). The magical number seven plus or minus two: some limits on our capacity for processing information. *Psychological Review, 63*, 81-97.

Moran, A. (1996). *The psychology of concentration in sport performers: A cognitive analysis.* East, Sussex, UK: Psychology Press.

Moran, A. (2003). Improving concentration skills in team sport performers: Focusing techniques for soccer players. In R. Lidor & K. Henschen (Eds.), *The psychology of team sports* (pp. 161-189). Morgantown, WV: Fitness Information Technology.

Motter, B. C. (1994). Neural correlates of feature selective memory and pop-out in extrastriate area V4. *Journal of Neuroscience, 14,* 2190-2199.

Navon, D. (1978). On a conceptual hierarch of time, space, and other dimensions. *Cognition, 6,* 223-228.

Peterson, L. R., & Peterson, M. J. (1959). Short-term retention of individual items. *Journal of Experimental Psychology, 58,* 193-198.

Posner, M. I., Nissen, M. J., & Odgen, W. C. (1978). Attended and unattended processing modes: The role of set for spatial location. In H. J. Pick & I. J. Saltzman (Eds.), *Modes of perception* (pp. 137-157). Hillsdale, NJ: Erlbaum.

Posner, M. I., Snyder, C. R., & Davidson, B. J. (1980). Attention and the detection of signals. *Journal of Experimental Psychology: General, 109,* 160-174.

Prinzmetal, W., & Millis-Wright, M. (1984). Cognitive and linguistic factors affect visual feature integration. *Cognitive Psychology, 16,* 305-340.

Proctor, R. W., & Dutta, A. (1995). *Skill acquisition and human performance.* Thousand Oaks: Sage.

Ripoll, H. (1979). Le traitement de l'information de donnes visuelles dans les situations tactiques en sport. L'exem;le du basketball. *Travaux et Recherches en ESP, 4,* 99-104.

Ripoll, H. (1988). Utilisation d'un dispositif videooculographique d'enregistrement de la direction du regard en situation sportive. *Science et Motricite, 4,* 25-31.

Rizzolatti, G., Riggio, L., Dascola, I., & Umilta, C. (1987). Reorienting attention across the horizontal and vertical meridians: Evidence in favor of a premotor theory of attention. *Neuropsychologia, 25,* 31-40.

Schmidt, R. A., & Lee, T. D. (2005). *Motor control and learning: A behavioral emphasis* (4th ed.). Champaign, IL: Human Kinetics.

Schmidt, R. A., & Wrisberg, C. A. (2004). *Motor learning and performance: A problem-based learning approach* (3rd ed.). Champaign, IL: Human Kinetics.

Schneider, W. (1993). Acquiring expertise: determinants of exceptional performance. In K. A. Heller, J. Monks, & H. Passow (Eds.), *International handbook of research and development of giftness and talent* (pp. 311-324). Oxford, UK: Pergamon.

Seiler, R. (2000). The intentional link between environment and action in the acquisition of skills. *The International Journal of Sport Psychology, 31,* 496-514.

Shall, J. D., Hanes, D. P., Thompson, K. G., & King, D. J. (1995). Saccade target selection in frontal eye field of macaque: I. Visual and premovement activation. *Journal of Neuroscience, 15,* 6905-6918.

Shulman, G. L., Remington, R. W., & McLean, J. P. (1979). Moving attention through physical space. *Journal of Experimental Psychology: Human Perception and Performance, 5,* 522-526.

Singer, R. N. (2001). Performance and human factors: Considerations about cognition and attention for self-paced and externally-paced events. *Ergonomics, 43,* 1661-1680.

Singer, R. N., Cauraugh, J. H., Murphey, M., Chen, D., & Lidor, R. (1991). Attentional control, distractors, and motor performance. *Human Performance, 4,* 55-69.

Singer, R. N., Lidor, R., & Cauraugh, J. H. (1993). To be aware or not aware? What to think about while learning and performing a motor skill. *The Sport Psychologist, 7,* 19-30.

Singer, R. N., Lidor, R., & Cauraugh, J. H. (1994). Focus of attention during motor skill performance. *Journal of Sports Sciences, 12,* 335-340.

Sloboda, J. A. (1976). Visual perception of musical notation: Registering pitch symbols in memory. Quarterly *Journal of Experimental Psychology, 28,* 1-16.

Sloboda, J. A. (1996). The acquisition of musical performance expertise: Deconstructing the italenti account in individual differences in musical expressivity. In K. A. Ericsson (Ed.), *The road to excellence: The acquisition of expert performance in the arts and sciences, sports, and games* (pp. 107-126). Mahwah, NJ: Erlbaum.

Smyth, M. M., & Pendleton, L. R. (1994). Memory for movement in professional ballet dancers. *International Journal of Sport Psychology, 25,* 282-294.

Starek, J., & McCullagh, P. (1999). The effect of self-modeling on the performance of beginning swimmers. *The Sport Psychologist, 13,* 269-287.

Starkes, J. L., & Allard, F. (1983). Perception in volleyball: The effects of competitive stress. *Journal of Sport Psychology, 5,* 189-196.

Starkes, J. L., & Deakin, J. M. (1984). Perception in sport: A cognitive approach to skill performance. In W. F. Straub & J. M. Williams (Eds.), *Cognitive sport psychology* (pp. 115-128). New York: Sport Science Associates.

Starkes, J. L., Caicco, M., Boutilier, C., & Sevsek, B. (1990). Motor recall of experts for structured and unstructured sequences in creative modern dance. *Journal of Sport and Exercise Psychology, 12,* 317-321.

Starkes, J. L., Deakin, J., Allard, F., Hodges, N. J., & Hayes, A. (1996). Deliberate practice in sports: What is it anyway? In K. A. Ericsson (Ed.), The road to excellence: *The acquisition of expert performance in the arts and sciences, sports, and games* (pp. 81-106). Mahwan, NJ: Erlbaum.

Starkes, J. L., Helsen, W., & Jack, R. (2001). Expert performance in sport and dance. In R. N. Singer, H. A. Hausenblas, & C. M. Janelle (Eds.), *Handbook of sport psychology* (2nd ed., pp. 174-201). New York: Wiley.

Tenenbaum, G., & Bar-Eli, M. (1993). Decision making in sport: A cognitive perspective. In R. N. Singer, M. Murphey, & L. K. Tennant (Eds.), *Handbook on research in sport psychology* (pp. 171-192). New York: McMillan.

Tenenbaum, G., & Bar-Eli, M. (1995). Personality and intellectual capabilities in sport psychology. In D. Sakulufske & M. Zeidner (Eds.), *International handbook on personality and intelligence* (pp. 687-710). New York: Plenum.

Tenenbaum, G., Levy-Kolker, N., Bar-Eli, M., & Weinberg, R. (1994). Information recall among skilled and novice athletes: The role of display complexity, attentional resources, visual exposure duration, and expertise. *Journal of Sport Psychology, 12,* 529-534.

Tenenbaum, G., Stewart, E., & Sheath, P. (1999). Detection of targets and attentional flexibility: Can computerized simulation account for developmental and skill-level differences? *International Journal of Sport Psychology, 30,* 261-282.

Tenenbaum, G., Sar-El, Z. & Bar-Eli, M. (2000). Anticipation of ball locations in low and high skill performers: A developmental perspective. *Psychology of Sport and Exercise, 1*, 117-128.

Tenenbaum, G., Tehan, G., Stewart, G., & Christensen, S. (1999). Recalling a floor routine: The effects of skill and age on memory for order. *Applied Cognitive Psychology, 13*, 101-123.

Treisman, A. M. (1982). Perceptual grouping and attention in visual search for features and for objects. *Journal of Experimental Psychology: Human Perception and Performance, 8*, 194-214.

Treisman, A. M., Kahneman, D., & Burkell, J. (1983). Perceptual objects and the cost of filtering. *Perception and Psychophysics, 33*, 527-532.

Vecera, S. P. (1997). Grouped arrays versus object-based representations: Reply to Kramer et al. (1997). *Journal of Experimental Psychology: General, 126*, 13-18.

White, A., & Hardy, L. (1998). An in-depth analysis of the uses of imagery by high-level slalom canoeists and artistic gymnasts. *The Sport Psychologist, 12*, 387-403.

Williams, M. A., & Grant, A. (1999). Training perceptual skill in sport. *International Journal of Sport Psychology, 30*, 194-220.

Wrisberg, C. A., & Anshel, M. H. (1989). The effect of cognitive strategies on free throw shooting performance of young athletes. *The Sport Psychologist, 3*, 95-104.

Wulf, G., Hob, M., & Prinz, W. (1998). Instructions for motor learning: Differential effects of internal versus external focus of attention. *Journal of Motor Behavior, 2*, 169-179.

Wulf, G., & Toole, T. (1998). Learning advantages of a self-controlled physical guidance schedule. *Journal of Sport and Exercise Psychology, 20*, S26.

Yantis, S. (1988). On analog movements of visual attention. *Perception and Psychophysics, 43*, 203-206.

Courtesy of Cpl. Julie A. Paynter/U.S. Marine Corps

2.3
Mental Skill Training Program for Children

PATSY TREMAYNE AND GLENN NEWBERY

Introduction

The term "mental skills training" or "psychological skills training" (PST) refers to "techniques and strategies designed to teach or enhance mental skills that facilitate performance and a positive approach to sport competition" (Vealey 1988, p. 319). Typically, these techniques and strategies include training in goal setting, arousal regulation, imagery, attentional focus, and appropriate self-talk.

Vealey (1988) observes that "most PST programs are geared to elite athletes" (p. 323). The reason for this applied bias toward elite performers is clear. Having reached the autonomous stage of motor learning (which is characterized by fast, parallel cognitive processing, such that the basic motor pattern runs off like a reflex, requiring little conscious effort), elite athletes need to devote little attention to the physical skills that constitute their sport; hence, it is the "mental game" that differentiates performers at this level. There is a substantial body of experimental evidence that demonstrates that PST is an effective way of enhancing the performance of elite athletes (Wrisberg & Anshel, 1989). However, most of the experimental evidence supporting the efficacy of PST

for athletic performance has been generated by studies involving non-elite athletes and recreational sport participants. As Whelan, Mahony, and Meyers (1991) point out, pragmatics dictate that this is so:

> Low to moderate skill level subjects are more likely to be available, and are often more willing participants than the limited population of elite athletes. In contrast to these elite athletes, volunteer participants from physical education courses or groups of recreational athletes allow the researcher greater experimental flexibility and control. (p. 309)

The practical convenience of obtaining participants from physical education courses may explain why controlled studies of PST tend to focus on young adults. Be this as it may, the fact remains that there is a paucity of studies exploring the viability of PST for children (Wrisberg & Anshel, 1989; Weinberg & Williams, 1998).

This under-representation of children in experimental studies of PST appears all the more anomalous in light of the fact that, since the early eighties, it has been widely advocated that PST should be provided for children involved in sport (Danish, Petitpas & Hale, 1992; Gould, 1983; Smoll, 1984; Vealey, 1988; Weiss, 1991). The Australian Bureau of Statistics, which investigated children's participation in cultural and leisure activities in 2003, found that 62% of children aged 5-14 years were involved in organized sport. If this percentage is extrapolated to children's involvement in sport in other Western countries, then it would appear that there is a need for PST for children because of the number of children involved in sport. Indeed, it has been argued that children are peculiarly suited to PST programs. Gould (1983), for instance, claims that "a... reason for the systematic development of psychological skills in young athletes is the ease with which psychological skills are learned by children" (p. 4), while Vealey (1988) says that "young athletes... are more ripe for PST interventions than older athletes who have already internalized dysfunctional responses to competition" (p. 323). Another rationale for PST training with children revolves around the stated positive socializing functions of sport participation (see FEPSAC, 1996). For instance, participation in sport provides opportunities to enhance not only the social attributes of cooperation and relating to others, but also the personal qualities of self-esteem, initiative, and independence. Children's moral development can also be positively affected through recognizing and abiding by common rules of behavior in sport. PST can foster such attributes by providing children with a variety of self-regulated individual learning strategies (such as imagery, arousal regulation, goal setting, self talk) that are fun, meaningful to the situation, and enhance their enjoyment of sport.

It is important to note that the terms "children" and "young athletes" specify different age ranges. The former is typically used to refer to those between 6 and 12 years of age; Weiss (1991) bears this out when she says that "during *childhood (about ages 7 to 12 years),* there is an increase in the use of peer comparison... (p. 342, our italics). The latter term, on the other hand, is typically applied to athletes between 6 and 18 years of age. For example, Gould (1983) states that "it is estimated that 20 to 30 million *young athletes between the ages of 6 and 17* take part in a variety of... sport programs" (p. 4, our italics). The term "young athletes," then, usually

includes both children (7 to 12 years) and adolescents (13 to 18 years). The following section reviews those experimental studies of PST which have involved both children and adolescents. The chapter then reviews anecdotal reports, and the relationship between psychological strategies, skills, and characteristics. This is followed by a synopsis of intrinsic motivation theory, the implications for children because of cognitive and motor developmental issues, and finally, the chapter concludes with recommendations regarding PST for children.

Review of experimental studies on children and adolescents

Most of the experimental studies that suggest that PST can be effective for young athletes have involved both children and adolescents within the same studies.

For instance, Hellstedt (1987) describes a sport psychology program conducted at a ski academy for a group of 43 competitive skiers in grades 8-12. The program involved four weekend workshops held once a month on the following topics: motivation in sport, anxiety and performance, mental imagery, and goal setting. Hellstedt found that, according to evaluations from participants and coaches, the workshops helped to develop both the sport specific skills and the general life-skills of young athletes at a ski academy (ages ranged from 12 to 18 years, $M = 15$).

Another study by Lee and Hewitt (1987) investigated the effects on performance of imagery training by 36 competitive gymnasts aged 9 to 17 years, who were pre-tested for facilitating and debilitating anxiety and skill levels. Based on these subgroups, gymnasts were randomly placed into three treatment conditions: once a week for six weeks practicing imagery in a flotation tank; practicing imagery at the end of a gym workout over the same time period; and a control group, which did not participate in any extra activity. Results, which were not all statistically significant, indicated that performance scores averaged across three State qualifying meets were highest when participants had practiced imagery in a flotation tank, compared to practicing imagery on a mat in a gymnasium.

There were several studies which investigated skating performance. In the first study, Palmer (1992) examined two self-talk interventions for improving performance of compulsory figures by young figure skaters (ages ranged from 12 to 17 years, $M = 13.4$). For the first intervention, skaters were asked to select key words to help them correct specific elements of each figure they were practicing, to use these key words during practice sessions on the ice, and to also walk through the figures on the floor away from the rink while rehearsing these key words. The second intervention involved skaters listing key words to help them concentrate on specific elements of each figure, and to trace their figures on paper while saying the key words aloud. The results indicated that only the second intervention was an effective strategy and limitations of the study included the fact that it was a pre-post design with no information provided on the session by session performance of the participants, and there were no procedures in place to ascertain whether the skaters actually used the self-talk during practices or during the pre and post assessments.

The next study by Ming and Martin (1996) corrected these limitations. They used a single-subject design to examine a self-talk package for improving performance of compulsory figures by four prenovice- and novice-level competitive figure skaters aged 11 to 13 years. The self-talk package consisted of: a) watching a videotape of national-level figure skaters using key words while performing, b) developing key words to aid concentration, and c) doing "off-ice walkouts" of compulsory figures. Objective behavioral observations confirmed that the skaters did utilize self-talk and that the self-talk package did improve performance during practices. A self-report follow-up one year later indicated that the skaters continued to utilize the self-talk during practices, and the results supported the view that planned self-talk could aid skill acquisition.

Another study by Wanlin, Hrycaiko, Martin, and Mahon (1997) found that a goal-setting package that consisted of several components increased the "on-task behavior" and improved the performance of young female skaters (ages ranged from 12 to 17 years) to work harder, and show less off-task behavior.

In 1998, a study by Garza and Feltz examined the effectiveness of mental practice techniques for improving not only figure skating performance, but also self-efficacy and self-confidence for competition.

Participants were 27 female competitive figure skaters aged between 10 and 18 years ($M = 12.37$). The results of this study indicated that a mental practice package involving a) the development of cue words to increase concentration, b) mental imagery, and c) a behavioral component, could improve the skating performance, self-efficacy expectations, and competition confidence of young competitive figure skaters (ages ranged from 10 to 18 years, $M = 12.37$).

The above studies involved the use of a variety of strategies, and the designs of the studies did not make it possible to ascertain whether one strategy was more effective than another. Even the Lee and Hewitt (1987) study, which appeared to use only one strategy, did not take into account the relaxation effect that may have occurred through use of a flotation tank. Nor does the fact that the participants in all of the studies were a mixture of children and adolescents allow for what may have been striking developmental differences. It is apparent, therefore, that the above studies do not adequately demonstrate the ages at which children can optimally benefit from PST and, despite the positive results attained, there is a lack of differentiation as to the effectiveness of any one strategy.

Review of experimental studies on children
Support for the notion that PST can be effective for children is provided by both experimental studies and by anecdotal reports.

Wrisberg and Anshel (1989) examined the effectiveness of relaxation and imagery techniques on the basketball free throw shooting performance of 40 boys aged between 10-12 years ($M = 11.6$), who were selected for their good basketball shooting skill. After obtaining baseline measures of free throw performance for all participants, they were divided into four groups. Group one learned and practiced mental imagery during the treatment period, group two learned and practiced an arousal regulation technique, group three practiced a combination of imagery and arousal regulation, while the fourth group was a control group and had no strategies. Results indicated that there was a significant improvement for the group that practiced a combination of imagery and arousal regulation. Of interest is the fact that the arousal regulation group performed the poorest during the trials, and this may have occurred because the instructions did not direct the participants to divert attentional focus back to the task after the relaxation response.

Another study by Zhang, Ma, Orlick and Zitzelberger (1992) examined the effect of mental imagery training on performance enhancement with 40 promising table tennis players aged 7 to 10 years, who were enrolled at a sport school in China. The participants were divided into three groups. The first group received mental training that included relaxation, video observation, and mental imagery sessions; the second group received only video observation sessions; and the third group was a control group that did not take part in any sessions. The intervention sessions continued for a period of 22 weeks, and all 40 participants participated in the same physical training during this time. Performance measures were taken before and after the experimental period. Results indicated that the mental training group was the only group to show significant increases in scores on the four performance measures, while the other two groups showed a significant improvement on only one of the performance measures.

Atienza, Balaguer, and Garcia Merita (1998) investigated the effects of imagery training and video modeling (i.e., an observational learning paradigm in which learners observe a videotape of models performing the motor skill) on tennis service performance in 12 female tennis players (aged 9-12 years, M=10.6). The players received training over 24 weeks and were divided into three groups: a physical practice group; a physical practice/video–modeling group; and a physical practice/video modeling/imagery group. Results indicated that the two groups given video-modeling, and video-modeling/imagery respectively, did not differ significantly from each other, but that tennis serves were significantly better for both of these groups than for the physical practice only group.

Although these were three empirical studies of the effectiveness of PST on children, there were limitations that need to be considered. First, no conclusions can be reached regarding the effectiveness of PST for a given age within the age ranges covered (10-12 years, 7-10 years, and 9-12, years respectively). Even though the groups did not include adolescents, there were still likely to be considerable developmental differences between the age groups as cognitive and motor skill development usually follows sequential patterns. Piaget (1952) is well known for his work on cognitive development, and in his theory he identifies four stages: the sensorimotor stage, the preoperational stage, the concrete operations stage, and the formal operations stage (these stages are discussed in more detail later in the chapter). Children who are at earlier stages of cognitive development may need simpler instructions in order to understand and effectively carry out tasks. With regard to motor development, children of 11 or 12 are able to perform movements of greater difficulty than younger children, and their motor skills have generally improved (Kirchner, 1992). Factors that affect this motor skill development may include not only environmental influences (Madill, 1993, Walleye, Holland, Tremor, & Robyn-Smith, 1993), but also individual differences, including children's state of "readiness to learn" (Gallahue & Omen, 1995).

A second limitation is that two of the studies again used a variety of strategies and no conclusions can be reached regarding the efficacy of any one strategy included in the packages tested. The Wrisberg and Anshel (1989) study was the exception, as there were separate groups for imagery and arousal regulation. However, the instructions given to the participants in the arousal regulation group may well have affected their poorer results, as their attention was not directed to the cues necessary for optimal performance after the act of releasing muscle tension. Another limitation in the studies by Zhang et al. (1992) and Atienza et al. (1998) is that there was a period of 22 and 24 weeks respectively between the pre- and the post-tests while children's physical training continued. It is possible that, because of the long period of time between the pre- and post- tests, a learning effect due to practice or "readiness to learn" may have occurred, rather than a performance effect due to the interventions.

Review of anecdotal reports

Given the paucity of informative experimental research on the efficacy of PST programs for children, guidelines for the development of such programs may be sought in anecdotal reports.

Some sport psychologists have, on the basis of their own practical experiences, proposed guidelines for developing psychological skills in young athletes (e.g., Gould, 1983; Orlick & McCaffrey, 1991; Weiss, 1991). There is clearly some substance to the standard caveat that such anecdotal reports do not have the same "scientific respectability" as controlled experimental studies. Admittedly, the observations which are reported anecdotally may, since the observational field is not systematically controlled, have greater ecological validity than well-controlled experiments; but this potential advantage is outweighed by the increased dubiousness of inferences concerning cause-effect relations. Nevertheless, the aforementioned anecdotal reports should not be overlooked; as will become apparent below, the guidelines these reports propose are grounded both in common sense and in established psychological theory (e.g., the emphasis placed on creating a positive and sincere approach to communication has an obvious connection to the humanistic theories of Maslow [1943] and Rogers [1961]). They provide, at the very least, a rich source of hypotheses which deserve to be tested under controlled conditions.

Gould (1983) proposed "strategies coaches can employ to develop psychological skills in young athletes, ranging in age from 6 to 17" (p. 5). Six such strategies are discussed: (1) determining and defining the objectives for psychological skills; (2) conveying the objectives for psychological skills to athletes via individual and/or team discussion; (3) implementing systematic goal-setting procedures; (4) the effective use of role models; (5) employing a positive and sincere approach to communication; and (6) developing educational programs for the parents of young athletes and other interested adults. Clearly, the first three strategies are interdependent and form the core of the program Gould proposes. These "core" strategies are unproblematic, for common-sense dictates that, if a sport psychologist (or a coach) is to help an athlete develop psychological skills, he/she must work with the athlete to determine what psychological skills are needed, what the objective characteristics of the needed skills are, and what specific steps must be taken to develop them. Strategies (4), (5), and (6) bear the influence of Smith and Smoll's (1982) ideas concerning both the role of coaches and the role of parents in creating a psychologically healthy environment for young athletes (see also Smoll & Smith, 1988). Gould also demonstrates an awareness of the developmental literature when he says that:

to be effective, the objectives and strategies identified for developing psychological skills must be appropriate for the developmental level of the athlete. It is essential that the developmental level of the athlete be considered since children of varying ages have been found to vastly differ in their ability to attend, comprehend, and retain information. (p. 9)

However, Gould does not detail the nature of the developmental levels to which he refers (i.e., the age range of each, the information processing limitations associated with each). Nor does he specify how each of the various strategies for developing psychological skills needs to be modified such that it is appropriate for a given developmental level.

Orlick and McCaffrey (1991) outline some of the "key ingredients" related to their "best successes with mental training for children." They recommend a flexible, individualized approach, that is, an approach whereby the psychologist first spends time with the child in order to establish a program which fits the child's needs, and then maintains ongoing contact with the child so that feedback concerning the program can be exchanged. This recommendation is, of course, similar to the "core" strategies proposed by Gould (1983). Indeed, Orlick and McCaffrey's proposals resemble Gould's in a number of respects. They too suggest that mental training with children is most likely to be effective if the person delivering the intervention takes a positive approach, if well chosen role models are used, and if the support of parents is solicited. They also reiterate Gould's claim that strategies for developing mental skills must be modified if they are to be effective for children:

We have found that many of the approaches we use with high performance athletes are relevant for children in sport, as long as the strategies and perspectives are explained, adapted, simplified, and presented in terms children understand. (p. 326)

Orlick and McCaffrey assume that each of the

various strategies for developing psychological skills will be appropriate for children of any age if they are made simple, concrete, and fun.

Weiss (1991) maintains that psychological skills training for children should focus on personal development rather than performance enhancement. Consistent with this is her belief that, rather than being directed only to those of high ability, psychological skills training should also be directed to children of non-elite sport skill. Weiss advocates an "integrated approach" to psychological development, according to which the child's development through sport is impinged upon by numerous interacting factors, including individual difference factors (e.g., body size, self-esteem), and social contextual factors (e.g., parents, peers, gender, race, structure of the sporting activity). She says that:

> The focus on an integrated approach to psychological development, as well as attention to both performance enhancement and personal development, naturally leads to the selection of particular psychological skills and the methods by which to facilitate the attainment of these skills. (p. 340)

The psychological skills selected by Weiss include: positive self-perceptions, intrinsic motivation, positive attitude toward physical activity, coping with anxiety and stress in sport, and sportsmanship or moral development. To facilitate the attainment of any one, or any combination, of these listed skills, she recommends both strategies that involve structuring the sport situation (i.e., "environmental influences"), and strategies that involve individual self-control (i.e., "individual control strategies"). Environmental influences include physical practice methods (e.g., providing optimal challenges), coach and parent education, positive communication styles (e.g., providing frequent, quality feedback), and effective modeling, while individual control strategies include biofeedback, self-talk and thought stopping, goal-setting, mental imagery, progressive or meditative relaxation, and attentional control. Weiss does not discuss how these strategies need to be modified to meet the needs peculiar to a given developmental stage; she merely comments that "children may

not always know exactly what you are talking about with psychological skills and methods," and that it is therefore "important not to take anything for granted with young athletes in the development of psychological skills and methods" (pp. 349-350).

The importance of this two-component approach has also been emphasized by anecdotal reports concerned specifically with stress management for children (Davis, 1991, Edwards & Hofmeier, 1991; Lang & Stinson, 1991; Smoll, 1984; Smoll & Smith, 1988). Smoll (1984), for example, recommends that attempts to reduce stress in youth sport should target both environmental influences and individual control factors. While he acknowledges the promise of "intervention programs that seek to teach specific physiological and cognitive coping skills" (p. 128), Smoll adds that "this kind of direct professional involvement is not always the most practical or economically justifiable approach" and, this being the case, "some economical and appropriate measures can be utilized at the situational level" (pp. 130-131).

Although the anecdotal reports reviewed here provide valuable suggestions about the form and content of psychological skills programs for children, they are quite vague with respect to several key issues. To their credit, Gould (1983), Orlick and McCaffrey (1991), and Weiss (1991) each observe that strategies aimed at developing psychological skills may need to be modified due to the capabilities of children. However, they do not provide answers to the questions their observation provokes: What are the relevant developmental considerations? What strategies need to be modified, why, and how? Until these questions are given detailed answers, it is not possible to conduct a meaningful experimental test of psychological skills programs for children. Two further questions warrant examination: Should psychological skills training for children focus on performance or personal development? and Should psychological skills programs focus exclusively on either "environmental control strategies" or "individual control strategies", or is a combination of both more likely to optimize outcomes? In later sections of this chapter, the abovementioned questions will be addressed via a consideration of established theory, especially self determination theory (Deci & Ryan, 1985; 1991; 1995; Ryan & Deci, 2000a; 2000b) and Piaget's (1952) stage theory of cognitive development. It is first necessary, however, to clarify the relationship between psychological strategies, psychological skills, and psychological characteristics.

Psychological Strategies, Skills, and States

Vealey (1988) suggests how sport psychologists can maximize the efficacy of psychological skills training; she says that, instead of becoming enamored of a particular method (i.e., strategy) and using it indiscriminately, sport psychologists should focus on the skills that the athlete needs to develop and then select an appropriate method, or combination of methods, to teach these skills. This is sound advice and, as Vealey herself points out, the first step in its application is to differentiate between psychological skills and methods. The need to define both the term "psychological skill" and the term "psychological method" becomes apparent upon consideration of the confusion that presently exists regarding each term's usage in the PST literature. For instance, Gould (1983) includes relaxation training and imagery in the set of psychological skills, whereas Vealey (1988) lists physical relaxation and imagery amongst the psychological methods. Clearly, Vealey is justified in identifying the differentiation of skills and methods as one of six needs "that represent viable future directions for PST" (Vealey 1988, p. 322).

Magill (1993) notes two ways in which the term "skill" can be used: it can be used to refer to an act or task, and it can be used as an indicator of quality performance. The term "skill," then, might be defined as "an act that is performed better than some normative standard." However, this definition cannot be used to differentiate between skills and methods, for a method is certainly something a person does voluntarily (i.e., an act), and it may also be something at which a person becomes proficient (and hence performs better than some normative standard). Weiss (1991) acknowledges this:

> some psychological methods can be considered to be psychological skills. For cxample, before goal setting can be implemented as a strategy that children can use to enhance motivation, they need to understand and learn how to write mastery rather than performance goals, and write strategies for achieving the goals. (p. 340)

Given her belief that goal setting can be a skill, Weiss must have some basis for calling goal setting a "strategy" (or "method") in the above passage. The basis is, of course, contextual; goal setting can be identified as a method in Weiss' example because the context makes it clear that it is employed as a means of attaining a certain end, in this case, enhanced motivation.

This "appeal to context" is evident in Vealey's (1988) attempt to differentiate between psychological skills and methods. In her view, "skills are qualities to be attained, as opposed to methods which are procedures or techniques athletes engage in to develop skills" (p. 326). Vealey's definition of "skills," however, is too broad; she specifies neither that the term refers to an act, nor that it indicates quality performance. On account of this, Vealey's (1988) model of psychological skills is somewhat confused. Consider, for instance, what she identifies as being "foundation skills," namely, volition, self-awareness, self-esteem, and self-confidence. While it is possible that a person may become better at self-awareness (inasmuch as he or she becomes more aware of his or her thoughts, feelings, etc.), it makes no sense to say that a person can "become better at volition," that a person is "good at self-esteem," or that a person is "proficient at self-confidence." This is because volition, self-esteem, and self-confidence are not psychological skills that a person may perform, but, in the case of self-esteem and self-confidence, psychological characteristics that a person possesses. Similarly, it makes no sense to say that a person can "become better at optimal physical arousal," that a person is "good at optimal mental arousal," or that a person is "proficient at optimal attention." Contrary to Vealey's claim, optimal physical arousal, optimal mental arousal, and optimal attention are not "performance skills;" rather, they are psychological characteristics that enhance performance and which may be achieved more readily by persons skilled at controlling both arousal and attention.

Differentiating between psychological skills and psychological characteristics is important, for the processes by which each develops are different. By acquiring an understanding of these different processes, the sport psychologist is able to be more discerning when attempting to select the psychological methods that are most appropriate for a given athlete's needs.

Skills, by definition, are not innate; as is the case with motor skills, mental skills must be learned, and they are learned (or "developed") primarily by doing. This is not to say that what might be broadly termed "education" (i.e., spoken instruction, written instruction, augmented feedback, etc.) plays no part in the development of mental skills. Rather, we would argue that such "education" typically plays a relatively minor role. Consider, for example, mental imagery. It has been demonstrated that the capacity to form and manipulate mental images—a capacity which is native to all normal human beings—can be strengthened if it is exercised frequently (Smith 1989, in Whelan, Mahoney, & Meyers, 1991). In other words, if a person wants to become skilled at mental imagery, the onus is on him/her to practice mental imagery. Once a person becomes skilled at mental imagery, he/she may use it as a method to develop further mental skills (e.g., arousal control). But in this instance too, the skill is developed by exercising the capacity in question, so the dominant "learning factor" remains individual activity or overt practice. That is to say, the person must practice controlling their arousal via mental imagery if he or she is to become skilled at controlling arousal. Since the directed actions of the learner contribute most to the development of mental skills, it is clear that the most appropriate methods for developing mental skills are what Weiss (1991) refers to as "individual control strategies," (i.e., methods that athletes implement themselves) which are, for example, goal-setting, mental imagery, relaxation, and thought control. Of course, the claim that these methods are implemented by the athletes themselves is not a denial of the important ongoing "educational" role of the coach and/or sport psychologist; rather, it points to the fact that nobody but the athlete can *do* his/her practice.

To the extent that the psychological characteristics of a young athlete are learned, they are primarily a product of environmental factors, factors which are largely, although not completely, outside the control of the athlete him/herself. Bandura's (1977) work on self-efficacy (i.e., self-confidence) bears this out particularly well. He claims that there are four factors that contribute to a psychological state of high self-efficacy: successful personal performances, exposure to the successful performances of personally relevant models, verbal persuasion from significant others, and the absence of aversive physiological states prior to performance. Obviously, none of these factors is completely within the control of the individual athlete: they can, however, be controlled to a relatively larger degree by certain external agents (e.g., parents, coaches, sport administrators). Given this, it is clear that the most appropriate psychological methods for developing positive psychological characteristics are those that Weiss (1991) calls "environmental influences," that is, "those psychological methods or strategies that pertain to how the sport situation is structured..." (p. 340).

While differentiating between psychological strategies (or methods), psychological skills, and psychological characteristics facilitates the selection of the psychological methods that best meet a given athlete's needs, it does little by way of establishing which psychological skills and/or psychological states do in fact need to be developed by children participating in sport. Deci and Ryan's self-determination theory provides some interesting suggestions relative to this latter issue. These suggestions will be examined in the following section.

Self-determination theory: Implications for psychological skills and states

It is generally assumed that children have a particularly strong tendency to engage in "intrinsically motivated" activity. Deci and Ryan (1985), for instance, say that

> The human organism is inherently active, and there is perhaps no place where this is more evident than in little children. They pick things up, shake them, smell them, taste them, throw them across the room, and keep asking, "What's this?" They are unendingly curious, and they want to see the effects of their actions. Children are intrinsically motivated to learn, to undertake challenges, and to solve problems. (p. 11)

Intrinsic motivation theory predicts that, when a child is intrinsically motivated to perform a task, (1) the quality of his or her performance is enhanced, and (2) it is more likely that he/she will continue to participate in that type of task. In order to establish the basis for these predictions, it is necessary to consider self-determination theory in more detail.

According to Deci and Ryan, who have advanced what is currently one of the most influential conceptualizations of intrinsic motivation within sport psychology (Deci & Ryan 1985, 1991, 1995; Ryan & Deci 2000a, 2000b), intrinsic motivation issues form the "intrinsic self," which "has at its core an energizing component that has been termed intrinsic or growth motivation" (Deci & Ryan 1991, p. 274). Since they claim that intrinsically motivated activity is energized by three innate psychological needs—namely, the need for competence, the need for self-determination, and the need for relatedness (see Deci & Ryan 1991, pp. 242-243)—it is clear that Deci and Ryan consider these needs to be the major constituents of the "intrinsic self" (and that the degree to which these three needs are met will dictate the extent of a person's self-determination). Because of the inherent desire to meet the innate psychological needs, people seek out activities which interest them; as Deci and Ryan (1985) put it, "interest plays an important directive role in intrinsically motivated behavior in that people naturally approach activities that interest them" (p. 34). Now, there exists a very close connection between interest and attention; when a person is interested in an activity, his/her attentional set for that activity is typically optimal. As Deci and Ryan themselves point out, interest "plays an important role in the amplification and direction of attention" (Deci & Ryan, 1985, p. 28). There also exists a close connection between attention and arousal such that, if a person's attentional set for a given task is optimal, then his/her level of arousal for that task must be optimal (see Cox 1998, p. 68). Hence, intrinsically motivated activity is characterized by both optimal attention and optimal arousal. Conversely, where an athlete's intrinsic motivation is undermined (e.g., relevant regulatory processes are not integrated with the "intrinsic self"), performance is characterized by greater negative affect (c.f. Vallerand, 2001). Given this, it is clear why intrinsic motivation is thought to bring about substantial enhancement of performance.

Although they acknowledge that there are other determining factors, Deci and Ryan (1985) maintain that "interest is, to a large extent, a function of optimal challenge" (p. 34). Not surprisingly, then, they also claim that "the intrinsic needs for competence

and self-determination motivate an ongoing process of seeking and attempting to conquer optimal challenges" (Deci & Ryan 1985, p. 32). An "optimal challenge" is, of course, a task that is neither too easy, nor too difficult, for a given participant. That is to say, a task that is optimally challenging for a person is a task that is ideally suited to that person's competencies. This being the case, a person attempting an optimally challenging task is likely to enjoy success, and this success will—as long as he/she perceives his or her behavior to be self-determined—enhance the person's perceived competence. Deci and Ryan (1985) say that "the more competent a person perceives him- or herself to be at some activity, the more intrinsically motivated he or she will be at that activity" (p. 58). An intrinsically motivated person, then, will continue to participate in an activity while they can find in that activity an optimal challenge.

Given the major tenets of the self determination framework outlined above, it would appear that children are in native possession of both key psychological skills (e.g., attentional control, arousal control, self-motivation) and key positive psychological characteristics (e.g., perceived competence, internal perceived locus of causality). Moreover, it would seem that they engage these skills and positive characteristics in an unselfconscious way. That is to say, it seems that children do not employ these skills and positive characteristics on account of a prior conscious belief in their efficacy; rather, their psychological skills and positive psychological characteristics come to the fore as a natural consequence of their interest. On the basis of this, it might be concluded that children are in no need of interventions designed to develop psychological skills and positive self perceptions. To reach this conclusion, however, is to overlook one crucial fact: while intrinsic motivation is considered to be innate, it is not considered to be immutable. Indeed, self-determination theory (SDT) specifies the factors within a social context which undermine, as well as the factors which promote, the intrinsic motivation of a child.

Deci and Ryan (1991) focus on three dimensions for assessing the social context: autonomy support, structure, and involvement. A social context is "autonomy supportive" when those within it believe they have the opportunity to choose what they do (i.e., believe they have the opportunity to be self-determined), and when the pressure to at-tain certain standards of performance is negligible. Autonomy support, then, is the opposite of "control." The "structure" dimension pertains to the quality of goals, behavior-outcome contingencies, and feed-back, whereas the "involvement" dimension pertains to the level of "task support" provided by significant others (i.e., coaches, parents, peers). A child's intrin-sic motivation is likely to be undermined by social contexts that are "controlling, that are unstructured or over-structured, or that do not provide involve-ment of significant others" (Deci & Ryan 1991, p. 246). For example, material rewards, such as money and trophies, can undermine a child's intrinsic mo-tivation if the child perceives them to be control-ling rather than informational. A child may also feel that his or her sporting efforts are controlled, rather than self-determined, if he or she is pressured to per-form at a certain standard. The structure of a social context may undermine intrinsic motivation if the child is exposed to activities that are not optimally challenging, or if the child is provided with no in-formational feedback about performance. Lastly, a child's intrinsic motivation may diminish if he or she receives no encouragement from significant others.

The notion that it is an unfavorable social con-text which undermines a child's intrinsic motivation suggests that, instead of needing to learn psycho-logical skills, and instead of needing to learn how to attain positive psychological characteristics, chil-dren actually need to have their native psychologi-cal skills and positive psychological characteristics nurtured. This, in turn, may lead one to conclude that programs designed to facilitate the psychologi-cal development of children must consist not of "in-dividual control strategies," but of "environmental control strategies." From what Weiss (1991) refers to as a "theory-to-practice" perspective, this position appears to be convincing. However, if a "practice-to-theory" approach (another term used by Weiss) is taken, it becomes apparent that the said position is seriously weakened by two considerations. First, it is practically impossible to achieve the necessary level of control over a given child's social context. For in-stance, parents may harbor unconscious hostilities toward one or more of their children (a fact which intrinsic motivation theory conveniently overlooks). Indeed, coaches are by no means exempt from this

dynamic. Moreover, while the hostilities directed to-ward a child by his or her peers are typically far more direct, they are no less difficult to control. Secondly, even if it were possible to achieve the necessary level of control over a given child's social context, the na-ture of optimally challenging sporting events is such that children participating in them will inevitably ex-perience some aversive affect (e.g., being break-point down in a tight tennis match; trying to progress to the next level of difficulty in a gymnastics routine).

In drawing attention to these two practical diffi-culties, it is not being suggested that "environmental control strategies" cannot facilitate the psychological development of children. They can. The claim being made is that "environmental control strategies" are necessarily limited in their effectiveness. Hence, it is desirable that they be supplemented with "individual control strategies" whose primary aim is to protect the child's intrinsic motivation. It is as the Stoic phi-losophers of Ancient Greece said; ultimately, the only thing a person can control is him- or herself. Children participating in sport must be "mentally tough," that is, they must develop "individual control strategies" to deal effectively with the various envi-ronmental cues attached to sport participation, for their interpretation of these cues has the potential to elicit negative thoughts and aversive effects, both of which threaten intrinsic motivation.

Earlier, the question was posed, Should psycho-logical skills programs focus exclusively on either "en-vironmental control strategies" or "individual control strategies", or is a combination of both more likely to optimize outcomes? In view of the foregoing discus-sion, it is evident that a combined approach is more promising. However, it is not presently clear which combination of strategies would be maximally effec-tive. As mentioned earlier, the experimental studies that purport to demonstrate the efficacy of "indi-vidual control strategies" for children in sport are problematic insofar as they report on performance averaged across a range of ages. As such, it is not clear whether the strategies in question are effective for all ages within the range. Similarly, because these studies involve multi-component interventions, it is not clear whether each component is effective for children. In the next section, the developmental lit-erature will be examined in an attempt to establish whether any ages within the range of 6 to 12 years need to be studied separately, and whether any of the recognized "individual control strategies" are inappropriate for children of a certain age because they exceed developmental limitations. The "performance versus personal development" issue will also be considered.

Cognitive development and motor development: Implications for PST for children

Piaget (1952) proposes what is perhaps the best known theory of cognitive development. He conceptualizes cognitive development as a progression through "stages," that is, periods of life which are qualitatively different inasmuch as they involve a distinct level of psychological organization. According to Piaget, these developmental stages are invariant (i.e., they proceed in a regular order) and universal (i.e., they occur in the same order for all individuals, regardless of culture). Four such stages are identified: the sensorimotor stage, the preoperational stage, the concrete operations stage, and the formal operations stage. It is during the sensorimotor stage (approximately birth-2 years) that the infant's concept of self emerges as a consequence of direct sensory experience and motor actions. The capacity for symbolic activity develops during the preoperational stage (approximately 2-7 years). Nonetheless, mental activity remains limited in certain important respects; for instance, the preoperational child cannot think of actions which he or she has not engaged in, or which he or she has not seen someone else perform. This "egocentricity" is overcome during the concrete operations stage (approximately 7-11 years). However, reasoning is limited to concrete things. In other words, a child at this developmental stage can only reason about what is, not what might be. It is not until the formal operations stage (approximately 11-15 years) that the child achieves relatively mature intellectual function and can engage in abstract thought .

Even this crude sketch of Piaget's theory makes it clear that it is of great relevance to both the application and the experimental evaluation of PST programs for children. Granting that there are substantial cognitive differences between 6 -7 year olds (pre-operational), 7-11 year olds (concrete operations), and 11-12 year olds (formal operations), it is reasonable to expect that a psychological skills program which is effective for one of these age ranges will not necessarily be effective for either of the other age ranges. Hence, the only studies that have been specific to the childhood age range so far (i.e. Wrisberg & Anshel, 1989; Zhang et al., 1992; and Atienza et al., 1998) are problematic insofar as they are, according to Piaget's theory, encompassing distinct developmental stages. For example, the study by Zhang et al. (1992) employs the same intervention for participants aged between 7 and 10 years, who may either be at the pre-operational stage or the concrete operations stage. The concern is, of course, that because these studies are reporting on performance data which is averaged across a given age range, their positive findings may reflect the efficacy of PST for just one, perhaps later, developmental stage within the age range.

A related problem with these three studies is that they each evaluated multi-component strategies. Specifically they evaluated strategies that were comprised of video modeling, relaxation, and imagery. Hence the positive findings of these studies do not indicate whether each of these component strategies was effective for the participants, or whether only one of these was effective. There are two considerations here. First, the developmental stages mentioned above may require different instructional approaches. For instance, introducing interventions via verbal instruction may be effective for those at the concrete operations stage and beyond, and yet ineffective for those at the pre-operational stage, especially given that the latter supposedly have difficulty thinking about things they either have not done or have not seen somebody else do (Rebok, 1987). The second consideration is that there may be age-related differences in the actual skill itself. Kosslyn, Margolis, Barrett, Goldknopf, and Daly (1990) found age differences for image generation. More specifically, participants aged 8 years were better at generating images than younger participants, aged 5 years. Indeed, the 5 year olds were said to have had a "very difficult time" in the image generation task (p.1001). Kosslyn et al. (1990) concede that the 5 year olds' difficulty may have had "nothing to do with imagery per se and that instead they may have had trouble interpreting the task cues" (p. 1001). Nevertheless this study does make it clear that it is important to explore the possibility that there are age-related differences in the various mental skills.

The motor development literature assists with the resolution of the performance versus personal development issue. It is well demonstrated that fundamental motor skills develop more rapidly than perceptual motor skills. Children achieve mature throwing (a fundamental motor skill) at approximately 5-6-1/2 years of age whereas they do not achieve mature striking (a perceptual motor skill) until approximately 10-12 years of age (Abernethy, Killers, Mackinnon, Neal & Hanrahan, 1996; Ulrich, 1987). Hence, it is likely that children will not reach the highest stages of motor learning for perceptual motor skills until they are at least at the latter stages of childhood. As a consequence, performance enhancement will not be a priority for these children. Rather facilitating motor learning will be the primary concern. There is no doubt that PST programs can facilitate motor learning. For example, the effective application of relaxation strategies will help a novice tennis player develop the correct movement patterns on his/her groundstrokes. However, fostering the learning of basic motor skills reflects a different agenda to performance enhancement (i.e., the agenda typically pursued with more accomplished athletes, where the consistent production of already well-learned movement patterns in pressure contexts is the primary concern). Therefore, facilitating motor learning comes under the general heading of personal development.

Recommendations regarding PST for children

Whether children can benefit from psychological skills training is an empirical question: there is nothing *a priori* to suggest that they cannot. Unfortunately, it is a question which has not, to date, been tested adequately. Those studies that have looked at the issue suffer because they collapse their findings over a relatively broad age range and disregard the possible developmental differences within those age ranges. Moreover, they neglect the possibility that not all strategies are appropriate for all developmental stages.

Currently, anecdotal studies provide some common sense, albeit somewhat vague, directives for the construction of effective PST programs. For instance, it is obvious that the cognitive processing capabilities of children should not be over-taxed by any intervention. However, the processing limitations pertaining to each age within the 6-12 years range have not been specified. Culbert, Kajander, and Reaney (1996) show more sensitivity to the established developmental stages when they suggest that biofeedback is particularly promising for very young children (i.e., those in the pre-operational stage) because it is a process that may be modeled and introduced to them "as a video game for your body" (p.343).

Of course, it is desirable to have the support of well-designed experimental studies in addition to such anecdotal evidence. The ideal experiment would separate the developmental stages within the 6-12 age range. That is to say, the effects of PST would be examined separately for pre-operational children and concrete operations children. Moreover, the effectiveness of single strategies would be examined in order to determine whether there are any age-related differences in the ability to employ certain mental skills. This is not to suggest that 6-7 year olds cannot, for instance, form mental images; it is only to suggest that when directed to employ such a strategy to achieve a specific end, they may not be able to do so as effectively as older children, either because their generation of the image is somehow lacking, or they cannot follow the instructions as well.

The general approach just outlined is suited to a variety of methodologies, each of which brings advantages and disadvantages. It would, for instance, be appropriate to employ a single-subject design study. This approach would certainly help to establish the best PST strategy for the subject in question; however, it does not allow the researcher to make legitimate generalizations from his/her observations to the wider population. On the other hand, a cross-sectional approach employing large samples permits more legitimate generalizations, but could at the same time mask potentially important individual difference factors.

Lastly, given the motor development literature, experimental studies of PST need to employ tasks that are maximally sensitive to improvement. That is, they need to employ motor tasks rather than perceptual motor tasks, as improvement in the latter may be constrained by maturational factors. Suppose, for example, that a perceptual-motor task—say, striking a ball with a bat—is used as the experimental task in an examination of a PST intervention's effect on the performance of 6 year olds (pre-operational stage), 8 year olds (concrete operations stage), and 11 year olds (formal operations stage); in such a case, the developmental constraints on children younger than 11 (which is, on average, the age at which children achieve mature functioning) may prevent them from evidencing any improvement on the task. This may, in turn, lead the experimenter to falsely conclude that the PST intervention is effective only for children 11 years or older. If, on the other hand, a motor task—a task which neither requires visual tracking, nor makes substantial demands on cognitive processes (e.g., running, throwing)—is employed to generate the dependent measure, then, since mature function on such tasks is typically achieved by the fifth or sixth year, it is less likely that the effect of the PST intervention would be masked by developmental constraints, and hence its efficacy across the said developmental stages could be more accurately gauged.

References

Abernethy, B., Kippers, V., Mackinnon, L. T., Neal, R. J., & Hanrahan, S. (1996). *The biophysical foundations of human movement*. South Melbourne: Macmillan Education Australia.

Atienza, F. L., Balaguer, I., & Garcia Merita, M. L. (1998). Video modeling and imaging training on performance of tennis serve of 9 to 12 year old children. *Perceptual and Motor Skills, 87*, 519-529.

Bandura, A. (1977). Self-efficacy: Toward a unifying theory of behavioral change. *Psychological Review, 84*, 191-215.

Cox, R. (1998). *Sport psychology: Concepts and applications*. 4th Ed. Boston: WCB McGraw Hill.

Culbert, T. P., Kajander, R. L., & Reaney, J. B. (1996). Biofeedback with children and adolescents: Clinical observations and patient perspectives. *Developmental & Behavioral Pediatrics, 17*, 342-350.

Danish, S. J., Petitpas, A. J., & Hale, B. D. (1992). A developmental-educational intervention model of sport psychology. *The Sport Psychologist, 6*, 403-415.

Davis, R. (1991). Teaching stress management in an elementary classroom. *The Journal of Physical Education, Recreation & Dance, 62*, 65-66, 70.

Deci, E. L., & Ryan, R. M. (1985). *Intrinsic motivation and self-determination in human behaviour*. New York: Plenum Press.

Deci, E. L., & Ryan, R. M. (1991). A motivational approach to self: Integration in personality. In R. Deinstbier (Ed.). *Nebraska Symposium on Motivation*, V38, pp. 237-288. Lincoln: University of Nebraska Press.

Deci, E. L., & Ryan, R. M. (1995) Human autonomy: The basis for true self-esteem. In M. H. Kernis (Ed.) *Efficacy, Agency, and Self-Esteem*. pp. 31-49. New York: Plenum Press.

Edwards, V. D., & Hofmeier, J. (1991). A stress management program for elementary and special-population children. *The Journal of Physical Education, Recreation & Dance, 62*, 61-64.

European Federation of Sport Psychology (1996). Position Statement of the European Federation of Sport Psychology (FEPSAC II): Children in sport. *The Sport Psychologist, 10*, 224-226.

Gallahue, D., & Ozmun, J. (1995). *Understanding motor development. Infants, children, adolescents, adults*. (3rd Ed) Madison: WCB.

Garza, D. L., & Feltz, D. L. (1998). Effects of selected mental practice on performance, self-efficacy, and competition confidence of figure skaters. *The Sport Psychologist, 12*, 1-15.

Gould, D. (1983). Developing psychological skills in young athletes. *Coaching Science Update*, 4-13.

Hellstedt, J. C. (1987). Sport psychology at a ski academy: Teaching mental skills to young athletes. *The Sport Psychologist, 1*, 56-68.

Kirchner, G. (1992). *Physical education for elementary school children*. (8th Ed.). Dubuque: WCB.

Kosslyn, S. M., Margolis, J. A., Barrett, A. M., Goldknopf, E. J., & Daly, P. F. (19990). Age differences in imagery abilities. *Child Development, 61*, 995-1010.

Lang, D. A., & Stinson, W. J. (1991). The young child: Stress management strategies to use. *The Journal of Physical Education, Recreation & Dance, 62*, 59-60, 69-70.

Lee, A. B., & Hewitt, J. (1987). Using visual imagery in a flotation tank to improve gymnastic performance and reduce physical symptoms. *International Journal of Sport Psychology, 18*, 223-230.

Magill, R. (1993). *Motor learning: Concepts and applications*. (4th Ed.). Dubuque: WCB.

Maslow, A. H. (1943). A theory of human motivation. *Psychological Review, 50*, 370-396.

Ming, S., & Martin, G. L. (1996). Single-subject evaluation of a self-talk package for improving figure skating performance. *The Sport Psychologist, 10*, 227-238.

Orlick, T., & McCaffrey, N. (1991). Mental training with children for sport and life. *The Sport Psychologist, 5*, 322-334.

Palmer, S. L. (1992). A comparison of mental practice techniques as applied to the developing competitive figure skater. *The Sport Psychologist, 6*, 148-155.

Piaget, J. (1952). Logic and psychology. In H. E. Gruber and J. J. Voneche (1977) *The Essential Piaget*. London: Routledge and Kegan Paul, pp. 445-477

Rebok, G. W. (1987). *Life-span cognitive development*. New York: Holt, Rinehart, & Winston.

Rogers, C. R. (1961) *On Becoming a Person: A Therapist's View of Psychotherapy*. London: Constable and Company.

Ryan, R. M., & Deci, E. L. (2000a) Intrinsic and extrinsic motivations: Classic definitions and new directions. *Contemporary Educational Psychology, 25*, 54-67.

Ryan, R. M., & Deci, E. L. (2000b) Self-determination theory and the facilitation of intrinsic motivation, social development, and well-being. *American Psychologist, 55*(1), 68-78.

Smith, R. E., & Smoll, F. L. (1982). Psychological stress: A conceptual model and some intervention strategies in youth sports. In R. A. Magill, M. J. Ash, & F. L. Smoll (Eds.), *Children in sport* (2nd ed.) pp. 178-195. Champaign, IL: Human Kinetics.

Smoll, F. L. (1984). Stress reduction strategies in youth sport. In Sport for children and youths. Weiss, M. R. & Gould, D. (Eds.). *The 1984 Olympic Scientific Congress Proceedings,* Vol. 10. Champaign, Ill.: Human Kinetics.

Smoll, F. L., & Smith, R. E. (1988). Reducing stress in youth sport: Theory and application. In Smoll, F. L., Magill, R. A., & Ash, M. U. (Eds.). *Children in Sport* (3rd Ed.). Champaign, Ill.: Human Kinetics.

Ulrich, B. D. (1987). Developmental perspectives of motor skill performance in Children. In D. Gould & M. R. Weiss (Eds.). *Advances in Pediatric Sport Sciences,* Vol 2. Behavioural issues. Champaign, Ill.: Human Kinetics.

Vallerand, R. J. (2001). A hierarchical model of intrinsic and extrinsic motivation in sport and exercise. In G. C. Roberts (ed.) *Advances in Motivation in Sport and Exercise.* pp. 263-319. Champaign, Illinois: Human Kinetics Books.

Vealey, R. (1988). Future directions in psychological skills training. *The Sport Psychologist, 2,* 318-336.

Walkley, J., Holland, B., Treloar, R., & Probyn-Smith, H. (1993). Fundamental Motor Skill Proficiency of Children. *The ACHPER National Journal, 40*(3) 11-14.

Wanlin, C. M., Hrycaiko, D. W., Martin, G. L., & Mahon, M. (1997). The effects of a goal-setting package on the performance of speed skaters. *Journal of Applied Sport Psychology, 89,* 212-228.

Weinberg, R. S., & Williams, J. M. (2001). Integrating and implementing a psychological skills training program. In J. M. Williams (Ed), *Applied sport psychology: Personal growth to peak performance.* (4th Ed.). Mountain View, CA: Mayfield.

Weiss, M. R. (1991). Psychological skill development in children and adolescents. *The Sport Psychologist, 5,* 335-354.

Whelan, J. P., Mahoney, M. J., & Meyers, A. W. (1991). Performance enhancement in sport: A cognitive behavioral domain. *Behavior Therapy, 22,* 307-327.

Wrisberg, C. A., & Anshel, M. H. (1989). The effect of cognitive strategies on the free throw shooting performance of young athletes. *The Sport Psychologist, 3,* 95-104.

Zhang L., Ma, Q., Orlick, T., & Zitzelsberger, L. (1992). The effect of mental-imagery training on performance enhancement with 7-10 year old children. *The Sport Psychologist, 6,* 230-241.

Courtesy of Lance Cpl. Virgil P. Richardson/U.S. Marine Corps

2.4

Learning Strategies in Motor Skill Acquisition: From the Laboratory to the Gym

RONNIE LIDOR AND ROBERT N. SINGER

Introduction

The learning of motor skills is a complex and multifaceted process that requires the optimal integration of motor, cognitive, and affective behaviors. Learning has been defined as an improvement in skill that is brought about as a function of practice (Magill, 1998; Schmidt & Lee, 2005). According to Lee, Chamberlin, and Hodges (2001), "learning is not a change in performance per se, but rather in an improved capability or potential to perform at a skill level that is higher than the skill level before practice was undertaken" (pp. 115-116). Educators attempt to communicate and to create learning environments that optimize the opportunity for learners to realize their potential to achieve.

Research in motor learning is abundant in certain areas. Some examples are (1) the ideal emphasis on practice conditions, such as massed versus distributed practice and blocked versus random practice (Lee et al., 2001); (2) the amount of variability that is introduced in a practice (Yan, Thomas, & Thomas, 1998); (3) the amount and timing of knowledge of results given to learners during or after performance (Magill, 2001); and (4) the role of the teacher or instructor in terms of modeling and demonstrating the learned task (McCullagh & Weiss, 2001). Relevant information from theoretical and practical perspectives on these issues, as well as on other essential instructional considerations, can be found in typical texts on motor skill acquisition (e.g., Schmidt & Lee, 2005; Schmidt & Wrisberg, 2004). Such information has been useful for instructors (e.g., physical educators and coaches) designing better instructional situations in which learners attempt to master skills related to the content of the activity.

During the past two decades, an attempt has been made by certain researchers in motor learning and educational sport psychology to study conscious and subconscious behaviors related to information processing and the development of movement skills (Singer, 2000, 2002). Research has also focused on how individuals can activate or inhibit appropriate cognitive processes during learning and how they can be provided with strategies for managing cognitive processes in order to improve performance.

The interest in cognitive aspects of motor skill acquisition has led to research on effective learning strategies and ways to teach these strategies to individuals who do not know how to use them effectively (Riding & Rayner, 1999). The prominent finding that has emerged from this research is that particular cognitive and metacognitive strategies can enhance the learning of motor skills. Research on strategies has been undertaken under laboratory conditions as well as in field settings.

The purpose of this chapter is threefold: (1) to examine the trends observed in one line of strategy research conducted in the motor domain during the past two decades under laboratory and field conditions; (2) to discuss knowledge based on strategy research that is useful for practitioners; and (3) to propose future studies that might increase the ecological validity of task-pertinent strategies.

There are seven parts of this chapter. The first part defines the term *learning strategy*. The second part is an overview of early strategy research, and the third part discusses the value of the five-step approach (5-SA) to the acquisition of self-paced motor tasks in laboratory settings. The fourth part discusses considerations about self-awareness and nonawareness when it comes to learning and performance. The fifth part provides evidence for strategy training in applied settings, such as in sport practice sessions and physical education classes. The sixth part summarizes what we have learned so far from strategy research in the motor domain, and the seventh part discusses research procedures from scholarly and applied perspectives with regard to potential future strategy research.

Strategic Behavior in Motor Learning: Cognitive and Metacognitive Strategies

Research has shown that task-pertinent learning strategies contribute to the acquisition and performance of self-paced motor tasks (e.g., Kim, Singer, & Radlo, 1997; Lidor, 2004). A self-paced task has been defined as an act that is executed in a relatively stable and predictable environment, with few time constraints on the initiation of the movement (Lidor & Singer, 2003; Singer, 2000, 2002). A performer is typically provided with a short preparation interval before the initiation of the act. In formal tennis competition, for example, the player is allowed about 25 seconds to initiate the serve and in basketball the player is allowed to spend 5 seconds at the free-throw line before executing a shot (in European basketball).

Individuals should use a preparatory procedure or a pre-performance routine, what we term a *general strategy* to improve learning and performance. A learning strategy can be self-initiated or externally imposed (e.g., by an instructor) with the intent of helping people to acquire a movement skill more efficiently and effectively than would be the case without its use (Kucan & Beck, 1997; Lidor & Singer, 2003; Singer, 2002; Woolfolk, 1998). Practically speaking, a learning strategy refers to the behaviors and thoughts that a learner activates deliberately or subconsciously to improve a skill or to accomplish a goal. Of primary interest in this chapter are strategies that are formally taught.

Another category of strategies has been termed metacognitive: strategies that can influence a variety of learning tasks and conditions (Weinstein & Van Mater Stone, 1996). Metacognition is related to self-monitoring, to the knowledge of one's self-evaluation, and to an understanding of how to achieve in various tasks. Metacognitive strategies help learners adjust to new conditions, transfer previous knowledge and skills to related learning situations, and cope with demands not previously experienced (Woolfolk, 1998). Learners are enabled to know more about how to manage their learning processes and how to analyze their progress with regard to situational demands (Riding & Rayner, 1999).

During the past two decades, the effectiveness of particular learning strategies has been investigated through performance of artificial tasks and sport-type tasks under laboratory conditions, as well as sport skills in "real" conditions. The general observation based on the data in these studies is that a variety of self-paced motor tasks have benefited with the use of particular learning strategies; tasks undertaken were as various as key pressing and modified dart throwing (i.e., artificial tasks), ball throwing at a target (i.e., an applied task), and free throws in basketball (i.e., a sport skill). Individuals who were exposed to specific strategy instructions were generally able to perform better than those who were provided with task instructions but without strategic guidelines.

A review of the research on the usefulness of learning strategies in self-paced motor skill acquisition is divided into four periods (see Figure 1): (1) early research on strategies, (2) laboratory studies on one general learning strategy, the 5-SA, (3) laboratory research on other learning strategies, and (4) strategy research in sport settings.

Table 1 presents a summary of 17 (11 laboratory and 6 field) studies conducted in one area of strategy research in the motor domain. It reflects the chronological approach that was adopted in this chapter: Early laboratory inquires are presented first, followed by laboratory studies that examined the usefulness of three learning strategies. Applied strategy studies are presented last.

Figure 1: Chronological Stages in Strategy on Self-Paced Motor Skills

Early strategy research: Task classification and task analysis → 5-SA laboratory inquiries: Establishment and development → Laboratory research on additional strategies: Awareness and nonawareness → Applied strategy research: Basketball, air gun shooting, and tennis

Early Strategy Research: Task Classification and Task Analysis

Studies on strategy use in the 1970s from a cognitive psychology perspective reflected the instructional-pedagogical assumptions that learners should learn how to learn, how to solve problems, and how to transfer knowledge and skills from one learning situation to another (Simon, 1975; Woolfolk, 1998). Empirical evidence for these assumptions was found in studies in education and educational psychology (e.g., Norman, 1976). Those individuals who acquired useful task-solving strategies when learning academic matter were able to achieve more adequately after the formal instructional program was completed. Due to the fact that verbal materials and skills were studied considerably more than motor skills, it was the purpose of researchers in the motor domain to use similar paradigms to determine if similar results would occur. In addition, there was very little impetus to study psychomotor activity from the perspectives of task analysis and information processing. Research on learning strategies most pertinent to directing cognitive processes associated with achievement in motor tasks was neglected as well. Therefore, one of the main objectives of early strategy research related to motor skills was to identify task-relevant strategies and to determine the influence of these strategies on achieving in self-paced motor skills. Controlled laboratory learning conditions and unique tasks were typical.

In an early study on the generalization of psychomotor learning strategies to related psychomotor tasks, Singer and Cauraugh (1984) used the task classification system proposed by Singer and Gerson (1981). It was postulated that psychomotor skills be categorized according to three factors: the information processing demands placed on the learner, environmental pacing conditions, and feedback availability. Based on this classification, Singer and Cauraugh (1984) taught learners to apply three strategic guidelines to a pursuit rotor learning task: (1) anticipatory (e.g., to be aware of potentially changing stimulus event conditions), (2) rhythmic (e.g., to develop a tempo and a feeling of the rhythmic movement), and (3) feedback

Table 1: Strategy Studies Conducted Under Laboratory and Field Conditions

Study	Learning Conditions	Participants	Strategy/ies	Motor Task/s	Results
Singer and Cauraugh (1984)	Laboratory	20 undergraduate and graduate students (8 females and 12 males)	Anticipatory strategy, rhythmic strategy, and feedback strategy	A Lafayette pursuit rotor task	1. Strategy groups attained greater performance on the primary task and under modified task conditions 2. Strategy groups showed greater use of cognitive strategies
Singer, Cauraugh, Lucariello, and Brown (1985)	Laboratory	16 university students (8 women and 8 men)	Imagery strategy, rhythmic pattering of movements strategy, and selective monitoring feedback strategy	A complex photoelectric maze task	Strategy groups completed the mazes faster than a control group
Brown, Singer, Cauraugh, and Lucariello (1985)	Laboratory	24 undergraduate and graduate female college students (mean age = 23 yrs)	Imagery strategy, rhythm strategy, and feedback strategy	A maze task	Strategies enhanced speed in both reflective and impulsive participants compared with control reflective and impulsive participants
Singer and Suwanthada (1986)	Laboratory	80 university students (ranging in age from 17 to 25 yrs)	Content-dependent 5-SA and content-independent 5-SA	Underhanded dart throwing, jart throwing, and soccer foul shooting tasks	1. Strategy learning conditions were more effective than a control condition for each task 2. Content-independent strategy group achieved better in the learning of the task most related to the primary task than the content-dependent strategy 3. Content-independent strategy group that was provided with reminders outperformed the other strategy groups in the less-related task
Singer, Flora, and Abourezk (1989a)	Laboratory	30 undergraduate student physical education majors	5-SA (a slightly modified version)	A novel complex motor task (touching targets in a sequenced order)	5-SA group performed faster than the other two groups, and not at the expense of a greater number of errors
Singer, DeFrancesco, and Randall (1989)	Laboratory	40 university students ranging in age from 18 to 31 years (mean age = 22.5 yrs)	5-SA	A complex laboratory motor task requiring speed and accuracy in movement, a modified table tennis serve (applied sport) task, and a seated underhand dart-throwing (transfer) task	1. 5-SA groups were faster than control groups during primary task performance 2. 5-SA groups outperformed the control groups during transfer performances

Study	Learning Conditions	Participants	Strategy/ies	Motor Task/s	Results
Singer, Flora, and Abourezk (1989b)	Laboratory	40 undergraduate students	5-SA	A novel complex motor task (touching targets in a sequenced order)	1. Participants who were provided with the 5-SA before practice began performed faster compared to participants who were provided with the 5-SA after practice began and participants who were not provided with the strategy 2. Preparation times were longer in the strategy groups compared with the control group
Kim, Singer, and Radlo (1996)	Laboratory	36 university students (18 females and 18 males; mean age = 24 yrs.) in Study 1; 48 university students (24 females and 24 males; mean age = 19.8 yrs) in Study 2	5-SA	Brain scrambler and golf-putting (Study 1); Card sorting, star tracing with mirror, and ball rolling to a target (Study 2)	1. 5-SA enhanced performances of a low cognitive demand task and a medium cognitive demand task 2. 5-SA did not facilitate high cognitive demand performances
Singer, Lidor, and Cauraugh (1993)	Laboratory	72 physical education and fitness students (36 females and 36 males; mean age = 20.13 yrs)	5-SA, an awareness strategy, a nonawareness strategy	Overhand throw at a target apparatus	1. Strategy participants were more accurate than control participants 2. 5-SA and nonawareness participants were more accurate than awareness participants
Singer, Lidor, and Cauraugh (1994)	Laboratory	64 university students (32 females and 32 males)	5-SA, an awareness strategy, a nonawareness strategy	A key pressing task	1. Strategy participants were faster than control participants 2. 5-SA and nonawareness participants were faster than awareness participants
Lidor, Tennant, and Singer (1996)	Laboratory	80 undergraduate students (40 females and 40 males; mean age = 23.2 yrs)	5-SA, an awareness strategy, a nonawareness strategy	A ball throwing task and a dart throwing task	5-SA participants were more accurate and consistent than awareness, nonawareness, and control participants in both throwing tasks
Lidor and Tenenbaum (1994)	Basketball gym	A 16-year-old basketball player	5-SA	Free throws in basketball	1. Accuracy of shooting was increased over time 2. Preperformance interval was increased (up to 5 sec)
Lidor, Arnon, and Bronstein (1999)	Basketball gym	28 basketball players (15 girls; mean age = 13.2 yrs and 13 boys; mean age = 14.1 yrs)	5-SA	Free throws in basketball	5-SA enhanced performance accuracy of foul throws in basketball for the boys and girls combined
Chung, Kim, Janelle, and Radlo (1996)	An international shooting site	24 experienced male shooters (mean age = 22.3 yrs)	5-SA	A target shooting task with an air gun pistol	5-SA participants were more accurate and consistent compared with control participants

Study	Learning Conditions	Participants	Strategy/ies	Motor Task/s	Results
Bouchard and Singer (1998)	Tennis court	63 recreational university tennis players (39 men and 24 women; mean age = 22.3 yrs)	5-SA with videotaped modeling and audiotape 5-SA plus written transcript	A tennis serve	Strategy and control participants improved across time on the dependent measures
Lidor (2004)	Basketball gym	56 female learners (mean age = 12.5 yrs.)	5-SA, an awareness strategy, a nonawareness strategy	Free throws in basketball	1. 5-SA and nonawareness learners were more accurate than the awareness and control learners 2. Strategy learners increased their preparation intervals compared with the control learners
Lidor (1997)	Basketball gym (Experiment 1); Team-handball gym (Experiment 2)	40 third-grade children (20 girls and 20 boys; mean age = 9.8 yrs) in Experiment 1; 33 seventh-grade children (15 girls and 18 boys; mean age = 12.6 yrs) in Experiment 2	Modified 5-SA (Experiments 1 and 2)	Bowling throw (Experiment 1); Overhand ball throwing (Experiment 2)	1. 5-SA group was more accurate than a control group (Experiment 1) 2. 5-SA group was more accurate than a control group (Experiment 2)

(e.g., to be aware of, in this case, the noise generated by the task). Participants were directed to perform a pursuit rotor task under different response-demand conditions, namely a pursuit rotor set at 60 rev/min and a set of randomly assigned speeds ranging from 35 to 85 rev/min. It was found that the strategy groups attained greater performance on the primary task and under the modified task conditions compared with the control group (no-strategy). In addition, the strategy groups reported greater use of cognitive strategies.

Similar strategic guidelines were introduced by Singer, Cauraugh, Lucariello, and Brown (1985). A task analysis procedure was used to determine the information processing demand of a maze task: information available, response demands, and feedback characteristics. Three strategies were administered, one for each task analysis process: imagery (i.e., an explicit mental picture of the correct pattern of movement), rhythmic patterning of movements, and selective monitoring of feedback. Two versions of the maze task were performed by university students. The usefulness of the strategies was compared to a control condition (no-strategy). It was found that the strategy groups completed the related maze tasks faster than the control group.

In a similar study using maze tasks, Brown, Singer, Cauraugh, and Lucariello (1985) introduced the imagery, rhythm, and feedback strategies to learners with different styles of responding, as classified by The Matching Familiar Figures test. Learners performing the maze task were classified as impulsive or reflective. It was found that for the maze task that emphasized speed, the performance of reflective and impulsive participants was facilitated by appropriate learning strategies compared with the control reflective and impulsive participants. No significant differences were observed for strategies introduced to reflective or impulsive learners.

The process of task classification applied in the early stage of strategy inquiry led these researchers to propose four forms of strategies: anticipatory, rhythmic, feedback, and imagery. It was argued that these strategies helped learners to become active, problem-solving strategy users (Singer & Cauraugh, 1984). The learners were able to activate relevant cognitive processes and manage their actions to effectively achieve the learning goals. Based on these strategies, a more global and structured learning strategy, namely the 5-SA, was developed. The idea of developing a global learning strategy composed of a set of mini cognitive and metacognitive strategies, was originated in the early stages of strategy research.

The Effectiveness of the 5-SA in Acquisition of Self-Paced Motor Tasks: Laboratory Settings

The 5-SA was proposed to enhance the learning and performance processes in self-paced skills (Singer, 1988, 2000). The strategy is composed of five substrategies, each of which has been subjected to a fair amount of scientific scrutiny (Lidor, 1999). The steps of the strategy are as follows (Singer, 2000): (1) readying—establishing a ritual that involves optimal positioning of the body, confidence, expectations, and emotion, (2) imaging—creating a vivid picture of

one's best performance, (3) focusing attention—concentrating intensely on one external feature which is most relevant to the act or environment, (4) executing—performing with a quiet mind; adopting a "just do it" approach, and (5) evaluating—if time permits, using self-feedback information on the quality of the performed act as well as on the implementation of the previous four steps. Specific guidelines for each step of the 5-SA are presented in Table 2.

The usefulness of the 5-SA has been investigated in both laboratory and field studies. In early stages of 5-SA research, the strategy was compared to a control condition in which no strategic instructions were introduced. The strategy instructions were presented either by the experimenter or audio cassettes under sterile learning conditions. Typically, the strategy instructions were presented before any practice or experience with the task. Practically speaking, participants listened to a short strategy explanation, were provided with a limited number of practice trials (i.e., 2 to 3 trials), and then performed the task. They were asked to use the strategy instructions as much as possible for each trial.

The first study that examined the effectiveness of the 5-SA on the learning of related closed motor skills was conducted by Singer and Suwanthada (1986). In this study, the 5-SA was introduced under four different strategy conditions, namely a content-dependent strategy (CDS), a content-dependent strategy plus reminders (CDSR), a content-independent strategy (CIS), and a content-independent strategy plus reminders (CISR). The CDS and CDSR participants were taught the strategy with specific reference to the explicit task at the very beginning of the learning session. The CIS and CISR participants were taught the strategy without reference to any one specific task, but rather were given a number of examples in the context of learning the strategy. The reminders groups were verbally cued by the experimenter to use the strategy and were also shown a chart containing strategy guidelines during intervals between each set of trials. All strategy conditions were compared to a control condition (no strategy). The participants were taught to perform three different laboratory tasks: (1) underhand dart throwing (a specific task), (2) jart throwing (a very related task), and (3) soccer foul shooting (a less related task). All tasks were classified as self-paced. The data analyses

---

Table 2: Specific Guidelines of the 5-SA (Lidor, 1997)

Readying
  Get comfortable physically
  Attain an optimal mental-emotional state
  Attempt to do things in preparation that are associated with
    previous best performances
  Try to be consistent in attaining the preparatory state
    for the act

Imaging
  Mentally picture yourself performing the act briefly as to how
    it should be done, from the result of the act to the initiation
    of the movement
  Think positively and feel confident
  Feel the movement

Focusing
  Concentrate intensely on one relevant feature of the situation
    such as the seams of a tennis ball to be hit
  Think only of this cue and block out all other thoughts

Executing
  Do it
  Do not think of anything about the act itself or the possible
    outcome

Evaluating
  If time permits, use available feedback information from
    which to learn
  Assess the performance outcome and the effectiveness of
    each step in the routine
  Adjust any procedure next time, if necessary

revealed that all of the strategy learning conditions were more effective than the control condition for each task. In addition, the CIS learning situation was more beneficial for the learning of the task most related to the specific task than the CDS learning situation. The CISR group outperformed the other strategy groups in the less-related task. The findings provided support for the significant role of meta-cognition in the acquisition of motor tasks. The participants probably succeeded in developing a plan for achieving a more ideal readiness and execution state for learning/performing. A more global task-referenced strategy has greater benefit than one which is learned specific to one task.

The effectiveness of the 5-SA was further examined under laboratory conditions. In one study, participants were asked to perform a novel complex motor task (Singer, Flora, & Abourezk, 1989a). The participants were assigned to one of three learning conditions: (1) 5-SA, (2) preview (participants were directed to preview or familiarize themselves with the location of the targets), and (3) control (participants received only the task procedure). It was found that the 5-SA participants performed faster than the preview and control participants, but not at the expense of a greater number of errors.

In another study, the transferability effect of the 5-SA was investigated across three tasks: (1) a novel but complex motor task requiring speed and accuracy in movement (a laboratory task), (2) a modified table-tennis serve (an applied sport task), and (3) a seated underhand dart throwing task (a transfer task; Singer, DeFrancesco, & Randall, 1989). Four strategy manipulations were applied: (1) a strategy group that initially practiced the strategy while learning the laboratory task, (2) a laboratory control group that began the experiment by learning the task without the strategy, (3) a strategy group that initially applied the strategy to learning the applied sport task, and (4) a control group that initially learned the sport task without the strategy. It was reported that both strategy groups performed better than their respective control groups in the laboratory tasks. Results of the transfer task indicated that the group that initially applied the strategy to learning the applied sport task performed at the same level as the group that initially practiced the strategy while learning the laboratory task. However, both strategy groups outperformed the control groups. The data provided further support for the use of the 5-SA; not only laboratory tasks but also applied self-paced tasks could be enhanced by the strategy. The researchers speculated that the strategy assisted the participants in effectively preplanning the task situation and facilitating the functioning of cognitive processes prior to, during, and after the actual movement.

In laboratory studies conducted by Singer, Flora, and Abourezk (1989a) and Singer, DeFrancesco, and Randall (1989), the 5-SA was introduced to the participants at the beginning of the learning process, namely before practice began. The participants listened to the strategy instructions, and were then asked to perform a few blocks of trials of the learned task or tasks. The argument made by the researchers was that the learners might benefit most from early exposure to the strategy guidance by preplanning their action in advance and efficiently allocating attention to the relevant cues most related to the task and environment. However, this assumption seems to be true only when the learner is engaged in learning a simple motor task. When attempting to learn a more complex motor task, task-simulation familiarization may be important at first, but afterward the strategy may be most meaningful in terms of the ability of the learner to make effective application.

This issue, namely the point of introduction of the 5-SA, was first studied by Singer, Flora, and Abourezk (1989b). In their study, the 5-SA was presented at one of three different intervals: (1) before any experience with the task, (2) after 12 trials (25% practice) of the task, or (3) after 24 trials (50% practice) of the task. The strategy conditions were compared to a control condition in which no strategy was introduced. The participants were asked to perform a complex novel motor task, as administered to the participants in Singer, Flora, and Abourezk's (1989a) study. It was found that the group that was provided with the 5-SA before any practice with the task attained a better overall movement time than the other three groups. The group that received the strategy instructions after 25% of practice performed faster than both the 50% practice and control groups. In addition, analyses of the preparation times (the duration of time from the illumination of the starting cue to the initiation of the movement sequence; the extent of each participant's information processing and strategy usage prior to performing) indicated an inverse trend between preparation times and movement times: longer preparation times seemed to be associated with shorter movement times. The researchers argued that in order to produce the correct movement sequence, the participants had to use cognitive processes in each trial to determine both the order and the direction of the specific sequence for the six targets. Therefore, they concluded that introducing the 5-SA prior to practice with motor tasks containing a heavy cognitive component led to the most favorable results.

From another cognitive perspective, the effects of the 5-SA on achievement in psychomotor tasks were investigated in two studies varying in the degree of cognitive activity involved (Kim, Singer, & Radlo, 1996). The 5-SA was compared to a control condition in which no strategy was introduced. In Study 1, participants were taught to perform a brain scrambler which was classified as a high cognitive demand task, and golf putting which was classified as a low cognitive demand task. The findings revealed that the 5-SA facilitated performance in the low cognitive demand task. In Study 2, in addition to a high cognitive demand task (i.e., a card-sort) and a low cognitive demand task (i.e., a ball roll), a medium cognitive task, namely a mirror draw, was introduced. It was indicated that skill in the low cognitive demand task and the medium cognitive demand task was improved by the use of the 5-SA. The findings that emerged from Studies 1 and 2 provided support for the assumption that performance in tasks containing a greater number of motor elements is enhanced more with the use of the 5-SA than those having a high number of cognitive elements. It was assumed that the more vivid an image of the action that can be created by the performer, the greater the chances that the image can be controlled and manipulated, and that the resulting motor sequence will be effectively planned and organized.

The laboratory studies that were discussed in this part of the chapter compared either one learning strategy, the 5-SA, to a control condition (a no learning strategy), or different conditions in which one strategy, the 5-SA, was introduced [e.g., task-dependent or task-independent (Singer & Suwanathada, 1986), or before practice began or after some experience with the task (Singer, Flora, & Abourezk,

1989b)]. At that point in the chronology of this line of strategy research, the strategy has not been compared to a different strategy or strategies. The next section presents laboratory investigations in which the 5-SA was compared to two other potential task pertinent learning strategies, namely an awareness strategy and a nonawareness strategy.

Additional Strategy Inquiries in Laboratory Skill Acquisition: Awareness and Nonawareness Approaches to Learning

Although the 5-SA had been the primary strategy of interest, two additional approaches to learning and performance have been investigated and compared with the 5-SA under experimental settings: awareness and nonawareness. The strategies will be described briefly. A rationale for the development of the awareness and nonawareness approaches, as well as suggested sets of instructions on how to administer them, can be found in Lidor (1999) and Lidor and Singer (2003).

An awareness strategy for learning and performance

Traditional instruction has emphasized that learners should be aware of their body parts as they act. In early studies on motor skill acquisition, beginners were usually taught to think about the way they execute the movements and how to use movement-produced feedback (Cox, 1933; Goodenough & Brian, 1929; Holding & Macrae, 1964; Parker & Fleishman, 1961). The awareness approach is associated with paying attention to kinesthetic cues, feeling of the movements, and thinking about the act while performing (Lidor, 1999; Lidor & Singer, 2003). This strategy directs learners to be aware of body sensations while the movement is carried out. Kinesthetic information is explained so learners can feel their movements and use self-feedback information for improving their attempts in executing the task. In effect, the strategy directs learners to feel their movements, think about what they are doing, and pay attention to small details.

A nonawareness strategy for learning and performance

In sport settings, skilled athletes have reported frequently that they did not pay attention to what they were doing when they executed at their best (Jackson & Csikszentmihalyi, 1999). They seemed to perform without awareness. They were relaxed and presumably let the movements flow. Their body seemed to take over and everything "just happened." The nonawareness approach instructs learners to imitate the mode of operation of skilled performers such as athletes, dancers, or musicians. The strategy asks them to preplan their actions, focus on one relevant cue that would block out thinking when performing, and trust themselves to let their movements flow during performance.

The first study that compared the 5-SA to the awareness and nonawareness strategies was conducted by Singer, Lidor, and Cauraugh (1993) in which participants were taught to perform a ball throwing task under laboratory conditions. Groups were instructed to use the components of the 5-SA, the awareness, or the nonawareness strategies. The awareness approach guided participants to consciously attend to the ball throwing act and to what one is doing during throwing. In addition, the strategy directed participants to feel their ball throwing movements and pay attention to small details which were relevant to the learned task and the learning environment (i.e., the target apparatus). The nonawareness approach instructed participants to preplan their ball throwing movements and to focus on the one external cue (i.e., the center of the target apparatus) that was most relevant to the performance. The participants were asked to "just do it" by clearing their mind during the throwing performances. The 5-SA participants were informed to apply the set of the five sub-strategies (readying, imagery, focusing attention, executing, and evaluating) when attempting to aim at the target. The 5-SA, the awareness, and the nonawareness strategy groups were compared to a control group which was provided with additional technical information on the ball throwing task.

The participants in Singer et al.'s (1993) study were administered 250 trials with a ball throwing task and 50 more trials in a dual-task situation. They were told to try to hit the center of a target apparatus, which was composed of 16 concentric circles.

During the additional 50 trials, besides to the throwing task, the participants were instructed to listen to a sequence of five 1-digit numbers and call out one of the numbers in the sequence. The data indicated that the 5-SA, awareness, and nonawareness learners were more accurate and consistent than the control learners, not only in the ball throwing task but also in the dual-task assignment. When comparing the effectiveness of the three strategies introduced in the two-phase study, the 5-SA and the nonawareness learners achieved better than the awareness learners. An important instructional observation can be made based on the data: strategy participants who were explained to focus attention on only one specific cue and to clear their mind during the throwing act achieved a higher level of performance compared with the participants who were taught to pay attention to performance details and think about what they were doing. In other words, it might be better not to think about anything while performing brief target-aiming self-paced tasks. Performance can be improved if the mind is not occupied with thoughts related to the act and the learning environment.

Supportive evidence for the results obtained in Singer et al.'s (1993) study was found in a similar laboratory study (Singer, Lidor, & Cauraugh, 1994) in which the same three strategies, the 5-SA, awareness, and nonawareness, were introduced to participants. They completed 250 trials of nine sequential key presses, and 50 trials of a dual task (key presses and verbal reports). Faster response times were found for the 5-SA and nonawareness strategies during both the key pressing task and the dual-task condition. It was concluded that learners should be instructed to preplan their movements in advance, trust themselves, and execute without being aware of the task and environment.

The data obtained in Singer et al.'s (1993, 1994) studies have shown that novices can successfully use an expert's mental approach during the execution of repetitive and brief self-paced acts, at least for the type of tasks administered in these studies, such as ball throwing and key pressing. Instructors may want to reconsider the orientation to learning/performance offered to beginning learners. Instead of telling them to be aware of what they are doing during performance and to feel the movements, it might be better to instruct them to preplan their actions and to try to execute with a quiet mind. As indicated by Singer et al. (1993), "the appropriate self-direction of thought processes during execution can indeed make a difference in how well one accomplishes" (p. 29).

The participants in the studies conducted by Singer and his colleagues (1993, 1994) were directed to perform a single motor task. After being introduced to the strategy, they practiced either a ball throwing task (Singer et al., 1993) or a key pressing task (Singer et al., 1994). However, the generalizability effect of the 5-SA, the awareness, and the nonawareness strategies across similar gross motor tasks had not yet been examined. One of important goals of learning is to provide learners with instructional tools so they will be able to transfer knowledge from one learning situation to another. Therefore, if a learning strategy is found to enhance acquisition of a particular self-paced task, its transferability across similar self-paced tasks should be examined as well. In this respect, an interesting question can be raised: Can learners benefit from the same strategy not only when learning a primary task but also across related self-paced tasks sharing similar characteristics?

In a study conducted by Lidor, Tennant, and Singer (1996), the participants were asked to apply the components of the 5-SA, awareness, and nonawareness strategies in a series of laboratory tasks. After being provided with strategy instructions, the participants were taught to perform a ball throwing task and a dart throwing task. Half of the participants performed the ball throwing task first and then the dart throwing task, and half performed the dart throwing task first and then the ball throwing task. This procedure was undertaken in order to eliminate task order influence. Of the four strategies applied, only the 5-SA was found to improve accuracy and consistency of both tasks. It was suggested that a global and well-structured learning strategy such as the 5-SA could assist learners to transfer cognitive knowledge from one task to another. It is not necessary to teach the same strategy for each learning situation as long as learners understand the applicability of the strategy across related learning tasks. One global strategy such as the 5-SA can be used effectively for this purpose. However, the tasks should share the same degree of similarity, as is the case with all types of target-aiming acts.

Strategy Use in Field Studies: Sport Settings and Physical Education Classes

The usefulness of the 5-SA, awareness, and nonawareness strategies has been studied not only under laboratory conditions but also in field settings. The instructional program differs greatly in field settings compared to the laboratory environment (Lidor, 1999). For example, under laboratory conditions, usually only one participant at a time is taught how to use the strategy. In contrast, during field settings such as sport practice sessions and physical education classes, many learners are taught at the same time.

One of the main objectives of field investigations is to increase the environmental (ecological) validity of the results obtained under highly controlled and artificial laboratory conditions (Thomas & Nelson, 2001). The effectiveness of the 5-SA, awareness, and nonawareness strategies in sport practice sessions and physical education classes is of interest in determining any confirmation of the laboratory data. In classes and practices learners are exposed to external distractors such as noise generated by others or weather conditions. These environmental conditions, which can hinder learning, may be avoided under laboratory conditions; however it would be very difficult to remove them in field settings.

In field settings, coaches and physical educators administer the strategy, not usually the researchers. Typically, the strategy is introduced as part of the technical instructions given by the coach or the physical educator at the beginning of the session (e.g., a practice or a physical education class). The learners are asked to apply the strategy when executing. Among the sport skills that have been studied in the line of strategy research discussed in this chapter are free throws in basketball, air gun shooting, and serving in tennis.

Sport settings

Four studies have been conducted in sport settings in which participants were asked to execute self-paced aiming events. In these studies, athletes were already very experienced, unlike the laboratory studies in which the tasks were novel and the participants had no prior experience with them. Athletes had been practicing these skills on a regular basis in almost every practice session. All were aware of the fact that in practice, game, and competition settings they are provided with a short period of time to ready themselves before executing. In this respect, the components of the strategy could be used effectively not only under practice conditions but also during games or competitions.

Free throw shots in basketball

In a single-subject study, Lidor and Tenenbaum (1994) examined the influence of the 5-SA on free throw shots in basketball in a real field situation. A 16-year-old male basketball player who was a member of the Israeli junior national team was chosen to participate. He took part in eight sessions in which 120 free throw shots were performed (15 in each). Baseline data on the player's shooting ability were collected during the first two sessions, in which no strategy was administered. The 5-SA was provided in each of the following six sessions. The player was explained how to use the five steps of the strategy —before taking the shot (i.e., Steps 1, 2, and 3), during the shot (i.e., Step 4), and after completing the shooting act (i.e., Step 5). Shooting accuracy and preparation times (the time which the participant took to shoot the ball, assessed from the moment the coach handed over the ball to when the shot was taken) were measured in each of the sessions. Success in free throw shooting was higher following the implementation of the strategy. In addition, the preparation time intervals increased linearly when the participant became more acquainted with the strategy. Interestingly, the preparation time intervals were equal prior to successful and unsuccessful shots.

In Lidor and Tenenbaum's (1994) single subject design, the basketball player was able to improve his shooting percentages with the use of the 5-SA. Although a case study approach may not be the best scientific method to generalize findings to others (Thomas & Nelson, 2001), it is of primary importance to the practitioner who encounters an individual (e.g., the athlete) on a one-to-one basis (Yin, 1994). Apparently, the player benefited from the total attention provided to him by the consultant, and the consultant benefited from the commitment of the player. In effect, the findings provide support for the notion that "sport psychologists can acquire knowledge much more rapidly by developing solutions to practical problems" (Martens, 1987, p. 53).

In another field study, 13-year-old female and male basketball players were exposed to the principles of the 5-SA (Lidor, Arnon, & Bronstein, 1999). Baseline data on accuracy and preparation times of free throw performances were collected during one practice session. Then, six strategy meetings were held. The strategy players listened to the strategy instructions in the locker room just before practices began, and then went to the gym to perform 15 free throw shots (15 in each strategy session; 90 in total). Two more retention sessions were administered in which 15 throws were performed in each one. No strategy instruction was given to the players during the retention sessions. When the data were analyzed for the boys and girls combined, it was observed that the 5-SA players performed with greater accuracy compared with the control players.

Air gun shooting

Chung, Kim, Janelle, and Radlo (1996) questioned whether experienced shooters would benefit from using the 5-SA while performing in their natural shooting environment. The shooters performed a target shooting task with an air pistol. They aimed at a standard international target consisting of nine concentric circles. The 5-SA shooters were provided with tape-recorded as well as written strategy instructions. The control shooters received irrelevant information regarding types of shooting errors. Shooters in the 5-SA group performed better than those in the control group in both accuracy and variability of shooting performance. Although a validation of the use of cognitive and metacognitive strategies for dealing with real-world sport skills was provided, it was argued that "researchers should continue to focus on the adaptability of the 5-SA in real-world sport situations, emphasizing specific environmental characteristics such as distractors that may impede cognitive functioning and decrease achievement" (Chung et al., 1996, p. 594).

Tennis serve

Bouchard and Singer (1998) designed a study in which the objective was to compare two methods of instructing the 5-SA and their effect on the learning and performance of a tennis serve. One strategy group was taught the strategy and the serve via a videotape. A television and VCR placed on a portable stand were positioned beyond the baseline of the court service area, directly in front of the participants. The instructions were to watch, listen, and follow the instructions described in the video. A second strategy group was introduced to the 5-SA with an audiotape version of the videotape instructions, while simultaneously reading a written version transcript. A control group watched a video segment that illustrated how to win serve and how to break serve while playing from the backcourt and at the net. The participants performed 10 tennis serves in each of seven blocks of serves into the appropriate return-side service court. All groups improved across time and maintained this improved performance on a subsequent retention test. However, no treatment differences were noted among groups.

The players in this study received the strategy instructions on the VCR and practiced the serve on the tennis court. This, in itself, may have produced a number of confounding effects while watching the video presentation, such as others playing on nearby courts, people passing by, and the time of day (e.g., position of the sun). The researchers argued that "at times, it was very difficult to view the video monitor clearly because of inclement weather conditions or position of the sun, thereby limiting the visual effectiveness of this treatment" (Bouchard & Singer, 1998, pp. 744-745).

Physical education settings

The physical education studies were designed to investigate the usefulness of learning strategies in school learning environments. Two studies are reported in which the strategies were introduced to elementary- and junior-high school students who enrolled in physical education classes. The physical education program was part of the curriculum offered by the school.

Free throw shots in basketball

In one physical education study on free throw shots, the usefulness of the 5-SA, awareness, and nonawareness strategies was examined in beginning junior-high female basketball players (Lidor, 2004). The participants took part in five physical education classes in which they learned the fundamentals of the free throw shot. In Class 1, the participants performed two blocks of 10 free throws using a self-selected style; neither technical information of the task nor strategy guidelines were provided during this session. In Classes 2 to 4, the physical education teacher provided the participants with specific instructions on the techniques of the free throw shots, combined with the strategy manipulations. In each strategy session, the participants performed two blocks of 10 trials with the shooting task. In Class 5, the participants performed three blocks of 10 trials with the shot. Neither strategy instructions nor strategy reminders were provided during the last session. Accuracy of shooting performances and preparation times (the time which the participants took before they actually shot the ball) were measured in each session. In addition, the standard deviations of the preparation times were calculated. It was found that the 5-SA and the nonawareness participants performed more accurately than the awareness and the control participants. The strategy participants increased their preparation intervals compared with the control participants. However, the three learning strategies failed to train the participants to use a fixed interval of preparation times prior to each shot.

Bowling and team-handball throw

In a second physical education study, two experiments were carried out to investigate the usefulness of the 5-SA as an instructional technique during actual class meetings (Lidor, 1997). In Experiment 1, third-grade children were asked to perform a bowling simulation task, namely to throw a ball at 10 bottles that had been placed on the floor. The 5-SA children were instructed how to use the components of the strategy, based on illustrated directions and fun games. Different throwing, catching, running, and jumping drills which were part of 10 activity stations were presented. The physical education teacher attempted to stimulate the children to apply the five sequential steps of the strategy during the 10-station workout. The control group performed the same drills in each of the stations but without being provided guidance regarding strategy. In Experiment 2, seventh-grade children were taught to throw balls at a rectangular target which simulated a handball goal of a team-handball game. The instructions of the strategy were taped, and the physical education teacher provided additional information on the 5-SA by using an easy-to-read illustrated colored poster. The poster presented the steps to be applied by the children and also provided practical examples of how to use them. The strategy instructions and the additional verbal explanations focused mainly on how to utilize the strategy during class activities. The control learners were given additional instructional information on the task, the physical education program in school, and the importance of learning throwing tasks in ball games. These learners were not exposed to any information about the strategy. In both experiments, the 5-SA children were more accurate than the control children. It was concluded that young children can effectively apply illustrated strategic instructions. In addition, the 5-SA can facilitate the learning of gross motor skills executed in school settings, such as the team-handball throw.

What We Have Learned So Far From Strategy Research? Instructional and Pedagogical Reflections

As discussed in the last four parts of this chapter, the effectiveness of learning strategies for self-paced aiming tasks has been investigated under well-controlled laboratory conditions as well as in sport and physical education settings. Six observations can be made based on this line of research. The observations are as follows:

1 Learning and performing can be enriched by the use of effective learning strategies such as the 5-SA and the nonawareness approach (e.g., Singer et al., 1993, 1994). Accuracy and speed in a variety of tasks were improved when learners were taught how to apply thought processes to the execution of tasks in a closed learning environment. It is suggested that the strategies helped individuals how to learn, how to remember, how to think, and what thought processes to inhibit (Riding & Rayner, 1999). Such strategies seem to provide learners with effective tools for organizing, controlling, and directing

thoughts before, during, and after execution.

2 Appropriate strategies (e.g., the 5-SA) can be positively used by learners not only in a single self-paced motor task condition but also for a series of self-paced tasks sharing similar characteristics (e.g., Lidor et al., 1996). The strategy instructions should be presented before practice begins with the primary task. Then, this strategic knowledge can be applied independently by learners when performing similar and related tasks if they understand how to make applicability.

3 Not only adult learners but also children can benefit from similar strategies (e.g., Lidor, 1997). From a cognitive development point of view, as soon as children are able to attend, imagine, and apply metacognitive processes, task-pertinent strategies can be introduced to them. Also, success depends on how strategies are communicated, with consideration for developmental stages.

4 The 5-SA can be presented in a variety of modes, such as a verbal explanation (e.g., Singer & Suwanthada, 1986), a written set of instructions (e.g., Bouchard & Singer, 1998), a short video demonstration (e.g., Bouchard & Singer, 1998), and game activities (e.g., Lidor, 1997). The selected mode of presentation should reflect the cognitive and emotional stages of development of the learners. Adult learners can benefit from an oral presentation of strategy instructions; for young learners it may be more beneficial to use an illustrated mode of strategy presentation. Also, group versus individual situations may favor one type of presentation over another one.

5 The effectiveness of the strategies studied has been realized in a relatively small number of strategy sessions (e.g., Kim et al., 1996). As can be seen in Table 3, in most studies—laboratory as well as field—only one strategy session was provided to the participants. They were asked to listen to

strategy instructions during a single session, and were then provided with strategy reminders at certain points during acquisition (e.g., Singer et al., 1994). Apparently, one session is effective. Of course, more sessions, especially for complex movement tasks, may be more beneficial.

6 Strategies can be presented in a short period of time. In most strategy studies, about 10 min were allocated to present the main points (see Table 3). The shortest period of time reported to introduce the strategy was 7 min and the longest one was 15 min. During these periods of time, participants were asked to sit on a chair and listen alone to strategy instructors (in laboratory investigations) or to sit within the group and listen to the strategy guidance (in field investigations).

These observations may provide practitioners with practical knowledge on how to administer the strategies. Learning environments can be designed in which strategy instructions are part of the instructional program for elementary, junior-high, and adult learners.

Table 3: Instructional Strategy Information: Number of Strategy Sessions, Length of Strategy Instructions, and Mode of Presentation

Study	Strategy	Number of strategy sessions	Length of strategy instructions	Mode of presentation
Laboratory Studies				
Singer and Suwanthada (1986)	5-SA	1	10 min	Verbal instructions
Singer, Flora, and Abourezk (1989a)	5-SA (a modified version)	1	10 min	Verbal instructions given by a well-trained experimenter
Singer, Flora, and Abourezk (1989b)	5-SA (a modified version)	1	10 min	Audio cassette
Singer, DeFrancesco, and Randall (1989)	5-SA	1	10 min	Audio cassette
Kim, Singer, and Radlo (1996)	5-SA	1	15 min (Study 1) and 10 min (Study 2)	Audio cassettes
Lidor, Tennant, and Singer (1996)	5-SA, awareness, nonawareness	1	8 min	Audio cassette
Field Studies				
Chung, Kim, Janelle, and Radlo (1996)	5-SA	1	20 min	Written and taped instructions
Lidor (1997)	5-SA	1	7 min (Experiments 1 and 2)	Illustrated verbal directions, fun games (Experiment 1); audio cassette and verbal explanation (Experiment 2)
Bouchard and Singer (1998)	5-SA with videotaped modeling and audiotape 5-SA plus written transcript	1	11 min for the video group, 14 min for the audiotape group, and 13 min for the control group	Video presentation, audio cassette, and written transcript
Lidor, Arnon, and Bronstein (1999)	5-SA	6	8 min + 2 min reviewing the principles of the strategy; total = 10 min	Audio cassette
Lidor (2004)	5-SA, awareness, nonawareness	3	12 min + 3 min reviewing the mechanics of the shot and the strategy guidelines; total = 15 min	Audio cassette and verbal emphases by the PE teacher

Critical Thinking on Strategy Research: What Needs to Be Done to Enhance Strategy Use in Applied Settings

Practitioners such as coaches and physical educators should consider teaching learning strategies more frequently. The components of effective strategies, such as the 5-SA, can be integrated within the instructional program provided to the learners at the initial phase of learning (Lidor, 2004; Lidor & Singer, 2003), thus complementing task-specific performance instructions. However, from both methodological and applied perspectives, a few steps should be taken in order to strengthen the implementation of strategies.

First, more variables that provide information on the extent of learning with the adoption of particular useful learning strategies should be determined in investigations. For example, self-paced skills, such as

nitive domain, students have been shown to learn more thoroughly from well-designed multimedia presentations than from more traditional modes of communication involving words alone (Kosslyn, 1989; Mayer, 2003). Although a variety of modes of strategy presentations has been used in different laboratory and field studies (see Table 3), in most studies only one mode of presentation was selected by the researcher/s, such as a verbal strategy presentation (e.g., Kim et al., 1996). In a few studies (e.g., Lidor, 1997), a combined-mode approach of strategy presentation was used. In order to increase strategy understanding and facilitate strategy learning, a number of modes might be used in the same study. The different modes of strategy presentations might enable more students with different learning styles and different learning preferences to master a particular strategy (Riding & Rayner, 1999).

Third, the number of sessions in which the strategies are presented to the participants might

Figure 2: Typical Type of Self-paced Tasks Administered in Strategy Research in Laboratory and Field Conditions

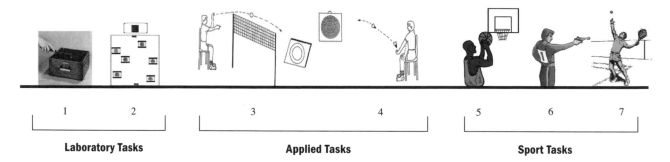

| Laboratory Tasks | Applied Tasks | Sport Tasks |

1   2   3   4   5   6   7

rifle shooting, archery, and golf, have been the subject of psychophysiological research to determine profiles of expert performers when they execute as well as when they perform at their best (Lidor & Singer, 2003; Radlo, 1997; Radlo, Steinberg, Singer, Barba, & Melnikov, 2002). Future strategy research might adopt one of the research paradigms used in psychophysiological research. In doing so, strategy implications may be derived as to how to perform better by being in an ideal internal state immediately prior to and during the act.

Second, more modes of strategy presentation should be administered and assessed as to effectiveness. For example, consideration should be given to multimedia messages consisting of words and pictures when introducing the strategy. In the cog-

be increased. Although a one-strategy exposure has been found to be effective in facilitating learning, a multisession approach might help learners much more. It is probably difficult to retain the information from a 10-min instructional session presented only once. Rarely in research is long-term retention measured. Therefore, distributed schedules of strategy sessions might be conducted to provide sufficient time between strategy sessions for learners to strengthen the learning process of a strategy (Riding & Rayner, 1999).

Fourth, the length of time for strategy instructions might be increased. Although it has been reported that learners were able to benefit from a 10-min strategy presentation in both laboratory (e.g., Singer & Suwanthada, 1986) and field (e.g., Lidor et al., 1999) studies, more time might be spent on instructing the nature and application of a strategy. A longer phase of instruction could conceivably help learners gain more understanding.

Fifth, more sport and recreational skills need to be studied with regard to strategy influence. Basically, three types of tasks have been administered in the strategy studies described in this chapter. They are laboratory (pure laboratory tasks such as the pursuit rotor), applied (simulated sport tasks such as bouncing a ball to a target), and sport (real sport skills such as free throws in basketball; see Figure 2). However, laboratory and applied tasks have been most often selected by researchers. Because the primary objective of strategy research is to make an impact on sport and physical education learning situations, much more research is needed with a focus on real-life skills learning.

During the past two decades, researchers in motor learning and educational sport psychology, as well as practitioners such as physical educators, coaches, and instructors, have realized more and more the desirability of teaching learners how to regulate thought processes while attempting to learn and perform self-paced motor skills. Novices and the highly skilled can benefit from such information. Learning how to learn, how to remember, how to problem-solve, and how to analyze one's progress are critical objectives. Relevant strategies for enriching learning and enhancing performance are challenging for researchers and practitioners to determine.

Future applied research on the effectiveness of various types of strategies for various tasks and situations should provide valuable theoretical and practical information.

References

Bouchard, L. J., & Singer, R. N. (1998). Effects of the five-step strategy with videotape modeling on performance of the tennis serve. *Perceptual and Motor Skills, 86*, 739-746.

Brown, H. J., Singer, R. N., Cauraugh, J. H., & Lucariello, G. (1985). Cognitive style and learner strategy interaction in the performance of primary and related maze tasks. *Research Quarterly for Exercise and Sport, 56*, 10-14.

Chung, S., Kim, J., Janelle, C. M., & Radlo, S. J. (1996). The five-step strategy and air gun shooting performance of experienced shooters. *Perceptual and Motor Skills, 82*, 591-594.

Cox, J. W. (1933). Some experiments on formal training in the acquisition of skill. *British Journal of Psychology, 24*, 67-87.

Goodenough, F. L., & Brian, C. R. (1929). Certain factors underlying the acquisition of motor skills by pre-school children. *Journal of Experimental Psychology, 12*, 127-155.

Holding, D. H., & Macrae, A. W. (1964). Guidance, restriction and knowledge of results. *Ergonomics, 7*, 289-295.

Jackson, S. A., & Csikszentmihalyi, M. (1999). *Flow in sport: The keys to optimal experiences and performances.* Champaign, IL: Human Kinetics.

Kim, J., Singer, R. N., & Radlo, S. J. (1996). Degree of cognitive demands in psychomotor tasks and the effects of the five-step strategy on achievement. *Journal of Human Performance, 2*, 155-169.

Kosslyn, S. M. (1989). Understanding charts and graphs. *Applied Cognitive Psychology, 3*, 185-226.

Kucan, L., & Beck, I. L. (1997). Thinking aloud and reading comprehension research: Inquiry, instruction and social interaction. *Review of Educational Research, 67*, 271-299.

Lee, T. D., Chamberlin, C. J., & Hodges, N. J. (2001). Practice. In R. N. Singer, H. A. Hausenblas, & C. M. Janelle (Eds.), *Handbook of sport psychology* (2nd ed.; pp. 115-143). New York: Wiley.

Lidor, R. (1997). Effeciveness of a structured learning strategy on acquisition of game-related motor tasks in school settings. *Perceptual and Motor Skills, 84*, 67-80

Lidor, R. (1999). Learning strategies and the enhancement of self-paced motor tasks: Theoretical and practical implications. In R. Lidor & M. Bar-Eli (Eds.), *Sport psychology: Linking theory and practice* (pp. 109-132). Morgantown, WV: Fitness Information Technology.

Lidor, R. (2004). Developing metacognitive behavior in physical education classes: The use of task-pertinent learning strategies. *Physical Education and Sport Pedagogy, 1*, 55-71.

Lidor, R., Arnon, M., & Bronstein, A. (1999). The effectiveness of a learning (cognitive) strategy on free-throw performance in basketball. *The Applied Research in Coaching and Athletics Annual, 14*, 59-72.

Lidor, R., & Singer, R. N. (2003). Preperformance routines in self-paced tasks: Developmental and educational considerations. In R. Lidor & K. P. Henschen (Eds.), *The psychology of team sports* (pp. 69-98). Morgantown, WV: Fitness Information Technology.

Lidor, R., & Tenenbaum, G. (1994). Applying learning strategy to a basketball shooting skill: A case study report. In R. Lidor, D. Ben-Sira, & Z. Artzi (Eds.), *Proceedings of the 1993 FIEP World Congress* (pp. 53-59). Netanya, Israel: Wingate Institute.

Lidor, R., Tennant, K. L., & Singer, R. N. (1996). The generalizability effect of three learning strategies across motor task performances. *International Journal of Sport Psychology, 27*, 22-36.

Magill, R. A. (1998). *Motor learning: Concepts and applications* (5th ed.). Boston: McGraw-Hill.

Magill, R. A. (2001). Augmented feedback in motor skill acquisition. In R. N. Singer, H. A. Hausenblas, & C. M. Janelle (Eds.), *Handbook of sport psychology* (2nd ed.; pp. 86-114). New York: Wiley.

Mayer, R. E. (2003). The promise of multimedia learning: using the same instructional design methods across different media. *Learning and Instruction, 13*, 125-139.

McCullagh, P., & Weiss, M. R. (2001). Modeling: Considerations for motor skill performance and psychological responses.

In R. N. Singer, H. A. Hausenblas, & C. M. Janelle (Eds.), *Handbook of sport psychology* (2nd ed.; pp. 205-238). New York: Wiley.

Martens, R. (1987). Science, knowledge, and sport psychology. *The Sport Psychologist, 1,* 29-55.

Norman, D. A. (1976). *Memory and attention.* New York: Wiley.

Parker, J. F., & Fleishman, E. A. (1961). Use of analytical information concerning task requirements to increase the effectiveness of skill training. *Journal of Applied Psychology, 45,* 295-302.

Radlo, S. (1997). *The effectiveness of Singer's five-step strategy during a competitive situation: A behavioral and psychophysiological investigation.* Unpublished doctoral dissertation, University of Florida, Gainesville.

Radlo, S., Steinberg, G. M., Singer, R. N., Barba, D. A., & Melnikov, A. (2002). The influence of an attentional focus strategy on alpha wave activity, heart rate, and dart-throwing performances. *International Journal of Sport Psychology, 33,* 205-217.

Riding, R., & Rayner, S. (1999). *Cognitive styles and learning strategies: Understanding style differences in learning and behavior.* London: David Fulton.

Schmidt, R. A., & Lee, T. D. (2005). *Motor control and learning: A behavioral emphasis* (4th ed.). Champaign, IL: Human Kinetics.

Schmidt, R. A., & Wrisberg, C. A. (2004). *Motor learning and performance: A problem-based learning approach* (3rd ed.). Champaign, IL: Human Kinetics.

Simon, H. A. (1975). The functional equivalence of problem-solving skills. *Cognitive Psychology, 7,* 268-288.

Singer, R. N. (1988). Strategies and metastrategies in learning and performing self-paced athletic skills. *The Sport Psychologist, 2,* 49-68.

Singer, R. N. (2000). Performance and human factors: Considerations about cognition and attention for self-paced and externally-paced events. *Ergonomics, 10,* 1661-1680.

Singer, R. N. (2002). Preperformance state, routines, and automaticity: What does it take to realize expertise in self-paced events? *Journal of Sport and Exercise Psychology, 24,* 359-375.

Singer, R. N., & Cauraugh, J. H. (1984). Generalization of psychomotor learning strategies to related psychomotor tasks. *Human Learning, 3,* 215-225.

Singer, R. N., Cauraugh, J. H., Lucariello, G., & Brown, H. J. (1985). Achievement in related psychomotor tasks as influenced by learning strategies. *Perceptual and Motor Skills, 60,* 843-846.

Singer, R. N., DeFrancesco., & Randall, L. E. (1989). Effectiveness of a global learning strategy practiced in different contexts on primary and transfer self-paced motor tasks. *Journal of Sport and Exercise Psychology, 11,* 290-303.

Singer, R. N., Flora, L. A., & Abourezk, T. (1989a). The effect of a five-step approach learning strategy on the acquisition of a complex motor task. *Journal of Applied Sport Psychology, 1,* 98-108.

Singer, R. N., Flora, L. A., & Abourezk, T. (1989b). The point of introduction of a learning strategy and its effect on achievement in a complex motor task. *Journal of Human Movement Studies, 6,* 259-270.

Singer, R. N., & Gerson, R. F. (1979). Learning strategies, cognitive processes, and motor learning. In H. F. O'Neil, Jr. &

C. D. Spielberger (Eds.), *Cognitive and affective learning strategies* (pp. 174-188). New York: Academic Press.

Singer, R. N., & Gerson, R. F. (1981). Task classification and strategy utilization in motor skill. *Research Quarterly for Exercise and Sport, 52,* 100-116.

Singer, R. N., Lidor, R., & Cauraugh, J. H. (1993). To be aware or not aware? What to think about while learning and performing a motor skill. *The Sport Psychologist, 7,* 19-30.

Singer, R. N., Lidor, R., & Cauraugh, J. H. (1994). Focus of attention during motor skill performance. *Journal of Sports Sciences, 12,* 335-340.

Singer, R. N., & Suwanthada, S. (1986). The generalizability effectiveness of a learning strategy on achievement in related closed motor skills. *Research Quarterly for Exercise and Sport, 57,* 205-214.

Thomas, J. R., & Nelson, J. K. (2001). *Research methods in physical activity* (4th ed.). Champaign, IL: Human Kinetics.

Weinstein, F. E., & Van Mater Stone, G. (1996). Learning strategies and learning to learn. In E. De Corte & F. E. Weinert (Eds.), *International encyclopedia of developmental psychology* (pp. 419-423). London: Pergamon.

Woolfolk, A. E. (1998). *Educational psychology* (7th ed.). Boston: Allyn and Bacon.

Yan, J. H., Thomas, J. R., & Thomas, K. T. (1998). Children's age moderates the effect of practice variability: A quantitative review. *Research Quarterly for Exercise and Sport, 69,* 210-215.

Yin, R. K. (1994). *Case study research: Design and methods* (2nd ed.). Thousand Oaks, CA: Sage.

Section III
Techniques to Improve Psychological Functioning and Foster Motivation

Introduction

The topic of motivation in sport is one that holds considerable appeal to practitioners and researchers alike. Athletes, coaches, and others involved in sport want to better understand what causes motivational levels to drop and what strategies can contribute to sustained motivation in the athletic milieu. Sport psychology scholars are interested in the study of the motivational processes impacting behavioral patterns in athletic settings.

In this section, the focus is on the enhancement of motivation and psychological functioning in the physical domain. First, Weinberg and Butt provide a clear and concise review of what arguably could be considered the most pervasive motivation-enhancement technique, namely goal setting. The major findings of studies assessing the effectiveness of goal setting in sport and exercise settings are summarized and the existent goal-setting work is analyzed from a theoretical and methodological perspective. Finally, drawing from the literature, principles of effective goal setting are offered.

In the second chapter, Hackfort and Schlattmann provide an intriguing synthesis of the concepts of self regulation of action and self presentation with particular reference to athletic performers. Emphasis is placed on intentional self-presentation strategies that athletes may use to impact their own motivation or emotional state while engaged in sport. Hackfort and Schlattmann also discuss the potential influence of athletes' self presentation on the inner state of others in the sport environment as well as the nature of their interactions with these individuals. New and innovative approaches to analyzing and modifying athletes' self presentation of emotions are presented.

The final chapter by Duda, Cumming, and Balaguer aims to link contemporary models of motivation with self regulation in the sport domain. A case is made to explain why greater self determination and task involvement should correspond to more positive and adaptive self-regulatory strategies use in athletes. Duda and colleagues also suggest that sport psychology researchers and consultants consider the impact of psychological skills training and self-regulation techniques on athletes' motivational processes, as well as their athletic performance.

Courtesy of John Bright Images

3.1

Goal Setting in Sport and Exercise Domains: The Theory and Practice of Effective Goal Setting

ROBERT WEINBERG AND JOANNE BUTT

Introduction

We know from anecdotal reports and quotes that coaches, athletes, and exercisers have been employing goal setting as a means to enhance motivation and increase performance for a long time. When the first author started to conduct empirical research on this area back in 1985, there were only five empirical studies found that were specially conducted in sport and exercise settings to test the effects of goal setting to enhance performance. Frankly, it was surprising that there were so few empirical studies regarding a technique that so many people were taking for granted and using as if it had been proven effective for enhancing performance and increasing motivation. It was at this time that Weinberg started empirically investigating the relationship between goals and performance, and others have appeared

to follow in this direction. Specifically, Kyllo and Landers (1995) conducted a meta-analysis (which will be discussed in more detail later) on goal setting in sport and exercise settings and found 36 studies in this area suitable for review (although 49 studies were identified, 13 were eliminated due to goal setting not being the independent variable, no comparison against a control group, or no objective measure of performance). More recently, in an article appearing in the *Handbook of Sport Psychology*, Burton, Naylor, and Holliday (2001) have noted that a large increase of goal setting research in sport has occurred in the seven years since the first edition of the *Handbook* was published. In fact, Burton et al. list approximately 250 references (of course, not all of these were empirically based and conducted in sport or exercise settings), which is another piece of evidence to document the widespread empirical attention that goal setting has recently been given in the sport and exercise domains.

In a quick perusal of the literature, it becomes evident that almost all athletes set goals, but they rate them as only being moderately effective. Thus, athletes appear to understand that goals can help them in many ways (e.g., improve motivation, enhance concentration, improve performance), yet they have trouble figuring out how to best set goals to maximize their effectiveness. But the researchers' literature can offer specific guidelines to help athletes, exercisers, and coaches in this regard. Thus, given the widespread use of goal setting and the explosion of empirically based studies, the purposes of this chapter are (a) to provide definitions of the different types of goals, (b) to review the goal-setting literature in industrial and organizational settings, (c) to review the goal-setting literature in sport and exercise, (d) to provide a theoretical and methodological analysis of the goal-setting literature, and (e) to provide some guidelines on effective goal-setting practices based on empirical findings. Let us begin with some definitions.

Definitions and Types

By definition, a goal is that which an individual is trying to accomplish; it is the object or aim of an action. For example, in most goal-setting studies, the term *goal* refers to attaining a specific level of proficiency on a task, usually within a specified time limit (Locke, Shaw, Saari, & Latham, 1981). However, it should be noted that although goals can help direct behavior, they do not necessarily work at a conscious level all the time. In fact, in a well automated skill like a pitcher throwing a baseball, goals help initiate action, but once initiated, little conscious control is needed to pursue the goal effectively. From a practical point of view, goals focus on standards of excellence such as improving one's first serve percentage in tennis by 5%, losing 10 pounds, lowering one's time in the mile run by 4 seconds, or improving one's batting average by 20 points. In addition, these goals would have to be reached within a given time frame, such as by the end of the season or within a certain number of days, weeks, or months.

In sport and exercise settings, the type of goals set by participants and coaches vary in their degree

of specificity and difficulty in measuring if the goal was accomplished. This has led sport psychologists to distinguish between outcome, performance, and process goals. More specifically, *outcome goals* usually refer to winning and losing such as a goal to come in first place in the swim meet or to win the state championship. Thus achieving your goal depends, at least in part, on the ability and play of your opponent. Essentially, the focus here is on social comparison (i.e., doing better than a particular player, team, or standard). *Performance goals* refer to one's actual performance in relation to his or her standard of excellence. For example, an athlete may wish to improve their free throw percentage from 70% to 80%, knock off two seconds in the 1,500 meters, or improve their high jump from 6 feet 2 inches to 6 feet 6 inches. These are all under the control of the athlete and do not depend on outcome goals like winning or losing. Finally, *process goals* are usually concerned with how an athlete or exerciser performs a particular skill; often the skills themselves are the focus of goals in practice or training. For example, a process goal in golf might be to relax when taking the club back on the back swing. Similarly, in baseball it might be trying to keep your bat straight up when waiting for the pitch (of course, percentages can be placed on these process goals to make them more specific). Although cases can focus on one type of goal or another, our position will be that all three types of goals can effectively enhance performance and have a positive effect on behavior. The upcoming sections of the chapter discuss these different types of goals.

Theoretical and Conceptual Underpinnings of Goal Effectiveness

For the sake of understanding the theory and concept of goal effectiveness, it is important to understand why and how goals have a positive influence on performance and other behaviors. Several different theories have been proposed. Two of the more cognitive-oriented theories are the *competitive goal-setting model*, which focuses on goal-setting styles (Burton, 1992, 1993), and *cognitive mediation theory* (Garland, 1985), which focuses on the interaction of task ability, performance valence (satisfaction gained by reaching certain goals), and performance expectancy (subjective probability of reaching certain goals). Although these approaches to goal setting have potential for enhancing our understanding of the goal-setting process, most of the research to date testing the goal-performance relationship has tested Locke's (1968) original theory, which is the focus of the next portion of the chapter.

Locke's Goal-Setting Theory

Much of the early work on goal setting originated from two major sources, one academic and one organizational. The academic source extends back to the early 1960s and focuses on the associated concepts of intention, task set, and level of aspiration (see Ryan, 1970, for a review). The organizational line of research can be traced to the work of Taylor (1967), in which the concept of task (a specific assignment or goal given to a worker each day) eventually led to the application of goal setting in the form of management-by-objectives programs, now widely used in industrial settings (Ordiorne, 1978).

Using these early sources as building blocks, Locke and his colleagues (Locke, 1966, 1968, 1978; Locke et al., 1981; Locke & Latham, 1990a, b) developed a theory of goal setting that has served as the stimulus for literally hundreds of studies in industrial and organizational settings, and more recently in sport and exercise settings. The basic assumption of goal-setting theory is that task performance is regulated directly by the conscious goals that individuals are trying for on a task. Essentially, goals are immediate regulators of human action. Goals operate largely through internal comparison processes and require internal standards against which to evaluate ongoing performance.

According to the theory, hard goals result in a higher level of performance and effort than easy goals, and specific hard goals result in a higher level of performance than no goals or generalized goals of "do your best." In addition, the theory states that a person's goals mediate how performance is affected by monetary incentives, time limits, knowledge of results, participation in decision making, degree of commitment, and competition. Locke argued that although goals can influence behavior, no simple correlation can be assumed because people make er-

rors, or lack the ability to attain their objectives, or subconsciously subvert their conscious goals. A brief synopsis of the goal-setting literature conducted in industrial and organizational settings will be presented below.

Goal-Setting Research in Industrial and Organizational Settings

The acceptance and use of goal setting to enhance performance and productivity has come in response to overwhelming evidence for its motivational and performance-enhancing effects in the organizational and industrial literature. In fact, many of the initial studies testing the effectiveness of goal setting in enhancing performance and productivity also assessed the basic tenets of Locke's goal-setting theory. There are now over 500 goal-setting studies testing various aspects of the goal-setting-performance relationship including such aspects as goal specificity, goal difficulty, goal proximity, goal commitment, and goal type. Reviews of this research (Locke & Latham, 1990a, b; 2002) confirm that specific, difficult goals lead to higher levels of task performance than do-your-best goals, easy goals, or no goals. In addition, of the 201 studies with over 40,000 participants reviewed by Locke and Latham (1990b), goal-setting effects were evident in 183, a 91% success rate. Furthermore, five meta-analyses of general goal-setting research have strongly supported the contention that specific, challenging goals lead to higher levels of task performance than do-your-best goals, easy goals, or no goals (Chidester & Grigsby, 1984; Hunter & Schmidt, 1983; Mento, Steel, & Karren, 1987; Tubbs, 1986; Wood, Mento, & Locke, 1987). Specifically, in the 192 studies reviewed in these meta-analyses, 175 (91%) provided support for harder goals producing higher levels of task performance than easy goals with effect sizes ranging from .42 to .82 as well as performance increases of 8-16%. Finally, Locke and Latham's (1990a) review of this literature documented the consistency and magnitude of goal-setting effects across a wide variety of tasks, settings, performance criteria, and types of participants. Thus, it has been repeatedly demonstrated that goals enhance performance and productivity in industrial and organizational settings.

Goal Setting in Sport and Exercise

While considerable research has been conducted on goal setting in industrial and organizational settings, only in the last 20 years have sport and exercise psychology researchers begun to examine the topic. A systematic and concerted effort to study this relationship began with the publication of Locke and Latham's (1985) article on the application of goal setting to sports. Locke and Latham suggested that goal setting could work even better in sports than in business because the measurement of an individual's performance is typically more objective in sports than in organizational settings. Following the emphasis in industrial psychology, goal-setting research in sport and exercise settings has focused on the areas of goal specificity, goal difficulty, and goal proximity (Weinberg, 1994).

Utilizing the survey approach, the perceived effectiveness of goal setting has been demonstrated in studies conducted with leading sport psychology consultants working with U.S. Olympic athletes. Specifically, results revealed that goal setting was one of the most-often-used psychological intervention in both individual athlete-coach and group consultations (Gould, Tammen, Murphy, & May, 1989; Sullivan & Nashman, 1998)). In addition, results from Orlick and Partington's (1988) extensive study of Canadian Olympic athletes also demonstrated the regular use of goal setting as athletes reported daily goal setting as part of their regular training regimen. Furthermore, Weinberg, Burton, Yukelson, and Weigand, (1993) found that collegiate athletes virtually all use goal setting, although they find it only moderately effective.

These surveys would tend to indicate that goal setting is effective in enhancing performance of athletes. A perusal of the literature would support this claim although the results are not quite as impressive as those found in the industrial and organizational literature. For example, the Kyllo and Landers meta-analysis (1995) revealed an effect size of .34 when comparing *no goals* or *do-your-best goals to specific goals,* which is somewhat smaller than the .42 to .80 effect sizes found in the industrial and organizational literature. More recently, Burton et al. (2001) conducted a review of 56 studies (Kyllo & Landers had

36 studies) and found that 44 demonstrated moderate or strong goal-setting effects for a 78% effectiveness rate. Interestingly, Burton (1993), in an earlier review, only found 14 empirical sport/exercise related studies, with positive goal-setting effects found in approximately 66%. Therefore, it appears that goal setting has been receiving increased attention in the sport and exercise psychology literature and that as more studies accumulate, the consistency of goal-setting effects are increasing, although still not up to the effects demonstrated in the more general psychological literature (see Burton et al., 2001; Burton & Naylor, 2002; Hall & Kerr, 2001, for detailed reviews).

Reconciling the Sport and Organizational Findings

As noted above, although the empirical data indicate that goals appear to positively influence performance in both sport/exercise and industrial/organizational settings, the results have been consistently larger in organizations (although results appear to be getting stronger in sport). Locke (1991; 1994) and Weinberg and Weigand (1993; 1996) have debated why the results appear to be somewhat different across these two settings, with Weinberg and Weigand arguing that the inconsistent findings are at least in part due to the different methodologies employed in sport and exercise settings along with moderator variables that mediate the goal-setting-performance relationship. Some of the methodological and design considerations include (a) spontaneous goal setting in control groups, (b) participant motivation and commitment, (c) task characteristics, (d) competition among participants, (e) individual differences, and (f) measurement of personal goals. More recently, Kyllo and Landers (1995) have argued that these differences might be due to smaller sample sizes being employed in sport and exercise settings, which would result in smaller statistical power to detect any potential differences. However, a review of the literature by Burton et al. (2001) found that the average sample size across all goal attributes was over 100 participants and most goal conditions had a minimum of 20 participants. These numbers would appear to be large enough to detect any goal-setting differences among groups and thus sample size does not appear to be a cogent explanation for the goal-setting differences across domains.

It is beyond the scope of the present chapter to fully discuss the potential methodological differences that might have led to the goal-setting differences across domains as these can be found in the references noted above. However, based on the recent trend finding more potent goal-setting effects in sport and exercise settings (which in part may be due to better methodologies), it seems that goal setting is an extremely powerful technique for enhancing performance. In addition, several intervention studies conducted across athletic seasons revealed that setting specific, obtainable, moderately difficult goals led to higher levels of performance than equivalent control conditions (Anderson, Crowell, Doman, & Howard, 1988; Galvan & Ward, 1998; Kingston & Hardy, 1997; Swain & Jones, 1995; Wanlin, Hrycaiko, Martin, & Mahon, 1997; Weinberg, Stitcher, & Richardson, 1994). Furthermore, recent studies using athlete populations (e.g., Burton, Weinberg, Yukeslson, & Weigand, 1998; Filby, Maynard, & Graydon, 1999; Weinberg, Burke, & Jackson, 1997; Weinberg, Burton, Yukelson, & Weigand, 2000) have demonstrated that there are certain positive goal-setting outcomes due to the impact of goal setting. These consistencies are listed below.

- Almost all athletes use some type of goal setting to enhance performance and find these goals to be moderately to highly effective.

- Athletes using multiple goal strategies exhibit the best performances.

- The primary reason for setting goals is to provide direction and focus.

- Goals should be moderately difficult, challenging, and realistic.

- Process goals appear to produce more positive outcomes than outcome goals. However, outcome, performance, and process goals are all important to enhancing performance and psychological skills.

- Short-term and long-term goals combined are more effective than short- or long-term goals employed alone.

- Goal commitment and acceptance is important in keeping motivation high over time.

- Action plans facilitate the effective implementation of goal-setting strategies.

Why Goals Work

Although different mechanisms have been proposed as to why and how goals work, the one that has received the most support is known as the *mechanistic explanation* (Locke et al., 1981; Locke & Latham, 1990a). This approach suggests that goals influence performance in four distinct ways: (a) directing attention, (b) mobilizing effort, (c) enhancing persistence, and (d) developing new learning strategies (Merritt, & Berger, 1998).

First, goals can influence performance through directing an individual's attention to the task at hand and focusing on the relevant cues in the athletic or exercise environment. In fact, research (Weinberg et al., 1993; Weinberg et al., 2000) found that college and Olympic athletes felt that the most important reason they set goals was to focus attention to the task at hand. For example, if a basketball player sets a goal to improve his field goal percentage, foul shot percentage, rebounds, and assists, then undoubtedly he would focus his attention in these specific game areas. Essentially, the basketball player's attention is focused on important elements of his game that need to be improved.

In addition to focusing attention, goals also increase effort and persistence by providing feedback on one's progress. For example, a long distance runner may not feel like putting in the required mileage day after day or feel bored with the repetitive routine of training. But by setting short-term goals and seeing progress toward her long-term goal, motivation can be maintained on a day-by-day basis as well as over time. Similarly, losing 60 pounds might seem like an impossible task for an obese person who has been overweight much of his life. However, by setting a goal to lose two pounds a week and charting this subgoal accomplishment, the individual can stay motivated and persist with the weight loss program for the time required.

The final mechanism by which goals can influence performance is through the development of relevant learning strategies. That is, when goals are set, strategies to help reach the goal should be put in place by coaches and/or athletes to help reach the goal. This is one of the areas in which both coaches and athletes could be more diligent and detailed in designing strategies to meet goals. For example, if a golfer had a goal to improve the percentage of drives hit the fairway from 80% to 90%, then she might invoke the strategy of hitting an extra 100 drives each day, or changing her pre-shot routine, or even changing the mechanics of her drive. In any case, new strategies are developed to help the player to obtain her driving-down-the-fairway goal.

Goal Setting and Coaches

Most recently, researchers (Weinberg, Butt, & Knight 2001 Weinberg, Butt, Knight, & Perritt, 2001) focused their work on the goal-setting practices of coaches since virtually all previous goal-setting research was oriented toward athletes and exercisers. Typically, in athletic competitions, it is the coaches who are responsible for setting goals and working with athletes to set both team and individual goals. Two qualitative investigations have been conducted employing high school and collegiate individual and team sport coaches focusing on their goal-setting practices both in competition and practice and both for team and individual goals. Although there were definitely differences between the two groups regarding their goal-setting practices, a number of consistent findings did emerge:

- Sometimes coaches set goals by dictating them to the team, while at other times they elicited input from the athletes. This depended on the situation and the maturity of the athletes' involvement.

- The emphasis in terms of the areas of goal setting was in the performance of skills and conditioning.

- Team and individual goals were measured both objectively and subjectively.

- Coaches were inconsistent in actually writing down their goals.

- Although coaches set both long- and short-term goals, the focus was generally on short-term goals.

- Coaches generally re-evaluated their goals, but the process of doing this varied widely among coaches.

- The major reason for setting goals was to provide and maintain focus and direction.

- Goal commitment was predominantly related to enjoyment and fun.

- Process, performance, and outcome goals were all used by coaches with their focus generally on process and performance goals.

- A variety of barriers got in the way of goal attainment. These barriers were generally considered physical (e.g., low ability), psychological (e.g., poor attitude), or external (e.g., social commitments).

- Coaches and athletes alike used goal setting extensively.

- The primary disadvantage of setting goals would come into play if the goals were set unrealistically high. Unrealistically high goals are likely to result in failure and, eventually, lower motivation.

- There was a good deal of variability in coaches' understanding of the principles of goal setting, and thus the frequency of use also varied significantly.

Goal-Setting Attributes

Although we have briefly reviewed the goal-setting research in both organizational and sport settings, it is instructive to briefly review the specific attributes that have been investigated. Essentially, we are in this section looking at the different aspects of the goal-setting process as opposed to whether goal setting is effective or not. Hence, the focus will be on the attributes that have received the greatest attention in the sport and organizational literatures.

Goal Specificity

Probably the most-often-researched aspect of goal setting has been the notion of *goal specificity*. In essence, this investigates the effectiveness of specific goals in relation to no goals or more general do-your-best goals. Several meta-analyses have focused on this issue and the overwhelming conclusion is that specific goals enhance performance. For example,

Locke and Latham (1990a) found that 51 of 53 goal specificity studies partially or completely support the notion that specific goals enhance performance more than no goals, general goals, or do-your-best goals. Similarly, Mento et al. (1987) found an effect size of .44 for goal specificity across 49 studies with almost 6000 participants, which translates into approximately a 9% increase in performance and/or productivity.

Although goal specificity was a clear focus of the goal-setting literature conducted in industrial and organizational settings, Locke and Latham (1990a,b) have revised their theory noting that goal specificity really works via goal difficulty. That is, goal specificity does not have a direct performance-enhancement effect; rather it contributes primarily to performance consistency (reducing performance variability) by providing the performer with specific feedback relating to the progress in meeting his or her goals. In fact, Locke and Latham argue that goal specificity effects are most prominent when combined with goal difficulty to maintain more stringent standards, which in turn promote performance consistency. Interestingly, Burton et al. (2001) found that 15 of 25 studies partially or strongly supported goal specificity predictions, although in many cases, goal specificity was confounded by goal difficulty (or goal proximity). Thus, more studies are needed that specifically test the goal specificity hypothesis and to determine if, in fact, goal specificity interacts with goal difficulty in sport and exercise settings.

Goal Difficulty

One of the most interesting relationships involves *goal difficulty* and performance. In the industrial and organizational literature, using Locke's (1968) initial goal-setting theory, results have produced impressive support for the positive relationship predicted between goal difficulty and performance. Specifically, Locke and Latham (1990a) found that 91% of the 192 studies they reviewed found a positive relationship between goal difficulty and performance, with harder goals producing higher performance than easier goals. In addition, four meta-analyses (see Burton et al., 2001 for a review) found effect sizes ranging from .52 to .82 supporting the goal difficulty-performance linear relationship. These effect sizes translated into performance increments ranging from approximately 10% to 16%. Although the meta-analytic and enumerative reviews have provided strong support for this linear relationship, there are some studies that have called this relationship into question. For example, Wright, Hollenbeck, Wolf, and McMahan (1995) found that when goals were operationalized in terms of absolute performance, a linear relationship was found. However, this relationship was not seen when individuals' perceived ability was considered. Specifically, an inverted-U relationship was found when goals were operationalized based on performance improvements. This underscores the notion that perceived ability appears to mediate the relationship between goal difficulty and performance.

Despite the overwhelming support for the goal difficulty hypothesis in the industrial and organizational literature, the sport and exercise psychology research is much more equivocal on this issue. In Burton et al.'s (2001) review, they found that just over 50% of the studies (10 of 19) supported a linear relationship between goal difficulty and performance. For example, in some of the initial research by Weinberg and his fellow researchers, (Garland, Weinberg, Bruya, & Jackson, 1988; Hall, Weinberg, & Jackson, 1987; Weinberg, Bruya, Jackson, & Garland, 1986; Weinberg, Fowler, Jackson, Bagnall, & Bruya, 1991) they did not find the linear relationship hypothesized by Locke and Latham (1990a). In addition, the researchers did not support the prediction that unrealistically high goals would be detrimental to performance.

For example, in the Garland et al. (1988) study, participants in the first experiment were divided into three goals groups (*easy, moderately difficult, and difficult*). Contrary to prediction, there were no significant differences among the groups. In the second experiment, participants were divided into do-your-best, difficult, and highly improbable goals with the highly improbable group given a goal of improving by 60 sit-ups over the course of the 10-week period. Prior to this, in testing over 1,200 participants, not one individual improved by as much as 60 sit-ups. Results again revealed no differences among the groups. However, interestingly, three individuals from the highly improbable goal group (out of 10 in the group) improved by at least 60 sit-ups. This fact alone was amazing since this amount of improvement had never been achieved before in over 1,200 participants. Additionally, this group was not significantly different from the other groups because some individuals actually had a detriment in performance. The critical point then appears to be that setting unrealistically high (difficult) is not necessarily detrimental to performance. In fact, it appeared to spur some people to extremely high levels of performance (while undermining the motivation of others). Thus, individual differences, which were not assessed in this study, would appear to be crucial moderating variables for future research when investigating the goal difficulty-performance relationship.

Another explanation for the somewhat discrepant findings between the sport and business literature regarding goal difficulty may lie in the difficulty of operationalizing goal difficulty. Specifically, what is a *difficult* goal and what is a *very difficult* goal? Unfortunately, these differ from study to study (both in business and sport) and thus it becomes difficult to compare results across studies. This is somewhat like the exercise adherence literature where *adhere* is defined differently in different studies. Locke (1991) has operationalized a *difficult goal* as one that can be achieved by only 10% of the participants. But a goal that can be accomplished by only 10% of the performers may be perceived as difficult (or not achievable), prompting low goal acceptance. This may in turn undermine motivation, and encourage people to start to set their own goals that they perceive as more challenging and perhaps more realistic. In fact, in our earlier research, it was found that many performers were setting goals on their own (i.e., spontaneous goal setting) as they were rejecting the goals that were set for them by the experimenter. Finally, it should be noted that other factors that have been identified as potential mediators of the goal difficulty-performance relationship include *self-efficacy* (Theodorakis, 1995; 1996) and *competition* (Lerner & Locke, 1995).

Goal Proximity

The third area that has received the most attention besides goal specificity and difficulty is *goal proximity*. There are no definitive predictions regarding short- versus long-term goals from Locke and Latham (1990a), and empirical results have been somewhat equivocal both in sport and business settings. One line of thinking emphasizes the effectiveness of short-term goals, as researchers such as Bandura (1986) argue that short-term goals are more effective because they provide feedback to the individual, which helps enhance their self-efficacy and keep motivation high. In addition, in the sport realm, Burton (1989) contends that short-term goals are more flexible and thus can be reevaluated to keep the challenge at an optimal level. Some early research supports the effectiveness of short-term goals (e.g., Bandura & Shunk, 1981; Bandura & Simon, 1977) as these goals offer consistent feedback to alter performance and change strategies.

In contrast, some researchers favor long-term goals, hypothesizing that they provide a roadmap of where an individual is going. Furthermore, short-term goals can prompt excessive evaluation, making it difficult to stay focused on the specific goal. Essentially, the short-term goal may begin to control one's behavior, which could lower intrinsic motivation (Deci & Ryan, 1985). Kirschenbaum (1984, 1985) provides data to support the effectiveness of long-term goals, especially if they are combined with specific planning and strategies to achieve these goals.

Of course it would make good intuitive sense that a combination of short- and long-term goals would produce the best performance. Research in the sport and exercise domains have found inconsistent results when comparing the effectiveness of short- versus long-term goals (e.g., Hall & Byrne, 1988; Weinberg, Bruya, & Jackson 1985; Weinberg, Bruya, Longino, & Jackson, 1988) although these appear to produce better performance than no goals or do-your-best goals (e.g., Boyce, 1992; Frierman, Weinberg, & Jackson, 1990). But the meta-analysis by Kyllo and Landers (1995) found an effect size of .48 for a combined effect of short- and long-term goals on performance. However, more studies are needed, especially employing athletic populations, to further investigate the relationship between goal proximity and performance. And similar to the goal difficulty area, definitions regarding timeframes are needed for short- and long-term goals. Specifically, if one sets daily and weekly goals, are the daily goals short-term and the weekly goals long-term? But if one sets weekly and monthly goals, are the weekly goals now short-term and the monthly goals long-term? Again, this makes it difficult to compare results across studies.

Effective Goal Setting

One of the consistent misconceptions regarding goal setting is that the mere fact that one sets goals would automatically make them effective. Because on the surface, there doesn't seem to be much to setting goals, many individuals do not understand that goal setting is a comprehensive process comprising a series of systematic steps. But goal-setting theory and research emphasize that goal setting is most definitely a process and that its implementation requires a systematic effort. Along these lines, Locke and Latham (1990a) have outlined a seven-step process that, if followed, should maximize the effectiveness of set goals. These seven steps will be briefly discussed below in the order in which the process should flow.

Set Appropriate Goals

The first step in any goal-setting process is to set goals that are congruent with empirical goal-setting principles. Along these lines the research would argue that goals should be specific, moderately difficult (although individual differences are important here), both short- and long-term, written down, and process oriented (although they should include performance and outcome goals where appropriate). One interesting point is how to determine the difficulty of one's goals (this problem was noted earlier). These approaches have varied from very objective (where a formula for setting difficult goals is provided; e.g., O'Block & Evans, 1984) to more subjective (Orlick, 1998), where individuals would put down their *dream goal* (a very difficult goal that might be achievable if the individual performs at their very best; e.g., a peak performance), their *realistic goal* (a goal of moderate difficulty that is challenging but definitely possible based on current levels of performance, capabilities, and situational factors; not as hard as a *dream goal*), and a *self-acceptance goal* (the lowest level of performance that an athlete could achieve and still feel somewhat successful and accepting of themselves). In any case, an individual needs to systematically develop their goal-setting plan based on their long-term objectives, current level of ability, and environmental constraints.

Develop Goal Commitment

It stands to reason that goal commitment would be a critical variable in determining goal achievement. In fact, in Locke's original (1968) model, it is emphasized that goal commitment is necessary if one is to employ the appropriate implementation strategies to reach the goal. In addition, two meta-analyses (Locke, 1996; Locke, Latham, & Erez, 1988) have found that goal commitment is most important when goals are specific and difficult, and goal commitment is enhanced when the goal is perceived to be important and attainable. In the general goal-setting literature, a number of variables have been associated with enhanced goal commitment including competition, public disclosure of goals, goal participation, incentives and rewards, peer influences, and the authority of the individual assigning the goals (see Burton et al., 2001, for a review). Along these lines, recent quantitative and qualitative research using high school, collegiate, and Olympic athletes as well as coaches (Weinberg et al., 2000; 2001) have indicated that goal commitment can be improved by a variety of factors including creating (and meeting) high standards and expectations for teams, enhancing the love and enjoyment of the sport, striving for success, receiving extrinsic factors (e.g., rewards, deals, endorsements), realizing intrinsic factors (e.g., participation in the goal-setting process), and receiving social support factors (support from others). Finally, more effective goal setters (Burton et al., 1998) appear to differ from less successful goal setters in terms of their commitment, especially as it relates to the social support they received from others. Obviously, we need to know more about what stimulates an individual's commitment in sport and what can we do as professionals to sustain this commitment.

Evaluate Impediments to Goal Attainment

After becoming committed to a goal, an athlete should be aware of potential barriers to reaching this goal. Along these lines, Weinberg et al. (2000) found that the most common barriers for Olympic athletes could be broken down into internal and external barriers. Specifically, examples of internal barriers include a lack of confidence in reaching the goal: lack of physical abilities or skills, lack of goal feedback, and setting goals that are too difficult. Illustrations of external barriers include lack of time to train properly, imposition of work commitments, lack of social support from friends and family, and an excess of personal and family responsibilities. In conducting in-depth interviews with high school coaches, Weinberg et al. (2001) found that some similarities and differences arose relating to goal barriers. Specifically, the most often cited themes relating to barriers were referred to as *psychological barriers* (e.g., lack of confidence, negative attitudes, lack of commitment, and moody teenagers—obviously a high school issue), *physical barriers* (e.g., injury/illness, lack of ability), *external barriers* (e.g., weather, ability of opponent, dating, parties, parents), and *motivational barriers* (e.g., lack of effort, losing interest). Finally, research (Burton et al., 1998) has found that more effective goal setters have fewer goal barriers (internal and external) than do less effective goal setters.

Develop Action Plans

Much of the research in industrial and organizational settings and in sport and exercise settings has focused on principles of effective goal setting along with mediators of the goal-setting-performance relationship. But of course, after goals are set, they need to be implemented. However, little research has focused on the implementation aspect of goal setting. In fact, research with high school, collegiate, and Olympic athletes and coaches (Weinberg et al., 2000; 2001) has consistently found that athletes are not very systematic in implementing their goal-setting strategies. In our interviews with coaches (Weinberg et al., 2001; in press), we have found a great deal of inconsistency among coaches in implementing goal setting within their programs. More specifically, although most coaches wrote down their goals, many were very inconsistent about actually putting these goals into practice. Many cited some of the barriers noted above with lack of time being a prime reason for not implementing and following through with a systematic goal-setting program. Coaches realized the importance of such a program but never got around to actually doing it. Or in some cases, they felt they lacked the specific knowledge to correctly or effectively implement a goal-setting regimen. But Burton et al. (1998) have found that more effective goal setters used action plans significantly more than did less effective goal setters. Thus, researchers and practitioners need to focus more on how to imple-

ment an effective program and on the principles that might guide or inform such a program.

Feedback on Goal Progress and Attainment

An essential part of any goal-setting program (and for that matter most intervention programs) is the provision of feedback regarding how well individuals are progressing toward their goals. To substantiate the important role that feedback plays in the goal-setting process, Locke and Latham (1990a) found that 17 of 18 studies revealed that goals plus feedback produced higher levels of task performance than goals alone. In addition, 21 of 22 studies indicated that goals plus feedback were significantly better than feedback alone. Furthermore, in their meta-analytic review, Mento et al. (1987) found that performance was improved by 17% when feedback was added to goal setting. Finally, in his meta-analytic review, Locke (1996) found that goal setting is most effective when feedback regarding one's progress is provided. Therefore, it is abundantly clear that feedback is an essential aspect of the goal-setting process.

It is interesting to note that despite the overwhelmingly positive effect that feedback has on performance, Locke (1996) cautions that feedback needs to be viewed positively by the recipient in order for it to be helpful to performance. Specifically, if feedback is viewed negatively by the recipient, then this could lead to lower levels of self-efficacy, effort, and motivation. This is consistent with the research on coaching behaviors and reinforcement, which has consistently demonstrated that positive feedback (as opposed to negative feedback) is associated with positive athlete outcomes such as increased intrinsic motivation, satisfaction, continued participation, enhanced self-esteem, and performance improvements (Amorose & Horn, 2000; Smith & Smoll, 1996; 1997). Thus, although feedback is definitely important to enhance goal-setting effects, this feedback needs to be positive and informational so that it can be integrated into strategies to continue to move toward achieving one's goal.

Evaluation of Goal Progress and Attainment

As with most behavior change programs, evaluation is a critical component in the goal-setting process and is integral toward goals enhancing motivation and self-confidence. Before athletes reach their ultimate goal, there is usually a re-evaluation process that helps them keep on track. For example, in our study with high school coaches (Weinberg et al., 2001) most coaches re-evaluated their goals on a somewhat regular basis with timeframes ranging from every practice to weekly to once every three weeks to once every 10 games to once at the end of the season. Some coaches simply stated they re-evaluated their goals as needed. The key point is that coaches repeatedly re-evaluated the goals of their teams and individual athletes and changed them accordingly. The most important reasons for changing goals were injury, illness, or the discovery that the goals had been set too high or too low. Interestingly, some coaches said they would only re-evaluate the goal if they were to set a higher goal, whereas other coaches stated that they would raise or lower the goal depending on the individual progress of the athlete.

In addition to re-evaluating goals along the way, it is also important to evaluate the end result of a particular goal-setting process. If an athlete's performance equals or exceeds the goal, then this typically would result in higher levels of self-confidence, perceived competence, and intrinsic motivation. If an athlete fails to meet a goal, then this should provide feedback, which should promote future goal achievement efforts. Of course, this relationship would probably be mediated by individual differences, such as an individual's perceived ability, self-confidence, and perceived environmental conditions. Therefore, from a practical point of view, goal evaluation provides critical information not only to the participant but also to the coach or teacher.

Reinforce Goal Achievement

The final step in the goal-setting process focuses on reinforcing achievement of the goal. Relying on the vast reinforcement literature (Smith, 2001), it is consistently emphasized that motivation and performance will be enhanced through positive reinforcement of appropriate behaviors. Achieving a goal certainly fits into the category of positive behaviors, and it is thus important to reward that achievement either through material or nonmaterial rewards. Rewards will encourage the individual to start a new goal-setting process (which would include the seven steps just discussed) and, hopefully, have the athlete start building toward higher, more challenging goals.

Future Directions for Goal-Setting Research in Sport/Exercise Domains

The goal-setting process outlined by Locke and Latham (1990a) should help provide more direction and focus to subsequent goal-setting research in general and in sport and exercise settings in particular. Similar to many other areas, the focus should turn to the process of goal setting and not simply if goals work or not, (although this is still important research). For example, we know very little about the implementation process in general, as few research studies have formally investigated this area of goal setting. As a result, we have little empirical evidence to help athletes implement their goal-setting programs. Therefore, understanding the process will help both researchers and practitioners help athletes develop a systematic goal-setting program that can be effectively implemented over time. Some of these future directions will be presented below.

Comparing Process, Performance, and Outcome Goals

A lot has been written about the interaction of these three types of goals in sport and exercise settings, but little empirical work (Kingston & Hardy, 1997 is a notable exception) has been conducted investigating how these interact with each other. There appears to be a strong push in the literature for emphasizing process or performance goals over outcome goals. But it would seem that all three goals can serve different purposes. The key is how these interact with each other and which is seen as most important. Certainly, many athletes are motivated to win (i.e., outcome goal is predominant) and you hear many athletes who have achieved individual success speak about the overwhelming desire to "play with a winner," even if it means a lesser role for them (A good example is David Robinson of the San Antonio Spurs accepting a lesser role to the younger and very talented Tim Duncan which resulted in an NBA championship). The goal orientation literature is also clear that task and ego-orientations are independent and that elite athletes tend to be high on both these attributes (see Duda & Hall, 2001 for a review). Therefore, how these three different goals interact to influence a variety of different behaviors (not only performance) would appear to be a fruitful area for future research.

Individual Differences Affecting Goal-Setting Effectiveness

Locke and Latham (1990a, b) suggest that individual differences should have a significant impact on how individuals react to goal setting. Unfortunately, there have been relatively few studies investigating how individual personality factors might affect goal setting. Factors such as goal orientation, self-efficacy, (Locke and Latham, 1990a particularly feel self-efficacy is an important variable, and have conducted a couple of studies investigating the relationship between self-efficacy and goal setting) hardiness, optimism/pessimism, locus of control, competitiveness, self-motivation, and intrinsic motivation are just some of the personality traits that could be investigated and offer promise to their potential. For example, in some of our earlier research noted earlier (e.g., Garland et al., 1988), it was found that the effectiveness of setting unrealistically high goals differed across individuals assigned to this group. Although this was an interesting finding in and of itself, why people reacted differently might be even more important. For example, if it was found that individuals with high self-motivation significantly improved performance given extremely difficult goals, whereas individuals low in self-motivation actually exhibited decreases in performance, then different coaching strategies might be employed to maximally motivate these different types of people.

More recently, a study by Brown, Cron, and Slocum (1998) found that individuals high in competitiveness set higher goals when they perceive the organizational climate as competitive, whereas individuals low in competitiveness set relatively low goals, regardless of their perceptions of competition in the organizational climate. In addition, as noted above, self-efficacy was directly related to goals and subsequent performance. Lambert, Moore, and Dixon (1999) found that locus of control was also an important individual difference variable. Specifically, participants having a higher internal locus of control spent relatively more time on-task under the self-set goal-setting condition, whereas those with a more external locus of control spent more time on-task when the coach set their goals. These two

studies, while underscoring the importance of individual differences, also demonstrate an interactional approach, which is central to the understanding of goal effectiveness. Finally, there is a vast amount of research indicating the importance of goal orientation to a wide variety of behaviors. Along these lines, recently, goal orientation as an individual difference factor that might affect the kind of goals that are set and their effectiveness has also proved to be fruitful (Duda & Hall, 2001). More research is obviously needed in this area to determine which individual difference variables exert the greatest influence on the goal-setting process.

Developing Action/Implementation Plans

A consistent finding from both quantitative and qualitative studies on goal setting is the idea that many athletes and coaches do not systematically plan or implement goal-setting strategies over the course of a season (or during the off-season if appropriate). Many are aware of the importance of following through and having a plan of action but many report simply thinking about their goals (or even imaging them) but they don't plan for goal implementation. In fact, in Locke's (1968) mechanistic approach, he proposes that one of the ways in which goals work is through the implementation of relevant learning strategies. For example, if a player sets a goal to improve his free throw percentage from 65% to 75% then Locke would argue that relevant learning strategies would be implemented such as focusing on the biomechanics of the shot (i.e., developing a smooth follow-through), or developing a pre-shot routine. Unfortunately, in many cases, these implementation and action plans are not developed and thus goals, at times, might be less effective than they might be. Therefore, research should focus on developing effective goal-setting implementation strategies such as seen in Orlick's (2000) applied work with Canadian Olympic athletes.

Determining Optimal Goal Difficulty

As noted in the earlier discussion of goal difficulty, one of the difficulties in studying this area has been the problems associated with operationalizing what exactly is a difficult goal. If, in fact, as the literature generally suggests, difficult goals lead to higher levels of performance than easy goals, no goals, or "do your best" goals, then what exactly is a difficult goal? A beginning point would be to ask the question, "how are difficult goals determined by coaches and athletes?" Some of our interviews with coaches (Weinberg et al, 2001, in press) indicate that previous performance accomplishments are the most often used informational source in determining goal difficulty although ability level of the opponent (especially in team sports) was another critical information source in determining goal difficulty. However, we really know very little about how to set goals of optimal difficulty and the precise goal difficulty-performance relationship (i.e., is it linear as was originally predicted or is it curvilinear as some sport/exercise research would tend to indicate?). In any case, this is an area deserving of future research attention.

Goal Reevaluation

There is no doubt that coaches and athletes often reevaluate their goals. But it is unclear as to the process of this reevaluation. For example, what would trigger a reevaluation of an athlete's goal? Would it be more likely to reevaluate a goal if the athlete is doing better than or worse than their initial goal? Along these lines, are goals more likely to be reevaluated upwards or downwards? Who is more likely to initiate a goal reevaluation, a coach or an athlete? A lot of time has been spent by researchers developing guidelines for setting goals, but little research exists regarding the reevaluation of goals. The process here is important to understand and would need a systematic research program to uncover these important aspects of goal setting. Along these lines, a recent study (Williams, Donovan, & Dodge, 2000) found that athletes tended to set goals too high although their goal revision during the season served to maintain rather than eliminate this goal discrepancy. How coaches and athletes resolve the discrepancy between the goals set and actual performance is still not very well understood and should be a focus of future research.

Summary

This chapter has focused on the effectiveness of setting goals in sport and exercise environments. A goal was defined as attaining a specific level of proficiency on a task, usually within a specified period of time,

and a distinction was made between different types of goals. Locke's theory of goal setting was presented, which indicated that specific, difficult, challenging goals lead to higher levels of task performance than easy goals, no goals, or "do your best" goals. More recent research investigating the goal-performance relationship in sport and exercise settings has also found support for the effectiveness of goals although the findings are not quite as robust as those in the industrial literature. Differences (particularly methodological and sampling) between these literatures which might account for these somewhat different results were discussed and some consistent findings in the sport/exercise literature was summarized. Locke's mechanistic approach was then presented to help explain why goals work. Specifically, it has been hypothesized that goals directly influence behavior by orienting performer attention to important elements of the task, increasing effort and persistence, and facilitating the development of relevant learning strategies.

Recent qualitative research on coaches and the process of goal setting was also presented followed by a synopsis of the research focusing on the most salient goal-setting attributes. Locke and Latham's (1990a, b) model of setting effective goals was then presented as a way to focus researchers and practitioners on the process of goal setting. Finally, future directions for research were offered, with a particular focus to help researchers understand the goal-setting process and how to make goals more effective. However, it should be remembered that the effectiveness of any goal-setting program will, in large part, rely on the interaction of the coach, exercise leader, or sport psychologist with the motivations of the specific participants and the specific environmental constraints. In essence, it is up to the practitioner to employ the science of goal setting (presented in this chapter) by using the art of goal setting. This means knowing when, how, and to whom to apply the research and principles noted throughout this chapter.

References

Amorose, A. J., & Horn, T. S. (2000). Intrinsic motivation: Relationships with collegiate athletes' gender, scholarship status, and perceptions of their coaches' behavior. *Journal of Sport and Exercise Psychology, 22*, 63-84.

Anderson, D. C., Crowell, C. R., Doman, M., & Howard, G. S. (1988). Performance posting, goal-setting, and activity-contingent praise as applied to a university hockey team. *Journal of Applied Psychology, 73*, 87-95.

Bandura, A. (1986). *Social foundations of thought and actions: A social cognitive theory.* Englewood Cliffs, NJ: Prentice Hall.

Bandura, A., & Schunk, D. H. (1981). Cultivating competence, self-efficacy, and intrinsic interest thought proximal self-motivation. *Journal of Personality and Social Psychology, 41*, 586-598.

Bandura, A., & Simon, K. M. (1977). The role of proximal intentions in self-regulation of refractory behavior. *Cognitive Therapy and Research, 1*, 177-193.

Boyce, A. (1992). The effects of goal proximity on skill acquisition and retention of a shooting task in a field-based setting. *Journal of Sport and Exercise Psychology, 14*, 298-308.

Brown, S. P., Cron, W. L., & Slocum, J. W. (1998). Effect of trait competitiveness and perceived intraorganizational competition on salesperson goal setting and performance. *Journal of Marketing, 62*, 88-98.

Burton, D. (1989). Winning isn't everything: Examining the impact of performance goals on collegiate swimmers' cognitions and performance. *The Sport Psychologist, 3*, 105-132.

Burton, D. (1992). The Jekyll/Hyde nature of goals: Reconceptualizing goal setting in sport. In T. Horn (Ed.), *Advances in Sport Psychology* (pp. 267-297), Champaign, IL: Human Kinetics.

Burton, D. (1993). Goal setting in sport. In R. N. Singer, M. Murphey, & L. K. Tennant (Eds.), *Handbook of research on sport psychology* (pp. 467-491). New York: Macmillan

Burton, D., & Naylor, S. (2002). The Jekyll/Hyde nature of goals: Revisiting and updating goal-setting in sport. In T. Horn (Ed.), *Advances in sport psychology* (2nd ed., pp 459-499). Champaign, IL: Human Kinetics.

Burton, D., Naylor, S., & Holliday, B. (2001). Goal setting in sport: Investigating the goal effectiveness paradox. In R. Singer, H. Hausenblaus, & C Janelle (Eds. *Handbook of sport psychology*, (pp.497-528), New York: John Wiley.

Burton, D., Weinberg, R., Yukelson, D., & Weigand, D. (1998). The goal effectiveness paradox in sport: Examining the goal practices of collegiate athletes. *The Sport Psychologist, 12*, 404-419.

Chidester, J. S., & Grigsby, W. C. (1984). A meta-analysis of the goal setting performance literature. In A. Pearce & R. B. Robinson (Eds.), *Proceedings of the 44th annual meeting of the Academy of Management* (pp. 202-206). Ada, OH: Academy of Management. Psychologist, 11, 277-293.

Deci, E. L, & Ryan, R. M. (1985). *Intrinsic motivation and self-determination in human behavior.* New York: Plenum Press.

Duda, J. L., & Hall, H. (2001). Achievement goal theory in sport: Recent extensions and future directions. In R. Singer, H. Hausenblaus, & C. Janelle (Eds.) *Handbook of sport psychology* (pp 417-443), New York: John Wiley.

Filby, C. D., Maynard, I. W., & Graydon, J. K. (1999). The effect of multiple-goal strategies on performance outcomes in training and competition. *Journal of Applied Sport Psychology, 11*, 230-246.

Frierman, S. H., Weinberg, R. S., & Jackson, A. W. (1990). The relationship between goal proximity and specificity in bowling: A field experiment. *The Sport Psychologist, 4*, 145-154.

Galvan, Z. J., & Ward, P. (1998). Effects of public posting on inappropriate on-court behaviors by collegiate tennis players. *The Sport Psychologist, 12,* 419-426.

Garland, H. (1985). A cognitive mediation theory of task goals and human performance. *Motivation and Emotion, 9*, 345-367.

Garland, H., Weinberg, R. S., Bruya, L. D., & Jackson, A. (1988) Self-efficacy and endurance performance: A longitudinal field test of cognitive mediation theory. *Applied Psychology: An International Review, 37*, 381-394.

Gould, D., Tammen, V., Murphy, S., & May, J. (1989). An examination of the U.S. Olympic sport psychology consultants and the services they provide. *The Sport Psychologist, 3*, 300-312.

Hall, H. K., & Byrne, A. T, J. (1988). Goal setting in sport: Clarifying recent anomalies. *Journal of Sport & Exercise Psychology, 10*, 184-198.

Hall, H. K., & Kerr, A. W. (2001). Goal setting in sport and physical activity: Tracking empirical developments and establishing conceptual direction. In G. C. Roberts (Ed.), *Advances in motivation in sport and exercise* (pp. 183-233), Champaign, IL: Human Kinetics.

Hall, H. K., Weinberg, R. S., & Jackson, A. (1987). Effects of goal specificity, goal difficulty, and information feedback on endurance performance. *Journal of Sport Psychology, 9*, 43-54.

Hunter, J. E., & Schmidt, F. L. (1983). Quantifying the effects of psychological interventions on employee job performance and work force productivity. *American Psychologist, 38*, 473- 478.

Kingston, K., & Hardy, L. (1997). Effects of different types of goals on processes that support performance. *The Sport Psychologist, 11*, 277-293.

Kirschenbaum, D. S. (1984). Self-regulation and sport psychology: Nurturing an emerging symbiosis. *Journal of Sport Psychology, 6*, 159-183.

Kirschenbaum, D. S. (1985). Proximity and specificity of planning: A position paper. *Cognitive Therapy and Research, 9*, 489-506.

Kyllo, L. B., & Landers, D. M. (1995). Goal setting in sport and exercise: A research synthesis to resolve the controversy. *Journal of Sport and Exercise Psychology, 17*, 117-137.

Lambert, S. M., Moore, D. W., & Dixon, R. S. (1999). Gymnasts in training: The differential effects of self- and coach-set goals as a function of locus of control. *Journal of Applied Sport Psychology, 11*, 72-82

Lerner, B. S., & Locke, E. A. (1995). The effects of goal setting, self-efficacy, competition, and personal traits, on the performance of an endurance task. *Journal of Sport and Exercise Psychology, 17*, 138-152.

Locke, E. A. (1978). The ubiquity of the technique of goal setting in theories of and approaches to employee motivation. *Academy of Management Review, 3*, 594-601.

Locke, E. A. (1968). Toward a theory of task motivation incentives. *Organizational Behavior and Human Performance, 3*, 157-189.

Locke, E. A. (1966). The relationship of intentions to level of performance. *Journal of Applied Psychology, 50*, 60-66.

Locke, E. A. (1991). Problems with goal-setting research in sports-and their solution. *Journal of Sport and Exercise Psychology, 8*, 311-316.

Locke, E. A. (1994). Comments on Weinberg and Weigand. *Journal of Sport and Exercise Psychology, 16*, 212-215.

Locke, E. A. (1996). Motivation through conscious goal setting. *Applied and Preventative Psychology, 5*, 117-124.

Locke, E. A., & Latham, G. P. (1985). The application of goal setting to sports. *Journal of Sport Psychology, 7*, 205-222.

Locke, E. A. & Latham , G. P. (1990a). *A theory of goal setting and task performance.* Englewood Cliffs, N.J.: Prentice Hall.

Locke, E. A., & Latham, G. P. (1990b). Work motivation and satisfaction: Light at the end of the tunnel. *Psychological Science, 1*, 240-246.

Locke, E. A., & Latham, G. P. (2002). Building a practically useful theory of goal setting and task motivation. *American Psychologist, 57*, 705-717.

Locke, E. A., Latham, G. W., & Erez, M. (1988). The determinants of goal commitment. *Academy of Management Review, 13*, 23-39.

Locke, E. A., Shaw, K. N., Saari, L. M., & Latham, G. P. (1981). Goal setting and task performance. *Psychological Bulletin, 90*, 125-152.

Mento, A. J., Steel, R. P., & Karren, R. J. (1987). A meta-analytic study of the effects of goal setting on task performance: 1966-1984. *Organizational Behavior and Human Decision Processes, 39*, 52-83.

Merritt, E. A., & Berger, F. (1998). The value of setting goals. *Cornell Hotel and Restaurant Administration Quarterly, 39*, 40-49.

O'Block, F. R., & Evans, F. H. (1984). Goal setting as a motivational technique. In J. M. Silva, & R. S. Weinberg (Eds.), *Psychological foundations of sport* (pp.188-196). Champaign, IL: Human Kinetics

Odiorne, G. S. (1978, Oct.) MBO: A backward glance. *Business Horizons, 21*(5), 14-24.

Orlick, T. (1998).*Enhancing your potential.* Champaign, IL: Human Kinetics

Orlick, T. (2000). *In search of excellence.* Champaign, IL: Human Kinetics

Orlick, T., & Partington, J. (1988). Mental links to excellence. *The Sport Psychologist, 2*, 105-130.

Ryan, T. A. (1970). *Intentional behavior: An approach to human motivation.* New York: Ronald Press.

Smith, R. E. (2001). Positive reinforcement, performance feedback, and performance enhnacement. In J. Williams (Ed.), *Applied sport psychology: Personal growth to peak performance* (pp.29-42), Mountain View, CA: Mayfield Publishers

Smith, R. E., & Smoll, F. L. (1996). *Way to go coach: A scientifically-proven approach to coaching effectiveness.* Portola Valley, CA: Warde Publishers.

Smith, R. E., & Smoll, F. L. (1997). Coach-mediated team building in youth sports. *Journal of Applied Sport Psychology, 9*, 114-132.

Sullivan, P. A., & Nashman, H. W. (1998). Self-perceptions of the role of USOC sport psychologists in working with Olympic athletes. *The Sport Psychologist, 12*, 95-103.

Swain, A., & Jones, G. (1995). Effects of goal setting interventions on selected basketball skills: A single-subject design. *Research Quarterly for Exercise and Sport, 66*, 51-63.

Taylor, F. W. (1967). *The principles of scientific management.* New York: Norton (Originally published, 1911).

Theodorakis, Y. (1995). Effects of self-efficacy, satisfaction, and personal goals on swimming performance. *The Sport Psychologist, 9*, 245-253.

Theodorakis, Y. (1996). The influence of goals, commitment, self-efficacy, and satisfaction on motor performance. *Journal of Applied Sport Psychology, 8,* 171-182

Tubbs, M. E. (1986). Goal setting: A meta-analytic examination of the empirical evidence. *Journal of Applied Psychology, 71*, 474-483.

Wanlin, C. M., Hrycaiko, D. W., Martin, G. L., & Mahon, M. (1997). The effects of a goal-setting package on the performance of speed skaters. *Journal of Applied Sport Psychology*, 212-228.

Weinberg, R. S. (1994). Goal setting and performance in sport and exercise settings: A synthesis and critique. *Medicine and Science in Sport and Exercise, 26*: 469-477.

Weinberg, R. S., Bruya, L. D., Jackson, A., & Garland, H. (1986). Goal difficulty and endurance performance: A challenge to the goal attainability hypothesis. *Journal of Sport Behavior, 10*, 82-92.

Weinberg, R., Bruya, L., & Jackson, A. (1985). The effects of goal proximity and goal specificity on endurance performance. *Journal of Sport Psychology, 7*, 296-305.

Weinberg, R. S., Bruya, L. D., Longino, J., & Jackson, A. (1988). Effect of goal proximity and specificity on endurance of primary-grade children. *Journal of Sport and Exercise Psychology, 10*, 81-91.

Weinberg, R., Burke, K., & Jackson, A. (1997). Coaches' and players' perceptions of goal setting in junior tennis: An exploratory investigation. *The Sport Psychologist, 11*, 426- 439.

Weinberg, R., Burton, D., Yukelson, D., & Weigand, D. (1993). Goal setting in competitive sport: An exploratory investigation of practices of collegiate athletes. *The Sport Psychologist, 7*, 275-289.

Weinberg, R. S., Burton, D., Yukelson, D., & Weigand, D. (2000). Perceived goal-setting practices of Olympic athletes: An exploratory investigation. *The Sport Psychologist 14*, 280-296.

Weinberg, R. S., Butt, J., & Knight, B. (2001). High school coaches' perceptions of the process of goal setting. *The Sport Psychologist, 15*, 20-47.

Weinberg, R. S., Butt, J., Knight, B., & Perritt, N. (2001). Collegiate coaches' perceptions of their goal setting practice: A qualitative investigation. *Journal of Applied Sport Psychology, 13*, 374-398

Weinberg, R. S., Fowler, C., Jackson, A., Bagnall, J., & Bruya, L. (1991). Effect of goal difficulty on motor performance: A replication across tasks and subjects. *Journal of Sport and Exercise Psychology, 13*, 160-173.

Weinberg, R. S., Stitcher, T., & Richardson, P. (1994). Effects of a seasonal goal setting program on lacrosse performance. *The Sport Psychologist, 8*, 166-175.

Weinberg, R. S. & Weigand, D. (1993). Goal setting in sport and exercise. A reaction to Locke. *Journal of Sport & Exercise Psychology, 15*, 88-95.

Weinberg, R. S. & Weigand, D. (1996). Let the discussions continue: A reaction to Locke's comments on Weinberg and

Weigand. *Journal of Sport and Exercise Psychology, 18,* 89-93.

Williams, K. J., Donovan, J. J., & Dodge, T. L. (2000). Self-regulation of performance: Goal establishment and goal revision processes in athletes. *Human Performance, 13,* 159-180.

Wood, R. E., Mento, A. J., & Locke, E. A. (1987). Task complexity as a moderator of goal effects: A meta-analysis. *Journal of Applied Psychology, 72,* 416-425.

Wright, P. M., Hollenbeck, J. R., Wolf, S., & McMahan, G. C. (1995). The effects of varying goal difficulty operationalizations on goal setting outcomes and processes. *Organizational Behavior and Human Decision Processes, 61,* 28-43.

Courtesy of Mark Turney/U.S. Marine Corps

3.2

Self-Presentation with a Special Emphasis on Emotion-Presentation: Concept, Methods, and Intervention Strategies

DIETER HACKFORT AND ANDREAS SCHLATTMANN

Introduction

Presentation of oneself is part of our every day behavior as well as our sport-related behavior. We will discuss self-presentation aspects connected with actions in sports, with a special focus on emotional presentation. The main purpose of this chapter is the explanation of the function of self-presentation with regard to action regulation in sports. We will analyze and evaluate theoretical consideration methods, as well as introduce modification methods and interventional strategies. Finally, an outline for future research will be presented.

Watzlawick, Beavin, and Jackson (1967) stated that it is impossible for a person to not behave. Following this logic for the topic of this chapter, it is impossible to not present oneself. Instead of a discussion of the term "self" or "self-concept," we use it (the term "self") in this chapter as a description of the cognitive representation of various aspects of oneself. As Arkin (1988, p. 8) explained,

> the term self-presentation refers to the process of establishing an identity through the appearance one presents to others. People are constantly engaged in presenting an appearance, either intentionally or unintentionally, honestly or deceitfully, to actual or imagined others.

The phenomenon "self-presentation" is realized as soon as a person steps into a situation with other persons. Indeed, even the anticipation of a social situation brings aspects of self-presentation into being.

Self-presentation is included in every action — sometimes it is emphasized and intentionally organized (e.g., in figure skating), in other situations it is not a central aspect and the acting subject is not aware of its occurrence (e.g., ice speed skater). Actions, as a special class of behavior (Nitsch & Hackfort, 1981; Hackfort & Munzert in this volume), namely goal-directed and purposive behaviors, are not only organized to realize a goal-oriented process but also connected with self-presentation. Sometimes we are not aware of the self-presentation and it is not under conscious control but sometimes it is, e.g. in gymnastics or dance, presentation of the self to others is a main aspect of the performance. In addition, we sometimes use a particular strategy of self-presentation to influence social partners in processes of communication and interaction (i.e., what is referred to as "inter-individual action-regulation"; Nitsch & Hackfort, 1984; Hackfort & Munzert in this volume). Moreover, sometimes we control our self-presentation to influence our inner state (e.g., modify our actions, emotions, or motivation). This functional aspect of self-presentation refers to the intra-individual action regulation with respect to tuning (see Hackfort & Munzert in this volume). "Tuning" refers to the psycho-physiological and psycho-social fundamentals or preconditions of the realization of a goal directed process, that is the psycho-physiological arousal, on one hand (intra-individual precondition), and the social atmosphere (inter-individual precondition), on the other.

In this chapter, we emphasize intentional self-presentation with respect to the functional meaning of intra- and inter-individual action regulation. Furthermore, we consider such sports in which self-presentation is a part of the performance (e.g., in figure skating) as well as sports in which self-presentation is not an aspect of performance-oriented evaluation (e.g., in sailing).

Theoretical Background

In his book "The Presentation of Self in Everyday Life," Goffman (1959) tries to prove that self-presentation is a necessary element of human life that operates according to pre-defined rules and under pre-defined controls. According to Goffman, in social situations, it is meaningful for the interacting persons to have influence on the definition of the situation to be able to form their inter-personal executions. Goffman points out that this is not at first reached by instrumental behaviors or communication between the individuals. Rather, the interacting persons try to influence the meaning of the context by expressing themselves in a way that creates an impression on others involved in the interaction. Each person hopes that such impressions will induce others to voluntarily go along with his or her plans; for example, when an ice hockey player starts to present aggressiveness.

The concept of "face" plays a central role in Goffman's theory (1959). We can have different faces for different audiences. We have a face for our parents, a different one for our children, and in turn a different one for friends. Somebody generally can be dominant and aggressive with friends, for example, but behave in a more restrained way with his/her parents or employer. Such changes of face do not represent an inconsistency of the person but merely different "faces" of an individual which are caused by different perceived situational requirements.

A participant, who builds a suitable "image" with others in the interaction and also receives information from the others that the self-presentation is suitable, is "in face." Opposite to this is a person whose projected image is rejected by others. This person would be "out of face." Goffman (1959) points out that a set of rules for such face-to-face situations can be detected. These rules determine which kind of behavior is suitable in a particular social situation.

Goffman (1959) suggests that participants in social interactions often use different techniques to help each other "keep the face." This process, called "face-work," can be observed in cases where excuses are given. For example, we sometimes offer excuses for others following a difficult circumstance to spare them social disgrace and personal defeat (e.g., "I probably also would have lost against that opponent"). "Accepting techniques" which assist others in keeping their face are also sometimes employed (e.g., "I agree with you that this opponent was unbeatable today").

But the preservation of the face isn't the only aim of social interaction. Rather, such preservation is held to be a necessary condition for the continuity of the social interaction. It is a basic assumption of Goffman's (1959) theory that self-presentation is necessary to build up and keep an effective interpersonal relation.

Self-presentation as conveyed via nonverbal behavior is connected with both the content of communication and the relational aspect of the communication (see Watzlawick, Beavin, & Jackson, 1969). This aspect refers to the regulation of inter-individual relations among interacting persons and is assumed to fulfill a social-regulative function. In addition, the presentation of an individual person in the interaction process can serve a self-regulative function.

The self-regulative function can support a social-regulative function, (e.g., an athlete attempting to reduce internal unrest by slowing gestures and body movements.) Such non-verbal behaviors signal "coolness" and can influence others and their behavior (reactions) in the interaction process.

The self-regulative function of a self-presentation refers to the operating psycho-physiological processes, e.g., reducing arousal in a stressful situation. In contrast, the social-regulative function refers to psycho-social processes, e.g., to demonstrate motivation and will-power and to intimidate an opponent as Boris Becker did it with his famous gesture, the "Beckerfaust." This theory-based analytical distinction in practical life often is confused, as when a tennis player tries to work off his/her frustration by emotional outbursts. In so doing, he/she presents himself/herself as angry; the outburst can work off physical tension (self-regulative function) and induce social tension (social-regulative function) at the same time.

The social-regulative aspect of self presentation was a prominent issue in social psychology research in the United States during the 1980s. The topic was discussed as in concepts of "impression formation" (Riggio & Friedman, 1986) and "impression management" (Schlenker, 1980). However, the self-regulative aspect remained neglected although concepts like "self monitoring" (Snyder, 1974, 1987) indicate awareness of a self-regulative meaning of self-presentation.

The outlined regulatory functions of self-presentation can be regarded more specifically, i.e., with respect to emotions. Our research and applied interest in sport psychology during the past decade have revolved around what is referred to as emotion-presentation (see Hackfort & Schlattmann, 1991). "Emotion-presentation" refers to the presentation of felt or not felt (see below) emotions by non-verbal behavior.

In our studies exploring the functional meaning of emotion-presentation (e.g., Hackfort & Schlattmann, 1991), we asked athletes whether they use the presentation of emotions and, if so, for what reasons. The content analyses of the interview data obtained can be summarized in two different levels, with two different purposes found in each level (see Figure 1). On the first level, strategies can be distinguished in terms of whether (a) the athlete shows an experienced emotion, or (b) the athlete does not show an actually felt emotion; e.g., he/she demonstrates pride or reveals that he/she actually felt anger, or he/she does not show anxiety or disappointment that was felt. On the second level, strategies can be distinguished in terms of whether athletes aim to (a) demonstrate emotions that they do *not* really feel in that situation, or (b) do *not* show emotions that they do *not* feel. The latter situation is an interesting case which will be explained in more detail below.

The self-regulative meaning of emotion-presentation is realized by demonstrating emotions and, in

Figure 1: Functional Meanings of Emotion-Presentation

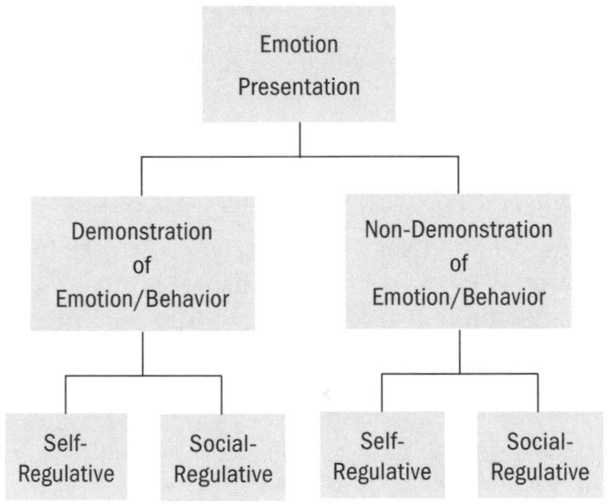

doing so, the quality of that emotion will be modified (e.g., having an outburst to reduce one's activation level). The purpose of demonstrating an emotion which is not truly felt in that situation is to overcome actually felt emotions; e.g., feeling anxious may be modified by acting confident.

The social-regulative meaning of emotion-presentation is realized, on one hand, by showing experienced emotions to provoke certain reactions of the opponent, e.g., sympathy. On the other hand, experienced emotions are not demonstrated in an effort to intimidate the opponent. Demonstrating emotions that are not really felt in that situation serves to deceive an opponent and to influence, e.g., his/her motivation or confidence.

Expressive behaviors accompany emotions and the question of their functional meaning has always been a central aspect in attempts to scientifically elucidate emotional processes (see Darwin, 1872). In the center of the current discussion on possible relations between physiological processes and emotionally expressive behavior, there are two contrary hypotheses. First, we have the catharsis- or diversion-hypothesis, which results from the fact that expressive behavior can lead to a diversion of excitement/arousal. This hypothesis assumes that an inner emotional pressure has to be discharged via a valve, the emotional expression ("steam boiler"). These ideas, which partly have their origins in psychoanalytical theories, correspond to everyday advice such as "Give vent to your tears, that will make you feel better" or "let him/her sow his/her wild oats, then he/she can be talked to again."

Buck, Miller, and Caul (1974) were able to find support for the existence of an inverse relation between emotional expression and physiological arousal: people who showed less expressive behavior when watching emotion-arousing slides had less strong reactions (changes in skin resistance) than people with a more pronounced expressive behavior (cf. also Jones, 1935, 1950, Lanzetta & Kleck, 1970). Schneider (1990, p. 421) described this effect as the expressive function of expressive behavior. By this he meant that expressive behavior is also used as a means to control and regulate emotional states, e.g. through diversion of tension, the intensity of the emotional experience is changed as well.

With respect to the second hypothesis, scientists are of the opinion that depending on proprioceptive feedback, expressive behavior does not reduce arousal but can actually increase it (cf. Gellhorn, 1970; Tomkins, 1962, 1963, 1984). Darwin (1872)

pointed to this possibility when he emphasized that the expression of emotional states can intensify emotions while the suppression of emotions can weaken them (i.e., serving a self-regulative function).

Furthermore, the expression of emotions can be regarded as the cause of emotional states. Facial expression is thought to affect or even determine the experience of emotions decisively (cf. Tomkins, 1962; Izard, 1971, 1977; Leventhal, 1980). Empirical findings on these considerations (the so-called "Facial-Feedback" Hypothesis) were presented by Lanzetta, Cartwright-Smith, and Kleck (1976). These investigators examined the effect of emotion-presentations on emotions. They asked subjects to either suppress or exaggerate the expression of pain felt by an electric shock. Contrary to the supposition that emotion suppression leads to an increase in intensity, they found that the degree of emotion (physiological measurements) corresponded with the emotional expression. These findings give rise to the assumption that in a person who expresses existing (or non-existing) emotions, physiological processes are affected in a way that these emotions can be generated or intensified (cf. also Baumeister & Cooper, 1981).

Hantas, Katkin, and Blascovich (1982) investigated the relation between the ability to perceive physiological processes precisely and the emotional state. Participants (N=63) were divided into good (n=17) and poor (n=46) "perceivers" by a test in which they had to determine their own heart rate. In the next step, the participants watched slides of seriously-injured victims of accidents. For each slide, they were asked to classify their individual state of arousal. The analysis of the actual heart rate showed no differences between the two groups, whereas people with a better ability to perceive physical processes classified themselves as significantly more aroused. These results point to a connection between the ability to perceive and differentiate one's own physiological processes and the emotional experience (cf. also Pennebaker, 1980; Katkin, 1985).

Obviously, it can be assumed that certain emotions can be induced by the perception of one's own emotional state. Similar processes may occur simply by observing the emotional states of other people. For example, the feelings of others can be "infectious." In sport, this phenomenon becomes particularly evident, if, for example, cheering players "infect" the audience with a desire to cheer or if aggressiveness on the playing field also extends to the fans. Similarly, athletes can be encouraged by the support of the audience and their feelings of confidence whereas fan boredom or remarks of displeasure may be demoralizing for some athletes.

While Sherman (1927) argued against universal emotion-typical facial expressions, Tomkins (1962, 1963) holds that universal patterns of facial expression can at least be differentiated in terms of so-called "basic emotions." Ekman and Izard support this proposition and have provided evidence for six to eight so-called basic emotions that are judged consistently in different cultures (cf. Ekman, Sorenson, & Friesen, 1969; Izard, 1971; Ekman, Friesen, & Ellsworth, 1972; Ekman & Friesen, 1975).

Evidence can also be found for socio-cultural differences in emotional expression (cf. Birdwhistell, 1970). In a given society at a particular point of time, people learn which emotions they (may) feel and show (e.g., the loss of a family member in different cultures arouses different reactions). This cultural determination of emotional experience and emotional expression does not always hold within a cultural group (as is shown by Ekman, 1972), as members of the same culture can differ in their subjective perception of "identical" events. Ekman (1972) distinguishes between different display rules to describe the meaning of social factors on the expression of feelings:

1. Amplification. An emotion is shown more distinctly than it is actually experienced.

2. De-amplification. An emotion is partly suppressed and is not shown as distinctly as it is actually experienced.

3. Neutralization. The person tries not to show an experienced emotion.

4. Disguise. An existing, mostly "negative" emotion is hidden by showing a different emotion. The non-existing emotion is pretended (e.g., exhibiting joy when one is anxious).

These rules are based on conventional agreements and are conveyed to children in the socialization process. There is a close connection between the existing values of a society and emotional expression.

In the view of Wallbott (1984), however, one also has to assume that not all emotion-presentations are intentionally communicative. Emotions are not necessarily directed towards other people from the onset. Information about inner processes is sometimes sent automatically or implicitly with the instrumental/goal directed behavior, even though it is often controlled. However, an arbitrary control of the expression becomes more likely as people become more conscious of the communicative meaning of the expression in social situations. Meanwhile, many people participate in training to improve not only verbal but also non-verbal communications, which is based on this insight. Argyle (1975) distinguished different forms of emotion-presentation:

1. physiological reactions with no intention to communicate something (e.g., facial expression of disgust);

2. expressive, social signals which have developed through human evolution (e.g., exhibiting anxiety);

3. social signals, used consciously (e.g., showing happiness, even though the person is annoyed).

In this chapter, we focus on this last aspect of emotion-presentation. In emotion-presentation, i.e., when showing or not showing emotions, self, and social regulative functions are perceived either intentionally or unintentionally (cf. figure 1). Thus, obvious expressions of joy after a successful goal can be differentiated according to the self-regulative (such as diversion of arousal) and the social regulative (such as trying to enhance the motivation of fellow players or rattle opponents) functions.

The self-regulative meaning of emotion-presentation is realized by demonstrating emotions to reduce activation and the intensity of that emotion, and, in so doing, modify the quality of the emotion. Sometimes emotions are exhibited that are different from those which are experienced in that situation. This strategy can serve to overcome those emotions (e.g., high anxiety). In contrast, not demonstrating experienced emotions can serve to prevent the athlete from losing concentration.

The social-regulative meaning of emotion-presentation is realized by demonstrating emotions to provoke particular reactions in the opponent (e.g., pity). Not demonstrating experienced emotions can serve to intimidate the opponent (e.g., not to show surprise about a lucky strike in tennis). Exhibiting emotions that are not actually experienced can serve to deceive opponents or to reduce their motivation or confidence.

Analyzing and Modifying Emotion-Presentation

Usually an observer perspective is used to analyze self-presentation and the presentation of emotions. In addition, methods such as the facial affect scoring technique can be used to quantitatively assess the intensity of emotional expressions (see Ekman, Friesen, & Tomkins, 1971 for discussion of scoring special aspects of the facial expression on the basis of photos). The idea of our methodological approach is to combine quantitative and qualitative data and to integrate the analysis of emotion-presentation with an interventional approach. This is accomplished by a multi-method strategy which includes a video-stimulated self-commentary method, the administration of a self-presentation scale, and video-assisted behavioral training.

Video-Stimulated Self-Commentary

Nisbett and DeCamp Wilson (1977) summarize their analyses on "verbal reports on mental processes" by stating that this method "suggests that though people may not be able to observe directly their cognitive processes, they will sometimes be able to report accurately about them" (p. 231). On one hand, it was proven that people are able to provide information about their cognitive processes or cognitions (thoughts), on the other hand, it is important to recognize that Nisbett and DeCamp Wilson (1977) are talking about "reports." We are referring here to self-commentary on cognitions that is cognitions about cognitions (metacognitions). In addition, Nisbett and

DeCamp Wilson (1977) refer to the relevance of the conditions at hand and mention that we will be correct in our verbal reports "when influential stimuli are ... available" (p. 253). We suggest that this is the case when using video tapes.

Nisbett and DeCamp Wilson (1977) also propose that "when people are asked to report how a particular stimulus influenced a particular response, they do so not by consulting a memory of the mediating processes, but by applying or generating causal theories about the effects . . ." (p. 248). Maybe being in a self-commentary situation (e.g., sitting in front of a monitor and watching oneself in action) provokes similar mental processes and similar cognitions and emotions as was the case when the individual was actually in the situation. Another process may be operating as well according to Nisbett and DeCamp Wilson. They refer to the so called "Heisenberg-type effect," and suggest that the assessment process "may suggest to the subject a connection that was not apparent to him before" (p. 253). Being aware that such reports are comments (meta-cognitions, explanations), this effect is not a methodological mistake but an intended strategy. "Telling more than we can know" (the title of the article by Nisbett & DeCamp Wilson, 1977) refers to the reports on cognitive processes and is true for so called self-confrontation strategy as a method of stimulated recall, but not for the video-assisted self-commentary method, as the logic of this method refers to "commentaries" as a special class of verbal data: cognitions about the taped self-presentations. These cognitions are not "meta-cognitions" as is the case with the data generated by stimulated recall strategies. The video-stimulated self-commentary procedure can be characterized by the following steps:

- The athletes perform under normal conditions (for example competition).

- Their behaviors are recorded by video.

- The athletes get the opportunity to view the videotapes and are then asked to comment on their own behavior. The comments are recorded and evaluated.

To analyze the videos, the athlete provides commentary upon the videotape without instruction (free commentary). Then he or she provides commentary following instructions on specified themes (theme-oriented commentary). The athlete provides further commentary on separate parts of the video. These parts are chosen either by the athlete, the coach, or the sport psychologist. An alternate possibility requires that the athlete provide commentary on a prepared videotape which is viewed in normal speed, in slow motion, in time-lapse photography, or as a series of static images. By using this technique, it is possible to identify "ticks" and other special behaviors (e.g., routines or stereotypes). The athletes' comments are structured with the help of the Self-Presentation Scale (SPS; Hackfort & Schlattmann, 2002).

Self-Presentation-Scale (SPS)

The Self-Presentation Scale (Hackfort & Schlattmann, 2002) includes three separate dimensions: ideal self-presentation (SPS-I: "How do I want to present myself"), real self-presentation (SPS-R: "How did I present myself"), and desired change (SPS-C: "How do I wish to change my self-presentation"). The three versions (SPS-I, SPS-R, SPS-C) are administered to the athlete (self-perspective) and to another person (e.g., the coach or other athletes) to gain a social-perspective. In this way the different perspectives on the specific aspect of self-presentation, e.g., emotion-presentation (items like "aggressiveness", "anxiety") can be compared and evaluated in terms of whether it should be modified or not.

At first, it is necessary to choose the relevant dimensions of self-presentation for each specific situation. Referring to the concept of "action situation" (Hackfort, 1986; Nitsch & Hackfort, 1981) it is important to consider the task-environment constellation and its subjective interpretation as well as the person and his or her self-concept. All this is done in cooperation with the athlete. The emotional responses provided in each of the versions of the SPS can be graded by a set of 44 items (e.g., "aggressive," "elegant," "friendly," "nervous," "disappointed," "vigorous"). This set of items can be used in full by having the athlete (or coach) respond to all of the 44 items or by choosing a selected set of items which are especially relevant for the situation.

The SPS includes three forms and each form contains special instructions:

a) Version SPS-I: Before analyzing the videotape the athlete classifies how he or she wants to present himself or herself in this situation. The athlete can classify each aspect on a Likert scale from 1 = "applies to me not at all" to 5 = "applies to me completely." The following items provide an illustration of this scale. In this example, the athlete wants to present himself as not at all anxious, mainly relaxed and somewhat aggressive. After that the athlete is asked to watch a video sample of his behavior (e.g., the last competition in which the athlete performed).

Figure 2: Self-Presentation-Scale, Version I

How I want to present myself?

	1	2	3	4	5
anxious	X				
relaxed				X	
aggressive			X		

1=not at all, 5=very much so

(b) Version SPS-R: After watching the video recordings, the athlete is asked to classify his or her self-presentation referring to the same dimensions. In the following illustration, the athlete classifies his or her real self-presentation to be a little anxious, somewhat relaxed and completely aggressive. Through a comparison of the two versions, differences between ideal and real self-presentation can be identified. The logical consequence of any identified difference would be that the athlete wishes to overcome the differential. Based on our experience of using this procedure with athletes, we have learned that this is not true in every case. Logical consequences are not always synonymous with psychological consequences. For further clarification of this point, SPS-C was developed.

Figure 3: Self-Presentation-Scale, Version R

How did I present myself?

	1	2	3	4	5
anxious		0			
relaxed			0		
aggressive					0

(c) Version SPS-C: To analyze the subjective meaning of differences in the ideal self-presentation and real self-presentation, the athlete is asked how much he or she wants to change his or her self-presentation. The athlete can classify his or her answers by selecting from a range of -2 (a strong desire to reduce aggressive self-presentation behavior) to +2 (a strong desire to intensify self-presentation behavior), with a selection of 0 meaning the athlete does not wish to modify self-presentation behavior.

In this example, the athlete wants to maintain his presentation of anxiousness but desires to present himself as being more relaxed and less aggressive.

Figure 4: Self-Presentation-Scale, Version C

How much do I wish to change?

	--	-	0	+	++
anxious			X		
relaxed				X	
aggressive	X				

At this stage, the data are transferred for evaluation into a two-dimensional grid which represents the differences between real and ideal self-presentation, as well as any desired change in the view of the athlete.

Positive differences arise if the real image has a greater numeric value than the ideal. For example, a positive difference will be reported if a person identifies that the video shows him to be more anxious than he would like. Negative differences would be reported if the person judges his behavior to be less anxious than he desires it to be. No differences will be reported if the appraisals are found to be identical.

The wish to change can be differentiated according to whether the self-presentation should be reduced (for example: "I like to present myself as being less relaxed.") or intensified (for example: "I like to present myself as being more relaxed."). In addition, the athlete can express a desire to keep the current status. Furthermore, two different constellations of real versus ideal self-presentation appraisals are possible: (1) There is no numeric difference between real and ideal self-evaluation but the athlete wants to change his or her self-presentation in such situations, and (2) There is a difference in the evaluation between real and ideal self-presentation but instead of wishing to change his or her self-presentation, the athlete adapts his or her self-concept (ideal self-presentation). For example, if his/her rating for an ideal self-presentation with regard to aggressiveness was lower than the rating for the real self-presentation observed on the videotape but the athlete regards it as appropriate as he/she showed it in the concrete action-situation, the athlete would not try to modify his/her real self-presentation but his/her ideal (concept of) self-presentation.

Figure 5: Evaluation-Scheme (self perspective)

Discrepances real-ideal		Reducing	Intensifying	Keeping
	+	5 aggressive (3)		2 anxious (1)
	-		3 relaxed (4)	
	0			

With the information gleaned from this methodological strategy, it is appropriate to start the training intervention. The training program is developed in cooperation with the athlete, and considers his or her interests and preferences. In addition, the perspective and opinion of others (e.g., the coach) may be of interest and can be considered in planning the strategy to optimize the athlete's behavior.

Video-Assisted Behavioral Training (VBT)

After establishing which aspects are to be changed, video-assisted self-presentation training is utilized. The most relevant steps of this training are:

Step 1: Videotapes are used to demonstrate the specific behaviors which are to be developed and performed by the athlete (optional techniques: presentation of printed graphic overlay or photo depicting the targeted behavior(s)). That is, goal setting or goal adaptation with special respect to self-presentation.

Step 2: To simulate the appropriate method and behaviors, the athlete is encouraged to practice the intended behavior/emotional response. This is videotaped to create a short self-model videotape. The athlete then observes it repeatedly.

Step 3: The athlete is asked to imitate this behavioral model until he or she gets the feeling for or sense of this behavior/emotional response and he or she is able to identify with the specific kind of presentation.

Step 4: Finally, the self-presentation is evaluated by the persons involved in the training program with regard to the identified dimensions. For example, if the athlete has to fight against his nervousness and to overcome anxious behavior by demonstrating calm movements/slow motions he is asked to judge the effectiveness of this kind of self-presentation with special emphasis on worry (task irrelevant cognitions) and emotionality (feelings of tension).

Figure 6: Self-Presentation-Scale, Version R

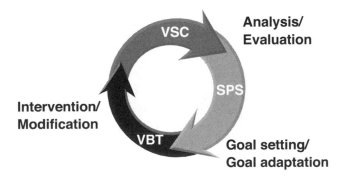

This intervention can be supplemented by other specialized training, e.g., assertiveness training, self-motivation training, or relaxation training. In addition, the emotion-presentation/self-presentation training can be included in a program to enhance self-management and social competence. The interventional process is summarized in Figure 6.

Final Remarks

Self-presentation and emotion-presentation is often neglected in counseling top athletes, but they have important functional meanings for action regulation. With regard to any action, the theoretical concept of self- and the social-regulatory meaning of emotion-presentation can be differentiated. A special procedure to develop appropriate emotion-presentation especially for competitive situations has been introduced here. VBT enables athletes to improve emotion-presentation and to optimize the (pre-) conditions for successful behavior.

This approach has been proven (case studies; Hackfort & Schlattmann, 1995) as a useful tool in counseling top class athletes of various sports (e.g., sailing, figure skating, tennis, boxing, soccer). Our experiences show that such a procedure (cooperating with the athlete in identifying relevant dimensions for emotion-presentation) can modify emotion-presentational actions and serve as a functional behavior to support the athletes' self-concept and self-management. Further quantitative research to evaluate the strategy is in progress.

References

Argyle, M. (1975). *Bodily Communication*. London: Methuen.

Arkin, R. M. (1988). Self-Presentation strategies and sequelae. In S.L. Zelen (Ed.), *Self-representation* (pp. 5-29). New York: Springer.

Asendorpf, J. (1983). Soziale Interaktion und Emotion (Social interaction and emotion). In H. A. Euler & H. Mandl (Eds.), *Emotionspsychologie (Psychology of emotions*; pp. 267-273). München: Urban & Schwarzenberg.

Baumeister, R. F., & Cooper, J. (1981). Can the public expectation of emotion cause that emotion? *Journal of Personality*, *49*, 49-59.

Birdwhistell, R. (1970). *Kinesics and context*. Philadelphia: University of Pennsylvania Press.

Buck, R. W., Miller, R. E., & Caul, W. F. (1974). Sex, personality, and physiological variables in the communication of emotion via facial expression. *Journal of Personality and Social*

Psychology, 30 (4), 587-596.

Darwin, C. (1872). *The expression of emotions in man and animals.* London: Murray.

Ekman, P. (1972). Universals and cultural differences in facial expression of emotion. In J. R. Cole (Ed.), *Nebraska Symposium on Motivation* (pp. 207-283). Lincoln: University of Nebraska Press.

Ekman, P., & Friesen, W. V. (1969). The repertoire of nonverbal behavior: Categories, origins, usage, and coding. *Semiotica, 1,* 49-98.

Ekman, P., & Friesen, W. V. (1975). *Unmasking the face.* Englewood Cliffs, NJ: Prentice Hall.

Ekman, P., Friesen, W. V., & Ellsworth, P. (1972). *Emotion in the human face: Guidelines for research and integration of findings.* New York: Pergamon Press.

Ekman, P., Friesen, W. V., & Tomkins, S.S. (1971). Facial affect scoring technique (FAST). *Semiotica, 3,* 37-58.

Ekman, P., Sorenson, E. R., & Friesen, W.V. (1969). Pan-cultural elements in the facial displays of emotion. *Science, 164,* 86-88.

Gellhorn, E. (1970). The emotions and the ergotropic and trophotropic systems. *Psychologische Forschung, 34,* 48-94.

Goffman, E. (1959). *The presentation of self in everyday life.* New York: Doubleday.

Hackfort, D. (1986). *Theorie und Analyse sportbezogener Ängstlichkeit (Theory and analysis of sport-related anxiety).* Schorndorf: Hofmann.

Hackfort, D., & Schlattmann, A. (1991). Functions of emotion presentation in sport. In D. Hackfort (Ed.), *Research on emotions in sport* (pp. 95-110). Köln: Strauss.

Hackfort, D., & Schlattmann, A. (2002). Self-presentation training for top athletes. *International Journal of Sport Psychology, 33* (1), 61-71.

Hantas, M., Katkin, E. S., & Blascovich, J. (1982). Relationship between heartbeat discrimination and subjective experience of affective state. *Psychophysiology, 19,* 563.

Izard, C. E. (1971). *The face of emotion.* New York: Appleton-Century-Crofts.

Izard, C. E. (1977). *Human emotions.* New York: Plenum.

Jones, H. E. (1935). The galvanic skin reflex as related to overt emotional expression. *American Journal of Psychology, 47,* 241-251.

Jones, H. E. (1950). The study of patterns of emotional expressions. In M.L. Reymert (Ed.), *Feelings and emotions* (pp. 161-168). New York: McGraw-Hill. Katkin, 1985

Katkin, E. S. (1985). Blood, sweat, and tears: Individual differences in automatic self-perception. *Psychophysiology, 22,* 125-137.

Lanzetta, J. T., Cartwright-Smith, J., & Kleck, R. E. (1976). Effects of non-verbal dissimulation on emotional experience and autonomic arousal. *Journal of Personality and Social Psychology, 33,* 354-370.

Lanzetta, J. T., & Kleck, R. E. (1970). Encoding and decoding of nonverbal affect in humans. *Journal of Personality and Social Psychology, 16,* 12-19.

Leventhal, H. (1980). Toward a comprehensive theory of emotion. In L. Berkowitz (Ed.), *Advances in experimental social psychology* (Vol. 13, pp. 140-207). New York: Academic Press.

Nisbett, R. E., & DeCamp Wilson, T. (1977). Telling more than we can know: Verbal reports on mental processes. *Psychological Review, 84* (3), 231-259.

Nitsch, J. R., & Hackfort, D. (1981). Stress in Schule und Hochschule - eine handlungspsychologische Funktionsanalyse (Stress at school and university: A functional analysis based on action theory). In J.R. Nitsch (Ed.), *Stress* (pp. 263-311). Bern: Huber.

Pennebaker, J. W. (1980). Self-perception of emotion and internal sensation. In D. M. Wegner & R. R. Vallacher (Eds.), *The self in social psychology* (pp. 80-101). New York: Oxford University Press.

Riggio, R. E., & Friedman, H. S. (1986). Individual differences and cues to deception. *Journal of Personality and Social Psychology, 45,* 899-915.

Schlattmann, A. & Hackfort, D. (1995). Interventionsbezogene Befindensanalyse (Intervention-oriented anlysis of mood). In J.R. Nitsch & H. Allmer (Eds.), *Emotionen im Sport (Emotions in sports;* pp. 348-352). Cologne: bps.

Schlenker, B. R. (1980). Impression management: The self-concept, social identity, and interpersonal relations. Monterey, CA: Brooks & Cole.

Schneider, K. (1990). Emotionen (Emotions). In H. Spada (Ed.), *Lehrbuch allgemeine Psychologie* (pp. 403-449). Bern: Huber.

Sherman, M. (1927). The differentiation of emotional responses in infants. *Journal of Comparative Psychology, 7,* 265-284.

Snyder, M. (1974). Self-monitoring of expressive behavior. *Journal of Personality and Social Psychology, 30,* 526-537.

Snyder, M. (1987). *Public appearances/private realities: The psychology of self-monitoring.* San Francisco: Freeman.

Tomkins, S. S. (1962). *Affect, imagery, consciousness. Vol. 1: The positive affects.* New York: Springer.

Tomkins, S. S. (1963). *Affect, imagery, consciousness. Vol. 2: The negative affects.* New York: Springer.

Tomkins, S. S. (1984). Affect theory. In K.R. Scherer & P. Ekman (Eds.), *Approaches to emotion* (pp. 163-196). Hillsdale, NJ: ErlbaumWallbott (1984),

Wallbott, H. G. (1984). Nonverbale Kommunikationsforschung. Befunde, Probleme und Perspektiven (Research on nonverbal communication: Results, problems, and perspectives). *Unterrichtswissenschaft, 4,* 295-307.

Watzlawick, P., Beavin, J. H., & Jackson (1967). *Pragmatics of human communication.* New York: Norton.

3.3

Enhancing Athletes' Self Regulation, Task Involvement, and Self Determination via Psychological Skills Training

JOAN L. DUDA, JENNIFER CUMMING, AND ISABEL BALAGUER

Introduction

Going back to its Latin derivative, "the word 'motivation' means 'to move'; hence, in this basic sense, the study of motivation is the study of action" (Eccles & Wigfield, 2002, p. 110). Although not always well understood, the concept of motivation is certainly salient and frequently evoked in athletic circles. This topic holds considerable practical relevance, as most athletes, coaches, and parents are interested in how to maintain or enhance motivated behavior within the sport domain. One would be hard pressed to find an applied book in sport psychology that does not contain a chapter or two concerning techniques and

strategies that should help foster a sport participant's motivation.

Motivation in the athletic milieu has also been the focus of considerable theoretical and empirical interest. Within this literature, motivation is typically linked to achievement striving and defined with respect to "those personality factors, social variables, and/or cognitions that come into play when a person undertakes a task at which he or she is evaluated, enters into competition with others, and/or attempts to attain some standard of excellence" (Roberts, 1992, p. 5). Indeed, if one considers the number of publications in scientific journals and attention allocated in major textbooks, research centered on the nature, measurement, antecedents, and/or consequences of motivation composes one of the most popular areas of inquiry in the field of sport psychology. Over the years, a number of theoretical perspectives have undergirded investigations of sport motivation, including Bandura's (1986, 1997) social cognitive theory, Harter's competence motivation framework (Harter, 1978, 1981), action theory (Nitsch, 2000; Nitsch & Hackfort, 1981), Eccles' expectancy x value model (Eccles, 1987; Eccles & Harold, 1991), Deci and Ryan's cognitive evaluation and self determination theories (Deci & Ryan, 1985, 2000), and achievement goal frameworks (e.g., Ames, 1992; Dweck, 1986, 1999; Elliot, 1999; Elliot & Church, 1997; Elliot & McGregor, 2001; Nicholls, 1984, 1989). Such work has enhanced understanding of the different motivational processes impacting learning, performance, and participation in sport.

In this chapter, we focus on two social cognitive models of sport motivation that formed the foundation for a plethora of studies over the past two decades, namely self determination theory (SDT; Deci & Ryan, 1985, 2000; Ryan & Deci, 2002) and contemporary achievement goal theories (AGT; Ames, 1992, Dweck, 1999; Elliot, 1999; Nicholls, 1984, 1999). These two conceptualizations of motivation center on the goal-directed behavior of individuals, emphasize the motivational significance of the meaning behind such striving, and consider how individuals interpret the social situations in which they are placed. SDT speaks to the positive motivational outcomes associated with self determination. Self-determined motivation is marked by behaviors that are volitional; i.e., internally endorsed by individuals and engaged in out of personal choice rather than because of coercion. AGT-based research has provided support for the motivational advantages associated with task-focused goals in sport (see Duda, 2001; Duda & Hall, 2000; Roberts, 2001). When task-involved, individuals strive to experience personal improvement and mastery and provide their best effort. When this is realized, they feel competent and successful.

With respect to applied implications that emanate from SDT and AGT, the trend in sporting contexts has been to propose or implement task- or situation-related intervention strategies that are assumed to fuel self determination and/or task involve-

ment. That is, this literature tends to concentrate on what coaches can do to alter tasks or modify the psychological environment they create to enhance athletes' motivation (e.g., see Biddle, 2001; Mageau & Vallerand, 2003; Pelletier, Fortier, Vallerand, & Briere, 2001; Reinboth, Duda, & Ntoumanis, 2004; Treasure, 2001).

This chapter takes a different tack and focuses on athlete-centered interventions that can be tied to the SDT and achievement goal frameworks (Green-Demers, Pelletier, Stewart, & Gushue, 1998). Such interventions fit comfortably in what is typically referred to as cognitive-behavioral psychological skills training (PST) among athletes (Meyers, Whelan, & Murphy, 1996; Whelan, Mahoney, & Meyers, 1991).

As conceptualized by Vealey (1988, p. 319), PST comprises the "techniques and strategies designed to teach or enhance mental skills that facilitate performance and a positive approach to sport." Vealey distinguishes between the skills that athletes work to develop (e.g., self-awareness, maintaining confidence) and the methods (e.g., goal setting, imagery training) utilized to enhance those skills. Murphy and Tammen (1998) extend this distinction by proposing a three-step process for the application of psychological skills for performance management in sport. In step one, referred to as self-analysis, athletes need to identify the cognitive and affective features of their ideal performance state. In step two, labeled self-monitoring, athletes are requested to monitor their psychological state across training and competitive sessions to discern whether changes (and which changes) are needed. Finally, in step three or the self-regulation phase, the athlete moves to becoming proficient in performance management by learning and then practicing the necessary psychological methods pertinent to fostering her or his ideal performance state.

More specifically, cognitive-behavioral PST programs focus on "helping athletes manage their thoughts and emotions so that they can perform optimally" (Beauchamp et al., 1996, p. 158). Congruent with Murphy and Tammen (1998), we couch our discussion of cognitive-behavioral PST methods (e.g., goal setting, imagery training, attentional training, thought control) to foster athletes' self determination and task involvement within the broader concept of self regulation. The study of self regulation entails the "analysis of psychological mechanisms underlying goal-directed movement" (Crews, Lochbaum, & Karoly, 2001, p. 566) or "goal striving mechanisms" (Lee, Sheldon, & Turban, 2003). In general, a consideration of self-regulation in sport revolves around the examination of athletes' performance standards, elicited actions, strategy employment, attentional foci, cognitive patterns, and emotional responses that are internal and self-conscious (or at least initially intentional) and that occur in interaction with the task/ environment as they attempt to move toward goal attainment. In our view, the occurrence of fundamental, positive self regulatory processes contribute to and perhaps are even indicative of athletes experiencing more self-determined and task-centered states of involvement in training and competition. Indeed, we propose that potential changes in self regulation mechanisms should be taken into account when there is interest in determining whether motivation-related interventions are efficacious. Most critically in this contribution though, we argue that outcome measures of the effectiveness of any PST intervention designed to foster self regulation of athletes should include more than performance or learning indicators and/or performance-related cognitions (e.g., state confidence) and emotions (e.g., state anxiety). Specifically, a measure of the success of any such PST intervention should also incorporate the corresponding effect on athletes' motivational regulations and achievement goals.

We begin with a review of three models of self regulation that have guided sport-related research and practice, namely Bandura's (1986) model of self-regulatory processes, Kirschenbaum's (1984, 1987; Kirschenbaum & Wittrock, 1984) five-stage model of self regulation, and Zimmerman's (1989, 1994: Zimmerman & Ritenberg, 1997) self-regulation learning model. These models are all social cognitive in perspective (i.e., they assume that cognitions mediate the influence of social environments on behavior) and place differential emphases on key self regulatory mechanisms that are assumed to lead to optimal task learning and performance and sustained task investment, such as awareness and self-monitoring, goal setting, cognitive (such as self talk) and imaginal strategies, planning and problem solving, intrinsic interest, and self-reward (Crews et al., 2001). We then turn to the major constructs and assumptions embedded in the self determination (Deci & Ryan, 1985, 2000) and achievement goal (Ames, 1992; Dweck, 1999; Elliot, 1999; Nicholls, 1989; Pintrich, 2000) theories of motivation. These frameworks, which are also grounded in a social cognitive perspective, point to the benefits associated with more intrinsic and autonomous involvement and a stronger task goal focus among athletes. The chapter then highlights some empirically supported links between key self regulatory mechanisms and more self-determined and task-involved motivational processes.

As the reader will readily discern, systematic and theoretically-based research on the effect of athlete-centered (and primarily cognitive-behavioral) strategies and techniques on self regulation, self determination, task involvement, and their interdependencies is limited. With an eye toward encouraging future cognitive-behavioral PST interventions that assimilate and aim to impact self regulation and motivational processes, an integrative model will be presented. The chapter will propose some measurement-related issues that need to be addressed before the proposed links can be appropriately and more extensively examined in work involving athletes. We close with a brief discourse on potential additional lines of applied research on the interplay between PST, self regulatory mechanisms, self determination, and task involvement.

Self Regulation in Sport

It is often said in sport, that when engaged in competition, "no one can do it" for an individual athlete. The coach, fellow team-mates, fans, and others can provide support and even overt assistance (depending on the sport and/or level of competition) during the competitive encounter. However, when it comes down to it, it is the athlete himself or herself that needs to "keep the eye on the prize" in terms of the goal(s) for which he or she is striving. Only the athlete can provide the effort, manage emotions, concentrate, execute, monitor how things are going and adjust if necessary, and perform up to his or her capability. That is, the athlete needs to be able to self-regulate thoughts, actions, and emotions with respect to the pursuit of the competitive goals at hand (Crews, et al., 2001). Indeed, research has indicated that the ability to self-regulate regarding competition is an important source of confidence among high level athletes (e.g., Vealey, Hayashi, Garner-Holman, & Giacobbi, 1998).

The capacity of athletes, especially as they gain in experience, to "guide behavior along a specific path to a directed aim or goal" (Behncke, 2004, p. 2) is pertinent to optimizing training as well. Depending on where they are in their development, athletes need to keep learning new techniques, strategies, mental skills, etc.; they primarily do this during practice. Training, especially once major learning has taken place, is often arduous, repetitive, tedious, and/or demanding of considerable investment and energy over time (Green-Demers et al., 1998). In other words, engaging in the necessary amount of sport practice with the needed level of intensity is a test of perseverance or sustained task involvement. As was the case for the athlete's competitive engagement, no one can do the training for the athlete although others can provide help and encouragement. Thus, self-regulation mechanisms are pertinent to athletes of all skill levels in terms of their continued learning and maximizing of practice.

In the following section, we briefly present three social cognitive models of self-regulation applicable to learning, competitive performance, and task involvement over time that have guided sport-related research and/or applied interventions involving athletes.

Bandura's Model of Self-Regulatory Processes

The capacity for self-regulation is one of the elemental features of human agency in the social cognitive framework proposed by Bandura (1986, 2001). According to Bandura's theory (Bandura, 1986, 1997), self-regulation depends on three interacting components, which are goals or standards of performance, self-evaluative reactions to performance, and self-efficacy beliefs. Among these mechanisms of human agency, it is assumed that none is more important or pervasive than beliefs of personal efficacy (Bandura & Locke, 2003).

With respect to goals and performance standards, athletes set goals for themselves, anticipate the likely consequences of their prospective actions, and select and create courses of action likely to produce desired outcomes and avoid detrimental ones (Bandura, 1991; Locke & Latham, 1990). Thus, goals

and performance standards are important to self-regulation because they contribute to the organization and direction of athletes' behaviors, thoughts, and emotions with respect to the achievement of preferred outcomes. Goals give athletes perspective regarding desired future events and allow them to construct incentives that motivate and guide their actions. In this way, proposed or planned future events are converted into current motivators and regulators of behavior (Bandura & Locke, 2003). Of course, the regulative efficiency of goals would be dependent on how close or distant the future goals are projected in time.

Bandura and Locke remind us that goals also provide standards to assess athletes' progress (Bandura & Locke, 2003). Another central feature of self regulation, in Bandura's view (Bandura, 1997, 2001), revolves around the self-evaluative reactions to one's efforts regarding goal attainment. Self-evaluative reaction provides the emotional component of the processes linked to goal pursuit(s). In sport, athletes are continuously confronting the degree of alignment between their expectations and the observed outcomes, so they have a lot of possibilities to examine their own functioning. In this process of evaluation and confrontation, athletes are expected to make adjustments of their exerted effort to achieve desired outcomes. Self-evaluations can also lead to positive (e.g., satisfaction, intrinsic pride) or negative (e.g., self-dissatisfaction, anxiety) emotional reactions that can improve or disturb the self-regulation process. When athletes consider that they are efficacious and making good progress toward a goal, this should result in constructive, positive emotional states that then contribute to cognitive and behavioral effectiveness and successful self-regulation. If there is a discrepancy between performance and the standards set, self-dissatisfaction can result. However, such a negative emotional response is assumed to correspond to heightened effort as long as the task is well-learned and the discrepancy is small (Bandura & Jourden, 1991). In contrast, self-dissatisfaction experienced with respect to activities that have high (particularly attentional) demands or entail large discrepancies between performance and the set goal can result in disrupted self-regulation and debilitated performance.

Finally, Bandura's model (1986, 1997, 2001) holds that self-efficacy beliefs play a central role in this process of self-management as they affect actions directly but also indirectly through their impact on cognitive, motivational, decisional, and affective determinants of goal attainment (Bandura, 2001). That is, according to Bandura and Jourden (1991, p. 942), perceptions of self-efficacy are "concerned with people's beliefs in their capabilities to mobilize the motivation, cognitive resources, and courses of action needed to exercise control over environmental events." In the sport domain, such beliefs would influence the goals set by athletes (e.g., higher perceived self-efficacy is linked to higher or more demanding standards). Self-efficacy beliefs also are predicted to influence athletes' choice of goal-directed activities, how much effort they invest in selected endeavors, how long they persevere in the face of challenge and difficulties, and whether failures are motivating or demoralizing. Bandura (1986, 1997) argues that the probability of individuals working hard in order to reach a prospective performance standard is a function of their beliefs about whether or not they can produce the behaviors endemic to this performance level. When athletes have strong efficacy beliefs, they are more likely to persevere and such perseverance is more likely to translate into successful performance (especially if contrasted with giving up or rescinding effort). Positive performance is held to then translate into enhanced subsequent perceptions of efficacy.

Bandura's model (1986, 1997, 2001) of self-regulatory mechanisms has formed the basis for numerous studies in organizational settings (e.g., Bandura & Jourden, 1991) and educational contexts (e.g., Schunk, 1995). Sport work has also been grounded in this framework and generally offers support for the model's major assumptions (e.g. Kane, Marks, Zaccaro, & Blair, 1996; Lee, 1988; Theodorakis, 1995; Williams, Donovan, & Dodge, 2000; Winfrey & Weeks, 1993). For example, Kane and colleagues (1996) examined facets of self-regulation processes among wrestlers engaged in a week of competitions at a wrestling camp. They examined the predictive utility of self-efficacy and personal goals with respect to performance as well as the effect that performance had on subsequent goal setting, self-efficacy beliefs, and satisfaction. In general, the results were congruent with Bandura's model of self-regulation (1986, 1997, 2001).

Williams and colleagues (2000) followed a sample of track and field athletes across a competitive season with respect to their goal establishment and goal revision processes. The athletes were requested to provide information regarding the goals set, progress toward reaching goals in terms of observed performance, and then subsequent goal revision. The findings provided evidence for Bandura's model in that discrepancy-production and discrepancy-reduction were evident in the athletes' self-regulation of their goals. Whether the athletes attributed their performance to controllable or uncontrollable causes and the phase of the season emerged as moderators of the current performance-goal revision relationship. Subsequent goals became more challenging when the previous goal-current performance difference was limited or the performance was attributed to a controllable cause. When the discrepancy was large and uncontrollable attributions were given, subsequence goals were reduced. Unfortunately, parallel changes in self efficacy across the competitive season were not assessed in the Williams et al. (2000) investigation.

In sum, drawing from Bandura's model (1986, 1997, 2001), athletes are expected to be not only agents of action, but also planners, self-examiners, and self-regulators of their own functioning. Moreover, in the course and direction of this dynamic process, self-efficacy beliefs are assumed to be fundamental.

Kirschenbaum's Five-Stage Model of Self Regulation

According to Kirschenbaum (1984), the regulation of goal-directed behaviors without immediate external constraints involves a complex interaction between cognitive (e.g., goal-setting, planning, evaluating), affective (i.e., emotional states), physiological (e.g., strength, physical condition), and environmental variables. To more fully explain the process of self-regulation in sport, Kirschenbaum and Wittrock (Kirschenbaum 1984, 1987; Kirschenbaum & Wittrock, 1984) developed a five-phase model. In Kirschenbaum's model, self-regulation includes problem identification, commitment, execution, environment management, and generalization.

In the first phase of problem identification, the athlete recognizes a problem via self-regulation.

Kirschenbaum (1984, 1987, 1997) pointed out that athletes, like most people, function in a semi-automatic fashion. For instance, they may have established routines or habits for how they approach training and competition. As part of the ongoing process of striving towards excellence, however, it is important for athletes to be aware of their own strengths and weaknesses, as well as to acknowledge areas that might need improvement. Moreover, Kirschenbaum suggests that athletes need to consider how they might take more responsibility for the quality of their performance in sport. One area that athletes tend to report as being problematic (Gould, Petlichkoff, Hodge, & Simons, 1990) concerns their use of psychological skills. Although athletes generally report using psychological skills such as imagery, they do not tend to use these skills in the regular and systematic fashion in which they approach physical practice (Barr & Hall, 1992; Hall, Rodgers, & Barr, 1990; Rodgers, Hall, & Buckolz, 1991). Consequently, they are unlikely to maximize the potential benefits of psychological skill utilization such as increased motivation, self-confidence, and overall improvements to performance. Thus, during the problem identification stage, the athlete recognizes the potential improvements they would be able to make by taking charge of their psychological skills training. Implicit within this stage is the notion that athletes must believe that a change in their behavior is possible and that working towards this behavioral change will bring desirable results.

After deciding that behavioral change is both necessary and plausible, the next step is for the athlete to make a commitment to that change. Within this second stage, the athlete might employ one or more of several strategies to increase his/her commitment and perseverance towards making the necessary alterations to training. Publicly expressing an intention to change and identifying a plan to achieve this outcome are two such strategies. To continue with the example of psychological skills training, athletes might commit themselves to engaging in additional imagery training in order to achieve more long term improvements to performance.

The execution phase follows commitment, and involves the athlete beginning an active process of behavioral change. Athletes will first begin this third phase by systematically monitoring their tar-

get behavior, a process referred to as self-monitoring. This is followed by self-evaluation, which involves comparing one's current level of performance with an established goal or standard. The loop is closed by self-consequation, which involves administering consequences or rewards to oneself depending on the outcome of the self-evaluation. If the self-evaluation is favorable, self rewards might occur. Such self rewards reflect personally directed positive feedback and indicate that behavioral change has been successful. In contrast, when self-evaluation is unfavorable, negative consequences can result in the form of self-punishment. This negative feedback suggests that more effort is needed on the part of the athlete for executing the behavioral change or informs the athlete that her/his plan to achieve the desired performance outcome needs to be modified.

The fourth stage of self-regulation is environmental management. Although self-regulation by nature is a solitary activity, Kirschenbaum (1984, 1987, 1997) recognizes that behavior does not occur in a vacuum. The pursuit of goals involves managing limitations from both the physical and social environment. For example, an athlete's practice session might be restricted by his/her current level of physical conditioning or by the amount of time she or he has access to training facilities and coaching. As a result, athletes may develop alternative methods of practicing when faced with these constraints (e.g., cross-training, imagery use). As another example, athletes need to be both physically and mentally prepared for unexpected situations that might disrupt their competitive performance (e.g., delay in the start time, unfavourable weather conditions, problems with equipment). Again, athletes might refine strategies (e.g., the use and content of pre-competition routines) to help them successfully cope with these problems. Thus, the self-regulation of sport performance involves careful planning and consideration of how to manage these environmental considerations.

The final phase is generalization, which involves maintaining the behavioral change over time and across different situations. This is the long term goal of self-regulation, but can be difficult to achieve because of the variety of competing demands from both internal and external sources. To prevent failure of generalization from occurring, Kirschenbaum

(1984) suggests that athletes need to engage in self-monitoring in a vigilant manner.

Kirschenbaum's (1984, 1987, 1997) model has received some initial support in the sport literature. In a study examining the extent to which swimmers used various components of the model, four of the five components were reported: problem identification, commitment, execution, and environment management (Anshel & Porter, 1995). Moreover, elite swimmers could be distinguished from their non-elite counterparts by their use of self-regulatory processes (Anshel & Porter, 1995, 1996). Using the model as a guide, Kirschenbaum, Owens, and O'Connor (1998) designed a self-regulatory training program entitled Smart Golf for five experienced golfers. The program involved attending four seminars on preparation, positive focusing (self-monitoring), and self-regulation planning principles. The acronym, PAR, was used to summarize these self-regulatory principles: Plan (e.g., plan a shot), Apply (e.g., consistently follow pre-shot routine), and React (e.g., respond constructively to shot). Golfers then applied their newly acquired knowledge by using an adapted score card that allowed them to record not only their performance score for each round, but to self-monitor the different elements of the Smart Golf program. After the intervention, all five golfers demonstrated improvements in their emotional control and positive self-talk, as well as their golf performance. More recently, Kirschenbaum, O'Connor, and Owens (1999) conducted a series of studies to examine whether following a more conservative and realistic planning strategy could effectively counter a golfer's tendency towards being overly optimistic when making shot selections. When golfers were given an opportunity to take a second shot off the tee, those who were provided with a more realistic and conservative plan (Smart Golf condition) tended to hit better shots than those who followed their own inclinations (i.e., those in the control condition).

In sum, Kirschenbaum's five-stage model suggests that self-regulation involves identifying a problem, making a commitment to resolving the problem by changing behavior, actively participating in planned changes, managing environmental concerns, and maintaining the changed behavior over time and generalizing this to other situations. Thus, the model not only accounts for relationships between behaviors, cognitions, emotions, and physiological aspects of training and performance, but also considers the role of environmental variables.

Zimmerman's Self Regulation Learning Model

Zimmerman's model (1986) of self regulation centers on the learning of skills rather than skill performance once proficiency has been realized. According to Zimmerman (1986), self-regulated learning is the degree to which an individual is meta-cognitively, behaviorally, and motivationally involved in his or her own learning process. For self-regulation to be achieved regarding the acquisition of new skills, a learner will progress through four sequential levels: observation, emulation, self-control, and self-regulation.

The first level, observation, involves learning by watching a model. The aim of the modeling experience is to provide the learner with a clear image of the motor skill to be performed; this guides further learning. Kitsantas and Zimmerman (2000) describe modeling as the process through which information is gained by observing another person's actions, hearing the descriptions of the actions, and observing the consequence of those actions. Indeed, modeling is considered to be one of the most powerful means of transmitting information about a specific behavior (Bandura, 1986). During this level, the observer's motivation is enhanced vicariously by rewards attained by the model.

The second level, emulation, consists of both modeling and social feedback. Here, the learner attempts to reproduce the model's performance of the skill, and this is often guided by feedback from an instructor regarding the accuracy of the response (e.g., the coach). This process of imitation or emulation provides the learner with a sense of how the skill feels to perform and allows him/her to internalize standards of correct performance that will be used for self-evaluation in subsequent phases of learning. By conveying information about the learning process, social feedback makes learners better equipped to practice effectively on their own. Furthermore, the social feedback provided, which is assumed to be the primarily source of motivation at this level, has been linked to both higher achievement and motivation to learn. For instance, Kitsantas, Zimmerman, and Cleary (2000) found that social feedback enhanced dart throwing performance and indices of self-motivation (self-efficacy, intrinsic motivation, and satisfaction with performance) among a sample of 60 high school age girls.

The first two phases of Zimmerman's model focus on social learning experiences, which in turn, prepare the learner for attaining higher levels of skills on her or his own in later phases. When the individual moves to the level of self-control, skill performance is now enhanced through self-directed practice until the goal of automaticity is achieved. Within sport, an athlete at the level of self-control no longer relies directly on the model to learn, but instead uses a mental representation of the model's standard of performance. Throughout this phase, the athlete would be expected to continuously compare his or her performance to the standards set by the model. Consequently, the primary source of motivation at this level stems from the self-reactions from having matched or surpassed the model's performance standard.

At the fourth and final level, namely self-regulation, the athlete acquires the ability to adapt performance to changing internal and external conditions. Attention now shifts from modeled processes to performance outcomes, and the skill can be performed without intentional thought. In other words, automatic skill performance has now been achieved. As a result of this shift in attention, Zimmerman and Kitsantas (1996) suggested that learners should be taught to focus on performance goals initially until automaticity has been achieved and then shift to outcome goals. Focusing on outcomes before fundamental process techniques are acquired is thought to impair learning. By contrast, focusing on the process will not only enhance the acquisition of the skill during the earlier phases, but also athletes' self-perceptions of progress, self-efficacy about future success, and intrinsic motivation to continue to mastery. This implication has been tested and supported by Zimmerman and Kitsantas (1997) regarding the acquisition of a dart throwing skill. Their findings also support the notion that two primary sources of motivation during self-regulation are self-efficacy beliefs and intrinsic interest in the motor skill being practiced.

Within this fourth level, Zimmerman and his colleagues (Kitsantas & Zimmerman, 1998; Zimmerman & Kitsantas, 1996, 1997) outlined how self-regulatory processes and these self-motivational processes interact in three cyclical phases: forethought (proceeds practice of a motor skill), performance control (occurs during practice of motor skill), and self-reflection (follows each practice effort). In addition to the goal-setting, self-observation, and self-evaluation processes embedded in models of self-regulation discussed previously in this chapter (Bandura, 1986, 2001; Kirschenbaum, 1984, 1997), the model of Zimmerman and colleagues also incorporates other self-regulatory mechanisms such as planning, use of strategies, attributions (Kitsantas & Zimmerman, 2002), and self-efficacy and self-satisfaction reactions (Cleary & Zimmerman, 2000). Zimmerman and his colleagues described the three cyclical phases in terms of how expert performers can be differentiated from their non-expert counterparts based on their self-regulatory behaviors. They suggest that experts do not necessarily display superior domain-specific knowledge, but instead demonstrate that they are better able to access and use this information to regulate their cognitions, affective responses and actions. Thus, self-regulation strategies become necessary for athletes to achieve high levels of performance.

The forethought phase of self-regulation discusses differences in expert-novice goal-setting and the establishment of plans to accomplish set goals, self-efficacy beliefs, outcome expectancy, and intrinsic motivation. More specifically, experts are predicted to set specific outcome and process goals and to plan how they will accomplish these goals. Moreover, experts are predicted to report higher levels of self-efficacy, outcome expectancy, and intrinsic motivation than their novice-level counterparts. In support of these predictions, Kitsantas and Zimmerman (2002) found that expert female volleyball players set more specific technique and process goals and structured their practice routine more than players at a lower performance standard. Furthermore, the expert players reported higher levels of self-efficacy, and more interest in the intrinsic properties of the task as well as the perceived instrumentality of perfecting the overhand volley serve.

During the performance control phase, expert performers are predicted to use more self-control (e.g., self-instruction, imagery, attention focusing, and task-specific strategies) and self-monitoring (i.e., deliberate tracking of one's behavior) strategies than novices. Kitsantas and Zimmerman (2002) again found support for these predictions by finding that expert female volleyball players used more specific technique strategies and reported monitoring their technique and service outcomes than was the case for less elite peers.

During the last phase, self-reflection, experts are predicted to self-evaluate, attribute causation, experience satisfaction, and adapt their performance in a systematic fashion. When compared to their less skilled counterparts, the expert volleyball players in Kitsantas and Zimmerman's (2002) study were more likely to self-reflect on their serving performance by engaging in evaluation processes, attributing failures to problems with technique, and then making subsequent changes to correct these deficiencies.

It has been pointed out that the literature on self regulation in the physical domain is far from systematic and consistent theoretically and/or methodologically (Behncke, 2004; Crews et al., 2001). The observed lack of consensus regarding the "definitions, methods, and procedures of self-monitoring" in sport psychology work has been particularly noted (Behncke, 2004). With that said, there are at least three bonafide, supported frameworks regarding self-regulatory mechanisms that stem from a social cognitive perspective (Bandura, 1986, 1997; Kirschenbaum, 1984, 1987; Zimmerman, 1986, 1989, 1994) and have laid the groundwork for sport psychology research and practice. Indeed, all three models of self regulation reviewed in this chapter provide insight into the learning and performance of sport skills and the maintenance of engagement in the task or activity at hand. Moreover, a closer look may indicate that these theoretical perspectives may be "more alike than they are divergent" (Crews et al., 2001, p. 567) in the key self-regulatory mechanisms emphasized. Under the "umbrella" of what is termed self-regulation (sometimes denoted by differing terminology) the literature keeps pointing to the relevance of the setting of self performance standards or personal goals, self-monitoring, self-evaluation of performance, self-efficacy, and self-satisfaction. Obviously, the central word here is self.

An intriguing question revolves around whether this emphasis on the self, that is integral to self-regulation, is functional or dysfunctional in terms of learning, performance, perseverance, and the overall quality of the experience. In the next section, we turn to two contemporary social cognitive models of motivation (namely self determination theory and the achievement goal frameworks) that have laid the basis for a plethora of studies in sport and other achievement settings. It is suggested that these two models provide considerable insight into the antecedents and nature of adaptive self-regulation.

Social Cognitive Theories of Motivation

Over the past several decades, social cognitive theories of motivation have dominated research efforts in sport psychology (Roberts, 1992, 2001). According to Roberts (1992, p. vii), the social cognitive perspective assumes that "motivation and achievement are manifestations of cognitions ... within dynamic social contexts; and it is these ... thought processes that govern motivated action." Two social cognitive frameworks that have been particularly popular in recent years are the achievement goal (AGT) (Dweck, 1999; Nicholls, 1989) and self-determination (SDT) (Deci & Ryan, 2001) theories of motivation. Both distinguish between the meaning and function of different goals of action and focus on how differential motivational processes and outcomes emanate from these goals. Besides fostering our understanding of achievement patterns, AGT and SDT also shed light on the mechanisms contributing to the development of the self and the promotion of quality involvement in activities (Deci & Ryan, 2000; Dweck, 1999; Nicholls, 1989). The major tenets and constructs of each framework will be briefly described here.

Self Determination Theory

Self-determination theory (SDT; Deci & Ryan, 1985; Ryan & Deci, 2000a, 2000b) addresses the degree to which behavior is deemed to be fueled by a sense of an individual's choice and personal volition. An essential assumption of SDT is that people are active organisms, with innate tendencies toward personal growth, optimal engagement, and efficacious interactions with the environment. SDT distinguishes between reasons that regulate action, namely intrinsic motivation, extrinsic motivation, and amotivation.

Intrinsic motivation represents the exemplar self-determined regulation because an intrinsically motivated athlete will participate due to feelings of enjoyment, interest, and satisfaction that are inherent in the activity (Deci & Ryan, 1985; Ryan & Deci, 2000a). In contrast, when extrinsically motivated, behavior is regulated by consequences that are separate from the activity per se and the activity in question is not deemed to be inherently rewarding in and of itself.

Deci and Ryan (1985; Ryan & Deci, 2002) have proposed that extrinsic motivation is not always controlling, but can also be self-endorsed (i.e., a personally-controlled motivational regulation directed toward attaining a desired consequence). Specifically, self-determination theory considers several distinct types of extrinsic motivation that vary in their degree of self-determination from low to high respectively, such as external regulation, introjected regulation, and identified regulation. External regulation refers to behaviors that are engaged in for extrinsic, instrumental reasons (e.g., to gain an external reward and/or to avoid punishment). Introjected regulation represents a form of extrinsic motivation which is characterized by the individual internalizing external regulations (Ryan & Deci, 2002). With introjected regulation, the impetus for action stems from self-imposed sanctions (i.e., shame, self-guilt, ego enhancement, pride) as opposed to some overt extrinsic contingencies. Although the "driving force" in introjected regulation is internal to the individual, his/her actions are not experienced as fully part of the self as the person is still governed by an external locus of causality (Ryan & Deci, 2000b). Reflecting greater self-determination, identified regulation refers to behaviors that are regulated by a conscious valuing of an activity in accordance with one's personal goals (Ryan & Deci, 2000a). However, although the actions are willingly performed in this case, they are not enjoyed for their own sake. Rather, activity engagement is deemed to be instrumental and aimed at achieving some personally valued outcome(s).

Amotivation is witnessed when individuals engage passively in activities without any sense of intention (Ryan & Deci, 2000a, 2000b, 2002). Such a motivational condition is assumed to occur when people feel incompetent and/or do not perceive any contingencies (internal or external) between their actions and desired outcome(s) (Ryan & Deci, 2000a, 2000b).

Deci and Ryan (1985, 2000) have proposed that intrinsic motivation and certain forms of extrinsic motivation (primarily identified regulation and, in some rare cases, introjected regulation) enhance motivational processes and psychological functioning (e.g., task absorption), and thus lead to positive motivational outcomes. On the other hand, it is proposed that motivational types low in self-determination (e.g., external regulation and amotivation) correspond to maladaptive cognitive, affective, and behavioral responses (e.g., greater anxiety, lack of persistence). Recent research in the physical domain has supported these propositions (e.g., Ntoumanis, 2001; Standage, Duda, & Ntoumanis, 2003; Vallerand, 2001).

True to its social cognitive underpinnings, SDT (Deci & Ryan, 1985) considers the potential influence of environmental factors on motivational processes. Characteristics of the social environment, such as its structure (or the degree to which clear expectations are conveyed, encouragement and informative feedback are provided) and particularly its autonomy-supportive features [i.e., the degree to which choice is given, extrinsic contingencies are minimized, and the perspectives, values and goals of the individual are considered by the significant other(s)] are assumed to contribute to greater self-determination. The impact of the social context on individuals' motivational regulations in that setting is held to operate via the environment's satisfaction of three basic psychological needs, namely people's needs to feel competent, autonomous, and connected to others in a meaningful way (Deci & Ryan, 2000; Ryan & Deci, 2000b).

Achievement Goal Theory

In contemporary achievement goal frameworks (e.g., Dweck, 1999; Elliot, 1999; Nicholls, 1984, 1989), it is assumed that the meaning of one's investment in achievement activities such as sport is colored by the achievement goals endorsed. These goals capture the criteria underlying subjective success (and failure) and influence how individuals interpret and cognitively, affectively, and behaviorally respond to achievement endeavors.

According to Nicholls (1984, 1989), there are at

least two major achievement goals operating, namely a task (or mastery) and ego (or performance) goal, which stem from how competence is construed. When task-involved, one's perceived level of competence is self-referenced and dependent on the individual's own demonstration of learning, performance improvement, exerted effort, and/or task mastery. If ego-involved, one feels competent and thereby successful if comparatively superior ability is demonstrated. That is, perceptions of competence are other-referenced when ego goals prevail.

With respect to achievement processes and behavioral patterns, AGT (Dweck, 1999; Nicholls, 1984) holds that it is not only the level of perceived competence (or self efficacy) that is pertinent to goal striving and resulting learning/performance, but also how such competence is judged. More specifically, it is proposed that a task goal focus will result in optimal learning and sustained performance as well as greater perseverance, regardless of whether the performer perceives his or her competence to be high or low (Dweck, 1999; Nicholls, 1984). This is because it is assumed that task involvement will translate into more concentrated effort and intrinsic interest in the activity, and a greater utilization of effective strategies to meet task demands. When task-involved, the individual's main concern is to "get the job done" and witness improvement if possible.

AGT (Dweck, 1999; Nicholls, 1984, 1989) holds that if perceived competence is high, an ego goal focus will also result in learning and good performance. In such circumstances, the ego-involved individual can display the superior competence that he or she desires and positive task engagement therefore should not be disrupted. However, in states of ego involvement in which questions about the adequacy of one's competence abound, learning difficulties and performance impairment are expected. The demonstration of superiority and, indeed one's sense of self, are threatened in this case and heightened anxiety, the occurrence of task-irrelevant thoughts, and the rescinding of effort are some likely consequences.

Achievement goal frameworks (Ames, 1992; Dweck, 1986, 1999; Nicholls, 1989) hold that individual differences and situational factors come into play with respect to the frequency and intensity of task and ego involvement manifested in achievement settings. Nicholls (1989) especially points to the significance of dispositional goal orientations. That is, individuals tend to vary with respect to their degree of task and ego orientation and these two dispositional goals tend to be orthogonal (Duda & Whitehead, 1998). Ames (1992) speaks to the role of the perceived motivational climate created by significant others in impacting observed differential emphases on task and/or ego achievement goals. More specifically, the social psychological environments created by coaches, teachers, parents, peers, etc., can be viewed as being more or less task- and/or ego-involving.

An extensive literature has examined the correlates and effects of dispositional and situational task and ego achievement goals in sport settings (see Biddle, Wang, Kavussanu, & Spray, 2003; Duda, 2001, in press; Duda & Hall, 2001; Roberts, 2001; Treasure, 2001, for reviews). All in all, this research provides evidence regarding the motivational advantages of a strong task goal emphasis, from the standpoint of dispositional tendencies or the motivational climate deemed to be operating.

With respect to the potential debilitating implications of an ego goal emphasis, the literature in the sport (Duda, 2001) and educational (Harackiewicz, Baron, Pintrich, Elliot, & Thrash, 2002) domain is equivocal. Without incorporating perceptions of competence (and usually in the short-term; Duda, 2001), ego orientation has been found to positively relate to, not correspond, or be negatively associated with achievement-related cognitions and behaviors. Moreover, any theoretically predicted negative achievement-related correlate of ego orientation tends to be suppressed when coupled with a high task orientation.

With an eye toward reconciling the observed ambiguities regarding the motivational implications of a strong ego orientation, Elliot (1999; Elliot & Church, 1997) has argued for an extension of the task/ego goal dichotomy epitomized in the work of Dweck (1999) and Nicholls (1989) by considering an approach and avoidance dimension of ego or performance goals. When focused on an ego approach goal, the individual desires to demonstrate high normatively-referenced ability. If centered on an ego avoidance goal, the concern is with avoiding the demonstration of low normatively-referenced competence. In this trichotomous framework (Elliot,

1999), perceived competence (typically defined as performance expectations) is held to be an antecedent of whether an approach (high perceived ability) or avoidance (low perceived ability) goal is adopted. Initial sport work grounded in this three goal conceptualization has been aligned with theoretical predictions (e.g., Cury, Da Fonseca, Rufo, Peres, & Sarrazin, 2003; Cury, Elliot, Sarrazin, Da Fonseca, & Rufo, 2002).

More recently, Elliot has assimilated the definition [i.e., centered on absolute/intrapersonal (task) or normative (ego) criteria] and valence (i.e., oriented toward the possibility of demonstrating high competence or avoiding the demonstration of low competence) aspects of goals to form a 2 x 2 achievement goal model (Elliot & McGregor, 2001). With respect to goal constructs, the major extension in the 2 x 2 framework is the consideration of what is termed a mastery (or task) avoidance goal perspective. In this case, the individual strives to avoid absolute and/or self-referenced incompetence. Sport research on the 2x2 model is in its infancy but results to date have been consonant with this multi-goal framework (Conroy, Elliot, & Hofer, 2003; Nien & Duda, 2004)

As goal setting processes (Bandura & Locke, 2003) are endemic to the models of self regulation reviewed above, it is important to note that there are important distinctions between discrete goals that one may set and achievement goals (whether approach or avoidance-oriented, self- or normatively-referenced) as conceptualized within AGT (see Duda, 2004, for further discussion of this point). Discrete goals are typically distinguished with respect to their process, performance, or outcome focus when linked to behavior (e.g., Kingston & Hardy, 1997) but this does not mean that their nature or function are the same as achievement goals (Duda, 2001). Hall and Kerr (2001) have pointed out that discrete goals regulate behavior by specifying the end state or objective standard of performance that one is trying to achieve at a particular task. They don't tell the performer how to get to this level of performance, how to decide whether he or she has demonstrated competence in so doing, and what it means to the performer if he or she does or does not reach the performance standard in question. In contrast, and as was the case with self determination, a consideration of the achievement goals emphasized is relevant to

the likelihood of self-regulation occurring during task engagement and the nature of the self-regulatory processes manifested.

SDT and AGT: Some Empirical and Conceptual Links

It probably is obvious to the reader that there are a number of commonalities between the self determination (Deci & Ryan, 1985, 2000) and achievement goal (Dweck, 1989; Elliot, 1999; Nicholls, 1989) frameworks. As indicated previously, both are social cognitive in perspective and center on variations in the meaning of behavior. Moreover, they hold that such differences in meaning have important ramifications for the quantity and quality of motivation. The tenets of and empirical findings associated with SDT and AGT also advocate the benefits of adopting more personally controllable, task-centered, and self-referenced approaches to task engagement. Not surprisingly then, previous research in educational and athletic settings has found task orientation/ mastery approach goals and perceptions of a task-involving climate to correspond to greater intrinsic motivation and other more self determined regulations (e.g., Nien & Duda, 2004; Elliot & Church, 1997; Kavussanu & Roberts, 1996; Smith, Duda, Allen, & Hall, 2002). Ego orientation/performance approach goals and perceptions of an ego-involving climate are positively associated with extrinsic motivation. Avoidance goals (both task/mastery and ego/performance) have been found to relate to amotivation in the classroom and sport (Nien & Duda, 2004; Smith et al., 2002).

Also embedded in both SDT (Deci & Ryan, 1985, 2000) and AGT (Dweck, 1999; Nicholls, 1984, 1989) is the assumption that variations in the meaning of achievement activities and ensuing motivational processes reflect aspects of and concerns about the self. When participating in an activity, an individual can be preoccupied with how one does in the activity in terms of what that performance will reveal (to the person himself/herself and others) about the self or more centered on self development via task engagement. The latter perspective, which is aligned with greater self determination and task involvement, should contribute to greater task absorption. The former approach, which reflects a more ego-involved and controlled type of engagement, seems amenable to heightened self absorption and more likely to result in the person taking his or her mind off of the task to be completed.

Self Regulatory Mechanisms, Self Determination, and Task Involvement

From a conceptual perspective, there are logical interdependencies between task involvement, self-determined regulations for behavior, and self regulatory mechanisms. According to SDT (Deci & Ryan, 1985, 2000), when intrinsically motivated or more self-determined, people tend to act out of personal choice and the rewards offered via participation are primarily experiential. They are more likely to be absorbed by the task, optimally challenged, and "in the moment," and less likely to feel pressured with respect to their engagement. That is, when self-determined, individuals are less likely to be driven by or concerned about things or people external to the task. Rather, they are motivated by the personal satisfaction of task completion and the inherent joy and captivation of the process "of doing" in and of itself. In essence, they are more likely to truly self-reward (Kirschenbaum, 1984, 1987) rather than look toward reinforcement outside the task. As a result, self determination is assumed to "naturally" lead to self-regulation and those self-regulatory processes should be more conducive to optimal learning and performance (Ryan & Deci, 2000c).

It makes sense to suspect that there would be a conceptually consonant congruence between achievement goals and self regulation as well. According to AGT (Dweck, 1999; Kaplan & Maehr, 1999; Nicholls, 1989), achievement goals are the organizing principle that guides subsequent action and provides the criteria underlying and processes by which we self-evaluate. Achievement goals would therefore be expected to play a role in the discrete performance standards that we strive to reach. When we desire task feedback and/or look to models for task-related information, achievement goals should influence the type of feedback we want and information we take from watching others perform. They also should impact what we self-monitor and how much we are concerned about proving (or protecting) self worth rather than improving and mastering the task at hand when we monitor task performance. As addressed in an earlier section of this chapter, goal

setting (Bandura & Jourden, 2003), observation (Kitsantas & Zimmerman, 2000), self-evaluation (Bandura & Locke, 2003) and self-monitoring (Behncke, 2004) are all fundamental self-regulatory processes. Achievement goals, therefore, are assumed to have a bearing on the discrete goals set and other such facets of self-regulation or goal striving mechanisms (Lee et al., 2003).

Beyond these conceptual linkages, the empirical literature to date reinforces the presumed correspondence between task involvement, self determination, and self regulation. For example, in the academic context, task or mastery goals have been found to correspond to deeper cognitive processing while the emphasis placed on ego or performance goals has been linked to more surface processing and lower levels of cognitive engagement (Ford, Smith, Weissbein, Gully, & Salas, 1998; Meece, Blumenfeld, & Hoyle, 1988; Nolen, 1988; Pintrich, 2000). In a recent study, Wolters (2004) found that mathematics students' mastery/task goal orientation and their perceptions of a mastery or task goal structure operating in their classroom to be positive predictors of their use of cognitive and meta-cognitive self-regulation learning strategies, persistence, task choice, and mathematics grade. Ablard and Lipschultz (1998) examined the associations between self-regulated learning and achievement goals among high-achieving students. Aligned with the perspective of Zimmerman (1986), Ablard and Lipschultz (1998, p. 94) defined self-regulated learners as individuals who "engage in ... tasks for personal interest and satisfaction and are metacognitively and behaviorally active participants in their own learning." Consistent with previous research and theoretical predictions, task or mastery goals emerged as a positive predictor of self-regulated learning strategies. Ego or performance (approach) goals related positively to SRL use, but only when coupled with a strong task orientation.

Research in the physical domain has indicated that variations in achievement goals and beliefs correspond to differential patterns of cognitive engagement and strategy use (Lochbaum & Roberts, 1993; Roberts & Ommundsen, 1996). A task orientation (or perceptions of a task-involving climate) has been found to positively predict task interest and satisfaction (e.g., Roberts, Treasure, & Kavussanu, 1996) and performance and skill development (e.g., Solmon &

Boone, 1993; Van Yperen & Duda, 1999) in sport settings. A task goal emphasis has been positively associated with reported attentional focus during skill execution (e.g., Papaioannou & Kouli, 1999) while an ego orientation coupled with low perceived ability and/or low task orientation has been linked to greater task-irrelevant and self-preoccupied thinking (e.g., Hatzigeorgeadis & Biddle, 1999; White, 1998). Thill and Brunel (1995) found task orientation to correspond to a greater use of deep processing strategies while ego orientation positively related to the reported employment of superficial strategies in sport.

In the physical education setting, Ommundsen (2003) examined the interplay between students' theories of ability and reported self-regulation strategies (e.g., planning, self monitoring, effort regulation, adaptive help seeking). The belief that one's physical ability level is changeable via effort and learning (which links to a task or mastery goal orientation) corresponded to greater employment of SR strategies. In contrast, the belief that ability levels are stable (which is associated with an ego or performance goal orientation) was negatively associated with self-regulation strategy use.

In a motivationally more comprehensive study that considered variations in self regulation within the educational domain and was grounded in both AGT (Dweck, 1999; Elliot, 1999; Nicholls, 1989) and SDT (Deci & Ryan, 1985; Ryan & Deci, 2000a, 2000b), Lee et al. (2003) examined the relationships between SDT-related individual differences (i.e., personal orientations toward autonomy, control, and amotivation), achievement goals (i.e., task/mastery, ego or performance approach, and ego or performance avoidance), goal striving processes (i.e., goal setting, attentional focus/task absorption), and enjoyment and performance (GPA) throughout a semester among university students. Consistent with the position advocated in this chapter, Lee et al. (2003) conceptualized achievement goals as "involving domain-specific self-regulation patterns" (p. 258). The results revealed autonomy orientation to positively predict mastery/task goals. Control orientation predicted both ego approach and ego avoidance goals. Amotivated orientation corresponded positively to the emphasis placed on ego or performance-avoidance goals. Mastery/task goals corresponded

directly to enjoyment while mastery/task and performance approach goals were linked indirectly to performance via attentional focus/task absorption. Performance-avoidance goals were negatively linked to attentional focus/task absorption and the setting of difficult goals. Taken in their totality, this study indicated that facets of self regulatory processes (as reflected in the students' achievement goals, goal difficulty, and reported attentional focus/task absorption) mediated the relationship of more global personality characteristics regarding self determination to achievement and affect. It would be interesting and important to try and replicate the Lee et al. (2003) study in the case of an athletic sample.

Besides such investigations relating motivational factors to self regulation and task engagement in sport and the classroom, sport research has revealed a link between motivational processes and the employment of psychological skills among athletes. For example, Cumming, Harwood, and colleagues (Cumming, Hall, Harwood, & Gammage, 2002; Harwood, Cumming, & Hall, 2003) investigated the role of achievement goals to young athletes' behavioral investments into imagery use. Cumming et al. (2002) argued that athletes with low levels of task and ego orientation would invest less time engaging in imagery. By contrast, individuals with higher levels of task orientation would maximize their opportunities for personal mastery by engaging in cognitive specific imagery (i.e., images of skill development and execution), cognitive general imagery (i.e., images of strategy development and execution), and motivational general-mastery imagery (i.e., images of being confident, focused, and mentally tough). Moreover, individuals who possess a higher ego orientation would likely engage in motivational specific imagery (i.e., images of outcome goals). Thus, athletes with higher levels of both task and ego orientation were predicted to engage in greater amounts of imagery use, with actual imagery content varying as a function of goal orientation (Harwood et al., 2002).

In the first study, Cumming et al. (2002) found that Canadian provincial level swimmers (N = 105) with a moderate task/higher ego goal profile reported a greater use of motivational specific imagery and motivational general-mastery imagery. To lend cross-cultural support to these previous findings, a second study involving an elite British youth sample (N = 290) was conducted (Harwood et al., 2003). Again, athletes with varying combinations of task and ego orientations could be distinguished by their imagery use. More specifically, athletes with a higher task/higher ego profile reported a significantly greater use of all types of imagery than did athletes with either a lower task/moderate ego profile or a moderate task/lower ego profile.

In a recent study, Harwood, Cumming, and Fletcher (2004) investigated the link between achievement goal orientations and a wider range of psychological skills, including the use of goal-setting, relaxation, self-talk, and imagery among 573 elite young athletes. Athletes with a higher task/moderate ego profile reported using significantly more imagery, goal-setting, and positive self-talk that athletes with either a lower task/higher ego or moderate task/lower ego profile.

Furthering Applied Work on PST, Self Regulation, and Motivational Processes

The proceeding discussions suggest that there are theoretical and empirical links between motivational processes, as addressed via the achievement goal and self determination frameworks, and self regulation. We also emphasize that cognitive behavioral psychological skills training (PST) is best conceptualized as a multi-faceted and multi-method process that contributes to self regulation and thus should have motivational consequences (if not also motivational determinants!). In terms of this second issue, we suggest that a limitation in the PST literature is that we rarely see theoretically-grounded motivation variables and self-regulatory processes examined as potential outcome measures.

One notable exception is the work of Beauchamp, Halliwell, Fournier, and Koestner (1996). Beauchamp and colleagues determined the effect of a 14-week cognitive-behavioral program (Boutcher & Rotella, 1987) on the pre-shot preparation (an aspect of self regulation), putting performance, and motivational regulations of novice golfers. This program consisted of the teaching and learning of pre-performance routines as well as training in stress management and relaxation, concentration, positive thought control, and imagery. Skills, knowledge, and aspects of the putting stroke were taught and the golfers instructed and encouraged to assess their strengths and weaknesses in the various psychological skills plus their ability to effectively self monitor. Goal setting was introduced in the motivational phase of program. Finally, the program emphasized the integration of the mental skills use, evaluation, and self-monitoring routine. The golfers in this cognitive-behavioral program were contrasted with a physical skills training only group and control group. Measures were taken at baseline and then every three weeks until the conclusion of the program. With respect to potential changes in motivational regulations, Beauchamp et al. (1996) focused on variations in intrinsic motivation and introjected regulation and expected the cognitive-behavioral program to enhance the former and lead to decreases in the latter (because the intervention should foster perceptions of competence and personal control, and diminish the focus on extrinsic contingencies in terms of the skill at hand). In contrast to the other two groups, novice golfers in the cognitive-behavioral condition exhibited greater IM, superior putting performance, and more consistent use of their pre-putt routines (an aspect of self regulation). These golfers were also significantly lower in introjected motivation.

In an interesting and innovative study, Greens-Demers et al. (1998) examined the use and motivational implications of "interest-enhancing strategies" (IESs) in the case of recreational and competitive figure skaters. This investigation did not entail an intervention per se but rather centered on the strategies spontaneously used by figure skaters to counter periods of boredom and enhance motivation. The four IESs that emerged were "creating challenges for oneself, adding variety to the task, providing oneself with self-relevant rationales for performing the task, and exploiting stimulation from other sources than the task itself" (e.g. daydreams, watching other people such as spectators) (Green-Demers et al., 1998, p. 251). The first three of these IESs were considered to reflect adaptive self-regulatory strategies. The frequency of use of each of the IESs was examined in terms of what the skaters deemed to be interesting tasks versus less interesting tasks. The creation of challenge, addition of variety, and provision of self-relevant rationales all positively related to higher interest during engagement in tasks that were more or less interesting. Such interest corresponded to greater self-determined motivation (intrinsic motivation in the case of interesting activities and self-determined extrinsic motivation in the case of less interesting activities). The use of stimulation from other sources to foster interest, which Green-Demers et al. (1998) reported to be a maladaptive self-regulatory strategy, was negatively linked to self-determined external regulations when engaged in less interesting activities. Finally, the degree to which the skaters reported self-determined extrinsic motivation when engaged in boring tasks positively predicted their level of intrinsic motivation when doing interesting skating tasks. In discussing these findings, Green-Demers et al. (1998) argue that, when trying to alter interest and motivation, the tendency (in research and practice) has been to focus on the impact of social environmental factors. In contrast, their research highlights the significance of targeting "self-influence" strategies which are really self-regulatory processes tied to interest and motivation enhancement.

A Proposed Integrative Model

Figure 1 provides a schematic of the proposed interplay between environmental and personality factors, motivational regulations and achievement goal orientations, cognitive-behavioral based psychological skills training, self-regulation mechanisms, and intervention outcomes. Pulling from the tenets of self determination theory (Deci & Ryan, 1985; Ryan & Deci, 2000c) and achievement goal frameworks (Ames, 1992; Elliot, 1999; Nicholls, 1989), this model indicates that characteristics of the social psychological environment and motivation-related personality factors can serve as antecedents to differences in motivational regulations and dispositional achievement goals and reflects the inter-relationship between these two facets of motivation. It also suggests that whether an athlete is more or less self-determined and oriented toward task and/or ego approach and/or avoidance goals will correspond to the likelihood of his/her engagement in psychological skills training. In this model, variability in athletes' motivational regulations and goal orientation will also influence the nature of the goal striving processes manifested during training and competition. The proposed interdependence between PST and self regulation is included in the model. Finally, Figure 1 reinforces the point that indices of the quality and quantity of

motivation should be incorporated when we examine the impact of PST and self regulatory skill interventions among athletic populations.

The testing of the proposed links embedded in Figure 1 will not be without challenges in the athletic milieu. With respect to the motivation-related constructs, valid and reliable assessments pertinent to the sport setting exist to capture dispositional differences and prevailing social environmental factors (e.g., see Duda & Whitehead, 1998; Vallerand, 2001; Vallerand & Fortier, 1998). At the situational or state level (Vallerand, 2001), measures of motivational regulations in sport-related settings exist (Standage, Treasure, Duda, & Prusak, 2003; Vallerand & Fortier, 1998). However, there are no established and agreed upon assessments of achievement goal states (Duda, 2001; Duda & Whitehead, 1998; Treasure, Duda, Hall, Roberts, Ames, & Maehr, 2002).

As pointed out by Crews and associates (2001), the measurement of cognitive and affective self regulatory mechanisms (e.g., ability to self-monitor) "has a long way to go." In classroom work, the tools of choice have been the Self-regulated Learning Interview (Zimmerman & Martinez-Pons, 1986) or the Motivated Strategies for Learning Questionnaire (MSLQ; Pintrich, Smith, Garcia, & McKeachie, 1993) and these measures have been adapted for use in the physical domain (e.g., Ommundsen, 2003). However, we are lacking consensus and theoretical grounding concerning which aspects of self regulation should be assessed as well as evidence regarding the validity and reliability of available assessments in sport settings. Moreover, we are faced with a measurement challenge when facets of self regulation become so well-learned and integrated into task engagement that they have become autonomatic. That is, how do we go about measuring unconscious self regulatory processes (Crews et al., 2001)?

Finally, in terms of PST, existing assessments of psychological skills have been criticized (Murphy & Tammen, 1998; Vealey & Garner-Holman, 1998). Specifically, these measures are often atheoretical and plagued by questionable psychometric properties. Moreover, there is no clear and consistent recognition of the relevant domain regarding psychological skills (Murphy & Tammen, 1998). Vealey and Garner-Holman (1998) emphasize the need for valid and reliable measures targeting professional practice

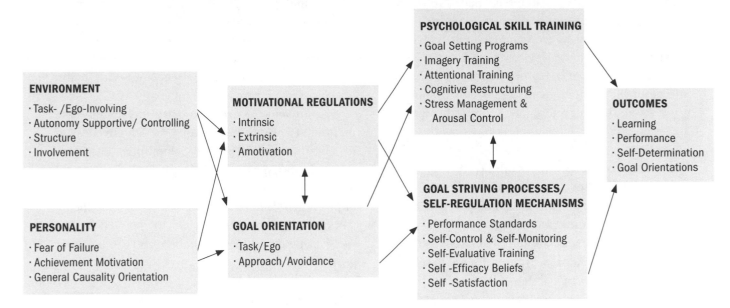

Figure 1: Proposed Model of the Inter-relationships Between Motivational Regulations, Goal Orientations, Psychological Skills Training, and Self-Regulation Mechanisms

in sport psychology and suggest that nomothetic research-based tools as well as idiographic assessments designed for individual applied work are warranted. Whether tapping psychological skills or self regulatory and motivational processes for that matter (Duda, 2001), it is not appropriate to readily use nomothetic, interpersonal measures to assess idiosyncratic, intra-individual responses.

Additional Directions to Consider

In terms of the diversity of methods, perspectives, and lines of inquiry evident in applied sport psychology, there are a multitude of directions that could be taken in the design and evaluation of PST interventions based on the model presented in Figure 1. We provide three possibilities below.

Self-Regulation of Emotional States

Drawing from Hanin's IZOF model (Hanin & Syrja, 1995), one interesting line of research and related applied work in sport psychology has revolved around identifying and then modifying emotional states that are associated with desired versus undesirable performances. Robazza, Pellizzari, and Hanin (2004) examined the effect of multi-modal and individualized self-regulation strategies upon emotions and bodily symptoms (+ and -, functional and dys-

functional) of eight male high level Italian athletes. The athletes were asked to recall the emotions and body symptoms associated with their best and worst performances and then identify the spontaneous, idiosyncratic psychological preparation and self-regulation strategies utilized especially during best performances (e.g., goal setting, imagery use, self-talk). The athletes were then taught to self-monitor emotions experienced in competitions across a competitive season, and develop and refine their own self-regulation program. These self-regulation procedures built on what the athletes were doing that had been effective and included specific strategies (use of routines, goal setting, self assessment, focusing, and relaxation techniques) that contributed to enhanced facilitative and decreased dysfunctional emotions and body symptoms. Robazza and colleagues (2004) reported that the observed patterns of emotions and symptoms, with-treatment when compared to pre-treatment, became more consistent with the patterns associated with best performances. Such change was associated with the athletes' ratings of their performance.

Besides assessing objective performance and other achievement-related responses of the athletes in the Robazza et al. (2004) study, measuring specific self regulatory processes (e.g., did the athletes improve in their ability to self-monitor which then contributed to greater regulation of their emotions and body symptoms?) would have added to the picture regarding the impact of the intervention on self regulation. Further, as we would expect such an intervention to have some motivational implications, did post-program athletes become more self-determined in the regulations underlying their sport enjoyment and/or self-referenced in how they tend to define success and judge their competence?

An Acceptance Model of PST

As alluded to above, the cognitive-behavioral approach has been the predominant perspective adopted in North American applied sport psychology. Recently, Gardner and Moore (2004) have proposed a Mindfulness-Acceptance-Commitment-Based Approach to performance enhancement in sport. This perspective challenges more traditional cognitive-behavioral skills programs that center on developing athletes' self-control (by eliminating or replacing) negative thoughts and emotions; e.g., via negative thought stopping, cognitive restructuring, stress management. It is assumed that suppression of negative thoughts and feelings can actually have a paradoxical effect, leading to an increase in primarily unwanted cognitive activity, unproductive emotional reactions, and the production of a task-irrelevant focus rather than an ideal performance state. Such a proposition is consistent with Hanin's position that positive and negative thoughts and feelings can facilitate or debilitate performance, depending on their intensity and meaning to the athlete (Hanin & Syrja, 1995). The advocated "alternative or supplemental" approach, in contrast, emphasizes "acceptance, rather than direct change, suppression, or control of cognitive and affective experiences" and physical sensations (Gardner & Moore, 2004, p. 707). Specifically, the Mindfulness-Acceptance-Commitment-Based model holds "optimal self regulation requires minimal self-judgment, minimal vigilance to external or internal threat, and minimal worry (i.e., scanning for threat) about possible performance consequences and ramifications". Athletes, in this manner, are taught to be mindful of the present, their overall purpose/goal, and less judgmental about how the situation is going at a particular moment of time. Rather, it is explained that tolerating negative psychological and behavioral states is a reflection of the athletes' commitment to

more distal goals. Further, the training aims to assist athletes in becoming more aware of the contingency between external cues and personal "contextually appropriate responses" that have been beneficial with respect to obtaining valued outcomes. In essence, they are taught to self-regulate with the aim of achieving a future important goal.

Gardner and Moore (2004) have presented some preliminary evidence regarding the effectiveness of the Mindfulness-Acceptance-Commitment-Based Approach in the sport setting. It would be most intriguing if subsequent work stemming from this model of performance enhancement could examine the effect of such an intervention on athletes' self regulatory capacities, self determination, and achievement goals.

Motivation, Self Regulation, and Well-Being

An appealing feature of AGT and SDT is that these frameworks aim to provide insight not only into achievement-related patterns but also the interplay between motivation and the optimal functioning and welfare of the individual in various contexts (Duda, 2001; Ryan & Deci, 2000a). Previous research in sport and educational settings has supported a link between achievement goals and well-being (e.g., Elliot, Sheldon, & Church, 1997; Kaplan & Maehr, 1999; Reinboth & Duda, 2004). In particular, a task goal focus has been positively associated with indices of psychological and physical health. The literature also has revealed a positive relationship between self-determination and well-being (e.g., Levesque, Blais, & Hess, 2004; Reinboth et al., 2004; Standage, Pensgaard, & Duda, in press).

Wrosch, Scheier, Miller, Schulz, and Carver (2003) have provided evidence for the interdependence between adaptive self regulation (as reflected in the capacity to disengage from unattainable goals and then reengage regarding more appropriate goals) and subjective well-being. A recent study by Ratelle, Vallerand, Chantal, and Provencher (2004) also suggests that self regulation processes are pertinent to mental health (in this instance, defined as low anxiety and reduced depressive symptoms).

Thus, another provocative and potentially potent direction for future PST work with athletes centers on considering health-related outcomes in our applied work. That is, might the fostering of psychological skills and self regulation not only impact the motivation and achievement of athletes but also the quality of the sport experience and their physical and mental welfare?

Conclusion

In the proceeding sections, we have attempted to illustrate that there are commonalities in the social cognitive-based sport psychology literature regarding key self-regulatory mechanisms. We have also tried to make the case that variations in motivation are relevant to whether self regulation is more or less likely to occur and the degree to which this self regulation is adaptive or optimally functional. Indeed, it was proposed that the motivational states of intrinsic motivation/self determination and task involvement underpin or can be considered reflective of positive self regulatory processes.

In this chapter, we have suggested that the training aspect of the preponderance of cognitive-behavioral psychological skills techniques and strategies in sport psychology concerns the fostering of self regulatory skills and capacities among athletes. As such, the major aim of this contribution was to encourage the assessment of self-regulation mechanisms (or goal striving processes; Lee et al., 2003) as well as relevant motivation-related variables (in particular, the athletes' motivational regulations and goal orientations) along with other behavioral, cognitive, and affective learning/performance-related outcomes when we assess the effectiveness of such interventions. With these proposals in mind, there is a lot of exciting and hopefully influential applied work to do in sport psychology centered on performance enhancement as well as the enrichment of athletes' sport experiences. Such efforts would reinforce what should be a natural interdependence between theory and practice and bridge areas of work in the field that are too often kept separated.

References

Ablard, K. E., & Lipschultz, R. E. (1998). Self-regulated learning in high-achieving students: Relations to advanced reasoning, achievement goals, and gender. *Journal of Educational Psychology, 90,* 94-101.

Ames, C. (1992). Classrooms, goal structures, and student motivation. *Journal of Educational Psychology, 84,* 261-274.

Anshel, M. H., & Porter, A. (1995). Self-regulatory characteris-

tics of competitive swimmers as a function of skill level and gender. *Journal of Sport Behavior, 19,* 91-110.

Anshel, M. H., & Porter, A. (1996). Efficacy of a model for examining self-regulation with elite and non-elite male and female competitive swimmers. International *Journal of Sport Psychology, 27,* 321-336.

Bandura, A. (1986). *Social foundation of thought and action: A social cognitive theory.* Englewood Cliffs, NJ: Prentice-Hall.

Bandura, A. (1991). Self-regulation of motivation through anticipatory and self-regulatory mechanisms. In R. A. Dienstbier (Ed.), *Perspectives on motivation: Nebraska Symposium on Motivation* (Vol.38, pp.69-164). Lincoln: University of Nebraska Press.

Bandura, A. (1997). *Self-Efficacy: The exercise of control.* New York: Freeman.

Bandura, A. (1999). A social cognitive theory of personality. In L. Pervin & O. John (Eds.), *Handbook of personality* (2nd ed.) (pp. 154-196). New York: Guilford.

Bandura, A. (2001). Social cognitive theory: An agentic perspective. *Annual Review of Psychology, 52,* 1-26.

Bandura, A., & Jourden, F. J. (1991). Self-regulatory mechanisms governing the impact of social comparison on complex decision making. *Journal of Personality and Social Psychology, 60,* 941-951.

Bandura, A., & Locke, E. (2003). Negative self-efficacy and goal effects revisited. *Journal of Applied Psychology, 88* (1) 87-99.

Barr, K., & Hall, C. (1992). The use of imagery by rowers. *International Journal of Sport Psychology, 23,* 243-261.

Beauchamp, P. H., Halliwell, W. R., Fournier, J. F., & Koestner, R. (1996). Effects of cognitive-behavioral psychological skills training on the motivation, preparation and putting performance of novice golfers. *The Sport Psychologist, 10,* 157-170.

Behncke, L. (2004). Self-regulation: A brief review. *Athletic Insight: The Online Journal of Sport Psychology.* http://www.athleticinsight.com/Vol4Iss1/SelfRegulation.htm

Biddle, S. J. H. (2001). Enhancing motivation in physical education. In G. C. Roberts (Ed.), *Advances in sport and exercise motivation* (pp. 101-128). Champaign, IL: Human Kinetics.

Biddle, S. J. H., Wang, J., Kavussanu, M., & Spray, C. (2003). Correlates of achievement goal orientations in physical activity. *European Journal of Sport Science, 3.*

Boutcher, S. H., & Rotella, R. J. (1987). A psychological skills educational program for closed-skill performance enhancement. *The Sport Psychologist, 1,* 127-137.

Cleary, T., & Zimmerman, B. J. (2000). Self-regulation differences during athletic practice by experts, non-experts, and novices. *Journal of Applied Sport Psychology, 13,* 61-82.

Conroy, D. E., Elliot, A. J., & Hofer, S. M. (2003). A 2 x 2 Achievement Goals Questionnaire for Sport: Evidence for factorial invariante, temporal stability, and external validity. *Journal of Sport and Exercise Psychology, 25,* 1-21.

Crews, D. J., Lochbaum, M. R., & Karoly, P. (2001). Self-regulation: Concepts, methods, and strategies in sport and exercise. In R. N. Singer, H. A. Hausenblas, & C. M. Janelle (Eds,), *Handbook of sport psychology* (pp. 566-584). New York: John Wiley.

Cumming, J., Hall, C., Harwood, C., & Gammage, K. (2002). Motivational orientations and imagery use: A goal profiling analysis. *Journal of Sports Sciences, 20,* 127-136.

Cury, F., Da Fonseca, D., Rufo, M., Peres, C., & Sarrazin, P.

(2003). The trichotomous model and investment in learning to prepare a sport test: A mediational analysis. *British Journal of Educational Psychology, 73,* 529-543.

Cury, F., Elliot, A., Sarrazin, P, Da Fonseca, D., & Rufo, M. (2002). The richotomous achievement goal model and intrinsic motivation: A sequential mediational analysis. *Journal of Experimental Social Psychology, 38,* 473-481.

Deci, E. L. & Ryan, R. M. (1985). *Intrinsic motivation and self-determination in human behavior.* N.Y. Plenum Press.

Deci, E. L., & Ryan, R. M. (2000). The "what" and "why" of goal pursuits: Human needs and the self-determination of behavior. *Psychological Inquiry, 11,* 227-268.

Duda, J. L. (2001). Goal perspectives research in sport: Pushing the boundaries and clarifying some misunderstandings. In G. C. Roberts (Ed.), *Advances in motivation in sport and exercise* (pp.129-182). Champaign, IL: Human Kinetics.

Duda, J. L. (2004). Goal setting and achievement motivation in sport. In C. Spielberger (Ed.), *Encyclopedia of Applied Psychology* (pp. 567- 582). San Diego, CA: Academic Press.

Duda, J. L. (in press). Motivation in sport: The relevance of competence and achievement goals. In A. J. Elliot & C. S. Dweck (Eds.), *Handbook of competence and motivation.* New York: Guildford Publications.

Duda, J. L., & Hall, H. (2001). Achievement goal theory in sport: Recent extensions and future directions. In R. Singer, H. Hausenblas, & C., Janelle (Eds.), *Handbook of sport psychology,* (2nd ed.) (pp. 417-443). New York: John Wiley & Sons.

Duda, J. L., & Whitehead, J. (1998). Measurement of goal perspectives in the physical domain. In J. Duda (Ed.), *Advances in Sport and Exercise Psychology Measurement* (pp. 21-48). Morgantown, WV: Fitness Information Technology.

Dweck, C. S. (1986). Motivational processes affecting learning. *American Psychologist, 41,* 1040-1048.

Dweck, C. S. (1999). *Self-theories: Their role in motivation, personality, and development.* Philadelphia: Psychology Press.

Eccles, J. S. (1987). Gender roles and women's achievement-related decisions. *Psychology of Women Quarterly, 11,* 135-172.

Eccles, J. S., & Harold, R. (1991). Gender differences in sport involvement: Applying the Eccles' expectancy-value model. *Journal of Applied Sport Psychology, 3,* 7-35.

Eccles, J. S., & Wigfield, A. (2002). Motivational beliefs, values, and goals. *Annual Review of Psychology, 53,* 109-132.

Elliot, A. J. (1999). Approach and avoidance motivation and achievement goals. *Educational Psychologist, 34,* 169-189.

Elliot, A. J., & Church, M. A. (1997). A hierarchical model of approach and avoidance motivation. *Journal of Personality and Social Psychology, 72,* 218-232.

Elliot, A. J., & McGregor, H. A. (2001). A 2 X 2 achievement goal framework. *Journal of Personality and Social Psychology, 80,* 501-519.

Elliot, A. J., Sheldon, R. M., & Church, M. A. (1997). Avoidance personal goals and subjective well-being. *Personality and Social Psychology Bulletin, 23,* 915-927.

Ford, J. K., Smith, E. M., Weissbein, D. A., Gully, S. M., & Salas, E. (1998). Relationships of goal orientation, metacognitive activity, and practice strategies with learning outcomes and transfer. *Journal of Applied Psychology, 83,* 218-233.

Gardner, F. L., & Moore, Z. E. (2004). A mindfulness-acceptance-commitment-based approach to athletic performance enhancement: Theoretical considerations. *Behavior Therapy, 35,* 707-723.

Gould, D., Petlichkoff, L., Hodge, K., & Simons, J. (1990). Evaluating the effectiveness of a psychological skills educational workshop. *The Sport Psychologist, 4,* 249-260.

Green-Demers, I., Pelletier, L. G., Stewart, D. G., & Gushue, N. R. (1998). Coping with the less interesting aspects of training: Toward a model of interest and motivation enhancement in individual sports. *Basic and Applied Social Psychology, 20,* 251-261.

Hall, C., Rodgers, W., & Barr, K. (1990). The use of imagery by athletes in selected sports. *The Sport Psychologist, 4,* 1-10.

Hall, H. K., & Kerr, A. W. (2001). Goal setting in sport and physical activity: Tracing empirical developments and establishing conceptual direction. In G. Roberts (Ed.), *Advances in sport and exercise motivation* (pp. 183-234). Champaign, IL: Human Kinetics.

Hanin, Y., & Syrja, P. (1995). Performance affect in junior ice hockey players: An application of the individual Zones of Optimal Functioning model. *The Sport Psychologist, 9,* 169-187.

Harackiewicz, J. M., Baron, K., Pintrich, P., Elliot, A. J., & Thrash, T. M. (2002). Revision of achievement goal theory: Necessary and illuminating. *Journal of Educational Psychology, 94,* 638-645.

Harter, S. (1978). Effectance motivation re-considered. *Human Development, 21,* 34-64.

Harter, S. (1981). A model of intrinsic mastery motivation in children: Individual differences and developmental change. In W. A. Collins (Ed.), *Minnesota symposium on child psychology* (Vol. 14, pp. 215-255). Hillsdale, NJ: Erlbaum.

Harwood, C., Cumming, J., & Fletcher, D. (2004). Motivational profiles and psychological skills usage within elite youth sport. *Journal of Applied Sport Psychology, 16,* 318-332.

Harwood, C., Cumming, J., & Hall, C. (2003). Imagery use in elite youth sport: Reinforcing the applied significance of achievement goal theory. *Research Quarterly for Exercise and Sport, 74,* 292-300.

Hatzigeorgeadis, A., & Biddle, S. B. J. (1999). The effects of goal orientation and perceived competence on cognitive interference during tennis and snooker performance. *Journal of Sport Behavior, 22,* 17 -28.

Kaplan, A., & Maehr, M. L. (1999). Achievement goals and student well-being. *Contemporary Educational Psychology, 24,* 330-358.

Kane, T. D., Marks, M. A., Zaccaro, S. J., & Blair, V. (1996). Self-efficacy, personal goals, and wrestlers' self-regulation. *Journal of Sport and Exercise Psychology, 18,* 36-48.

Kavussanu, M., & Roberts, G. C. (1996). Motivation in physical activity contexts: The relationship of perceived motivational climate to intrinsic motivation and self-efficacy. *Journal of Sport and Exercise Psychology, 18,* 254-280.

Kingston, K. M., & Hardy, L. (1997). Effects of different types of goals on processes that support performance. *The Sport Psychologist, 11,* 277-293.

Kirschenbaum, D. S. (1984). Self-regulation and sport psychology: Nurturing an emerging symbiosis. *Journal of Sport Psychology, 6,* 159-183.

Kirschenbaum, D. S. (1987). Self-regulation and sport performance. *Medicine and Science in Sports and Exercise, 19,* S106-S113.

Kirschenbaum, D. S. (1997). *Mind matters: Seven steps to smarter sport performance*. Carmel, IN: Cooper.

Kirschenbaum, D. S., O'Conner, E. A., & Owens, D. (1999). Positive illusions in golf: Empirical and conceptual analyses. *Journal of Applied Sport Psychology, 11*, 1-27.

Kirschenbaum, D. S., Owens, D., & O'Conner, E. A. (1998). Smart golf: Preliminary evaluation of a simple, yet comprehensive, approach to improving and scoring the mental game. *The Sport Psychologist, 12*, 271-282.

Kirschenbaum, D. S., & Wittrock, D. A. (1984). Cognitive-behavioral interventions in sport: A self-regulatory perspective. In J. M. Silva & R. S. Weinberg (Eds.), *Psychological foundations of sport* (p. 81-90). Champaign, IL: Human Kinetics.

Kitsantas, A., & Zimmerman, B. J. (2000). Self efficacy, activity participation, and physical fitness of asthmatic and non-asthmatic adolescent girls. *Journal of Asthma, 32*(2), 163-174.

Kitsantas, A., Zimmerman, B. J., & Clearly, T. (2000). The role of observation and emulation in the development of athletic self-regulation. *Journal of Educational Psychology, 92*(4), 811-817.

Lee, C. (1988). The relationship between goal setting, self efficacy, and female field hockey team performance. *International Journal of Sport Psychology, 20*, 147-161.

Lee, F. K., Sheldon, K. M., & Turban, D. B. (2003). Personality and the goal-striving process: The influence of achievement goal patterns, goal level, and mental focus on performance and enjoyment. *Journal of Applied Psychology, 88*, 256-265.

Levesque, M., Blais, M. R., Hess, U. (2004). Motivation, comportements organisationnels discrÈtionnaires et bien-Ître en milieu Africain: Quand le devoir oblige? Canadian *Journal of Behavioral Science, 36*(4), 321-332.

Lochbaum, M. R., & Roberts, G. C. (1993). Goal orientations and perceptions of the sport experience. *Journal of Sport and Exercise Psychology, 15*, 160-171.

Locke, E. A. & Latham, G. P. (1990). *A theory of goal setting and task performance*. Englewood Cliffs, NJ: Prentice-Hall.

Mageau, G. A., & Vallerand, R. J. (2003). The coach-athlete relationship: A motivational model. *Journal of Sports Sciences, 21*, 883-904.

Meece, J. L., Blumenfeld, P., & Hoyle, R. H. (1988). Students' goal orientations and cognitive engagement in classroom activities. *Journal of Educational Psychology, 82*, 60-70.

Meyers, A., Whelan, J., & Murphy, S. (1996). Cognitive behavioral strategies in athletic performance enhancement. In M. Hersen, R. Eisler, & P. Miller (Eds.), *Progress in behavior modification* (p. 196-219). New York: Brooks/Cole Publishing.

Murphy, S., & Tammen, S. (1998). In search of psychological skills. In J.L. Duda (Ed.), *Advances in sport and exercise psychology measurement* (pp. 195-211). Morgantown, WV: Fitness Information Technology.

Nicholls, J. G. (1984). Achievement motivation: Conceptions of ability, subjective experience, task choice, and performance. *Psychological Review, 91*, 328-346.

Nicholls, J. G. (1989). *The competitive ethos and democratic education*. Cambridge, MA: Harvard University Press.

Nien, C., & Duda, J. L. (2004). *A test of the 2 x 2 achievement goal framework in sport: Antecedents and consequences*. Manuscript under review.

Nitsch, J. R. (2000). Handlungstheoretische Grundlagen der Sportpsychologie (Action theory fundamentals for sport psychology). In H. Gabler, J.R. Nitsch, & R. Singer (Eds.), *Einführung in die Sportpsychologie, Teil 1 (Introduction to sport psychology, Part 1* pp. 43-164). Schorndorf: Hofmann.

Nitsch, J. R., & Hackfort, D. (1981). Stress in Schule und Hochschule - eine handlungspsychologische Funktionsanalyse (Stress in school and university - an action psychology functional analysis). In J. R. Nitsch (Ed.), *Stress* (pp. 263-311). Bern: Huber.

Nolen, S. (1988). Reasons for studying: Motivational orientations and study strategies. *Cognition and Instruction, 5*, 269-287.

Ntoumanis, N. (2001). Empirical links between achievement goal theory and self-determination theory in sport. *Journal of Sports Sciences, 19*, 397-409.

Ommundsen, Y. (2003). Implicit theories of ability and self-regulation strategies in physical education classes. *Educational Psychology, 23*, 141-157.

Papaioannou, A., & Kouli, O. (1999). The effect of task structure, perceived motivational climate, and goal orientations on students' task involvement and anxiety. *Journal of Applied Sport Psychology, 11*, 51-71.

Pelletier, L. G., Fortier, M. S., Vallerand, R. J., & Briere, N. M. (2001). Associations among perceived autonomy support, forms of self-regulation, and persistence: A prospective study. *Motivation and Emotion, 25*, 279-306.

Pintrich, P. (2000). The role of goal orientation in self-regulated learning. In M. Boekaerts, P. R. Pintrich, & M. H. Zeidner (Eds.), *Handbook of self regulation*. (pp. 452-502). San Diego, CA: Academic Press.

Pintrich, P., Smith, D., Garcia, T., & McKeachie, W. (1993). Predictive validity and reliability of the Motivated Strategies for Learning Questionnaire (MLSQ). *Educational and Psychological Measurement, 53*, 801-813.

Ratelle, C. F., Vallerand, R. J., Chantal, Y., & Porvencher, P. (2004). Cognitive adaptation and mental health: A motivational analysis. *European Journal of Social Psychology, 34*, 459-476.

Reinboth, M., & Duda, J. L. (2004). Relationship of the perceived motivational climate and perceptions of ability to psychological and physical well-being in team sports. *The Sport Psychologist, 18*, 237-251.

Reinboth, M., Duda, J. L., Ntoumanis, N. (2004). Dimensions of coaching behavior, need satisfaction, and the psychological and physical welfare of young athletes. *Motivation and Emotion, 28*, 297-313.

Robazza, C. Pellizzari, M., & Hanin, Y. (2004). Emotion self-regulation and athletic performance: An application of the IZOF model. *Psychology of Sport and Exercise, 5*, 379-404.

Roberts, G. C. (1992). Motivation in sport and exercise: Conceptual constraints and convergence. In G. C. Roberts (Ed.), *Motivation in sport and exercise* (pp. 3-29). Champaign, IL: Human Kinetics.

Roberts, G. C. (2001). Understanding the dynamics of motivation in physical activity: The influence of achievement goals on motivational processes. In G. C. Roberts (Ed.), *Advances in sport and exercise motivation* (pp. 1-50). Champaign, IL: Human Kinetics.

Roberts, G. C., & Ommundsen, Y. (1996). Effect of goal orientation on achievement beliefs, cognition, and strategies in team sport. *Scandinavian Journal of Medicine and Science in Sports, 6*, 46-56.

Roberts, G. C., Treasure, D., & Kavussanu, M. (1996). Orthogonality of achievement goals and its relationship to beliefs about success and satisfaction in sport. *The Sport Psychologist, 10,* 398-408.

Rodgers, W., Hall, C., & Buckolz, E. (1991). The effect of an imagery training program on imagery ability, imagery use, and figure skating performance. *Journal of Applied Sport Psychology, 3,* 109-125.

Ryan, R. M., & Deci, E. L. (2000a). Self-determination theory and the facilitation of intrinsic motivation, social development, and well-being. *American Psychologist, 55,* 68-78.

Ryan, R. M., & Deci, E. L. (2000b). The darker and brighter sides of human existence: Basic psychological needs as a unifying concept. *Psychological Inquiry, 11,* 319-338.

Ryan, R. M., & Deci, E. L. (2000c). When rewards compete with nature: The undermining of intrinsic motivation and self-regulation. In C. Sansone & J. M. Harackiewicz (Eds.), *Intrinsic and extrinsic motivation: The search for optimal motivation and performance* (pp. 13-54). New York: Academic Press.

Ryan, R. M., & Deci, E. L. (2002). An overview of self-determination theory. In E. L. Deci & R. M. Ryan (Eds.), *Handbook of self-determination research* (pp. 3-33). Rochester, NY: University of Rochester Press.

Schunk, D. (1995). Self-efficacy and education and instruction. In J.E. Maddux (Ed.), *Self-efficacy, adaptation, and adjustment: Theory, research, and application* (pp. 281-303). New York: Plenum Press.

Smith, M. L., Duda, J. L., Allen, J., & Hall, H. K. (2002). Contemporary measures of approach and avoidance goal orientations: Similarities and differences. *British Journal of Educational Psychology, 72,* 155-190.

Solmon, M., & Boone, J. (1993). The impact of student goal orientation in physical education classes. *Research Quarterly for Exercise and Sport, 64,* 418-424.

Standage, M., Duda, J. L., & Ntoumanis (2003). Predicting motivational regulations in physical education: The interplay between dispositional goal orientations, motivational climate, and perceived competence. *Journal of Sport Sciences, 21,* 631-47.

Standage, M., Duda, J. L., & Pensgaard, A.M. (in press). The effect of competitive outcome and the motivational climate on the psychological well-being of individuals engaged in a coordination task. Motivation and Emotion.

Standage, M., Treasure, D., Duda, J. L., & Prusak, K. A. (2003). Validity, reliability, and invariance of the Situational Motivation Scale (SIMS) across diverse physical activity contexts. *Journal of Sport and Exercise Psychology, 21*(8), 631-647.

Theodorakis, Y. (1995). Effects of self-efficacy, satisfaction, and personal goals on swimming performance. *The Sport Psychologist, 9,* 245-253.

Thill, E., & Brunel, P. (1995). Ego involvement and task involvement: Related conceptions of ability, effort, and learning strategies among soccer players. *International Journal of Sport Psychology, 26,* 81-97.

Thomas, P. R., Murphy, S. M., & Hardy, L. (1999). Test of performance strategies: Development and preliminary validation of comprehensive measure of athletes' psychological skills. *Journal of Sports Sciences, 17,* 697-711

Treasure, D. C. (2001). Enhancing young people's motivation in youth sport: An achievement goal approach. In G.C. Roberts (Ed.), *Advances in motivation in sport and exercise* (pp. 79-100). Champaign, IL: Human Kinetics.

Treasure, D. C., Duda, J. L., Hall, H. K., Roberts, G. C., Ames,

C., & Maehr, M. L. (2001). Clarifying misconceptions and misrepresentations in achievement goal research in sport: A response to Harwood, Hardy, and Swain. *Journal of Sport and Exercise Psychology, 23*(4), 317-329.

Vallerand, R. J. (2001). A hierarchical model of intrinsic and extrinsic motivation in sport and exercise. In G. C. Roberts (Ed.), *Advances in sport and exercise motivation* (pp. 263-320). Champaign, IL: Human Kinetics.

Vallerand, R. J., & Fortier, M. S. (1998). Measures of intrinsic and extrinsic motivation in sport and physical activity: A review and critique. In J. L. Duda (Ed.), *Advancements in Sport and Exercise Psychology Measurement* (pp. 81-104). Morgantown, WV: Fitness Information Technology.

Van Yperen, N., & Duda, J. L. (1999). Goal orientations, beliefs about success, and performance improvement among young elite Dutch soccer players. *Scandinavian Journal of Medicine and Science in Sports, 9,* 358-364.

Vealey, R. S. (1988). Future directions in psychological skills training. *The Sport Psychologist, 2,* 318-336.

Vealey, R. S., & Garner-Holman, M. (1998). Applied sport psychology: Measurement issues. In J. L. Duda (Ed.), *Advances in sport and exercise psychology measurement* (pp. 433-446). Morgantown, WV: Fitness Information Technology.

Vealey, R. S., Hayashi, S. W., Garner-Holman, M., & Giacobbi, P. (1998). Sources of sport-confidence: Conceptualization and instrument development. *Journal of Sport and Exercise Psychology, 20,* 53-80.

Whelan, J., Mahoney, M., & Meyers, A. (1991). Performance enhancement in sport: A cognitive-behavioral domain. *Behavior Therapy, 22,* 307-327.

White, S. A. (1998). Adolescent goal profiles, perceptions of the parent-initiated motivational climate, and competitive trait anxiety. *The Sport Psychologist, 12,* 16-28.

Williams, K. J., Donovan, J. J., Dodge, T. L. (2000). Self-regulation of performance: Goal establishment and goal revision processes in athletes. *Human Performance, 13,* 159-180.

Winfrey, M. L., & Weeks, D. L. (1993). Effects of self-modeling on self-efficacy and balance team performance. *Perceptual and Motor Skills, 77,* 907-913.

Wolters, C. A. (2004). Advancing achievement goal theory: Using goal structures and goal orientations to predict students' motivation, cognition, and achievement. *Journal of Educational Psychology, 96,* 236-250.

Wrosch, C., Scheier, M. F., Miller, G. E., Schulz, R., & Carver, C. S. (2003). Adaptive self-regulation of unattainable goals, goal disengagement, goal reengagement, and subjective well-being. *Personality and Social Psychology Bulletin, 29,* 1491-1508.

Zimmerman, B. J. (1986). Becoming a self-regulated learner: Which are the key subprocesses? *Contemporary Educational Psychology, 11,* 307-313.

Zimmerman, B. J. (1989). A social cognitive view of self-regulated academic learning. *Journal of Educational Psychology, 81,* 329-339.

Zimmerman, B. J. (1994). Dimensions of academic self-regulation: A conceptual framework for education. In D. H. Schunk & B. J. Zimmerman (Eds.), *Self-regulation of learning and performance: Issues and educational applications* (pp. 3-21). Hillsdale, NJ: Erlbaum.

Zimmerman, B. J., & Kitsantas, A. (1996). Self-regulated learning of a motor skill: The role of goal setting and self-monitoring. *Journal of Applied Sport Psychology, 8,* 69-84.

Zimmerman, B. J., & Kitsantas, A. (1997). Developmental phases in self-regulation: Shifting from process goals to outcome goals. *Journal of Educational Psychology, 89*, 29-36.

Zimmerman, B. J., & Martinez-Pons, M. (1986). Development of a structured interview for assessing student use of self-regulated learning strategies. American *Educational Research Journal, 23*, 614-628.

Zimmerman, B. J., & Risemberg, R. (1997). Self-regulatory dimensions of academic learning and motivation. In G. D. Phye (Ed.), *Handbook of academic learning: Construction of knowledge* (pp. 105-125). New York: Academic Press.

Section IV
Stress Management Techniques

Introduction

The chapters in this section highlight, on one hand, one of the most common and elaborated techniques of stress management—biofeedback. On the other hand, anxiety is viewed as probably the most common stress emotion, and strategies for prevention and management are discussed with respect to this example.

In the first chapter, Boris Blumenstein and Michael Bar-Eli elaborate on biofeedback as a technology developed for the treatment of stress-related disorders and how to adopt this method in a careful and appropriate manner for more general purposes in sport psychology interventions. The authors describe the current state of applied biofeedback research in sport and provide several examples of biofeedback-based training programs recently used to enhance athletic performance.

The author of the second chapter, Mark Anshel, addresses psychosocial stress, as opposed to biological or somatic stress, and competitive state anxiety, in contrast to trait anxiety, a predisposition. The author examines the antecedents and underlying personal and situational causes of appraisals that lead to stress and anxiety in sport, and describes how the athlete can help manage these feelings.

Both of the contributions address issues of utmost importance in high-performance sports, in which it is viewed today that most of the top athletes are similar with respect to their physical preconditions but differ considerably with regard to their ability to manage stress induced by the perception of the significance of the competition situation and the psychophysiological phenomena evoked by these perceptions and constitutive for the stress experience.

4.1

Biofeedback Applications in Sport

BORIS BLUMENSTEIN AND MICHAEL BAR-ELI

Introduction

The discipline of sport psychology offers much practical information, primarily in terms of performance enhancement. Despite its substantive involvement in enhancing elite athletes' performance, the full potential of sport psychology has yet to be attained. One possible reason that this is the case may be the somewhat premature application of stress management techniques for other purposes in the sport/exercise domain. Biofeedback (BFB)—a technological advance in the treatment of stress-related disorders—has not always been used by practicing sport psychologists in a careful, appropriate manner. The main purpose of this chapter is to describe the current state of applied BFB research in sport, as well as provide several examples of BFB-based training programs used to enhance athletic performance.

The relevance of BFB interventions to athletic preparation is evident in the "psychophysiological principle" presented by Green, Green, and Walters (1970). According to this principle, every physiological change is accompanied by a parallel change in one's mental-emotional state and conversely, every mental-emotional change—conscious or unconscious—is accompanied by a physiological change. Thus, BFB can be a powerful tool for initiating physiological change, such as increasing individual awareness and/or control over the body and reducing habitual physiological tension.

The first BFB applications were limited to medical-clinical practices. For example, Kamiya (1968) demonstrated that participants could voluntarily control their brainwaves, and Basmajian (1977) showed that participants could learn to control single motor units in their spinal cord. At that time, the possibilities offered by BFB—e.g., controlling bodies through brainwaves—seemed fascinating. In fact, BFB applications became popular in the medical-clinical area and in other domains of interest, such as education (LaVaque, 1998).

A large amount of good BFB research was conducted in sport and exercise during the 1980s and early 1990s (e.g., Blumenstein, Bar-Eli, & Tenenbaum, 1995; Collins, 1995; Hatfield & Landers, 1987; Pettruzzello, Landers, & Salazar, 1991; Zaichkowsky & Fuchs, 1988). Most of this research found positive effects for various BFB interventions on performance. However, we agree with Crews, Lochbaum, and Karoly (2001, p. 578), who stated that "one of the criticisms of biofeedback training has been the ability to transfer the learned response to performance in the real world." In other words, the research-based applicability of BFB in terms of its contribution to athletic performance enhancement needs further explanation, which we will attempt in the remainder of this chapter.

First, we will review the existing research on BFB applications in sport. Following this review, we will present a specific recent application, the "Wingate 5-step approach."

Review of Research on Biofeedback Applications in Sport

In this section, the effects of BFB interventions on athletic performance in different sports will be described in terms of research and practical work. We will review several studies that have investigated the performance-enhancement effects of combining different BFB modalities with different psychological techniques in various athletic settings.

Several BFB modalities have been used in sport, such as muscle tension electromyography (muscle feedback—EMG), peripheral skin temperature as an index of peripheral blood flow (thermal feedback, often referred to as "temperature"—Temp.), electrodermal or sweat gland activity (electrodermal feedback—EDA), electrical activity of the brain (electroencephalographic feedback—EEG), and electrocardiography, including heart rate (cardiovascular or heart rate feedback—HR) and blood pressure feedback—BP). Applied BFB research in sport, using these modalities, demonstrated that BFB can often be effective in reducing anxiety as well as in improving muscle and athletic performance in different sport disciplines. The following review will focus on these major issues.

BFB and anxiety

High anxiety levels can be detrimental to motor learning, performance, and participation in competition (Gould, Greenleaf, & Krane, 2002). One way of building self-confidence and reducing competition anxiety is to improve performance skills. This can be accomplished by continually providing athletes with feedback on their efforts, skill improvement, and

performance outcomes (Anshel, 2003). Accordingly, BFB training in sport psychology has been used most extensively in the treatment of performance anxiety (Blumenstein, 2002).

Reducing state anxiety and improving balancing performance on a stabilometer was studied by Teague (1976). During four 60-minute sessions both systematic desensitization and EMG BFB training were used; 20 college students were found to reduce state anxiety and improve balancing performance. French (1978) reported similar results, stating that training significantly improved balancing performance and reduced muscle tension. In a study conducted by Sabourin and Rioux (1979), participants significantly reduced tension and improved task performance after five EMG BFB training sessions (30 min. each). Blais and Vallerand (1986) found that six EMG BFB training sessions (30 min. each) reduced EMG tension and improved balancing performance.

Zaichkowsky, Dorsey, and Mulholland (1979) as well as Griffiths, Steel, Vaccaro, and Karpman (1981) examined the effects of EMG BFB training on reducing state anxiety and improving performance. Zaichkowsky et al. (1979) found that in six EMG BFB and systematic desensitization training sessions (each 15-20 min.), no significant reduction in state anxiety or improvement in gymnastic performance was demonstrated. Griffiths et al. (1981) found a reduction in state anxiety after six EMG BFB and relaxation training sessions (each 20 min.), but found no significant effect on performance. Similar findings were reported by Weinberg and Hunt (1976) as well as by Tsukomoto (1979). De Witt (1980) revealed a reduction in competitive anxiety and an improvement in basketball and football performance after EMG BFB training (basketball - 11 sessions X 60 min.; football - 12 sessions X 30 min.). Finally, Daniels and Landers (1981) successfully applied BFB (HR, respiration) training to help elite rifle shooters deal effectively with performance anxiety.

The studies noted above indicate that BFB training (usually frontalis EMG) does have some positive effects, although it is not always successful in reducing muscular tension, thereby reducing anxiety and improving performance. It seems that any positive effects are conditioned upon factors such as the task to be performed, the specific BFB modalities used, the length of BFB treatment (sessions X time), and the combination of BFB training with other psychological techniques.

Biofeedback and muscle performance

The attempt to improve muscle performance with BFB training (usually with EMG) is well-documented in clinical practice (Basmajian, 1983; Schwartz, 1987) and sport (Landers, 1988; Zaichkowsky & Fuchs, 1988). For example, Croce (1986) found that a combined training program, which consisted of an isokinetic exercise and EMG BFB training, resulted in significant gains in maximal force and electromyographic activity of key extensor muscles. In another study, Lucca and Recchiuti (1983) demonstrated the practical application of EMG BFB training for increasing muscle strength. In this study, the experimental group showed significantly greater gains in average peak torque (in comparison to the control group) after a 19-day program of EMG BFB training. Peper and Schmid (1983) found that among members of the U.S. rhythmic gymnastics team, BFB (EMG, Temp., EDA) had significant training effects on voluntary control over peripheral temperature, EMG activity, heart rate, and skin conductance. Dorsey (1976) and Goodspeed (1983) revealed that following an application of various BFB training programs (using EMG, GSR, and Temp.), improved motor control and performance in gymnastics were evident. Ren's (1995) study demonstrated improved consistency of archers with muscle exertion and enhanced postural consistency. Similar positive effects of EMG BFB training were reported by Krueger, Ruehl, Scheel, and Franz (1988), who used EMG BFB to optimize technique with "wing" kayak paddles.

The effects of BFB training on muscle endurance and perceived pain have been examined in several investigations. For example, McGlynn, Laughlin, and Filios (1979) found significant reductions in the perceived mean pain level in an EMG BFB training group. However, in Lloyd's (1972) study, auditory BFB training with EMG did not increase endurance time or decrease the degree of perceived pain. Edwards and Lippold (1956) argued that in order to sustain a given level of tension, EMG BFB needs to be increased, which may indicate more efficiency in muscular contraction during the fatigue regimen (Middaugh, Miller, Foster, & Ferdon 1982).

The studies reviewed above have attempted to increase muscle strength, improve muscle control, and reduce muscle fatigue and pain through the use of various BFB training programs. Results have indicated that BFB training effects were not always conclusively positive. In general, BFB is considered an important tool for stress control and management. However, it is sometimes difficult to prove a direct relation between BFB and muscle performance, a relation which is conditioned on factors such as the number and length of training sessions, the type of task to be performed, and the specific modality/ies used.

Combined techniques of mental preparation with BFB

The principle of combining several mental preparation procedures in order to investigate their integrated impact on athletic performance was reflected in much of the earlier applied BFB research in sport and exercise (e.g., Petruzzello et al., 1991), as well as in a more recent studies (for review, see Blumenstein, Bar-Eli, & Tenenbaum, 2002). Essentially, BFB involves the voluntary and autonomic branches of the central nervous system and provides the individual with typically inaccessible information about his or her biological state. BFB consists of training the individual to change various physiological indices (e.g., muscle tension, heart rate, brain activity) and to regulate physiological states with instrumentation. These abilities are expected to be transferred to performance settings, in which the individual is expected to function in the absence of BFB (Basmajian, 1983; Green & Green, 1977). Despite Dishman's (1987) statement that BFB should be included among the somatic performance enhancement procedures, which minimize the role of cognitions in determining human behavior, it was also proposed that in order to strengthen BFB effects, other mental techniques—mainly of a cognitive nature—be applied in combination with BFB (Petruzzello et al., 1991).

In the early 1980s, Goodspeed (1983) examined the efficacy of using electrodermal and temperature BFB as part of a comprehensive mental training program (which included imagery, relaxation, and several other cognitive strategies) with gymnasts. Goodspeed (1983) found improved motor control and performance among his participants. Similarly, Peper and Schmid (1983) found positive effects when temperature, EMG, and HR BFB were used in conjunction with progressive relaxation, autogenic training, and imagery to enhance athletic performance among members of the U.S. rhythmic gymnastic team. In addition, Scartelli (1984) has revealed some positive effects when EMG BFB was combined with sedative music. Finally, several other studies conducted in the 1980s (Blais & Vallerand, 1986; Costa, Bonaccorsi, & Scrimali, 1984; Daniels & Landers, 1981) described positive effects when BFB was used in conjunction with other psychological intervention techniques (e.g., relaxation and imagery) to control non-optimal states (e.g., anxiety) that precede athletic competition.

Blumenstein, Bar-Eli, and Tenenbaum's (1995) study looked at using three psychoregulative procedures of relaxation and excitation in combination with BFB to examine their effect on physiological and athletic performance variables. Participants were randomly assigned to three groups of psychoregulatory treatment (autogenic and imagery training, AT + IT; music and imagery training, M + IT; autogenic, music and imagery training, AT + M + IT), one placebo group and a control group. Imagery was related to a 100-m run. Treatment was provided accompanied by frontalis EMG BFB. Heart rate, galvanic skin response, EMG, breathing frequency (f_b), and athletic task (100-m run) were used as dependent variables. BFB was found to have a significant augmenting effect on physiological components and athletic performance when accompanied by autogenic, imagery, and music training. Thus, when BFB is used as part of a larger intervention package (e.g., imagery, relaxation), its most substantial effect seems to be an augmenting one. Similar findings were reported by Caird, McKenzie, and Steivert (1999), who revealed improved running economy among trained long distance runners as a result of HR BFB operated together with relaxation techniques.

Taken together, the above studies support the principle of combining BFB modalities with mental preparation procedures such as relaxation and imagery to enhance athletic performance. It seems that the major effect of BFB as a part of a comprehensive mental preparatory package is an augmenting one, although this conclusion needs further elaboration in future research.

In target sports such as shooting (e.g., Hatfield

et al., 1987; Landers, 1985), archery (e.g., Landers, Petruzzello, Salazar, Crews, Kubitz, Gannon, & Han, 1991; Salazar, Landers, Petruzzello, Crews, Kubitz, & Han, 1990), and golf (e.g., Crews, 1991; Crews & Landers, 1993), positive effects of EEG BFB on performance have been repeatedly demonstrated. For example, Hatfield, Landers, and Ray (1984) found that as shooters prepare to compete, there is a marked shift from left to right hemispheric activation, which facilitates enhanced performance. Similarly, Crews (1991) reported substantial left/right hemisphere changes in EEG spectral densities, which are associated with performance enhancement in golf. Landers et al. (1991) reported similar effects in archery. However, Kavussanu, Crews, and Gill (1998) found no relationship between EEG, EMG, and HR BFB during six 30-minute training sessions, and performance (as measured pre- and post-shooting by 60 basketball free throws) in all three experimental conditions: single (i.e., EMG) BFB training, multimodal (i.e., EEG, EMG, HR) BFB training, and control.

Dorsey (1976) and Zaichkowsky (1983) found that a BFB training with EMG, GSR, and Temp. helped gymnasts control stress and improve performance. Similarly, positive effects were demonstrated on athletic performance among members of the U.S. rhythmic gymnastic team in a study conducted by Peper and Schmid (1983). After a two-year BFB training program which included EMG, GSR, and Temp. BFB training with progressive relaxation, autogenic training, and imagery, gymnasts reported enhancing their performance and utilizing relaxation to reenergize and control their arousal states.

The "Wingate 5-step approach" (Blumenstein, Bar-Eli, & Tenenbaum, 1997) is a mental preparation program which incorporates BFB training in conjunction with other techniques and is intended to enhance athletes' performance in applied sports settings. To examine the effectiveness of this program, Bar-Eli, Dreshman, Blumenstein, and Weinstein (2002) investigated the relationship between an adapted version (with the program's first three steps), used for mental preparation, and swimming performance among 11-14 year-old children. Participants were randomly assigned to one of two conditions: (a) experimental—regular training plus three stages of the original training program, and (b) control—regular training plus relaxing activities. After

Sport discipline categories	Authors	Combination of BFB modalities and mental techniques
TARGET SPORTS		

Shooting
  Rifle
  Pistol
Archery
 	
Golf
	Landers, 1985; Hatfield et al., 1984; 1987; Hatfield & Landers, 1987
	Daniels & Landers, 1981
	Salazar et al., 1990;
	Landers et al., 1991; Ren, 1995
	Crews, 1991;
	Crews et al., 1991;
	Crews & Landers, 1993
		HR, EEG, Respir. + MR
		
		EMG, GSR + Br, IM
		EEG, HR
		EEG, EMG
		HR + R, IM
		EEG
		EEG

TEAM SPORTS		
Basketball Basketball and American Football Handball	Kavussanu, Crews, & Gill, 1998 De Witt, 1980 Costa et al., 1984	EEG, HR, EMG + IM EMG, HR + MR, IM GSR + R, C
COMBAT SPORTS		
Karate Judo	Collins, Powell, & Davies, 1990 Blumenstein, 1999	EEG EMG, GSR + AT, IM
ARTISTIC SPORTS		
Gymnastics Rhythmic Gymnastics Synchronized Swimming	Dorsey, 1976; Zaichkowsky, 1983; Goodspeed, 1983; Tsukomoto, 1979;Wilson & Bird, 1981 Peper & Schmid, 1983 Wentz & Strong, 1980	EMG, GSR, Temp. + MR, AT, IM, D EMG + MR EMG, HR +MR EMG, Temp. + R, IM
ENDURANCE SPORTS		
Swimming Track & Field Long Distance Running Canoeing, Kayaking	Blumenstein, Tenenbaum et al., 1995; Blumenstein, 1996; Bar-Eli, Dreshman, Blumenstein & Weinstein (2002) Blumenstein, Bar-Eli, & Tenenbaum, 1995 Caird et al., 1999 Blumenstein & Bar-Eli; 1998; Krueger et al., 1988	EMG, GSR + AT, IM HR + MR EMG, GSR + AT, IM EMG
TRACK & FIELD		
Sprint 100m	Blumenstein, Bar-Eli, & Tenenbaum, 1995	EMG + AT, IM
WINTER SPORTS		
	Kappers & Chapman, 1984; Kappers & Mills, 1982	Temp. + AT

* Note: EMG – Electromyography (muscle feedback); GSR – Galvanic Skin Response (electrodermal feedback); Temp. – Thermal feedback; EEG – Electroencephalogram; HR – Heart Rate (cardiovascular feedback); AT – Schultz' Autogenic Training, MR – Jacobsen's Progressive Muscular Relaxation; R – Relaxation; IM – Imagery; Br. – Breathing techniques; C – Concentration; D – Systematic Desensitization.

a baseline measurement, participants were tested on evaluation scores and actual performance twice during a 14-week period. Results indicated that the experimental group exhibited substantially greater increases in performance after 3.5 months of training in terms of their results in real competitions as well as coaches' evaluations concerning their swimming technique. The control group also displayed some minor improvements.

In another study, Bar-Eli and Blumenstein (2004a) used a similar research design and paradigm with 16-18 year-old adolescent physical education pupils. Results indicated that the experimental group exhibited a substantial increase in short running performance, whereas the control group remained relatively stable.

It should be noted that these studies (Bar-Eli et al., 2002; Bar-Eli & Blumenstein, 2004a) are part of a series of investigations conducted to test the effectiveness of the "Wingate 5-step approach" in different contexts. One of the primary purposes of the training process with child swimmers and/or pupils is the acquisition of the technical skills required for adequate performance. Therefore, in order to apply the program for this purpose, it was sufficient to use only the first three steps of introduction, identification, and simulation. These steps are connected more to the instructional, coach-child athlete process, whereas transformation and realization (i.e., the last two steps) are more appropriate for higher-level athletes preparing for competition.

In a recent study conducted with lower-level athletes, Bar-Eli and Blumenstein (2004b), using all five steps, investigated 16-18 year-old pre-elite swimmers. Results indicated that the experimental group improved its performance (swimming, running) over time, with improvement being most substantial during steps four and five (transformation and realization). In contrast, the control group remained relatively stable on both dependent measures. In general, Bar-Eli and Blumenstein (2004b) found a similar pattern of results in comparison to the one revealed in Bar-Eli et al.'s (2002) and Bar-Eli and Blumenstein's (2004a) studies, namely, a consistent superiority of the experimental groups in all the field experiments conducted.

Together with previous studies (for review, see Blumenstein & Bar-Eli, 2001), these three recent studies strongly indicate that a mental preparation program, which is based on the principles of the "Wingate 5-step approach" (Blumenstein, et al., 1997), may indeed substantially contribute to the enhancement of athletes' performance in competition, provided it is appropriately adapted to their specific needs. This conclusion is further strengthened by elite athletes' reports (e.g., Blumenstein, 1999; Blumenstein & Bar-Eli, 1998), as well as by the objective evaluation of their own performances in top-level contests such as the World Championships and the Olympic Games (Blumenstein, 1996). Thus, it can be concluded that the "Wingate 5-step approach" is a useful mental training program, and is well-grounded in both scientific research and applied experience in elite sport.

BFB research and practice offer many promising opportunities for enhancing athletic performance. HR, EEG, and respiratory BFB training appear to be related to performance in aiming tasks; Temp., EDA (GSR), and EMG BFB induce relaxation in sports where mental relaxation and concentration are crucial (i.e., gymnastics); EMG, GSR BFB training should be used in combat sports; and EMG, GSR, and breathing BFB may be applied in sports such as swimming or biathlon. Most importantly, BFB-training shows real promise when used as part of larger intervention packages, such as BFB in conjunction with a relaxation and/or imagery technique.

BFB-based Training in Sports: The "Wingate 5-step Approach"

Traditionally, BFB training has been used for clinical purposes in a laboratory setting to reduce psychological stress, anxiety, and/or muscular tension. Building on this principle, the "Wingate 5-step approach" (Blumenstein, et al., 1997) enables athletes to transfer the psycho-regulative skills acquired in the laboratory to real training and competition, utilizing testing and different simulative material. Thus, the goal of this method is to improve athletic self-regulation, optimize competitive behavior, and improve athletic performance. The "Wingate 5-step approach" includes: (a) introduction (i.e., learning various self-regulation techniques); (b) identification (i.e., identifying and strengthening the most efficient BFB response modality); (c) simulation (i.e.,

BFB training with simulated competitive stress); (d) transformation (i.e., proceeding mental preparation from laboratory to field); and (e) realization (i.e., obtaining optimal regulation in competition). We will describe these steps in more detail here.

(a) Introduction: takes place in laboratory settings, includes 10-15 sessions, each session lasting about 50 minutes, 2-3 times a week. The goal of step 1 is to learn various self-regulation techniques: relaxation, imagery, BFB (at the end of this step). Before and after terminating each step, the athlete undergoes a self-regulation test (SRT) to indicate his or her psycho-regulative level and to observe the specific modalities pertaining to his or her individual responses (more details in Blumenstein et al., 1997, pp. 444-445).

(b) Identification: takes place in laboratory, includes about 15 sessions, each session lasting 45-50 minutes, twice a week. The goal of step 2 is to identify and strengthen the athlete's most efficient response modality on BFB (see conclusions). In this step, relaxation-excitation speed and relaxation-excitation level are highly important—for example, in judo, to achieve EMG relaxation in limits 0.8-1.0µV and during 1-3 minutes of excitation with imagery in limits 1.8-2.2 µV during 1 minute.

(c) Simulation: takes place in laboratory, includes about 15 sessions, each session lasting 45-50 minutes, twice a week. All mental training programs are accompanied by different simulative material (competitive situations, VCR-fragments, competitive noises, etc.).

(d) Transformation: takes place in training conditions, includes about 15 sessions and is characterized by an intense use of portable BFB and VCR devices in the field before, during, and after training. The goal of step 4 is to transform the preceding mental preparation procedures acquired by the athlete from lab to training conditions.

(e) Realization: takes place in competitive situations, includes about 10-15 competitions. The goal of step 5 is to obtain optimal regulation in competitive conditions. In a combat sport (judo, wrestling, taekwondo, fencing, boxing) 20-25 minute sessions were held before each match (relaxation-excitation pattern with imagery of a tactical plan for an upcoming event), as well as between matches (relaxation with analysis of past match—5-10 minutes and excitation before next match—1-3 minutes).

Each training course with the "Wingate 5-step approach" lasts about 70-75 training sessions, held over a period of about 7-8 months. In Table 2, the general principles of a mental training program based on this approach, developed for and applied in elite judo and taekwondo, is presented.

In line with this general mental program, daily, weekly, and monthly mental training sessions are developed.

A general pre-competition weekly mental training program applied to elite Israeli judo and taekwondo athletes is presented here, based on steps 4 and 5 of the program.

Table 2: Principles of the "5-step Approach", Applied in Judo and Taekwondo

Steps	Step 1*	Step 2*	Step 3*	Step 4	Step 5
Goal	**Introduction** (learning)	**Identification** (of most efficient BFB response)	**Simulation** (training with simulated stress)	**Transformation** (from laboratory to field)	**Realization** (optimal regulation in competition)
Content	Psychophysiological diagnosis (self-regulation test, reaction time test, muscle and time reproduction); mental techniques: AT, muscle relaxation, imagery and concentration training, BFB training	BFB training with EMG and GSR modalities; Self-regulation test	BFB training with imagery and VCR system (planning competition situations and recovery between matches). - BFB training with EMG, GSR modalities after VCR demonstration; - Self-regulation test with VCR	Mental practice in training (e.g., in hall, between training matches): - brief relaxation in pre-start preparation, - recovery between fights; - relaxation after training; Self-regulation test with VCR	Pre-start competition support: - planning competition versions; - recovery between matches; - concentration before matches. Self-examination and analysis after competition with analysis of VCR films
Mode and Length of Treatment	group - individual	individual	individual	individual - group	individual
	10-15 times x 45-50 min	10-15 times x 30-35 min	30-35 times x 20-25 min 20-25 times x 5-10 min	20-30 times x 1-3 min 20-30 times x 1-5 min 10-15 times x 10-15 min	20-25 times x 3-5 min 20-25 times x 5-10 min 10-15 times x 1-3 min

*Homework for Steps 1-3:
Mental relaxation with music; special relaxation program with portable GSR_{BFB}; 10-15 times x 10-15 min; daily relaxation practice with portable GSR_{BFB}; EMG_{BFB}; extended relaxation, 4-5 times x 15 min; brief relaxation 7-10 times x 5 min; brief relaxation 6-9 times x 1 min.

Saturday   Extended relaxation with music accompanied with portable GSP modalities—15 minutes

Sunday   Concentration exercises in warm-up with portable EMG-GSR_{BFB} + IM fragments of competitive match (excitation and concentration)—1-2 times x 2-3 minutes
Muscle relaxation and rest between fights with portable EMG-GSR_{BFB}—2-3 minutes
BFB relaxation after training—5 minutes with portable GSR_{BFB}

Monday   Homework with portable GSR_{BFB} and analysis of VCR films
with competition fights—3-4 times x 5-10 minutes

Tuesday   In warm-up: Relaxation + Imagery (excitation) with concentration on concrete competition fight and next relaxation (EMG in limit 0.8-0.9 µV): 1 time x 5 minutes, 1 time x 3 minutes, 1 time x 1 minutes
Mental recovery after training (group): 10-15 min with portable GSR_{BFB}

Wednesday   Concentration exercises in warm-up: 2 times x 1-3 minutes
Imagery with portable GSR_{BFB} after training (individual): 5-10 minutes

Thursday   During training—brief relaxation during performance (special exercises): 2-3 times x 1 minute, 2-3 times x 30 seconds, 2-3 times x 10 seconds
Homework with portable GSR_{BFB}—brief relaxation: 3-4 times x 1 minute

Friday   Brief relaxation—excitation during performance (special exercises): 3-4 times x 30 seconds
Mental recovery after training (group): 10-15 minutes with portable GSR_{BFB}

27.6	BFB training with EMG-GSR—relaxation: times x 3-5 minutes BFB training with EMG-GSR and audio-visual stimulation - (athlete listens to competition noise from previous competitions)—3-5 minutes. Preview of his previous match and thus relaxation with EMG-GSR$_{BFB}$ and imaging competition fragments of this match with corrections.
1.7	Relaxation with EMG-GSRBFB accompanied with a special music relaxation program—10-15 minutes (EMG in limit—0.8-0.9 µV) Homework with VCR collection film (special exercises)
3.7	BFB training with EMG (in limit 0.6-0.9 µV) BFB training with EMG-GSR—relaxation-excitation (IM competition fragments) 2 times x 5 minutes Preview of match and imagery based on this match, including corrections and planning. Relaxation with EMG-GSR$_{BFB}$—3-5 minutes—preparation for next match. Analysis of this fight together with coach. Relaxation with EMG-GSR$_{BFB}$—5-10 minutes
4.7	BFB training with portable EMG-GSR—relaxation-excitation-relaxation—3 times x 3-5 minutes Preview of match: and imagery based on this match, including corrections and planning.
6.7	Relaxation exercises with portable EMG-GSR 2 times x 5 minutes at the end of training.

In the above, a concrete example of an individual pre-competition BFB training plan with a specifically prepared VCR collection of previous competitions is presented (for a judoka participating in an event).

It should be noted that this mental program is derived from extensive experience with athletes successfully participating in top-level events such as three Olympic Games (1996, 2000, 2004), two World and three European championships, in which three gold, two silver, and three bronze medals were achieved.

Conclusions

This review of the current state of applied BFB research in sport includes a discussion of several examples of BFB-based training programs that have been used to enhance athletic performance.

We conclude that to successfully apply BFB-based mental preparation programs in sport in the future, the transition from laboratory to field should be continued and strengthened. The applicability of programs such as the "Wingate 5-step approach," should be further examined with various athlete populations (e.g., children, adolescents, and adults), differing tasks (i.e., various sport disciplines) and in diverse situations (e.g., training vs. top competitions). This principle reflects the transactional approach to BFB in sport described elsewhere (Bar-Eli, 2002).

The review of both basic and applied work conducted with the Wingate 5-Step approach between 1995 and 2001 reveals that research and application of the method has developed over time. These developments prove that the approach can be useful for both athletes and applied sport psychologists. In Table 3 the various development stages of the program are presented.

Table 3 offers an overview of the various studies and events associated with the Wingate 5-step approach. In the left two columns, research publications are presented; the right two columns present applications of the approach, including the major events in which the approach was used, and the various published reports. The various steps of development of this approach are presented chronologically.

We suggest that future research in this area could include the following:

- Further empirical research into the adequate content and composition of BFB-based psychological skills training programs is needed.

- New BFB devices need to be developed that are comfortable and user-friendly for athletes in both laboratory and field settings, including BFB telemetric systems, internet BFB versions, and other devices.

- Further evaluation of the effects of psychological skills training with BFB interventions in various sports is required.

- Development of treatment standards and guidelines for BFB-based training in sport is necessary.

Table 3: The "Wingate 5-step Approach": Stages of Development

Year	Research		Application	
	Basic	Applied	Major Events	Publications
1992 **1993** **1994** **1995**	Blumenstein, Bar-Eli, Tenenbaum, 1995 – BFB augmentation of physiological components and improvement of athletic performance	Blumenstein, Tenenbaum, Bar-Eli, & Pie, 1995 – development of two steps	1992-1996 Participation in preparation for European and World Championships in judo, wrestling, sailing, windsurfing (1 silver medal, 2 bronze medals)	
1996			1996 - Olympic Games, Atlanta	Blumenstein, 1996 – report on Atlanta Olympic Games
1997 **1998**		Blumenstein, Bar-Eli, & Tenenbaum, 1997 – development of 5 steps	1996-2000 Participation in preparation for European and World Championships in judo, taekwando, sailing, track & field, (2 silver medals, 1 bronze medal)	Blumenstein, Bar-Eli, 1998 – Use of 5-step approach in canoe/kayak
1999				Blumenstein, 1999 – 5-step approach in combat sports
2000			2000 – Olympic Games, Sydney	
2001			Participation in preparation for European and World Judo Championships (1 gold medal, 1 silver medal)	Blumenstein, Bar-Eli, 2001 – 5-step approach in different sports Blumenstein, 2001 – BFB and mental preparation in cross-cultural perspective
2002		Bar-Eli, Dreshman, Blumenstein, & Weinstein, 2002 – investigation augmentation of child swimmers, using 3 steps	2000-2004 – Participation in preparation for European and World Championships in judo, taekwondo, canoe/kayak, track & Field (2 gold medals, 1 silver medal, 1 bronze medal)	
2004	Bar-Eli & Blumenstein, 2004a –investigation of adolescent physical eduation pupils, using 3 steps Bar-Eli & Blumenstein, 2004b – performance enhancement in swimming with 5-steps		2004 – Olympic Games, Ahens	Blumenstein & Bar Eli, 2005 - From participation to Olympic Medals: Israel Approach (in preparation)

Future research and events
-Double feedback procedure and application, 5-step approach in different sports and special populations
 (e.g., children, adolescents, elderly).
-Participation in preparation for major elite sport events.

- Development of BFB training models for various sport disciplines and different training preparation periods (e.g., for general and specific training preparation, prestart preparation or recovery stages after competition and after competition season) are recommended.

- Detailed training protocols for BFB interventions (including session duration; session order; different exercises with BFB channels in visual and auditory versions; motivation support during BFB training; and combining BFB with other psychological techniques in different sports, etc.) should be developed and elaborated upon, taking into consideration cumulative experience in applied work with athletes.

- BFB applications for rehabilitation of sport injuries should be promoted.

- Interpretation tools, including useful recommendations for coaches and athletes, should be provided.

The advancement of BFB-based mental preparation in sport should encourage the application of such programs in other areas of interest, such as education, driving safety, or aviation. We are hopeful that these possibilities will indeed be translated from vision to reality.

References

Anshel, M. (2003). *Sport psychology: from theory to practice* (4th ed.). San Franciso, CA: Benjamin Cummings.

Basmajian, J. V. (1977). Motor learning and control: A working hypothesis. *Archives of Physical Medicine and Rehabilitation, 58*, 38-41.

Basmajian, J. V. (1983) (Ed.). *Biofeedback: Principles and practice for clinicians* (2nd ed.). Baltimore: Williams & Wilkins.

Bar-Eli, M. (2002). Biofeedback as applied psychophysiology in sport and exercise: Conceptual principles for research and practice. In B. Blumenstein, M. Bar-Eli, & G. Tenenbaum (Eds.), *Brain and body in sport and exercise: Biofeedback applications in performance enhancement* (pp. 1-14). London: Wiley.

Bar-Eli, M., & Blumenstein, B. (2004a). The effect of extra-curricular mental training with biofeedback on short running performance of adolescent physical education pupils. *European Physical Education Review, 10*, 123-134.

Bar-Eli, M., & Blumenstein, B. (2004b). Performance enhancement in swimming: The effect of mental training with biofeedback. *Journal of Science and Medicine in Sport, 7*, 454-464.

Bar-Eli, M., Dreshman, R., Blumenstein, B., & Weinstein, Y. (2002). The effects of mental training with biofeedback on the performance of young swimmers. *Applied Psychology - An International Review, 51*, 567-581.

Blais, M. R., & Vallerand, R. J. (1986). Multimodal effects of electro-myographic biofeedback: Looking at children's ability to control pre-competitive anxiety. *Journal of Sport Psychology, 8*, 283-303.

Blumenstein, B. (1996). Psychological aspects of Olympic preparations. *Proceedings, 2nd Post-Olympic International Symposium, "The Process of Training and Competition in View of he Atlanta '96 Games"* (pp. 97-105). Netanya: Wingate Institute.

Blumenstein, B. (1999). Mental training with biofeedback in combat sport. In V. Hosek, P. Tilinger and L. Bilek (Eds.), *Proceedings of the X European Congress of Sport Psychology, Part I* (pp. 119-121). Prague, Czech Republic.

Blumenstein, B. (2001). Sport psychology practice in two cultures: similarities and differences. In G. Tenenbaum (Ed.), *The practice of sport psychology* (pp. 231-240). Morgantown, WV: Fitness Information Technology.

Blumenstein, B. (2002). Biofeedback applications in sport and exercise: Research findings. In B. Blumenstein, M. Bar-Eli, & G. Tenenbaum (Eds.), *Brain and body in sport and exercise: Biofeedback applications in performance enhancement* (pp. 37-54). London: Wiley.

Blumenstein, B., & Bar-Eli, M. (1998). Self-regulation training with biofeedback in elite canoers and kayakers. In V. Issurin (Ed.), *Science and practice of canoe/kayak high-performance training* (pp. 124-132). Elite Sport Department. Netanya: Wingate Institute.

Blumenstein, B., & Bar-Eli, M. (2001). A five-step approach for biofeedback training in sport. *Sportwissenschaft, 4*, 412-424.

Blumenstein, B. & Bar-Eli, M. (2005) *From participation to Olympic medals: Israel approach* (in preparation).

Blumenstein, B., Bar-Eli, M., & Tenenbaum, G. (1995). The augmenting role of biofeedback: Effects of autogenic, imagery, and music training on physiological indices and athletic performance. *Journal of Sports Sciences, 13*, 343-354.

Blumenstein, B., Bar-Eli, M., & Tenenbaum, G. (1997). A five-step approach to mental training incorporating biofeedback. *The Sport Psychologist, 11*, 440-453.

Blumenstein, B., Bar-Eli, M., & Tenenbaum, G. (2002). *Brain and body in sport and exercise: Biofeedback applications in performance enhancement*. London: Wiley.

Blumenstein, B., Tenenbaum, G., Bar-Eli, M., & Pie, J. (1995). Mental preparation techniques with elite athletes using computerized biofeedback and VCR. In W. Simpson, A. Le Unes, & J. Picou (Eds.), *Applied research in coaching and athletics, annual* (pp. 1-16). Boston, MA: American Press.

Caird, S. J. A., McKenzie, A., & Sleivert, G. (1999). Biofeedback and relaxation techniques improve running economy in sub-elite long distance runners. *Medicine and Science in Sports and Exercise, 31*, 717-722.

Collins, D. (1995). Psychophysiology and sport performance. In S. J. H. Biddle (Ed.), *European perspectives on exercise and sport psychology* (pp. 154-178). Leeds, UK: Human Kinetics.

Collins, D., Powell, G., & Davies, I. (1990). An electroencephalographic study of hemispheric processing patterns during karate performance. *Journal of Sport and Exercise Psychology, 12,* 223-234.

Costa, A., Bonaccorsi, N., & Scrimali, T. (1984). Biofeedback and control of anxiety preceding athletic competition. *International Journal of Sport Psychology, 15,* 98-109.

Crews, D. J. (1991). *The influence of attentive states on golf putting as indicated by cardial and electrocortical activity.* Eugene, OR: Microform.

Crews, D. J., & Landers, D. (1993). Electroencephalographic measures of attentional patterns prior to the golf putt. *Medicine and Science in Sport and Exercise, 25,* 116-126.

Crews, D. J, Lochbaum, M., & Karoly, P. (2001). Self-regulation: Concepts, methods and strategies in sport and exercise. In R. Singer, H. Hausenblas, & C. Janelle (Eds.), *Handbook of sport psychology* (pp. 566-581) (2nd ed.). New York: Wiley.

Crews, D. J., Martin, J. J., Hart, E. A., & Piparo, A. J. (1991). The effectiveness of EEG biofeedback, relaxation and imagery training on golf putting performance. Paper presented at the *North American Society for the Psychology of Sport and Physical Activity* (NASPSPA) Annual Conference, Asilomar, California.

Croce, R. V. (1986). The effects of EMG biofeedback on strength acquisition. *Biofeedback and Self-Regulation, 11,* 299-310.

Daniels, R., & Landers, D. M. (1981). Biofeedback and shooting performance: A test of disregulation and systems theory. *Journal of Sport Psychology, 3,* 271-282.

De Witt, D. J. (1980). Cognitive and biofeedback training for stress reduction with university athletes. *Journal of Sport Psychology, 2,* 288-294.

Dishman, R.K. (1987). Psychological aids to performance. In R.H. Strauss (Ed.), *Drugs and performance in sports* (pp. 121-146). Philadelphia, PA: Saunders.

Dorsey, J. A. (1976). *The effects of biofeedback assisted desensitization training on state anxiety and performance of college age gymnasts.* Unpublished doctoral dissertation, Boston, University, Boston, MA.

Edwards, R. G., & Lippold, O. C. (1956). The relationship between force and integrated electrical activity in fatigued muscle. *Journal of Physiology, 132,* 677.

French, S. N. (1978). Electromyographic feedback for tension control during five motor skill acquisitions. *Perceptual Motor Skills, 47,* 883-889.

Goodspeed, G. A. (1983). *The effects of comprehensive self-regulation training on state anxiety and performance of female gymnasts.* Unpublished doctoral dissertation, Boston University, Boston, MA.

Gould, D., Greenleaf, C., & Krane, V. (2002). Arousal-anxiety and sport behavior. In T. Horn (Ed.), *Advances in sport psychology* (2nd ed.) (pp. 207-241). Champaign, IL: Human Kinetics.

Green, E., & Green, A. (1977). *Beyond biofeedback.* New York: Delacorte.

Green, E., Green, A., & Walters, E. (1970). Voluntary control of internal states: Psychological and physiological. *Journal of Transpersonal Psychology, 2,* 1-26.

Griffiths, J.J., Steel, D.H., Vaccaro, P,. & Karpman, M.B. (1981). The effects of relaxation techniques on anxiety and underwater performance. *International Journal of Sport Psychology, 12,* 176-182.

Hatfield, B. D., & Landers, D. M. (1987). Psychophysiology in exercise and sport research: An overview. *Exercise and Sport Science Reviews, 15,* 351-388.

Hatfield, B. D., Landers, D. M., & Ray, W. (1984). Cognitive processes during self-paced motor performance: An electroencephalographic study of elite rifle shooters. *Journal of Sport Psychology, 6,* 42-59.

Jacobson, E. (1938). *Progressive relaxation.* Chicago: University of Chicago Press.

Kamiya, J. (1968). Conscious control of brain waves. *Psychology Today, 1,* 56-60.

Kappers, B. M., & Chapman, S. J. (1984). The effect of indoor versus outdoor thermal biofeedback training in cold weather sports. *Journal of Sport Psychology, 6,* 305-311.

Kappers, B. M., & Mills, W. (1982). Thermal biofeedback in the treatment of frostbite and cold injuries: A preliminary report. *American Journal of Clinical Biofeedback, 5,* 88.

Kavussanu, M., Crews, D., & Gill, D. (1998). The effects of single versus multiple measures of biofeedback on basketball free throw shooting performance. *International Journal of Sport Psychology, 29,* 132-144.

Kruger, K. M., Ruehl, M., Scheel, D., & Franz, U. (1988). Die Anwendbarkeit von EMG Biofeedback zur optimierung sportlicher Techniken im motorischen Lerprozess von Ausdauersportarten am Beispiel des Kanurennsports [The application of EMG-Biofeedback for optimizing athletic techniques in motor learning processes of endurance sport disciplines, using the example of Kanu]. *Theorie, Praxis, und Leistungssport* (Leipzig), 26, 128-142.

Landers, D. M. (1985). Psychophysiological assessment and biofeedback. In J. Sandweiss & S. Wolf (Eds.), *Biofeedback and sport science* (pp. 63-105). New York: Plenum.

Landers, D. M. (1988). Improving motor skills. In D. Druckman & J. A. Swets (Eds.). *Enhancing human performance* (pp. 61-101). Washington, DC: National Academy Press.

Landers, D. M., Petruzzello, S. J., Salazar, W., Crews, D. L., Kubitz, K. A., Gannon, T. L., & Han, M. (1991). The influence of electrocortical biofeedback on performance in pre-elite archers. *Medicine and Science in Sport and Exercise, 23,* 123-129.

La Vaque, T. J. (1998). School-based EEG programs for ADD/ADAD. *Biofeedback, 26,* 5A-6A.

Lloyd, A. J. (1972). Auditory EMG feedback during sustained submaximum isometric contractions. *Research Quarterly, 43,* 39-46.

Lucca, J. A., & Recchuiti (1983). Effect of electromyographic biofeedback on an isometric strengthening program. *Physical Therapy, 63,* 200-203.

McGlynn, G.H., Laughlin, N.T., & Filios, S.P. (1979). The effect of electromyographic feedback and static stretching on artificially induced muscle soreness. *American Journal of Physical Medicine, 58,* 139-148.

Middaugh, S. J., Miller, M. C., Foster, G., Ferdon, M. B. (1982). Electromiographic feedback: Effects of voluntary muscle contractions in normal subjects. *Archives of Physical and Medical Rehabilitation, 63,* 254-260.

Peper, E., & Schmid, A. (1983). The use of electrodermal biofeedback for peak performance training. *Somatics, 4,* 16-18.

Petruzzello, S. J., Landers, D. M., & Salazar, W. (1991). Biofeedback and sport/exercise performance: Applications and limitations. *Behavior Therapy, 22,* 379-392.

Ren, W. D. (1995). A study of EMG biofeedback for improving archery postural consistency. In F. H Fu & M. L. Ng (Eds.), *Sport psychology: Perspectives and practices toward the 21st century* (pp. 261-265). Hong Kong: Baptist University.

Sabourin, M., & Rioux, S. (1979). Effects of active and passive EMG biofeedback training on performance of motor and cognitive tasks. *Perceptual and Motor Skills, 49*, 831-835.

Salazar, W., Landers, D., Petruzzello, S., Crews, D., Kubitz, K., & Han, M. (1990). Hemispheric asymmetry, cardiac response and performance in elite archers. *Research Quarterly for Exercise and Sport, 61*, 351-359.

Scartelli, J. P. (1984). The effect of EMG biofeedback and sedative music, EMG biofeedback only, and sedative music only on frontalis muscle relaxation ability. *Journal of Music Therapy, 21*, 67-78.

Schwartz, M.S. (1987). *Biofeedback: A practitioner's guide.* New York: Guilford.

Teague, M. A. (1976). *A combined systematic desensitization and electromyograph biofeedback technique for controlling state anxiety and improving motor skill performance.* Unpublished PhD Dissertation, University of Northern Colorado, Greeley, CO.

Tsukomoto, S. (1979). *The effects of EMG biofeedback assisted relaxation on sport competition anxiety.* Unpublished master's thesis. University of Western Ontario, London, Ontario.

Weinberg, R. S., & Hunt, V. V. (1976). The interrelationships between anxiety, motor performance and electromyography. *Journal of Motor Behavior, 9*, 219-224.

Wenz, B. J., & Strong, D. J. (1980). An application of biofeedback and self-regulation procedures with superior athletes. In R. W. Suinn (Ed), *Psychology in sports: Methods and applications* (pp. 328-333). Minneapolis: Burgess.

Wilson, V., & Bird, E. (1981). Effects of relaxation and/or biofeedback training upon flexion in gymnasts. *Biofeedback and Self-Regulation, 6*, 25-34.

Zaichkowsky, L. D. (1983). The use of biofeedback for self-regulation of performance states. In L. E. Unestahl (Ed.), *The mental aspects of gymnastics* (pp. 95-105). Orebro, Sweden: Veje.

Zaichkowsky, L.D., Dorsey, J.A., & Mulholland, T.B. (1979). The effects of biofeedback assisted systematic desensitization in the control of anxiety and performance. In M. Vanek (Ed.), *IV Svetovy Kongress,* ISSP (pp. 809-812). Prague: Olympia.

Zaichkowsky, L. D., & Fuchs, C. Z. (1988). Biofeedback applications in exercise and athletic performance. In K. B. Pandolf (Ed.), *Exercise and sports sciences reviews* (pp. 381-421). New York: Macmillan.

4.2

Strategies for Preventing and Managing Stress and Anxiety in Sport

MARK H. ANSHEL

Introduction

Competitive athletes spend many hours learning and practicing skills and strategies in anticipation of transferring their talent to the competitive event. Often, however, the content of an athlete's thoughts and emotions prevents this outcome. Negative thoughts and emotions result in reduced effort and inefficient information processing prior to and during skill execution (Wrisberg, 2001). The result may be unexpectedly poor performance quality and performance outcomes. The underlying cause of this problem can be summed up in one word, *appraisal*—also referred to as interpretation or perception—of a stimulus or an event. The result may be stress and anxiety. As Shafer (1996) notes, consistent with the vast stress literature, the normal demands placed on the individual in daily life are stressful. However, the "harmful effects (of stress) result from the person's *interpretation* of those demands" (p. 6). The purposes of this chapter are to examine the

antecedents and underlying personal and situational causes of appraisals that lead to stress and anxiety in sport, and how the athlete can help manage these feelings. In particular, this chapter will be addressing psychosocial stress (PS), as opposed to biological or somatic stress, and *competitive state anxiety* (CSA), in contrast to *trait anxiety*, a predisposition, or anxiety occurring in nonsport situations.

As negative emotions, PS and CSA form an array of psychological barriers in athletic performance that inhibit successful performance. These interacting feelings and emotions include uncertainty, worry, threat, and the perceived loss of self-control (Hackfort & Schulz, 1989; Weinberg, 1989). Often, within the context of competitive sport, the result is reduced confidence, concentration, perceived competence, optimism, and the poor use of self-regulation techniques (Hackfort & Schwenkmezger, 1993). Perhaps not surprisingly, then, PS and CSA form arguably the most common and important areas of intervention among sport psychology consultants (Wann,

1997). However, apparently there has been a paucity of intervention research on the effective use cognitive and behavioral techniques in preventing and managing PS and CSA (Hackfort & Schwenkmezger, 1993; Naylor, Burton, & Crocker, 2002).

This chapter will consist of four sections: (a) an overview and definitions of stress and anxiety in sport, (b) a discussion of the personal and situational factors that influence the athlete's perception of stress and anxiety, (c) an examination of the coping process in responding effectively to stress and anxiety, and (d) a review of the cognitive-behavioral strategies and interventions in managing stress and anxiety.

Overview and Definitions of Stress and Anxiety in Sport

To understand the ways in which stress and anxiety affect sport performance, and the cognitive and behavioral strategies that athletes and coaches can use to control these factors, it is necessary to define these concepts. Although often used interchangeably, the concepts of stress and anxiety, sometimes (and erroneously) juxtaposed with the concept of fear, are quite different. Stress, anxiety, and fear, however, do share common misconceptions. For example, it is often assumed that each of these feelings is necessarily 'bad' and must be avoided or eliminated. Not true. In fact, stress and anxiety actually contribute to high quality sports performance. Instead, the goal of every athlete (and coach) is to control or manage, not extinguish, these feelings. Some degree of both stress and anxiety contribute to certain, desirable cognitive processes (e.g., attentional focusing, concentration, speed of decision making) and emotions (e.g., confidence, enthusiasm, excitement, optimism) (Landers & Arent, 2001).

Psychosocial Stress

While a full review of the stress literature goes well beyond the scope of this chapter, traditionally, stress has been defined in psychophysiological terms. For instance, Schafer (1996), reflecting the traditional stress literature, defines stress as "arousal of mind and body in response to demands made on them" (p. 6). By this definition, stress can be either positive or negative. Positive forms of stress—*eustress*—in sport

consist of any type of mental (e.g., planning a strategy, focusing attention on the task at hand) or physical demand (e.g., tackling a ball carrier, running toward an opponent's goal). *Distress*, on the other hand, is any mental or physical demand resulting in harm to mind or body. Thus, while most physical, mental, and emotional demands in sport are harmless or positive, other demands are—or can become—negative. Stressors may become distressors.

Shafer's (1996) definition of stress differs from the often-cited definition of Lazarus and Folkman (1984), which focused primarily on the negative features of stress. To Lazarus and Folkman, stress is "a particular relationship between the person and the environment that is appraised by the person as taxing or exceeding his or her resources and endangering his or her well-being" (p. 19). Lazarus and Folkman's definition, published in the general psychology literature, warrants attention in the context of competitive sport in two ways. First, the environmental factors are central to perceiving stress; stress is not experienced in a vacuum. The ability to manage stress, then, includes attending to environmental factors that cause or contribute to it. Second, an athlete's perception, or appraisal, of the situation or stimulus is a prominent feature of experiencing stress. Thus, because athletes must first interpret the situation as taxing or exceeding their resources, managing stress is controllable. In other words, if the athlete perceives a situation as harmless or positive, rather than as threatening or harmful, no stress should be perceived.

Perceiving an event or stimulus as challenging, one type of appraisal from the Lazarus and Folkman model, usually creates positive forms of stress, resulting in greater confidence and effort to combat the potentially threatening situation. Relatively little negative stress (e.g., threat or harm) accompanies a *challenge appraisal*. For example, a challenge appraisal in response to thoughts of an upcoming contest against highly skilled opponents or in response to opponents' successful performance will more likely produce heightened feelings of self-control and confidence than an appraisal of threat or harm. Challenge appraisals induce greater effort, whereas harm or threat appraisals may create defensiveness and anxiety (Lazarus, 1999). Successfully managing stress, then, primarily consists of three processes:

managing the environment (e.g., avoiding known unpleasant situations or people), building resourcefulness (e.g., confidence, optimism, self-control, mental toughness, coping skills), and influencing the athlete's interpretation—his or her cognitive appraisal—of situations to be able to move from interpreting situations as harmful or threatening to interpreting them as challenging, or even an appraisal of no stress, which Lazarus characterizes as benign or positive. Thus, the concept of psychosocial stress includes a *stressor*, situations or circumstances that the individual characterizes as dangerous to their physical or mental well being, and a *stressful reaction*, usually based on the individual's interpretation, or appraisal, of the unpleasant situation.

Another important issue in defining stress concerns its short-term (acute) versus its long-term nature (chronic). An event interpreted by the athlete as stressful is called acute (sudden) stress (Anshel, 1996). Examples of sources of *acute stress* include a coach reprimand, comments from others, pain or injury, or making an error. In contrast, a situation interpreted as stressful experienced over a prolonged period of time is called *chronic stress* (e.g., a poor relationship with a coach, daily pressure to succeed, unpleasant personal interactions). This differentiation is important because acute and chronic stress require different types of coping strategies for optimal effectiveness in reducing the intensity of perceived stress (Gottlieb, 1997).

Competitive State Anxiety

Anxiety is the perception of threat about a *future* event or experience and is generally viewed as an inherently unpleasant emotion, not unlike anger, tension, apprehension, nervousness, or jealousy (Hackfort & Schwenkmezger, 1993; Spielberger, 1989; Woodman & Hardy, 2001). State anxiety is defined in the *Dictionary of the Sport and Exercise Sciences* (Anshel et al., 1991) as a "subjective feeling of apprehension or perceived threat, sometimes accompanied by heightened physiological arousal" (p. 9). As Spielberger (1989) notes, "the concept of threat refers to an individual's perception or appraisal of a situation as potentially dangerous or harmful" (p. 5).

While state anxiety is transitory, lasting relatively short periods of time, *trait anxiety*, on the other hand, is permanent. The *Dictionary of the Sport and Exercise Sciences* defines trait anxiety as the "relatively permanent personality predisposition to perceive certain environmental situations as threatening or stressful, and the tendency to respond to these situations with increased state anxiety" (p. 154). Thus, trait anxiety reflects an individual's susceptibility, or likelihood, to feel anxious in a given situation. According to Eysenck (1992), "the state-trait distinction relates mainly to temporal duration: States typically last for relatively short periods of time, whereas traits remain essentially unchanged for considerably longer" (p. 38).

Although state anxiety has somatic properties such as increased heart rate, blood pressure, and sweating (Martens, Vealey, & Burton, 1990), it is commonly held throughout the literature that these physiological responses are a manifestation of the individual's feelings of worry or threat. Thus, the emotion of competitive state anxiety is primarily cognitive; it is a result of thoughts and feelings that are mediated by previous experiences involved in the appraisal process. In sport, then, the athlete experiences stress as an integral part of the competitive event (i.e., a demand on the mind or body), which is then interpreted as threatening and causes an emotional state called anxiety, more specifically, competitive state anxiety.

Another emotion that is commonly cited interchangeably, but wrongly, with anxiety is *fear*. As described by Hackfort and Schwenkmezger (1993), fear reflects what the athlete is experiencing *now*. To these authors, "Fear is regarded as a biological, self-protective, adaptive mechanism, whereas anxiety is associated with learning and socialization processes" (p. 329). Fear, then, is related to feelings experienced while engaging in the competitive event (e.g., facing an opponent's successful performance or receiving a penalty), whereas anxiety reflects thoughts of a *future* event (e.g., concerns about losing the contest or desires not to experience an injury).

Stress Postulates

Stress researchers and theorists have generated two postulates, or assumptions, in describing the processes of perceiving and coping with stress (e.g., Anshel, 2003; Lazarus & Folkman, 1984; Smith, 1986; Wheaton, 1997).

Postulate 1: **An extreme or unusual external stimulus perceived as threatening or harmful will be stressful and cause significant changes in psychological, physiological, and behavioral responses**. In the context of competitive sport, this means that athletes will think and act differently under highly stressful than under less stressful situations. For instance, the athletes' thoughts and actions and their speed and accuracy of information processing (e.g., perception, retention, decision-making, autonomous performance) will be affected in response to an event that is perceived as a highly intense stressor. The use of effective coping strategies builds the athlete's resourcefulness in dealing with the stressor or reduces environmental demands. On the other hand, improper or maladaptive coping often contributes to the intensity of perceived stress, and has more deleterious emotional and performance outcomes (Anshel et al., 1993; Lazarus, 1990; Wheaton, 1997).

Postulate 2: **The failure to cope effectively with short-term, sudden stress leads to long-term, chronic stress and burnout**. Examples include ongoing harassment, poor communication, unpleasant relationships, and chronic physical discomfort or pain. Chronic stress reduces efficient information processing, leading to slower and less accurate decision-making. It also contributes to poorer emotional control, which heightens unpleasant emotions such as anxiety, depression, and anger. Long-term effects include reductions in self-esteem, confidence, and perceived self-control (Gottlieb, 1997; Smith, 1986). Unless the athlete enacts proper coping strategies, reduced participation satisfaction, poor performance, mental withdrawal, and even cessation from further engagement in sport results. Thus, athletes who use maladaptive coping skills (e.g., excessive anger or aggression, drug use, smoking, overeating) or fail to interpret sport-related events accurately and react in a rational manner will likely experience chronic stress and, eventually, may dropout of further sport participation (Smith, 1986).

Taken together, these stress postulates provide a foundation on which to understand the meaning of stress in sport and how to cope with sport-related stress through effective stress and anxiety management.

Positive Stress

To many athletes and coaches, *positive stress* is an oxymoron; the two terms simply do not seem compatible. Not according to Shafer (1996), however. Shafer, reflecting a plethora of other literature, contends "stress can be helpful as well as harmful. Positive stress can provide zest and enjoyment, as well as attentiveness and energy for meeting deadlines, entering new situations, coping with emergencies, achieving maximum performance, and meeting new challenges" (p. 16). Loehr (1994) views positive forms of stress as "anything that causes energy to be expended . . . physically, mentally, and emotionally" (p. 67). Stress, then, can be a form of *positive energy* because it may also produce growth, achievement, and excellence. Without taxing the system physically, mentally, or emotionally, the athlete cannot reach nor maintain an optimal performance state (Loehr, 1994).

Inherent in understanding the role of positive stress in sport is the concept of *voluntary recovery*. As Selye (1974) noted, and Loehr (1994) supported more recently, all forms of stress are alleviated when the individual engages in voluntary recovery. Voluntary recovery is a planned action or thought process. Recovery is anything that causes energy to be renewed or recaptured. Recovery consists of two characteristics. First, it has a re-energizing effect, so that after the recovery period, the person feels more invigorated. Second, the recovery strategy distracts the performer from the task at hand. Thus, a tennis player would not recover from hitting groundstrokes by immediately hitting a series of serves. Instead, he or she would disconnect physically, mentally, and emotionally by drinking water, having an informal conversation, or thinking about anything *except* the next task. Balancing stress and recovery is fundamental to preventing distress and being able to maintain desirable cognitive, emotional, and biological processes (Selye, 1974; Loehr, 1994; Schafer, 1996). Exposure to stress, followed by planned, voluntary recovery periods is called *oscillation* (Loehr, 1994) and prolongs the athlete's ability to sustain high performance on demand under pressure.

Failure to engage in voluntary recovery often results in *involuntary recovery*. Involuntary recovery consists of a breakdown, or deterioration, of the human organism. Biological breakdown manifests as sickness, disease, and physical fatigue. Emotional breakdown may result in anxiety, depression, feelings of helplessness, or reduced confidence or self-control. Examples of mental breakdowns include loss of concentration, forgetfulness, and mental fatigue.

CSA is not inevitable for every athlete under identical circumstances. Athletes differ on their susceptibility and intensity of anxious feelings in given situations. Each athlete possesses numerous previous experiences, feelings, and personal dispositions that are antecedents to anxiety. Examples of personal factors include trait anxiety, confidence, self-esteem, and perceptions about task complexity, importance of the contest or situation, the athlete's competence as compared to the opponent's competence, and self-control. Situational factors include the particular source of stress, situational conditions (e.g., time remaining, present score), and the opponent's skills. For a review of ways to measure anxiety and the personal and situational factors that influence perceived stress and anxiety in sport, see Hackfort and Schulz (1989); Hackfort and Schwenkmezger (1993); and Martens, Vealey, and Burton (1990).

The Process of Coping With Stress and Anxiety

Experiencing stressful events during sports competition often leads to reduced psychological functioning, such as misdirected attentional focus, poor concentration, negative self-talk, and heightened state anxiety, and, from a somatic perspective, increased muscle tension (Anshel, Brown, & Brown, 1993; Krohne & Hindel, 1988). Therefore, it is imperative that athletes use all available resources to deal with the inevitable experience of stress in order to achieve optimal performance. The conscious and purposeful reaction to stressful events in order to reduce their perceived intensity and frequency or to enhance the athlete's personal resources in dealing with the situation is called *coping*.

Coping

Coping is a multidimensional process. It consists of a vast array of thoughts, emotions, and actions, often executed in a very rapid, sometimes parallel, manner and is influenced by various personal and situational factors. The failure to cope effectively with acute stress often leads to reduced performance quality and, eventually, mental burnout and dropout from sport. It is surprising, then, that the area of coping is still in its infancy in the sport psychology literature. This section will consist of a brief overview of the coping process, followed by suggested cognitive and behavioral strategies for coping with acute and chronic forms of sport-related stress.

Coping Myths

There are three areas of contention or misunderstanding in the literature related to common definitions of coping. These concern whether coping is a conscious or an automatic process, whether the concept of coping implies effectiveness in the stress response, and differences between coping strategies and coping styles.

Coping is a conscious process. Researchers (e.g., Carver, Scheier, & Weintraub, 1989; Krohne, 1993; Lazarus, 1990) generally agree that coping consists of *conscious* psychological and physical efforts to improve one's resourcefulness in dealing with stressful events (e.g., building self-confidence, reinterpreting the situation, increasing perceptions of self-control or optimism) or to reduce external demands (e.g., managing the environment). Researchers and theorists, however, differ on whether coping is necessarily a conscious process. For example, while Lazarus and Folkman (1984) argue that coping is a conscious attempt at reducing or managing stress, others (e.g., Hardy, Jones, & Gould, 1996) argue that coping strategies can be initiated with minimal cognition. There is debate as to whether automated responses to stress constitute coping. To Compas et al. (1997), coping begins with conscious and effortful attempts to manage stress, and through repeated practice, becomes automated. The authors contend "some responses to stress that initially require effortful control may become automatic as a result of overlearning and, thus, are no longer considered coping" (p. 109). Thus, for example, an athlete might learn to cope with unpleasant input from the crowd by focusing on the task at hand and filtering out noise, which the athlete appraises as irrelevant. If the athlete then learns to perform this function automatically, as many athletes do, they are no longer coping with crowd noise, according to Compas et al.

Coping as a conscious process has two important

implications that have heretofore been ignored in the sport psychology literature. First, enacting a coping strategy is accompanied by the individual's awareness of their cognitive or behavioral responses to stress. For example, while anger is a frequent response to frustration following stressful events in sport, it is not necessarily a coping strategy when the athlete's anger is impulsive and in the virtual absence of planning or thinking. If, however, the athlete acknowledges that anger has a cathartic, stress-reducing effect, or improves his or her ability to confront the stressor, then anger might be considered a coping strategy.

The second implication is that coping is not necessarily an effective or adaptive response to stress. A particular coping strategy may lead to chronic stress or result in reduced concentration, higher tension, or anxiety (Anshel et al., 1993). This makes the coping strategy maladaptive, or counterproductive. As Aldwin and Revenson (1987) assert, coping strategies can be either effective or ineffective in terms of reducing perceived stress intensity, depending on the short-term and long-term outcomes of using the coping strategy. A coping strategy may do more harm than good. Examples of ineffective, or *maladaptive*, coping strategies include the intake of banned substances or alcohol, smoking, uncontrolled anger, seeking revenge, mental disengagement—resulting in reduced concentration—or quitting sport.

Coping Styles and Strategies

Researchers and practitioners have often failed to differentiate between coping styles and coping strategies. The result has been the use of inappropriate measures and inaccurate conclusions. A *coping style* is a disposition that reflects behavior over time. It refers to the athlete's preference, or tendency, to use certain types of coping strategies across time in response to the same type of stressor, or following different types of stressful events (Krohne, 1993). A *coping strategy*, on the other hand, is a state or situational measure. It consists of the athlete's use of one or more cognitive or behavioral attempts at reducing perceived stress intensity. An athlete's coping style consists of several coping strategies that can be categorized according to similar characteristics. Examples include problem-focused and emotion-focused strategies (Lazarus & Folkman, 1984), approach and

avoidance (Anshel, 1996; Suls & Fletcher, 1985), monitoring and blunting (Miller, 1989), attention and distraction (McCrae, 1992), sensitization and desensitization, and engagement and disengagement (Carver et al., 1989). The following coping model reflects the athlete's use of coping strategies, not coping style, in response to stressful events in sport.

The Coping Process: A Brief Overview

Although numerous coping models exist in the general psychology literature that illustrates the coping process in response to nonsport stress, there appears to be widespread agreement among theorists and researchers about the general sequence in which coping occurs. Anshel et al. (2001) generated a coping model, also confirmed in a qualitative study (Anshel, 2001), that illustrates the coping process following acute stress in competitive sport. The following is a brief overview of this model.

Stimuli or events

First, an external stimulus or event must be encoded upon entering the information processing system. Ignoring or filtering out this input will prevent the appraisal (perceptual) process. Thus, if the athlete does not detect or perceive the incoming information, it cannot be interpreted as stressful, and therefore, stimuli are not perceived and no coping eventuates. However, if incoming data are detected and encoded, it enters the next (second) phase of the coping process, cognitive appraisal.

Cognitive appraisal

Typically, using the ubiquitous Lazarus and Folkman (1984) model, individuals make one of three types of appraisals: benign/positive, harm/threat, or challenge. Again, coping is unnecessary if the appraisal is benign or positive. Appraisals that are perceived as threatening, harmful, or challenging, however, require coping. This stage may be considered the *pre-coping* process. Whether athletes possess an *appraisal style* has apparently not been studied and remains an area of needed future research.

Harm/loss appraisals reflect perceived stress or damage that has already occurred. Harm/loss appraisals are typical when the athlete has experienced a physical or mental error, a reprimand, injury, or pain. One potential problem with harm/loss appraisals is that individuals are more likely to use less mature, more passive coping strategies (McCrae, 1992). Harm/loss appraisals may be preferred under conditions of low controllability (Dewe, 1992). For example, the stress associated with an opponent's successful performance or a bad call—'bad' as in one that goes against the athlete—from the referee or umpire must often be either quickly forgotten or discounted. This is especially true in continuous sports in which the cognitive and physical demands require ongoing monitoring, while not being distracted from the task at hand (Anshel et al., 1997; Roth & Cohen, 1986). Lehrer and Woolfolk (1993) contend that effective stress management consists of controlling what is controllable and forgetting about or minimizing the importance of stressful experiences that cannot be controlled.

Threat. A threat appraisal reflects the athlete's state anxiety because it reflects worry about how the situation might turn out (McCrae, 1992). It consists of expectations of possible future harm or danger often accompanied by unpleasant self-statements such as "What if... " or "I hope... " One potentially harmful and threatening source of stress for athletes, for example, is an opponent's ability or previous success (Anshel et al., 1997). A threat appraisal reflects the situation's uncertainty, the chances that an opponent will demonstrate superior performance, or whether the athlete's health or physical well being will be at risk, particularly in contact sports. Sometimes threat appraisals are irrational, based on the athlete's thoughts about worst case scenarios (e.g., "What if I lose the contest?" "What if I get injured?") or a reflection of low confidence (e.g., "I hope I can outscore my opponent"). Threat is an appropriate appraisal when there is concern about how a particular situation might influence the contest, especially if the event is associated with the athlete's previous experience.

Challenge appraisals reflect the view that the person will benefit from overcoming the stressful experience. An important component of challenge appraisals is the anticipation that unpleasant events are inherent in sport and must be overcome in order to achieve a desirable outcome (Peacock & Wong,

1990). Challenge appraisals might result in less intense stress because they tend to increase the person's sense of control over the situation, and they might be more productive in keeping the athlete focused on the task at hand and maintaining confidence, alertness, and proper arousal level.

There are other forms of appraisal, however, that go beyond the Lazarus and Folkman (1984) model. Terry (1991), for example, used controllability as her form of appraisal. Stressful events appraised as highly controllable will produce different types of coping strategies than low-control stressful events. In their work with child athletes, Anshel and Delany (1999) used the appraisal categories of *positive* and *negative* based on the idea that younger athletes would have more difficulty identifying their appraisals using more complex dimensions.

Coping strategies

At the heart of the coping process is the person's use of cognitive or behavioral strategies that are intended to reduce the perceived stress intensity following the athlete's stressful appraisal. One construct that accurately reflects coping in the context of competitive sport is *approach and avoidance* (Krohne, 1993, 1996). Unlike other coping constructs, approach-and-avoidance coping has received conceptual and empirical support in the general psychology (e.g., Carver et al., 1989; Holahan, Moos, & Schaefer, 1996; Leventhal, Suls, & Leventhal, 1993; Tobin, Holroyd, Reynolds, & Wigal, 1989) and sport psychology literatures (e.g., Anshel, 1996; Anshel et al., 1997; Anshel & Wells, 2000; Krohne, 1993, 1996). In addition, approach-and-avoidance coping includes cognitive and behavioral subdimensions that reflect sport situations unlike the problem-focused and emotion-focused coping (Lazarus & Folkman, 1984) framework that is often cited in nonsport research. Leventhal et al. (1993) provide a critical analysis of the problem- and emotion-focused coping framework.

Before describing the approach-avoidance coping framework, however, it is important to note that coping is not a required response following perceived stress (Lazarus, 1999). The athlete may not enact a coping strategy. In fact, not coping with a stressful event has the benefit of ignoring it, consciously or subconsciously, and to continue attending to the next task at hand. However, the "costs" of not coping after making a stress appraisal might be experiencing continued stress, while maintaining unpleasant feelings. The result may be poor performance and negative affect.

Approach coping strategies reflect the intensified intake and processing of unpleasant or threatening information. Main objectives of approach coping are to improve one's understanding or control of the stressful situation, or to improve one's personal resourcefulness in dealing with it. This can occur through thoughts (approach-cognitive coping) such as planning or analyzing, or by actions (approach-behavioral coping) such as asking for information or confrontation.

Approach coping is usually preferred when the athlete views the situation as controllable, knows the source of stress, is receptive to discussing the situation, has good communication skills, has adequate time to resolve or at least address the issue, will be disadvantaged by failing to resolve the issue, and is highly confident in his or her ability to resolve the problem (Roth & Cohen, 1986).

Approach-behavioral coping refers to an athlete's actions taken in trying to resolve a stressful situation (e.g., interacting with or confronting the source stress, actively obtaining information, seeking social support, setting goals in attempting to resolve the situation, discussing feelings with others). *Approach-cognitive coping* consists of thoughts that improve one's emotional status and reduces stress intensity (e.g., thinking about or analyzing the stressful event, planning an effective response, or using cognitive strategies such as psyching-up or positive self-talk).

Avoidance coping strategies reflect a conscious attempt at physically or mentally turning away from the stressful source (Krohne, 1993). There are different objectives in using avoidance coping, depending on the situation. One objective, discussed earlier with respect to making threat appraisals, is to distract the individual from the stress source, particularly important when the situation does not allow for a more involved, reflective response. Avoidance coping is also preferred when the athlete wants to replace unpleasant, nonconstructive thoughts with more positive ones.

Roth and Cohen (1986) have suggested that avoidance coping is preferred when the situation is uncontrollable (e.g., a bad call from the referee or a coach's reprimand, bad in the sense that it goes against the athlete); emotional resources are limited (e.g., low self-confidence, reduced energy, less sense of urgency); the person must deal with a great deal of information very quickly, and therefore, must reduce information load in short-term memory (e.g., rapid decision-making is required); the source of stress is not clear or unknown (e.g., the origin of a spectator's abusive comment); the outcome measures are immediate or short-term (e.g., the ball is in play; movement is continuous); more time is needed, but unavailable, to assimilate stressful information (e.g., no time to obtain information from the referee to explain the call); or there is little chance of resolving the stressful issue (e.g., dealing stress associated with a hostile coach, a 'bad' call from the referee or umpire, or abusive spectators or opponents). Krohne and Hindel (1988) found that more successful elite table tennis players used avoidance coping and suffered lower anxiety after committing performance errors than their less successful counterparts.

Avoidance-cognitive coping strategies include *psychological distancing* (e.g., "He or she is young and does not know better;" "The coach is having a bad day"); *discounting* (e.g., "That person is too angry to make any sense;" "The person's views are off target;" "The person doesn't know what they are saying"); *self-deprecating humor* (e.g., "I can't believe I said/did that"); *cognitive reappraisal*, which is an attempt at reinterpreting the stressor (e.g., "I learned something from that experience"); and *rationalization* ("Everyone makes mistakes; I'm not perfect;" "Some days I play better than others").

Avoidance-behavioral coping comprises actions that physically remove the athlete from the stress source (Anshel, 1996; Anshel et al., 1997). Examples include engaging in exercise (e.g., jogging, walking, strength training, yoga); social engineering, which consists of avoiding an individual or the stressful situation; or quickly moving ahead to the next task at hand. Exercise, in particular, has at least two stress-reducing benefits related to avoidance coping. First, it distracts the individual from thinking about past stressful experiences, also referred to as the *distraction or timeout hypothesis*. Second, exercise may improve one's tolerance to stress, called the buffer hypothesis (see McAuley, 1994, for a review of these explanations). Since exercise may actually prevent stress, athletes should engage in a regularly scheduled exercise program that they find enjoyable and rewarding. Examples of maladaptive avoidance-behavioral coping strategies include drug or alcohol abuse, prolonged use of tobacco, and overeating—food as a vehicle to replace or reduce stressful feelings—or food avoidance (e.g., anorexia nervosa, bulimia).

Often, the athlete's selection of a coping strategy is a function of the type of stressful event and other situational characteristics (e.g., perceived control of the situation, predictability of the stressor, the time at which stress is experienced during the contest), depicted by the *transactional coping* model (Lazarus, 1990; Lazarus & Folkman, 1984). If, however, the athlete uses similar coping responses—strategies or styles—following different types of stressors, or copes similarly over repeated experiences of the same type of stressor, then the *trait coping model* is supported (Lazarus, 1990; Lazarus & Folkman, 1984). To date, the transactional model has gained more research support than the trait model in the sport psychology literature (e.g., Anshel, 1996; Anshel & Wells, 2000; Kaissidis-Rodafinos et al., 1997).

Post-coping Processes

Briefly, the process of coping also includes post-coping thoughts or behaviors. These include *remaining on task, assessing coping effectiveness*, and *cognitive reappraisal*. Stress management training for remaining on task requires the athlete to focus on external events (e.g., "Where is the ball/opponent?" "What is my strategy?" "What is the next task at hand?") to minimize negative thoughts by reducing internal attentional focusing and, instead, to focus on external cues, while ignoring the previous stressful event. The content of post-coping thoughts might be task-specific, in which the athlete associates or dissociates thoughts with bodily responses, motivational positive self-talk (e.g., "Stay with it," "I can do this; I'm ready"), or evaluating performance quality following the coping attempt. *Cognitive reappraisal* is more likely to occur after the coping strategy has been enacted. Athletes are now ready to initiate a new, different interpretation of the stressful situation. Reappraisals, which reflect ongoing reassessments of the resources available for dealing with the stressful event, give athletes an opportunity to

change initial appraisals, perhaps view the stressful event as a learning opportunity, and reduce the intensity of subsequent, similar stressors (Lazarus & Folkman, 1984).

Assessing coping effectiveness is accompanied by defining the criteria for effective coping outcomes. In differentiating between coping effectiveness and coping efficacy, Aldwin and Revenson (1987) contend that coping effectiveness is "the relation between coping and some outcome measure . . . ." Coping efficacy, on the other hand, "refers to the perception that the coping effort was successful in achievement the individual's goals in a particular situation" (p. 339). See Zeidner and Saklofske (1996) for a discussion of eight criteria for assessing coping outcomes. Taken together, the selection of post-coping activity is a function of task (e.g., closed versus open), cognitive (e.g., active or passive), and situational demands (Singer, 2000).

Strategies for Preventing and Managing Stress and Anxiety

Perhaps the most effective approach to managing stress in sport settings is to prevent stressful appraisals in response to a stimulus or event in the first place. Meichenbaum (1977, 1985) refers to this process as *stress inoculation*. This first section will describe factors that are likely to prevent perceptions of stress and anxiety.

Approaches to Stress and Anxiety Prevention

Although athletes rarely have control over the sport environment, they can control their own thoughts, emotions, and reactions to various stimuli and situations. The primary approaches to preventing stress and anxiety (i.e., stress innoculation) are avoiding stress or minimizing appraisals and building mental toughness.

Eliminate Actual Stressors

This strategy has been advanced by Hepburn, Loughlin, and Barling (1997) in the job stress literature. It may appear to be common sense to suggest the best stress management technique is to eliminate the sources of stress that induces stress in the first place. Yet, this strategy is often ignored in sport because athletes—and their coaches—wrongly assume that most common sources of stress in sport are natural, typical, and even desirable. Studies report that the sources of stress in sport—chronic and acute—are often unavoidable (e.g., making an error, receiving a reprimand from the coach, spectator booing; see Anshel et al., 2001, for a review of this literature). Some sources, however, may be far more controllable. Examples include not allowing a call from the referee or umpire upset or distract the athlete from the task at hand. Athletes who automatically assume responsibility for receiving a penalty are closer to eliminating this common source of stress than athletes who become defensive and upset about the call. Even making external causal attributions in response to performance errors or an opponent's success to uncontrollable factors (e.g., task difficulty/superior opponent) is less likely to become a stressor. Athletes should think about common sources of stress and try to eliminate as many as possible before they arise during the contest.

Avoid Stress Appraisals

As depicted earlier in describing the coping process, experiencing stress and anxiety begins with an interpretation, or appraisal, of a stimulus or event. Benign, irrelevant, or positive appraisals, which do not lead to stress and anxiety, can replace appraisals of threat or harm. The apparent advantage to nonstressful appraisals is that they do not require coping. Coping is necessary only in response to situations or events interpreted as adverse or unpleasant. Thus, a potentially stressful situation, such as being hit by a pitch in baseball, receiving a hard block in football, or being out-jumped in basketball, might be interpreted as simply a part of the game.

If an appraisal must, or even should, cause stress, then the issue becomes which appraisal is most beneficial given particular situational demands for effective stress management. *Challenge* appraisals are ideal in sport because they represent confidence to deal directly with, learn from, or even benefit from the stressor. Lazarus (1990) contends that challenge appraisals provide an opportunity to achieve growth, mastery, or profit by using more than routine resources to meet a demand. For example, competing against a superior team or highly skilled opponent might be interpreted as threatening; however, it can

also be viewed as an opportunity to demonstrate competence, gain recognition, provide information about areas for further improvement, or enhance one's stature on the team. Whether challenge appraisals lead to particular types of coping strategies, as opposed to threat or harm appraisals, has apparently not been explored in the sport psychology research literature. It is plausible to surmise, however, that highly skilled athletes should enter the contest viewing the opponent as a challenge, an opportunity and obligation to demonstrate their own competence, not as a threat.

Probably the most common stress appraisal in sport is threat. Threat appraisals, commonly associated with state anxiety (Meichenbaum, 1985), consist of expectations of future harm (e.g., batting against a superb pitcher, competing in sport after experiencing an injury, or returning to competition after rehabilitation).

Threat appraisals have advantages and disadvantages. One advantage of harm appraisals is that it allows athletes to make appropriate psychological and behavioral adjustments and increases readiness, thereby preventing the stressor from occurring or from doing optimal damage, not unlike looking both ways before crossing a dangerous road. Perceived threat also allows athletes to raise their personal resources in meeting future demands. Threat appraisals, per se, are not deleterious to performance success. However, Gottleib (1997) contends that the failure to use positive personal resources to meet and overcome threatening stressful events, such as confidence, arousal, positive expectancies, high self-esteem, optimism, and self-control will increase the likelihood of experiencing chronic stress, burnout, reduced performance quality, and eventually quitting. Features of the athlete's personality, previous experiences, and situational factors should be taken into account before using threat appraisals as a productive stress management technique (Lehrer & Woolfolk, 1993; Mace, 1990).

Build Mental Toughness

Stress inoculation is concerned with strategies in which athletes can both prevent and deal with the inevitable feelings of stress and anxiety that is inherent in competitive sport. One approach to helping athletes resist or deal effectively with stressful feelings is to build mental toughness. Mental toughness is the ability to ignore elements of interference during competition.

Loehr (1982, 1991, 1994) generated the term *mental toughness* to mean reaching and sustaining high performance in sport—the athlete's ideal performance state—under pressure by expanding capacity physically, mentally, and emotionally. Loehr contends that mental toughness is learned, not inherited. One common, but false, view of many athletes (and coaches) is that we are born with the right 'competitive instincts,' and that not being able to handle failures is due to lacking the genetic predisposition to be mentally tough. Loehr contends that this view—the belief in a mental toughness gene—is very tempting because it absolves the athlete of feeling responsible for failure performance. This is self-destructive thinking, because the athlete is more likely to feel helpless, a loss of self-control over developing this skill, and lacking in the self-motivation to learn the proper mental skills to become more competitive.

Mentally tough competitors are self-motivated and self-directed (their energy comes from internal sources, not forced from the outside), positive but realistic (they are builders and optimists, not critics, faultfinders, and pessimists), in control of their emotions (they have "tamed the lion inside" in response to frustration and disappointment), calm and relaxed under fire (rather than avoiding pressure, they are challenged by it), highly energetic and ready for action (capable of getting themselves pumped up and energized for optimal effort and performance), determined (they have a strong will to succeed and relentless in the pursuit of goals), mentally alert and focused (capable of long and intensive periods of full concentration), doggedly self-confident (a high belief in their ability to perform well), and fully responsible (taking full responsibility for their own actions).

Strategies for Building Mental Toughness

Although mental toughness is partly composed of selected dispositions (e.g., high levels of self-control, confidence, self-esteem, hardiness, and low levels of trait anxiety, negative perfectionism, and helplessness), Loehr (1982, 1991, 1994) suggests several cognitive and behavioral strategies to build mental toughness in sport (also see Anshel, 2003, for a review of this area). The value of these techniques is their relevance for controlling chronic and acute stress and anxiety.

Increase fitness. Loehr (1994) contends that exercise, in general, and aerobic exercise, in particular, expands the capacity of an individual to perform optimally under pressure, given occasional periods of recovery, that is, any activity that distracts or reenergizes the individual.

Practice to improve mental skills. To resist anxiety and other negative thought patterns in response to sudden adversity, athletes should rely on cognitive skills to maintain self-control.

Set realistic but challenging goals. One outcome inherent in goal setting is to create challenges that induce effort and, when accomplished, foster intrinsic motivation based on feelings of competence and task satisfaction.

Think positively and create enthusiasm. Positive thinking (e.g., confidence, optimism, self-control, enthusiasm) and positive expectancies increase effort and the likelihood of success.

Repeat positive self-affirmations. Positive self-affirmations promote high self-expectancies, while reducing the likelihood of engaging in negative thinking. Therefore, a stressful experience is less likely to distract the athletes, inhibit information processing, and impede progress toward achieving desirable goals.

Increase self-discipline (maintain control). Mentally tough athletes have established consistent routines that block out distractions, call for backup plans following adversity, and encourage persistent effort. Plan B, that is, an alternative to initial planned performance, has been practiced and mastered in response to unexpected barriers and situational demands.

Use positive visualization. The use of mental visualization overcomes errors, allows more efficient responses to unpleasant and unexpected events, and fosters desirable responses. This strategy consists of mentally imaging a vast array of situations that the athlete is likely to experience before or during competition, each of which is performed with perfect skill and a desirable outcome.

Review film/video of best performances-or recall them. Reviewing previous high quality performance allows the athlete to rehearse desirable skills and to build and maintain confidence, especially after experiencing unpleasant or disappointing outcomes. The mentally tough athlete knows that failure is inevitable in sport, and that to combat inaccurate perceptions of competence, it is important to acknowledge success regularly.

Think practice. Succumbing to pressure, a condition called *choking*, is usually accompanied by severe anxiety: the perception of worry and threat about the competitive event. Mental toughness may be facilitated by thinking about practice conditions, rather than self-defeating thoughts (e.g., "What if I make an error or lose?"), which may be overcome by saying to oneself, "think practice."

See competition and opponents as a challenge, not as a threat. Stressful events begin with the appraisal process. Interpreting situations, events, or stimuli as threatening or harmful, rather than as benign or challenging, will heighten anxiety. Mentally tough athletes say, "throw me the ball" or "hit the ball to me." They observe opponents and conclude "I'm better!"

Reduce cognition during skill execution. While thinking is inherent in performance success, the mentally tough athlete engages in mental preparation prior to skill execution. The planning and initial executing of sport skills should occur in the virtual absence of thinking primarily for two reasons: (a) so that negative thoughts and other distractions do not interfere with performance quality, and (b) so that the athlete is able to ignore physical response demands and, instead, attend to more meaningful environmental cues. Reduced cognition during performance will allow the performer to engage in important cognitions such as pre-cueing (detecting environmental cues or stimuli prior to performance initiation), anticipation, rapid (internal-external) attentional focusing, and being able to ignore interfering thoughts and emotions.

Stay externally focused on the task at hand. Particularly with respect to open-skill sports, it is important to ignore distractions and maintain attentional focus to relevant cues in the environment. For most sports, this means remaining vigilant to external, not to internal, stimuli.

Attribute success to internal causes. The mentally tough athlete uses accurate causal attributions that increase motivation. They take responsibility for most performance outcomes, learn from mistakes, are receptive to and integrate feedback from their coach, and never stop learning.

Use thought-stopping when having a negative thought. High quality athletes do not allow ill-timed negative thoughts to continue. A technique called thought-stopping (i.e., saying to oneself, "stop" or "focus" while thinking the unpleasant thought) is used immediately.

Have positive role models. Read about and listen to other athletes who have stories of overcoming adversity and maintaining self-control. These individuals have a mentoring role in teaching the skills needed for mental toughness.

Avoid thoughts of helplessness and hopelessness. Helplessness consists of feeling a lack of control about the present, while hopelessness is a perception that the situation will not improve. The mentally tough athlete maintains self-control about the present and a sense of optimism, confidence, and improvement about the future.

Routines. Routines are thoughts and behaviors that are automatically integrated into our day. We have routines before we go to sleep, when we wake up in the morning, and yes, just before the event in competitive sport. In sport, as in life, routines serve many valuable purposes. These include reducing the amount of in-depth thinking (e.g., creating, decision-making, problem-solving), which saves a good deal of time, maintaining emotional control, particularly under pressure, and regulating our physical, mental, and emotional performance preparation, both before and during competition. Finally, rituals help athletes move from the cognitive stage to the automatic stage of performing sport skills. The cognitive stage is characterized by a considerable amount of thinking (e.g., planning, decision-making), typical of novice performers. The automatic stage is more advanced, in which sport skills are performed with minimal thinking.

Rituals help the competitor maintain self-control and concentration under conditions of high duress and pressure, not uncommon in competitive sport (Lidor & Singer, 2000).

Stress and Anxiety Management Strategies

A brief overview of stress is important in understanding how to manage it. First, stress is inherent in sport. Therefore, the athlete should anticipate it and plan in advance how to control it. Second, some stress is good, even necessary, for optimal performance and successful outcomes. Therefore, the key objective in experiencing stress in sport is not to attempt to eliminate it, but to manage its frequency and intensity. Here are some ways for athletes to accomplish this goal.

Acknowledging predispositions. It is in the athletes' best interest to know if they are susceptible to experiencing stress and making stress appraisals. Although evidence of appraisal style has not been studied in sport psychology, clearly some athletes are more likely than others to make stress appraisals (e.g., harm/loss, threat) than non-stress appraisals (e.g., irrelevant/benign/positive,). Coping style is another factor that may predispose that athlete toward stressful feelings. For example, 'approachers' are more susceptible to thinking about stimuli or information that is labeled stressful as opposed to 'avoiders,' who are more likely to discount or not be as sensitive to such input (Krohne, 1993). Other orientations such as learned resourcefulness, optimism, self-esteem, perfectionism, self-control, and confidence each influence the athlete's susceptibility and response to stress. Athletes who acknowledge their typical reactions to situational factors of the competitive event can take precautions toward planning for and learning proper stress management skills.

Controlling environmental factors. The belief that athletes have little control over their environment is a myth (Anshel, 2003). While coaches can be part of the problem or the solution in helping athletes to manage their stress and anxiety, athletes are capable of manipulating their environment to help manage their stress. Examples include, what Greenberg (1993) calls, *social engineering* in which the individual takes the initiative to move toward or away from a location that is known, in advance, to either foster or reduce stress. For instance, an athlete who knows that being in the presence of his or her coach or a teammate will increase the athlete's negative emotion, may want to use a social engineering technique to avoid close proximity with the coach or teammate. We use social engineering every day when we try to avoid driving in rush hour or in certain high-traffic locations.

Another strategy that serves a similar function is *social support.* Social support consists of building relationships that benefit the individual (Schafer, 1996). Social support can be expressive (emotional support) or instrumental (task-related support). Athletes need to become acquainted with the competitive environment in advance and then plan to use the proper behavioral strategies to control it.

Anxiety Management

According to Romas and Sharma (1995), managing anxiety should be approached by listing the worries to be faced (there is no use worrying about over things over which the athlete has no control, such as the opponent's skill level), *worries to be solved immediately* (e.g., quickly comparing one's skills with the effectiveness of strategies for overcoming an opponent's skills; the opponent's performance strategies), *worries to be postponed* (e.g., a highly talented but injured teammate cannot play today; hopefully he or she can play in the next contest), and *worries to be ignored* (e.g., crowd noise or remarks, being unfairly judged by a referee or umpire). Anxiety management is about replacing thoughts that produce threat with thoughts that encourage optimism, confidence, and optimal effort. One approach toward meeting these goals is to develop precompetitive and competitive performance routines.

Coping

As indicated earlier, coping consists of two processes, either *building personal resources*, that is, improving one's resourcefulness, or *reducing external demands* in dealing with events that have been appraised by the athlete as stressful (e.g., harmful, threatening, or challenging). Building personal resources is represented by desirable predispositions (e.g., self-esteem, learned resourcefulness, optimism, hardiness, competitiveness, low trait anxiety) and thinking styles that are preferred in most sport situations (e.g., confidence, the appropriate coping style, self-control, self-regulation skills, reappraisal) that allow the individual to persevere and attend to the task at hand in response to adversity. Reducing external demands reflects the athlete's skills at managing the environment so that stressful events are either avoided or dealt with efficiently. Strategies in response to stress and anxiety will reflect the coping model depicted earlier.

Approach Coping (Cognitive and Behavioral)

Addressing or confronting the source of stress, psychologically or behaviorally, is warranted under numerous circumstances in competitive sport. However, this form of coping can also be counterproductive to regaining emotional control and performing optimally. Approach coping can also take adaptive (e.g., asking for clarification of a referee's call, increasing emotional intensity, changing game strategy) and maladaptive forms (e.g., arguing, fighting, continued thinking of the unpleasant event, continuous self-criticism). As indicated earlier, in general, athletes should consider using approach coping when there is time to address the source of stress (e.g., during a break in play, after the contest), when something can be done about the stressful situation (e.g., confronting an abusive opponent, changing performance strategy, mentally rehearsing the correct technique following an error), when relationships with others is secure (e.g., asking the coach to provide information), when the athlete is highly confident or possesses superb communication skills, when failure to confront the stressor may result in a long-term or permanent problem (e.g., experiencing pain or injury), or when the athlete's personality (i.e., coping style) is compatible with an approach orientation.

Examples of adaptive forms of approach coping following acute stress include problem-solving, social support, verbal communication of feelings, information-seeking, self-pacing, asking others to alter their behavior, practice, thinking about the problem and the appropriate response, time management, and managing actions (e.g., effective listening, assertiveness, taking action). Coping strategies that are usually considered maladaptive (undesirable) forms of approach coping include fighting, arguing, over-

eating, catastrophizing (i.e., chronic complaining or thinking the worst), thinking about the unpleasant experience when there is insufficient time, and negative self-talk (Schafer, 1996). The reason these are often considered ineffective approach coping strategies is that, at times, physical confrontation is needed to establish a sense of authority or respect, such as in ice hockey and other contact sports, or to overcome an opponent's abusive treatment. It is important, however, that the cure is not worse than the disease, in other words, that the coping strategy does not cause additional problems for the athlete.

Avoidance Coping (cognitive and behavioral)

Experiencing adversity in sport is psychologically distracting, reducing concentration, misdirecting the athlete's attentional focus, and generating negative thinking, all of which are potentially deleterious to sport performance. Therefore, the ability to remove oneself psychologically or behaviorally from unpleasant events experienced during the contest sometimes is very desirable for optimal performance. Avoidance coping is often more appropriate when there is not sufficient time to address the stressor (e.g., while the ball is in play), when it is early in the contest and the stressor is not perceived as important, when the situation is perceived as uncontrollable (e.g., bad luck, an opponent's superior performance, a coach's reprimand), when the athlete does not have an expressive personality, confidence is low, or has an avoidance coping style.

Schafer (1996) and Anshel et al. (2001) suggest that avoidance coping strategies following acute stress include engaging in physical exercise, performing various relaxation techniques, using positive self-talk, altering thoughts from irrational to rational beliefs, remembering your skills and other positive qualities, taking a time break, engaging in mental distraction, seeing an unpleasant event as temporary, praying, and using psychological distancing and discounting, which involves not taking the source of stress seriously or being able to rationalize it (e.g., "that's part of the game," "my opponent is just doing their job," "I can't take them seriously; it's just trash talk"). Examples of maladaptive avoidance coping, while not necessarily enacted during the contest, include excessive use of alcohol or drugs, use of tobacco products, over-consumption of food, displaced aggression (i.e., becoming upset with another person who is not responsible for the problem), unnecessary risk-taking, and use of medications.

Conclusions and Future Directions

Surprisingly little is known about the effective use of preventing (prestress) and managing stress and anxiety (post-stress) in competitive sport. One reason for this is the dearth of intervention research in the related sport psychology literature. Another reason includes the lack of a coherent understanding of the coping process in competitive sport, in which there is a dearth of conceptual frameworks, theories, and models in sport contexts. In addition, measures often used to measure the intensity and frequency of chronic and acute stress and anxiety experienced during and immediately following the competitive event lack psychometric scrutiny. Better, more reliable and valid, instruments are needed to measure each phase of the coping process, while controlling for the various personal (e.g., appraisal style, coping style, self-esteem, self-confidence, optimism, perfectionism, resourcefulness, hardiness, cognitive appraisals, self-control, cultural differences) and situational factors (e.g., sources of stress, measuring chronic versus acute stress, performer's role in the contest, perceived game importance), that can influence the athlete's anxiety, perceptions of stress, and coping responses.

Stress management research and interventions have both been criticized for their reliance on canned programs. Such programs have ignored the individual's preferences for using certain types of coping strategies and have omitted personal and situational characteristics that accompany certain coping techniques (Lehrer & Woolfolk, 1993). For example, most of these programs extol the virtues of relaxation training, yet ignore the fact that relaxation may be counterproductive in many circumstances or may not be effective for individuals with particular needs, preferences, or previous experiences (Anshel, 2003). For example, Fillinghim and Blumenthal (1993), in their review of related literature, found equivocal findings on the effects of aerobic exercise on reducing stress. In reference to individual differences, they concluded that exercise *may* reduce

stress and improve mood state for individuals who enjoy the exercise experience, have a history of exercise participation, and are already fit, as opposed to their less experienced, less fit counterparts.

With respect to competitive sport, there continues to be some degree of uncertainty about how an athlete's thoughts influence his or her performance. Several studies by Jones and Swain (1995) and Kerr (1985) on facilitative anxiety and reversal theory, respectively, demonstrate that the athlete's thoughts and emotions, including anxiety, actually improve cognition and performance. It is likely that anxiety, similar to other emotional states, have optimal levels that facilitate, rather than inhibit, sport performance. Research is needed to identify the personal and situational factors that lead to and maintain each athlete's level of optimal anxiety. As Lehrer and Woolfolk (1993) conclude, "Stress management techniques do not make stress vanish, nor do they confer permanent immunity to stressors; they are tools that aid individuals in work that is perennial" (p. 521). Because stress and anxiety are inherent in competitive sport, it is imperative that athletes learn to apply the cognitive and behavioral tools that will allow their talent, not the inevitable exposure to stress and feelings of anxiety, to determine their level of optimal performance.

References

Aldwin, C. M. (1994). *Stress, coping, and development: An integrative perspective.* New York: Gifford.

Aldwin, C. M., & Revenson, T. A. (1987). Does coping help? A reexamination of the relation between coping and mental health. *Journal of Personality and Social Psychology, 53,* 337-348.

Anshel, M. H. (1990). Toward validation of the COPE model: Strategies for acute stress inoculation in sport. International *Journal of Sport Psychology, 21,* 24-39.

Anshel, M. H. (1996). Examining coping style in sport. *Journal of Social Psychology, 136,* 311-323.

Anshel, M. H. (2001). Qualitative validation of a model for coping with acute stress in sport. *Journal of Sport Behavior, 24,* 223-246.

Anshel, M. H. (2003). *Sport psychology: From theory to practice* (4th ed). San Francisco, CA: Benjamin Cummings.

Anshel, M. H., Brown, M., & Brown, D. (1993). Effectiveness of an acute stress coping program on motor performance, muscular tension, and affect. *Australian Journal of Science and Medicine in Sport, 25,* 7-16.

Anshel, M. H., & Delany, J. (1999). Sources of acute stress, cognitive appraisals, and coping strategies of male and female child athletes. *Journal of Sport Behavior, 24,* 329-353.

Anshel, M. H. (1991) (editor & lexicographer), Freedson, P., Hamill, J., Haywood, K., Horvat, M., & Plowman, S. *The dictionary of the exercise and sport sciences*. Champaign, IL: Human Kinetics.

Anshel, M. H., & Kaissidis, A. N. (1997). Coping style and situational appraisals as predictors of coping strategies following stressful events in sport as a function of gender and skill level. *British Journal of Psychology, 88,* 263-276.

Anshel, M. H., Kim, K. W., Kim, B. H., Chang, K. J., & Eom, H. J. (2001). A model for coping with stressful events in sport: Theory, application, and future directions. *International Journal of Sport Psychology, 32,* 43-75.

Anshel, M. H., & Wells, B. (2000). Sources of acute stress and coping styles in competitive sport. *Anxiety, Stress, and Coping: In International Journal, 13,* 1-26.

Anshel, M. H., Williams, L. R. T., & Hodge, K. (1997). Cross-cultural and gender differences on coping style in sport. *International Journal of Sport Psychology, 28,* 141-156.

Beck, A. T. (1976). *Cognitive therapy and emotional disorders.* New York: International Universities Press.

Burton, D. (1998). Measuring competitive state anxiety. In J. L. Duda (Ed.), *Advances in sport and exercise psychology measurement* (pp. 129-148). Morgantown, WV: Fitness Information Technology.

Carver, C. S., Scheier, M. F., & Weintraub, J. K. (1989). Assessing coping strategies: A theoretically-based approach. *Journal of Personality and Social Psychology, 56,* 267-283.

Compas, B. E., Connor, J., Osowiecki, D., & Welch, A. (1997). Effortful and involuntary responses to stress. In B. H. Gottlieb (Ed.), *Coping with chronic stress* (pp. 105-130). New York: Plenum.

Dewe, P. (1992). The appraisal process: Exploring the role of meaning, importance, control and coping in work stress. *Anxiety, Stress, and Coping, 5,* 95-109.

Eysenck, M. W. (1992). *Anxiety: The cognitive perspective.* Hove, England: Erlbaum.

Frost, R. O., Marten, P., Lahart, C., & Rosenblate, R. (1990). The dimensions of perfectionism. *Cognitive Therapy and Research, 14,* 449-468.

Gottlieb, B.H. (1997). Conceptual and measurement issues in the study of coping with chronic stress. In B. H. Gottlieb (Ed.), *Coping with chronic stress* (pp. 3-42). New York: Plenum.

Greenberg, J. S. (1993). *Comprehensive stress management* (4th ed.). Dubuque: Brown and Benchmark.

Hackfort, D., & Schulz, P. (1989). Competence and valence as determinants of anxiety. In D. Hackfort & C. D. Spielberger (Eds.), *Anxiety in sports: An international perspective* (pp. 29-38). New York: Hemisphere.

Hackfort, D., & Schwenkmezger, P. (1993). Anxiety. In R. N. Singer, M. Murphey, & L. K. Tennant (Eds.), *Handbook of research on sport psychology* (pp. 328-364). New York: Macmillan.

Hardy, L., Jones, G., & Gould, D. (1996). *Understanding psychological preparation for sport: Theory and practice of elite performers.* New York: John Wiley & Sons.

Hepburn, C. G., Loughlin, C. A., & Barling, J. (1997). Coping with chronic work stress. In B. H. Gottlieb (Ed.), *Coping with chronic stress* (pp. 343-366). New York: Plenum.

Hewitt, P. L., & Flett, G. L. (1991). Perfectionism in the self and social contexts: Conceptualization, assessment and associa-tion with psychopathology. *Personality and Social Psychology, 60,* 456-470.

Holahan, C. J., Moos, R. H., & Schaefer, J. A. (1996). Coping, stress resistance, and growth: Conceptualizing adaptive functioning. In M. Zeidner & N. S. Endler (Eds.), *Handbook of coping: Theory, research, applications* (pp. 24-43). New York: John Wiley & Sons.

Jones, G., & Swain, A. (1995). Predispositions to experience debilitative and facilitative anxiety in elite and nonelite performers. *The Sport Psychologist, 9,* 201-211.

Kaissidas-Rodafinos, A., Anshel, M. H., & Porter, A. (1997). Personal and situational factors that predict coping strategies for acute stress among basketball referees. *Journal of Sports Sciences, 15,* 427-436.

Kerr, J. H. (1985). The experience of arousal: A new basis for studying arousal effects in sport. *Journal of Sports Sciences, 3,* 169-179.

Krohne, H. W. (1993). Attention and avoidance: Two central strategies for coping with aversiveness. In H. W. Krohne (Ed.), *Attention and avoidance* (pp. 3-18). Seattle, WA: Hogrefe & Huber.

Krohne, H. W. (1996). Individual differences in coping. In M. Zeidner & N. S. Endler (Eds.), *Handbook of coping* (pp. 381-409). New York: John Wiley & Sons.

Krohne, H. W., & Hindel, C. (1988). Trait anxiety, state anxiety, and coping behavior as predictors of athletic performance. *Anxiety Research, 1,* 225-234.

Landers, D. M., & Arent, S. M. (2001). Arousal-performance relationships. In J. M. Williams (Ed.), *Applied sport psychology: Personal growth to peak performance* (4th ed; pp. 206-228). Mountain View: Mayfield.

Lazarus, R. S. (1990). Theory-based stress measurement. *Psychological Inquiry, 1,* 3-13.

Lazarus, R. S., & Folkman, S. (1984). *Stress, appraisal, and coping.* New York: Springer.

Lehrer, P. M., & Woolfolk, R. L. (1993). Research on clinical issues in stress management. In P. M. Lehrer & R. L. Woolfolk (Eds.), *Principles and practice of stress management* (2nd ed.; pp. 521-538). New York: Guilford.

Leventhal, E. A., Suls, J., & Leventhal, H. (1993). Hierarchical analysis of coping: Evidence from life -span studies. In H. W. Krohne (Ed.), *Attention and avoidance* (pp. 71-99). Seattle, WA: Hogrefe & Huber.

Lidor, R., & Singer, R. N. (2000). Teaching preperformance routines in beginners. *Journal of Physical Education, Recreation, and Dance, 71,* 34-37.

Mace, R. (1990). Cognitive-behavioral interventions in sport. In G. Jones & L. Hardy (Eds.), *Stress and performance in sport* (pp. 203-230). New York: John Wiley & Sons.

Martens, R., Vealey, R. S., & Burton, D. (1990). *Competitive anxiety in sport.* Champaign, IL: Human Kinetics.

McAuley, E. (1994). Physical activity and psychosocial outcomes. In C. Bouchard, R. J. Shephard, & T. Stephens (Eds.), *Physical activity, fitness, and health: International proceedings and consensus statement* (pp. 551-568). Champaign, IL: Human Kinetics.

McCrae, R. R. (1992). Situational determinants of coping. In B. N. Carpenter (Ed.), *Personal coping: Theory, research, and application* (pp. 65-76). Westport, CT: Praeger.

Meichenbaum, D. (1985). *Stress inoculation training.* Elmford, NY: Pergamon Press.

Meichenbaum, D. (1977). *Cognitive-behavior modification: An integrative approach*. New York: Plenum Press.

Miller, S. M. (1989). Cognitive informational styles in the process of coping with threat and frustration. *Advances in Behavior Research and Therapy, 11*, 223-234.

Naylor, S., Burton, D., & Crocker, P. (2002). Competitive anxiety and sport performance. In J. M. Silva & D. E. Stevens (Eds.), *Psychological foundations of sport* (pp. 132-154). Boston: Allyn & Bacon.

Peacock, E. J., & Wong, P. T. P. (1990). The stress appraisal measure (SAM): A multidimensional approach to cognitive appraisal. *Stress Medicine, 6*, 227-236.

Rosenbaum, M. (1990). *Learned resourcefulness on coping skills, self-control, and adaptive behavior*. New York: Springer.

Roth, S., & Cohen, L. J. (1986). Approach, avoidance, and coping with stress. *American Psychologist, 41*, 813-819.

Schafer, W. (1996). *Stress management for wellness* (3rd. ed). New York: Harcourt Brace.

Scheier, M. F., & Carver, C. S. (1985). Optimism, coping, and health: Assessment and implications of generalized outcome expectancies. *Health Psychology, 4*, 219-247.

Scheier, M. F., Weintraub, J. K., & Carver, C. S. (1986). Coping with stress: Divergent strategies of optimists and pessimists. *Journal of Personality and Social Psychology, 51*, 1257-1264.

Selye, H. (1974). *Stress without distress*. Philadelphia: Lippincott.

Singer, R. N. (2000). Performance and human factors: Consideration about cognition attention for self-paced and externally-paced events. *Ergonomics, 43*, 1661-1680.

Smith, R. E. (1986). Towards a cognitive-affective model of athletic burnout. *Journal of Sport Psychology, 8*, 36-50.

Spielberger, C. D. (1989). *Stress and anxiety in sports*. In D. Hackfort & C. D. Spielberger (Eds.), Anxiety in sports: An international perspective (pp. 3-17). New York: Hemisphere.

Suls, J., & Fletcher, B. (1985). The relative efficacy of avoidant and nonavoidant coping strategies: A meta-analysis. *Health Psychology, 4*, 249-288.

Terry, D. J (1994). Determinants of coping: The role of stable and situational factors. *Journal of Personality and Social Psychology, 66*, 895-910.

Terry, D. J. (1991). Coping resources and situational appraisals as predictors of coping behavior. *Personality and Individual Differences, 12*, 1031-1047.

Tobin, D. L., Holroyd, K. A., Reynolds, R. V., & Wigal, J. K. (1989). The hierarchical factor structure of the coping strategies inventory. *Cognitive Therapy and Research, 13*, 343-361.

Wann, D. L. (1997). *Sport psychology*. New York: Prentice-Hall.

Weinberg, R. S. (1989). Anxiety, arousal, and motor performance: Theory, research, and applications. In D. Hackfort & C. D. Spielberger (Eds.), *Anxiety in sports: An international perspective* (pp. 95-116). New York: Hemisphere.

Wheaton, B. (1997). The nature of chronic stress. In B. H. Gottlieb (Ed.), *Coping with chronic stress* (pp. 43-73). New York: Plenum.

Williams, J. M., & Andersen, M. B. (1998). Psychosocial antecedents of sport injury: Review and critique of the stress and injury model. *Journal of Applied Sport Psychology, 10*, 5-25.

Woodman, T., & Hardy, L. (2001). Stress and anxiety. In R. N. Singer, H. A. Hausenblas, & C. M. Janelle (Eds.), *Handbook of sport psychology* (2nd ed.; pp. 290-318). New York: John Wiley & Sons.

Wrisberg, C.A. (2001). Levels of performance skill: From beginners to experts. In R. N. Singer, H. A. Hausenblas, & C. M. Janelle (Eds.), *Handbook of sport psychology* (2nd ed.; pp. 3-19). New York: John Wiley & Sons.

Zeidner, M. & Saklofske, D. (1996). Adaptive and maladaptive coping. In M. Zeidner & N. S. Endler (Eds.), *Handbook of coping: Theory, research, applications* (pp. 505-531). New York: John Wiley & Sons.

Section V
Social/Educational Strategies

Introduction

This section comprises six chapters which refer to social, psychosocial, educational, and moral issues. The contributions focus on psychosocial intervention and counseling, educational strategies, training, and the assessment of training outcomes. The scope of the fields of application is from mass sport to elite sports.

The first chapter, by Mark Eys, Michelle Patterson, Todd Loughead, and Albert Carron, is on team building. Team chemistry/teamwork/team cohesion is regarded to be important to team success. The focus of this contribution is on team building—the process of enabling a team to function together more smoothly and effectively—and the role that team building can play in developing team cohesion. A special emphasis is given to introduce and discuss intervention strategies that can be used to increase team cohesion.

The next two chapters of this section are on career issues. Sandy Gordon, David Lavallee, and Robert Grove describe various career assistance programs, report on studies to evaluate different programs, and provide informations from athletes on the the most useful aspects of the programs. Dieter Hackfort and Zhijian Huang reflect on the theoretical and methodological approaches in research on career counseling and report on evidences with a special focus on transition from the career in elite sports to the post-sports career. Both contributions are designed to complement each other.

In the fourth chapter of this section, Bryan Blissmer, David Marquez, Gerald Jerome, and Jay Kimiecik deal with exercise behavior. They discuss major theoretical approaches and applications to promote exercise behavior, the implementation across different levels of intervention, and their basic efficacy in exercise behavior change.

In the fifth chapter, Brenda Light Bredemeier and David Light Shields refer to the construct of character. To explain the development of character, they highlight the theoretical, empirical, and programmatic roots of sociomoral work in sport psychology and argue for a new framework. It is demonstrated how this conceptual framework can lead to new avenues of applied research, coaching and consulting strategies, and educational programs.

Coach training programs designed to enhance the instructional and interpersonal competencies of coaches are discussed in the sixth chapter of this section, written by Ronald Smith and Frank Smoll. In their review, they focus on the evaluation of programs that are designed to have a positive impact on psychosocial outcome variables and provide the current status of knowledge.

This is the most voluminous section of the book. It is anticipated that it will touch on the interest of various colleagues and be of particular interest to those who are looking for information to counsel and enhance performance in teams and/or those who are more engaged in pedagogical settings as well as those who like to reflect on methodological, evaluative, or ethical issues of the programs.

Courtesy of the University of British Columbia Athletic Department

5.1

Team Building in Sport

MARK A. EYS

MICHELLE M. PATTERSON

TODD M. LOUGHEAD

ALBERT V. CARRON

When asked what key ingredient was found in championship teams, University of North Carolina women's soccer (16-time national championship team) coach Anson Dorrance replied, "It's tied into team chemistry, really. And it's tied into a philosophy that we've encouraged from the beginning—the concept of playing for each other... team chemistry is perhaps the most critical element in a championship season" (as cited in Packer & Lazenby, 2001, p. 1). The difference between success and failure often comes down to the effectiveness of teamwork (Hardy & Crace, 1997). Developing team chemistry, harmony, and/ or cohesion is desired in many sport teams and is often the focus of team building programs. Not only is performance affected by team chemistry but team chemistry affects individual effort. Orlick (2000, p. 199) stated, "one of the most satisfying experiences in sport and the workplace is to be a member of a team that gets along well and works as a cohesive unit."

Team chemistry/teamwork/team cohesion all develop naturally and are inevitably present *to some extent* in every group—a fact that was pointed out by Donnelly, Carron, and Chelladurai (1978) almost 37 years ago when they observed, "[I]f a group ex-

ists it is to some extent cohesive" (p. 7). However, because team chemistry/teamwork/team cohesion is so important to team success, there is considerable interest in increasing the amount present. Any program designed to promote "an increased sense of unity and cohesiveness [to enable a team to] function together more smoothly and effectively" (Newman, 1984, p. 62) is called *team building*. In this chapter, the role that team building can play in developing team cohesion is explored. Initially, the nature of team building in a sport context is outlined. Then, recent literature regarding team building in sport is presented. Finally, intervention strategies that can be used to increase team cohesion are introduced. At the onset it should be noted that team building is not a single protocol; a variety of approaches can be used to enhance team cohesion. In this chapter, four correlates of group cohesion—team goals, group norms, group leadership, and role clarity—are explored.

The Nature of Team Building

Definition

Team building has been defined from a number of perspectives (Hardy & Crace, 1997). One approach has been to define it from a structural standpoint. From this perspective, team building involves gathering or amalgamating the necessary resources to form a new entity or team (Adair, 1986). A second, more common perspective has been to view team building as a process of enhancing team performance and/or interpersonal dynamics (Hardy & Crace, 1997). In fact, in a study examining expert coaches' perceptions of what constitutes team building, Schinke, Draper, and Salmela (1997) found that expert coaches viewed the incorporation of both structural (i.e., pre-season athlete selection) and performance enhancement (e.g., developing cohesion, utilizing goal setting, etc.) components as important to the team building process.

Brawley and Paskevich (1997) argued that current team building definitions do not provide a good foundation for developing operationalizations. They also summarized definitions within the organizational development literature and stated that team building is a method of "helping the group to a) increase effectiveness, b) satisfy the needs of its members, or c) improve work conditions. . . . [T]he process might be more accurately characterized as team enhancement or team improvement for task and social purposes" (p. 14).

A similar approach was taken by Widmeyer and Ducharme (1997). They pointed out that the two major objectives of groups (teams) are group locomotion and group maintenance (Lewin, 1935). Locomotion refers to the performance of the group (i.e., goal achievement) and maintenance refers to the ability of the group to stay functioning (i.e., cohesion). Team building, therefore, could be looked at as attempts to enhance both of these outcomes for the group.

Benefits of Team Building

Since the objectives of team building are to enhance both social and task aspects of the group, there are a number of processes that benefit from having an effective team building program. Woodcock and Francis (1994) described six potential benefits:

1. team leadership is seen as being coherent, visionary, and acceptable;

2. team members understand and accept their responsibilities and roles within the team;

3. members dedicate their efforts to the collective achievements;

4. there is a positive, empowering climate surrounding the group;

5. members make good use of their time and resources during team meetings; and

6. the team is able to conduct self-diagnosis to identify and correct weaknesses within the team.

Team-Building Research

There have been a number of studies and reviews on team building conducted in the industrial and organizational psychology literature (e.g., Buller & Bell, 1986; Salas, Rozell, Mullen, & Driskell, 1999). Unfortunately, research within sport psychology has been somewhat limited (Hardy & Crace, 1997). However, in 1997, a special issue of the *Journal of Applied Sport Psychology* was dedicated specifically to team building in sport. A number of researchers prominent in the area of team building and group dynamics contributed to this issue and two general concerns should be highlighted. One pertains to the approaches taken; the second to problems that have plagued team building research.

Team-building protocols. Two protocols have been used by team psychological skills advisors to facilitate team building: direct or indirect (Carron & Hausenblas, 1998). In the *direct approach*, the individual responsible for introducing the team building intervention (i.e., psychological skills advisor) works directly with the team members to implement the strategies. This represents a hands-on approach. One example is illustrated in the work of Yukelson (1997). He noted his team building approach with Pennsylvania State University athletic teams consisted of four stages: a) assessment of the situation (i.e., finding out as much about the dynamics of the team as possible); b) education of the team members regarding the purposes of team building interventions; c) collective brainstorming for ideas to enhance the team's performance; and d) development of goals, mission statements, and action plans.

With an *indirect approach,* the consultant works with the coach or leader, not the team (Carron & Hausenblas, 1998). Therefore, the implementation of ideas for developing a more effective team becomes the direct responsibility of the coach who is in consultation with the psychological skills advisor. One example is illustrated in the work of Prapavessis, Carron, and Spink (1996). This protocol incorporated four stages; a) an introductory stage to provide an overview of benefits of team building; b) a conceptual stage to educate the leader on group dynamics; c) a practical stage to brainstorm strategies to use in team building sessions; and d) an intervention stage where the leader/coach introduces and maintains the team building procedures.

Problems with team-building research. Brawley and Paskevich (1997) stated that there are a number of areas for concern in team-building research undertaken to date. One is that team building definitions have been plagued by a lack of clarity. Second, there have been a number of different models that examine different areas of group dynamics—all under the general rubric of "team building." Third, the relationships between the different variables have not been described properly. Finally, reporting within some studies has been somewhat vague (i.e., sample size, statistical techniques used, etc.)

Team Building Through Development of Cohesion

Many strategies have focused on cohesion as a method of team building (i.e., Prapavessis, Carron, & Spink, 1996). Since the ultimate goal of most sport teams is to enhance performance, it is not surprising that this is the case. Carron, Colman, Wheeler, and Stevens (2002), in their meta-analysis examining the cohesion-performance relationship, found a link between performance and both task (i.e., the group's unity surrounding task aspects) and social cohesion (i.e., the group's unity surrounding social issues). More specifically, an increased perception in cohesion was associated with higher performance. While this meta-analysis utilized studies that examined the cohesion/performance relationship drawing on individual perceptions of cohesion, Carron, Bray, and Eys (2002) examined the same relationship using composite team cohesion scores. They found that, firstly, cohesion was a shared perception (i.e., one could distinguish between teams based on collective cohesion perceptions) and, secondly, there was a strong positive relationship (r = 0.55-0.67) between cohesion and success.

With cohesion as a focus, Carron and Spink (1993) developed a conceptual framework that could be used as a basis for selecting intervention areas for a team building program. The framework designated cohesion as an output that was affected by three features; a) group processes (i.e., team goals, cooperation, and sacrifice), b) group structure (i.e., leadership, role clarity, and conformity to norms), and c) group environment (i.e., distinctiveness). The conceptual framework proposes that the group environment and group structure are inputs that influence group processes (a throughput) that in turn influences group cohesion.

The focus of the remainder of the chapter will be to highlight four important components of the above conceptual framework. Each section will give general information regarding the definition of each construct, previous literature describing how each construct relates to cohesion, and practical suggestions/ideas to implement as interventions within a team building program. The first component is team goal-setting, which is considered a group process. The remaining three components come from the group structure area and contain the under-researched topics of *adherence to norms* and *role ambiguity* as well as the more heavily researched area of *leadership.*

Group Goals

A team goal can be defined as "a future state of affairs desired by enough members of a group to motivate the group to work toward its achievement" (Johnson & Johnson, 1987, p. 132). When team goals are set, a number of positive benefits result including increased motivation, increased clarity of expectation, increased interest in the task, increased personal and collective confidence, and, last but not least, improved team performance/productivity.

A highly consistent positive relationship between goals and productivity has been observed (discussed in more detail below). This has led theoreticians and researchers to search for underlying mechanisms. Why does group goal setting work? Weldon and Weingart (1988) suggested that six processes play a mediating role in the relationship between group goals and the group's productivity. One of these is increased *effort and persistence.* When goals are established, individuals are motivated to achieve them. In order to do so, they work with greater intensity and over longer durations than they would otherwise. A second mediator is *group planning and strategy development.* Goals serve to highlight what is important for collective success. Therefore, once they are established, members must determine how to achieve the group's goals. Third, the existence of group goals leads members to *monitor performance* and assess progress. As a consequence, motivation is improved. Having group goals also leads to *morale-building communications,* a fourth mediator. When goals are present, they stimulate group interactions that are emotional and enthusiastic. Fifth, with the introduction of group goals, members are likely to engage in *extra-role behaviors.* These are behaviors that improve the performance of others or facilitate coordination among group members. Finally, Weldon and Weingart also proposed that a sixth mediator, *reduced quality of performance,* could come into play in those instances where the group's goal is to increase quantity of performance. Quality may become secondary to achieving more quantity.

Participation in individual goal setting

Although it does not directly bear on the question of goal setting and cohesion, research on participation in *individual* goal setting is illuminating. In a

meta-analysis undertaken by Kyllo & Landers (1995), the effect size[1] (ES) found for assigned goals was .30. When participants set their own goals, the ES was .49 and when goals were set cooperatively by the coach and athlete the ES was .62. So, assigning goals to athletes leads to better individual performance but when athletes are consulted the effect is twice as large. As will be pointed out subsequently, these findings have implications for team goal setting programs.

Team goal setting and cohesion

A team goal-setting program has the potential to enhance team cohesion if team members are involved in the goal-setting process. Some of the evidence supporting this suggestion comes from research on athletes' preferences for leadership behavior. In a study with (North American) high school football players, Westre and Weiss (1991) found that a higher degree of democratic (participative) leadership behavior on the part of coaches was associated with a higher level of task cohesion. Subsequently, Kozub (1993), in a study with high school basketball teams, and Lee, Kim, and Lim (1993), in a study using a random stratified sample of high school athletes, reported identical findings. Also, Brawley, Carron, and Widmeyer (1993) found that participation by athletes in setting team goals was positively associated with stronger perceptions of goal clarity, goal influence on behavior, and task cohesiveness.

Team vs. individual goal setting

Research on collective (group) goal setting provides considerable evidence that the presence of group goals contributes to enhanced group performance (Becker, 1978; Buller & Bell, 1986; Klein & Mulvey, 1989; Latham & Yukel, 1975; Pritichard, Jones, Roth, Stuebing, & Ekeberg, 1988; Weingart, 1992; Weingart & Weldon, 1991; Weldon, Jehn, & Pradhan, 1991). Also, considerable research on individual goal setting provides evidence that the presence of individual goals contributes to enhanced individual performance (Kyllo & Landers, 1995). There is less research bearing on the question of whether *groups* are better served by emphasizing individual goals for all members or group goals for the collective. The research evidence that is available, however, from a laboratory (Matsui, Kakuyama, & Onglatco, 1987) and a bowling field study (Johnson, Ostrow, Perna,

& Etzel, 1997) show that group goals are superior to individual goals for group outcomes.

Optimal Conditions for Effective Group Goal Setting

A large body of literature on individual goal setting (Carron & Colman, 2000; Kyllo & Landers, 1995; Locke, Shaw, Saari, & Latham, 1981) provides empirical support for four generalizations pertaining to conditions that maximize the effectiveness of a team goal-setting program. They are :

• athletes should have input into the type and magnitude of goals set,

• goals should be set in specific behavioral terms,

• long-term goals should be established with short-term goals used as a link to them, and

• coach supportiveness is essential.

These four conditions provide an empirical basis for a team-goal setting program designed to enhance group cohesion and group performance (see Carron & Colman, 2000; Widmeyer & McGuire, 1996).

A Team Goal Setting Program

The following sections highlight a team building process outlined by Widmeyer & Ducharme (1997). For purposes of communication, it is useful to consider the initiation and maintenance of the team goal-setting program to comprise three stages. In Stage 1, the rationale for the program is provided and specific team goals and targets/standards for those goals are determined. Stage 2 represents game-by-game monitoring and feedback—usually provided by the coach. Stage 3 is where feedback and short-term evaluation are provided by the sport psychologist in conjunction with the coach and team captain.

Initially, in Stage 1, the rationale for the program is discussed. Then the athletes as a collective determine appropriate long-term and short-term *outcome* goals. Typically, the former is reflected in overall team standing (e.g., finish among the top two teams in the conference) while the latter is reflected in outcomes in an upcoming game or series of games (e.g., obtain at least 4 wins in the next 5 games). Once the short- and long-term outcome goals are set, the question, "what do you have to do especially well as a team on a game-to-game basis to maximize your chances of reaching your short-term and long-term goals?" is addressed. At this point, athletes are provided with a list of performance (game) indices that are specific and measurable (e.g., steals, rebounds). Each athlete *independently* picks 5 or 6 performance indices that s/he thinks are most important for team success. Athletes are then assigned to *subgroups* of 5 individuals and asked to discuss and negotiate until each subgroup has consensus on 5-6 performance indices. Working in subgroups prior to working in an *open forum* (i.e., the total team) increases the likelihood that each athlete's views are heard. Finally, the choices emanating from the various subgroups are discussed in an open forum. Through negotiation, if necessary, the 5-6 performance indices considered most important for team success are established.

Once the specific team goals are established, the specific level—the target to strive for in each game—is established. To this end, athletes are provided with pertinent statistics from the previous year. Then the process described above is repeated. That is, first, each athlete, working independently, determines the level or target he/she thinks is appropriate. When all athletes have made their independent decisions, they are assigned to the same subgroup of five people to discuss and negotiate appropriate levels or targets for each of the team goals. Finally, the decisions made in the various subgroups are discussed in an open forum and a collective decision is made.

In Stage 2, the game-by-game monitoring, the specific levels targeted are placed in the locker room and results are posted for the athletes to examine. Also, depending upon the dynamics of the situation, the coach discusses some or all of the performance indices and highlights those that require attention.

In Stage 3, summary feedback is provided to the team and the goals and their levels are discussed (i.e., to possibly modify for future games). Also, a specific team goal no longer considered by the athletes to be essential to team success can be replaced with another goal.

Group Norms

Group norms are standards that describe appropriate and inappropriate behavior for a given situation (Forsyth, 1999). Norms reflect existing values pertaining to matters considered important to the group (Carron & Hausenblas, 1998). These generalized expectations are informal rules of conduct that help maintain behavioral consistency among group members and provide a basis for predicting the behavior of all members (Johnson & Johnson, 2000). Thus, group norms assist in creating a structured and effective group environment.

Organizational psychologists and sport psychologists agree on the value of norms in the development and performance of groups. Organizational psychologists often discuss the contribution of norms in creating a corporate culture and propose that norms tell people what they are supposed to be doing, saying, and believing (e.g. Armstrong, 2001; Jones, 2001; Wheelan, 1999). As Armstrong (2001) stated, "norms exert very powerful pressure on behavior" (p. 207).

Sport psychologists have also theorized about the impact of norms in sport teams. In 1981, Carron proposed that the development and collective acceptance of team norms contributes to a team's success for two reasons. First, athletes who accept team norms join together to ensure the continuation of the group. Second, norms provide knowledge regarding the team's reality and offer standards against which individuals can evaluate themselves and others.

Although norms have not been extensively examined in sport, researchers have found support for the proposition that norms do exist in sport teams and that when highly endorsed norms exist within a highly cohesive team, these norms ultimately have a positive influence on team success.

Norms in Sport Teams

Munroe, Estabrooks, Dennis, and Carron (1999) conducted a qualitative study examining norms prevalent in sport. Munroe and her colleagues (1999) found that norms develop in four contexts: practice, competition, off-season, and team social functions. Furthermore, within these contexts, prevalent norms evolve in relation to the two major group processes identified by Lewin (1935)—locomotion and maintenance. Specifically, the norm for productivity and the norm to attend training and competition directly relate to the task objectives (i.e. group locomotion). The maintenance of the group is reinforced by norms to maintain contact with team members during the off-season, to attend and include all team members in team social functions, and to positively interact with team members.

Team Norms and Performance

Kim (1995), examining the relationship between performance norms and team success, found that more successful basketball teams had stronger performance norms than did less successful basketball teams. Thus, teams that more highly endorsed performance norms were more successful. Likewise, Shields, Bredemier, Gardner, and Bostrom (1995) examined leadership, cohesion, and team norms regarding cheating and aggression and found that athletes on winning teams endorsed team norms to a greater degree.

Team Norms and Cohesion

Using a sample of Japanese sport teams, Kim (1992) found a significant positive correlation between performance norms and cohesion. As well, when Prapavessis and Carron (1997) examined athletes' sacrifice behavior, perceptions of cohesion, and conformity to team norms, they found that perceptions of sacrifice contributed to group cohesion, and in turn, cohesion contributed to perceptions of team members' conformity to group norms.

Further, after conducting a meta-analysis of the cohesion-performance relationship, Mullen and Copper (1994) proposed that the salience and legitimacy of norms in sport teams might moderate the cohesion-performance relationship. This proposition was tested and supported by Gammage, Carron, and Estabrooks (2001). Their findings supported the suggestion that high cohesion and high norms for productivity lead to the best performance, high cohesion and low norms lead to the worst performance, and low cohesion with high or low norms lead to intermediate levels of performance.

Developing Team Norms

Although theory in group dynamics suggests that group norms are critical in the effective functioning of groups, and initial empirical evidence supports the contribution of group norms to successful team performance, the formation and empirical testing of interventions to facilitate the development and enforcement of group norms is negligible.

Fortunately, based on group dynamic theory and their vast experience in putting theory into practice, Johnson and Johnson (2000) have provided guidelines for interventions to establish and support group norms. They proposed that group members will accept and internalize group norms when they: (1) feel a sense of ownership for the norms; (2) recognize that the norms exist when other members are seen accepting and following them; (3) understand how the norms help accomplish the group's goals; and (4) experience enforced sanctions when the norms are violated.

Using these guidelines as a basis, the following intervention program was developed and successfully implemented with university athletic teams (Colman, 2001).

Create a sense of ownership. Johnson and Johnson's (2000) first guideline suggests that team members will accept, internalize, and comply with norms if they feel a sense of ownership. This guideline is the foundation of this team norm intervention program. It is critical that athletes and coaches be involved in every stage of the program to ensure that they have a meaningful experience and increase their compliance and commitment to the program.

Clarify expectations with team captains. In order for individuals to accept group norms, they must recognize that they exist and see others following them. Therefore, a meeting is scheduled so that coaches and team captains can determine how the captains can set an example for other team members. Ideally this meeting occurs at the beginning of the season; and focuses on three outcomes. First, team captains are asked to identify three characteristics that best describe the team when it is successful. Second, team captains are asked to identify behaviors that represent these characteristics. Finally, coaches discuss with the team captains what their role is in endorsing the identified behavioral expectations.

Clarify expectations with the team. For individuals to internalize norms, they must see how norms relate to the goals and tasks to which they are committed to achieving. Therefore, a meeting is set up with the whole team to clarify behavioral expectations for the team and discuss how the behaviors will assist in achieving team goals. As was the case above, three outcomes are targeted. First, team members are asked to individually identify three characteristics that best represent the team when it is successful. The athletes then get into small groups to discuss the characteristics identified and come to a consensus on the three most critical. Then the whole team comes together and decides on the three most important characteristics. Second, team members identify the behaviors that represent the characteristics. Finally, coaches and athletes discuss how the characteristics and their respective behaviors will help the team achieve their goals. The resulting behavioral expectations often are formalized by organizations and sport teams into a code of conduct, which can be posted as a reminder of the behaviors that will help the team be successful.

Implement sanctions and rewards. In order to encourage compliance to the team norms, sanctions must be enforced if a norm is violated. Therefore, the suggested intervention again requires a team meeting to discuss (a) the nature of the consequences if team norms are violated, (b) who is responsible (e.g. the team, captains, coaches) for monitoring behaviors throughout the season, and (c) who is responsible (e.g. the team, captains, coaches) for implementing consequences for norm violations. Consequences could range from using public apologies to assigning extra physical training. Coaches may also want to consider developing a reward system for recognizing compliance to team norms. Positive reinforcement of appropriate behaviors helps to ensure that compliance is maintained.

Role Ambiguity

Role ambiguity has been defined as a lack of clear, consistent information regarding one's position (Kahn, Wolfe, Quinn, Snoek, & Rosenthal, 1964). However, it has also often been referred to by its antonym, role clarity; the degree to which an individual understands what is expected of him/her (Carron & Hausenblas, 1998). These terms can be used interchangeably as they represent two ends of a continuum.

Role Ambiguity In Sport

A plethora of anecdotal evidence is available which describes the necessity for all members of the group or team to recognize and understand their roles. It also highlights the importance for teams/groups to a) develop roles (i.e., what are the individual's responsibilities?), b) effectively communicate those roles (i.e., have the team leaders transmitted those responsibilities to the athlete?), and c) ensure that athletes understand their roles (i.e., does the athlete understand what has been transmitted?).

For example, in an address to Roger Neilson's Coaches Clinic (2001), former NHL hockey coach Mike Keenan stated:

> In the past, I have developed a very team oriented philosophy that incorporates individual roles among the group. As an example, some specific methods which I have utilized successfully include one-on-one meetings with the players to employing particular on-ice techniques during practice sessions themselves. (p. 49)

Keenan's methods would go a long way to alleviating the uncertainty that might arise in athletes about their specific responsibilities. A recent conceptualization highlights that role ambiguity could arise in any one of four areas.

Conceptualization of the nature of role ambiguity

Beauchamp, Bray, Carron, and Eys (2002) have recently developed a conceptual model of role ambiguity for a sport setting based on conceptualizations emanating from business and industry. In this conceptualization for interactive teams such as hockey, basketball, or soccer, role ambiguity is viewed as a multidimensional construct that can occur on both offense and defense.

One dimension, *scope of responsibility,* refers to the individual's knowledge of the extent of his or her responsibilities. For example, a point guard in basketball would have to understand the general fact that he or she occupies that position. A second dimension, *behavior to fulfill responsibilities,* pertains to the individual's understanding of what behaviors are necessary to successfully carry out the role. Therefore, does this same point guard understand that his or her duties are to dribble the ball up the court, distribute the ball to teammates, and conduct off the court responsibilities such as weight lifting or extra running. *Evaluation of responsibilities,* a third dimension, represents the individual's knowledge of what criteria the coaches use to evaluate the individual's role performance. For example, does the point guard know whether the coaches are looking for leadership ability or statistical information (i.e., shooting percentage)? A final dimension, *consequence of not fulfilling responsibilities,* has to do with whether the individual understands the consequences of inadequate role performance (i.e., loss of playing time, reduced responsibilities). One caveat noted by Beauchamp et al. is that their conceptualization is associated with roles specifically assigned to team members (i.e., formal roles); not those that occur spontaneously from naturally occurring player interaction (i.e., informal roles).

Role ambiguity empirical research. Research has linked role ambiguity to other important group constructs. For example, Beauchamp and Bray (2001) examined perceptions of role ambiguity, role efficacy, and role conflict within interdependent sport teams (i.e., basketball, soccer, field hockey, etc.). Role conflict was defined as "the presence of incongruent expectations placed on a role incumbent (Kahn, Wolfe, Quinn, Snoek, & Rosenthal, 1964) while role efficacy was defined as the individual's belief that he/she is able to successfully carry out required responsibilities. Beauchamp and Bray (2001) found that role ambiguity was negatively associated with role efficacy. That is, as role ambiguity increased, the individual's belief that he/she could successfully complete required responsibilities decreased. Also, role ambiguity mediated the role conflict-role efficacy relationship.

Beauchamp, Bray, Eys, & Carron (2002) conducted another study that examined the relationship between role ambiguity and both role related efficacy and role performance of male rugby players. As in the previous study, role ambiguity was found to have a negative relationship with role efficacy. Also, role ambiguity was found to be negatively related to role performance. Finally, a greater understanding of one's role is related to higher athlete satisfaction (Eys, Carron, Bray, & Beauchamp, 2003), less cognitive anxiety (Beauchamp et al., 2003), and stronger intentions of the athlete to return to their current team (Eys et al., in press).

Similar to the previous areas discussed (i.e., team goal setting and team norms), research also shows that role ambiguity has a relationship with cohesion. Eys and Carron (2001) conducted a study that examined the relationship between the four manifestations of role ambiguity described above and task cohesion. They found that the more ambiguity athletes experienced, the more likely they were to perceive their team as being a less cohesive unit regarding task issues.

Reducing Role Ambiguity in Sport

Although it has never been empirically tested, research evidence provides support for the proposition that team-building interventions designed to reduce individual role ambiguity will have a beneficial effect on team cohesion and team performance. Three approaches are offered here (Eys, 2001).

Coach/athlete interview. The first method involves the use of a coach/athlete interview to open up communication channels. Although this suggestion may seem self-evident or frivolous, the purposeful use of such meetings is employed at the highest levels (i.e., professional) of sport as was indicated in the earlier quote by Mike Keenan. The first step in conducting these interviews is to have the athlete outline in detail his/her responsibilities prior to attending the meeting. The focus should be on formal functions (i.e., sport related); not informal or social responsibilities. Also prior to the meeting, the coach should outline what he/she believes are the role responsibilities of the athlete. At the meeting, the player and coach can discuss the congruency of the perceptions each of them had and any misconceptions by the athlete can be rectified. The athlete should be able to leave the meeting with a clearer sense of purpose. One major disadvantage of this approach is the extra workload for the coach. For example, if there are 22 athletes on the team, the responsibilities have to be spelled out for each one. One possibility for time reduction would be to have the coach simply use the athlete's list of perceived responsibilities and either add or delete functions as is appropriate.

Anonymous teammate feedback. The second method to reduce role ambiguity is through the use of anonymous feedback from the athlete's teammates. Each team member is given a form containing the names of all his/her teammates. At the top of the sheet is the phrase "In order for us to be successful, XXXX must...". Each team member is required to independently and confidentially write statements about every other person on the team. After this process is completed, the statements are compiled and each team member receives a personal feedback sheet that contains all the statements from the rest of the team.

The "hot seat." A third method to reduce role ambiguity—one that should be used only with mature athletes in a supportive environment—is referred to as the hot seat. In this method, all members are given an opportunity to publicly list their responsibilities to their teammates. Each member is required to stand or sit in front of the group (i.e., the hot seat) and explain to the rest the team what s/he believes his or her formal functions are. Following the presentation, teammates and coaches are allowed a chance to agree with, modify, dispute, or add to the responsibilities listed by the athlete. The head coach has the final authority.

One benefit of this technique is that the athlete must publicly state what he or she is prepared to do for the team. Thus, every member becomes familiar with who is responsible for what and when. A second benefit is that the athletes receive feedback from the coach as well as fellow teammates.

Leadership

Leadership can be defined as "a process whereby an individual influences a group of individuals to achieve a common goal" (Northouse, 2001, p. 3). Based on this definition, it is clear that leadership can be viewed as a style of behavior (Johnson & Johnson, 2000). In fact, Chelladurai and Saleh (1980) developed the Leadership Scale for Sport (LSS), which identified five dimensions of leader behavior in sport: training and instruction, democratic behavior, autocratic behavior, social support, and positive feedback. The coaching behavior of training and instruction is described as improving an athlete's performance by instructing the skills, techniques, and tactics of the sport; by clarifying relationships among team members; and managing team members' activities. Democratic behavior is the coaching behavior that allows the athletes to participate in the decision making process on issues such group goals, practice methods, tactics and strategies. Autocratic behavior is the coaching behavior whereby the coach is independent in the decision making process. The coaching behavior of social support is characterized by a concern for the well being of the athletes and developing positive interpersonal relations with team members. Finally, positive feedback is a behavior whereby the coach reinforces the athletes by recognizing and rewarding good performance.

The LSS is based on Chelladurai's (1978) *multidimensional model of leadership*. The multidimensional model is concerned with the influence of leader behavior on performance and satisfaction of athletes. Therefore, one of its central tenets is that the higher the congruency between a coach's behavior and the situational requirements, the higher the group satisfaction. Westre and Weiss (1991) argued that a similar effect would also be present between coaching behaviors and team cohesion.

Coaching Behaviors and Team Cohesion

The rationale suggesting that coaching behaviors would be related to cohesion is based on the supposition that coaches can affect the team's processes (i.e., cohesion). In fact, Widmeyer and Williams (1991) examined the importance that coaches attach to cohesion and how coaches developed this property on their team. The results revealed that coaches' efforts to foster cohesion were positively related ($r = .22$-$.26$) to both task and social cohesiveness.

What is the importance of studying the relationship between leader behaviors and team cohesion? According to Gardner, Shields, Bredemeier, and Bostrom (1996) there are two essential reasons. First, as noted previously, group cohesion has an important influence on team performance (Carron et al., 2002). Second, in comparison with personal factors, environmental factors, and team factors (Carron, 1982) leadership is perhaps the most influential factor affecting cohesion. Williams (1993) has suggested that the coach has the strongest basis from which to exert change on factors such as team cohesion.

The first study to examine the relationship between cohesion (using the GEQ) and leader behavior (using the LSS) was by Westre and Weiss (1991).

Using male high school football players, Westre and Weiss found that players who perceived their coaches to engage in higher levels of training and instruction, democratic behavior, social support, and positive feedback perceived higher levels of task cohesion. Due to an unacceptably low reliability score on the autocratic behavior scale, the relationship between task cohesion and this scale could not be tested. Along the same lines, low reliability scores (alpha < .70) on the social cohesion scales precluded testing the relationship between social cohesion and leader behaviors.

Replicating the Westre and Weiss (1991) study, Pease and Kozub (1994) examined female high school basketball players. In general, their results showed certain coaching behaviors were positively related to task cohesion. More specifically, the coaching behaviors of training/instruction and democratic behavior were positively associated with the cohesion measure of group integration-task. In addition, training and instruction were positively related to the cohesion measure of attraction to the group-task. In other words, athletes who perceived that their coaches displayed higher levels of these coaching behaviors also perceived that their team was more task cohesive. On the other hand, none of the coaching behaviors from the LSS were related to the social manifestations of cohesion.

Gardner, Shields, Bredemeier, and Bostrom (1996) also examined the leader behavior-cohesion relationship. The results revealed that the coaching behaviors of training and instruction, democratic behavior, social support, and positive feedback were positively related to task cohesion. On the other hand, the coaching behavior of autocratic behavior was negatively related to task cohesion. However, unlike Pease and Kozub (1994), the coaching behaviors of training and instruction as well as social support were positively related to *social cohesion*.

Modifying Coaching Behavior

While there is empirical support for the notion that coaching behaviors are related to team cohesion, there have been no intervention studies conducted that have utilized Chelladurai and Saleh's (1980) Leadership Scale for Sport (LSS) to evaluate the effects of leader behavior change on group cohesion. However, Smith, Smoll, and Curtis (1979) have developed a coach-mediated approach to team building, known as Coach Effectiveness Training (CET), for youth sports. The guidelines offered by Smith et al. could be used to improve cohesion.

The Coach Effectiveness Training (CET) program is based on two techniques that are used to change behaviors: self-monitoring and behavioral feedback. Self-monitoring involves observing and recording one's own behavior (Smoll & Smith, 1993). The objective of self-monitoring is to increase the awareness of behavioral patterns of the coaches. One method that is used to assist coaches in self-monitoring selected behaviors is the completion of a form immediately following games and/or practices (Smith & Smoll, 1997). For example, a coach who wants to increase the level of task cohesion on his/her team may adopt more positive feedback behaviors. This assumption is based on empirical evidence that the coaching behavior of positive feedback is positively related to task cohesion. Following the game or practice, the coach assesses the selected behavior using the self-monitoring form. In the present example, the coach has selected the behavior of positive feedback to monitor. The following are sample questions that may appear on the self-monitoring form: To what extent did you respond with positive feedback behaviors? Describe a situation when you responded with positive feedback behaviors. Describe a situation when you should have responded with positive feedback behaviors but didn't. How do you plan to implement positive feedback behaviors in the future under similar circumstances?

A second behavioral change technique involves behavioral feedback. Coaches can obtain feedback from their assistants (Smith & Smoll, 1997) during regularly scheduled meetings (e.g., once a week meetings). To give the meetings a focus, coaches are encouraged to proceed through each section of the above mentioned self-monitoring form. Therefore, coaches have an opportunity to discuss different methods of coping with difficult athletes or situations and how to effectively deal with them in the future (Smith & Smoll, 1997). Other sources of feedback include the input from athletes using the LSS (Smith & Smoll, 1997).

Summary

The general focus of this chapter has been to outline recent literature in the area of team building in sport. Empirical research into group dynamics and team building is relatively underdeveloped in comparison to other areas in sport psychology, typically more individual oriented (i.e., anxiety, self-efficacy). However, the influence of group processes on individual and collective outcomes cannot be overstated. The development of group cohesion is one effective way to build a sense of team. Four general areas (i.e., group goals, norms, role ambiguity, and leadership) were discussed in terms of how they could be influential in contributing to greater team cohesion with the ultimate goal being enhanced performance.

References

Adair, J. (1986). *Effective Team building*. Brookfield, VT: Gower Publishing Company Ltd.

Armstrong, M. (2001). *A handbook of human resource management practice* (8th ed.). London: Kogan Page.

Beauchamp, M. R., & Bray, S. R. (2001). Role ambiguity and role conflict within interdependent teams. *Small Group Research, 32*(2), 133-157.

Beauchamp, M. R., Bray, S. R., Eys, M. A., & Carron, A. V. (2002). Role ambiguity, role efficacy, and role performance: Multidimensional and mediational relationships within interdependent sport teams. *Group Dynamics: Theory, Research, and Practice, 6*, 229-242.

Beauchamp, M. R., Bray, S. R., Eys, M. A., & Carron, A. V. (2003). The effect of role ambiguity on competitive state anxiety. *Journal of Sport and Exercise Psychology, 25*, 77-92.

Becker, L. J. (1978). Joint effect of feedback and goal setting on performance: A field study of residential energy conservation. *Journal of Applied Psychology, 23*, 428-433.

Brawley, L. R., Carron, A. V., & Widmeyer, W. N. (1993). The influence of the group and its cohesiveness on perceptions of group-related variables. *Journal of Sport and Exercise Psychology, 15*, 245-260.

Brawley, L.R. & Paskevich, D.M. (1997). Conducting team building research in the context of sport and exercise. *Journal of Applied Sport Psychology, 9*, 11-40.

Buller, P., & Bell, C. (1986). Effects of team building and goal setting on productivity: A field experiment. *Academy of Management Journal, 23*, 23-40.

Carron, A.V. (1981). Processes of group interaction in sport teams. *Quest, 33*, 245-270.

Carron, A. V. (1982). Cohesiveness in sports: Interpretations and considerations. *Journal of Sport Psychology, 4*, 123-138.

Carron, A. V., Bray, S. R., & Eys, M. A. (2002). Team cohesion and team success in sport. *Journal of Sports Sciences, 20*, 119-126.

Carron, A. V. & Colman, M. M. (2000, May). *A team goal setting program for elite sport: From research to practice.*

Presentation at the Sport Psychology in the New Millennium Conference, University of Halmstead, Halmstead, Sweden.

Carron, A. V., Colman, M. M., Wheeler, J., & Stevens, D. (2002). Cohesion and performance in sport: A meta-analysis. *Journal of Sport & Exercise Psychology, 24,* 168-188.

Carron, A.V. & Hausenblas, H.A. (1998). *Group Dynamics in Sport* (2nd ed.). Morgantown, WV: Fitness Information Technology Inc.

Carron, A. V. & Spink, K. S. (1993). Team building in an exercise setting. *The Sport Psychologist, 7,* 8-18.

Chelladurai, P. (1978). *A contingency model of leadership in athletics.* Unpublished doctoral dissertation, Department of Management Sciences, University of Waterloo, Canada.

Chelladurai, P. & Saleh, S. D. (1980). Dimensions of leader behavior in sports: Development of a leadership scale. *Journal of Sport Psychology, 2,* 34-45.

Cohen, J. (1969). *Statistical power analysis for the behavioral sciences.* New York: Academic Press.

Cohen, J. (1992). A power primer. *Psychological Bulletin, 112,* 155-159

Colman, M. M. (2001). *Group Norms:* Theory to Practice. Paper presented at the meeting of the Association for the Advancement of Applied Sport Psychology, Orlando, Fl.

Donnelly, P., Carron, A. V., & Chelladurai, P. (1978). Group cohesion and sport. *CAHPER Sociology of Sport Monograph.* University of Calgary, Calgary, AB.

Eys, M. A. (2001). *Role Ambiguity: Theory to Practice.* Paper presented at the meeting of the Association for the Advancement of Applied Sport Psychology, Orlando, FL.

Eys, M. A. & Carron, A. V. (2001. Role ambiguity, task cohesion, and task self-efficacy. *Small Group Research, 32* (3), 356-373.

Eys, M. A., Carron, A. V., Bray, S. R., & Beauchamp, M. R. (2003). Role ambiguity and athlete satisfaction. *Journal of Sports Sciences, 21,* 391-401.

Eys, M. A., Carron, A. V., Bray, S. R., & Beauchamp, M. R. (in press). The relationship between role ambiguity and intention to return. *Journal of Applied Sport Psychology.*

Forsyth, D. R. (1999). *Group Dynamics* (3rd ed). Belmont, CA: Brooks/Cole Wadsworth.

Gammage, K. L., Carron, A. V., & Estabrooks, P. A. (2001). Team cohesion and individual productivity: The influence of the norm for productivity and the identifiability of individual effort. *Small Group Research, 32* (1), 3-18.

Gardner, D. E., Shields, D. L., Bredemeier, B. J., & Bostrom, A. (1996). The relationship between perceived coaching behaviors and team cohesion among baseball and softball players. *The Sport Psychologist, 10,* 367-381.

Hardy, C. J. & Crace, R. K. (1997). Foundations of team building: introduction to the team building primer. *Journal of Applied Sport Psychology, 9,* 1-10.

Johnson, D. W. & Johnson, F. P. (1987). *Joining together: Group theory and group skills* (3rd ed.). Englewood Cliffs, NJ: Prentice-Hall.

Johnson, D. W. & Johnson, F. P. (2000). *Joining together: Group theory and group skills* (7th ed.). Needham Heights, MA: Allyn & Bacon.

Johnson, S. R., Ostrow, A. C., Perna, F. M., & Etzel, E. F. (1997). The effects of group versus individual goal setting on bowling performance. *The Sport Psychologist, 11,* 190-200.

Jones, G. R. (2001). *Organizational theory: Text and cases* (3rd ed). Upper Saddle River, NJ: Prentice Hall.

Kahn, R. L., Wolfe, D. M., Quinn, R. P., Snoek, J. D., & Rosenthal, R. A. (1964). *Organizational stress: Studies in role conflict and ambiguity.* New York: John Wiley.

Keenan, M. (2001, June). *A philosophical position paper on player motivation.* Paper presented at Roger Neilson's Coaches' Clinic, Windsor, ON.

Kim, M. (1992). The relation of performance norms and cohesiveness for Japanese school athletic teams. *Perceptual and Motor Skills, 74,* 1096-1098.

Kim, M. (1995). Performance norms and performance by teams in basketball competition. *Perceptual and Motor Skills, 80,* 770.

Klein, H. J., & Mulvey, P. W. (1989, August). *Performance goals in group settings: An investigation of group and goal processes.* Paper presented at the 48th Annual Meeting of the Academy of Management, Washington, DC.

Kozub, S. A. (1993). *Exploring the relationships among coaching behavior, team cohesion, and player leadership.* Unpublished doctoral dissertation, University of Houston, TX.

Kyllo, L. B., & Landers, D. M. (1995). Goal setting in sport and exercise: A research synthesis to resolve the controversy. *Journal of Sport and Exercise Psychology, 17,* 117-137.

Latham, G. P., & Yukel, G. A. (1975). Assigned versus participative goal setting with educated and uneducated wood workers. *Journal of Applied Psychology, 60,* 299-302.

Lee, H. K., Kim, B. H., & Lim, B. J. (1993). The influence of structural characteristics on team success in sport groups. *Korean Journal of Sport Science, 5,* 138-154.

Lewin, K. (1935). *A dynamic theory of personality.* New York: McGraw-Hill.

Locke, E. A., Shaw, K. N., Saari, L. M., & Latham, G. P. (1981). Goal setting and task performance: 1969-1980. *Psychological Bulletin, 90,* 125-152.

Matsui, T., Kakuyama, T., & Onglatco, M. L. (1987). Effects of goals and feedback on performance in groups. *Journal of Applied Psychology, 72,* 407-415.

Mullen, B. & Copper, C. (1994). The relation between group cohesion and performance: An integration. *Psychological Bulletin, 115* (2), 210-227.

Munroe, K., Estabrooks, P., Dennis, P., & Carron, A. V. (1999). A phenomenological analysis of group norms in sport teams. *The Sport Psychologist, 13,* 171-182.

Newman, B. (1984). Expediency as benefactor: How team building saves time and gets the job done. *Training and Development Journal, 38,* 26-30.

Northouse, P. G. (2001). *Leadership: Theory and practice* (2nd ed.). Thousand Oaks, CA: Sage Publications, Inc.

Orlick, T. (2000). *In pursuit of excellence: How to win in sport and life through mental training* (3rd ed.). Champaign, Il: Human Kinetics.

Packer, B. & Lazenby, R. (2001). Dorrance leads UNC dynasty. *Championship Performance, 5* (57), 1-7.

Pease, D. G., & Kozub, S. A. (1994). Perceived coaching behaviors and team cohesion in high school girls basketball teams. *Journal of Sport & Exercise Psychology, 16,* S93.

Prapavessis, H., & Carron, A. V. (1997). Sacrifice, cohesion, and conformity to norms in sport teams. Group Dynamics: *Theory, Research, and Practice, 1* (3), 231-240.

Prapavessis, H., Carron, A. V., & Spink, K. S. (1996). Team building in sport. *International Journal of Sport Psychology, 27,* 269-285.

Pritchard, R. D., Jones, S. D., Roth, P. L., Stuebing, K. K., & Ekeberg, S. E. (1988). Effects of group feedback, goal setting, and incentives on organizational productivity. *Journal of Applied Psychology, 73,* 139-145.

Salas, E., Rozell, D., Mullen, B., & Driskell, J. E. (1999). The effect of team building on performance: An integration. *Small Group Research, 30*(3), 309-329.

Schinke, R. L., Draper, S. P., & Salmela, J. H. (1997). A conceptualization of team building in high performance sport as a season-long process. *Avante, 3,* 57-72.

Shields, D.L.L., Bredemeier, B.J.L., Gardner, D.E., & Bostrom, A. (1995). Leadership, cohesion, and team norms regarding cheating and aggression. *Sociology of Sport Journal, 12,* 324-336.

Smith, R. E. & Smoll, F. L. (1997). Coach-mediated team building in youth sports. *Journal of Applied Sport Psychology, 9,* 114-132.

Smith, R. E., Smoll, F. L., & Curtis, B. (1979). Coach effectiveness training: A cognitive-behavioral approach to enhancing relationships skills in youth sport coaches. *Journal of Sport Psychology, 1,* 59-75.

Smoll, F. L., & Smith, R. E. (1993). Educating youth sport coaches: An applied sport psychology perspective. In J. M. Williams (Ed.), *Applied sport psychology: Personal growth to peak performance* (2nd ed., pp. 36-57). Mountain View, CA: Mayfield.

Weingart, L. R. (1992). Impact of group goals, task component complexity, effort, and planning on group performance. *Journal of Applied Psychology, 77,* 682-693.

Weingart, L. R. & Weldon, E. (1991). Processes that mediate the relationship between a group goal and group member performance. *Human Performance, 4,* 33-44.

Weldon, E. & Weingart, L. R. (1988, August). *A theory of group goals and group performance.* Paper presented at the Annual Meeting of the Academy of Management, Anaheim, CA.

Weldon, E., Jehn, K. A., & Pradhan, P. (1991). Processes that the relationship between a group goal and improved group performance. *Journal of Personality and Social Psychology, 61,* 555-569.

Westre, K. R. & Weiss, M. R. (1991). The relationship between perceived coaching behaviors and group cohesion in high school football teams. *The Sport Psychologist, 5,* 41-54.

Wheelan, S.A. (1999). *Creating effective teams: A guide for members and leaders.* Thousand Oaks, CA: SAGE Publications, Inc.

Widmeyer, W. N. & Ducharme, K. (1997). Team building through team goal setting. *Journal of Applied Sport Psychology, 9,* 97-113.

Widmeyer, W. N. & McGuire, E .J. (1996, May). *Sport psychology for ice hockey.* Presentation to Ontario Intermediate Coaching Clinic, Waterloo, ON.

Widmeyer, W. N. & Williams, J. M. (1991). Predicting cohesion in a coaching sport. *Small Group Research, 22,* 548-570.

Williams, J. M. (1993). *Applied sport psychology: Personal growth to peak performance* (2nd ed.). Mountain View, CA: Mayfield.

Woodcock, M., & Francis, D. (1994). *Teambuilding strategy.* Cambridge: University Press.

Yukelson, D. (1997). Principles of effective team building interventions in sport: a direct services approach at Penn State University. *Journal of Applied Sport Psychology, 9,* 73-96.

Footnotes

1. Cohen (1969, 1992) has suggested that effect sizes of .20, .50, and .80 be considered small, medium, and large, respectively.

Courtesy of www.bigphoto.com

5.2

Career Assistance Program Interventions in Sport

SANDY GORDON

DAVID LAVALLEE

J. ROBERT GROVE

Introduction

This chapter presents a brief rationale for career assistance programs in contemporary elite sport followed by an overview of existing programs, their target populations, their content, and their style of delivery. The next section describes three sport-career assistance program evaluation studies and concludes with brief comments on work-career assistance interventions that have potential implications for sport. Finally, the chapter makes recommendations and directions for evidence-based research on career assistance programs in sport settings.

Rationale for Career Assistance Programs

Recent reviews of sport career transition processes (Lavallee, Sinclair, & Wylleman, 1998; Lavallee, Wylleman, & Sinclair, 1998) and conceptual models of adaptation to sport retirement (Gordon & Lavallee,

2004; Taylor & Ogilvie, 2001) have identified three factors that are most likely to determine whether experiences will be positive or negative: voluntary or involuntary reasons for transitions, developmental experiences, and coping resources. Recurring themes from that research have been useful for designing career assistance programs and directing further research. Patterns from the evidence suggest that athletes are unprepared for some transitions and that they desire more support from career assistance programs. There also appears to be a need for gradual resocialization out of athletic identities and into non-sport-related or more balanced roles in society through education or second careers or both.

In the future it is anticipated that career assistance programs as primary prevention strategies will continue to target problems prior to their occurrence and to facilitate organizational structures that make prevention programs possible and offer the most efficient use of limited human service resources (Pearson & Petitpas, 1990; Petitpas, Champagne,

Chartrand, Danish, & Murphy, 1997; Ungerleider, 1997). By adopting a primary prevention model in youth sport, parents, coaches, and administrators can foster a holistic approach to sport participation that emphasizes personal growth and social development instead of success and winning. Rather than promote single-minded pursuit of excellence and socialize unidimensional and cognitively simple young athletes, prevention-oriented career assistance programs can use sport participation as a vehicle to learn general life skills. As a consequence, experience with psychological and social phenomena in sport will enable young athletes to grow personally and socially and to function in diverse situations.

Lee and Johnston (2001) have acknowledged that, in the adult work-world, career management will be full of uncertainty as a result of forces such as globalization, downsizing, advancing technology, and increasingly diverse workplaces. Similarly, in elite and professional sport, athletes will likely become global celebrities whose lives will more closely resemble film and rock music stars (Coakley, 2001; Reinhart, 1998). Sport organizations will become increasingly global, especially those involved with power and performance sports with an increasing ability to attract corporate sponsors. The benefits, for some athletes, may be greater autonomy and power to enhance their careers, but these may be accompanied by incessant pressures for measurable achievement and successful competitive outcomes. Sport organizations, whose principles will reflect entertainment and consumption motives in the quest for profit and economic expansion, will also prosper. However, concerns may be raised in regard to the use of technology, the increased chances of injuries and ethical problems associated with pushing human limits, and other potentially exploitive practices.

In view of these forecast developments in elite and professional sport, the need for primary prevention-oriented career assistance programs, increasingly acknowledged by player unions, becomes even more apparent.

Sport Career Transition Programs: Overview

The growth of career assistance programs for athletes has, to some extent, coincided with the growth in size and popularity of high-level competitive sports. As presented in Table 1, numerous programs have been developed in countries around the world to help resolve the conflict that many individuals face in having to choose between pursuing their sport and post-sport career goals. The formats of existing programs vary and often include workshops, seminars, educational modules, and individual counseling. As described in Wylleman, Lavallee, and Alfermann (1999), most programs focus on lifestyle management and the development of transferable skills that can assist individuals in making the transition from life in sport into a post-sport career. As such, these programs provide athletes with an introduction to career planning and development by focusing on values and interest exploration, career awareness and decision-making, curriculum vitae and resumé preparation, interview techniques, and job search strategies.

Career development programs for athletes are primarily managed by national sports governing bodies, national Olympic Committee player unions within specific sport federations (e.g., National Basketball Players Association), academic institutions (e.g., Springfield College), and independent organizations linked to sport settings (e.g., Women's Sports Foundation). While some programs address the needs of professional athletes (e.g., the United States National Football Leagues Career Transition Program), the majority have been developed for elite amateur sports participants (Gordon, 1995).

The following section provides a brief description of some of the most advanced career development programs for athletes. These programs include the international Olympic Job Opportunities Program, United States Career Assistance Program for Athletes, Canadian Olympic Athlete Career Centre, and Athlete Career and Education Program that operates in both Australia and the United Kingdom.

Olympic Job Opportunities Program

The Olympic Job Opportunities Program (OJOP) is an international program that has been initiated in Australia, South Africa, and the United States. Sponsored by the company Ernst and Young, the principal goal of OJOP is to develop and source career opportunities for Olympians and potential Olympians. Eligible athletes are either current or Olympic-caliber athletes who need to be certified as such by their respective national federations. In addition to providing direct employer contacts and identifying job positions, OJOP provides career analysis services, personality aptitude testing, and interview skills training (Gordon, 1995).

Initially, in the United States, a grant from the US Olympic Foundation was awarded to OJOP in 1988 to create a program to assist elite athletes in coping with the transition out of active sport competition. Following a survey with approximately 1,800 Olympic and other elite-level athletes, the Career Assistance Program for Athletes (CAPA) was established to introduce individuals to the career development process while they were competing. This program was based on the lifespan development model of Danish and D'Augelli (1980), and focused on increasing athletes' sense of personal competence through understanding and identifying transferable skills. A number of one-day workshops were organized around three main themes: managing the emotional and social impact of transitions, increasing understanding and awareness of personal qualities relevant to coping with transitions and career development, and introducing information about the world of work. Although these workshops were well-received by athletes (Petitpas, Danish, McKelvain, & Murphy, 1992), funding for the CAPA Program was terminated in 1993.

Olympic Athlete Career Centre

One of the first career development programs to be developed for athletes was the Canadian Olympic Athlete Career Centre (OACC), which was launched in 1985 following a series of needs-based surveys conducted in 1983-1984 by the Canadian Olympic Association (COA). The original center, based in Toronto, had a mandate to assist athletes through the transition process to a second career, primarily through career and education planning (Sinclair & Hackfort, 2000). Athletes who had achieved approved rankings by way of their performances at Olympic, Commonwealth, and Pan Pacific Games had access to the OACC (Anderson & Morris, 2000). Sinclair and Hackfort (2000) outlined the following

career development services that were initially offered through the OACC:

- Clarification of career planning needs, self-assessment, aptitude/interest assessment to assist in identification of specific occupations of interest, decision-making, and action-planning skills.

- Booklets were made available to all eligible athletes on the topics of curriculum vitae preparation, interview preparation, job search techniques, and information interviewing.

- Retirement planning focused on what athletes should expect during the adjustment period. Transition workshops and peer support groups were established to help athletes deal effectively with the career transition process.

- Reference letters of support were provided by the COA as well as personalized business cards bearing the COA logo for networking purposes.

In addition, a shadow program was developed in 1990 to provide athletes with the opportunity to explore career options by shadowing professionals in the field of their choice.

In recent years, the COA has initiated a reorganization process that has resulted in an increase in the number of centers operating within Canada, as well as additions to the career development services provided. There are currently Olympic Athlete Career Centres operating in Calgary, Montreal, Ottawa, Toronto, and Vancouver, with each employing consultants to work with athletes living in or around these locations (Anderson & Morris, 2000). The standardization of service provision across centers is ongoing and is influenced by the need and utility of the services for the athlete population in each region.

Athlete Career and Education Program

The Athlete Career and Education (ACE) Program was developed in Australia by the Victorian Institute of Sport in Melbourne in 1990, and was later amalgamated with the Lifeskills for Elite Athletes Program (SportsLEAP) in 1995. SportsLEAP was originally established in 1989 by the Australian Institute of Sport based on the results of a needs-based survey following the 1988 Seoul Olympics (Fortunato, Anderson, Morris, & Seedsman, 1995). This program was highly successful, but the scope and content of each program varied according to athlete demand in each State Institute or Academy of Sport. Consequently, a decision was made to integrate SportsLEAP and the ACE Program (under the ACE name) to form a national program.

The overall objective of the ACE program is to assist athletes in balancing the demands of their sporting careers while enhancing their opportunities to also develop their educational and vocational skills (Anderson & Morris, 2000). A major component of the program is to assist individuals in developing a career plan that integrates both sporting and nonsporting components. The philosophy is to create an environment where athletes can be encouraged to be independent, be self-reliant, and have a capacity to meet the demands associated with elite sport.

Anderson and Morris (2000) have outlined the following services provided through the Australian ACE Program:

- Individual athlete assessments are used to provide a structured process in which to assess individual athletes' educational, vocational, financial, and personal development needs.

- Over thirty personal development training courses are structured to assist athletes in meeting their sporting, educational, and career aspirations. Many of these courses provide individuals with nationally accredited, competency-based education programs.

- A nationally consistent career and education planning process is employed to enable athletes to manage their own individual vocational requirements. Career development is provided in the form of direct assistance in finding employment through career advice, training paths, and vocational training. Secondary and tertiary education support is provided through networking with individuals in secondary schools, technical and further education colleges (TAFE), and universities that can offer unit- or course-selection advice, as well as assistance in negotiating appropriate academic and residential arrangements for athletes. Also available are computerized programs of information on all tertiary, TAFE, and community courses in Australia; Austudy information (mature-age student funding scheme); and Courscan, which assists Year 11 and 12 students to match secondary school subjects to tertiary and TAFE courses (Gordon, 1995).

- A specific transition program provides career and education guidance for elite athletes undergoing transitions to a post-sporting career.

- Training opportunities and supervised practice for ACE staff is provided through a Graduate Certificate in Athlete Career and Education Management that has recently been developed by Victoria University of Technology in Melbourne.

- Direct athlete needs-based assessments provide a structured process to assess athletes' eligibility for support.

Currently ACE services are available to over 3,000 elite-level athletes throughout Australia. The United Kingdom Sports Institute has also recently initiated the ACE UK Program across England, Scotland, Wales, and Northern Ireland. To be eligible for assistance in Australia, athletes must be scholarship holders with the Australian Institute of Sport, state institutes or academies of sport, or participants in the Olympic Athlete Program. ACE managers and advisors are employed in each state institute or academy of sport in Australia, and a national manager co-ordinates the program.

Evaluation of Program Interventions

While systematic program evaluation in career management in nonsport settings is fairly common (e. g., Dedmond, 1996; McCharen, 1996), very few investigations have been conducted in sport. Recent exceptions are examinations of the ACE program in Australia (Gorely, Lavallee, Bruce, Teale, & Lavallee, 2001) and the UK (UK Sport, 2001), and an assessment of a career assistance program designed specifically for youth-aged cricketers (Bobridge, Gordon, Walker, & Thompson, 2003).

ACE Australia

The specific aim of Gorely, Lavallee, Bruce, Teale, and Lavallee's (2001) research was to determine usage levels of the program, identify athletes' perceived needs, determine overall satisfaction with the program, and identify athletes' suggestions for the future. Focus groups with athletes, coaches, and administrators were initially formed to develop an understanding of the key issues. A survey instrument was then developed and distributed to every athlete (more than 3,000 across 48 sports) eligible to receive ACE services in Australia.

Results revealed that the majority of athletes (70.7%) reported contact with the ACE program during the 12-month period prior to data collection. The most-used services were career guidance/planning, help with school or university, professional development workshops in finding/establishing a job, time management, and goal setting. The career transition service center was the least used, with less than one percent of the athletes indicating that they accessed this service.

The most frequently cited reason for using ACE services was *they may help my life outside sport.* Other reasons included *they may help my sporting career, they may help my sporting performance,* and *a coach/administrator suggested it.* Athletes also indicated that suitable program mechanics such as low costs and the availability of ACE representatives influenced their use of ACE services.

The main reasons for athletes not using the program were classified as *aspects of the program, lack of perceived need,* and *personal factors.* Aspects of the program inhibiting usage included *lack of awareness of the services offered and unsuitable venues or timing of services. Lack of perceived need* was reported by some athletes and reasons for this included *having other priorities, using alternative resources,* or simply *having no need for the services ACE provides.* Personal factors such as *not getting around to it* and *laziness* indicated perhaps a lack of motivation on behalf of the individual to utilize the ACE program.

Analysis of the explanations for non-use of ACE services provides program managers with a number of strategies to address them. Reluctance to participate in aspects of the program can be overcome by ensuring that services are available at times (including after hours and weekends) and locations (preferably close to training sites) convenient to the athletes and to increasing athlete awareness (Petitpas & Champagne, 2000). The athletes indicated that their preferred method for receiving information was by personal contact with an ACE representative or by mailings. However, some athletes mentioned that a system to make sure athletes were receiving the mailings would be useful.

Lack of perceived need can be addressed by targeting existing services to specific groups of athletes more closely, ensuring that the benefits of services are clearly explained, and adding services to meet the specific needs of different athlete groups. This suggestion approximates that of Taylor (1997) in a school setting who determined that students needed to be formally oriented to career planning services. Personal issues may be overcome to a large extent by the previous two strategies. Greater perceived benefits and easier access may reduce the inertia experienced by athletes, but the challenge to ACE may be to find ways of enhancing athletes' personal motivation before having the opportunity to teach them relevant skills, such as goal setting and time management. Successfully addressing this challenge may rest on creating an environment, in conjunction with coaches and parents, that promotes balanced personal and social development.

ACE United Kingdom

Recent research in the United Kingdom (UK Sport, 2001) assessed how career transition programs can be more effective by investigating potential users of the ACE UK program who are still active elite athletes. The specific aims of the study were to examine (a) planning age for athletic retirement among elite athletes in the United Kingdom (representatives of different sports and genders, as well as able-bodied and disabled athletes), (b) short-term plans used by athletes to balance sport commitments and other activities, and (c) long-term plans in regard to activities after sport career termination.

Employing a census approach, all 988 athletes who were registered in the ACE UK program up to June 2000 were sent an introductory letter, questionnaire, and postage-paid reply envelope for instrument return. The introductory letter explained the purpose of the study and assured confidentiality and anonymity. Respondents were invited to return completed questionnaires to an independent agency.

The questionnaire was four pages long and consisted primarily of closed questions focusing on such topics as athletes' expected years until career termination, short-term plans, and plans about life after sport. Some open-ended questions (e.g., "If you have made plans, what are they?") were also included to allow athletes to expand on issues related to their post-sporting career. A total of 561 valid and completed questionnaires were returned by the athletes. There were slightly more males (54%) than females (46%) in the sample, and more able-bodied athletes (83%) than athletes with disabilities. The average age of the overall sample was 26.0 years old. A total of 37 individual and team sports were represented.

Results on *planning age of retirement* indicated that athletes intended to retire from competitive sport at the average age of 34 (*SD*=7.84); however, average retirement age was found to vary significantly across sports. Female athletes intended to retire significantly earlier than males, and able-bodied athletes intended to retire significantly earlier than disabled athletes. A number of particular ages at which athletes in the sample were planning to retire from sport were also identified. While athletes' retirement from sport first starts to occur at 25 years, percentage peaks also appeared around 30, 35, and 40 years, suggesting that athletes may plan their sport and post-sport careers around five-year periods.

When the number of years before the athletes were expected to retire was examined in more detail, results showed that 13% were considering retiring from competitive sport in the next 1-2 years, 30% were planning to retire in the next 3-5 years, and 57% were not planning to retire for another six years at least. Overall, the athletes in the sample were eight years away from retiring so it may be inferred that in any one year approximately 5-7% of competitive athletes in the UK are thinking about retiring from sport in that year.

Results from *short-term plans* for the twelve months immediately following the study suggested that the most important issue was increasing the amount of time they spend training and competing.

Over half of the respondents (56%) revealed they would increase the amount of time they spend sport training over the next twelve months, 28% intended to enter education, and 21% stated that finding work was a priority.

Short-term plans were found to vary significantly for the athletes across the following four age categories: under 21 years (*N*=115); 21-24 years (*N*=121); 25-29 years (*N*=118); and over 30 years (*N*=118). Compared to older athletes, younger athletes would more likely enter education and spend more time in sport training, while older athletes were more likely to suggest that they would be looking for work.

The length of time before athletes plan to retire from sport (i.e., next 1-2 years, next 3-5 years, and 6 years or more) was also found to be influential on their plans over the next twelve months. Athletes who suggested that they intended to retire from sport in the next one or two years were less likely to suggest that they were going to increase the amount of time devoted to sports training over the next year (27%) and more likely to be trying to find work (31%). Athletes who suggested that they did not intend to retire from sport for six years or more were very likely to be increasing the amount of time they spend on training (72%), more likely than average to be looking to enter education (31%), and less likely to be looking for work (20%).

Overall, the results from *long-term plans* revealed that 53% of the respondents had made plans, and 47% had not. When the data were analyzed according to the time until their planned retirement, 79% of athletes who were retiring in the next one or two years had made plans compared to 45% who were not retiring for six years or over. However, 21% who were planning to retire in the next one or two years did not have an idea about what they were going to do after they finished competitive sport. These athletes included 22 individuals who were 30 years or over, 16 who were not in education or employment (i.e., they were full-time athletes), and six who had no work experience.

Those respondents who had made plans were also asked about what they intended to do after their sporting careers had ended. Developing a career was foremost in the athletes' minds, with 81% suggesting that they intended to start, or increase the amount of time devoted to, work. Thirty-two percent were working, or intended to work, in an area connected to sport after they retire.

In conclusion, it appears that while competitive athletes in the UK are increasing the amount of time they devote to training and competition, most are content with the balance between sport and nonsporting activities. However, as the demands of the performance environment increase, the tendency to pursue sport in all its senses may also increase, affecting younger athletes coming through the elite athlete system even more. The need is apparent, therefore, for career transition programs that provide younger athletes with a focus with which to consider their longer-term career development needs.

Youth Sport Research

While the previous two studies evaluated the perceptions of mature athletes who were potential ACE program users, Bobridge, Gordon, Walker, and Thompson (2003) set out to assess the effects of a career assistance program on youth-aged athletes. Specifically, the Western Australian Cricket Association (WACA) wished to examine the outcomes of a third-party intervention delivered by TMP Worldwide (2001) on particular self-identity characteristics of selected male cricketers under 17 years old.

The participants ($N=31$) were male athletes identified by the WACA as talented junior cricketers. The experimental group ($N=20$) consisted of those selected in a preliminary squad for a State cricket carnival. Ages ranged from 15 to 16 with a mean age of 15.78 years ($SD=.42$). The control group ($N=11$) consisted of cricketers also identified as talented by the WACA, but who missed out on selection for the State squad. Ages for the control group were between 15 and 16 with a mean age of 15.64 years ($SD=.50$).

The AIMS questionnaire (Brewer, Van Raalte, & Linder, 1993) was used to assess Athletic Identity, with participants indicating their extent of agreement for each of the 10 items on a 7-point Likert scale. Scores for each item were then summed to provide an index of Athletic Identity, with high scores representing strong or exclusive athletic identity. Identity Foreclosure was measured using the 6 items relating to Foreclosure in the Objective Measurement of Ego Identity Scale (OM-EIS; Adams, Shea, & Fitch, 1979). These items also used a 7-point Likert scale with

the same ranges as the AIMS. A score for Identity Foreclosure was determined by summing the scores from each item, with high scores representing high Identity Foreclosure. Career thoughts were assessed using the Career Thoughts Inventory (CTI; Sampson, Peterson, Lenz, Reardon, & Saunders, 1996a; 1996b), which relies on the premise that while dysfunctional career thinking cannot be measured directly, such thinking can be inferred from an individual's endorsement of the test statements that reflect a variety of dysfunctional career thoughts (Sampson et al., 1996a). Specifically, the test measures four factors. There is a global indicator of dysfunctional career thinking, CTI Total, which is the total amount of negative career thoughts determined by summing the scores on each item of the CTI ($N=48$ items). Second, there is Decision-Making Confusion (DMC; 14 items), which relates to the inability to initiate or sustain the decision-making process. Third, Commitment Anxiety (CA; 11 items) measures the inability to make a commitment to a specific career choice, accompanied by general anxiety about the decision-making process. Finally, there is External Conflict (EC; 5 items), which relates to the inability to balance the importance of input from significant people with self-perceptions (Sampson et al., 1996b). An intervention evaluation questionnaire, Player Feedback Inventory, was also administered to the experimental group to assess participants' opinions of the career assistance program.

Pre-intervention (Time 1) both groups completed the AIMS, Identity Foreclosure, and CTI instruments. While the control group pursued normal attendance at school and club cricket, the experimental group additionally participated in the career assistance program for a period of 14 weeks (6 sessions plus a summary session). Post-intervention (Time 2) both groups again completed the same instruments and the experimental group was administered the Player Feedback Inventory. The TMP Worldwide (2001) career assistance program explored issues such as career models, confidence, values, goal setting, skills and qualities, ideal jobs, study choices, resumé and interview preparation, networking, and applying for jobs.

Contrary to expectations and hypotheses generated from previous research, results showed no significant changes from pre- to post-intervention for Athletic Identity, Identity Foreclosure, and for three of the four measures of Career Thoughts (CTI). There were, however, significant and positive changes evident in the area of External Conflict suggesting that the program helped players become better at balancing their own judgments with those of significant others. This is related to the construct of Identity Foreclosure and suggests that changes in research design may be necessary to more directly examine the relationship between identity development and career maturity and the effect of career assistance on career development.

Participants also reported that the program helped them with career development in a number of significant ways. They reported an increased awareness of need for a career outside of sport, and that they could see themselves in other important roles besides being a sportsperson. They became more aware of career options available to them and reported that they were more likely to pursue these options. Although there was no change in Athletic Identity, self-reports suggested that players became more open-minded about careers outside of sport.

According to participants, the most useful aspects of the program were the practical elements such as creating resumés, preparing for interviews, assessing skills and qualities, setting goals, and understanding work choices. Players also reported increasing confidence about their decision-making abilities and developing the resources and skills to pursue career goals. Finally, they acknowledged that gaining practical skills and confidence in regard to career goals can enable them to develop career opportunities outside of sport.

Work-Career Intervention Research

Historical perspectives (e. g., Herr, 2001) and reviews of intervention research in nonsport careers (e. g., Arbona, 2000; Spokane, 1991; Whitson, Sexton, & Lasoff, 1998) have identified distinct theoretical approaches, career assistance programs, and assessment instruments that appear to have both potential and relevance to sport career research. For example, a social cognitive approach to career development has been proposed (Lent & Brown, 1996) both for unifying existing career theories and for conceptualizing developmental and remedial career interventions. In addition, Kidd (1998) has argued that greater attention should be given to the role of emotion in understanding career development. She believes that the literature on emotion generally, and emotional labor in particular, has potential in understanding the challenging dynamics of career counseling and coping with change in contemporary employment contexts.

In regard to experimental designs, Lougheed and Black (1990) provided a *futures* perspective of job change designed to stimulate further thinking in a changing world of work. Whan (1995) and Marko and Savickas (1998) also examined *career time perspective* that included a future orientation in their career assistance program. In terms of program outcomes, various dependent measures have been investigated, and those that appear particularly relevant to sport include *life satisfaction* (Perna, Ahlgren, & Zaichkowsky, 1999), *career maturity and decidedness* (Dagley, 1999), *career indecision* (Larson & Majors, 1998), *career progress* (Barnes & Herr, 1998), *career decision-making self-efficacy* (Cox, 1997) and *vocational cognitive complexity* (Mau, Calvert, & Gregory, 1997).

Future Directions

Although increased attention has been devoted to career transitions and career assistance programs in the past decade, the research in this area remains limited in a number of important ways. These limitations include issues related to the transition process in general, the specific nature of transitions within the domain of competitive sport, and the implementation and evaluation of career assistance programs. The focus here is on research related to career assistance programs. See Gordon and Lavallee (2004) for a broader discussion that includes consideration of the other areas.

Firstly, it must be acknowledged that research on career assistance programs in sport is not only scant but also highly descriptive. Analyses have consisted mainly of profiling the extent to which athletes have used (or not used) the services and the program components they found to be most (or least) helpful (e. g., Gorely et al., 2001). These types of descriptive studies need to be complemented with a stronger evidentiary base that includes information about the

Table 1: Selected Career Transition Programs

Program	Institution	Country
Athlete Career and Education Program (ACE)	Australian Institute of Sport	Australia
Athlete Career and Education Program (ACE UK)	United Kingdom Sports Institute	UK
Career Assistance Program for Athletes	U.S. Olympic Committee	USA
CD Sports	Coyne Didsbury Sports	Australia
Making the Jump Program	Advisory Resource Centre for Athlete	USA
Olympic Athlete Career Centre—National Sports Centre	Olympic Athlete Career Centre	Canada
Olympic Job Opportunities Program	Australian Olympic Committee	Australia
Study and Talent Education Program	Vrije Universiteit Brussels	Belgium
The Retiring Athlete	Dutch Olympic Committee	Netherlands
Whole-istic	American College Athletic Association	USA
Women's Sports Foundation Athlete Service	Women's Sports Foundation	USA

impact of program participation on outcomes such as retirement planning, career adjustment, and life satisfaction.

The contribution of specific program components in producing favorable outcomes should also be examined. For example, programs that provide opportunities for mentoring (cf. Perna et al., 1996) and/or account-making (cf. Grove, Lavallee, Gordon, & Harvey, 1998) could be compared to those that do not provide such opportunities. These program components have the potential to assist both athletes and coaches in making successful transitions, but no empirical evaluations of their impact have been undertaken.

Stage considerations also need to be incorporated into future research on the impact of career assistance programs. An adequate treatment of these issues will require analyses of both stage-of-career factors and stage-of-change factors. With respect to stage-of-career factors, Wylleman et al. (1999) have identified stages in a sport career involving increased specialization, more intensive training, higher levels of participation (e. g., amateur to elite/professional), changes in performance capabilities, and termination of involvement. Each of these career stages is likely to involve unique transition experiences, and the relevance and impact of various program components may therefore be stage dependent.

With respect to stage-of-change factors, future research into the effectiveness of career assistance programs could benefit from a career-orientation approach that considers the readiness of athletes for career assistance (e. g., Hewett , 1994). This approach is based on the transtheoretical model of behavior change (Prochaska & Diclemente, 1986) and suggests that some coaches and athletes are ready for input from career assistance programs while others are not. Thus, appropriate outcome goals for some individuals may be to change their beliefs about the value of such assistance, while appropriate outcome goals for others may be to develop better life management skills. For maximum effectiveness, program structure as well as evaluation protocols need to be sensitive to these differences.

Finally, there is a need for research employing longitudinal designs and a multimethod approach. Data collected from athletes and/or coaches before, during, and after their exposure to career assistance programs will not only enhance our understanding of the career transition process but will also improve our ability to detect meaningful changes that result from this exposure. These are worthwhile and important objectives, and a blending of quantitative and qualitative methodologies will help us to achieve them.

References

Adams, G. R., Shea, J., & Fitch, S. A. (1979). Towards the development of an objective measurement of ego identity status. *Journal of Youth and Adolscence, 8*, 223-237.

Anderson, D. K., & Morris, T. (2000). Athlete lifestyle programs. In D. Lavallee & P. Wylleman (Eds.), *Career transitions in sport: International perspectives.* (pp. 59-80). Morgantown, WV: Fitness Information Technology.

Arbona, C. (2000). Practice and research in career counselling and development - 1999. *Career Development Quarterly, 49*(2), 98-134.

Barnes, J. A., & Herr, E. L. (1998). The effects of interventions on career progress. *Journal of Career Development, 24*(3), 179-193.

Bobridge, K., Gordon, S., Walker, A., & Thompson, R. (2003 Winter). Evaluation of a career transition program for youth-aged cricketers. *Australian Journal of Career Development, 12,* 19-27.

Brewer, B. W., Van Raalte, J. L., & Linder, D. E. (1993). Athletic identity: Hercules' muscles or Achilles' heel? *International Journal of Sport Psychology, 24,* 237-254.

Coakley, J. J. (2001). *Sport and society: Issues and controversies* (7th ed.). Sydney: McGraw-Hill.

Cox, S. H. (1997). The effectiveness of career planning courses in enhancing career decision-making self-efficacy. *Dissertation Abstracts International, A (Humanities and Social Sciences), 57,* 4272.

Dagley, J. C. (1999). The restoration of group process in career counseling groups. *International Journal of Action Methods, 15*(4), 141-157.

Danish, S. J., & D'Augelli, A. R. (1980). *Helping skills II: Life development intervention.* New York: Human Sciences.

Dedmond, R. M. (1996). Evaluation of the career planning program. *Journal of Career Development, 23*(1), 83-93.

Fortunato, V., Anderson, D., Morris, T., & Seedsman, T. (1995). Career transition research at Victoria University of Technology. In R. Vanfraechem-Raway & Y. Vanden Auweele (Eds.), *Proceedings of the 9th European Congress on Sport Psychology* (pp. 533-543). Brussels: European Federation of Sport Psychology.

Gordon, S. (1995). Career transitions in competitive sport. In T. Morris and J. Summers (Eds.) *Sport Psychology: Theory Applications and Current Issues.* (pp. 474-501) Brisbane: John Wiley & Sons.

Gordon, S., & Lavallee, D. (2004). Career transitions in competitive sport. In T. Morris and J. Summers (Eds.), *Sport Psychology: Theory Applications and Current Issues,* (2nd ed.) (pp. 584-610). Brisbane: John Wiley & Sons.

Gorely, T., Lavallee, D., Bruce, D., Teale, B., & Lavallee, R. (2001). A sampling of perceptions of potential users of the Australian Athlete Career and Education program. *Academic Athletic Journal, 15,* 11-21.

Grove, J. R., Lavallee, D., Gordon, S., & Harvey, J. (1998). Account-making as a treatment model for distressful reactions to retirement from sport. *The Sport Psychologist, 12,* 52-67.

Herr, E. L. (2001). Career development and its practice: A historical perspective. *Career Development Quarterly, 49,* 196-211.

Hewett, K. (1994). *Career orientation of elite amateur athletes.* Unpublished honours thesis, The University of Western Australia: Perth.

Kidd, J. M. (1998). Emotion: An absent presence in career theory. *Journal of Vocational Behaviour, 52,* 275-288.

Larson, L. M., & Majors, M. S. (1998). Applications of the Coping with Career Indecision instrument with adolescents. *Journal of Career Assessment, 6,* 163-179.

Lavallee, D., Sinclair, D. A., & Wylleman, P. (1998). An annotated bibliography on career transitions in sport: 2. Empirical references. *Australian Journal of Career Development, 7*(3), 32-44.

Lavallee, D., Wylleman, P., & Sinclair, D. A., (1998). An annotated bibliography on career transitions in sport: 1.

Counselling-based references. Australian *Journal of Career Development, 7*(2), 34-42.

Lee, F. K., & Johnston, J. A. (2001). Innovations in career counselling. *Journal of Career development, 27*(3), 177-185.

Lent, R. W., & Brown, S. D. (1996). Social cognitive approach to career development: An overview. *Career Development Quarterly, 44,* 310-321.

Lougheed, T. A., & Black, D. R. (1990). Job change in the future. *Journal of Career Development, 17*(1), 71-76.

Marko, K. W., & Savickas, M. L. (1998). Effectiveness of a career time perspective intervention. *Journal of Vocational Behaviour, 52*(1), 106-119.

Mau, W-C., Calvert, C., & Gregory, R. (1997). Effects of career interventions on vocational cognitive complexity. *Journal of Career Development, 23,* 279-293.

McCharen, B. (1996). Measuring the effects of career planning: The seventh C-Competency. *Journal of Career Development, 23*(1), 73-82.

Pearson, R. E., & Petitpas, A. J. (1990). Transitions of athletes: Developmental and preventive perspectives. *Journal of Counseling and Development, 69,* 7-10.

Perna, F. M., Ahlgren, R. L., & Zaichkowsky, L. (1999). The influence of career planning, race, and athletic injury on life satisfaction among recently retired collegiate male athletes. *The Sport Psychologist, 13,* 144-156.

Petitpas, A. J., & Champagne, D. (2000). Practical considerations in implementing sport career transition programs. In D. Lavallee & P. Wylleman (Eds.), *Career transitions in sport: International perspectives* (pp. 81-94). Morgantown, WV: Fitness Information Technology.

Petitpas, A. J., Champagne, D., Chartrand, J., Danish, S., & Murphy, S. (1997). *Athlete's guide to career planning.* Champaign, IL: Human Kinetics.

Petitpas, A., Danish, S., McKelvain, R., & Murphy, S. (1992). A career assistance program for elite athletes. *Journal of Counseling and Development, 70,* 383-386.

Prochaska, J., & DiClemente, C. (1986). Toward a comprehensive model of change. In W.E. Miller & N. Heather (Eds.), *Treating addictive behaviours* (pp. 3-27). London: Plenum Press.

Reinhart, R. E. (1998). *Players all: Performances in contemporary sport.* Bloomington: Indian University Press.

Sampson, J. P., Peterson, G. W., Lenz, J. G., Reardon, R. C., & Saunders, D. E. (1996a). *Career Thoughts Inventory.* Odessa, FL. Psychological Assessment Resources.

Sampson, J. P., Peterson, G. W., Lenz, J. G., Reardon, R. C., & Saunders, D. E. (1996b). *Career Thoughts Inventory: Professional manual.* Odessa, FL: Psychological Assessment Resources.

Sinclair, D. A. & Hackfort, D. (2000). The role of the sport organisation in the career transition process. In D. Lavallee & P. Wylleman (Eds.), *Career transitions in sport: International perspectives* (pp. 131-142). Morgantown, WV: Fitness Information Technology.

Spokane, A. R. (1991). *Career intervention.* Upper Saddle River, NJ: Prentice-Hall.

Taylor, S. C. (1997). Workshop to orient students to career planning services. Career *Development Quarterly, 45*(3), 293-296.

Taylor, J., & Ogilvie, B. C. (2001). Career transitions among athletes: Is there life after sports? In J. M. Williams (Ed.),

Applied sport psychology: Personal growth to peak performance (5th ed., pp. 480-496). Mountain View, CA: Mayfield.

TMP Worldwide (2001). *Proposal for career management for the players of the Western Australian Cricket Association.* Perth: A. Walker.

UK Sport (2001). *Athletes' lifestyle and ACE UK: A survey of athletes' experience of sport, education and work, and the role of the ACE UK programme.* Author: London.

Ungerleider, S. (1997). Olympic athletes' transitions from sport to workplace. *Perceptual and Motor Skills, 84,* 1287-1295.

Whan, K. A. (1995). Modifying career time perspective. *Dissertation Abstracts International Section B: Sciences and Engineering, 55*(10-B), 4596.

Whitson, S. C., Sexton, T. L., & Lasoff, D. L. (1998). Career intervention outcome: A replication and extension of Oliver and Spokane (1988). *Journal of Counseling Psychology, 45*(2), 150-165.

Wylleman, P., Lavallee, D., & Alfermann, D. (Eds.). (1999). *Career transitions in competitive sports.* FEPSAC Monograph Series: European Federation of Sport Psychology.

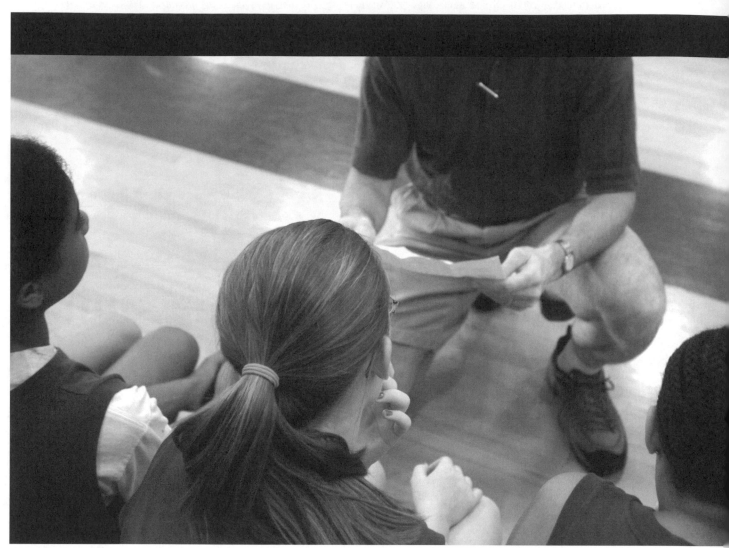

Courtesy of iStockphoto Inc.

5.3

Considerations for Research on Career Counseling and Career Transition

DIETER HACKFORT AND ZHIJIAN HUANG

Introduction

The development, transition, and termination of the careers of elite athletes, as well as their personal development, are attracting attention from the pedagogical and social sciences. Sport psychologists who counsel elite athletes have focused their attention on athletic careers, retirement, and success in life (Danish & Hale, 1981; Danish, Petitpas, & Hale, 1993; Hackfort & Schlattmann, 1994; Hackfort, Emrich, & Papathanassiou, 1997; Murphy, 1995; Ogilvie & Taylor, 1993; Sinclair & Orlick, 1993). Several concepts have been stressed and various methodological strategies have been followed to analyze career transition, athletes' crises, and lifespan development interventions. Career education programs, counseling, and assistance have been adapted or developed in the

sport domain itself. The purpose of this chapter is to reflect on the fundamental issues of this research, to discuss some ideas for further progress in the field, and to supplement the information provided by Gordon, Lavallee, and Grove in another chapter of this volume.

Theory Perspective

The theories and models used in athletic career transition studies are heterogeneous. Due to the absence of sport-specific concepts, studies in this field are based on research paradigms from related domains such as organizational psychology and sociology (Haerle, 1975; Hill & Lowe, 1974; Ingham, 1975; Lerch, 1982; McPerson, 1980; Reynolds, 1981; Rosenberg, 1981). However, studies of the career transitions of elite athletes developed in the domain of career counseling have become increasingly interesting (Crook & Robertson, 1991). The theoretical perspectives offered in the past decade (see Sinclair & Orlick, 1993) on career termination (e.g., thanatology, social gerontology, career transition, or lifespan development) lack a holistic understanding. They treat retirement as a singular event or neglect the contextual aspect, including the person's environment. A brief overview of two alternative approaches is provided in Tables 1 and 2.

The action theory perspective offers a holistic approach including goal-directed and purposeful behavior in a person-environment-task constellation (Nitsch & Hackfort, 1981; Nitsch, 2000; Hackfort, Munzert, & Seiler, 2000). Such a broad understanding can include the integration of special concepts, such as lifespan development. According to the lifespan development intervention (LDI) perspective (Super, 1980), stages in an individual lifespan are hierarchically dependent. Thus, to understand the process of athletic career transition, it is necessary to consider the processes and stages of an athlete's lifespan. In addition, it is useful to study athletic career transition across different cultures and sport systems to better understand the process.

It is assumed that "action theory offers a conceptual framework and language for understanding career development and career counseling that is close to human experience" (Young, 1995). One fundamental characteristic of the action theory perspective that we embrace is the interactive relationship between three components in an action situation: The task, the person, and the environment (Nitsch & Hackfort, 1981; Hackfort, 1986, Hackfort, Munzert, & Seiler, 2000; Nitsch, 2000). The interaction of

Table 1: Gerontology Theories in Research on Athletic Career

Gerontology theories	Concept of retirement	Implication for athletic career	Merits and shortcomings
Activity/ substitution theory (e.g., Havighurst & Albrecht, 1953	High activity and maintenance of role will positively influence the self-concept and life satisfaction.	Do not provide mechanisms to predict whether activity or disengagement will result.	In fact, athletes who significantly decrease their activities will usually have negative experiences
Disengagement theory (Cummings et al., 1960)	Both the person and society withdraw benefit and satisfaction from the individual retirement.	To accept the disengagement notion or not, is the key of successful athletic career retirement.	From this approach we learn that it is important for a successful adjustment after retirement to find a new area of activity and engagement to overcome the loss that is the result of the end of the sport career.
Subculture theory (Rose, 1965)	In a certain subculture, older people may enjoy the decrease of activity.	Competitive athletes have obvious and distinguishable subcultural characteristics.	The influence of athletic subcultures on their post-athletic life in "regular" culture should be discussed further.
Continuity theory (Atchley, 1980)	The time and energy of the prior role will be either redistributed among remaining roles or redirected towards the new role of individual.	Explaining why athletes do not voluntarily withdraw from sport position	Limited meaning for research on athletic career.
Social breakdown theory (Kuypers & Bengston, 1973)	Retirement will make individual susceptible to the external evaluation.	"Social reconstruction" for retired athletes is important in career counseling.	Limited meaning for research on athletic career
Social exchange theory (e.g., Thibaut & Kelley, 1959)	A subjective assessment of the costs and benefits of activities will influence individual to continue, reduce, or withdraw the current activity.	According to Rosenberg (1981), exchange theory can help athletes to understand the relationship between sport and themselves over time provides a perspective on what will happen to that relationship over time.	In research on athletic career, this theory perspective has its merits in pre-retirement counseling programs.

Table 2: Lifespan Development Interventions Across Time

Point in time	Before critical life event	During critical life event	After critical life event
Intervention strategies	Enhancement strategies	Supportive strategies	Counseling strategies
Function/ contents	to help (athlete) to anticipate normative events; to assist and facilitate transfers of life-skills across phases; to teach coping skills.	to listen to and build rapport with on-event athletes; to organize support environment for the transitional events; to link athletes to possible organizational resources.	to help to confront the impact or the aftermath of the event; to assist individuals in coping with and growing through critical events; to help to build up connections between life phases before and after the (critical) events.
Main approach	educational workshop; goal setting skill.	communication with successful-transferred athletes; emotional support. (Rosenfeld et al., 1989)	Rapport; goal-setting strategy; other counseling interventions.

these components is influenced by external (social, ecological, etc.) and internal (a person's thoughts) factors. A person organizes and regulates his or her actions according to his or her subjective definition of the situation. Understanding this process is crucial when analyzing careers.

"Career" is defined differently in sociology and psychology. Schein (1978) defined two basic categories of a career conception: *External career* and *internal career*. External career refers to "the objective categories used by society and organizations to describe the progression of steps through a given occupation" (p. 10). Internal career refers to "the set of steps or stages that make up the individual's own concept of his own progression within an occupation" (p. 11). Thus, "the career can be considered as a naïve biographical concept. Similarly, we have used several concepts, such as manifest career, cognitive steering, and social meaning, to describe career," (Valach, 1990, p. 119).

The action theory framework integrates the aspects emphasized in social gerontology such as transition concepts, LSD, and LDI approaches. It also includes the influence of the social and cultural environment especially in the process of retirement, the person-environment interaction, the influence of various factors in the transition process, and the meaning of the transition regarded as a developmental task. Such aspects are related to the (self-) organization and (self-) control (regulation) of intentional behavior (actions), which is based on the objective influences (causes of behavior), as well as on subjective concepts: the perception and understanding of objective factors, personal factors (ability and motivation), environmental factors (affordances and opportunities), and factors of the task (difficulty, attractiveness). From this point of view, not only is the objective social or cul-

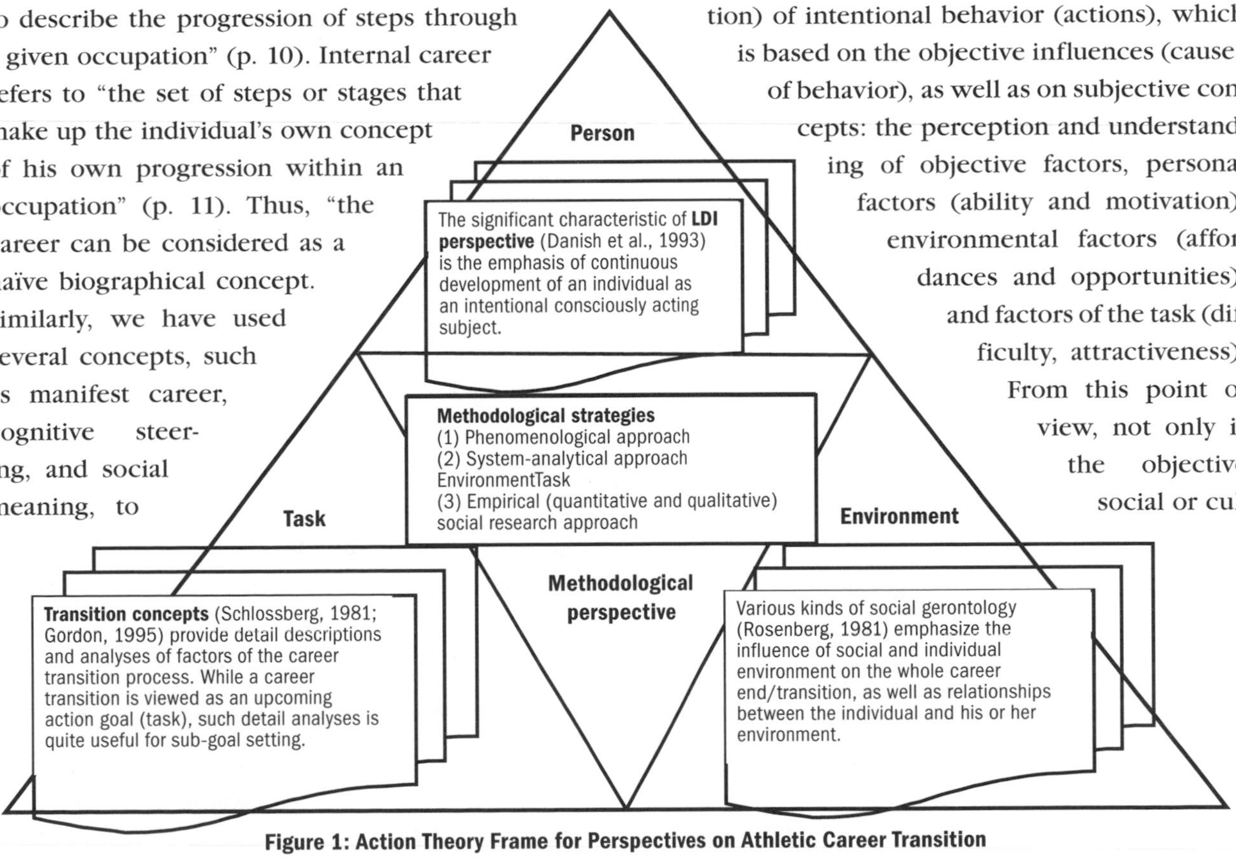

Figure 1: Action Theory Frame for Perspectives on Athletic Career Transition

Person

The significant characteristic of **LDI perspective** (Danish et al., 1993) is the emphasis of continuous development of an individual as an intentional consciously acting subject.

Methodological strategies
(1) Phenomenological approach
(2) System-analytical approach
EnvironmentTask
(3) Empirical (quantitative and qualitative) social research approach

Task

Environment

Methodological perspective

Transition concepts (Schlossberg, 1981; Gordon, 1995) provide detail descriptions and analyses of factors of the career transition process. While a career transition is viewed as an upcoming action goal (task), such detail analyses is quite useful for sub-goal setting.

Various kinds of social gerontology (Rosenberg, 1981) emphasize the influence of social and individual environment on the whole career end/transition, as well as relationships between the individual and his or her environment.

tural environment of interest but also the individual perception and understanding of this environment. These concepts are the basis for intentional organization and regulation of actions. Each action is organized to handle the task at hand, and the transition can be regarded as a complex task subdivided into various goals. From this perspective, goal setting is an important aspect in career counseling.

The action theory frame for the integration of various perspectives is illustrated in Figure 1. Methodological aspects will be discussed below.

Main Issues and Methodological Perspectives

Over the past two decades, numerous studies have analyzed the processes of athletic career development, termination, retirement, and transition. An overview and exploration of this research will be helpful to understanding the processes as well as the development of future empirical research in this field.

Lavallee, Wylleman, and Sinclair (2000) provided an annotated bibliography of studies on sport career transition. A total of 226 references from 1950 to 1998 were included; 96 were theoretical and/or applied studies and 132 were empirical. We will discuss the research objectives, the factors emphasized in the studies, and the methodological considerations.

Existing studies in sport career development, retirement, and transition mainly address three issues: (a) the reasons and consequences of sport career termination; (b) various interacting and mediating factors that possibly differentiate the concepts of sport career development and transition; and (c) the effectiveness of sport career assistance strategies and interventions.

Reasons and consequences of athletic career termination

The transition from high-level performance to retirement is inevitable for competitive athletes. What happens to individuals during this process? Studies on this topic have drawn in very different conclusions.

A number of studies focus on the emotional trauma and adjustment difficulties experienced by retiring athletes. Significant problems have been reported by world-class amateur and professional athletes (Mihovilovic, 1968; Arviko, 1976; Weinberg

& Around, 1952; Harris & Eitzen, 1971), including identity crises (Ball, 1976; Pollack, 1956), attempted suicide (Beisser, 1967; Hare, 1971), and behavior problems like alcohol and drug abuse (Arviko, 1976; McPherson, 1980; Newman, 1991; Ogilvie & Howe, 1986). Werthner and Orlick's study with high performance amateur athletes (1986) revealed that two thirds of the athletes encountered some degree of difficulty when leaving their sport careers, and one third had a relatively smooth transition. Greendofer and Kleiber (1982) described three potential negative outcomes of retirement from sports: (a) downward mobility, that is, a perception of failure or loss of social status; (b) alcohol or drug dependency; and (c) emotional and psychosocial difficulties.

On the other hand, some studies (Blinde & Greendorfer, 1985; Coakley, 1983; Greendorfer & Blinde, 1985) found evidence that leaving high-level competitive sport can be a positive experience. Retirement may actually relieve athletes of the pressure and time commitment of sport and allow them to explore new opportunities for personal growth and development. In a study by Allison and Meyer (1988), 10 of 20 female tennis professionals expressed relief upon retirement, while seven reported initial adjustment problems (e.g., loss of identity, isolation).

Grove, Lavallee, Gordon, and Harvey (1998) reviewed 11 studies that specifically examine reactions to retirement from sport. Over 2,000 athletes in a wide range of sports and ability levels are included in these studies. Taken together, the studies indicate that more than 19% (n=410) of the participants experienced considerable emotional disturbances.

These inconsistent and sometimes conflicting results indicate that athletic retirement affects individuals differently. The nature of the retirement/adjustment process is mainly influenced by two factors: (a) the reason(s) for the termination of the career; and, (b) the interaction of mediating factors, including personal characteristics and institutional/social environment (Ogilvie & Taylor, 1993; Alfermann, 2000).

Chronological age, deselection, injury or health problems, and choice are the main reasons that an athletic career ends. Different causes appear to exert different influences on psychological, social, and developmental issues related with career transition and adaptation processes.

Age

A significant difference between the termination of an athletic career and the retirement process in a "regular" career is that most individuals in competitive sport finish their sport career in their adolescence or early middle adulthood and have to adapt to a dramatically different career and living situation in their post-sport life. Empirical results have also emphasized the relationship between chronological age and elite athletes' retirement (Allison & Meyer, 1988; Mihovilovic, 1968; Svoboda & Vanek, 1982).

Age influences the termination of an athletic career physiologically, psychologically, and socially (Taylor & Ogilvie, 1998). Since some physical capabilities deteriorate with age, (Fisher & Conlee, 1979) athletes in sports like gymnastics and figure skating usually end their competitive careers during adolescence due to increases in height and weight. In other sports like football, rowing, wrestling, and track and field, athletes may compete competitively into their 30s. As a natural result of aging, their athletic performance will eventually decline, and their careers will end. The age at which an athlete must end his or her career will influence how well he or she will adapt to a post-sport career. The older a person is when their sport career ends, the less social mobility and educational opportunities they will have (Coakley, 1986).

Older athletes may lose motivation in competitive sport either because they feel that they have reached their athletic goals (Werthner & Orlick, 1986) or because they know that their goals can no longer be reached. Their focus may also change from winning to family, friends, and social partners (Svoboda & Vanek, 1982).

Age also influences the social lives of individuals in competitive sport. On the one hand, more social connections and experiences provide older athletes with more opportunities for involvement outside of sport. On the other hand, they may face pressure to quit from their manager, coach, younger teammates, fans, and the media, especially when their performance begins to diminish. This type of termination is connected with a loss of status that may cause further difficulties in the career transition process (Sinclair & Orlick, 1993).

Deselection

It is well known that in competitive sport, athletes must face competition and challenge not only from opponents, but also from their teammates. There is a harsh deselective mechanism, especially in elite sports when athletes strive to be chosen for important events (e.g., Olympic Games) or run for a higher level team/competition (change from local team to national team). One study (Ogilvie & Howe, 1986) indicated that 5% of North American high school football players can receive university scholarships, and only 1% of these athletes have an opportunity to play in the National Football League (professional level). Those who aren't chosen usually receive less attention from both inside and outside the sport system, compared with individuals who "survive" (Ogilvie & Howe, 1982).

Injury/Health Problems

Serious injuries and health problems also cause career termination. In competitive sport, injury is a natural problem (Ford, Eklund, & Gordon, 2000; Sperryn, 1994). Athletes in competitive sport commonly experience serious sport injuries more than once during their career. Most can be overcome, but some athletes experience a loss in physical or psychological abilities that make it difficult or impossible to continue their sport career. Taylor & Ogilvie (1998) indicate that 14%-32% of participants were forced to retire from competitive sport prematurely due to injury. A retirement forced by physical disabilities is usually associated with negative consequences, as outlined in the Grieving Model by Kübler-Ross (see Baillie, 1993).

Table 3: Differences Between Voluntary and Involuntary Sport Career Termination (Reported by Alfermann and Gross, 1998)

Reasons of sport career termination	Emotional response	Coping strategy	Social support
Voluntary termination	More positive emotions	More active strategies	More independence
Involuntary termination	More negative emotions	Higher number of coping strategies and more passive strategies	More need of social support

Free Choice

Athletes' free choice to leave competitive sport is another important cause of career termination, and has been neglected in most studies to date. Sinclair and Orlick (1993) polled 199 retired elite athletes and found that their four main reasons for retirement were: (a) they were tired of the circuit or lifestyle/time; (b) they had achieved their goals; (c) they had difficulties with coaching staff; or (d) they wanted more time for personal relationships. The first, the second, and the fourth reasons can be regarded as free choice retirement. Authors like Werthner and Orlick (1986), Greendorfer and Blinde (1985), and Svoboda and Vanek (1982) have also reported similar reasons for a career termination given by elite athletes.

In a study by Alfermann and Gross (1998), the responses and adjustment process of sport career termination were analyzed in 132 former German athletes. Several differences between athletes with voluntary and involuntary retirement have been observed. The effects of voluntary or involuntary sport career termination are summarized in Table 3.

Interacting Factors in the Adaptation to Career Transition

Sinclair and Orlick (1993) reported on the period of time it takes former athletes to adjust to retirement. They found that this period varies from one month to more than two years. Another study by Baillie and Danish (1992) with 260 elite and professional athletes indicated that the process of adjustment took an average of two years. Some athletes, however, were still struggling ten years after their athletic retirement. During this process, athletes may face life challenges in social, psychological, financial, and occupational aspects. Taylor and Ogilvie (1998) propose some factors that influence the adaptation process of athletes in transition based on a review of various studies. The factors they highlight include (a) self-identity; (b) social identity; (c) perceptions of control; and (d) some tertiary contributing factors like socioeconomic status, minority status, gender and the health of athletes at the time of retirement, etc.

Most of the studies mentioned above were designed from the perspective of the career transition model. Two processes of sport career development are emphasized. The first is the transition within different phases of a sport career, and the second is the process of sport career termination and post-sport career development. Few studies have analyzed the process of entering a career in elite sports. (Those who quit in the middle of their sport career cannot be included.) It is necessary for future studies to compare the differences between two sample groups (athletes and normal population) to compare the effects of factors such as social and family relations, expectations for the sport career, and academic degrees on all aspects of the sport career (Hackfort, Emrich, & Papathanassiou, 1997).

A look at methodology across studies reveals both quantitative and qualitative approaches. The questionnaire and the interview are the most popular methods used in the studies. The single-case design, which is sensitive to the individual's issues (e.g., self-concept, goals) and the complexity of the action situations, should be used more often, especially in research on elite athletes. In recent years, a research strategy that combines quantitative and qualitative approaches has become a favored methodological approach in this field (see e.g., Chamalidis, 1998; Hackfort, Emrich, & Papathanassiou, 1997; Hawkins & Blann, 1993, 1994; Huang, Schmidt, Hackfort, & Si, 2001). However, an appropriate theoretical framework is badly needed to provide a sufficient background for the interpretation and reconstruction of the abundant information that has been obtained through the interview and other qualitative methods. The action theory, as mentioned above, refers also to subjective concepts and provides a framework for the interpretation of qualitative data (Huang, Hackfort, & Schmidt, 2001) and a triangulation with quantitative data (Hackfort & Birkner, 2003).

Goal-directed behavior cannot be sufficiently analyzed by using trait oriented measurement or observations of behavior and its consequences. Both the subjective meaning of actions taken as a part of the career process and their relation to the circumstances of life outside of sport should be considered. Instead of regarding events as isolated units, they need to be considered as meaningful episodes in the course of life, with emotional consequences as well as consequences in the developmental process.

It is inadequate to analyze an athlete's career only in terms of what occurred during his or her career. The implications of future situations and individual developments are equally important in understanding the athlete's actions. As the ecological social-psychology field has shown, these past- and future-oriented perspectives must be combined (Carroll, Haveman, & Swaminathan, 1992).

Social circumstances (social environmental conditions) are a basic component of an action situation. Although a sport career is usually considered a personal project, actions are largely based on psychological processes established by learning and socialization, including rules, conventions, norms, and social representations. The social environment includes family, peer group, teammates, and members of relevant organizations. These social factors combine with the individual's subjective perceptions to make up the action situation. In addition, a career is the result of actions organized in a number of situations over a longer period of time.

Further Aspects

Various career counseling programs developed in different countries are discussed by Gordon et al. in another chapter of this book. It becomes evident that the organizational structure determines the design of the program, its realization, and its effectiveness. An example is the establishment of career assistance interventions and environmental management for elite athletes in Germany.

Since 1986 there have been sections for social-pedagogical support at each Olympic Training Center (OTC, 20 at present) in Germany. The OTCs are organizational units of the German Sports Federation, and the career counseling and environmental management services are a part of systematic services provided for elite athletes in the OTCs (Hackfort & Schlattmann, 1994; see also Emrich, Altmeyer, & Papathanassiou, 1994). Most career development assistance exists in the form of individual counseling. The services have been developed by a bottom-up strategy toward an educational (social-pedagogical) and lifespan developmental career assistance and environmental management service (Hackfort & Schlattmann, 1994). The environmental management aspect focuses on persons who (regarded as representing a pedagogical position) find suitable jobs for, help students figure out how to pay off student loans or apply for scholarships, offer advice on the coordination of military service with the sport

career, etc. These people are employees of the sport organization and are required to follow the objectives and interests of the organization. The potential for conflict is great, and such conflicts may be accompanied by ethical dilemmas.

With respect to commercialization in elite sport, the interdependent relationship between the elite athlete and the sport system is obvious yet complex. This relationship can be looked at from two sides: (1) the dependence of an individual performer on the sport system, and (2) the reliance of the sport system on the commitment of individual athletes.

Traditionally, this relationship operated on a principle of utilitarianism. However, criticism has arisen in response to growing concerns regarding personal development and perceived benefit for the individual. In the field of elite sport, Thomas and Ermler discussed that

> based on one of the severest criticisms of utilitarianism, specifically that it appears to justify the imposition of great suffering on a few people (athletes) for the benefit of many people (the athletic establishment and the general public), a pluralistic deontology will be utilized in developing institutional obligations related to the athlete. Deontology argues for the identification of a set of duties of obligation appropriate to a context. (1988, p. 143)

From the pluralistic deontological perspective, the individual athlete is "an informed and autonomous decision maker whose individual welfare comes before institutional outcomes" (Thomas & Ermler, 1988). Based on this premise, Thomas and Ermler have held that *autonomy*, *beneficence*, and *nonmaleficence*, which are interrelated and mutually dependent, should be highlighted in the development and practice of future sport career programs.

Autonomy, which emphasizes self-determination and self-governance, is a concept that has been well covered by the basic assumptions of action theory (e.g., the actor as a reflexive subject). Under any organizational setting, everyone should be treated as an autonomous decision maker, whose welfare is more important than the overall success of the organization.

Figure 2: Action Theory Perspective on Career Assistance Program Design

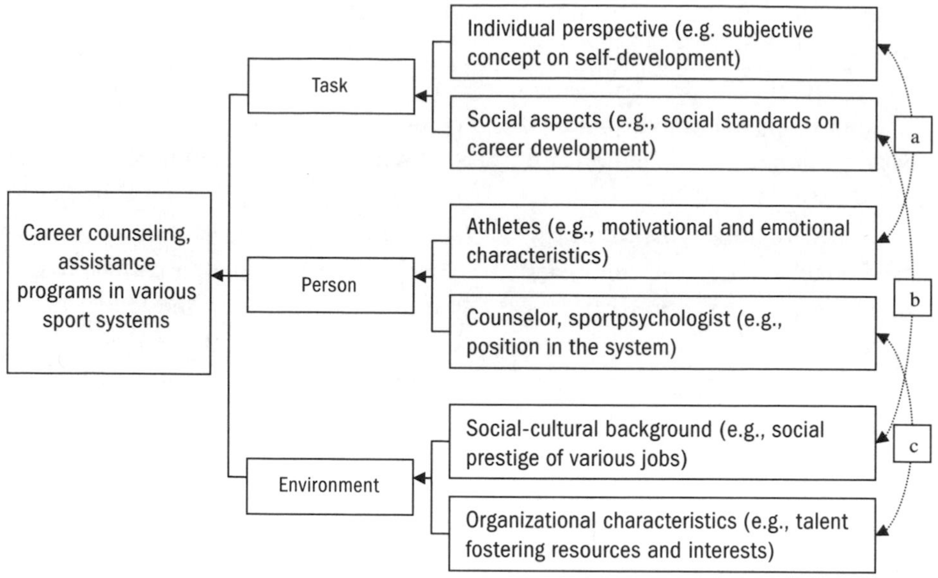

Connected with autonomy, *beneficence* is an effort to help others to realize their interests. It includes both the provision of benefit and the prevention and removal of harm. However, a conflict exists between autonomy and beneficence. Indeed, Childress (1980, p.17) stated that "one of the most pervasive and perplexing moral dilemmas in health care results when the moral principles of benefiting the patient and respecting the patient's autonomy come into conflict."

Providing beneficence to athletes might be associated with a kind of paternalism. Career assistance approaches such as education during the sport career, post-athletic job arrangement, and so on could be viewed as *strong paternalism*. These paternalistic behaviors on the part of the institution are intended to provide beneficence to athletes, but they also have a high potential to disturb an athlete's individual autonomy and personal development.

In contrast to *strong paternalism, weak paternalism* (Hodson, 1977) is viewed as a justifiable and practicable approach for providing institutional beneficence. However, more research is needed in elite sport to define an appropriate weak paternalistic attitude from an ethical perspective.

Nonmaleficence is a principle that is widely recognized in medicine and public health care ethics. It is an obligation not to intentionally inflict harm.

Nonmaleficence is discussed mainly in situations when harm seems inevitable. Nonmaleficence may also arise from single actions that have both good and bad effects. This principle is related to the concept of autonomy. Who should make action decisions in these types of situations—the individual or the authority? In the athletic field, the principle of nonmaleficence is seldom discussed, but it must be considered in career counseling and psychological interventions.

Perspective

Consequences of the arguments outlined in this chapter are summarized and illustrated in Figure 2.

When analyzing the three components of an action situation to design career counseling and assistance programs, the task, the person, and the environment should be considered in the context of social-cultural backgrounds, particular sport systems, and an individual's characteristics. Furthermore, the relationships among these different aspects (see a, b, c in Figure 2) should also be considered in order to provide appropriate support for athletes in their sport career, personal development, career transition, and life after sport.

References

Alfermann, D. (2000). Causes and consequences of sport career termination. In D. Lavallee & P. Wylleman (Eds.), *Career Transitions in Sport: International Perspectives,* pp. 45-58. Morgantown, WV, USA: Fitness Information Technology, Inc.

Alfermann, D., & Gross, A. (1998). Erleben und bewaeltigen des kareereendes im hochleistungssport [How elite athletes perceive and cope with career termination]. *Leistungssport, 28* (2), 45-48.

Allison, M. T., & Meyer, C. (1988). Career problems and retirement among elite athletes: The female tennis professional. *Sociology of Sport Journal, 5,* 212-222.

Arviko, I. (1976). Factors influencing the job and life satisfaction of retired baseball players. Unpublished master's thesis, University of Waterloo, Ont., Canada.

Atchley, R. C. (1980). *The social forces in later life.* Belmont, CA. Wadsworth.

Baillie, P. H. F. & Danish, S. J. (1992) Understanding the career transition of athletes. *The Sport Psychologist, 6,* 77-98.

Baillie, P. H. F. (1993). Understanding retirement from sports: Therapeutic ideas for helping athletes in transition. *The Counseling Psychologist, 21* (3), 399-410.

Ball, D. W.(1976). Failure in sport. *American Sociological Review, 41,* 726-739.

Beisser, A. (1967). *The madness in sport.* New York: Appleton-Century-Crofts.

Blinde, E. M., & Greendorfer, S. L. (1985). A reconceptualization of the process of leaving the role of competitive athlete. *International Review for the Sociology of Sport. 20*(1/2), 87-94.

Carroll, G. R., Haveman, H., & Swaminathan, A. (1992). Careers in organization: An ecological perspective. In D. L. Featherman, R. M. Lerner, & M. Perlmutter (Eds.), *Life-span Development and Behavior* (pp. 111-145). Hillsdale, NJ: Lawrence Erlbaum Associates, Inc. Publishers.

Chamalidis, P. (1998). *Masculine identity in high-level sport: The glory and grief of the champion.* Unpublished doctoral dissertation, University of Rene Descartes, Paris, France.

Childress, J. F. (1980). *Priorities in biomedical Ethics.* Philadelphia: Westminster Press.

Coakley, J. J.(1983). Leaving competitive sport: Retirement or rebirth? *Quest, 35,* 1-11.

Coakley, J. J.(1986). *Sport in Society.* USA: Mosby College Publishing.

Crook, J. M., & Robertson, S. E. (1991). Transition out of elite sport. *International Journal of Sport Psychology, 22,* 115-127.

Cummings, E., Dean, L. R., Newell, D. S., & McCaffrey, I. (1960). Disengagement: A tentative theory of aging. *Sociometry, 13,* 23.

Danish, S. J., & Hale, B. D. (1981). Toward an understanding of the practice of sport psychology. *Journal of Sport Psychology, 3,* 90-99.

Danish, S. J., Petitpas, A. J., & Hale, B. D. (1993). Life development intervention for athletes: Life skills through sports. *The Counseling Psychologist, 21*(3), 352-385.

Emrich, E., Alltmeyer, L., & Papathanassiou, V. (1994). Career counseling in an Olympic Center - A German experience? In D. Hackfort (Ed.), *Psycho-social issues and interventions in elite sports.* (pp.199-235). Frankfurt: Peter Lang.

Fisher, A. G., & Conlee, R. K. (1979). *The complete book of physical fitness* (pp.119-121). Provo, UT: Brigham Young University Press.

Ford, I. W, Eklund, R. C., & Gordon, S. (2000). An examination of psychosocial variables moderating the relationship between life stress and injury time-loss among athletes of high standard. *Journal of Sports Sciences, 18,* 301-312.

Gordon, S. (1995). Career transitions in competitive sport. In T. Morris & J. Summers (Eds.), *Sport Psychology: Theory, applications and issues* (pp.474-501). Brisbane: Jacaranda Wiley.

Greendorfer, S. L., & Blinde, E. M. (1985). "Retirement "from intercollegiate sport: Theoretical and empirical considerations. *Sociology of Sport Journal, 2,* 101-110.

Greendorfer, S. L., & Kleiber, D. A. (1982). *Sport retirement as social death: The college athlete.* Paper presented at the Third Annual conference of the North American Society for the Sociology of Sport, Toronto.

Grove, J. R., Lavallee, D., & Gordon S. (1998). Coping with retirement from sport: The influence of athletic identity. *Journal of Applied Sport Psychology, 9,* 191-203.

Grove, J. R., Lavallee, D., Gordon S., & Harvey, J. H. (1997). Account-Making: A model for understanding and resolving distressful reactions to retirement from sport. *The Sport Psychologist, 1998, 12,*52-67.

Haerle, R. (1975). Career patterns and career contingencies of professional baseball players: An occupational analysis. In Ball and Loy (Eds.), *Sport and Social Order.* Reading, MA: Addison-Wesley.

Hackfort, D. (1986). *Theorie und Analyse sportbezogener Ängstlichkeit (Theory and analysis of sport-related trait anxiety).* Schorndorf: Hofmann.

Hackfort, D. (1990). Empirical social science oriented research in sport science. *International Journal of Physical Education. 27* (1), 25-32.

Hackfort, D., & Birkner, H. A. (2003). Triangulation as a basis for diagnostic judgements. *International Journal of Sport and Exercise, 1,* 82-94.

Hackfort, D., Emrich, E., & Papathanassiou, V. (1997). *Nachsportliche Karriereverläufe (Post sports courses of career).* Schorndorf: Hofmann.

Hackfort, D., Munzert, J., & Seiler, R. (2000). *Handeln im Sport als handlungspsychologisches Modell (Acting in sports as an action-psychology model).* Heidelberg: Asanger.

Hackfort, D., & Schlattmann, A. (1994). Career counseling and environmental management for elite athletes. In D. Hackfort (Ed.), *Psycho-social issues and interventions in elite sports.* (pp. 132-199). Frankfurt: Peter Lang.

Hare, N. (1971). A study of the black fighter. *The Black Scholar, 3,* 2-9.

Harris, D. S., & Eitzen, D. S. (1971). The consequences of failure in sport. *Urban Life, 7*(2), 17-188.

Havighurst, R. J., & Albrecht, R. (1953). *Older people.* New York: Longmans.

Hawkins, K., & Blann, F. W. (1993). *Athlete/coach career development and transition.* Canberra: Australian Sport Commission.

Hawkins, K., & Blann, F. W. (1994, June). *Coping with the end of an athletic career.* Paper presented at the annual meeting of the International Association for Physical Education in Higher Education, Berlin.

Hill, P., & Lowe, B. (1974). The inevitable metathesis of the retiring athlete. *International Review of Sport Sociology, 4,* 5-29.

Hodson, J. D. (1977). The principle of paternalism. *American Philosophical Quarterly. 14*(1), 61-65.

Huang, Z., Schmidt, U., Hackfort, D., & Si, G. (2001). Career transition of former elite athletes: Preliminary results of a cross-cultural study between China and Germany. In A. Papaioannou, M., Goudas, & Y. Theodorakis (Eds.), *In the dawn of the new millennium: Programme and Proceedings of the 10th World Congress of Sport Psychology (Vol. 5, pp. 8-10).* Skiathos, Hellas, 28, May - 2, June, 2001. Thessaloniki: Christodoulidi.

Huang, Z., Hackfort, D., & Schmidt, U. (2001). Transition from elite sports: A cross-cultural study from an action theory perspective. In J. Mester, G., King, H. Strüder, E. Tsolakidis, & A. Osterburg (Eds.), *Perspectives and profiles: Proceedings of the 6th Annual Congress of the European College of Sport Science.* Cologne, Germany, 24-28 July, 2001.

Ingham, A. G. (1975). Occupational subcultures in the work world of sport. In Ball and Loy (Eds.), *Sport and Social Order.* Reading, MA.: Addison-Wesley

Kübler-Ross, E. (1969). *On death and dying.* New York: Macmillan.

Kuypers, J. A., & Bengston, V. L. (1973). Social breakdown and competence: A model of normal aging. *Human Development, 16,* 181-220.

Lavallee, D., Wylleman, P., & Sinclair, D. (2000). Career transitions in sport: An annotated bibliography. In D. Lavallee & P. Wylleman (Eds.), *Career Transitions in Sport: International Perspectives (pp. 207-258).* Morgantown, WV: Fitness Information Technology.

Lerch, S. H. (1982). Athlete retirement as social death. In N. Theberge & P. Donnelly (Eds.), *Sport and the sociological imagination* (pp259-272). Fort Worth, TX: Texas Christian University Press.

McPherson, B. D. (1980). Retirement from professional sport: The process and problems of occupational and psychological adjustment. *Sociological Symposium, 30,* 126-143.

Mihovilovic, M. (1968). The status of former sportsman. *International Review of Sport Sociology, 3,* 73-96.

Murphy, S. M. (1995). Transitions in competitive sport: Maximizing individual potential. In S. M. Murphy (Ed.). *Sport Psychology Interventions.* (pp. 331-346). Champaign, IL : Human Kinetics.

Newman, B. (1991, March 11). The last return. *Sports Illustrated* pp. 38-42.

Nitsch, J. R. (2000). Handlungstheoretische Grundlagen der Sportpsychologie (Action theory fundamentals for sport psychology). In H. Gabler, J.R. Nitsch, & R. Singer (Eds.), *Einführung in die Sportpsychologie, Teil 1 (Introduction to sport psychology, Part 1,* pp. 43-164). Schorndorf: Hofmann.

Nitsch, J. R., & Hackfort, D. (1981). Stress in Schule und Hochschule—eine handlungspsychologische Funktionsanalyse (Stess in school and university—an action psychology functional analysis). In J. R. Nitsch (Ed.), *Stress* (pp. 263-311). Bern: Huber.

Ogilvie, B. C., & Howe, M. (1982). Career crisis in sport. In T. Orlick, J. T. Partington, & J. H. Salmela (Eds.), *Proceedings of the Fifth World Congress of Sport Psychology* (pp. 176-183). Ottawa, Canada: Coaching Association of Canada.

Ogilvie, B. C., & Howe, M. (1986). The trauma of termination from athletics. In J. M. Williams (Ed.), *Applied sport psychology* (pp365-382), Palo Alto, CA: Mayfield.

Ogilvie, B. & Taylor,J.(1993). Career termination issues among elite athletes. In Singer, R., Murphey, M., Tennant, L.K.(Eds.), *Handbook of Research on Sport Psychology* (pp.761-775). New York, NY: Macmillan Publishing Company.

Pollock, O. (1956). *The social aspects of retirement.* Homewood, III.:Irwin.

Reynolds, M. J. (1981). The effects of sports retirement on the job satisfaction of the former football player. In S. L. Greendorfer & A. Yiannakis (Eds.) *Sociology of sport: Diverse perspectives* (pp. 127-137). West Point, NY: Leisure Press.

Rosenberg, E. (1981). Gerontological theory and athletic retirement. In S. L. Greendorfer & A. Yiannakis (Eds.), *Sociology of sport: Diverse perspectives* (pp. 119-126). West Point, NY: Leisure Press.

Rosenfeld, L. B., Richman, J. M., & Hardy, C. J. (1989). Examining social support networks among athletes: Description and relationship to stress. *The Sport Psychologist, 3,* 23-33.

Schein, E. H. (1978). Career development: theoretical and practical issues for organisations. In. *Career planning and development, Management Development Series No. 12.* 3rd impression (pp. 9 - 48). Geneva: International Labour Office

Schlossberg, N. K. (1981). A model for analysing human adaptation to transition. *The Counseling Psychologist, 9*(2), 2-18.

Sinclair, D. A., & Orlick T. (1993). Positive transitions from high-performance sport. *The Sport Psychologist, 7,* 138-150.

Sinclair, D. A., & Orlick T. (1994). The effects of transition on high performance sport. In D. Hackfort (Ed.), *Psycho-social issue and interventions in elite sports* (pp. 29-55). Frankfurt: Peter Lang.

Sperryn, P. (1994). Sports medicine on the line? (editorial). *British Journal of Sport Medicine, 28* (3).

Super, D: E. (1980). A life-span, life-space approach to career development. *Journal of Vocational Behavior, 13,* 282-298.

Svoboda, B., & Vanek, M. (1982). Retirement from high level competition. In T. Orlick, J.T. Partington, & J.H. Salmela (Eds.), *Proceedings of the Fifth World Congress of Sport Psychology* (pp. 166-175). Ottawa, Canada: Coaching Association of Canada.

Taylor, J. & Ogilvie, B. C. (1998). Career transition among elite athletes: Is there life after sport? In J. Williams (Ed.), *Applied sport psychology: Personal growth to peak performance* (3rd ed.) (pp. 429-444). Palo Alto, CA: Mayfield.

Thibaut, J. W., & Kelley, H. H. (1959). *The social psychology of groups.* New York: Wiley.

Thomas, C. E., & Ermler, K. L. (1988). Institutional Obligations in the athletic retirement process. *QUEST, 40,* 137-150.

Valach, L. (1990). A theory of goal-directed action in career analysis. In R. A. Young, & W. A. Borgen (Eds.), *Methodological approaches to the study of career* (pp. 107-126). New York: Praeger.

Weinberg, K., & Around, H. (1952). The occupational culture of the boxer. *American Journal of Sociology, 57,* 460-469.

Werthner, P., & Orlick, T. (1986).Retirement experiences of successful Olympic athletes. *International Journal of Sport Psychology.17,* 337-363.

Young, R. (1995). An action approach to career counseling. *ERIC Digest.* Ottawa: Canadian Guidance and Counselling Foundation. (Online material: www.de.gov/databases/ERIC_Digests/ed404579.html)

Courtesy of WVU Photographic Services

5.4

Theory and Applications in Promoting Exercise Behavior

BRYAN BLISSMER

DAVID X. MARQUEZ

GERALD J. JEROME

JAY C. KIMIECIK

Introduction

The first of many questions that one must address when attempting to promote exercise behavior is exactly what behavior to promote. The two major exercise recommendations that are currently promoted are also highly debated by the scientific community. The first recommendation is that to improve fitness, everyone should exercise 3-5 days per week for 20-60 minutes at 60-90% of their maximum heart rate (American College of Sports Medicine, 1998). The other recommendation suggests that everyone should accumulate 30 minutes or more of moderate intensity activity on most or all days of the week to reduce health risks (Pate et al., 1995). As there is credible evidence to support both recommenda-

tions, the choice should be driven by the desired outcomes, whether they are related to general fitness, health, or specific diseases.

Regardless of the exact exercise dose that is being promoted, evidence suggests that there is a great deal of work to be done in the field of exercise promotion. For example, in the United States only 22% of the population is engaging in regular moderate activity for 30 minutes on five or more days per week, suggesting that approximately three-quarters of the population may have increased health risks due to inadequate activity levels (U.S. Department of Health and Human Services, 1996). The World Health Organization estimates that approximately 60% of the world's population does not exercise enough to benefit their health. Even fewer individuals are meeting the more rigorous fitness requirement suggested by the ACSM (1998) with estimates ranging from 10-15% (U.S. Department of Health and Human Services, 1996). The need to increase the number of people that engage in regular physical activity has been highlighted as a major health objective around the world (World Health Organization, 2001; U.S. Department of Health and Human Services, 2000). There is an obvious need to place greater emphasis on developing more effective physical activity interventions.

There is a large body of literature on both exercise determinants and interventions, enough to fill a book of its own (e.g., Dishman, 1994). The focus of this chapter is to provide an overview of the theories and practices in the promotion of exercise. Specifically, we will examine the major theoretical approaches and frameworks, namely social cognitive theory and the transtheoretical model, which have been adopted to promote exercise. We will then examine how each of these approaches has been implemented across different levels of intervention (i.e., environmental, community, and individualized) and their basic efficacy for promoting exercise behavior change. A special section highlights the need to use multicultural approaches for promoting exercise behavior among culturally diverse populations. There are also several recommendations for areas requiring further research and newly developing areas of inquiry.

Theoretical Approaches to Promoting Exercise

Much of the theoretical work that has been conducted in exercise promotion has been focused on behavioral prediction and determinants. Thus, we have relatively well-established theories for the prediction of exercise behavior, yet there is frustratingly little research that has clearly applied that knowledge to the actual promotion of exercise. The major theoretical approaches that are referenced in exercise interventions can typically be grouped into *social cognitive approaches, the transtheoretical model,* or *basic cognitive-behavioral strategies.* Most major exercise promotion interventions have identified theoretical bases. However, too often they use a collection of different theories and/or never truly investigate the

proposed theoretical framework. As we will discuss in more detail in the new directions section, there is a greater need to include assessments of the theoretical constructs that are guiding the intervention in an effort to examine mediator relationships (Baranowski, Anderson, & Carmack, 1998).

Social Cognitive Approaches

Social cognitive approaches are based on Bandura's (1986) social cognitive theory. Social cognitive theory postulates that behavior, cognitive factors, and environmental influences all operate as interacting determinants of each other in what is termed *triadic reciprocal causation.* Thus, an individual's environment (e.g., safety, pathways) and cognitions (e.g., self-efficacy) interact to influence behavior (e.g., exercise). The concept of *reciprocal determinism* is reflected in the fact that self-efficacy is an important predictor of who exercises regularly and is also an important outcome associated with regular exercise. Although this approach does allow for the explanation of many behaviors, it may be so inclusive that it can be claimed to be the theoretical framework behind nearly any study. Most contemporary theories of human behavior are social cognitive in nature because they involve the interplay between the person, their behavior, and their environment. For example, theories such as the Theory of Reasoned Action and the Theory of Planned Behavior, which have been responsible for a great deal of work on the determinants of exercise participation (Hausenblas, Carron, & Mack, 1997), can be categorized as social cognitive theories.

However, the unique variable developed in Bandura's theory is self-efficacy (1986, 1997a). Self-efficacy is an individual's belief in their ability to successfully execute a desired course of action. Self-efficacy has been identified as an important outcome and determinant of exercise behavior (McAuley, 1992; McAuley & Blissmer, 2000). Self-efficacy has been linked to the affective outcomes associated with both acute and chronic exercise, with greater levels of efficacy being associated with greater satisfaction and enjoyment (e.g., McAuley, Blissmer, Katula, & Duncan, 2000). Self-efficacy has also been shown to be an important consequence of engaging in regular exercise across a number of studies (e.g., McAuley et al., 1999). In keeping with social cognitive theory's tenet of reciprocal determinism, self-efficacy has also been shown to be an important determinant of exercise adoption (e.g., Oman & King, 1998) and maintenance after termination of a formal program (Sallis et al., 1986).

The sources of self-efficacy that have been identified by Bandura (1986, 1997a) can provide the framework for promoting exercise behavior change. Studies may be designed that manipulate mastery experiences, social modeling, verbal persuasion, and interpretation of physiological states in a manner that are designed to enhance self-efficacy (Bandura, 1997a). For example, McAuley, Courneya, Rudolph, and Lox (1994) developed an intervention that focused on enhancing the sources of efficacy in middle-aged males and females. They found that the intervention group had greater levels of exercise adherence compared to an attentional control group after five months. There have also been a number of studies that have examined the effects of manipulating the exercise environment through the use of different instructional techniques, differential feedback, and changes to the physical environment that have resulted in changes in levels of exercise self-efficacy (e.g., Katula, McAuley, Mihalko, & Bane, 1998; McAuley, Talbot, & Martinez, 1999; Turner, Rejeski, & Brawley, 1997).

Another social cognitive approach to promoting exercise behavior is the use of social support. Social support has been examined in numerous populations, using a variety of measures, and consistently demonstrates a positive relationship with physical activity. Social support has been operationally defined in a number of ways, ranging from social networks that examine the number and nature of the participant's relationships (e.g., Leon et al., 1999) to measures that differentiate between types of social provisions (e.g., McAuley et al., 2000) or identify the sources of social support, such as family, friends, or significant others (e.g., Carron, Hausenblas, & Mack, 1996; Castro, Sallis, Hickman, Lee, & Chen, 1999; Eyler et al., 1999).

This positive correlation between social support and physical activity has been reported across a diverse number of populations, including adults from Europe (Stahl et al., 2001), Sweden (Lindstrom, Hanson, & Ostergren, 2001), and Canada (Courneya, Plotnikoff, Hotz, & Birkett, 2000; Spanier & Allison, 2001). This relationship has also been identified in Eastern European young adults (Steptoe & Wardle, 2001); rural, urban, and blue-collar women from the United States (Kelsey et al., 2000; Wilcox, Castro, King, Housemann, & Brownson, 2000); and older adults from Canada (Cousins, 1995), Australia (Patterson & Chang, 1999) and the United States (Chogahara, Cousins, & Wankel, 1998). These studies emphasize that the positive relationship between social support and an active lifestyle is generalizable across cultures and age groups.

Although there is substantial evidence for the relationship between social support and physical activity, less is known about how or why social support works. It is important to understand how social support works in order to develop intervention strategies that improve support. Researchers have examined social support within the context of behavioral change theories such as the social cognitive theory (e.g., Duncan, 1993; McAuley et al., 2000), the theory of planned behavior (e.g., Courneya et al., 2000), and the stages of change (e.g., Ronda, Van Assema, & Brug, 2001). These studies attempt to better understand how social support works in relation to other determinants of exercise.

There have been a few attempts to examine physical activity interventions designed to increase social support. For example, King and Fredericksen (1984) found that a brief intervention discussing social support techniques was not effective in increasing jogging behavior, although it is important to note that they did not specifically provide social support in their study. Wallace, Raglin, and Jastremski (1995) did find that people who joined a fitness program with their spouse had greater adherence rates than individuals who joined alone. A study of weight loss in Mexican American women found that an intervention that included the entire family was more effective at promoting exercise and weight loss than an intervention targeting the women alone (Cousins et al., 1992). Continued theory-based research is needed, including controlled interventions that examine the effect of different types of support (e.g., instrumental versus emotional, or perceived versus received) and different providers of support including friends, family, and instructors.

In general, the inclusiveness of the social cognitive approaches have, to date, not made for specific recommendations or strategies for promoting behavior change such as increasing levels of physical activity and exercise. The only variable in social cognitive theory that has well-developed behavior change implications is self-efficacy. Not surprisingly, self-efficacy has been adopted for use in other theories such as the transtheoretical model. The use of social support is also apparent in the processes of change in the transtheoretical model.

Transtheoretical Model

The transtheoretical model was developed as a framework for understanding behavior change and is arguably the most popular approach for promoting exercise behavior. The popularity of the use of stages of change from the transtheoretical model stems from the intuitive appeal that individuals are at different stages of readiness to make behavioral changes and thus require tailored interventions. The stages and processes of change were developed by Prochaska and colleagues from their work observing the patterns of behavioral change among those attempting to quit smoking (Prochaska & DiClemente, 1983). These observations led to the identification of five stages of change and ten processes of change. The current classification scheme includes five stages, varying from precontemplation (no intention to be active in the next six months) to contemplation (intending to be active in the next six months) to preparation (intending to be active in the next thirty days) to action (regularly active for less than six months) and, finally, to maintenance (regularly active for more than six months; Richards Reed, Velicer, Prochaska, Rossi, & Marcus, 1997). As individuals attempt to change their behavior they may move linearly through these stages, but the model allows for the possibility of repeated relapse and successful change may end up resembling a recursive relationship, with several unsuccessful attempts to change, rather than a straight line.

Associated with these stages of change are ten processes of change, as well as decisional balance and self-efficacy measures. The processes are intended to illustrate the strategies used by individuals in attempting to advance through the stages of change. For ease of discussion and to parallel the propensity of individuals to use multiple processes simultaneously (Prochaska, Velicer, DiClemente, & Fava, 1988), the

ten processes can be broken down into two second-order factors: experiential (consciousness-raising, dramatic relief, self-reevaluation, social reevaluation, and social liberation) and behavioral (self-liberation, counterconditioning, stimulus control, contingency management, and helping relationship). Work has been done to define the processes that are most effectively used to facilitate progression through the stages in general (Prochaska, DiClemente, & Norcross, 1992) and, specifically, for exercise (Marcus, Rossi, Selby, Niaura, & Abrams, 1992).

Physical activity research has documented the stages of change and their psychosocial correlates among adolescents (e.g., Myers & Roth, 1997; Nigg & Courneya, 1998), adults (e.g., Herrick, Stone, & Mentler, 1997), rural and inner-city communities (e.g., Potvin, Gauvin, & Nguyen, 1997), and older adults (e.g., Lee, 1995). A recent meta-analysis (Morris & Biddle, 2001) identified 71 published studies that have examined some components of the transtheoretical model in exercise. Much of the research was cross-sectional in nature (54 of 71 studies) and there was support that activity levels, process use, confidence, and decisional balance did differ by the stages of change. However, there is a clear need to move beyond the descriptive level of analysis. Critics of the transtheoretical model (e.g., Bandura, 1997b) argue that exercise is a complex, continuous behavior that should not be broken down into discrete stages. Weinstein, Rothman, and Sutton (1998) have argued that a randomized, controlled trial involving both stage-matched and mismatched interventions is necessary to truly test the stage nature of exercise behavior.

Cognitive-Behavioral Approaches

Cognitive-behavioral approaches encompass techniques such as behavioral contracting, goal setting, self-monitoring, stimulus-response work, etc. Rooted in cognitive-behavior therapy, they involve relatively simple techniques for promoting physical activity. Cognitive-behavioral approaches are often integrated in other theories as techniques for promoting behavior changes, such as several of the processes in the transtheoretical model or the sources of self-efficacy in social cognitive theory (Bandura, 1986, 1997a). However, these approaches have also been frequently used as stand-alone interventions to influence exercise behaviors. These interventions may include things such as giving prizes for participation in exercise (e.g., Courneya, Estabrooks, & Nigg, 1997), signs directing individuals to use the stairs instead of the elevators (e.g., Brownell, Stunkard, & Albaum, 1980) or simply the provision of new facilities for exercising (Linenger , Chesson, & Nice, 1991). Despite their relatively low complexity, cognitive-behavioral interventions were found in a review by Dishman and Buckworth (1996) to be among the most effective at increasing physical activity levels.

Different Levels of Promotion

The approach used in this chapter to categorize the exercise promotion literature is to examine the theories and approaches used at varying levels of intervention, ranging from environmental to individual approaches. These are analogous to Marcus and Forsyth's (1999) downstream (individual), midstream (community, worksite), and upstream (environmental/policy) intervention levels. Each of the different levels has typically relied on different approaches with varying degrees of theory implementation. Although the efficacy of the interventions may vary by level of implementation, it is important to consider that the potential impact of the intervention on population activity levels is a function of both efficacy and reach. We need to weigh the need to have sophisticated, highly effective interventions that help only a few people make significant changes in their exercise behavior against the use of environmental or community interventions that are not as effective but have the potential to reach many more individuals.

Environmental/Policy Level

Although we may hope for the day when governments legislate that being a couch potato is illegal, it is not likely to happen. At the policy level, it may be more feasible to advocate for policies such as the regulation of physical education requirements for children and tax breaks to encourage communities or corporations to build and maintain public exercise facilities (Sallis, Bauman, & Pratt, 1998). There are some smaller environmental changes that may be effective at increasing physical activity levels and do not require years of lobbying. Often these interventions rely on simple cognitive-behavioral approaches.

A common approach that has proven quite effective is the use of signs near the elevator suggesting that individuals take the stairs instead of the elevator to benefit the health of their heart. Across a number of different studies, this simple point-of-contact behavioral prompt has been effective at increasing the number of individuals that take the stairs by about 5% (e.g., Blamey, Mutrie, & Aitchison, 1995; Titze, Martin, Seiler, & Marti, 2001). Due to their extremely low cost, this type of intervention was recently recommended by the Task Force on Community Preventive Services (Centers for Disease Control and Prevention, 2001) as an effective strategy for increasing physical activity levels. Different environmental situations may suggest different prompts; it is up to the innovative researcher to envision what might work best in their situation.

A newly emerging area of research does not involve the explicit prompts to exercise discussed previously, but rather involves making changes to the environment such as the creation of walking paths, parks, shopping within walking distance, etc. (Sallis et al., 1998). These urban design and landscaping interventions adopt a "Field of Dreams" framework, with the thought that "If you build it, they will come." The research that is used to support these interventions is based in part on geographical surveys that have found that people who live closer to parks and fitness facilities (e.g., Lee, Castro, Albright, Pruitt, & King, 2000) or perceive their environment as safe (Centers for Disease Control and Prevention, 1999) are more likely to engage in regular physical activity than others (Brownson, Baker, Housemann, Brennan, & Bacak, 2001). However, we still do not know the causal direction in those relationships. Social cognitive theory would suggest that individuals that already exercise would choose to live in an environment that supports their activity.

To determine causal direction would require the completion of randomized trials that are difficult to conceive on such a large scale over the time required to implement the environmental changes. We may gain some insight from the efforts at worksite exercise promotion that have involved the creation of an on-site exercise facility. The typical long-term rates of use in these facilities are approximately 20-30% of eligible employees, paralleling the natural rates we find in epidemiological studies (Dishman,

Oldenburg, O'Neal, & Shephard, 1998; Shephard, 1996). Thus, the facilities may simply be attracting the people that already exercise and now have a convenient and free place to do so. These interventions may not be attracting the sedentary people who were the original target.

There has been relatively little systematic investigation of how changing environments on a large, community scale affects activity patterns. One study that involved the addition of bike paths and extended hours at recreation centers on two military communities found that the community with the exercise-friendly environment did have improved levels of fitness, although there were no significant differences in total energy expenditure (Linenger et al., 1991). A study conducted in Finland attempted to encourage active commuting to work (e.g., bicycling, jogging) by provision of changing facilities and found a 7% increase in the percentage of people that actively commuted to work (Vuori, Oja, & Paronen, 1994). A study of the creation of walking paths in a rural community found that 39% of the individuals with access did use the walking trails (Brownson et al., 2000). However, one of the predictors of trail use was the classification of the individual as a regular walker, suggesting that the trails may not have attracted many new individuals to exercise. There are currently several ongoing projects that should help further elucidate the efficacy of these environmental restructuring approaches. However, with no clear theoretical framework behind these studies, it will remain difficult to fully examine why they are or are not effective. When a theory is espoused in these studies, it is typically ecological theory, which conceptualizes the environment as the primary predictor of behavior (Moos, 1979). However, placing these types of studies in a social cognitive framework would allow the investigators to examine how these environmental changes not only affect behavior, but also how their use is both determined by and affects the cognitions of the individuals in the communities.

Population/Community

Population and community interventions have the ability to reach a relatively large number of individuals but typically must sacrifice some of the theoretical rigor of the individualized approaches. Some of

the largest community-level campaigns, such as the Stanford Five City Project (Young, Haskell, Taylor, & Fortmann, 1996), the Minnesota Heart Health Program (Leupker et al., 1994), and the Pawtucket Heart Program (Eaton et al., 1999), included exercise but also involved multiple behavioral targets. Typically, these interventions were based on large-scale media campaigns promoted at education. The results indicate that these types of intervention have some success at increasing knowledge but have modest effects, at best, on actually changing behaviors such as exercise (Iverson, Fielding, Crow, & Christenson, 1985).

Community-based programs that involve more than simply educational messages and offer better access to facilities, special workshops to teach new exercises, etc., are truly multilevel in design and have been more effective at increasing levels of physical activity (Centers for Disease Control and Prevention, 2001; Marcus, Owen, et al., 1998). These multilevel interventions shall be discussed more fully in the new directions section.

Schools have been the target for a large number of exercise promotion messages, although they are often combined with other health-related messages. There is clear support to suggest the requirement that every child engages in regular physical education as both a way to get them active and teach skills they can use throughout their lifetime (Stone, McKenzie, Welk, & Booth, 1998; Centers for Disease Control and Prevention, 2001). However, interventions that simply focus on educational lectures (e.g., Osler & Jespersen, 1993; Walter, 1989), while effective at increasing knowledge, are not likely to be very effective at increasing behavior (Centers for Disease Control and Prevention, 2001).

Worksites have been a popular place to target health behavior change including exercise (Dishman et al., 1998). As discussed previously, the simple addition of on-site facilities does appear to attract users, but they are likely those that were already active. The worksite has also been the population targeted for several interventions that are truly individualized in nature and therefore are discussed in the following section.

Interventions at the community—or population-level, including schools and worksites, do appear to be effective for the promotion of exercise behavior.

There is even evidence to suggest that church-based programs may also be effective (e.g., Simmons et al., 1998). However, the most effective interventions appear to be those that implement individualized approaches and simply use the community or population as the target for the intervention in order to take advantage of existing structures and relationships.

Individualized Approaches

We have conceptualized, individualized approaches as those that are tailored and/or delivered on a person-by-person basis. Thus, an individualized approach may be implemented at a worksite, but is individualized in our definition because different individuals receive different messages. We are purposefully not including the large body of literature that exists on exercise interventions that are tests of the efficacy of different intensities, dosages, and modalities. Although these are certainly important studies that serve as the foundation for our behavioral recommendations, their primary purpose is not necessarily the promotion of physical activity. Not surprisingly, the most commonly applied individualized approach used for large-scale studies have involved the application of the transtheoretical model or at least its concept of stages of change. This approach has been used in a variety of settings and has been delivered using several modalities.

Worksite

One of the first studies that attempted to use the stages of change as an intervention tool to promote physical activity participation was conducted by Marcus and colleagues (Marcus, Rossi, et al., 1992). Stage-specific manuals based on the processes of change were utilized in the intervention in an attempt to assist individuals' transitions to higher levels of physical activity. In this six-week intervention, 62% of individuals in the contemplation stage as well as 61% in the preparation stage became more active. Although this study was rather short and utilized no control conditions, it did offer early evidence that relatively simple exercise interventions based on the stages of change might be effective in increasing individual's exercise stage.

Peterson and Aldana (1999) examined the effectiveness of stage-based materials versus standard physical activity information and a control condition over a six-week period in a sample of 527 adults in a worksite setting. Results indicated that in the tailored, stage-based group, 33% of the study participants progressed towards maintenance, versus 19% and 14% in the informational and control conditions, respectively. A larger study by Marcus and colleagues (Marcus, Emmons, et al., 1998) obtained similar results in a worksite sample of 1,559 adults over a three-month period. They found that tailored, stage-based advice was able to outperform a standard care intervention in which participants received typical exercise promotion materials developed by the American Heart Association. Stage-matched materials resulted in 37% of participants increasing their stage of change while only 11% regressed. In the standard care condition, 27% progressed and 15% regressed.

Physician Counseling

Due to both their level of contact with their patients and their authority position, physicians often find physician-based physical activity counseling an attractive approach to promoting physical activity. However, most physicians report that they do not have the time or knowledge to properly advise their patients about exercise, so the typical approach has been to provide the physicians with the tools necessary to make stage-based activity recommendations (Pender, Sallis, Long, & Calfas, 1994). One of the first studies that helped train physicians in the delivery of stage-based exercise promotion methods was Project PACE (Calfas, Sallis, Oldenburg, & Ffrench, 1997). A brief stage-tailored intervention was delivered by the physician with a telephone follow-up two weeks later. The results supported the effectiveness of this intervention with study participants increasing their self-reported levels of exercise after six weeks.

Similar interventions have been successful or are currently in testing (e.g., Albright et al., 2000; Pinto, Goldstein, DePue, & Milan, 1998), but challenges remain (for a review see Pinto, Goldstein, & Marcus, 1998). There are unique challenges to recruiting both the physicians' practices and their patients in these studies (Margitic et al., 1999). One of the greatest barriers is the lack of time and monetary incentives for the physician. With only a few minutes spent with a patient, the counseling typically is focused on the problem that precipitated their visit to the physician.

Mail-Based

Based on the transtheoretical model, there have been several studies that have been successful at increasing physical activity levels using a mail-based approach. For example, Cardinal and Sachs (1996) utilized three conditions (lifestyle-activity manual, structured-exercise manual, control) that were mailed to participants in an effort to experimentally examine the effectiveness of two types of physical activity recommendations on exercise behavior when compared to a control condition. The authors reported that both transtheoretical conditions, regardless of the activity recommendations, significantly increased their physical activity behavior. Although this study was relatively short in duration, it does offer support for the effectiveness of mailed activity manuals based on transtheoretical constructs. This technique has been used in a number of similar studies with equal success (e.g., Owen, Lee, Nacerrella, & Hagg, 1987).

The benefits of this approach are that it allows the researcher to deliver relatively long messages in a format that allows for illustration and diagrams that can be saved and reviewed. Unfortunately, they are static messages of a type that individuals are used to getting everyday in the mail. Therefore, care must be taken in the development of these materials to make sure they are not lost in the mix of junk mail that individuals receive every day.

Telephone

The telephone has also been successfully used in the promotion of regular physical activity. For example, King and colleagues (King., Taylor, Haskell, & DeBusk, 1988) used a variety of cognitive-behavioral strategies such as self-monitoring and goal-setting as a replacement for face-to-face contact. Their results show that the use of telephone counseling and prompting can be effective at increasing program adherence. These studies have now begun to incorporate stage-based approaches to delivering the exercise promotion messages. This allows for the instant, tailored feedback versus having to complete a questionnaire and waiting for a reply. The advantage of the telephone over mail-based interventions is that it can allow for counselor relationships to help support behavior change and allows individuals to call in for help when they need it to help overcome specific exercise barriers.

Internet/Computer

Because of its increasing prevalence in daily life and its flexibility as a communication tool, the Internet has been identified as an ideal medium for the development of large-scale exercise and physical activity interventions (Marcus, Nigg, Riebe, & Forsyth, 2000; Mockenhaupt, 2001). More than half of the houses in the United States have a computer and approximately 89% of children under the age of 18 have access to a computer either at home or school (U.S. Census Bureau, 2001). Moreover, approximately 40% of all U.S. households have Internet access, up from only 26% in 1998 (U.S. Census Bureau, 2001). The Internet connects the most remote individual with interpersonal contact through email, chat, or video-conferencing and 24-hour access to online information. However, only a handful of published studies have used the Internet for exercise or physical activity research.

The Internet has been used to survey physical activity participants through activity news-groups to examine the relationship between negative affect, inactivity, and anxiety (Szabo, Frenkl, & Caputo, 1996). Although the Internet was shown to be effective in gathering cross-sectional data, it promises a greater return by supporting physical activity interventions. For example, an Internet-based physical activity intervention helped to increase the activity levels of adults with Non-Insulin Dependent Diabetes Mellitus (Type 2 diabetes) (McKay, King, Eakin, Seeley, & Glasgow, 2001). There appeared to be no difference in physical activity levels between the intervention condition that included goal setting and personalized feedback and the control condition that included Internet information only. However, those participants who accessed the online materials more frequently derived more benefit. Similarly, a group of overweight adults was randomized into either an online education condition or an online behavioral therapy condition (Tate, Wing, & Winett, 2001). The participants in the online education condition were provided with a face-to-face weight loss session and access to a website with links to Internet weight loss materials. Participants in the behavioral therapy condition had the addition of ongoing behavioral lessons and individualized feedback via email. After six months, the behavioral therapy group had significantly greater weight loss and decreases in waist circumference than the education condition. In the PACE+ study, computer stations at physician's offices utilized the transtheoretical model as tool for promoting exercise and dietary change in adolescents (Patrick et al., 2001). The computer-based intervention was successful at increasing moderate-intensity exercise participation, but did not influence vigorous activity. These studies provide support for the continued use of computers and the Internet for delivering exercise and physical activity interventions.

The Internet is multifaceted and a systematic approach combining theory and various Internet features, such as email, chat, and message posting, is needed to determine not only the best way to induce behavioral change, but to determine why different features are more effective. One study examining computer use among adolescents in Hong Kong determined that boys who use the computer for surfing and email engaged in more social-physical activities than boys who used the computer to play games, yet this pattern was not found for girls (Ho & Lee, 2001). Ho and Lee also reported that computer users in general, engage in more exercise and social behaviors than noncomputer users. This suggests that developing exercise interventions for adolescents that encourage participants to use the computer for email and information gathering would not detract from time spent actually exercising. This is an important contribution to our understanding of computer-human interactions and continued research should be conducted integrating these interactions within a theoretical exercise adherence framework.

Multicultural Approaches

An important area of exercise promotion is the proper tailoring of interventions to promote exercise behavior across diverse populations that each present unique challenges. For example, physical inactivity of African-Americans may be due not only to environmental constraints but also to cultural beliefs. A focus group study examining urban African-Americans' perceptions of exercise found that study participants believed resting during leisure time was as important as exercising (Airhihenbuwa, Kumanyika, Agurs, et al., 1995). These same participants were less likely to recognize exercise as a possible treatment for hypertension and, in fact, were more likely to view activity as a cause of high blood pressure.

In the past decade, increasing attention has been paid to implementing interventions focusing on increasing physical activity in U.S. minority populations, namely African-Americans and Latinos/Hispanics. This is important, given that participation of African-Americans in prevention trials has been low (Fitzgibbon et al., 1998). Also, physical activity participation rates for African-Americans are consistently lower than Caucasians (Crespo, Keteyian, Heath, & Sempos, 1996). These rates are discouraging considering the numerous health issues which could be improved by physical activity participation for which African-Americans have high prevalence rates such as hypertension, obesity, coronary heart disease (Duey et al., 1998; Jones, 1999). In addition, 36% of Latino adults report no participation in leisure time physical activity (National Center for Health Statistics, 1999), and Latina women have the lowest rate of exercise participation in the United States (Coleman, Gonzalez, & Cooley, 2000). Given that Latinos are the fastest growing minority segment of the U.S. population (U.S. Census Bureau, 2001), effective exercise promotion is a necessity.

Taylor, Baranowski, and Young (1998) have published a review of physical activity interventions for ethnic minorities. Up to 1997, only ten interventions had been identified, six targeting African-Americans and four targeting Latinos. Of these ten, only four were randomized controlled trials (i.e., Nader et al., 1983; Nader et al., 1986; Baranowski et al., 1990; Chen et al., 1998).

Perhaps the most important distinguishing characteristic of interventions that target different ethnic groups is being culturally tailored and sensitive. One common, erroneous, assumption is that only the materials used in an intervention, such as brochures or public service announcements, need to be culturally tailored (Pasick, D'Onofrio, & Otero-Sabogal, 1996). Pasick et al. state that superficial tailoring such as this is not adequate, and there must be an in-depth knowledge and understanding of the population. They suggest that this can be best achieved through meaningful involvement of community members and through research conducted by representatives of the culture.

Several studies involving African-Americans

have done just that. "Hip Hop to Health" is a four-year randomized controlled trial aimed at dietary fat reduction and increased exercise among 6-10 year olds and their inner city African-American families (Fitzgibbon et al., 1998). An effort was made in order to hire an African-American staff that would 'match' the target population, given that this staff would have an increased knowledge of African-American culture and family networks. In addition, the African-American staff, due to their affiliation with the participants, would receive increased trust among the participants.

Ard, Rosati, and Oddone (2000) evaluated the impact of culturally sensitive modifications to the Duke University Rice Diet weight loss program for African-American dieters, given that the dietary and behavioral needs of non-White populations are rarely considered in traditional weight loss programs. The culturally sensitive modifications included decreasing the cost of the program, using ethnic recipes in the cooking classes, and including family members in the program. In addition, an African American instructor led the lectures. Perhaps most importantly, 90% of participants agreed or strongly agreed that the modified diet therapy suited their needs as African-Americans.

Culturally tailored interventions have also been developed for Latinos. "Cuidando el Corazon" (CEC; Taking Care of Your Heart) was designed to assess the efficacy of a culturally adapted weight-reduction and exercise program for achieving long-term weight loss in Mexican Americans (Foreyt, Ramirez, & Cousins, 1991). As was hypothesized, weight loss was greatest in the family-involvement group and least in the information-only control group. This was expected due to the importance of family in Latino cultures. Foreyt et al. note that focusing on the family was extremely important. For example, Mexican American women are often uncomfortable doing things for themselves, such as losing weight, so a persuasive approach was used that focused on the benefits of losing weight for the family.

The exercise component of CEC involved brisk walking, which appears to be an activity that is cross-cultural and doesn't step out of cultural norms. However, some participants reported that their husbands were jealous and kept them from walking around the neighborhood. Thus, a church hall was regularly used for walking, exemplifying how cultural needs can be addressed.

In an attempt to acquire an in-depth knowledge and understanding of a population, focus groups have been used to assist in the development of messages and strategies for interventions. For example, the National Heart, Lung, and Blood Institute (NHLBI) conducted seven focus groups to develop Salud para su Corazon, a heart-disease prevention and education program (Moreno et al., 1997). The information from these groups helped raise awareness of cultural concepts that could have been misunderstood and not considered by health professionals when developing interventions with needs and preferences that differ from that of the majority population.

An important element of Salud para su Corazon was a community-agency partnership for implementing the intervention. This partnership was developed based on the need to involve community members in the planning and implementation of research, training, and development of educational materials and activities, and incorporating cultural beliefs, practices, and concerns of the community during all stages of the intervention (Lenfant, 1995).

Two other projects based in California were tailored to the community. La Vida Caminando was a community-based physical activity intervention that was designed by and for Latino families living in rural cities. A local advisory committee was formed in each community, and walking clubs were established which were free of charge and provided materials and information in both Spanish and English. In addition, information sessions were held that focused on risk reduction for chronic disease, especially diabetes, which is highly prevalent in Latinos.

A second intervention in California, La Vida Buena, was a culturally tailored physical activity program for Latina women (Whitehorse, Manzano, Baezconde-Garbanati, & Hahn, 1999). A community coalition was formed, made up of representatives from major health care providers in the area, churches, schools, advocacy organizations, other community members, and others. Focus groups were formed, interviews were conducted, and community forums were used to shape the program. Lay health advisors, or *promotores*, were trained to assist in recruitment and program implementation. This intervention demonstrated success in recruiting underserved adults, and the authors recommend that collaboration between academic groups and community groups increase to enhance the number of members of underserved adults in health promotion research.

These studies illustrate the importance of culturally tailored interventions in order to acquire positive outcomes. Taylor et al. (1998) state that there are several salient issues in cultural tailoring including avoiding the superficiality of tailoring an intervention to a community characterized by a racial or ethnic description; not relying solely on the broad concept of ethnic background in identifying attributes related to health behavior; defining groups by attitudes, beliefs, behaviors, cultural concepts, and cultural dimensions relevant to health practices; and tailoring interventions by culture as needed but being applicable across cultures when appropriate/possible. When these issues are well thought out, positive results can be expected.

New Directions

Multilevel Approaches

After examining the types of interventions that are used at various levels of implementation, the obvious question is whether or not simultaneous interventions at different levels can be effective. One might even hope that there may be synergistic effects among the different levels. For example, there may be an intervention to make the environment more inviting to exercisers by the addition of walking paths in conjunction with a community-wide advertising campaign promoting physical activity and the use of such paths for an individualized, stage-tailored intervention designed to help people at all stages of exercise adoption. As exciting as these opportunities may be, they are equally challenging to implement and assess.

There have been some initial attempts to implement these large-scale exercise interventions. For example, in the Johnson and Johnson Live for Life program, the goal was to reach more than just the highly motivated individuals through the use of health assessments, seminars, exercise classes, and health education (Blair, Piserchia, Wilbur, & Crowder, 1986). After two years, participation in vigorous activity more than doubled in those sites that

received the intervention, supporting the efficacy of these multilevel interventions. Future interventions may wish to examine the addition of stages and processes of change as a mechanism to help those individuals that are not ready to begin a program of regular exercise.

Multiple Outcomes

As exercise researchers we are often concerned with simply increasing an individuals' level of fitness. Unfortunately, with the less stringent activity recommendations and the push towards large-scale studies, we have limited opportunities to observe large changes in individual fitness levels. We must recognize the multitude of other health benefits that are associated with physical activity beyond fitness changes. One of the major initiatives in the United States' Healthy People 2010 is to increase the quality of life (U.S. Department of Health and Human Services, 2000). We should concern ourselves with how our interventions are affecting health-related quality of life, healthy days, and mental health outcomes. These are all very important intervention outcomes that are too often ignored in favor of an increase in VO2max or a greater level of caloric expenditure. The appeal of a physical activity intervention is that it has been shown to have far-reaching effects on a number of important outcomes beyond increasing longevity and fitness (Dubbert, 1992). We need to continue to document the effectiveness of our interventions at enhancing these other outcomes. In particular, are certain interventions more effective than others at enhancing these mental health outcomes because of their level of social interaction? Do environmental or higher-level interventions that more subtly influence activity levels have the same effect as an intervention that requires the individual to make a conscious choice to engage in a program of regular activity?

Multiple Behavior Approaches

A recent study conducted in the U.S. state of Michigan found that while only 26% of the population was getting enough regular exercise, remarkably only 3% of the population was engaging in all of the healthy behaviors of not smoking, proper diet, and exercise (Reeves, Rafferty, McGee, & Miller, 2001). These are alarming rates, implying that nearly 88% of individuals that exercise for health benefits are still either smoking or eating improper diets. Recently there has been a push to examine intervening on multiple behaviors such as smoking, diet, and exercise (King, 1994). Typically, these interventions may be considered *modular*, that is, they involve simply stacking interventions for each target behavior together. Although the answer to how many interventions individuals can complete at once is certainly important, the real challenge in the future will be determining how best to integrate interventions for multiple behaviors. Is there a synergistic effect where one can build on past successes in another behavioral domain to enhance self-efficacy levels? Since the processes necessary to transition between stages are relatively constant across behavior, can teaching people the patterns and strategies be an effective tool for creating change across multiple behaviors? A study of changes in dieting behavior that were associated with an exercise intervention found that individuals in the intervention did make changes in their diet, although they were not directly associated with changes in activity levels (Wilcox, King, Castro, & Bortz, 2000).

Much as with the need to examine multiple outcomes discussed above, exercise researchers need to form interdisciplinary teams that create and test theoretical interventions designed to facilitate changes in multiple behaviors. The health impact of changing one behavioral risk factor is significant, but changing multiple risk factors promises to have much greater impacts for health care costs and will be the challenge for behavioral medicine in the coming decades.

Systematic Theoretical Evaluation

A concern raised early in the chapter that has been echoed throughout each section is the need to systematically evaluate the theoretical relationships in our intervention work. There has been a call to conduct more thorough investigations of the mediators of change (Baranowski et al., 1998; Sallis, 2000). Basing an intervention on the transtheoretical model and then not examining changes in the processes of change or decisional balance does not shed any light onto the reasons behind whether or not the intervention was successful. Too often we simply assume that it was the theory at work when the intervention succeeds and that it was a design flaw when the intervention failed. A thorough investigation of the theoretical relationships will help enhance the efficacy of the interventions and also help advance the theory.

There has been some research in this area that has begun to paint a picture of what is changing when we are intervening to promote exercise behavior. Calfas et al. (1997) examined changes in activity behavior and predictors of behavior change following a six-week physician-based, exercise stage matched intervention. Sedentary adults were counseled in how to enhance their levels of physical activity based on their current stage of exercise behavior change by their physician during an office visit, whereas controls received no such counseling. Those in the intervention group also received written materials and a telephone prompt after two weeks to help encourage behavior change. After six weeks, participants in the intervention condition significantly increased their levels of physical activity compared to the controls. Of particular interest is that this study attempted to use changes in use of the processes of change, self-efficacy, and perceived social support as predictors of changes in activity levels. Both changes in self-efficacy and the behavioral processes of change were significant in predicting changes in activity levels. This study is the first to examine how changes in the use of processes of change can predict subsequent exercise behavior change.

Recently other investigators have begun to examine the mediators of behavior change as a tool to advance our understanding of both the theory and intervention (e.g., Bock, Marcus, Pinto, Forsyth, 2001; Pinto, Lynn, Marcus, DePue, & Goldstein, 2001). More research of this nature is a necessary step if we are to reach the physical activity goals that we are setting for the population.

Applied Research into Practice

As is discussed in Kimiecik and Blissmer (1997), a major challenge of turning our research into practice is getting practitioners to adopt our theories and interventions. Often these are complex theories that require multiple assessments with lengthy, seemingly repetitive measures. Including practitioners and the people that will actually deliver the interventions in the initial planning stages may be a strategy worth adopting. Interestingly, it appears that some of the best efforts in this area are being done in the multicultural studies where extensive effort is made to secure community input. This can serve to both inform both the researcher and practitioner about potential implementation problems and moves us closer towards the final goal, that of sustainability.

Sustainability is necessary because our involvement in exercise promotions eventually must end and there are only so many that we can reach. For any interventions to achieve long-term success we need to ensure that they are adopted by the individuals and communities that are involved. We must not create a dependency on our expertise, services, or money if the intervention will truly be successful. Green and Kreuter's (1991) text on health promotion planning may serve as an excellent source for information on how to help create and foster effective, sustainable interventions.

Conclusion

Robert Butler stated, "If exercise could be packed in a pill, it would be the single most widely prescribed and beneficial medicine in the nation." This sentiment is echoed in the World Health Organization's (2001) description of exercise promotion as a "best buy." Unfortunately, that pill isn't being produced and there isn't a big rush to buy the WHO's bargain of the millennium. Therefore, there remains a great deal of work to be done in the field of exercise promotion. There is a great need to continue to develop and refine theoretical approaches to exercise approaches across all of the levels of intervention for use in the diverse populations around the world. We also must continue efforts to examine multiple level interventions, multiple outcomes, and multiple behaviors in our efforts to create sustainable exercise interventions.

References

Airhihenbuwa, C. O., Kumanyika, S., Agurs, T. D., & Lowe, A. (1995). Perceptions and beliefs about exercise, rest, and health among African-Americans. *American Journal of Health Promotion, 9,* 426-429.

Albright, C. L., Cohen, S., Gibbons, L., Miller, S., Marcus, B., Sallis, J., Imai, K., Jernick, J., & Simons-Morton, D. G. (2000). Incorporating physical activity advice into primary care: Physician-delivered advice with the Activity Counseling Trial. *American Journal of Preventive Medicine, 18,* 225-234.

American College of Sports Medicine (1998). Position statement: The recommended quantity and quality of exercise for developing and maintaining cardiorespiratory and muscular fitness in healthy adults. *Medicine and Science in Sports and Exercise, 30,* 975-991.

Ard, J. D., Rosati, R., & Oddone, E. Z. (2000). Culturally-sensitive weight loss program produces significant reduction in weight, blood pressure, and cholesterol in eight weeks. *Journal of the National Medical Association, 92*(11), 515-523.

Bandura, A. (1986). *Social foundations of thought and action.* Englewood Cliffs, NJ: Prentice Hall.

Bandura, A. (1997a). *Self-efficacy: The exercise of control.* New York: W. H. Freeman and Company.

Bandura, A. (1997b). The anatomy of stages of change. *American Journal of Health Promotion, 12*(1), 8-10.

Baranowski, T., Anderson, C., & Carmack, C. (1998). Mediating variable frameworks in physical activity interventions: How are we doing? How might we do better? *American Journal of Preventive Medicine, 15*(4), 266-297.

Baranowski, T., Simons-Morton, B., Hooks, P., Henske, J., Tiernan, K., Dunn, J. K., Burkhalter, H., Harper, J., & Palmer, J. (1990). A center-based program for exercise change among black-American families. *Health Education Quarterly, 17*(2), 179-196.

Blair, S. N., Piserchia, P. V., Wilbur, C. S., & Crowder, J. H. (1986). A public health intervention model for worksite health promotion: Impact on exercise and physical fitness in a health promotion plan after 24 months. *Journal of the American Medical Association, 255,* 921-926.

Blamey, A., Mutrie, N., & Aitchison, T. (1995). Health promotion by encouraged stair use. *British Journal of Medicine, 311,* 289-290.

Bock, B. C., Marcus, B. H., Pinto, B. M., & Forsyth, L. H. (2001). Maintenance of physical activity following an individualized motivationally tailored intervention. *Annals of Behavioral Medicine, 23,* 79-87.

Brownell, K. D., Stunkard, A. J., & Albaum, J. M. (1980). Evaluation and modification of exercise patterns in the natural environment. *American Journal of Psychiatry, 137,* 1540-1545.

Brownson, R. C., Baker, E. A., Housemann, R. A., Brennan, L. K., & Bacak, S. J. (2001). Environmental and policy determinants of physical activity in the United States. *American Journal of Public Health, 91,* 1995-2003.

Brownson, R. C., Housemann, R. A., Brown, D. R., Jackson-Thompson, J., King, A. C., Malone, B. R., & Sallis, J. F. (2000). Promoting physical activity in rural communities: Walking trail access, use, and effects. *American Journal of Preventive Medicine, 18,* 235-241.

Calfas, K. J., Sallis, J. F., Oldenburg, B., & Ffrench, M. (1997). Mediators of change in physical activity following an intervention in primary care: PACE. *Preventive Medicine, 26,* 297-304.

Cardinal, B. J., & Sachs, M. L. (1996). Effects of mail-mediated, stage-matched exercise behavior change strategies on female adults' leisure-time exercise behavior. *Journal of Sports Medicine and Physical Fitness, 36,* 100-107.

Carron, A., Hausenblas, H., & Mack, D. (1996). Social influence and exercise: A meta-analysis. *Journal of Sport & Exercise Psychology, 18,* 1-16.

Castro, C. M., Sallis, J. F., Hickman, S. A., Lee, R. E., & Chen, A. H. (1999). A prospective study of psychological correlates of physical activity for ethnic minority women. *Psychology and Health, 14,* 277-293.

Centers for Disease Control and Prevention (1999). Neighborhood safety and the prevalence of physical inactivity-selected states. *Morbidity and Mortality Weekly Report, 48,* 143-146.

Centers for Disease Control and Prevention (2001). Increasing physical activity: A report on the recommendations of the Task Force on Community Preventive Services. *Morbidity and Mortality Weekly Report, 50,* 1-18.

Chen, A. H., Sallis, J. F., Castro, C. M., Lee, R. E., Hickmann, S. A., William, C., & Martin, J. E. (1998). A home-based behavioral intervention to promote walking in sedentary ethnic minority women: Project WALK. *Women's Health, 4*(1), 19-39.

Chogahara, M., Cousins, S., & Wankel, L. (1998). Social influences on physical activity in older adults: A review. *Journal of Aging and Physical Activity, 6,* 1-17.

Coleman, K. J., Gonzalez, E. C., & Cooley, T. (2000). An objective measure of reinforcement and its implications for exercise promotion in sedentary Hispanic and Anglo women. *Annals of Behavioral Medicine, 22*(3), 229-236.

Courneya, K.S., Estabrooks, P.A., & Nigg, C.R. (1997). A simple reinforcement strategy for increasing attendance at a fitness facility. *Health Education and Behavior, 24,* 706-713.

Courneya, K. S., Plotnikoff, R. C., Hotz, S. B., & Birkett, N. J. (2000). Social support and the theory of planned behavior in the exercise domain. *American Journal of Health Behavior, 24*(4), 300-308.

Cousins, S. O. (1995). Social support for exercise among elderly women in Canada. *Health Promotion International, 10*(4), 273-282.

Cousins, J. H., Rubovits, D. S., Dunn, J. K., Reeves, R. S., Ramirez, A. G., & Foreyt, J. P. (1992). Family versus individually oriented intervention for weight loss in Mexican American women. *Public Health Reports, 107*(5), 549-555.

Crespo, C. J., Keteyian, S. J., Heath, G. W., & Sempos, C. T. (1996). Leisure-time physical activity among US adults. Results from the Third National Health and Nutrition Examination Survey. *Archives of Internal Medicine, 156*(1), 93-98.

Dishman, R. K. (1994). *Advances in exercise adherence.* Champaign, IL: Human Kinetics.

Dishman, R. K., & Buckworth, J. (1996). Increasing physical activity: A quantitative synthesis. *Medicine and Science in Sports and Exercise,* 706-719.

Dishman, R. K., Oldenburg, B., O'Neal, H., & Shephard, R. J. (1998). Worksite physical activity intervention. *American Journal of Health Promotion, 15,* 344-361.

Dubbert, P. M. (1992). Exercise in behavioral medicine. *Journal of Consulting and Clinical Psychology, 60,* 613-618.

Duey, W. J., O'Brien, W. L., Crutchfield, A. B., Brown, L. A., Williford, H. N., & Sharff-Olson, M. (1998). Effects of exercise training on aerobic fitness in African-American females. *Ethnic Discourse, 8*(3), 306-311.

Duncan, T. E., & McAuley, E. (1993). Social support and efficacy cognitions in exercise adherence: A latent growth curve analysis. *Journal of Behavioral Medicine, 16*(2), 199-218.

Eaton, C. B., Lapanne, K. L., Garber, C. E., Gans, K. M., Lasater, T. M., & Carleton, R. A. (1999). Effects of a community-based intervention on physical activity: The Pawtucket Heart Health Program. *American Journal of Public Health, 89,* 1741-1744.

Eyler, A. A., Brownson, R. C., Donatelle, R. J., King, A. C., Brown, D., & Sallis, J. F. (1999). Physical activity social support and middle- and older-aged minority women: Results from a US survey. *Social Science & Medicine, 49,* 781-789.

Fitzgibbon, M. L., Prewitt, T. E., Blackman, L. R., Simon, P., Luke, A., Keys, L. C., Avellone, M. E., & Singh, V. (1998). Quantitative assessment of recruitment efforts for prevention trials in two diverse black populations. *Preventive Medicine, 27*(6), 838-845.

Foreyt, J. P., Ramirez, A. G., & Cousins, J. H. (1991). Cuidando El Corazon: A weight reduction intervention for Mexican Americans. *American Journal of Clinical Nutrition, 53,* 1639-1641.

Green, L. W., & Kreuter, M. W. (1991). *Health Promotion Planning: An Educational and Environmental Approach* (2nd Ed.). Toronto: Mayfield Publishing Company.

Hauesenblas, H. A., Carron, A. V., & Mack, D. E. (1997). Application of the theories of reasoned action and planned behavior to exercise behavior: A meta-analysis. *Journal of Sport & Exercise Psychology, 19,* 36-51.

Herrick, A. B., Stone, W. J., & Mettler, M. M. (1997). Stages of change, decisional balance, and self-efficacy across four health behaviors in a worksite environment. *American Journal of Health Promotion, 12*(1), 49-56.

Ho, S. M. Y., & Lee, T. M. C. (2001). Computer usage and its relationship with adolescent lifestyle in Hong Kong. *Journal of Adolescent Health, 29*(4), 258-266.

Iverson, D. C., Fielding, M. E., Crow, R. S., Christenson, G. M. (1985). The promotion of physical activity in the United States population: The status of programs in medical, worksite, community, and school settings. *Public Health Reports, 100,* 212-224.

Jones, D. W. (1999). What is the role of obesity in hypertension and target organ injury in African Americans? *American Journal of Medical Sciences, 317*(3), 147-151.

Katula, J. A., McAuley, E., Mihalko, S. L., & Bane, S. M. (1998). Mirror, mirror on the wall. . . exercise environment influences on self-efficacy. *Journal of Social and Behavioral Personality, 13,* 219-332.

Kelsey, K. S., Campbell, M. K., Tessaro, I., Benedict, S., Belton, L., Fernandez, L. M., Henriquez-Roldan, C., & DeVellis, B. (2000). Social support and health behaviors among blue-collar women workers. *American Journal of Health Behavior, 24*(6), 434-443.

Kimiecik, J. C., & Blissmer, B. (1998). Applied exercise psychology: Measurement issues. In J. L. Duda (Ed.), *Advances in Sport and Exercise Psychology* (pp. 447-460). Morgantown, WV: Fitness Information Technology, Inc.

King, A. C. (1994). Clinical and community interventions to promote and support physical activity participation. In R. K. Dishman (Ed.), *Advances in Exercise Adherence* (pp. 183-212). Champaign, IL: Human Kinetics.

King, A. C. & Fredericksen, L. W. (1984). Low-cost strategies for increasing exercise behavior: Relapse prevention training and social support. *Behavior Modification, 8,* 3-21.

King, A. C., Taylor, C. B., Haskell, W. L., DeBusk, R. F. (1988). Strategies for increasing early adherence to and long-term maintenance of home-based exercise training in healthy middle-aged men and women. *American Journal of Cardiology, 61,* 628-632.

Lee, C. (1993). Attitudes, knowledge, and stages of change: A survey of exercise patterns in older Australian women. *Health Psychology, 12*(6), 476-480.

Lee, R. E., Castro, C. M., Albright, C. A., Pruitt, L. A., & King, A. C. (2000). Neighborhood topography and physical activity in ethnic minority women. *Annals of Behavioral Medicine, 22,* S80.

Lenfant, C. (1995). Enhancing minority participation in research. The NHLBI experience. *Circulation, 92*(3), 279-280.

Leupker, R. V., Murray, D. M., Jacobs, D. R. et al. (1994). Community education for cardiovascular disease prevention: Risk factor changes in the Minnesota Heart Health Program. *American Journal of Public Health, 84,* 1383-1393.

Lindstrom, M., Hanson, B. S., & Ostergren, P. O. (2001). Socioeconomic differences in leisure-time physical activity: The role of social participation and social capital in shaping health related behaviour. *Social Science & Medicine, 52*(3), 441-451.

Linenger, J. M., Chesson, C. V., & Nice, D. S. (1991). Physical fitness gains following simple environmental change. *American Journal of Preventive Medicine, 7,* 298-310.

Marcus, B. H., Banspach, S. W., Lefebvre, R. C., Rossi, J. S., Carleton, R. A., & Abrams, D. B. (1992). Using stages of change model to increase the adoption of physical activity among community participants. *American Journal Health Promotion, 6*(6), 424-429.

Marcus, B. H., Emmons, K. M., Simkin-Silverman, L. R., Linnan, L. A., Taylor, E. R., Bock, B. C., Roberts, M. B., Rossi, J. S., & Abrams, D. B. (1998). Evaluation of motivationally tailored vs. standard self-help physical activity interventions at the workplace. American *Journal of Health Promotion, 12*(4), 246-253.

Marcus, B. H., & Forsyth, L. H. (1999). How are we doing with physical activity? *American Journal of Health Promotion, 14,* 118-124.

Marcus, B. H., Nigg, C. R., Riebe, D., & Forsyth, L. H. (2000). Interactive communication strategies: Implications for population-based physical-activity promotion. *American Journal of Preventive Medicine, 19*(2), 121-126.

Marcus, B. H., Owen, N., Forsyth, L. H., Cavill, N. A., & Fridinger, F. (1998). Physical activity interventions using mass media, print media, and information technology. *American Journal of Preventive Medicine, 15*(4), 362-378.

Marcus, B. H., Rossi, J. S., Selby, V. C., Niaura, R. S., & Abrams, D. B. (1992). The stages and processes of exercise adoption and maintenance in a worksite sample. *Health Psychology, 11*(6), 386-395.

Margitic, S., Sevick, M. A., Miller, M., Albright, C., Banton, J., Callahan, K., Garcia, M., Gibbons, L., Levine, B. J.,n Anderson, R., & Ettinger, W. (1999). Challenges faced in recruiting patients from primary care practices into a physical activity intervention trial: Activity Counseling Trial Research Group. *Preventive Medicine, 29,* 277-286.

Marshall, S. J., & Biddle, S. J. H. (2001). The transtheoretical model of behavior change: A meta-analysis of applications to physical activity and exercise. *Annals of Behavioral Medicine, 23,* 229-246.

McAuley, E. (1992). Understanding exercise behavior: A self-efficacy perspective. In G.C. Roberts (Ed.), *Motivation in sport and exercise* (pp. 107-128). Champaign, IL: Human Kinetics.

McAuley, E., & Blissmer, B. (2000). Social cognitive determinants and consequences of physical activity. *Exercise and Sports Science Reviews, 28*(2), 85-88.

McAuley, E., Blissmer, B., Marquez, D. X., Jerome, G. J., Kramer, A. F., & Katula, J. (2000). Social relations, physical activity, and well-being in older adults. *Preventative Medicine, 31,* 608-617.

McAuley, E. Courneya, K. S., Rudolph, D. L., & Lox, C. L. (1994). Enhancing exercise adherence in middle-aged males and females. *Preventive Medicine, 23,* 498-506.

McAuley, E., Katula, J. A., Blissmer, B., & Duncan, T. E. (1999). Exercise environment, self-efficacy, and affective responses to acute exercise in older adults. *Psychology and Health: An International Journal, 15,* 1-15.

McAuley, E., Katula, J., Mihalko, S. L., Blissmer, B., Duncan, T. E., Pena, M., & Dunn, E. (1999). Mode of physical activity and self-efficacy in older adults: A latent growth curve analysis. *Journals of Gerontology: Psychological Sciences, 54B,* P238-P292.

McAuley, E., Talbot, H. M., & Martinez, S. (1999). Manipulating self-efficacy in the exercise environment in women: Influences on affective responses. *Health Psychology, 18*(3), 288-294.

McKay, G. H., King, D., Eakin, E. G., Seeley, J. R., & Glasgow, R. E. (2001). The diabetes network internet-based physical activity intervention: A randomized pilot study. *Diabetes Care, 24*(8), 1328-1334.

Mendes de Leon, C. F., Glass, T. A., Beckett, L. A., Seeman, T. E., Evans, D. A., & Berkam, L. F. (1999). Social networks and disability transitions across eight intervals of yearly data in the New Haven EPESE. *Journal of Gerontology, 54B*(3), S162-S172.

Mockenhaupt, R. (2001). National blueprint for increasing physical activity among adults age 50 and older: Creating a strategic framework and enhancing organizational capacity for change. *Journal of Aging & Physical Activity, 9*(S), S1-S28.

Moos, R. H. (1979). Social-ecological perspectives on health. In G. C. Stone, F. Cohen, & N. E. Adler (Eds.), *Health Psychology: A Handbook* (pp. 523-548). San Francisco: Josey-Bass.

Moreno, C., Alvarado, M., Balcazar, H., Lane, C., Newman, E., Ortiz, G., & Forrest, M. (1997). Heart disease education and prevention program targeting immigrant Latinos: Using focus group responses to develop effective interventions. *Journal of Community Health, 22*(6), 435-450.

Myers, R. S., & Roth, D. L. (1997). Perceived benefits of and barriers to exercise and stage of exercise adoption in young adults. *Health Psychology, 16*(3), 277-283.

Nader, P. R., Baranowski, T., Vanderpool, N. A., Dunn, K., Dworkin, R., & Ray, L. (1983). The family health project: Cardiovascular risk reduction education for children and parents. *Journal of Developmental and Behavioral Pediatrics, 4*(1), 3-10.

Nader, P. R., Sallis, J. F., Patterson, T. L., Abramson, I. S., Rupp, J. W., Senn, K. L., Atkins, C. J., Roppe, B. E., Morris, J. A., Wallace, J. P., & et al. (1989). A family approach to cardiovascular risk reduction: Results from the San Diego Family Health Project. *Health Education Quarterly, 16*(2), 229-244.

Nader, P. R., Sallis, J. F., Rupp, J., Atkins, C., Patterson, T., & Abramson, I. (1986). San Diego family health project: Reaching families through the schools. *Journal of School Health, 56*(6), 227-231.

National Center for Health Statistics. (1999). *Healthy People 2000 Review,* 1998-1999. Hyattsville, MD: Public Health Service.

Nigg, C. R., & Courneya, K. S. (1998). Transtheoretical model: Examining adolescent exercise behavior. *Journal of Adolescent Health, 22,* 214-224.

Oman, R. F., & King, A. C. (1998). Predicting the adoption and maintenance of exercise participation using self-efficacy and previous exercise participation rates. *American Journal of Health Promotion, 12,* 154-161.

Osler, M., & Jespersen, N. B. (1993). The effect of a community-based cardiovascular disease prevention project in a Danish municipality. *Danish Medical Bulletin, 40,* 485-489.

Owen, N., Lee, C., Naccarella, L., & Haag, K. (1987). Exercise by mail: A mediated behavior-change program for aerobic exercise. *Journal of Sport Psychology, 9,* 346-357.

Pasick, R. J., D'Onofrio, C. N., & Otero-Sabogal, R. (1996). Similarities and differences across cultures: Questions to inform a third generation for health promotion research. *Health Education Quarterly, 23,* s142-s161.

Pate, R.R., Pratt, M.P., Blair, S.N., Haskell, W.L., Macera, C.A., Bouchard, C., Buchner, D., Ettinger, W., Heath, G. W., King, A.C., Kriska, A., Leon, A.S., Marcus, B.H., Morris, J., Paffenbarger, R.S., Patrick, K., Pollock, M.L., Rippe, J.M., Sallis, J., & Wilmore, J.H. (1995). Physical activity and public health: A recommendation from the Centers for Disease Control and Prevention and the American College of Sports Medicine. *Journal of the American Medical Association, 273,* 402-207.

Patrick, K., Sallis, J. F., Prochaska, J. J., Lydston, D. D., Calfas, K. J., Zabinski, M. F., Wilfley, D. E., Saelens, B. E., & Brown, D. R. (2001). A multicomponent program for nutrition and physical activity change in primary care: PACE+ for adolescents. *Archives of Pediatric Adolescent Medicine, 155,* 940-946.

Patterson, I., & Chang, M. L. (1999). Participation in physical activities by older Australians: a review of the social psychological benefits and constraints. *Australian Journal on Ageing, 18*(4), 179-185.

Pender, N. J., Sallis, J. F., Long, B. J., & Calfas, K. J. (1994). Health-care provider counseling to promote physical activity. In R. K. Dishman (Ed.), *Advances in Exercise Adherence* (pp. 213-235). Champaign, IL: Human Kinetics.

Peterson, T. R., & Aldana, S. G. (1999). Improving exercise behavior: An application of the stages of change model in a worksite setting. *American Journal of Health Promotion, 13*(4), 229-232.

Pinto, B. M., Goldstein, M. G., DePue, J. D., & Milano, F. B. (1998). Acceptability and feasibility of physician-based activity counseling: The PAL project. *American Journal of Preventive Medicine, 15,* 95-102.

Pinto, B. M., Goldstein, M. G., & Marcus, B. H. (1998). Activity counseling by primary care physicians. *Preventive Medicine, 27,* 506-513.

Pinto, B. M., Lynn, H., Marcus, B. H., DePue, J., & Goldstein, M. G. (2001). Physician-based activity counseling: Intervention effects on mediators of motivational readiness for physical activity. *Annals of Behavioral Medicine, 23,* 2-10.

Potts, M. K., Hurwicz, M., Goldstein, M. S., & Berkanovic, E. (1992). Social support, health-promotive beliefs, and preventative health behaviors among the elderly. *Journal of Applied Gerontology, 11*(4), 425-440.

Potvin, L., Gauvin, L., & Nguyen, N. M. (1997). Prevalence of stages of change for physical activity in rural, suburban and inner-city communities. *Journal of Community Health, 22*(1), 1-13.

Prochaska, J. O., & DiClemente, C. C. (1983). Stages and processes of self-change of smoking. *Journal of Consulting and Clinical Psychology, 51,* 390-395.

Prochaska, J. O., DiClemente, C. C., & Norcross, J. C. (1992). In search of how people change: Applications to addictive behaviors. *American Psychologist, 47*(9), 1102-1114.

Prochaska, J. O., Velicer, W. F., DiClemente, C. C., & Fava, J. (1988). Measuring processes of change: Applications to the cessation of smoking. *Journal of Consulting & Clinical Psychology, 56*(4), 520-528.

Reeves, M. J., Rafferty, A., McGee, H., & Miller, C. (2001). Prevalence of healthy lifestyle characteristics: Michigan, 1998 and 2000. *Morbidity and Mortality Weekly Report, 50,* 758-761.

Richards Reed, G., Velicer, W. F., Prochaska, J. O., Rossi, J. S., & Marcus, B. H. (1997). What makes a good staging algorithm: Examples from regular exercise. *American Journal of Health Promotion, 12*(1), 57-66.

Ronda, G., Van Assema, P., & Brug, J. (2001). Stages of change, psychological factors and awareness of physical activity levels in the Netherlands. *Health Promotion International, 16*(4), 305-314.

Sallis, J. F. (2001). Progress in behavioral research on physical activity. Annals of Behavioral Medicine, 23, 77-78.

Sallis, J. F., Bauman, A., & Pratt, M. (1998). Environmental and policy interventions to promote physical activity. *American Journal of Preventive Medicine, 15,* 379-397.

Sallis, J. F., Haskell, W. L., Fortman, K. M., Vranizan, K. B., Taylor, C. B., & Solomon, D. S. (1986). Predictors of adoption and maintenance of physical activity in a community sample. *Preventive Medicine, 15,* 331-341.

Shephard, R. J. (1996). Worksite fitness and exercise programs: A review of methodology and health impact. *American Journal of Health Promotion, 10,* 436-452.

Simmons, D, Fleming, C., Voyle, J, Fou, F., Feo, S., & Gatland, B. (1998). A pilot urban church-based programme to reduce risk factors for diabetes among Western Samoans in New Zealand. *Diabetes Medicine, 15,* 136-142.

Spanier, P. A., & Allison, K. R. (2001). General social support and physical activity: An analysis of the Ontario health survey. *Canadian Journal of Public Health, Revue Canadienne de Sante Publique. 92*(3), 210-213.

Stahl, T., Rutten, A., Nutbeam, D., Bauman, A., Kannas, L., Abel, T., Luschen, G., Rodriquez, D. J. A., Vinck, J., & Zee, J. v. d. (2001). The importance of the social environment for physically active lifestyle-Results from an international study. *Social Science and Medicine, 52,* 1-10.

Steptoe, A., & Wardle, J. (2001). Health behaviour, risk awareness and emotional well-being in students from Eastern Europe and Western Europe. *Social Science & Medicine, 53*(12), 1621-1630.

Stone, E. J., McKenzie, T. L., Welk, G. J., & Booth, M. L. (1998). Effects of physical activity interventions in youth: Review and synthesis. *American Journal of Preventive Medicine, 15,* 298-315.

Szabo, A., Frenkl, R., & Caputo, A. (1996). Deprivation feelings, anxiety, and commitment in various forms of physical activity—a cross-sectional study on the Internet. *Psychologia, 39*(4), 223-230.

Tate, D. F., Wing, R. R., & Winett, R. A. (2001). Using Internet technology to deliver a behavioral weight loss program. *Journal of the American Medical Association, 285*(9), 1172-1177.

Taylor, W. C., Baranowski, T., & Young, D. R. (1998). Physical activity interventions in low-income, ethnic minority, and populations with disability. *American Journal of Preventive Medicine, 15*(4), 334-343.

Titze, S., Matin, B. W., Seiler, R., & Marti, B. (2001). A worksite intervention module encouraging the use of stairs: results and evaluation issues. *Soz Praventivemed, 46,* 13-19.

Turner, E. E., Rejeski, W. J., & Brawley, L. R. (1997). Psychological benefits of physical activity are influenced by the social environment. *Journal of Sport and Exercise Psychology, 19,* 119-130.

U. S. Census Bureau. (2001). *The Hispanic Population.* Retrieved November 23, 2004, from http://www.census.gov/prod/2001pubs/c2kbr01-3.pdf

U. S. Census Bureau. (2001). *Home Computers and Internet use in the United States*: August 2000: U.S. Department of Commerce, Economics and Statistics Administration.

U.S. Department of Health and Human Services (1996). *Physical Activity and Health: A Report of the Surgeon General. Atlanta,* GA: U.S. Department of Health and Human Services, Centers for Disease Control and Prevention, National Center for Chronic Disease Prevention and Health Promotion.

U. S. Department of Health and Human Services (2000). *Healthy people 2010* (2nd Ed.). Washinton, DC: US Government Printing Office.

Vuori, I. M., Oja, P., & Paronen, O. (1994). Physically active commuting to work: Testing its potential for exercise promotion. *Medicine and Science in Sports and Exercise, 26,* 844-850.

Wallace, J. P., Raglin, J. S., & Jastremski, C. A. (1995). Twelve month adherence of adults who joined a fitness program with a spouse vs. without a spouse. *Journal of Sports Medicine and Physical Fitness, 35,* 206-213.

Walter, H. J. (1989). Primary prevention of chronic disease among children: The school-based "Know Your Body" intervention trials. *Health Education Quarterly, 16,* 201-214.

Weinstein, N. D., Rothman, A. J., & Sutton, S. R. (1998). Stage theories of health behavior: Conceptual and methodological issues. *Health Psychology, 17*(3), 290-299.

Whitehorse, L. E., Manzano, R., Baezconde-Garbanati, L. A., & Hahn, G. (1999). Culturally tailoring a physical activity program for Hispanic women: Recruitment successes of La Vida Buena's Salsa Aerobics. *Journal of Health Education, 30*(2), s18-s24.

Wilcox, S., Castro, C., King, A. C., Housemann, R., & Brownson, R. C. (2000). Determinants of leisure time physical activity in rural compared with urban older and ethnically diverse women in the United States. *Journal of Epidemiology & Community Health, 54*(9), 667-672.

Wilcox, S., King, A. C., Castro, C., & Bortz, W. (2000). Do changes in physical activity lead to dietary changes in middle and old age? *American Journal of Preventive Medicine, 18,* 276-283.

Young, D. R., Haskell, W. L., Taylor, C. B., & Fortmann, S. P. (1996). Effect of community health education on physical activity knowledge, attitudes, and behavior. *American Journal of Epidemiology, 144,* 264-274.

Courtesy of iStockphoto Inc.

5.5

Sport and the Development of Character

BRENDA LIGHT BREDEMEIER AND DAVID LIGHT SHIELDS

Introduction

Over the past few decades, sport participation and sociomoral development, functioning, and education have become more central to the field of sport psychology. Applied researchers have made significant theoretic and empirical advances, and practitioners have used these findings, together with their personal intuitions and experience, to promote the sociomoral development of participants in sports and physical education programs. Yet despite this theory-based research and practice, our understanding and programs remain limited by the lack of a shared and coherent understanding of moral agency that is defensible both psychologically and philosophically.

What integrates and coordinates the specific attitudes, discreet skills, and isolated behaviors we try to influence and assess? In the end, sport psychologists are probably more interested in educating and supporting the whole person, not merely developing particular competencies or encouraging a precise "right action." We suggest that the construct of character, the embodiment of moral agency, is the key to animating various sociomoral components of thought and action. Character, in brief, is that dimen-

sion of human agency that enables the individual to know, desire, and do that which is good or right.

In this chapter, we seek to accomplish two interrelated goals. First, we highlight the theoretical, empirical, and programmatic roots of sociomoral work in sport psychology. Second, we propose a conceptual framework that can lead to new avenues of applied research, coaching and consulting strategies, and educational programs. This new approach focuses on the construct of character as a way to integrate and extend previous work.

The chapter begins with a brief description of the two theoretical approaches, social learning and constructivist, that have most influenced sociomoral praxis in sport psychology. The next major section of the chapter features brief reviews of five seminal studies designed to assess sociomoral aspects of physical education and sports programs, and five contemporary models of sociomoral programs. Each of these programs is aimed at altering one or more discrete behaviors, attitudes, or competencies, but none offers a way to conceptualize and integrate the goals of sociomoral education in the physical education or sport realms. We conclude this section with a discussion centered on evolving sociomoral praxis in sport psychology. The third major section of the chapter introduces the construct of character as one way to provide a comprehensive model for sociomoral development, functioning, and education. It elaborates on character development, the role of will and desire, and the dynamics of moral motivation. The chapter concludes with an integrative discussion of the *communities of character* approach to developing moral character and athletic excellence.

Theoretical Foundations

In this opening section, we briefly review the two theoretical orientations that informed most of the early work on moral development, functioning, and education in the sport psychology literature. Necessarily, the review is selective and brief; those interested can consult more detailed reviews of the literature elsewhere (Shields & Bredemeier, 1995, 2001; Shields, Bredemeier & Power, 2002; Weiss & Smith, 2002).

The Social Learning Approach
Early social learning theorists adopted from behaviorism the premise that psychology is designed to describe and predict observable and measurable behavior, and that explanations for findings must be based on observable environmental influences. Thus, social learning theorists sought to identify learning principles that define how behavior is acquired, maintained, modified, or extinguished through contingencies operating in the social environment. They focused on modeling and reinforcement as two primary stimulants to learning.

More recently, social learning theorists have incorporated an emphasis on cognition as a mediator of behavior. Albert Bandura, for example, has proposed a "social cognitive theory" of morality (Bandura, 1986, 1991). According to this approach, moral cognitions, affective self-regulations, moral behavior, and environmental factors all operate as interacting determinants that influence each other. The moral judgments that help determine one's behavior involve two separate processes. First, a person selects the relevant moral information from a multitude of situational cues, and then prioritizes the moral values at stake by applying learned moral rules. With increasing experience, moral reasoning evolves from knowing and being able to apply simple rules to highly complex ones. For example, a young football player might first learn the rule "don't cheat," and later learn that certain types of holding are typically judged legitimate, even if they are technically rule-violating.

The relationship between moral cognition and moral action is mediated, according to Bandura, by two affective processes that operate in consort (Bandura, 1986; 1991; 2001). The first is *self-regulatory mechanisms;* these mechanisms, in combination with social sanctions, inhibit transgressive behavior and promote prosocial behavior. Self-regulatory mechanisms essentially translate the concepts of rewards and punishments into internal affective mechanisms; thus athletes' behavior is heavily influenced by how they believe they will feel after engaging in the behavior that they are contemplating. For example, a high school shot-putter might think about using an underweight shot in a situation where there will not be a weigh-in. In the face of this temptation, however, she may experience anticipatory guilt, leading her to use the proper weight shot. In this case, anticipatory guilt acts as a negative reinforcement. Similarly, anticipatory pride can act as a positive inducement for behavior.

The effective use of self-regulatory mechanisms requires not only well established affective self-reactions, but belief in one's capabilities to achieve personal control. *Perceived efficacy* in self-regulation is the second major construct regulating the relationship between moral cognition and moral action. According to Bandura, the stronger one's perceived self-regulatory efficacy, the more he will persevere in efforts to maintain moral conduct. Thus, the more our shot-putter believes she can control her temptation, the more likely she will be to do so.

On moral motivation, Bandura writes, "After people adopt a standard of morality, their negative self-sanctions for actions that violate their personal standards, and their positive self-sanctions for conduct faithful to their moral standards serve as the regulatory influences" (2001, p. 9). Ultimately, Bandura holds that moral action is self-interested; one's conviction that a particular act or principle is right, so important in constructivist theory, is not a significant motivator for social learning theorists.

Bandura's valuable theory is comprehensive,

and many of its key constructs have received empirical support. In many respects, it has moved social learning theory much closer to the constructivist approach that we will describe next. Most importantly, it has come to embrace a more creative, dynamic, and agentic view of the person (Bandura, 2001).

The Constructivist Approach

During the formative period of moral psychology, the primary alternative to the social learning perspective was the constructivist viewpoint articulated initially by Piaget (1932). Piaget's approach was largely ignored in American psychology until Lawrence Kohlberg (1981, 1984) began his pioneering work on moral development, work that dominated moral psychology research in the latter part of the twentieth century.

The unifying dimension of constructivist theory is an epistemology which focuses on human beings' abilities and tendencies to construct meaning, to organize and structure information. Constructivists theorize that we assimilate our environmental experiences to pre-existing patterns of interpretation, and that we accommodate existing cognitive schema to novel experiences. Learning takes place when our assimilatory tendency is disrupted by events or cues that don't conform to our expectations. Over time, such disruptive experiences, usually referred to as "cognitive conflict" or "cognitive dissonance," cause the learner to dissolve old cognitive meaning structures and reconstruct more adequate ones. Because learning takes place through an alternating process of disruption and consolidation of meaning structures, constructivists describe learning as more than a gradual accumulation of cultural information and rules. While learning does have a quantitative, additive dimension, it also takes place through qualitative transformations.

If the person-as-meaning-maker represents one pole of the interaction that leads to learning and development, the environment—in all its dimensions —represents the other. The environment, however, is not a buzzing blur of stimuli and cues; it has patterns and regularities that correspond to different domains of knowledge or information. Observing gravity's influence on a basketball can lead one to conclusions about the physical properties of things; playing pick-up ball and league play can reveal information about how games are organized and regulated; experiencing unfair play and broken promises can enable one to draw conclusions about the nature and importance of morality, and so on.

The environment is organized, but also complex. Sometimes a person encounters unexpected occurrences. The interaction between the person's innate tendency to assimilate experience into coherent meaning patterns, and an environment that provides disruptive information leads to development through a series of stages or phases. Each new stage represents something of a plateau, a consolidated approach to interpreting information that remains relatively stable until it, in turn, is eventually disrupted by information that cannot be readily assimilated. The precise characteristics of these stages, phases, or levels, their degree of invariance and university, and their relations to other aspects of mental functioning are conceptualized differently in different renderings of constructivist theory.

Because constructivists are concerned with the meaning that people attach to experience, they highlight learning dynamics that are likely to engage processes of meaning construction. In particular, the process of constructing shared meanings with others is likely to stimulate development. For example, peer dialogue is viewed as critically important because it is through dialogue that people are confronted with interpretations of experience that don't match their own. Other important learning dynamics emphasize problem-solving, personal reflection, autonomous judgment, cooperative learning, simulation and role playing, and other group processes.

Within the domain of moral development, Kohlberg's (1981, 1984) landmark work has framed most of the discussion. Kohlberg challenged social learning theorists, arguing that moral behavior cannot be reduced to socially conforming behavior. For Kohlberg, morality is fundamentally about *reasons* why actions are appropriate or inappropriate. According to Kohlberg's theory, the heart of moral growth takes place through a sequence of moral stages, with each succeeding stage reflecting a more adequate understanding of justice. In Kohlberg's early work, he and his colleagues demonstrated that moral growth could be stimulated through group discussions of hypothetical moral dilemmas (e.g., Blatt & Kohlberg, 1975). In his later work, he focused more on transforming the culture of schools so that morality could be learned through participation in "just communities" (e.g., Power, Higgins & Kohlberg, 1989). This approach relied on the use of a cooperative, democratic process to develop shared moral norms.

Empirical Foundations

Theoretically-based, empirically tested strategies and programs designed to foster sociomoral development and functioning are becoming more visible in contemporary sport psychology. We can trace some of the roots of these innovative efforts back to seminal studies conducted in the 1980s.

Five Seminal Studies

Empirical studies of sociomoral issues in physical education and sport contexts began appearing in the sport psychology literature in the 1980s. We briefly review five of these innovative studies. Each reports on the implementation and assessment of various strategies suggested by social learning and constructivist theorists. Together, these studies and others paved the way for a burst of interest in sociomoral intervention in sport and physical education contexts.

Kleiber and Roberts (1981) used an experimental design to examine whether sport experiences caused participants to be more or less altruistic. In a field experiment inspired by social learning theory, 54 fourth and fifth grade boys and girls were given a test of generosity before and after participating in a two-week sport competition, the "Kick-Soccer World-Series." At the time of the pretest, it was found that those children with the most sports experience were significantly less altruistic. After controlling for the initial differences in scores, Kleiber and Roberts found mixed results following the intervention. If all "trials" of the generosity test were examined, the kick-ball experience had no reliable impact on the giving pattern of participants. However, if only the last trial was counted (arguably the most significant), then the boys (but not the girls) displayed a significant decrease in generosity. For boys, at least, the study suggested a weak causal relationship between sport participation and decreased altruism.

Bredemeier, Weiss, Shields and Shewchuk (1986) compared the effects of coaching strategies based on constructivist and social learning theories in a summer sports camp. The camp participants (ages 5-7) were randomly placed into one of three groups. Coaches in the constructivist group employed pedagogical strategies that relied on peer dialogue and interpersonal negotiation to promote the young participants' moral development. Coaches in the social learning group implemented strategies emphasizing modeling and reinforcement. Control group coaches simply encouraged campers to follow safety precautions and conform to game rules. For six weeks, the three different groups employed a curriculum that featured a different moral theme each week. All participants were pre- and post-tested on moral reasoning maturity. Within-group analyses showed that both experimental groups gained in moral reasoning, but the control group did not. Between group analyses only approached significance ($p < .07$), with the constructivist group's moral reasoning only slightly more mature than that of the social learning group.

Drawing from constructivist theory, Romance, Weiss, and Bockoven (1986) conducted a study with older children (ages 10-11) in a public school physical education setting. Sixty-four children were equally divided into two classes; one served as a control group and one an experimental group. The latter group featured constructivist strategies designed to promote moral reasoning. For example, in one exercise, balls were placed out, but there were not enough balls for everyone to engage in the activity. Consequently, the children needed to negotiate over how to use the limited resources. The two classes were equivalent on pretest measures. After the eight-week session, however, the experimental group's moral reasoning improved significantly while the control group's did not. Moreover, the experimental group's moral reasoning was significantly more mature at posttest than the control group's reasoning. Finally, there were no differences in physical skill development between the two classes.

Wandzilak, Carroll, and Ansorge (1988) also used experimental and control groups in a field experiment designed to determine the effectiveness of an intervention program. In this study, however, the researchers combined both constructivist and social learning strategies into a values program for 20 male junior high basketball players in the experimental group. Moral thought (moral reasoning and perceptions of sportsmanship) and prosocial behavior measures were administered during the first and last weeks of the boys' nine-week season, and three boys from each group were systematically observed through the entire season. Statistical analyses revealed no significant between-group differences, yet within-group gains were significant for the experimental group on all variables; there were no significant within-group gains for the control group. Also, observations of the three boys from the experimental group suggested an emerging sportsmanlike behavioral pattern.

Finally, DeBusk and Hellison (1989), using a case study methodology with 10 at risk fourth-grade boys, also employed a hybrid of social learning and constructivist strategies. In the context of a physical education class, they used direct instruction, student sharing, reflection, modeling, praise, dialogue, and negotiation strategies to improve student cognitions, attitudes, and behavior. Their qualitative data suggested that the strategies were successful.

Five Contemporary Models

These five seminal studies, combined with a growing interest in the whole sociomoral domain, gave rise to a number of innovation programs. It is beyond the scope of this chapter to identify the multitude of local and national programs, many of them outstanding, which have been designed to promote sociomoral development and functioning in physical education and sports contexts. Nor will we discuss programs, such as those focused on promoting "life-skills," that only tangentially relate to sociomoral development. Rather, we highlight five programs that have undergone at least preliminary empirical evaluation and that have been published in refereed sport psychology or pedagogy journals.

Responsibility Model

Over the past two decades, Don Hellison has refined a model for developing self- and social-responsibility through physical education. First proposed in 1978 (Hellison, 1978), the model has benefited from continual refinement in response to extensive use in the field (Hellison, 1985, 1986, 1988, 1995; Hellison et al., 1996; Hellison & Georgiadis, 1992; Martinek & Hellison, 1997; see also Cutforth, 1997; Georgiadis, 1990), particularly with marginalized, inner-city populations.

At the core of the model is a set of heuristic levels through which program participants can move as they progress toward full responsibility for themselves and other participants in the program. After Level 0—Irresponsibility, each level reflects personal/social goals toward which students can progressively work (Level 1: Self-control, Level 2: Involvement, Level 3: Self-direction, Level 4: Caring). In addition to outlining these levels, Hellison has identified sub-levels and has recommended specific teaching strategies that can be used across levels. These strategies are drawn from various theories, and include such student experiences as making choices, solving problems, and offering feedback.

Hellison's personal and social responsibility model has received unparalleled praise from curriculum and pedagogy experts (e.g., Bain, 1988; Jewett & Bain, 1985; Siedentop, Mand, & Taggart, 1986; Winnick, 1990) as one of the best illustrations of a well-conceived and implemented program; it has also received significant empirical support (Hellison & Walsh, 2002). Future researchers might seek to investigate how the model's promotion of responsibility relates to other sociomoral processes and outcomes.

Fair Play for Kids

The Fair Play for Kids program originated when the Canadian Commission for Fair Play joined with Sport Canada to develop curricular materials for children in grades 4 through 6 (Gibbons et al., 1995). The program was launched in 1990, and was designed to be implemented across the entire education curriculum, though some used it solely in physical education classes. The curriculum featured five key ideals: (1) respect for rules; (2) respect for officials; (3) respect for opponents, (4) equal participation; and (5) self-control.

The pedagogical strategies were rooted theoretically in both constructivist and social learning approaches. For example, teachers were given materials to stimulate moral discussion; they were encouraged to use simulations and role plays, and were encouraged to facilitate value-based discussions. These constructivist strategies were complemented by rewards for "fair players" and visits from high profile athletes who could serve as role models. In two separate studies, Gibbons and her colleagues sought to test the effectiveness of the Fair Play program. Three groups were compared in the first study (Gibbons et al., 1995): (a) fair play across the curriculum; (b) fair play in physical education only; and (c) a control group that did not use the fair play curriculum. During the seven-month intervention, the fair play exercises were implemented weekly. Researchers found that both experimental groups improved significantly on a measure of moral functioning, while the control group did not. Significantly, there were no discernable differences between the two experimental groups.

For the second study, Gibbons and Ebbeck (1997) created a control group and two groups that employed the Fair Play program only in physical education classes: one group that utilized constructivist components of the program, and a second that utilized social learning components. Data was collected before the intervention, midway through the intervention, and at the end of the intervention. Analyses revealed that differences between the experimental groups and the control group were already apparent by mid-intervention, with both experimental groups demonstrating significant gains. Results also suggested that the constructivist strategies were more efficacious than the social learning strategies in promoting elevated moral functioning. Future research may help determine whether an intervention employing strategies drawn from both constructivist and social learning theories (like that in Gibbon's first study) is more efficacious than an intervention featuring single theory strategies (found in Gibbon's second study).

Sociomoral Education Program

Based on a 12-component model of moral action (Shields & Bredemeier, 1995), Miller, Bredemeier, and Shields (1997) implemented this sociomoral education program in a physical education class for underserved fourth and fifth graders. The program had four goals: promoting empathy, moral reasoning maturity, task motivation, and self-responsibility among the students. Moral education strategies involved providing opportunities for cooperative learning, building moral community, creating a mastery motivational climate, and increasing students' personal and social responsibilities. Interviews and observations revealed that the program was effec-

tive in promoting students' sociomoral development in each of the four targeted areas. More systematic qualitative and quantitative research with a control group design would offer stronger evidence of the efficacy of this program.

Sociomoral Curricular Model

Gloria Solomon's (Solomon, 1997a, 1997b, 1999) sociomoral curricular model for elementary physical education contexts is based on constructivist theory. It features communication skills, cooperation, and sharing; lesson plans are designed to directly teach social values and skills. She demonstrated impressive results by implementing a version of the curriculum in a 13-week program focused on trusting, helping, problem-solving, and body awareness. A pre- and posttest design with experimental and control groups revealed the program's efficacy in stimulating advances in moral reasoning development. Though this preliminary research looks promising, further modification and assessment of the model is crucial if it is to become more widely used.

Sports for Peace Program

Much like Hellison's responsibility model, the Sports for Peace program was designed primarily for urban students faced with the challenges of poverty and limited physical and social resources. Designed and evaluated by Catherine Ennis (1999), the program focuses on the development of responsibility, conflict-resolution skills, and a supportive community. Implemented by 12 teachers in six urban schools, the program combined comprehensive teacher training with maximum curricular flexibility, allowing teachers to draw from the Sports for Peace exercises as they saw fit. The program was implemented in a nine-week unit on basketball. The well-designed qualitative investigation of the program demonstrated that, despite some initial resistance from the more athletically skilled youth, the program was generally quite successful. As with any omnibus program, however, it is difficult to know which program elements are responsible for what specific outcomes.

Evolving Research and Practice

The cumulative impression left by the various intervention efforts reviewed here is that physical education and sport programs, when deliberately designed to do so, can be used to improve the moral functioning of participants. The Kleiber and Roberts (1981) study, however, sounds a cautionary note. It suggests that without an explicit effort to promote positive change, sports may actually foster undesirable outcomes. This caution is reinforced by several studies that have found lower levels of moral reasoning to be associated with participation in some sports (Beller & Stoll, 1995; Bredemeier & Shields, 1984, 1986; Hall, 1986; Priest, Krause, and Beach, 1999; Stevenson, 1998).

Perhaps what is most important to emphasize is that this is a relatively new domain of research and much work remains to be done. Even when interventions are successful, it is often unclear which component of the program, or which combination of components, is responsible for the gains. Methodologically, most studies to date have not examined the fidelity of program implementation, and so outcomes cannot be tethered to specific program elements. Moreover, there are significant problems with assessment tools (Bredemeier & Shields, 1998) that will need to be addressed before we can reach necessary levels of confidence in assessment.

Future researchers and practitioners can address a number of questions that stem from the pioneering efforts described above. One set of questions pertain to the degree of behavioral specificity. If a program succeeds in altering an athlete's tendency toward aggression, for example, is there any "spill over" into other morally-relevant behaviors, such as cheating? If so, under what conditions? Similar questions can be asked about the ability to generalize concerning changes that may be observed in the sport realm. Do positive changes in sport attitudes and behaviors transfer to life outside of sports? Does involvement in team decision-making, for example, lead to civic activity in the community outside sports? Might the transfer of values and behaviors be mediated by such variables as an athlete's sense of responsibility or assignment of importance to a particular value or behavior? What role is played by one's sense of self or valuing of sports?

Another set of questions pertains to the nature and role of various relationships operative in the sport setting. How do these relationships impact on, or interact with, different intervention strategies? How, for example, does the quality of the coach-player relationship mediate sociomoral outcomes? What relational competencies are needed to foster the type of relationships that will facilitate such behaviors as team loyalty or fair play? Weiss and Smith (2002) highlight the need to test a theory of how peers (friends and associates) influence one another's moral functioning.

The relationship between various aspects of moral functioning and achievement motivation is another area that needs to be explored more fully in applied settings. There is significant evidence to suggest a correlation between less than optimal moral functioning and high ego orientation and/or low task motivation (Duda, Olson, & Templin, 1991; Dunn & Dunn, 1999; Kavussanu & Roberts, 2001; Lemyre, Roberts, & Ommundsen, 2002; Stephens, 2000; Stephens & Bredemeier, 1996). Unfortunately, our professional literature does not yet reveal causal relationships between these variables, nor does it report on the efficacy of interventions based on moral-motivational links. This area of research promises a fruitful harvest with significant practical implications.

A related area of promising research involves determining correlational and causal relations between a team's culture and the sociomoral development, functioning, and behavior of its members. Miller, Roberts, and Ommundsen (2003) conducted one of the few studies in this new area of inquiry. They found that when soccer coaches emphasized ego goals over task goals, their players were more likely to have negative sportspersonship attitudes. Others have found that a coach's emphasis on performance criteria for success is associated with athletes' lower moral functioning (Ommundsen et al., 2003) and a team atmosphere that sanctions aggression and cheating (Kavussanu & Ntoumanis, 2003).

Team moral norms are a second aspect of team culture that may be as important as motivational climate in helping sport psychology researchers and practitioners understand the team culture-sociomoral functioning relationships (Guivernau & Duda, 2002; Kavussanu, Roberts, & Ntoumanis, 2002; Miller & Roberts, 2004; Shields et al., 1995; Smith, 2003; Stephens, 2000, 2001; Stephens & Bredemeier, 1996; Stephens, Bredemeier, & Shields, 1997; Stephens & Kavanagh, 2003; Stornes, 2001; Stuart & Ebbeck, 1995). Both researchers and practitioners may wish to explore such intriguing questions as: How can team moral culture best be conceptualized and operationalized? How do teams create, modify, and enforce moral norms? Can moral norms be influenced by changing the motivational climate? The answers to these questions have great theoretical import and practical significance.

As we move toward developing new interventions, we need to remember the old adage that there is nothing more practical than a good theory. In the moral domain, Jim Rest (1984) moved the field a major step forward when he proposed his four-component model of moral action. The model divided morally-relevant psychological constructs and research into theoretically relevant clusters, providing a way of seeing how diverse psychological theories and constructs might fit within a single, integrated model of moral action. Rest's model, and the expanded 12-component model featuring social and ego-processing influences on Rest's four original components (Shields & Bredemeier, 1995), also opened new, systematic ways for sport psychology researchers and practitioners to ask questions and conceive intervention strategies.

According to Rest's model, moral action involves four distinguishable sets of processes: interpretation, judgment, choice, and implementation. Let's consider how a sport psychology consultant might find the model helpful. Imagine that a basketball coach has requested a consultant's help with her star player, Beth, whose displays of aggression have become more frequent and intense; her last victim spent several weeks in the hospital. This type of aggression falls into the category of moral transgression, so we can assume that Beth experienced a breakdown in one or more of the four processes that underlie moral behavior. Thus, our hypothetical consultant could use Rest's model as a heuristic framework to consider four clusters of psychological processes to better understand and attempt to modify Beth's aggressive behavior.

First, Rest claimed that to act morally, one must identify moral issues in the situation. Our consultant may try to learn whether Beth has sufficient empathy and sensitivity to recognize such moral issues as fairness and intentional harm in the context of her athletic aggression. Did Beth perceive the act of intentionally hurting another during sport competition as behavior with moral implications? In other words, is Beth's aggression a result of not recognizing aggression involving moral issues?

Second, if Beth seems to recognize the moral issues at stake, our consultant may explore Beth's moral reasoning about these issues. Perhaps Beth felt her aggression was justified when her opponents were aggressive, because retaliation in her mind was a fair response. She may have decided, after weighing the contrasting values of fairness through retaliation and protecting her opponents' welfare, that an eye-for-an-eye interpretation of fairness was most important. Alternately, perhaps Beth was aware of the moral issues involved (Process I), judged athletic aggression to be wrong (Process II), and yet acted aggressively because of prioritizing other non-moral values (Process III) or problems implementing her choices (Process IV).

Moral decisions don't occur in a vacuum and moral values must be weighed against other values. Thus, our consultant may explore what other values are important to Beth in situations where she is aggressive. Is she most interested in winning? Does she want the emotional satisfaction of displaying dominance or getting even? Beth had to make a choice between her moral judgment and other competing values like these. Let's say that Beth chose, in the end, not to aggress against her opponents. Why, then, did she end up hurting them?

Rest's fourth process, implementation, focuses on what is necessary to act in a way that is consistent with one's choice. Beth may have wanted to avoid athletic aggression, but failed to do so because of problems in managing temptations and distractions. Our sport psychologist can now attempt to design a strategy for helping Beth successful carry out her intentions. Perhaps she needs training in anger management, for example, because of a problem controlling her irrational anger.

Rest's model provides a valuable means of ordering the various psychological processes tethered to the production of moral action. What the model lacks, however, is a coherent understanding of moral agency. Ultimately, morality belongs to the person, not to a set of processes. While Rest was clear that the four components of the model do not function mechanically, but interactively, he did not provide a theory about what gives coherence and unity to the separate components. One can reasonably ask, what animates the model? What coordinates the separate processes?

This question is critical. To date, most researchers have adopted the strategy of focusing on a specific, discrete aspect of morality or prosocial behavior tied to an underlying competence, an attitude or set of attitudes, or a specific type of behavior, or examining the impact of an intervention on a particular variable or set of variables. Of course, this is a completely valid strategy that can yield important insights. The strategy is limited, however, in that it does not address how the various components of moral functioning are interrelated, nor does it address the thorny issue of moral motivation. These limitations have led us to seek a more comprehensive and integrated approach, because ultimately one wants to do more than merely improve discrete competencies or impact isolated behaviors or particular attitudes. One wants to educate the whole person.

Moral Character

Character is that dimension of human agency that enables us to know, desire, and do what is good or right. It is agentic in the sense that it comes from and gives form to our inner sense of self in its moral or ethical aspects. Character is the agentic core that animates and coordinates the separate sociomoral processes organized in Rest's four component model (Shields, Bredemeier, & Power, 2002). Character incorporates a vision of what is good, right, and worthy, and when we seek to achieve that vision it gives coherence to our various sociomoral processes. Often, the language that gives expression to this vision is the language of virtues.

This section of the chapter is dedicated to the topic of character: of what it is comprised, how it develops, and how it motivates. Our inspiration for the following reflections come most especially from Blasi (1983, 1984, 1985, 1988, 1989, 1990a, 1990b, 1993, 1995, 1999; in press-a, in press-b; Blasi & Glodis, 1995; Blasi & Milton, 1991; Blasi & Oresick, 1986, 1987), but we have also been influenced by Colby and Damon (1992), Damon (1984), and Power (2004).

Character as Desire and Willpower

Character has two fundamental dimensions: moral desire and willpower (cf. Blasi, in press-a). The ontogenetic source of the desire dimension of character is the infant's primitive experiences of impulse and longing. Every infant is unique, and while there is significant overlap in what infants desire, each child has a unique configuration of primitive longings and inner urges. These are the early foundations on which the desire dimension of character is built. Importantly, even prior to the development of language, the child experiences his or her desires as personally owned. Much as the child experiences his or her body as uniquely "mine," so, too, the child experiences the inner landscape of desire as uniquely his or hers. Throughout life, these desires will undergo modifications, elaborations, and transformations, but they will remain a consistent and significant dimension of the self experience.

Character is reflective of what one comes to embrace as fundamentally desirable. To a significant extent, we are what we desire. Our desires "pull" us in certain directions; they provide us with certain goals, values, and life trajectories. Because of our moral desires, we come to embrace certain virtues. When we speak of desire in this context, of course, we are not referring to immediate or superficial desires, such as desiring victory for a favorite team. Rather, we are talking about moral desires, deep convictions about what is ultimately most desirable.

Morality is inherent in human relationships and it is nearly impossible to avoid having moral desires. Still, people vary considerably in terms of how salient morality is to their sense of self. For some people, moral desires are subordinate to other desires, while for others moral desires are preeminent. Also, people choose different virtues to express the ideals of their moral desire. While some people may deeply cherish justice, others may embrace the virtue of compassion. Character is shaped both by the relative salience of moral desire and by its content.

The second dimension of character is willpower. It refers to the ability to exercise control over inner psychological processes so as to sustain commitment to desired goals. Willpower is a collective term referring to a number of discreet, mostly cognitive, psychological processes. Willpower consists of such processes as the ability to delay gratification, to sustain attention, to break down longer term goals into a sequential set of manageable steps; it includes the ability to cognitively reframe obstacles as challenges, and to tolerate ambiguity when necessary. While these various self-control skills are conceptually distinct, they are highly correlated so we refer to them collectively as *willpower* (cf., Blasi, in press-a).

Moral desire is at the heart of character. It defines what one genuinely wants. It responds to what one believes is good, and it sets a trajectory for one's moral commitments. Willpower as self-control enables one to act consistently with one's considered desires. It enables one to manage and control inner impulses, and "say no" to impulses that would deviate from what one believes is right, true, good, or worthy. Moral agency involves the joint operation of these two dimensions of character.

Both moral desire and willpower can be influenced through experience. The unique set of virtues that we eventually come to embrace, giving order and form to our moral desires, evolve through experience in valued communities. Also, we can gain in proficiency at the cognitive skills associated with willpower. Building such proficiencies, in fact, is within the repertoire of most applied sport psychologists, though most do not take advantage of applying these to the moral domain. To better understand how these processes can be influenced, however, we need to probe more deeply into how character develops.

Character Development

Sport psychologists who wish to intervene effectively in the sociomoral domain require both a theory of character, and an understanding of how character is influenced by environmental experiences. As stated above, character has two dimensions. It reflects what one most deeply desires, and the ability to exercise willpower to achieve those desires. We reflect first on the development of moral desire.

As infants and young children, before we have developed the capacity to reflect introspectively, we simply embrace impulses in their immediacy. But as we develop, we gain the capacity to not only have desires, but to have "desires about our desires," or what Frankfurt (1982) calls second-order desires. This is a critical advance in the development of character. For example, a five-year old boy might desire to play for

the Yankees. By high school, the young man may still want to play professional ball, but over the years he may have reflected on the personal and social costs of single-mindedly pursuing a pro career. As a result, he may have decided to subordinate that desire to others. Second-order desires require that we create cognitive distance from our immediate wants and impulses so that they can be examined and evaluated. We can then desire (second-order) which desires (first-order) to pursue or cultivate. Character evolves as we intentionally choose which first-order wants and impulses to extend into action, which ones to nurture, which ones to suppress, and so on. Character entails establishing an inner hierarchy of desires.

Of course, our emerging moral desires evolve not only out of immediate impulses, but also in response to environmental experience and cultural content. Society, in a myriad of ways, offers images of what is desirable. Our culture supplies ordered ways of thinking, feeling, and acting. It provides systematized rules and roles to guide action. It proffers various norms and values embedded into its linguistic and semiotic systems. It holds up ideals and human projects worthy of pursuit. Cultural experiences influence, but do not determine, which virtues we ultimately embrace.

As children, we did not passively internalize the norms or values we were exposed to through culture. Rooted in the immediacy of "me-ness," we resisted some, modified some, and accepted some. Initially, these determinations about what and how to appropriate cultural contents were largely preconscious and reflected primitive impulses, desires, and inchoate longings. But as the capacity for reflective thought developed, these choices became more conscious. Eventually, in adolescence, we developed the capacity to turn inward and exercise discerning judgment over the very impulses and desires that had heretofore served as the criteria that governed opposition and appropriation. Through this process, we formed second-order desires. At this point, we were able to exercise critical judgment in response to social influences, utilizing more objective, interpersonally-valid criteria. As we constructed our sense of identity, various desires were prioritized into a more-or-less coherent self-system.

It is important to emphasize that with development, the appropriation process through which cultural content becomes "owned" becomes increasingly self-reflective and responsive to intersubjective reality and truth. Character becomes increasingly chosen, and chosen for moral and rational reasons. The criteria by which appropriation operates will never become fully conscious and rational, but with healthy development they become increasingly so.

Rather than operate through some more-or-less automatic process, moral socialization works largely through imagination. Imagination mediates the formation of desire, and imagination is influenced both by environmental and internal processes. For example, sports offers affectively compelling images of what "can be" and "should be"; what is truly valuable; what is virtuous. How we recreate these images in our imagination, however, is influenced by personal meaning structures, such as the content and competence of our moral reasoning. Equally important, imagination is both stimulated by and limited by what is actually experienced in the real communities of which we are a part. For sport psychologists, this means that developing athletes' moral reasoning competence is important, but so is enhancing the moral quality of the team environment; it is the latter that may influence athletes' perceptions of what is desirable and attainable in the sport realm.

Willpower also has its origins in infancy. Intentional activity, erupting from inchoate longings, is the foundation for development of willpower. As we mature, our ability to engage in intentional activity expands. With maturation and experience, a host of closely related skills develop, giving us the ability to exercise control over inner processes and direct our lives toward sustained projects. These skills tend to develop gradually and are enhanced with repetition and practice. We develop and exercise willpower without self-awareness. But as we advance cognitively, we become able to turn reflection inward and deliberately cultivate willpower skills. Once again, this ability to turn inward opens a critical new phase of character development.

In later adolescence and early adulthood, the process of self-construction becomes more overt and self-aware. This phase of development simultaneously features a level of unconscious processing of self-conceptions, a conscious effort to establish and confirm identity, and an ability to think critically and introspectively about the kind of person one wants to become. At this stage, genuinely moral motivation becomes possible.

Character and Moral Motivation

A young child's moral motivation is purely external. She or he is motivated to behave in socially-sanctioned ways in order to please others or avoid punishment. The child might also be motivated by primary impulses, such as empathically sharing a ball with a crying sibling. While these latter types of actions are intentional and prosocial, they are not genuinely moral since they are spontaneous and do not arise from an evaluation of the rightness or wrongness of the action. Somewhat later, the child comes to believe that moral prescriptions are necessary and are grounded in objective reality. Moral motivation then stems from an appreciation of their intrinsic worthiness. At this phase, however, the child experiences tension between personal desires and perceived moral demands. Morality may define what is right, but it is still not perceived as intrinsically desirable. Finally, for those who develop a character centered on virtue, morality becomes that which is desired, and failure to live up to moral ideals is experienced as self-betrayal. According to Blasi (in press-a), "The apex of moral motivation, it could be said, is to desire the morally good in the same way one desires what satisfies one's most intimate and deepest needs."

We have offered a view of character that integrates various strands of literature on moral development and moral functioning. Clearly, moral reasoning plays a central role in character because of the way it influences and shapes desire. But in addition to moral reasoning capacity, specific virtues, representing moral ideals, also play a critical role in the formation of character. The various components of Rest's model can be represented as means through which character-as-desire and character-as-willpower operate, with moral desire anchoring the moral meanings of the components.

Obviously, what we have provided here is more an outline than a comprehensive theory. There are a number of key questions that still need to be addressed. One in particular is worth highlighting. The model presumes a relatively unified approach to identity and selfhood. But we also know that people have multiple identities. To the extent that this is true, people may have variant moral perspectives associated with different identities. This could be, for example, one explanation for the divergence that we have found between a person's moral reasoning about sport issues and their reasoning about parallel issues in everyday life (Bredemeier, 1995; Bredemeier & Shields, 1984). Blasi (1985), seeking to avoid the modern tendency in psychology toward fragmentation, suggests that beneath the diversity of roles and identities is a core self. In the moral realm, he suggests that beneath the diversity of moral perspectives that may arise in response to varying contexts is the *good will,* a general tendency toward acting morally (Blasi, 1985). Clearly, the dynamic relationship between the core self and contextualized selves, including the athletic self, still needs to be carefully examined.

Communities of Character

One program that translates our insights on character into a comprehensive plan for promoting both athletic excellence and good character through sports teams is the *communities of character* approach (Bredemeier, 2001). This approach, inspired by the "just community" movement in education (cf. Power, Higgins, and Kohlberg, 1989), was designed to integrate an "athlete-in-community" focus with an emphasis on athletes as moral agents.

The success of the *communities of character* approach depends on participating teams' commitment to the concurrent athletic goals of skill development, personal and team effort, and performance excellence. Without these athletic goals, sport teams lose their unique benefits as a context for character development. Thus, a key strategy in the *communities of character* approach is to help everyone recognize character virtues that can simultaneously support athletic and character goals.

Performance and Relational Sport Virtues
Character virtues may be performance or relational in nature. Performance virtues include self regulatory qualities such as perseverance and self control. Behaviorally, perseverance can be seen when an athlete doesn't give up when behind in a competition, stays with challenging training regimens, keeps self-talk and emotions positive, etc. The virtue of self-control might require refraining from retaliation or other activities that interfere with the spirit of the game.

Performance virtues are not intrinsically good; they become good only when they serve good ends. One can persevere, for example, in trying to master a new throwing technique, in practicing patience with an irritating teammate, or in trying to injure an opponent. In this example, the same performance virtue can enhance athletic prowess (a non-moral goal), and also serve a moral and immoral purpose. Put in the service of bad ends, performance virtues lose their virtuous quality even though they are still part of one's character. Performance virtues are typically associated with good character in sports because they readily support athletic excellence and can support moral ends as well.

Relational virtues are qualities that nurture moral relations among people. The twin moral principles of justice (or fairness) and care are at the heart of these virtues. Relational virtues such as respect and responsibility play an important role in organizing goals and influencing behavior of athletes and their sport teams. These and other relational virtues can be thought of as core ethical virtues that help to express fairness and care in concrete ways.

When relational virtues are to be used to guide efforts at character formation, it is important to remember that they should be directed both outward toward others and inward toward the self. Fairness, for example, entails playing within the rules and spirit of the game, and avoiding the pressure of unrealistic goals or unfair expectations. The virtue of care may be embodied by making sure all teammates are included in team activities, and forgiving one's self for making mistakes.

In the *communities of character* approach, teams help define themselves by selecting those virtues they find especially valuable and helpful from among the plethora of those available. Sport psychologists and coaches can help facilitate this process of choosing a unique team identity. They also can play an important role in sustaining this identity by helping the team practice their core relational and performance virtues. Habituation is an important part of virtue formation, so even though habit should never replace reason, virtues should become habitual behaviors. This is best done in the context of a supportive team community.

Sport Teams as Communities

Building a supportive team community is crucial to the *communities of character* approach (Shields & Bredemeier, 2005). Durkheim used the word "community" to mean a social group through which moral education takes place. In Durkheim's view, it is the group that gives life and energy to the individual. This should not only be taken figuratively, but literally. Durkheim showed in his studies of suicide that when people become detached from meaningful connection to groups, they wither and die (Durkheim, 1897/1951). In *Moral Education* (1925/1973), he invited teachers to transform their classrooms into moral communities that prepare young people for membership in their society and in smaller voluntary organizations. In Durkheim's view, this type of moral education involves a feeling of attachment to the group, a sense of discipline, and a degree of autonomy.

Durkheim's approach may be faulted for being overly authoritarian and insufficiently interactional. The "just community" leaders sought to address these problems by providing a democratic process for faculty and students who worked together to make and enforce school rules and policies. We advocate these strategies in the *communities of character* approach to character education through sports.

The cornerstone of the *communities of character* approach is the development of collective team norms through a cooperative, participatory process. Team members are given a high level of responsibility for team governance, discipline, and other matters pertaining to the life of the group. Through open dialogue and negotiation, team norms evolve, reflecting such relational virtues as trust, openness, and respect. Additionally, by cooperatively building a mastery achievement climate, the team emphasizes self-referenced and progressive goals that require the marshalling of performance virtues. Thus, the team, experienced as a community, takes on qualities that can lead to athletic excellence and moral character.

In practice, the *community of character* approach focuses much attention on team meetings where team rules and goals are established, strategies are taught, and performances are assessed. The meetings are designed to accentuate sociomoral dimensions of athletes' sport experiences. Athletes fully participate, discussing and deciding upon disciplinary rules and punishments, and offering suggestions and feedback about strategies and performances. This democratic involvement is intended to help athletes develop shared norms that express and realize ideals of cooperation, fair play, and respect for officials and opponents. Moreover, in team meetings, players learn the democratic skills of self-expression, listening, and deliberating about the common good. In the same spirit, sport psychologists, coaches, and players respond to play-related mistakes and misbehavior in ways that are instructive and supportive of the athletes and their community.

When individual athletes are invited to exercise agency in shaping the life of the group, the team becomes a vehicle for developing the self-in-community, rather than imposing unidirectional peer pressure. Sport psychologists and coaches have an important role to play in helping athletes use the team as a social context for refining the criteria involved in self-construction; they can help facilitate athletes' processes for developing willpower and desire.

Finally, the *communities of character* approach features two complimentary ways for athletes to value their team. Typically, sport psychologists and coaches are motivated to help athletes appreciate the concept of team, to recognize ways that the team can meet needs and accomplish goals that cannot be achieved by individual athletes. This instrumental valuing of team, being grateful for others who can help you accomplish what no individual can do alone, can be a realistic, healthy, cohesion-generating perspective. By itself, however, it can turn into a narrow focus on the team as a means to an end (usually winning). To the extent that the team becomes a genuine community, it will be valued intrinsically as well as instrumentally. When athletes experience the other members of their team as valuable, regardless of their teammates' athletic prowess, then they are valuing the team intrinsically. Team members should be valued because they are who they are, not only because they can help the team win. If the team has only instrumental value, the team's moral norms lose their genuinely moral quality and become subservient to other goals.

Summary

In this chapter we have reviewed theoretical and empirical foundations for sociomoral praxis in sport psychology. We have also suggested that an integrative framework is needed to bring the various constructs related to moral development and functioning together, and we have suggested that the construct of character can provide such a framework. After highlighting aspects of character formation that are especially relevant to sport psychology practitioners, including willpower and desire, relational and performance virtues, and moral motivation, we described the *communities of character* approach as an integrative approach to promoting character in the context of sport teams.

References

Bain, L. L. (1988). Curriculum for critical reflection in physical education. In R. S. Brandt (Ed.), *Context of the curriculum: 1988 ASCD yearbook* (pp. 133-147). Washington, D.C.: Association for Supervision and Curriculum Development.

Bandura, A. (1986). *Social foundations of thought and action: A social cognitive theory.* Englewood Cliffs, NJ: Prentice-Hall.

Bandura, A. (1991). Social cognitive theory of moral thought and action. In W. M. Kurtines & J. L. Gerwitz, (Ed.), *Handbook of moral behavior and development, Vol. 1: Theory* (pp. 45-103). Hillsdale, NJ: Lawrence Erlbaum Associates.

Bandura, A. (2001). Social cognitive theory: An agentic perspective. *Annual Review of Psychology, 52,* 1-26.

Beller, J. M., & Stoll, S. K. (1995). Moral reasoning of high school student athletes and general students: An empirical study versus personal testimony. *Pediatric Exercise Science, 7,* 352-363.

Blasi, A. (1983). Moral cognition and moral action: A theoretical perspective. *Developmental Review, 3,* 178-210.

Blasi, A. (1984). Moral identity: Its role in moral functioning. In W. Kurtines & J. Gewirtz (Eds.), *Morality, moral behavior, and moral development* (pp. 128-39). New York: Wiley.

Blasi, A. (1985). The moral personality: Reflections for social science and education. In M. Berkowitz & F. Oser (Eds.), *Moral education: Theory and application* (pp. 433-444). Hillsdale, N.J.: Lawrence Erlbaum.

Blasi, A. (1988). Identity and the development of the self. In D. K. Lapsley and F. C. Power (Eds.), *Self, ego, and identity: Integrative approaches* (pp. 226-242). New York: Springer-Verlag.

Blasi, A. (1989). The integration of morality in personality. In I. E. Bilbao (ed.), *Perspectivas acerca de cambio moral: Posibles intervenciones educativas.* San Sebastian: Servicio Editorial Universidad del Pais Vasco.

Blasi, A. (1990a). Connected, unconnected, disconnected: A response to Linn and Gilligan, *New Ideas in Psychology, 8,* 209-213.

Blasi, A. (1990b). Kohlberg's theory of moral motivation. *New Directions for Child Development, 47,* 51-57.

Blasi, A. (1993). The development of identity: Some implications for moral functioning. In G. G. Noam and T. Wren (Eds.), *The moral self: Building a better paradigm* (pp. 99-122). Cambridge, MA: MIT Press.

Blasi, A. (1995). Moral understanding and the moral personality: The process of moral integration. In W. M. Kurtines and J. L. Gerwitz (Eds.), *Moral development: An introduction* (pp. 229-253). Boston: Allyn and Bacon.

Blasi, A. (1999). Emotions and moral motivation. *Journal for the Theory of Social Behaviour, 29,* 1-19.

Blasi, A. (In press-a). Moral character: A psychological approach. In D. Lapsley & F.C. Power (Eds.), *Character psychology and character education.* University of Notre Dame Press.

Blasi, A. (In press-b). Moral motivation and society: Internalization and the development of the self.

Blasi, A., & Glodis, K. (1995). The development of identity: A critical analysis from the perspective of the self as subject. *Developmental Review, 15,* 404-433.

Blasi, A., & Milton, K. (1991). The development of the sense of self in adolescence. *Journal or Personality, 59,* 217-242.

Blasi, A., & Oresick, R. (1986). Emotions and cognitions in self-inconsistency. In D.J. Bearison & H. Zimiles (Eds.), *Thought and emotion: Developmental perspectives.* Hillsdale, NJ: Erlbaum.

Blasi, A., & Oresick, R. (1987). Self-inconsistency and the development of self. In P. Young-Nisendrafth & J. Hall (Eds.), *The book of the self: Person, pretext, and process* (pp. 69-87). New York: University Press.

Blatt, M., & Kohlberg, L. (1975). The effects of classroom moral discussion upon children's moral judgment. *Journal of Moral Education, 4,* 129-161.

Bredemeier, B. (1995). Divergence in children's moral reasoning about issues in daily life and sport specific contexts. *International Journal of Sport Psychology, 26,* 453-463.

Bredemeier, B. (2001 November). *Courts of justice, fields of dreams.* Paper presented at the annual meeting of the North American Society for the Sociology of Sport, Colorado Springs, CO.

Bredemeier, B., & Shields, D. (1984). Divergence in moral reasoning about sport and everyday life. *Sociology of Sport Journal, 1,* 348-357.

Bredemeier, B., & Shields, D. (1986). Moral growth among athletes and nonathletes: A comparative analysis. *Journal of Genetic Psychology, 147,* 7-18.

Bredemeier, B., & Shields, D. (1998). Moral assessment in sport psychology. In J. L. Duda (Ed.), *Advances in sport and exercise psychology measurement* (pp. 257-276). Morgantown, WV: Fitness Information Technology.

Bredemeier, B., Weiss, M., Shields, D., & Shewchuk, R. (1986). Promoting moral growth in a summer sport camp: The implementation of theoretically grounded instructional strategies. *Journal of Moral Education, 15,* 212_220.

Colby, A., & Damon, W. (1992). *Some do care: Contemporary lives of moral commitment.* New York: Free Press.

Cutforth, N.J. (1997). What's worth doing? Reflections on an after-school program in a Denver elementary school. *Quest, 49,* 130-139.

Damon, W. (1984). Self-understanding and moral development from childhood to adolescence. In W. M. Kurtines &

Gewirtz (Eds.), *Morality, moral behavior, and moral development* (pp. 109-127). New York: Wiley.

DeBusk, M., & Hellison, D. (1989). Implementing a physical education self-responsibility model for delinquency-prone youth. *Journal of Teaching in Physical Education, 8,* 104-112.

Duda, J.L., Olson, L.K., & Templin, T.J. (1991). The relationship of task and ego orientation to sportsmanship attitudes and the perceived legitimacy of injurious acts. *Research Quarterly for Exercise and Sport, 62,* 79-87.

Dunn, J.G.H., & Dunn, J.C. (1999). Goal orientations, perceptions of aggression, and sportspersonship in elite male youth ice hockey players. *The Sport Psychologist, 13,* 183-200.

Durkheim, E. (1897/1951). *Suicide.* New York: Free Press.

Durkheim, E. (1925/1961). *Moral education.* New York: Free Press.

Ennis, C.D. (1999). Creating a culturally relevant curriculum for disengaged girls. *Sport, Education and Society, 4,* 31-49.

Frankfurt, H. (1982). The importance of what we care about. *Synthése, 53,* 252-272.

Georgiadis, N. (1990). Does basketball have to be all W's and L's? An alternative program at a residential boys' home. *Journal of Physical Education, 62,* 42-43.

Gibbons, S.L., & Ebbeck, V. (1997). The effect of different teaching strategies on the moral development of physical education students. *Journal of Teaching in Physical Education, 17,* 85-98.

Gibbons, S.L., Ebbeck, V., & Weiss, M.R. (1995). Fair Play for Kids: Effects on the moral development of children in physical education. *Research Quarterly for Exercise and Sport, 66,* 247-255.

Guivernau, M., & Duda, J. (2002). Moral atmosphere and athletic aggressive tendencies in young soccer players. *Journal of Moral Education, 31,* 67-85.

Hall, E.R. (1986). Moral development levels of athletes in sport-specific and general social situations. In L. Vander Velden & J. H. Humphrey (Eds.), *Psychology and sociology of sport: Current selected research* (Vol. 1), (pp. 191-204). New York: AMS Press.

Hellison, D. (1978). *Beyond balls and bats: Alienated (and other) youth in the gym.* Washington, D.C.: AAHPERD.

Hellison, D. (1985). *Goals and strategies for teaching physical education.* Champaign, IL: Human Kinetics.

Hellison, D. (1986). Cause of death: Physical education. *Journal of Physical Education, Recreation, and Dance, 57,* 27-28.

Hellison, D.R. (1988). Cause of death: Physical Education-a sequel. *Journal of Physical Education, 59,* 18-21.

Hellison, D. R. (1995). *Teaching personal and social responsibility through physical activity.* Champaign, IL: Human Kinetics.

Hellison, D., & Georgiadis, N. (1992). Teaching values through basketball. *Strategies, 5,* 5-8.

Hellison, D. R., Martinek, T. J., & Cutforth, N. J. (1996). Beyond violence prevention in inner city physical activity programs. Peace and Conflict: *Journal of Peace Psychology, 2,* 321-337.

Hellison, D.R., & Walsh, D. (2002). Responsibility-based youth programs evaluation: Investigating the investigations. *Quest, 54,* 292-307.

Jewett, A. E., & Bain, L. L. (1985). *The curriculum process in physical education.* Dubuque, IA: Brown.

Kavussanu, M., & Ntoumanis, N. (2003). Participation in sport and moral functioning: Does ego orientation mediate their relationship? *Journal of Sport and Exercise Psychology, 25,* 1-18.

Kavussanu, M., & Roberts, G. (2001). Moral functioning in sport: An achievement goal perspective. Journal of Sport and Exercise *Psychology, 23,* 37-54.

Kavussanu, M., Roberts, G., & Ntoumanis, N. (2002). Contextual influences on moral functioning of college basketball players. *Sport Psychologist, 16,* 347-367.

Kleiber, D.A., & Roberts, G.C. (1981). The effects of sport experience in the development of social character: An exploratory investigation. *Journal of Sport Psychology, 3,* 114-122.

Kohlberg, L. (1981). *Essays on moral development: Vol. 1: The philosophy of moral development.* San Francisco: Harper & Row.

Kohlberg, L. (1984). *Essays on moral development: Vol. 2: The psychology of moral development.* San Francisco: Harper & Row.

Lemyre, P. N., Roberts. G. C., & Ommundsen, Y. (2002). Achievement goal orientations, perceived ability, and sportspersonship in youth soccer. *Journal of Applied Sport Psychology, 14,* 120-136.

Martinek, T. J., & Hellison, D. R. (1997). Fostering resiliency in underserved youth through physical activity. *Quest, 49,* 34-49.

Miller, B., & Roberts, G.C. (2004). *Long term exposure to a motivational emphasis on winning in competitive youth sport and its effect on moral functioning, reasoning, and behavior.* Manuscript submitted for publication.

Miller, B.W., Roberts, G.C., & Ommundsen, Y. (2003). Effect of motivational climate on sportspersonship among competitive youth male and female football players. *Scandinavian Journal of Medicine and Science in Sports, 13,* 1-14.

Miller, S.C., Bredemeier, B.J.L., & Shields, D.L.L. (1997). Sociomoral education through physical education with at-risk children. *Quest, 49,* 114-129.

Ommundsen, Y., Roberts, G.C., Lemyre, P.N., & Treasure, D. (2003). Perceived motivational climate in male youth soccer: relations to social-moral functioning, sportspersonship and tem norm perceptions. *Psychology of Sport and Exercise, 25,* 397-413.

Piaget, J. (1954). *The construction of reality in the child* (M. Cook, Trans.). New York: Basic Books.

Power, F. C. (2004). *The responsible moral agent: Extra and Intrapersonal perspectives.* Manuscript submitted for publication.

Power, F. C., Higgins, A. & Kohlberg, L. (1989). *Lawrence Kohlberg's approach to moral education.* New York: Columbia University Press.

Priest, R. G., Krause, J. V., & Beach, J. (1999). Four-year changes in college athletes' ethical value choices in sports situations. *Research Quarterly for Exercise and Sport, 70,* 170-178.

Rest, J. R. (1984). The major components of morality. In W. Kurtines & J. Gewirtz (eds.), *Morality, moral behavior, and moral development* (pp. 356-629). New York: John Wiley & Sons.

Romance, T.J., Weiss, M.R., & Bockoven, J. (1986). A program to promote moral development through elementary school physical education. *Journal of Teaching in Physical Education, 5,* 126-136.

Shields, D., & Bredemeier, B. (1995). *Character development and physical activity*. Champaign, IL: Human Kinetics.

Shields, D., & Bredemeier, B. (2001). Moral development and behavior in sport. In R. Singer, H. Hausenblas, & C. Janelle (Eds.), *Handbook of sport psychology* (2nd Ed.) (pp. 585-603). New York: John Wiley.

Shields, D., & Bredemeier, B. (2005). Can sports build character? In D. Lapsley & F. C. Power (Eds.), *Character psychology and character education* (pp. 121-139). University of Notre Dame Press.

Shields, D., Bredemeier, B., Gardner, D., & Bostrom, A. (1995). Leadership, cohesion and team norms regarding cheating and aggression. *Sociology of Sport Journal, 12,* 324-336.

Shields, D., Bredemeier, B., & Power, F. C. (2002). Character development and children's sport. In F. Smoll & R. Smith (Eds.), *Children and youth in sport: A biopsychosocial perspective* (2nd ed.) (pp. 537-559). Dubuque, IA: Kendall/Hunt.

Siedentop, D., Mand, C., & Taggart, A. (1986). *Physical education: Curriculum and instruction strategies for grades 5-12.* Palo Alto, CA: Mayfield.

Smith, A. L. (2003). Peer relationships in physical activity contexts: A road less traveled in youth sport and exercise psychology research. *Psychology of Sport and Exercise, 4,* 25-39.

Solomon, G. B. (1997a). Character development: Does physical education affect character development in students? *The Journal of Physical Education, Recreation and Dance, 68,* 38-41.

Solomon, G. B. (1997b). Fair play in the gymnasium: Improving social skills among elementary school students. *Journal of Physical Education and Recreation, 68,* 22-25.

Stephens, D.E. (2000). Predictors of likelihood to aggress in youth soccer: An examination of coed and all-girls teams. *Journal of Sport Behavior, 23,* 311-325.

Stephens, D. (2001). Predictors of aggressive tendencies in girls' basketball: An examination of beginning and advanced participants in a summer skills camp. *Research Quarterly for Exercise and Sport, 72,* 257-266.

Stephens, D. E., & Bredemeier, B. J. L. (1996). Moral atmosphere and judgments about aggression in girls' soccer: Relationships among moral and motivational variables. *Journal of Sport & Exercise Psychology, 18,* 158-173.

Stephens, D., & Bredemeier, B., & Shields, D. (1997). Construction of a measure designed to assess players' descriptions and prescriptions for moral behavior in youth sport soccer. *International Journal of Sport Psychology, 28,* 370-390.

Stephens, D., & Kavanagh, B. (2003). Aggression in Canadian youth ice hockey: The role of moral atmosphere. *International Sports Journal, 7,* 109-119.

Stevenson, M. J. (1998). *Measuring the cognitive moral reasoning of collegiate student-athletes: The development of the Stevenson-Stoll Social Responsibility Questionnaire.* Unpublished doctoral dissertation, University of Idaho.

Stornes, T. (2001). Sportspersonship in elite sports: On the effects of personal and environmental factors on the display of sportspersonship among elite male handball players. *European Physical Education Review, 7,* 283-304.

Stuart, M., & Ebbeck, V. (1995). The influence of perceived social approval on moral development in youth sport. *Pediatric Exercise Science, 7,* 270-280.

Wandzilak, T., Carroll, T., & Ansorge, C. (1988). Values development through physical activity: Promoting sportsmanlike behaviors, perceptions, and moral reasoning. *Journal of Teaching in Physical Education, 8,* 13-22.

Weiss, M., & Smith, A. (2002). Moral development in sport and physical activity: Theory, research, and intervention. In T. Horn (Ed.), *Advances in sport psychology* (2nd Ed.) (pp. 243-280). Champaign, IL: Human Kinetics.

Winnick, J. (Ed.) (1990). *Adapted physical education and sport.* Champaign, IL: Human Kinetics.

Courtesy of Cpl. Joe Lindsay/U.S. Marine Corps

5.6

Assessing Psychosocial Outcomes in Coach Training Programs

RONALD E. SMITH AND FRANK L. SMOLL

Introduction

Coaches occupy a central and influential role within the athletic environment, and their influence often extends far beyond this domain into other areas of the athlete's life. A great deal of anecdotal and scientific evidence points to the coach's ability to have both positive and negative impact on the lives of participants at all levels of competition (e.g., Cote, 2002; Ewing, Seefeldt, & Brown, 1997; Scanlan & Lewthwaite, 1986; Smith & Smoll, 1997). Recognition of this fact has stimulated the development of training programs designed to enhance the instructional and interpersonal competencies of coaches so that they are capable of providing a positive athletic experience and environment. Some of these programs are national in scope; others are far more limited in their range of application. Content in these programs varies widely. Some are broad-spectrum programs that cover such diverse and important topics as instructional strategies, safety and risk management, developmental and biological factors, sport psychology, and biomechanical principles. Others are briefer and more focused, directed at improving pedagogical and strategic skills or focused on helping coaches create a positive interpersonal environment. Whatever their focus, however, it is important to know what effects these programs have on coaches and athletes and how well they achieve their objectives. Unfortunately, relatively little formal evaluative research has been done on these programs, causing some to question their effectiveness (e.g., Douge & Hastie, 1993; Gilbert & Trudel, 1999; Woodman, 1993). Indeed, given that coach training has become a large-scale commercial enterprise, it is surprising that it has not received more empirical attention. Developers of such programs have been focused primarily on development and dissemination, rather than evaluation. Yet, evaluative research is not only desirable, but essential. In the words of Lipsey and Cordray (2000), "... the overarching goal of the program evaluation enterprise is to contribute to the improvement of social conditions by providing scientifically credible information and balanced judgment to legitimate social agents about the effectiveness of interventions intended to produce social benefits" (p. 346).

In this review we focus on the evaluation of programs that are designed to have a positive impact on psychosocial outcome variables. We do not address the voluminous literature on sport pedagogy or technical skill enhancement of athletes (see Gilbert, 2002 for a comprehensive bibliography of such studies). Given that limited work has been done in the psychosocial domain, our focus will be on relevant evaluation principles and methods, and will include a review of the current status of knowledge. It is our hope that this discussion will stimulate additional evaluation research.

Links Between Theory, Research, and Coach Interventions

A distinction is sometimes made between basic and applied science. Basic science is usually defined as the development of theories and the discovery of knowledge for its own sake, whereas applied science involves the application of knowledge derived from basic science for the solution of practical problems. This dichotomy is convenient from a conceptual perspective, but the distinction blurs when we consider relations among theory development and testing, empirical research, and interventions designed to have practical impact. These relations do not simply involve a one-way causal path from knowledge or theory to application. Instead, they are more likely to involve the kinds of interactions shown in Figure 1 (Smith, 1999). This model shows reciprocal interactions between theory, research, and interventions, meaning that each of the three facets has a causal impact on the others and is, in turn, influenced by them.

Figure 1: Reciprocal Relations Involving Theory, Research, and Interventions in Sport Psychology

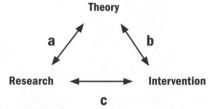

To illustrate the implications of the reciprocal influence model, let us apply it to the domain of coaching behaviors. Sport psychologists have long been interested in the antecedents and consequences of coaching behaviors, and the mechanisms whereby such behaviors affect psychosocial and performance outcome measures. They have also developed measurement tools for assessing both coaching behaviors and their effects (e.g., Gilbert & Trudel, 1999; Martin & Tkachuk, 2000; Rushall, 1977; Smith, Smoll, & Christensen, 1996). Such research has provided building blocks for the development of several theoretical models of coaching behavior (e.g., Chelladurai, 1990; Cote, Salmela, Trudel, Baria, & Russell, 1995; Smoll & Smith, 1989). To varying degrees, these models have been empirically tested to evaluate the hypothesized relations among constructs, so that theories have stimulated further research. Thus Link A is a reciprocal one, with theory and research affecting one another.

Our theories also inform the coach training interventions that we develop (e.g., Smith & Smoll, 1997). There is always some underlying rationale for building and structuring an intervention, and we believe it is preferable to base the intervention on a formal conceptual model that specifies the relevant constructs and assumed relations among them. The evaluation of these interventions, if properly performed, can affect theory development, for the success of these interventions reflect in part on the adequacy of our theory. That is, if our theory predicts that a particular intervention will work and it does not, either the theory needs to be revised or the intervention was not carried out correctly. Thus, Link B is also reciprocal, as is Link C, which connects intervention and research. Our body of research provides leads for intervention, and sound outcome research allows us to assess the efficacy of the interventions and, perhaps, to identify which aspects of the intervention are responsible for its success. In turn, the nature of the intervention dictates the outcome variables on which we focus and the way the evaluation is conducted.

This reciprocal-influence model not only provides a schema for conceptualizing scientific and applied aspects of sport psychology, but attending to the three basic linkages helps to ensure that our conceptual frameworks, research, and applied activities support one another and advances our field as a scientific and applied discipline. Where interventions are concerned, adherence to the model helps ensure that they are based on firm theoretical and research foundations and that they will be evaluated in a manner that conforms to standards of scientific accountability.

Research Designs and Program Evaluation Issues

Advances in coach training require the development and evaluation of programs to determine: (a) their overall effectiveness in accomplishing training goals, and (b) the specific program elements that mediate their effects on coaches.

Research to assess the comparative efficacy of alternate programs is highly desirable but virtually unheard of in the psychosocial coach intervention literature.

Addressing these questions is a challenging enterprise. In the course of designing and evaluating programs, researchers must first determine needs and articulate goals for the program in question. This may entail formative evaluations, in which potential consumers of the programs identify problems and indicate a desired end state. This information can be used to design the program, drawing upon past research that has identified effective procedures for attaining the particular program's goals or proceeding on an intuitive basis in the absence of data. Once the program is designed, an often-neglected step is to determine if the intervention is being delivered in a standardized fashion in accordance with prescribed procedures when administered by different trainers or even by the same trainer on different occasions. In evaluating the program, outcome variables and measures must be selected that are psychometrically sound and that operationalize constructs that are congruent with the program's goals. These measures

may assess different classes of outcome variables, including coaching behaviors, perceptions of such behaviors by coaches and athletes, coaches' mastery of factual and procedural knowledge components, environmental measures, and a myriad of self-report measures of psychological constructs.

Selecting Outcome Measures

The selection of outcome measures is a natural outgrowth of carefully specifying a training program's goals. In research on coaching, trainers may be interested in transmitting principles and behavioral guidelines to coaches; helping them understand the "why's" of technical, strategic, and behavioral guidelines; enhancing decision making, planning, or other cognitive functions; modifying observed coaching behavior in certain specific ways; influencing how coaches are perceived by their athletes or by themselves; enhancing individual athletes' or the team's performance and success; reducing athlete program attrition; creating a more positive (or less negative) sport environment (from the perspectives of coaches, athletes, parents, and administrators); preventing injuries or other negative outcomes; changing internal psychological factors (e.g., achievement orientation, self-esteem, performance anxiety, intrateam attraction); and a myriad of other variables.

Broadly speaking, outcome variables may be cognitive, behavioral, or physiological. They may be obtained through direct measurement or through self-report. Direct measurement includes physiological measures (e.g., of indices of emotional arousal or of brain functions involved in performance) and statistical performance measures. It also involves assessment of the observable behaviors and competencies of coaches, as well as the behaviors of athletes or others involved in the sport environment, such as parents or spectators. Self-report measures can be used to measure various aspects of knowledge acquisition; perceptions of self, others, and the environment; attitudes and values; expectancies (e.g., behavior-outcome and self-efficacy expectations); motivational, affective, and personality variables; and many other relevant variables.

The selection of existing measures should be based on an analysis of the constructs targeted by the intervention and the psychometric properties of the measure in question. In some instances, there may not be an adequate existing measure, requiring the investigator to develop one specifically for the evaluation. This should occupy primary attention prior to the intervention, for an inadequate measure may cloud the evaluation, adding nonsystematic (in the case of an unreliable measure) or systematic (in the case of an invalid one) error variance.

All coaching interventions are designed to help coaches acquire expertise and behave more effectively. This is accomplished by the transmission of two types of knowledge (Anderson, 1990; Gallagher, French, Thomas, & Thomas, 2002). Declarative knowledge is the knowledge of facts, concepts, and principles—the "whats" and "whys" of understanding. Technical or strategic knowledge and understanding of behavioral guidelines and their rationales are examples of declarative knowledge. Declarative knowledge is necessary for coaching effectiveness, but it is not sufficient. To translate declarative knowledge into effective behavior, procedural knowledge is required, the "doing" or "how" knowledge. Both types of knowledge are represented in the mind as schemas, organized cognitive or motoric structures that form the basis for expertise (Chi, Glaser, & Farr, 1988). Experts in any field, including coaching, develop knowledge structures that contain easily accessible and highly organized declarative and procedural knowledge.

These two kinds of knowledge can be measured in a variety of ways. Declarative knowledge can be assessed by knowledge tests of general coaching principles and specific knowledge concerning the sport in question. More often, specific knowledge is assessed in technical/strategic education concerning a particular sport. The desirability of training and assessing both domains of declarative knowledge is illustrated by the number of former star athletes (with outstanding knowledge of their sport) who fail as coaches because they have not acquired more general organizational and interpersonal coaching expertise. Given that every coach training program transmits declarative knowledge, it seems highly desirable that program-specific declarative knowledge assessment be part of any evaluation.

A recent qualitative analysis of focus group interviews conducted with 25 youth sport coaches provided insight concerning the relative value of declarative versus procedural coaching knowledge (Wiersma & Sherman, 2003). The results indicated that declarative knowledge of practice drills and skill techniques is not what leads to a good season. Rather, the theme that emerged emphasized the need for procedural knowledge on building and maintaining positive interpersonal relationships ("the interpersonal stuff and the team stuff"). Such knowledge is most directly assessed by observing coaches, either in situational simulations of relevant circumstances or in actual naturalistic situations and coding behaviors that are assumed to reflect that form of expertise. However, in the majority of coach interventions based on behavior modification, behavioral measures of focal coaching behaviors have only been used to establish that the coach carried out the procedures designed to enhance athlete performance (see Martin & Tkachuk, 2000 and Smith et al., 1996 for summaries of this work).

Developing comprehensive behavioral assessment systems is a challenging task, because coaches can engage in an infinite number of possible behaviors, and the situations they respond to are many and varied. Most current behavioral assessment instruments, such as the Coaching Behavior Assessment System (CBAS; Smith, Smoll, & Hunt, 1977) and the computerized Coaching Assessment Instrument (CAI; Franks, Johnson, & Sinclair, 1988) assess rather broad categories of behavior. Although the behaviors coded relate to other variables, particularly psychosocial ones (Smith & Smoll, 1990), the CBAS may well be missing more subtle behaviors and distinctions within categories that could account for significant additional variance in outcome measures (Abraham & Collins, 1998). As the developers of the CBAS have emphasized, it is possible to expand the system by adding new subcategories to capture nuances within the 12 original categories. As an example, Horn (1984) added a new combination category consisting of Reinforcement and Technical Instruction that is intuitively as well as empirically appealing. Unanswered is the question of whether a significantly expanded system can maintain the high level of interrater reliability currently achieved with the CBAS, particularly if behaviors are coded live, rather than from videotaped recordings. Both the CBAS and the CAI categories are linked to situational variables, and it is important to enhance such linkage to capture significant interacts between the coach and the situation in which s/he is behaving.

Athlete-perception measures have been used to assess a number of important outcome variables. One might argue that athletes' perceptions of coaching behaviors, motivational climate, and other variables are the true determinants of outcome measures. In other words, it is ultimately the athlete's subjective experience of the coach that is important. Yet, observed behaviors also account for unique variance on some psychosocial measures, such as attitudes toward the coach. For example, selecting coaches at the extremes of factor analytically derived behavioral coaching dimensions, such as Supportiveness and Instructiveness, yielded significant positive attitudes toward coaches, particularly among children who were low in self-esteem (Smith & Smoll, 1990).

In an early regression-based study of 51 youth coaches for whom more than 57,000 behaviors had been recorded, Smoll, Smith, Curtis, and Hunt (1978) found that factor scores derived from observed CBAS behaviors and from athletes' perceptions of those same behaviors accurately predicted attitudes toward the coach. In fact, the amount of variance accounted for an increase from 21% to 42% when perception measures were added to CBAS measures as a second block of predictor variables. However, a more sophisticated analysis of this data set using structural equation modeling (SEM) revealed the mediational importance of athlete-perception measures. Because of the sample size requirements of SEM, Leffingwell, Smoll, & Smith (2000) restricted their analysis to the positive and aversive control categories. They found that in the case of both supportive (Reinforcement and Mistake-Contingent Encouragement) and punitive (Punishment and Punitive Technical Instruction) behavior classes, athlete perceptions strongly mediated the relation between the CBAS behaviors and athletes' attitudes toward the coaches. Although more research of this type is needed to inform a strong recommendation, this pattern of results would suggest that behavioral observation is important in verifying differences or changes in the behaviors that are targeted by a coach intervention, but that athlete perception measures are essential in predicting psychosocial outcome measures. Thus, it would appear desirable to assess both behaviors and athlete perceptions, although behavioral assessment is resource-intensive if one wishes to assess the role of behaviors on other outcome variables.

The selection of behavioral categories to be used in observational and/or perceptual studies should be either theoretically derived or tailored to the specific behavioral targets of the coach training program. In the case of the CBAS, the basis was a theoretical one, as the categories were based on social learning theory antecedents shown to be important influences of behavior (Smith et al., 1977). The intervention that was later developed (and described below) was to be based on the same theoretical model, so that the CBAS was used in initial basic research to establish relations between coaching behaviors and athletes' reactions that could be used as the basis for the CET behavioral guidelines. It is conceivable that a coach training program based on a different theoretical model could have different coding categories. We hope that advances will be made in the development of additional behavioral measurement systems.

Evaluation Research Designs

A variety of different research designs have been used in evaluative research on coach training. A useful way to evaluate research designs is in terms of their ability to address threats to internal validity. Internal validity is the extent to which a research design can rule out alternative explanations of results. Among the threats to internal validity are the following (Campbell & Stanley, 1963; Kazdin, 1980):

History: any event occurring inside or outside of the study that could account for its results. For example, a coach in a control condition may, without the knowledge of the investigator, read a book on positive coaching techniques.

Maturation: process changes that occur in a participant over time, such as increased coaching experience.

Testing: the possibility that completing a self-report measure or being observed may change future responses on the same measure.

Instrumentation: changes in measurement procedures over time, as might occur if an observational measure is used differently over time (reliability drift).

Statistical regression: the tendency of extreme scores on a measure to regress toward the group mean upon retesting.

Selection biases: systematic differences in groups based upon the selection or assignment of participants to different conditions (e.g., to treatment and control groups).

Attrition: modifications in group composition as a result of participants dropping out of the study.

Diffusion or imitation of treatment: the possibility that elements of the intervention given to one group may be provided to some or all participants in a control group as well, reducing differences between groups on outcome measures. This might occur if coaches in a training condition share information with control group coaches.

Ideally, evaluations should be designed to address these threats to internal validity and common evaluation designs should take them into consideration.

As noted by the American Psychological Association's Task Force on Psychological Intervention Guidelines (1995), the randomized clinical trial remains the gold standard of outcome research. In this traditional experimental design, coaches are randomly assigned to one or more treatment and control conditions to eliminate selection biases and in the hope that intragroup variation on variables that could influence or interact with treatment effects, including history, maturation, and statistical regression, will be equalized by randomization. Several types of control conditions can be employed. No-treatment control conditions are methodologically sound, but they deprive coaches in the experimental group (and their athletes) of the potential benefits of the intervention. A waiting-list control may be feasible if the sport season or the coach's involvement in coaching extends over a long period, but this is seldom the case in most agency or scholastic programs.

If the study can be extended over a long enough period, a very desirable repeated-measures design can be employed. In this design, the experimental and control groups are created by random assignment and pretested on the dependent variable measures. Alternatively, the participants can be pretested and matched pairwise as closely as possible, then randomly assigned to conditions in order to create highly similar groups. The intervention is then administered to the experimental group and the two groups are tested a second time on the outcome measures, providing a test of treatment effects in the experimental group. At this point the intervention is administered to the wait-list control condition, after which the outcome measures are administered a third time. This final assessment provides within-group repeated measures analyses through which the durability of treatment effects in the experimental group can be assessed by comparing their Time 3 (followup) measures with Time 1 and Time 2 measures, and the former control group can be similarly compared with their previous measures, creating a replication test of treatment effects. This design provides a series of informative analytic possibilities and has been successfully employed in several intervention studies (e.g., Weitlauf, Smith, & Cervone, 2000).

Attention-placebo control conditions are attractive to intervention researchers because they control for contact and expectancy factors, but they must be well-designed so that they do not differ from the intervention in credibility. In the evaluation of a psychologically-oriented intervention, a sport-skills or techniques control condition conducted by an acknowledged expert can meet the equal-credibility requirement. In one study, for example, a psychologically-oriented coach training program was the focal intervention. Coaches in the control condition attended a workshop on the teaching of baseball skills conducted by the coaching staff of a Major League Baseball team, which was, like the experimental condition, rated very high on credibility and perceived value (Smoll, Smith, Barnett, & Everett, 1993) Assumed "placebo control" conditions should always be established as similar in ratings of credibility and expected benefits. In addition to failing to control for expectancy factors, a noncredible control condition can also result in selective attrition from the control condition.

Though the randomized experimental design is the gold standard of intervention evaluation, it is not without its practical problems when applied to coaching interventions. Random assignment of coaches from the same program to treatment and control conditions can create several difficulties. One is the possible leakage of information from members of the coach training condition to control group coaches, resulting in diffusion or imitation of the treatment condition that can reduce differences between groups on outcome measures. Admonishments to experimental group coaches not to reveal what they have learned or to share materials they have received with their friends or fellow coaches have not always proved successful. Additionally, it is difficult to maintain participants' awareness of the experimental design. Awareness on the part of control group coaches that they have not received the intervention may evoke some degree of resentment or reduce their enthusiasm for completing post-treatment outcome measures. Finally, random assignment may result in unintended differences between groups on important variables, such as seasonal won-loss record, that could affect outcome variables.

Quasi-experimental designs can be a desirable alternative to the classic randomized design. If two programs can be found that are very similar in variables that might affect outcome, one program can be randomly assigned to the intervention condition and the other can serve as a no-treatment, wait-list, or placebo control group. If the programs can be shown in *a priori* comparisons to not differ in variables such as social class and years of coaching experience, as well as other relevant variables, we have intrinsic control for another critical variable, namely won-loss record, which of necessity will be .500 in both conditions. If the programs have no contact with one another, concerns about leakage of information from experimental to control coaches are no longer a concern. This design has been successfully used in assessment of a coach training program (see Smith and Smoll, 1997).

One important statistical consideration merits discussion at this point. The reason that group equivalence should be established *a priori* in quasi-experimental designs is that if group differences are discovered after the study, there is no way of "correcting" for them statistically. Many researchers believe that analysis of covariance (ANCOVA) is appropriate for such correction, but this is not correct. ANCOVA can be appropriately applied for statistical control of covariates only if individual participants have been randomly assigned to conditions (see Cohen & Cohen, 1975; Miller & Chapman, 2001 for extended discussion of this issue). Such use may obscure part of the treatment effect or may create spurious ef-

fects because "treatment effects and pretreatment differences among the populations are confounded" (Huitema, 1980, p. 109). Because random assignment to conditions is carried out in the traditional randomized design, ANCOVA is an appropriate analytic tool in such designs.

Perhaps the simplest design, the pretest-posttest or single group design, has no control condition. Coaches are tested on the criterion measures before and after the intervention. In the absence of a control condition, positive changes could occur as a result of maturation, testing, or statistical regression in the absence of any real treatment effect. To address these problems, within-subject and intrasubject-replication designs evaluate the effects of treatment by presenting treatment and control conditions to the same coaches. This principle is seen in the switching-replications design described above, as the wait-list control condition is eventually given the intervention. In behavioral research, the reversal design is often employed to assess the effects of an experimental variable. This ABAB approach entails re-establishing the pretreatment baseline condition (A) after the experimental manipulation (B) has been applied for a period of time. However, this design is not feasible in instances where the experimental treatment brings about an enduring change in the participant. In coach intervention programs, learning of principles and behavioral guidelines is likely to make it impossible to "return" coaches to their pretreatment state.

Treatment Specificity and Integrity

If we view coach training program evaluations from an experimental perspective, the issue of a standardized experimental setting becomes an important consideration. As in a formal experiment, it is essential that all participants in a coach intervention be exposed to a standardized treatment if reasonable conclusions are to be drawn from the assessment. In the psychotherapy outcome literature, the emphasis on treatment specificity has fostered the development of "manualized" therapy procedures that are delivered to clients in a highly standardized fashion. Researchers also record treatment sessions so that treatment integrity, the administration of the program according to the manual, can be assessed. These measures are now routinely followed in psychotherapy research, and they should be adopted for coaching interventions as well.

The American Psychological Association Task Force's emphases on treatment specificity and the assessment of treatment integrity emerged from findings that therapists in psychotherapy outcome studies routinely departed from procedures even when doing relatively standardized cognitive-behavioral procedures (Chambless & Hollon, 1998; DeRubeis & Crits-Christoph, 1998). Several recent studies, to be discussed in greater detail below, indicate that the same lack of standardization can exist in the case of several large-scale coach training programs, with trainers failing to adhere to the procedures (Allen, 1999; Gilbert & Trudel, 1999). This research is a welcome addition to the coach training literature and

ought to alert future researchers to the need for standardization of training procedures.

We now review research focusing on psychosocial outcomes of participation in coach training programs. Reviews of research on technically-oriented coach training can be found in Gilbert (2002), Martin and Tkachuk (2000), and Smith et al. (1996).

Programs Designed to Enhance Psychosocial Outcomes

Regrettably, little systematic work has been done in relating theory, intervention, and evaluation. In this section, we focus on two research programs that have sufficient empirical bases to illustrate the linkages. One line of work involves the data-based development and evaluation of a psychosocial coach intervention program known as Coach Effective-

Figure 2: A theoretical model of coaching behaviors, their antecedents, and their effects on athletes, with hypothesized relations among situational and individual difference variables that are thought to influence the base relations.
(Smoll et al., 1978; Smoll & Smith, 1989)

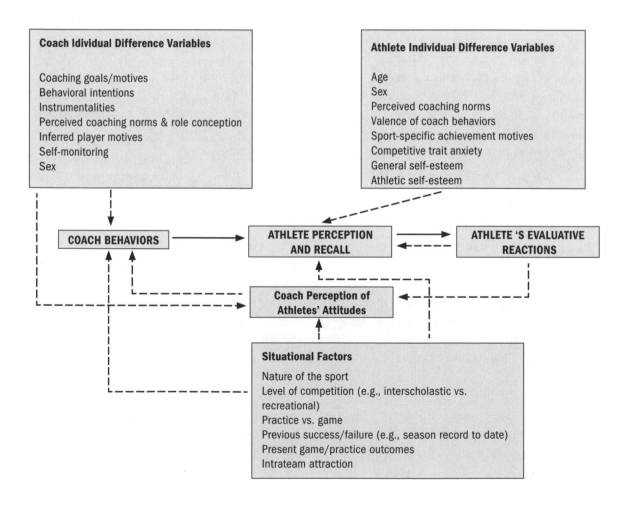

ness Training (Smith, Smoll, & Curtis, 1979; Smoll & Smith, 2001). The other is recent work on altering motivational climate that is based on achievement goal theory (Ames, 1992b; Dweck, 1999; Nicholls, 1989).

Coach Effectiveness Training (CET): A Social-Cognitive Approach

This coach training program is based on nearly 25 years of basic and applied research in the youth sport environment. The empirical work has focused on coach-athlete relationships and the development and assessment of an intervention designed to assist coaches in creating a healthy psychological environment for athletes—one that fosters youngsters' personal, social, and athletic development. The development and evaluations of the program help illustrate the reciprocal links between theory, research, and intervention discussed earlier.

Theoretical Underpinnings

The research program has focused on coaching behaviors, their determinants, and their effects on child athletes. The work has been guided by a social-cognitive framework that emphasizes interactions between situational and individual difference factors related to important cognitive-affective processes (Bandura, 1986, 1997; Mischel, 1973; Mischel & Shoda, 1995). This cognitive-behavioral framework has guided the choice of constructs, measurement approaches, and intervention techniques.

Mediational model of coaching behavior

Figure 2 presents a broad conceptual model of coaching behaviors and other situational and individual difference variables that are assumed to influence athletes' reactions to their athletic experience (Smoll et al., 1978; Smoll & Smith, 1989). We refer to this model as a mediational model because it assumes that athletes' evaluative reactions to overt coaching behaviors are mediated by their perceptions and recall of the behaviors. Likewise, as indicated by the bidirectional arrows between the perception/ memory component of the model and the evaluative component, we assume that athletes' evaluative reactions help color their perceptions and memories of

coaching behaviors. To test this aspect of the model, we developed behavioral assessment and self-report measures for coaching behaviors, athletes' perceptions of the behaviors, and athletes' evaluative reactions. We have garnered empirical support for the proposition that athletes' perceptions mediate the effects of overt coaching behaviors on athletes' evaluative reactions (e.g., Leffingwell et al., 2000; Smoll et al., 1978).

The model also includes situational factors and individual difference factors in coaches and children that are thought to affect the three central components (coach behaviors, athletes' cognitions, and athletes' evaluative reactions). In the course of our research, we have developed measures for many of the individual difference variables and tested the influence of some of these measures as moderator variables (e.g., Smith, Smoll, & Curtis, 1978; Smoll & Smith, 1989). Likewise, we have found that in addition to athletes' evaluative reactions, several of the individual difference variables, namely, self-esteem and competitive trait anxiety, are influenced by differences in coaching behaviors attributable to the coach intervention program (Smith at al., 1979; Smith, Smoll, & Barnett, 1995; Smoll et al., 1993).

The model has influenced not only our basic research on coaching behaviors, but also the approaches we took in designing and evaluating an intervention program for coaches known as Coach Effectiveness Training. Based on results obtained in the basic research, we focused on coaching behaviors and individual difference variables that related strongly to athletes' evaluative reactions (attitudes toward their experience, the coach, and teammates). For example, we found that a child's level of self-esteem strongly moderated their reactions to supportive and technical coaching behaviors, with low self-esteem children reacting much more strongly to variations in these observed behaviors (Smith & Smoll, 1990). We used cognitive-behavioral social influence techniques such as modeling, role playing, behavioral feedback, and self-monitoring in our attempts to modify coaching behaviors and thereby affect children's perceptions and evaluative reactions. An overview of our basic and applied research is presented below. A more detailed account appears elsewhere (Smoll & Smith, 2002).

Empirical Underpinnings

Several questions served as an impetus for our preliminary work. For example, what do coaches do, and how frequently do they engage in such behaviors as encouragement, punishment, instruction, and organization? What are the psychological dimensions that underlie such behaviors? And, finally, how are observable coaching behaviors related to children's reactions to their organized athletic experiences? Answers to such questions are not only a first step in describing the behavioral ecology of one aspect of the youth sport setting, but they also provide an empirical basis for the development of psychologically-oriented intervention programs. In accordance with our model, we have sought to determine how observed coaching behaviors, athletes' perception and recall of the coach's behaviors, and athlete attitudes are interrelated. We have also explored the manner in which athlete and coach individual difference variables might serve as moderator variables and influence the basic behavior-attitude relations.

Relating coaching behaviors to children's evaluative reactions

The Coaching Behavior Assessment System (CBAS; Smith et al., 1977) was developed to permit the direct observation and coding of coaches' actions during practices and games. Following development of the CBAS, field studies were conducted to assess relations between coaching behaviors and athletes' reactions to their sport experiences (Curtis, Smith, & Smoll, 1979; Smith & Smoll, 1990; Smith, et al., 1978; Smith, Zane, Smoll, & Coppel, 1983; Smoll et al., 1978). We found that the typical baseball or basketball coach engages in more than 200 coded actions during an average game. By collecting observational data on 4 to 5 occasions, we were thus able to generate behavioral profiles of up to several thousand responses for each coach over the course of a season. In large-scale observational studies, we coded more than 85,000 behaviors of some 80 male baseball and basketball coaches, then interviewed and administered questionnaires to nearly 1,000 of their athletes after the season to measure their recall of their coaches' behaviors and their evaluative reactions to the coach, their sport experience, and themselves (e.g., Curtis et al.,1979; Smith et al., 1983).

At the level of overt behavior, three independent behavioral dimensions were identified through factor analysis—supportiveness (comprised of Reinforcement and Mistake-contingent Encouragement), instructiveness (General Technical Instruction and Mistake-contingent Technical Instruction *versus* General Communication and General Encouragement), and punitiveness (Punishment and Punitive Technical Instruction *versus* organizational behaviors). Relations between coaches' scores on these behavioral dimensions and player measures provided clear evidence for the crucial role of the coach. The most positive outcomes occurred when children played for coaches who engaged in high levels of reinforcement (for both desirable performance and effort) and who responded to mistakes with encouragement and technical instruction. Not only did the children who had such coaches like their coaches more and have more fun, but they also liked their teammates more. Although only about 3% of the coded behaviors were punitive and critical in nature, they correlated more strongly (and negatively) than any other behavior with children's attitudes. Notably, the team's won-lost record was essentially unrelated to how well the players liked the coach and how much they wanted to play for the coach in the future. On the other hand, players on winning teams felt that their parents liked the coach more and that the coach liked them more than did players on losing teams. Apparently, winning made little difference to the children, but they knew that it was important to the adults. It is worth noting, however, that winning assumed greater importance beyond age 12, although it continued to be a less important attitudinal determinant than coach behaviors.

Another important issue concerned the degree of accuracy with which coaches perceive their own behaviors. Correlations between CBAS observed behaviors and coaches' ratings of how frequently they performed the behaviors were generally low and nonsignificant. The only actions on their self-report measure that correlated significantly (around .50) with the observational measures were the punitive behaviors. Overall we found that children's ratings on the same perceived behavior scales correlated much more highly with CBAS measures than did the coaches' own reports. It thus appears that coaches were, for the most part, blissfully unaware of how they behaved and that athletes were more accurate perceivers of actual coach behaviors. Because behavior change requires an awareness of how one is currently behaving, this finding clearly indicated the need to increase coaches' self-awareness when developing an intervention program.

Coach Effectiveness Training (CET) Principles and Procedures

Data from the basic research indicated clear relations between coaching behaviors and the reactions of youngsters to their athletic experience. These relations provided a foundation for developing a set of coaching guidelines that constitute the core of the CET program (Smith & Smoll, 2002). The empirically derived behavioral guidelines (i.e., coaching *do's* and *don'ts*) are based primarily on social influence techniques that involve principles of positive control rather than aversive control, and the conception of success or "winning" as consisting of giving maximum effort.

Five key principles are emphasized in a CET workshop, and behavioral guidelines are presented for implementing each principle. The first principle deals with a developmentally-oriented philosophy of winning. Coaches are urged to focus on athletes' effort and enjoyment rather than on success as measured by statistics or scoreboards. They are encouraged to emphasize "doing your best," "getting better," and "having fun" as opposed to a "win at all costs" orientation (Smith & Smoll, 2002; Smoll & Smith, 1981). Although formulated prior to the emergence of achievement goal theory (Ames, 1992a; Dweck, 1999; Nicholls, 1989), this principle is clearly consistent with a task or mastery orientation. It attempts to reduce the ultimate importance of winning relative to other prized participation motives (e.g., skill development and affiliation with teammates) and takes into account the inverse relation between enjoyment and competitive anxiety (Scanlan & Lewthwaite, 1984; Scanlan & Passer, 1978, 1979). Moreover, coaches are instructed to help promote separation of athletes' feelings of self-worth from game outcomes or won-lost records. Focusing on effort rather than outcome is consistent with Dweck's (1975) highly successful attributional retraining program with low-achieving children.

Our second principle emphasizes a "positive approach" to coaching. In such an approach, coach-athlete interactions are characterized by the liberal use of positive reinforcement, encouragement, and sound technical instruction that help create high levels of interpersonal attraction between coaches and athletes. Punitive and hostile responses are strongly discouraged, as they have been shown to create a negative team climate and to promote fear of failure in athletes (Scanlan & Lewthwaite, 1984; Scanlan & Passer, 1978, 1979). We emphasize that reinforcement should not be restricted to the learning and performance of sport skills. Rather, it should also be liberally applied to strengthen desirable responses (e.g., mastery attempts and persistence, teamwork, leadership, sportsmanship). CET also includes several "positive approach" guidelines pertaining to the appropriate use of technical instruction. For example, when giving instruction, we encourage coaches to emphasize the good things that will happen if athletes execute correctly rather than focusing on the negative things that will occur if they do not. This approach is designed to motivate athletes to make desirable things happen (i.e., helps develop a positive achievement orientation) rather than building fear of making mistakes.

The third coaching principle is to establish norms that emphasize athletes' mutual obligations to help and support one another. Such norms increase social support and attraction among teammates and thereby enhance cohesion and commitment to the team, and they are most likely to develop when coaches (a) are themselves supportive models, and (b) reinforce athlete behaviors that promote team unity. We also instruct coaches in how to develop a "we're in this together" group norm. This norm can play an important role in building team cohesion, particularly if the coach frequently reinforces athletes' demonstrations of mutual supportiveness.

A fourth principle is that compliance with team roles and responsibilities is most effectively achieved by involving athletes in decisions regarding team rules and by reinforcing compliance with them rather than by using punitive measures to punish noncompliance, a principle consistent with Ames's (1992a) and Epstein's (1989) guidelines for shared decisional responsibility in the task-oriented motivational climate of the classroom. By setting explicit guidelines that the athletes help formulate and by using positive reinforcement to strengthen desirable responses, coaches can foster self-discipline and often prevent athlete misbehaviors from occurring.

A fifth principle is that coaches should become more aware of their own behavior and its consequences. To enhance awareness, CET coaches are taught the use of behavioral feedback and self-monitoring, which are described below.

In a CET workshop, which lasts approximately 2.5 hours, behavioral guidelines are presented both verbally and in written materials (a printed outline and a 24-page manual) given to the coaches. The manual (Smoll & Smith, 1997) supplements the guidelines with concrete suggestions for communicating effectively with young athletes, gaining their respect, and relating effectively to their parents. Also, visual aids (content slides and cartoons illustrating important points) are used to facilitate comprehension and retention of the guidelines as well as to add to the organizational quality of the session.

One notable finding from our basic research was that coaches had very limited awareness of how they behaved, as indicated by low correlations between observed and coach-rated behaviors (Smith et al., 1978). Similar findings occurred in another observational study (Burton & Tannehill, 1987). Thus, an important goal of CET is to increase coaches' awareness of what they are doing, for change is unlikely to occur without this awareness. CET coaches are taught the use of two proven behavioral-change techniques, namely, behavioral feedback (Edelstein & Eisler, 1976; Huberman & O'Brien, 1999) and self-monitoring (Kanfer & Gaelick-Buys, 1991; McFall, 1977). To obtain feedback, coaches are encouraged to work with their assistants as a team and share descriptions of each others' behaviors. Another feedback procedure involves coaches soliciting input directly from their athletes.

With respect to self-monitoring, CET coaches are given a brief form that they are instructed to complete immediately after practices and games (see Smoll & Smith, 2001, pp. 396-397). On the form, they indicate approximately what percentage of the time they engaged in the recommended behaviors in relevant situations. For example, coaches are asked, "Approximately what percentage of the times they occurred did you respond to mistakes/errors with encouragement?" Coaches are encouraged to engage in self-monitoring on a regular basis in order to achieve optimal results.

CET also includes information on coach-parent relationships and provides instructions on how to organize and conduct a sport orientation meeting with parents. Such meetings are designed to inform parents about their responsibilities for contributing to the success of the sport program and to guide them toward working cooperatively and productively with the coach (see Smoll, 2001).

Program Evaluation Research on CET

Five important outcome questions have been the focus of CET program evaluation studies. First, does the CET program affect the behaviors of trained coaches in a manner consistent with the behavioral guidelines? Second, how does the program affect athletes' reactions to their sport experience? Third, does exposure to a positive interpersonal environment created by trained coaches result in an increase in general self-esteem, particularly among low self-esteem children? Fourth, does CET training help reduce performance anxiety among young athletes? And, finally, do positive changes in the first four outcomes increase the likelihood that young athletes will choose to return to the sport program?

All five of these desirable outcomes have been demonstrated in a series of outcome studies in which experimental groups of youth coaches exposed to the CET program were compared with untrained or attention-placebo control groups. Coaches exposed to CET differed from controls in both observed (CBAS) and athlete-perceived behaviors in a manner consistent with the behavioral guidelines. Trained coaches were more reinforcing, more encouraging, gave more technical instruction, and were less punitive and controlling than were control group coaches. In turn, the athletes who played for the trained coaches indicated that they enjoyed their experience more and liked their coach and teammates more. Such children also demonstrated significant increases in general self-esteem and significant decreases in performance anxiety over the course of the season (Smith et al., 1979; Smith et al., 1995; Smoll et al., 1993). We also found that athletes who are low in self-esteem are the ones who react most positively to trained coaches, indicating that the program has a salutary impact on the children who are most in need of a positive sport experience. Finally, a study of attrition showed a dropout rate of 26% among children who played for control group coaches, a figure that is quite consistent with previous reports of 30% to 40% annual attrition rates in youth sport programs (Gould, 1987). In contrast, only 5% of the children who had played for CET-trained coaches failed to return to the program the next season (Barnett, Smoll, & Smith, 1992). These positive psychosocial outcomes are all the more noteworthy in light of the fact that experimental and control groups have not differed in average won-lost percentages in any of the studies.

In summary, CET has proven to be an economical and effective program that alters coaching behaviors in a desirable fashion and thereby has positive psychosocial effects on youngsters who play for trained coaches. Five classes of outcome variables have been significantly influenced by the training program—coaching behaviors, young athletes' attitudes, self-esteem, performance anxiety, and attrition. We attribute the consistently positive results derived from our relatively brief intervention to the fact that our basic research helped to identify a set of core principles that are relatively easy for coaches to learn and that have a strong impact on young athletes.

Achievement Goal Theory and Coaching

Because the sport environment is inherently a competence and achievement context, motivational factors play an important role in the ultimate effects of participation on psychosocial development. A potentially useful formulation for understanding variations in young people's interpretations of and responses to the youth sport setting is the achievement goal framework (Ames, 1992b; Dweck, 1999; Nicholls, 1989). Achievement goal theory focuses on understanding the function and the meaning of goal directed actions, based on how participants define success and how they judge whether or not they have demonstrated competence. The two central constructs in the theory are individual *goal orientations* that guide achievement perceptions and behavior, and the *motivational climate* created within adult-controlled achievement settings.

Goal Orientations

Nicholls (1984, 1989) identified two different ways of defining success and construing one's level of competence, labeling them task involvement and ego involvement. When people are *task-involved*, subjective success and perceived competence are processed in a *self-referenced* manner. Task-involved people feel successful and competent when they have learned something new, witnessed skill improvement, mastered the task at hand, and/or given their best effort. Importantly, even if people perceive themselves as possessing lower ability than others, they can still feel competent and successful if focused on task-involved criteria (Nicholls, 1989). On the other hand, when individuals are in a state of *ego involvement*, their definitions of personal success and demonstrated competence are *other-referenced*. The goal here is to show that one is superior to relevant others (approach ego orientation), or to avoid appearing inferior to others (avoidance ego orientation; Elliott & Church, 1997).

As a result of their experiences in achievement contexts, particularly exposure to the conceptions of success emphasized by significant adults such as teachers, coaches, and parents, children come to develop relatively stable task and ego goal orientations that represent "interpretive lens" through which they process and respond to achievement situations (Dweck & Leggett, 1988; Nicholls, 1989). As a result, children differ in the conception of ability they emphasize and in their personal criteria for "successful" achievement. With respect to individual differences in goal orientations, Nicholls (1989) initially proposed that people vary in the tendency to be task- and/or ego-involved in achievement settings. However, research in both educational and sport domains suggests that these two goal orientations are not bipolar but rather orthogonal (Duda, 1996). That is, children can be high or low in both ego and task orientations as well as either high in one of the goal dimensions and low in the other. Within an ego orientation, they can have varying degrees of approach and avoidance motivation, also assumed to be orthogonal to one another (Elliott & Church, 1997).

Motivational Climate

Whether a person is task- and/or ego-involved at a given time is influenced by individual differences in goal orientations and by situational factors that make definitions of success more salient (Treasure et al., 2001). For example, Harwood (2002) found that athletes tend to report higher ego orientation than task orientation when they are actually in competition, suggesting that orientations may be different in games than in practices.

The social context or *motivational climate* can vary in the degree to which task- and/or ego-involving goals are emphasized by significant others in that context (Ames, 1992b; Maehr, 1983). Like the classroom setting, sport is an environment in which evaluation, recognition, and organizational practices of adult figures and athletes' motivation for learning and participation are often intertwined. Thus, researchers in the sport domain have highlighted the relevance of considering the role of adult significant others (such as coaches and parents) when explaining the achievement behaviors of young participants (Brustad, 1992; Duda, 1987).

Research in the educational domain indicates that children are more likely to invest in learning and adopt adaptive achievement strategies in task-involving environments, where the emphasis is on learning, personal improvement, and developing new skills rather than on interpersonal evaluation and social comparison (Ames & Archer, 1988). On the other hand, maladaptive achievement strategies and motivational problems tend to occur in predominantly performance-oriented or ego-involving climates, where mistakes are punished, children with greater ability receive more encouragement and rewards, and social comparison is emphasized (Ames, 1992a; Midgley et al., 1998).

Relations between task and ego-involving motivational climate and such variables as students' perceived causes of success and failure, perceptions of ability, reasons for participation, and indicators of the quality of experience have received considerable attention in educational settings (e.g., Ames & Archer, 1988; Nicholls, Cheung, Lauer, & Patashnick, 1989). Research in sport has replicated and extended the findings from many of these classroom-based studies. Sport studies have shown an association between athletes' goal orientations and the situational goal structure created by coaches and parents (e.g., Duda & Hom, 1993; Ebbeck & Becker, 1994; Papaioannou, 1994;).

Considered as a whole, the current literature on motivational climate in both academic and sport domains strongly supports the hypothesis that a task-orientated climate is associated with a wide range of salutary motivational, self-evaluative, affective, and behavioral outcomes (see McArdle & Duda, 2002). In the sport domain, however, the vast majority of the studies are correlational in nature, making causal inferences difficult. We therefore consider attempts to experimentally alter the motivational climate and assess the effects of such treatments.

Altering the Motivational Climate

In the academic realm, Ames (1992a), Dweck (1986), and Epstein (1988, 1989) have described specific methods that can be used to create a motivational climate that supports a task-orientation (also termed a mastery or learning orientation). These principles are designed to foster an orientation toward developing new skills, intrinsic motivation for learning, a focus on effort rather than social comparison, reduced fear of failure, and improved competence based on self-referenced standards. Among the most important principles are the following:

• Design learning tasks that are novel, diverse, challenging, and engaging. Help students establish short-term self-referenced mastery goals. Focus on the meaningful aspects of learning the activity, and support the development and use of effective learning strategies.

• Allow children to participate in decision making regarding aims and regulations that affect their actions and encourage them to take shared ownership of the learning process. Support the development and use of self-management and self-monitoring skills.

• Focus on individual improvement, progress, and mastery. Tailor the rate of personal instruction to the individual student where possible. Recognize effort exerted, performance improvement in relation to individual goals, and learning from mistakes. Encourage a view of mistakes as a natural and necessary part of the learning/mastery process rather than as something to be feared.

• Involve the student in the evaluation process. Minimize social comparison and ability distinctions in favor of individual progress.

Consistent with the above, Epstein (1988, 1989) coined the acronym **TARGET** to describe structures of the learning environment that are relevant to understanding and influencing motivational processes. The dimensions include **T**ask design, use of **A**uthority, learner **R**ecognition, implementation of **G**roup structure, **E**valuation procedures, and performance **T**imetable. Ames (1992a) translated the **TARGET** principles into specific classroom strategies/practices and tested their influence on children who were motivationally and academically at risk. Students in a task or mastery-oriented **TARGET** intervention condition were compared with control classrooms on measures of intrinsic motivation, academic attitudes, and self-perceived competence. By the end of the semester, the children in the mastery condition were higher in intrinsic motivation and had more favorable attitudes toward learning than did the children in the control classrooms.

Ames (1992b) argued that the principles of achievement goal theory developed in the classroom are readily applicable to the sport environment. Both environments are characterized by adult-defined authority and reward structures, and both are based on ability grouping, normative and social comparisons, and public individual performance. Accordingly, several researchers have applied the principles to physical activity settings. Theeboom, De Knop, and Weiss (1995) assigned children attending a summer sports program to one of two conditions (i.e., a task-involving climate versus an ego-involving climate). Consistent with achievement goal theory, participants in the task-involving program expressed greater enjoyment, and they demonstrated better motor skills than children assigned to the ego-involving condition. Although quantitative analysis did not show any significant difference between the groups with respect to perceived competence and intrinsic motivation, the investigators reported that qualitative analyses of interviews taken at the end of each lesson indicated a higher level of intrinsic motivation in the task-involved group.

Another study examined the effect of two different teaching styles on children's motivation in a physical education course (Goudas, Biddle, Fox, & Underwood, 1995). One class of 24 girls was taught track and field for 10 weeks, each lesson being taught with either a direct or a differentiated teaching style. In the lessons using the direct style, most of the decisions were made by the teacher. In the differentiated style, students were provided with a number of choices, such as the pace they wanted to work, and the activities they wanted to practice. After each lesson, the girls completed self-report measures of intrinsic motivation and goal involvement. On completion of the course, eight girls were interviewed to assess their perceptions of the lessons. The results indicated that students reporting higher levels of competence, autonomy, and task orientation had higher intrinsic motivation scores throughout the course. However, teaching style was also found to have an independent effect. Specifically, the differentiated style was associated with higher levels of intrinsic motivation and task goal involvement and lower levels of work avoidance involvement. The investigators concluded that a differentiated teaching style can positively influence young girls' reactions to a sport activity independent of perceptions of goal orientations, autonomy, and competence.

In a sample of young school children, Solmon (1996) created gender specific juggling classes with either a task-involving or ego-involving goal structure. The results of the study showed that individuals in the task-involving condition demonstrated greater persistence in learning difficult juggling tasks. Those children in the ego-involving condition had less resolve on troublesome tasks and tended to attribute success to ability. In a similar manner, Papaioannou and Kouli (1999) instructed teachers of 10 physical education classes in junior high schools in Greece to change strategies employed while students engaged in volleyball drills. Results showed that students in the ego-involving physical education class reported greater somatic anxiety and less state self-confidence than in the task-involving climate. In comparison with students in the task-involving class, those in the ego-involving climate more highly valued winning with minimum effort and perceived their classmates as more worried, less predisposed to learning, and more competitive.

Harwood and Swain (2002) recently investigated the effects of a season-long player, parent, and coach intervention program on goal involvement responses, self-regulation, competition cognitions, and goal orientations of three junior tennis players. The design combined case study reporting for the intervention outcomes with features of a pre-post A/B multiple-baseline across-participants design for examining changes in levels of self-regulation and competitive cognitions. The three treatment players, plus their parents and personal coach, engaged in extensive educational sessions and cognitive-motivational tasks over a three-month competition and training period. The three players were then compared with a matched control participant. A major component of the intervention focused on understanding the motives and reasons behind playing tennis. For parents and coaches, the consequences of different achievement goal profiles were explored, followed by an identification of the factors contributing to the development and activation of task and ego involvement. The principles of **TARGET** (Ames, 1992b; Epstein, 1988, 1989) were taught to parents and coaches to emphasize the role played by their verbal and nonverbal behaviors and the passive or active nature of their involvement. Additionally, the participants were introduced to a motivational approach to competition known as the Competitive Performance Mentality (CPM). The CPM reflected a goal involvement profile of both high self-directed task and ego involvement and a decreased emphasis on social approval goal involvement. The postintervention assessment yielded positive directional changes in all players except the control participant. Specifically, the multidimensional intervention program resulted in (a) positive changes in players' task and ego-involvement profiles in response to highly ego-involving competition scenarios, (b) enhanced self-regulation relative concerning the degree to which players self-assessed achievements in the performance components of tennis for feedback purposes, and (c) positive effects on players' competitive cognitions (i.e., increased self-efficacy, perceptions of lower threat and higher challenge). Moreover, the three participants either maintained or slightly increased their task orientation with the opposite occurring for their ego orientation.

Though derived independently from different theoretical systems, striking similarities exist in the goals and behavioral guidelines derived from CET and achievement goal theory. Both are designed to create a task-oriented motivational climate that focuses on the learning process rather than on outcome. Sport is viewed as a personal development arena, and the emphasis is on becoming "your best" rather than "the best." CET guidelines explicitly define "winning" as exerting maximum effort and commitment to learning the skills of the sport, a position that is highly consistent with a mastery-based motivational climate. Likewise, mistakes are conceived as steppingstones to achievement that provide the feedback needed to improve performance, i.e., as an important part of the learning process, rather than something to be feared. CET guidelines emphasize that to the extent that athletes are focused on effort and preparation and freed from unnecessary performance anxiety, winning as an outcome will take care of itself within the limits of their abilities. A desired outcome of both CET and achievement goal theory is the creation of a positive interpersonal and athletic environment that fosters intrinsic enjoyment of the activity.

A recent entry into the psychologically-oriented coach intervention domain is a coach training program developed in 1998 by Jim Thompson, founder of the Positive Coaching Alliance. Like CET, this Stanford University-based program has important links with achievement goal theory and with social-cognitive approaches to behavior change. The Positive Coaching program appears promising, but to this point, it has not been systematically evaluated in terms of its ability to change coaching behaviors or affect athletes' sport outcomes.

National Multifaceted Coach Training Programs

National coaching associations of many countries have developed educational programs with specific teaching modules designed to enhance the competencies of coaches (cf. Australia [Olderhove, 1996]; Canada [Wankel & Mummery, 1996]; Finland [Laakso, Telama, & Yang, 1996]; Japan [Yamaguchi, 1996]; Portugal [Goncalves, 1996]; Scotland [Hendry & Love, 1996]; and the Netherlands [Buisman & Lucassen, 1996]). In reviewing the structure and content of programs offered around the world, Campbell (1993) observed that "a national coach education strategy is largely determined by the culture, politics, and traditions of the nation concerned. As a result, there is no single system that can be considered an ideal model for others to copy" (p. 62). There are, however, certain commonalties among the programs that can be identified. Specifically, most programs provide training centered around two key areas: (a) sport-specific knowledge related to skills, techniques, and strategies, and (b) performance-related knowledge in sport sciences, such as biomechanics, exercise physiology, growth and development, nutrition, sports medicine, and sport psychology. Information pertaining to sport pedagogy, program planning, and risk management is commonly included as well. Many countries operate four- or five-level certification programs, the lower levels delivered outside of academia and the top levels presented as a university-level course. Additionally, certification courses typically place emphasis on practical coaching experience, the amount required to move to a higher level varying considerably from one country to another. As one might expect, the balance of the various components and the relative importance placed on each reflects the particular needs of the sport and the level at which the coach functions.

Unlike other countries, the United States does not have a national coaching association that provides a unified system for training and certification of coaches. Rather, three commercially distributed programs are widely available that include curricular components designed to influence coach-athlete interactions. The American Coaching Effectiveness Program (ACEP, Martens, 1997) was established in 1976 and first offered courses in 1981. ACEP was founded by Rainer Martens; its national center is located in Champaign, Illinois; and it is generally regarded as the largest coaching education program in the world (Douge & Hastie, 1993). The National Youth Sports Coaches Association (NYSCA, Brown & Butterfield, 1992) was founded in 1981 by Fred Engh, and it is located in West Palm Beach, Florida. The Program for Athletic Coaches' Education (PACE, Seefeldt, Clark, & Brown, 2001) was founded in 1991 by Vern Seefeldt, and it is administered by the Institute for the Study of Youth Sports at Michigan State University.

ACEP, NYSCA, and PACE are relatively lengthy (8- to 16-hour) programs. They offer broad-spectrum workshops that cover an array of topics, including those subsumed under the rubric of sport psychology (e.g., goal setting, motivation, stress management). Unfortunately, however, these three programs share two shortcomings in common. First, they lack a core theoretical and/or empirical foundation upon which their sport psychology components are based. Rather, the eclectic nature of their content is generally derived by borrowing principles from educational and psychological literature. Second, there is an absence of systematic research attempting to validate the efficacy of these programs. Consequently, very little is known about their impact on coaches or the athletes who play for them. Weiss and Hayashi (1996) noted that ACEP, NYSCA, and PACE "have provided coaching workshops to thousands of individuals involved in community-based and school-sponsored sports, but evaluation research is essential to determine the effectiveness of these training programs on increasing sport science knowledge and applications" (p. 53). Unfortunately, Coach Effectiveness Training is the only program that has been subjected to systematic evaluation to determine its influence on coaches' behaviors and the effects of such behaviors on youngsters' psychosocial development (Brown & Butterfield, 1992). The scant evaluation research that has been conducted on national coach training programs is reviewed below. It should be noted that coverage does not include studies published in non-English language journals.

Canada's National Coaching Certification Program (NCCP)

The NCCP is based on a five-level, three-component model, including technical, practical, and theory aspects. The program is designed to meet the educational needs of coaches from the grassroots level to the high-performance level. The NCCP for Hockey was established in 1974 and is broadly concerned with coaching attitudes, training procedures, skill instruction, and strategy. Graham and Carron (1983) examined the impact of NCCP-Hockey certification on coaching attitudes. Specifically, coaches who had 0, 1, and 2 levels of certification and those who had achieved certification at Levels 3, 4, and 5 were compared on attitudes toward important social psychological correlates of sport participation (e.g., emphasis that should be placed on winning, having fun, playing fair, sportsmanship). Two levels of competition (house league versus competitive league coaches) were also compared. Questionnaire data were obtained via mail from 249 minor hockey coaches (55% return rate). The results revealed that coaches with greater certification were older and more experienced. Also, coaches in competitive leagues were shown to be more experienced, and to attach more importance to setting realistic objectives and playing well, but less importance to providing a recreational experience for players than were house league coaches. With increasing certification, coaches in competitive leagues attached increased importance to beating an opponent and having a winning team while house league coaches showed a decrease. Finally, the emphasis placed upon providing equal ice time for all players remained low over the two levels of certification in the competitive league coaches; it showed a decrease with greater certification in the house league coaches.

Haslam (1990) examined the theory component of the NCCP (Levels 1 through 3) to determine whether its educational objectives represented the important and necessary skills needed to be an effective coach. A modification of the Delphi technique was used to elicit the opinions of experienced NCCP course conductors and provincial coaching coordinators from across Canada. The Delphi technique involves the successive questioning of individual experts, without face-to-face contact, interspersed with controlled feedback of the group's opinions and reasons in support of the opinions. In Haslam's study, 75 experts responded to three questionnaires (one on each level of the theory program) on three separate occasions. The respondents focused on a list of items concerning the educational objectives of the NCCP. (Typically, a Delphi technique is used to generate, rather than validate, items.) Each round of questioning was followed by feedback of the group's responses to each question, both in terms of written comments and statistical results of the group's opinions (the mean and standard deviation of the importance of each objective). The data confirmed the validity of most of the educational objectives at all three levels of the program. Further, the experts generally agreed that more time should be devoted to the social psychological aspect of the curriculum

at Levels 1 and 2, and a balance should be established between the social psychological and biophysical modules at Level 3.

To respond to the lack of program evaluation research, Gilbert and Trudel (1999) developed and applied a multimethod, content-specific evaluation strategy with one coach in a coaching course in Canada. Three questions guided the evaluation, including: (a) Was the course delivered as designed? (b) Did the coach acquire any new knowledge? and (c) Was any change found in the use of course concepts in the field? The participant was a male coach of a boys' Peewee (13- to 14-year-old) competitive hockey team. During the study, the coach attended and received credit for the NCCP Level 2 Theory course, which is designed to cover seven content areas (modules), requiring 21 hours and 40 minutes. The evaluation model focused on three stages relative to (a) course learning, (b) knowledge gain, and (c) knowledge use. In the first stage, the goal was to compare course conduct with course design. The coach and one of the investigators attended the NCCP course, and the researcher assumed the role of participant observer. Notes were taken to record the time allotted to each module, the content of discussions, and the coach's participation. The data were compared to guidelines in the course conductor's handbook. The goal of the second stage was to determine if the coach gained any sport science knowledge from the course. A background interview was conducted to determine the coach's knowledge of course concepts prior to attendance. To evaluate the coach's learning after the course two procedures were used: a written knowledge test and a summary interview conducted to solicit comments on the course. A content analysis of the background and postcourse summary interview transcripts was done to determine the coach's knowledge gain. In the third stage of the evaluation, three methods were used to evaluate knowledge transfer and reference to course content: (a) analysis of the coach's decision-making factors; (b) systematic observation (videotaping and coding) of the coach's instructional behaviors; and (c) a content analysis of transcripts from semistructured and stimulated recall interviews conducted prior to and following practices and games, plus two days after the event.

The evaluation strategy showed that the course was not delivered as designed, indicating poor treatment integrity. Moreover, there was no change in the coach's knowledge, which was possibly due to the inadequacy of the course delivery and/or the coaches' previous high knowledge base. Coding of the recall interviews provided insight into categories of factors that influence coaching decisions made during practices and games. For example, decision-making factors during practices included objective and subjective field information (e.g., drill setup, team performance) and coach knowledge of player characteristics (e.g., physical and psychological attributes) and knowledge of the game (e.g., rules, practice plan). The results revealed that coaches increased their reference to factors concerning player characteristics in making coaching decisions, which was regarded as a favorable outcome of course participation. Finally, although there was very little change in the coach's instructional behaviors, small changes were reported in his use of course concepts in the field. In commenting on their evaluation strategy, Gilbert and Trudel concluded that "it provides valuable in-depth information on course conduct and course impact, while using a small sample" (p. 248). Obviously, the approach is very labor-intensive and time consuming, which severely limits its practical utility.

American Coaching Effectiveness Program (ACEP)

ACEP, developed in the 1970s, is the oldest and most widely disseminated of the comprehensive commercial programs. The program is very comprehensive, and sport psychology is only one of its numerous modules. Live presentation of the material by trained workshop leaders is supplemented with well-constructed written and audiovisual instructional materials.

Despite the fact that ACEP has been in use for more than two decades, we were able to find only one formal evaluation study of its sport psychology component. Burton and Tannehill (1987) evaluated the 16-hour Level 1 program, comparing 12 youth basketball coaches who had taken the program with 12 controls. A quasi-experimental design was employed, with coaches from two different programs being assigned to the ACEP and control conditions. Subsequent analyses indicated that the two groups of coaches were very similar as to demographic and background variables, success expectancies, and coaching philosophy.

The evaluation was based on a conceptual and measurement model that took into account three classes of variables: (a) coaches' attitudes and philosophy; (b) observed, athlete-perceived, and coach-perceived coaching behaviors; and (c) coaches' and athletes' evaluative reactions. The conceptual model was hierarchical, predicting the most powerful effect of training on coaches' knowledge and attitudes, and the least impact on coaches' and athletes' evaluative reactions. A behavioral coding system, the Coaching Behavior Observational Rating System (CBORS) was developed that took into account the setting, the nature of the coach-athlete interactions, and 17 coaching behavior categories. High interrater reliability was demonstrated and the coding system was applied to record coaching behaviors during practices and games. Coaches were assessed from 4 to 6 times during the season. Data were obtained from 130 athletes at the end of the season.

Following ACEP training, coaches became less win-oriented than the control coaches and reported that they did more seasonal and daily planning than did the control coaches. Behavioral observations indicated that ACEP coaches spent more time in instructional activities early in the season and more time in actual practice later in the season, whereas the relation was reversed for untrained coaches. ACEP coaches also gave less instruction during games. As the season progressed, ACEP coaches increased encouragement and "hustle" prompts, whereas control coaches did the opposite. In general, ACEP coaches were more positive toward athletes during both practices and games. Nonetheless, both groups of coaches used approximately 20 times more criticism and 4 times more punishment than praise, a result that diverges sharply from the results of the CET outcome research. Whether this is attributable to different measurement procedures or to different program effects is unclear.

As in the Smith et al. (1978) research, little relation was found between coaches' ratings of how often they used particular behaviors and behavioral observations of those behaviors, with punitive behaviors being most accurately self-perceived. Athletes were somewhat more accurate than coaches, particularly for punitive and positive feedback behaviors.

Most importantly, in comparison with athletes who played for untrained coaches, those who played for ACEP-trained coaches rated them as using more general-positive feedback and less general-negative feedback. The two groups of coaches did not differ in athletes' perceptions of positive or negative specific feedback or in encouragement. No differences were found on more global evaluative athlete reactions, such as satisfaction, fun experienced, changes in liking for basketball, or desire to have the same coach again next year.

This comprehensive evaluation is the only one done to date with ACEP. The coach and athlete sample sizes were limited, affecting the ability to find group differences. The CBORS system demonstrated good rater reliability and is more specific in nature than the CBAS, and it is deserving of future attention from researchers. Hopefully, additional research will be done to evaluate the effects of the well-designed ACEP program.

Program for Athletic Coaches' Education (PACE)

PACE is a 12-hour program, designed in accordance with a set of national standards for athletic coaches (National Association for Sport and Physical Education, 1995). The course provides instruction on 14 modules, covering topics such as guidelines for interscholastic athletics; legal responsibilities of coaches; emergency procedures for victims of accidents and injuries; prevention, care, and rehabilitation of sport injuries; role of the coach; skill instruction and game strategy; motivating athletes; personal and social skills; positive coaching; and maintaining discipline. The instruction within each module is scripted; it is based on learning objectives; and it utilizes workbooks, assignments and videos interspersed with lectures, discussions, and reviews. PACE instructors complete a course designed to provide them with information on using the instructor's guide and other pedagogical material.

Allen (1999) conducted a study to determine the degree to which instructors implemented the PACE program as intended by its developers. During the program's 1993-1994 academic year, 13 PACE instructors were observed at least once by trained research assistants. The observers used recording forms that paralleled the prescribed instructional plan to monitor its implementation. Additionally, 226 coaches who participated in the sessions were asked to complete parallel tests covering the intended outcomes associated with each module prior to and at the conclusion of instruction. Their opinions on the content's usefulness were also collected immediately after the presentation of each topic. The results showed increases in the coaches' knowledge in some areas, and they generally provided positive feedback concerning the usefulness of the course content. However, the implementation of the sessions varied greatly across instructors. Indeed, some instructors presented 80% to 100% of the module segments as prescribed, while others completely ignored the protocol and presented content other than that in the guide. The findings thus suggest problems with treatment fidelity and the need to alter the PACE training process for instructors. Poor treatment fidelity would severely limit the ability to draw conclusions about program effects in future evaluation research.

Malete and Feltz (2000) conducted a study to determine the effect of participation in PACE on coaches' perceived coaching efficacy. Following a quasi-experimental design, 46 high school coaches and 14 university-level coaching preparation students were recruited for the experimental ($n = 36$) and control groups ($n = 24$). The male and female participants completed pretest and posttest administrations of the Coaching Efficacy Scale (CES, Feltz, Chase, Moritz, & Sullivan, 1999), a questionnaire that assessed how confident they were in influencing the learning and performance of their athletes in four dimensions of coaching: character building, motivation, strategy, and technique. Coaches in the experimental group attended two weekend PACE sessions with a one-week interval between the sessions (i.e., a two-day program with six contact hours per day). Pretest data were obtained at the beginning of the first session, and administration of the posttest took place at the end of the PACE program.

Analysis of pretest to posttest CES subscale scores revealed that the control group coaches did not significantly change. However, a small but statistically significant increase was found for the PACE group, with changes in strategy efficacy and technique efficacy contributing most to the increase. In commenting on this effect, the investigators referred to it as a "statistically significant finding, but not practically significant when applied to the original scale" (p. 417). Moreover, whether enhancement of perceived coaching efficacy causes desirable changes in coaching practices is unknown in the absence of formal behavioral assessment or measures of perceived behaviors administered to the athletes. Likewise, the impact of the intervention on psychosocial outcomes of athletes who play for the coaches remains an important topic for future research.

Conclusion

Program evaluation research is not only essential for assessing the effects of social interventions, such as coach training programs, but is also a means of testing theories. By their very nature, intervention programs manipulate variables thought to make a difference in designated outcome variables. In a sense, they are like independent variables in traditional experiments. Whether the underlying hypotheses are formal or informal, and whether the theory on which the intervention is based is formal or intuitive, the results of the evaluation should have relevance to the model if the intervention was carried out appropriately. This, of course, can become an important issue in the event of negative results. Is the theory wrong, or was the performed intervention not successful in influencing the theoretical variables assumed to be important?

As noted above, several widely-used multifaceted programs, such as ACEP, PACE, and NYSCA, have achieved wide circulation, but have undergone little formal evaluation. It is our hope that this situation will be remedied in the years to come. The content of these programs seems intuitively valid, yet we know little about their influence on either coaching behaviors or their impact on the children who play for trained coaches. It is also unclear whether the methods used to deliver course content have their intended effects on coaches. In multifaceted programs of this type, each component (e.g., pedagogy, sport psychology) or module should be subjected to empirical evaluation, using appropriate outcome measures tailored to each domain. There are welcome signs of increased attention to evaluation methods for such programs (e.g., Abraham & Collins, 1998; Gilbert & Trudel, 1999), and new qualitative approaches have appeared that could be applied to program development and evaluation (e.g., Cote et al., 1995; Wiersma & Sherman, 2003). Hopefully, these new models and methodological advances will help stimulate an increase in evaluative research. The coaches who spend time and money to expose themselves to these programs and the athletes who are affected by coaching behaviors deserve no less.

References

Abraham, A., & Collins, D. (1998). Examining and extending research in coach development. *Quest, 50,* 59-79.

Allen, H. R. (1999, May). *Program for athletic coaches' education (PACE): An implementation evaluation.* Poster session presented at the conference on Youth Sports in the 21st Century, East Lansing, MI.

American Psychological Association Task Force on Psychological Intervention Guidelines. (1995). *Template for developing guidelines: Interventions for mental disorders and psychological aspects of physical disorders.* Washington, DC: American Psychological Association.

Ames, C. (1992a). Classrooms: Goals, structures, and student motivation. *Journal of Educational Psychology, 84,* 261-271.

Ames, C. (1992b). Achievement goals and adaptive motivational patterns: The role of the environment. In G. C. Roberts (Ed.), *Motivation in sport and exercise* (pp. 161-176). Champaign, IL: Human Kinetics.

Ames, C., & Archer, J. (1988). Achievement goals in the classroom: Students' learning strategies and motivation processes. *Journal of Educational Psychology, 80,* 260-267.

Anderson, J. R. (1990). *Cognitive psychology and its implications.* New York: Freeman.

Bandura, A. (1986). *Social foundations of thought and action: A social cognitive theory.* Englewood Cliffs, NJ: Prentice-Hall.

Bandura, A. (1997). *Self-efficacy: The exercise of control.* New York: Freeman.

Barnett, N. P., Smoll, F. L., & Smith, R. E. (1992). Effects of enhancing coach-athlete relationships on youth sport attrition. *The Sport Psychologist, 6,* 111-127.

Brown, B. R., & Butterfield, S. A. (1992). Coaches: A missing link in the health care system. *American Journal of Diseases in Childhood, 146,* 211-217.

Brustad, R. J. (1992). Integrating socialization influences into the study of children's motivation in sport. *Journal of Sport and Exercise Psychology, 14,* 59-77.

Buisman, A., & Lucassen, J. M. H. (1996). The Netherlands. In P. De Knop, L-M. Engstrom, B. Skirstad, & M. R. Weiss (Eds.), *Worldwide trends in youth sport* (pp. 152-169). Champaign, IL: Human Kinetics.

Burton, D., & Tannehill, D. (1987, April). *Developing better youth sport coaches: An evaluation of the American Coaching Effectiveness Program (ACEP) Level 1 training.* Paper presented at the meeting of the American Alliance of Health, Physical Education, Recreation and Dance, Las Vegas, NV.

Campbell, D. T., & Stanley, J. C. (1963). Experimental and quasi-experimental designs for research and teaching. In N L. Gage (Ed.), *Handbook of research on teaching* (pp. 78-103). Chicago: Rand-McNally.

Campbell, S. (1993). Coaching education around the world. *Sport Science Review, 2*, 62-74.

Chambless, D. L., & Hollon, S. D. (1998). Defining empirically supported therapies. *Journal of Consulting and Clinical Psychology, 66*, 7-18.

Chelladurai, P. (1990). Leadership in sports: A review. *International Journal of Sport Psychology, 21*, 328-354.

Chi, M. T. H., Glaser, R., & Farr, M. J. (Eds.). (1988). *The nature of expertise.* Hillsdale, NJ: Erlbaum.

Cohen, J., & Cohen, P. (1975). *Applied multiple regression/correlation in the behavioral sciences.* Hillsdale, NJ: Erlbaum.

Cote, J. (2002). Coach and peer influence on children's development through sport. In J. M. Silva III & D. E. Stevens (Eds.), *Psychological foundations of sport* (pp. 520-540). Boston: Allyn and Bacon.

Cote, J., Salmela, J., Trudel, P., Baria, A., & Russell, S. (1995). The Coaching Model: A grounded assessment of expert gymnastic coaches' knowledge. *Journal of Sport and Exercise Psychology, 17*, 1-17.

Curtis, B., Smith, R. E., & Smoll, F. L. (1979). Scrutinizing the skipper: A study of leadership behaviors in the dugout. *Journal of Applied Psychology, 64*, 391-400.

DeRubeis, R. J., & Crits-Christoph, P. (1998). Empirically supported individual and group psychological treatments for adult mental disorders. *Journal of Consulting and Clinical Psychology, 66*, 37-52.

Douge, B., & Hastie, P. (1993). Coach effectiveness. *Sport Science Review, 2*, 14-29.

Duda, J. L. (1987). Toward a developmental theory of children's motivation in sport. *Journal of Sport Psychology, 9*, 130-145.

Duda, J. L. (1996). Maximizing motivation in sport and physical education among children and adolescents: The case for greater task involvement. *Quest, 48*, 290-302.

Duda, J. L., & Hom, H. L. (1993). The interrelationships between children's and parent's goal orientations in sport. *Pediatric Exercise Science, 5*, 234-241.

Dweck, C. S. (1975). The role of expectations and attributions in the alleviation of learned helplessness. *Journal of Personality and Social Psychology, 31*, 674-685.

Dweck, C. S. (1999). *Self-theories and goals: Their role in motivation, personality, and development.* Philadelphia: Taylor & Francis.

Dweck, C. S., & Leggett, E. L. (1988). A social-cognitive approach to motivation *Psychological Review, 95*, 256-273.

Ebbeck, V., & Becker, S. L. (1994). Psychosocial predictors of goal orientations in youth soccer. *Research Quarterly for Exercise and Sport, 65*, 335-362.

Edelstein, B. A., & Eisler, R. M. (1976). Effects of modeling and modeling with instructions and feedback on the behavioral components of social skills. *Behavior Therapy, 7*, 382-389.

Elliott, A. J., & Church, M. A. (1997). A hierarchical model of approach and avoidance achievement motivation. *Journal of Educational Psychology, 72*, 218-232.

Epstein, J. (1988). Effective schools or effective students? Dealing with diversity. In R. Haskins & B. MacRae (Eds.), *Policies for America's schools* (pp. 89-126). Norwood, NJ: Ablex.

Epstein, J. (1989). Family structures and students motivation: A developmental perspective. In C. Ames & R. Ames (Eds.), *Research on motivation in education: Vol. 3. Goals and Cognitions* (pp. 259-295). New York: Academic Press.

Ewing, M. E., Seefeldt, V. D., & Brown, T. P. (1997). Role of organized sport in the education and health of American children and youth. In A. Poinsett (Ed.). *The role of sports in youth development* (pp. 1-157). New York: Carnegie Corporation.

Feltz, D. L., Chase, M. A., Moritz, S., & Sullivan, P. (1999). Development of the multidimensional coaching efficacy scale. *Journal of Educational Psychology, 91*, 765-776.

Franks, I. M., Johnson, R. B., & Sinclair, G. D. (1988). The development of a computerized coaching analysis system for recording behavior in sporting environments. *Journal of Teaching in Physical Education, 8*, 23-32.

Gallagher, J. D., French, K. E., Thomas, K. T. & Thomas, J. R. (2002). Expertise in youth sport: Relations between knowledge and skill. In F. L. Smoll & R. E. Smith (Eds.). *Children and youth in sport: A biopsychosocial perspective* (pp. 475-500). Dubuque, IA: Kendall/Hunt.

Gilbert, W., & Trudel, P. (1999). An evaluation strategy for coach education programs. *Journal of Sport Behavior, 22*, 234-250.

Gilbert, W. D. (2002, June). *An annotated bibliography and analysis of coaching science:* 1970-2001. (Available from Wade D. Gilbert, Department of Kinesiology, 5275 N. Campus Drive, M/S SG28, California State University, Fresno, Fresno, CA 93740-8018)

Goncalves, C. (1996). Portugal. In P. De Knop, L-M. Engstrom, B. Skirstad, & M. R. Weiss (Eds.), *Worldwide trends in youth sport* (pp. 193-203). Champaign, IL: Human Kinetics.

Goudas, M., Biddle, S., Fox, K., & Underwood, M. (1995). It ain't what you do, it's the way that you do it! Teaching style affects children's motivation in track and field lessons. *The Sport Psychologist, 9*, 254-264.

Gould, D. (1987). Understanding attrition in children's sport. In D. Gould & M. R. Weiss (Eds.), *Advances in pediatric sport sciences* (pp. 61-85). Champaign, IL: Human Kinetics.

Graham, R. H., & Carron, A. V. (1983). Impact of coaching certification on coaching attitudes. Canadian *Journal of Applied Sport Sciences, 8*, 180-188.

Harwood, C. (2002). Assessing achievement goals in sport: Caveats for consultants. *Journal of Applied Sport Psychology, 14*, 106-119.

Harwood, C., & Swain, A. (2002). The development and activation of achievement goals within tennis: II. A player, parent, and coach intervention. *The Sport Psychologist, 16*, 111-137.

Haslam, I. R. (1990). Expert Assessment of the National Coaching Certification Program (NCCP) theory component. *Canadian Journal of Sport Sciences, 15*, 201-212.

Hendry, L. B., & Love, J. G. (1996). Scotland. In P. De Knop, L-M. Engstrom, B. Skirstad, & M. R. Weiss (Eds.), *Worldwide trends in youth sport* (pp. 204-221). Champaign, IL: Human Kinetics.

Horn, T. S. (1984). Expectancy effects in the interscholastic athletic setting: Methodological considerations. *Journal of Sport Psychology, 6*, 60-76.

Huberman, W. L., & O'Brien, R. M. (1999). Improving therapist and patient performance in chronic psychiatric group homes through goal-setting, feedback, and positive reinforcement. *Journal of Organizational Behavior Management, 19*, 13-36.

Huitema, B. (1980). *Analysis of covariance and alternatives.* New York: Wiley.

Kanfer, F. H., & Gaelick-Buys, L. (1991). Self-management methods. In F. H. Kanfer & A. P. Goldstein (Eds.), *Helping people change: A textbook of methods* (4th ed., pp. 305-360). New York: Pergamon.

Kazdin, A. E. (1980). *Research design in clinical psychology.* New York: Harper & Row.

Laakso, Telama, R., & Yang, X. (1996). Finland. In P. De Knop, L-M. Engstrom, B. Skirstad, & M. R. Weiss (Eds.), *Worldwide trends in youth sport* (pp. 126-138). Champaign, IL: Human Kinetics.

Leffingwell, T., Smoll, F. L., & Smith, R. E. (2000). *Perceptions mediate the impact of coaching behaviors on young athletes.* Unpublished manuscript, University of Washington.

Lipsey, M. W., & Cordray, D. S. (2000). Evaluation methods for social intervention. *Annual Review of Psychology, 51,* 345-376.

Maehr, M. L. (1983). On doing well in science. Why Johnny no longer excels; why Sarah never did. In S. G. Paris, G. M. Olson, & H. W. Stevenson (Eds.), *Learning and motivation in the classroom.* Hillsdale, NJ: Erlbaum.

Malete, L., & Feltz, D. L. (2000). The effect of a coaching education program on coaching efficacy. *The Sport Psychologist, 14,* 410-417.

Martens, R. (1997). *Successful coaching.* Champaign, IL: Human Kinetics.

Martin, G. L., & Tkachuk, G. A. (2000). Behavioral sport psychology. In J. Austin & J. E. Carr (Eds.), *Handbook of applied behavior analysis* (pp. 399-422). Reno, NV: Context Press.

McArdle, S., & Duda, J. L. (2002). Implications of the motivational climate in youth sports. In F. L. Smoll & R. E. Smith (Eds.), *Children and youth in sport: A biopsychosocial perspective* (2nd ed., 409-434). Dubuque, IA: Kendall/Hunt.

McFall, R. M. (1977). Parameters of self-monitoring. In R. B. Stuart (Ed.), *Behavioral self-management: Strategies, techniques and outcomes* (pp. 196-214). New York: Brunner/Mazel.

Midgley, C., Kaplan, A., Middleton, M., Maehr, M. M., Urdan, T., Anderman, L. H., & Roeser, R. (1998). The development and validation of scales assessing students' achievement goal orientations. *Contemporary Educational Psychology, 23,* 113-131.

Miller, G. A., & Chapman, J. P. (2001). Misunderstanding analysis of covariance. *Journal of Abnormal Psychology, 110,* 40-48.

Mischel, W. (1973). Toward a cognitive social learning reconceptualization of personality. *Psychological Review, 80,* 252-282.

Mischel, W., & Shoda, Y. (1995). A cognitive-affective system theory of personality: Reconceptualizing situations, dispositions, dynamics, and invariance in personality structure. *Psychological Review, 102,* 246-268.

National Association for Sport and Physical Education. (1995). *National standards for athletic coaches.* Reston, VA: Author.

Nicholls, J. G. (1984). Achievement motivation: Conception of ability, subjective experience, mastery choice, and performance. *Psychological Review, 91,* 328-346.

Nicholls, J. G. (1989). *The competitive ethos and democratic education.* Cambridge, MA: Harvard University Press.

Nicholls, J. G., Cheung, P. C., Lauer, J., & Patashnick, M. (1988). Individual differences in academic motivation: Perceived ability, goals, beliefs and values. *Learning and Individual Differences, 1,* 63-84.

Oldenhove, H. (1996). Australia. In P. De Knop, L-M. Engstrom, B. Skirstad, & M. R. Weiss (Eds.), *Worldwide trends in youth sport* (pp. 245-259). Champaign, IL: Human Kinetics.

Papaioannou, A. (1994). The development of a questionnaire to measure achievement orientations in physical education. *Research Quarterly for Exercise and Sport, 65,* 11-20.

Papaioannou, A., & Kouli, O. (1999). The effect of task structure, perceived motivational climate and goal orientations on students' task involvement and anxiety. *Journal of Applied Sport Psychology, 11,* 51-71.

Rushall, B. S. (1977). Two observation schedules for sporting and physical education environments. *Canadian Journal of Applied Sport Sciences, 1,* 138-150.

Scanlan, T. K., & Lewthwaite, R. (1984) Social psychological aspects of competition for male youth sport participants: I. Predictors of competitive stress. *Journal of Sport Psychology, 6,* 208-226.

Scanlan, T. K., & Lewthwaite, R. (1986). Social psychological aspects of competition for male youth sport participants: IV. Predictors of enjoyment. *Journal of Sport Psychology, 8,* 25-35.

Scanlan, T. K., & Passer, M. W. (1978). Factors related to competitive stress among male youth sports participants. *Medicine and Science in Sports, 10,* 103-108.

Scanlan, T. K., & Passer, M. W. (1979). Sources of competitive stress in young female athletes. *Journal of Sport Psychology, 1,* 151-159.

Seefeldt, V., Clark, M. A., & Brown, E. W. (Eds.). (2001). *Program for athletic coaches' education* (3rd ed.). Traverse City, MI: Cooper.

Smith, R. E. (1999). The sport psychologist as scientist-practitioner: Reciprocal relations linking theory, research, and intervention. In R. Lidor & M. Bar-Eli (Eds), *Sport psychology: Linking theory and practice* (pp. 15-34). Morgantown, WV: Fitness Information Technology.

Smith, R. E., & Smoll, F. L. (1990). Self-esteem and children's reactions to youth sport coaching behaviors: A field study of self-enhancement processes. *Developmental Psychology, 26,* 987-993.

Smith, R. E., & Smoll, F. L. (1997). Coaching the coaches: Youth sports as a scientific and applied behavioral setting. *Current Directions in Psychological Science, 6,* 16-21.

Smith, R. E., & Smoll, F. L. (2002). *Way to go, coach! A scientifically-proven approach to coaching effectiveness* (2nd ed.). Portola Valley, CA: Warde.

Smith, R. E., Smoll, F. L., & Barnett, N. P. (1995). Reduction of children's sport performance anxiety through social support and stress-reduction training for coaches. *Journal of Applied Developmental Psychology, 16,* 125-142.

Smith, R. E., Smoll, F. L., & Christensen, D. S. (1996). Behavioral assessment and interventions in youth sports. *Behavior Modification, 20,* 3-44.

Smith, R. E., Smoll, F. L., & Curtis, B. (1978). Coaching behaviors in Little League Baseball. In F. L. Smoll & R. E. Smith (Eds.), *Psychological perspectives in youth sports* (pp. 173-201). Washington, DC: Hemisphere.

Smith, R. E., Smoll, F. L., & Curtis, B. (1979). Coach Effectiveness Training: A cognitive-behavioral approach to enhancing relationship skills in youth sport coaches. *Journal of Sport Psychology, 1,* 59-75.

Smith, R. E., Smoll, F. L., & Hunt, E. B. (1977). A system for the behavioral assessment of athletic coaches. *Research Quarterly, 48,* 401-407.

Smith, R. E., Zane, N. W. S., Smoll, F. L., & Coppel, D. B. (1983). Behavioral assessment in youth sports: Coaching behaviors and children's attitudes. *Medicine and Science in Sports and Exercise, 15,* 208-214.

Smith, R. E., & Smoll, F. L. (1990). Self-esteem and children's reactions to youth sport coaching behaviors: A field study of self-enhancement processes. *Developmental Psychology, 26,* 987-993.

Smoll, F. L. (2001). Coach-parent relationships in youth sports: Increasing harmony and minimizing hassle. In J. M. Williams (Ed.), *Applied sport psychology: Personal growth to peak performance* (4th ed., pp. 150-161). Mountain View, CA Mayfield.

Smoll, F. L., & Smith, R. E. (1981). Developing a healthy philosophy of winning. In V. Seefeldt, F. L. Smoll, R. E. Smith, & D. Gould, *A winning philosophy for youth sports programs* (pp. 17-24). East Lansing, MI: Institute for the Study of Youth Sports.

Smoll, F. L., & Smith, R. E. (1989). Leadership behaviors in sport: A theoretical model and research paradigm. *Journal of Applied Social Psychology, 19,* 1522-1551.

Smoll, F. L., & Smith, R. E. (1997). *Coaches who never lose: Making sure athletes win, no matter what the score.* Portola Valley, CA: Warde.

Smoll, F. L., & Smith, R. E. (2001). Conducting sport psychology training programs for coaches: Cognitive-behavioral principles and techniques. In J. M. Williams (Ed.), *Applied sport psychology: Personal growth to peak performance* (4th ed., pp. 378-400). Mountain View, CA: Mayfield.

Smoll, F. L., & Smith, R. E. (2002). Coaching behavior research and intervention in youth sports. In F. L. Smoll & R. E. Smith (Eds.), *Children and youth in sport: A biopsychosocial perspective* (2nd ed., pp. 211-231). Dubuque, IA: Kendall/Hunt.

Smoll, F. L., Smith, R. E, Curtis, B., & Hunt, E. (1978). Toward a mediational model of coach-player relationships. *Research Quarterly, 49,* 528-541.

Smoll, F. L., Smith, R. E., Barnett, N. P., & Everett, J. J. (1993). Enhancement of children's self-esteem through social support training for youth sport coaches. *Journal of Applied Psychology, 78,* 602-610.

Solmon, M. A. (1996). Impact of motivational climate on students' behaviors and perceptions in a physical education setting. *Journal of Educational Psychology, 88,* 731-738.

Theeboom, M., De Knop, P., & Weiss, M. (1995). Motivational climate, psychological responses and motor skill development in children's sport: A field-based intervention study. *Journal of Sport and Exercise Psychology, 3,* 294-311.

Treasure, D. C., Duda, J. L., Hall, H. K., Roberts, G. C., Ames, C., & Maehr, M. L. (2001). Clarifying misconceptions and misrepresentations in achievement goal research in sport: A response to Harwood, Hardy, and Swain. *Journal of Sport and Exercise Psychology, 23,* 317-329.

Wankel, L. M., & Mummery, W. K. (1996). Canada. In P. De Knop, L-M. Engstrom, B. Skirstad, & M. R. Weiss (Eds.), *Worldwide trends in youth sport* (pp. 27-42). Champaign, IL: Human Kinetics.

Weiss, M. R., & Hayashi, C. T. (1996). The United States. In P. De Knop, L-M. Engstrom, B. Skirstad, & M. R. Weiss (Eds.), *Worldwide trends in youth sport* (pp. 43-57). Champaign, IL: Human Kinetics.

Weitlauf, J., Smith, R. E., & Cervone, D. (2000). Generalization effects of coping skills training: Influence of self-defense training on women's efficacy beliefs, assertiveness, and aggression. *Journal of Applied Psychology, 85,* 625-633.

Wiersma, L. D., & Sherman, C. P. (2003). *Attitudes of volunteer youth sport coaches toward coaching education/certification and parental codes of conduct.* Unpublished manuscript, California State University, Fullerton.

Woodman, L. (1993). Coaching: A science, an art, an emerging profession. *Sport Science Review, 2,* 1-13.

Yamaguchi, Y. (1996). Japan. In P. De Knop, L-M. Engstrom, B. Skirstad, & M. R. Weiss (Eds.), *Worldwide trends in youth sport* (pp. 67-75). Champaign, IL: Human Kinetics.

Section VI
Special Topics

Introduction

The three chapters of this section are quiet heterogeneous but there is also a link—health and well being in and through physical activity. Thus, the section is representing the state of the art in exercise psychology.

In the first chapter, Britton Brewer and Dean Tripp refer to injuries in sport. The issue of prevention and rehabilitation of sport injuries is quite popular and there are a lot of applications, but only recently have these interventions been subjected to empirical scrutiny. The psychological application is in need of elaborated concepts for a sufficient understanding, and sophisticated strategies are also especially in need of an evidence-based approach.

The second chapter, by Gershon Tenenbaum, addresses a central issue in sport and exercise psychology, in spite of the fact that the study of perceived effort has not been among the mainstream topics in the sport and exercise psychology research. As a consequence of the author's review of dominant, traditional trends in the study of perceived effort, a new conceptual framework is offered that consists of recent social cognitive theories and advances in methodology.

In the final chapter of this section, Dieter Hackfort and Hans-Albert Birkner review the most influential concepts in exercise psychology out of a specific theoretical perspective. Based on their action-theory perspective, they argue for a framework which is able to integrate the significant insights by the various approaches, to detect and complement neglected aspects, and to contribute to a more holistic and sophisticated action orientation.

Each chapter includes discussions on theoretical, methodological, and applied issues. The authors introduce new perspectives and approaches. With each contribution, a step toward a more holistic understanding and evidence-based action orientation is realized.

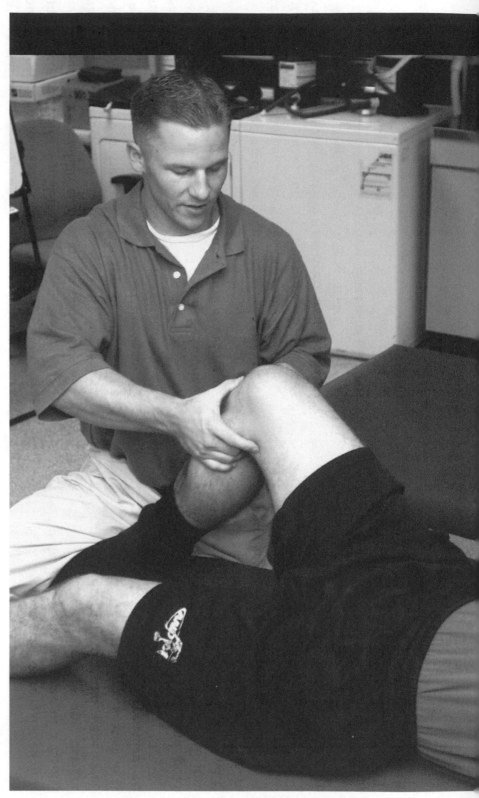

Courtesy of Cpl. Cindy L. Pray/U.S. Marine Corps

6.1

Psychological Applications in the Prevention and Rehabilitation of Sport Injuries

BRITTON W. BREWER AND DEAN A. TRIPP

Despite technological advances in sports equipment, improved coaching techniques, and activity-specific physical conditioning, injury is still prevalent in contemporary sport. Conservative estimates place the number of sport and recreation injuries at 3 to 6 million per year in the United States alone (Bijur et al., 1995; Burt & Overpeck, 2001; Kraus & Conroy, 1984). The severity of sport injuries can range from bruises and minor cuts requiring stitches to more devastating injuries such as spinal cord damage and paralysis (Smith, Scott, & Wiese, 1990). The costs associated with sport-related injuries are substantial in terms of medical expenses (e.g., diagnostic tests, surgery), impairment of sport performance, and daily

functioning. Annual health care costs associated with one of the more severe and debilitating sport injuries, an acute tear of the anterior cruciate ligament (ACL), have been estimated at 1 billion dollars in the United States (Griffin et al., 2000). Surveys of intercollegiate varsity sport participants suggest that as many as 35% of athletes may sustain injuries of sufficient severity to interfere with continued involvement in sport competition (Meeuwisse & Fowler, 1988). Sport injuries result in the restriction of life activity and the experience of significant pain for nearly half of all injured amateur athletes (Garrick & Requa, 1978; Hardy & Crace, 1990).

For more than three decades, researchers have

examined sport injury from a psychological perspective. Augmenting the traditional emphasis of sports medicine on identifying physical factors that contribute to the prevention and treatment of sport injuries, investigators have studied the psychological antecedents and consequences of sport injury. Scientific inquiry on psychological aspects of sport injury has provided a strong foundation for application. Psychological interventions designed to reduce injury risk and enhance recovery from injury have long been recommended (e.g., Astle, 1986; Gordon, 1986; Rotella, 1984; Weiss & Troxel, 1986), but have only recently been subjected to empirical scrutiny. The purpose of this chapter is to review research on psychological applications in the prevention and rehabilitation of sport injuries. For each aspect of sport injury—prevention and rehabilitation—relevant psychological theory and research are summarized, intervention studies are examined, and future directions for research and practice are provided.

Sport Injury Prevention

Theory and Research on Psychological Antecedents of Sport Injury

Although physical factors undoubtedly contribute to the occurrence of sport injuries, research strongly suggests that psychological factors also exert influ-

ence on injury outcomes. Following the lead of Holmes (1970), who documented a positive association between life stress and time loss due to injury in football players, investigators have examined the potential role of numerous psychological variables as risk factors for sport injury. Life stress is the psychological factor most consistently related to the occurrence of sport injury, with 30 of 35 studies reviewed by Williams (2001) documenting associations between life stress and sport injury. Although the strength of the stress-injury relationship and the types of life stress (e.g., positive, negative) associated with the occurrence of sport injuries have varied across studies (Williams, 2001), the robustness of the link between stress and sport injury prompted Andersen and Williams (1988) to develop a stress-based model of sport injury occurrence. In this recently revised model (Williams & Andersen, 1998; see Figure 1), the dynamic interplay between athletes' cognitive and physiological/attentional responses to potentially stressful sport situations has clear influence on sport injury vulnerability. Personality, history of stressors, coping resources, and interventions are posited to moderate the relationship between the stress response and injury.

Research has provided general support for hypotheses generated from the stress-injury model (Andersen & Williams, 1988; Williams & Andersen,

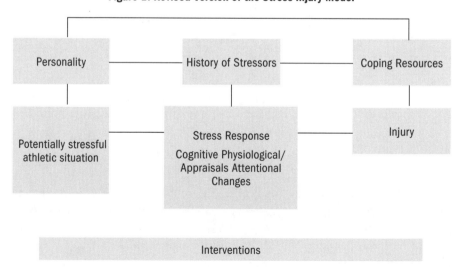

Figure 1: Revised Version of the Stress Injury Model

1998). With respect to personality, dispositional factors such as competitive trait anxiety (Blackwell & McCullagh, 1990; Hanson, McCullagh, & Tonymon, 1992; Lavallee & Flint, 1996; Passer & Seese, 1983; Petrie, 1993), locus of control (Dalhauser & Thomas, 1979; Kolt & Kirkby, 1996; Pargman & Lunt, 1989), tough mindedness (Wittig & Schurr, 1994), and Type A behavior (Fields, Delaney, & Hinkle, 1990) have been found to correlate directly with sport injury occurrence or severity. Competitive trait anxiety (Petrie, 1993) and sensation seeking (Smith, Ptacek, & Smoll, 1992) have been shown to moderate the relationship between life stress and time loss to injury. Mood states, which have a strong dispositional quality that is more transitory than that of personality characteristics, have also been associated with sport injury outcomes (Lavallee & Flint, 1996; Van Mechelen et al., 1996; Williams, Hogan, & Andersen, 1993). As noted above, history of stressors (i.e., accumulated life stress) has been consistently documented as a predictor of sport injury (Williams, 2001). Regarding the hypothesized influence of coping resources on vulnerability to sport injury, social support has been found to predict the frequency or severity of sport injury (Hardy, Richman, & Rosenfeld, 1991; Maddison, 2004; Williams, Tonymon, & Wadsworth, 1986) and both social support and psychological coping skills have been found to moderate the life stress-sport injury relationship (Andersen & Williams, 1999; Maddison, 2004; Petrie, 1992; Patterson, Smith, & Everett, 1998; Smith, Smoll, & Ptacek, 1990).

In terms of the proposed role of the stress response in affecting sport injury outcomes, research has shown that: (a) athletes with high levels of life stress experienced greater narrowing of peripheral vision on laboratory perceptual tasks than athletes with lower levels of life stress (Williams, Tonymon, & Andersen, 1990, 1991); (b) athletes with high-risk injury profiles in terms of history of stressors and coping resources performing a laboratory perceptual task under stressful conditions were more distractible in the center of the visual field than those without lower-risk profiles (Williams & Andersen, 1997); (c) injury vulnerability was elevated for athletes with high levels of life stress whose vigilance was impaired (i.e., broad, external attention, Thompson & Morris, 1994) ; and (d) athletes low in social support,

high in negative life event stress, and high in narrowing of peripheral vision during a stressful perceptual task sustained more injuries than athletes high in social support, low in negative life event stress, and low in peripheral narrowing (Andersen & Williams, 1999). Presumably, narrowed peripheral vision and impaired vigilance, along with the hypothesized but undocumented factor of elevated muscular tension, increase one's vulnerability to sport injuries.

Preventive Intervention Studies

The portion of the Andersen and Williams (1988; Williams & Andersen, 1998) model involving interventions has been largely ignored by researchers. Despite the demonstrated utility of the model in predicting sport injuries, very few studies have examined the effectiveness of psychological interventions in reducing vulnerability to sport injury. In accord with the model, interventions aimed at altering the stress response—by modifying cognitive appraisals of potentially stressful events, decreasing muscle tension, enhancing attentional focus, or some other method—would be expected to reduce injury risk. Interventions targeting moderators of the stress-injury relationship (e.g., competitive trait anxiety, psychological coping skills, social support) could also produce favorable effects on the occurrence of sport injuries (Williams, 2001).

The earliest support for using psychological interventions to reduce vulnerability to sport injury came from studies in which performance enhancement or general stress reduction, not injury prevention, was the primary focus of the intervention. In general, these studies were conducted with small samples and lacked formal statistical comparisons. Nevertheless, the results of the investigations suggested that interventions such as cognitive and physiological (biofeedback) training (DeWitt, 1980), relaxation training (Murphy, 1988), attentional control and imagery training (May & Brown, 1989), and attentional focusing (Schomer, 1990) could conceivably have a favorable impact on subsequent sport injury outcomes.

Studies by Davis (1991) and Kerr and Goss (1996) provided more substantial evidence in support of using psychological interventions to decrease vulnerability to sport injury. Although Davis' study lacked control groups and tests of statistical significance, he found that injuries to intercollegiate swimmers and football players were reduced by 52% and 33%, respectively, following the introduction of a program of progressive relaxation and sport-specific imagery. Addressing the methodological shortcomings of Davis, Kerr and Goss, experimental investigation of elite gymnasts showed that athletes who participated in a stress management intervention using a stress inoculation training framework (Meichenbaum, 1985) reported significantly less negative athletic stress and negative total stress than athletes who did not receive the intervention. Although the effect of the intervention on injury incidence was not statistically significant, likely due to insufficient statistical power rather than the strength of the effect, an injury-reducing effect size in the medium range was obtained (Andersen & Stoove, 1998).

Extending the work of Davis (1991) and Kerr and Goss (1996), a pair of recent randomized, controlled clinical trials assessing the impact of psychological interventions on injury-related time loss in competitive athletes have shown statistically significant effect (Maddison, 2004; Perna, Antoni, Baum, Gordon, & Schneiderman, 2003). Perna et al. found that collegiate rowers who received a cognitive-behavioral stress management (CBSM) program had significantly fewer injury (and illness) days than those who received no intervention. Similarly, Maddison reported that among rugby players deemed to be at elevated risk for injury based on their previous injury history, high level of life stress, and low levels of coping skills and social support, players who received a CBSM intervention experienced significantly less time loss due to injury than those who were not administered a CBSM program. Together, the Perna et al. and Maddison studies have raised the standard for methodological rigor of psychologically oriented preventive intervention research in the realm of sport injury.

Future Directions for Research and Practice
Preliminary research (Davis, 1991; DeWitt, 1980; Kerr & Goss, 1996; Maddison, 2004; May & Brown, 1989; Murphy, 1988; Perna et al., 2003; Schomer, 1990) suggests that stress management interventions (e.g., cognitive restructuring, imagery, relaxation) can decrease susceptibility to sport injury. Although encouraging, these data do not fully explicate the role of psychological interventions in preventing sport injury. Randomized controlled trials with larger samples of athletes at elevated risk for injury (based on their involvement in a sport with a high incidence of injury and their profile on empirically documented psychological antecedents of sport injury) are sorely needed to evaluate the utility of psychological interventions in the reduction of sport injury (Cupal, 1998). Optimally, interventions considered in future investigations should be grounded in relevant theory (cf. Andersen & Williams, 1988; Williams & Andersen, 1998). One aim of future research could be to identify the characteristics of the most effective interventions in various athlete populations and to determine the most efficient ways of implementing the interventions. The fact that psychological interventions targeting outcomes other than injury prevention may help reduce the occurrence of injuries and injury-related time loss from sport (Davis, 1991; DeWitt, 1980; Maddison, 2004; May & Brown, 1989; Murphy, 1988; Perna et al., 2003; Schomer, 1990) suggests that preventive interventions can be combined with performance enhancement interventions to save time and increase efficiency. Another potential avenue for implementing preventive psychological interventions is to include them as part of physical training programs that have been developed to prevent anterior cruciate ligament tears and other sport injuries.

Sport Injury Rehabilitation

Theory and Research on Psychological Factors in Sport Injury Rehabilitation

Psychological responses to sport injury
Just as the role of psychological factors in the occurrence of sport injuries has been recognized by researchers and practitioners, so, too, has the role of psychological factors in the rehabilitation of sport injuries. Little (1969) was among the first to document empirically the psychological consequences of sport injury, showing that neurotic symptoms were preceded by injury (or illness) to a significantly greater extent in athletic men than in nonathletic men. Following Little's seminal work, early attempts to provide theoretical guidance for inquiry on the psychological effects of sport injury involved adapting models of

grief and loss to the sport injury context. For example, noting that sport injury may involve loss of an aspect of the self (Peretz, 1970), several researchers (e.g., Astle, 1986; Lynch, 1988; Rotella, 1985) applied a stage model of adjustment to terminal illness (Kübler-Ross, 1969) to sport injury. In the adapted Kübler-Ross model, athletes are thought to progress through a sequential series of stages—denial, anger, bargaining, depression, and acceptance—after sustaining an injury. Other similar stage models, varying in the content and number of stages, have also been applied to sport injury (Evans & Hardy, 1995).

Although responses consistent with a grief reaction have been observed following sport injury (Macchi & Crossman, 1996) and athletes tend to display more adaptive emotions over time after injury (e.g., McDonald & Hardy, 1990; Smith, Scott, O'Fallon, & Young, 1990; Uemukai, 1993), research has not supported the notion that athletes follow a predictable sequence of psychological responses to injury (Brewer, 1994). As with responses to traumatic events in general (Silver & Wortman, 1980), psychological reactions to sport injury vary extensively across individuals and do not tend to follow any particular stereotypic, stage-like pattern (Brewer, 1994). As an alternative to stage models, researchers (e.g., Gordon, 1986; Weiss & Troxel, 1986) have proposed models that are based largely upon stress and coping theory and highlight the myriad factors that contribute to individual differences in psychological responses to sport injury. The most elaborate and well-developed of these models, which have been labeled "cognitive appraisal models" for the key role ascribed to cognitive interpretations of injury situation in influencing reactions to sport injury (Brewer, 1994), is that of Wiese-Bjornstal, Smith, Shaffer, and Morrey (1998). In their "integrated model," which was designed to incorporate elements of grief models within a cognitive appraisal framework, Wiese-Bjornstal et al. posited that preinjury variables (e.g., personality, history of stressors, and coping resources) and postinjury variables jointly affect athletes' responses to injury. More specifically, characteristics of the person (e.g., the nature of the injury, personality, demographic features, physical attributes) and the situation in which rehabilitation is occurring (e.g., sport-specific factors, social aspects, environmental variables) are thought to interact in the formation of injury-related cognitive appraisals. The cognitive appraisals, in turn, are thought to affect and be affected by emotional and behavioral responses to injury, with the reciprocal relationships of cognitive, emotional, and behavioral factors ultimately contributing to physical and psychological rehabilitation outcomes.

Research has provided support for hypotheses generated from cognitive appraisal models. A thorough review of the many studies in which such support was obtained is beyond the scope of this chapter, but a summary of the empirical literature on cognitive, emotional, and behavioral responses to sport injury is warranted. Although relatively few investigations have examined cognitive responses to sport injury, there is evidence that athletes with injuries report lower self-esteem than athletes without injuries (Chan & Grossman, 1988; Kleiber & Brock, 1992; Leddy, Lambert, & Ogles, 1994; McGowan, Pierce, Williams, & Eastman, 1993) and that self-esteem decreases following sport injury (Leddy et al., 1994). A personal factor—psychological investment in playing sport professionally—has been negatively correlated with postinjury self-esteem (Kleiber & Brock, 1992) and a situational factor—time since injury occurrence—has been associated with postinjury sport self-confidence (Quinn & Fallon, 1999). Further, athletes with injuries have been shown to readily generate attributions for the occurrence of their injuries (Brewer, 1991; Laurence, 1997; Tedder & Biddle, 1998) and use an abundance of cognitive coping strategies, including accepting injury, focusing on recovery, thinking positively, and using imagery (Bianco, Malo, & Orlick, 1999; Gould, Udry, Bridges, & Beck, 1997; Rose & Jevne, 1993; Udry, Gould, Bridges, & Beck, 1997). Coping strategy use has been shown to vary as a function of personality characteristics (Grove & Bahnsen, 1997) and stage of rehabilitation (Udry, 1997), which constitute personal and situational variables, respectively.

Of the various types of psychological response to sport injury, emotional reactions have garnered the most attention in research investigations. Results of qualitative studies have suggested that athletes experience a host of negative emotions following injury, including anger, confusion, depression, fear, and frustration (e.g., Bianco et al., 1999; Johnston & Carroll, 1998; Udry et al., 1997). These emotions are reportedly influenced by: (a) cognitive appraisals

(Johnston & Carroll, 1998a); (b) personal factors such as athletic identity (Sparkes, 1998) and previous injury experience (Bianco et al., 1999); and (c) situational factors such as injury severity and type, rehabilitation progress, and time of the season (Bianco et al., 1999; Johnston & Carroll, 1998). Numerous quantitative studies have verified the qualitative findings and provided additional details about the emotional responses of athletes to injury. As noted in a recent review of the literature (Brewer, 2001), quantitative research has indicated that (a) approximately 5 to 24% of athletes with injuries experience clinically meaningful emotional disturbances; (b) athletes with injuries report greater emotional distress than athletes without injuries; (c) emotional distress increases following sport injury; (d) personal factors such as age, athletic identity, and hardiness are correlated with postinjury emotions; (e) situational factors such as injury severity and type, life stress, rehabilitation progress, social support, and time of the season are related to postinjury emotions; and (e) postinjury emotions are associated with a variety of cognitive factors, including cognitive appraisals of injury coping ability and causal attributions for injury occurrence.

Adherence to sport injury rehabilitation programs and coping behaviors are the main types of behavioral responses to sport injury that have been examined empirically. Research on sport injury rehabilitation adherence has provided strong support for the cognitive appraisal perspective. A recent review of the literature (Brewer, 1999) revealed that investigators have documented associations between rehabilitation adherence and personal factors (e.g., internal health locus of control, pain tolerance, self-motivation, tough mindedness), situational factors (e.g., belief in the efficacy of treatment, comfort of the clinical environment, convenience of rehabilitation scheduling, perceived injury severity, social support for rehabilitation), cognitive responses (e.g., perceived ability to cope with injury, attribution of recovery to stable and personally controllable factors, goal setting, use of imagery and positive self-talk), and emotional responses (e.g., mood disturbance). With regard to coping behaviors, qualitative and quantitative studies have shown that athletes with injuries tend to adopt coping strategies that involve actively dealing with rehabilitation obstacles through

such methods as vigorously pursuing rehabilitation goals and seeking information or support from others (Bianco et al., 1999; Gould et al., 1997; Grove & Bahnsen, 1997; Udry, 1997). There is some disagreement, however, as to whether the coping behavior of athletes with injuries does (Bianco et al., 1999; Quinn & Fallon, 1999) or does not (Udry, 1997) vary over the course of rehabilitation.

Psychological factors and sport injury rehabilitation outcomes.

Although it is proposed in the integrated model of psychological response to sport injury (Wiese-Bjornstal et al., 1998) that physical and psychosocial recovery are influenced by the combined effects of cognitive, emotional, and behavioral responses to sport injury, the model does not specify the ways rehabilitation outcomes are affected. The biopsychosocial model of sport injury rehabilitation (Brewer, Andersen, & Van Raalte, 2002) was developed to identify potential pathways from biological, psychological, and social variables to sport injury rehabilitation outcomes. As shown in Figure 2, psychological factors are thought to be affected by injury characteristics and sociodemographic factors following sport injury and subsequently to share reciprocal relationships with biological and social/contextual factors. Psychological factors are also proposed to influence and be influenced by intermediate biopsychosocial outcomes and sport injury rehabilitation outcomes, two groups of conceptually similar variables that are considered together as "rehabilitation outcomes" for the purposes of this discussion.

A growing body of correlational findings has demonstrated that psychological factors of central importance to the integrated model are associated with rehabilitation outcomes. Personal/sociodemographic factors related to outcomes include personality (Wise, Jackson, & Rocchio, 1979), gender (Johnson, 1997), athletic identity (Brewer, Van Raalte, et al., 2000), and optimism (LaMott, 1994). With respect to situational and social/contextual variables, social support has been positively related to rehabilitation outcomes in two studies (Gould et al., 1997; Tuffey, 1991). Among the many cognitive factors that have been linked to rehabilitation outcomes are attribution of recovery to stable and personally controllable factors (Brewer, Cornelius, et

Figure 2: A Biopsychosocial Model of Sport Injury Rehabilitation

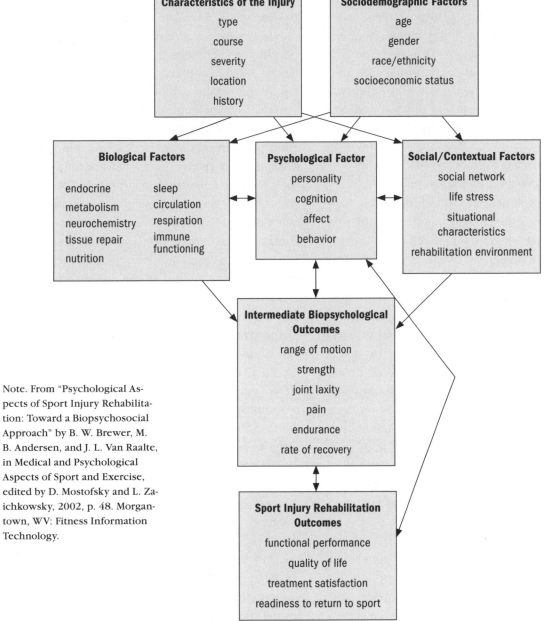

Note. From "Psychological Aspects of Sport Injury Rehabilitation: Toward a Biopsychosocial Approach" by B. W. Brewer, M. B. Andersen, and J. L. Van Raalte, in Medical and Psychological Aspects of Sport and Exercise, edited by D. Mostofsky and L. Zaichkowsky, 2002, p. 48. Morgantown, WV: Fitness Information Technology.

al., 2000; Laubach et al., 1996), injury-related cognitive appraisals (Johnson, 1997), pain coping (Morrey, Stuart, Smith, & Wiese-Bjornstal, 1999), number of rehabilitation goals, attitude toward rehabilitation, and use of goal setting (Gould et al., 1997; Ievleva & Orlick, 1991), healing/recovery imagery (Ievleva & Orlick, 1991), and imagery/visualization (Gould et al., 1997).

Negative emotional factors correlated with rehabilitation outcomes include injury rehabilitation anx-

iety (Johnson, 1997), psychological distress (Brewer, Van Raalte, et al., 2000), anger (de Heredia, Munoz, & Artaza, 2004; LaMott, 1994), mood disturbance (de Heredia, Munoz, & Artaza, 2004; Morrey et al., 1999), depression, fatigue, tension (de Heredia, Munoz, & Artaza, 2004), fear, and frustration (LaMott, 1994). Behaviors associated with favorable rehabilitation outcomes include higher levels of adherence to sport injury rehabilitation (de Heredia, Munoz, & Artaza, 2004; Brewer, Cornelius et al., 2003; Brewer,

Van Raalte, et al., 2000; Derscheid & Feiring, 1987; Treacy, Barron, Brunet, & Barrack, 1997; Tuffey, 1991), lower levels of physical inactivity (Gould et al., 1997), and higher levels of seeking social support (Gould et al., 1997; Johnson, 1997). Although causal inferences regarding the relationship between psychological factors and rehabilitation outcomes cannot be drawn from the results of the correlational studies, the findings nonetheless provide a strong foundation for experimental research on the topic.

Psychological interventions to enhance sport injury rehabilitation.

The logical applications of research on psychological responses to sport injury and the role of psychological factors in sport injury rehabilitation are to develop, implement, and evaluate psychological interventions to enhance sport injury rehabilitation processes and outcomes. In theory, manipulating variables that are correlated with rehabilitation processes and outcomes has the potential to elicit changes in these factors. Experimental investigations of the efficacy of psychological interventions in the realm of sport injury rehabilitation have provided the strongest evidence of causal links between psychological factors and sport injury rehabilitation outcomes. Psychological interventions that have been examined experimentally in the context of sport injury rehabilitation include biofeedback, goal setting, relaxation/imagery, self-talk, modeling, and multimodal treatment packages.

Biofeedback, which entails providing the recipient with physiological information (e.g., amount of electromyographic [EMG] activity in the quadriceps), has been used as a rehabilitative intervention in four studies that have included experimental controls (Draper, 1990; Draper & Ballard, 1991; Krebs, 1981; Levitt et al., 1995). Participants in all four of the studies were individuals undergoing postsurgical rehabilitation of knee injuries. Across the four studies, biofeedback produced significant gains in knee/leg strength (Draper, 1990; Draper & Ballard, 1991; Krebs, 1981; Levitt et al., 1995), EMG output (Krebs, 1981; Levitt et al., 1995), and range of motion (Draper, 1990). Although the mechanisms responsible for the success of biofeedback treatment in sport injury rehabilitation are not well understood, biofeedback is thought not only to enhance motivation for rehabili-

tation activities but also to improve the processing of proprioceptive information (Levitt et al., 1995).

Goal setting, an intervention in which the recipient generates short- and long-term personal standards to achieve during rehabilitation, has been evaluated experimentally in four studies (Evans & Hardy, 2002a; Penpraze & Mutrie, 1999; Theodorakis, Beneca, Malliou, & Goudas, 1997; Theodorakis, Malliou, Papaioannou, Beneca, et al., 1996). In one of the studies (Penpraze & Mutrie, 1999), athletes with injuries who were given specific rehabilitation goals demonstrated greater understanding of and adherence to their rehabilitation protocols than athletes with injuries who were assigned nonspecific rehabilitation goals. Similarly, Evans and Hardy found that a goal setting intervention produced greater rehabilitation adherence and rehabilitation self-efficacy than social support control and no treatment control conditions among athletes with injuries. In the other two studies, Theodorakis and his colleagues found that goal setting enhanced knee strength in individuals undergoing rehabilitation for knee injuries. In the four studies, goal setting is presumed to exert a favorable influence on sport injury rehabilitation by focusing the rehabilitative efforts of athletes with injuries, increasing their persistence in rehabilitative activities, and enabling them to develop new strategies in rehabilitation (Locke & Latham, 1990).

Although they are technically two separate interventions, relaxation and imagery are commonly combined in professional practice. Cupal and Brewer (2001) examined the effects of a relaxation and guided imagery intervention on individuals undergoing rehabilitation following anterior cruciate ligament reconstructive surgery. Participants who received the intervention demonstrated significantly greater knee strength and significantly less pain and reinjury anxiety at six months postsurgery than participants who received no intervention or a placebo intervention. Relaxation interventions calm the mind and the body, and imagery interventions facilitate mental rehearsal of various aspects of rehabilitation (e.g., motivation, healing, and performance). In combining relaxation and imagery, Cupal and Brewer hypothesized that the intervention may have enhanced rehabilitation outcomes by increasing motivation and, possibly, altering physiological processes (e.g., tissue regeneration/repair, immune/inflammatory responses) in a manner conducive to healing.

Only one study has examined the effects of self-talk on sport injury rehabilitation outcomes. Theodorakis, Beneca, et al. (1997) reported that athletes with injury who received a positive self-talk program presented by multimedia increased their leg strength to a significantly greater extent than those not given the positive self-talk intervention. As with the other interventions, the mechanisms for the obtained effect are not known, although it is possible that positive self-talk enhances motivation to engage in rehabilitation activities and stay focused on the tasks at hand.

Two studies have examined the effects of modeling—an intervention in which athletes with injuries learn vicariously from other athletes who are coping effectively with their injuries—on sport injury rehabilitation outcomes. Flint (1991) found that athletes who viewed a videotape of coping models following ACL reconstruction surgery experienced significantly greater self-efficacy and a trend toward more rapid achievement of progress in functional performance than those who did not view a videotape of coping models. Similar results were obtained by Maddison (2004), who reported that relative to a control condition, a coping models video produced significantly lower levels of expected postoperative pain and significantly greater rehabilitation self-efficacy and significantly better functional outcomes among athletes who were recovering from ACL surgery.

Multimodal treatment packages involve combining multiple psychological strategies to create more comprehensive interventions. The impact of such treatments on sport injury rehabilitation outcomes has been investigated in two studies. Ross and Berger (1996) examined the effects of stress inoculation training (Meichenbaum, 1985) on postsurgical pain, anxiety, and physical functioning among men with knee cartilage injuries. Members of the experimental group received training in self-monitoring signs of pain and distress, deep breathing, progressive muscle relaxation, imagery, positive coping statements, and self-reinforcement statements. Participants who received the treatment package (in two 1-hr sessions shortly after arthroscopic surgery) achieved a strength-based return to physical functioning criterion more rapidly and reported less pain and anxiety over the first 10 sessions of physical therapy than

control participants, who received no psychological intervention. Johnson (2000) investigated the effects of a short-term, 3-session psychological intervention on the mood of competitive athletes with various injuries. The intervention consisted of training in stress management/cognitive control, goal setting, and relaxation/guided imagery. Participants who received the intervention reported more positive mood, rated themselves as more physically restored and ready to return to physical activity, and were rated by their physiotherapist as having a more positive attitude and a more successful result at the end of rehabilitation than those who did not receive the intervention. Although a thorough component analysis is needed to determine the most effective elements of a multimodal treatment package, the subjective postrehabilitation responses of participants in Johnson's study suggested that the relaxation/guided imagery aspect contributed most strongly to the treatment effect.

Future Directions for Research and Practice

Over the past decade, major advances have been made in research on psychological aspects of sport injury rehabilitation. Summarizing recent empirical progress on the topic, Brewer (2001) cited the following areas in which the quality of research had improved: (a) identification of cognitive and emotional responses to injury that are characteristic of athlete populations; (b) investigation of the effects of psychological interventions on sport injury rehabilitation; (c) theoretical developments; (d) inclusion of both psychological *and* physical variables in research studies; (e) assessment of the prevalence of clinical levels of psychological distress among athletes with injuries; (f) implementation of prospective, longitudinal research designs; (g) use of qualitative methods; (h) use of control groups of athletes without injuries where relevant; (i) use of experimental research designs; and (j) examination of groups of athletes that are homogeneous with respect to injury type, severity, and prognosis. From an applied standpoint, however, these advances represent only a point of departure. There is much more to be done in terms of identifying the athletes who will benefit most from a particular intervention, delivered by whom and toward what goal, and under which specific circumstances (Paul, 1967).

Despite the growing body of research on the use of psychological interventions to enhance sport injury rehabilitation outcomes, little is known about how the interventions work. Understanding the mechanisms responsible for the salubrious effects of the interventions is essential to tailoring treatment to the many personal, situational, and psychological variables that have an impact on the sport injury rehabilitation process. Toward this end, intervention researchers should implement longitudinal designs that facilitate analysis of the underlying process of change. Theory provides guidance on the selection of variables to measure. For example, from a biopsychosocial perspective (see Figure 1), a particular psychological intervention could bring about changes in circulation and adherence to the rehabilitation protocol, both of which could ultimately influence rehabilitation outcomes. Only by measuring prospective mediating variables over time will the bases of intervention effects be uncovered. Frequent assessment of hypothesized mediators and outcomes will facilitate examination of the fluid, dynamic process by which rehabilitation outcomes unfold (Evans & Hardy, 1999). Qualitative follow-up studies such as that conducted by Evans and Hardy (2002b) can also be useful in identifying the mechanisms of observed effects of psychological interventions in the context of sport injury rehabilitation.

Another important target for future research on psychological applications in sport injury rehabilitation is to assess the full range of outcomes identified in the biopsychosocial model (see Figure 1) over longer periods of time than the relatively short (i.e., six months or less) time span that has been typical. Although physical functioning has justifiably been a primary outcome in most intervention studies, outcomes such as quality of life and, to a lesser extent, pain have been largely neglected and, consequently, warrant additional empirical attention. Sizable shifts in quality of life have been documented over the rehabilitation period following anterior cruciate ligament reconstructive surgery (Shapiro, Richmond, Rockett, McGrath, & Donaldson, 1996). Preliminary evidence suggests that how athletes cope with pain can influence not only how they feel following knee surgery, but also the level of disability that they experience (Morrey et al., 1999; Tripp, 2000).

Pain has been described as the most pervasive and debilitating obstacle to effective rehabilitation experienced by athletes with injuries, with substantial physical and psychological effects across many aspects of recovery (Heil, 1993). Both coaches and physicians currently acknowledge that athletes differ in their capacity to "handle" pain following an injury (e.g., Heil, 1993; Taylor & Taylor, 1998). There is also a growing awareness among sports medicine providers of the need to consider psychological factors as important not only in sport performance, but also in sport injuries, postoperative rehabilitation, and pain management (Flint, 1998; Wiese-Bjornstal et al., 1998). It has been suggested that pain intensity is the most powerful predictor of pain tolerance, particularly within the context of rehabilitation from injuries (Taylor & Taylor, 1998). Recent pain research with athletes has examined catastrophizing (i.e., negative, pain-related cognitive appraisals) as a variable related to the prediction of pain intensity in both experimental and clinical settings. Tripp (2000) found that catastrophizing is not only a significant predictor of experimental pain in athletes, but also a predictor of athlete postoperative pain over and above demographic variables, medication consumption, and ratings of affective distress following ACL surgery.

Researchers should be attuned to ways in which psychological interventions interact with medical factors, as the effectiveness of psychological interventions is likely to vary across injuries and medical treatments. Healing imagery, for example, might prove difficult to implement with athletes who have injuries of indeterminate etiology. Similarly, goal setting and other motivational interventions might work especially well when the rehabilitation protocol requires an extensive series of discrete tasks (e.g., exercises) for athletes with injury. Given that some athletes with injuries end up deriving perceived benefits such as improved life satisfaction, personal growth, and academic performance from their injuries (Udry, 1999), the possibility that psychological interventions can facilitate perceptions of benefit in athletes with injuries also merits exploration in future research.

With regard to practice, there is enormous potential for applying psychology in sport injury rehabilitation. Issues pertaining to the most effective and efficient ways of delivering psychological interventions to athletes with injuries abound, however. Although sport injury rehabilitation practitioners (e.g., physicians, physiotherapists, athletic trainers) have direct access to athletes with injuries and may be generally aware of and interested in psychological aspects of rehabilitation (e.g., Brewer, Van Raalte, & Linder, 1991; Gordon, Milios, & Grove, 1991; Larson, Starkey, & Zaichkowsky, 1996), they may not feel sufficiently qualified to implement psychological interventions. With relevant education and training (Gordon, Potter, & Ford, 1998), sport injury rehabilitation practitioners can increase their proficiency in communicating clearly, initiating simple psychological interventions (e.g., goal setting to boost motivation for rehabilitation), and identifying appropriate candidates for referral to mental health practitioners for athletes with injuries who demonstrate elevated levels of psychological distress or show signs of maladjustment. Although sport psychology consultants may be competent to deliver psychological interventions to athletes with injuries, they are not typically full-fledged members of the treatment team (Larson et al., 1996). To function more actively and effectively in the rehabilitation of athletes with injuries, sport psychology consultants must establish connections with sport injury rehabilitation practitioners and overcome potential barriers that include, but are not limited to: (a) a prospective lack of financial remuneration for services; (b) an absence of a standard protocol for referring athletes to receive psychological services (Larson et al., 1996); and (c) a possible reluctance of athletes with injuries to participate in psychological treatment even when such treatment is credible (Brewer, Jeffers, Petitpas, & Van Raalte, 1994).

Conclusions

Over the past 30 years, sizable scientific literatures documenting the role of psychological factors in the occurrence of sport injuries and detailing the psychological consequences of sport injuries have emerged. Preliminary research suggests that psychological applications have potential utility in the prevention and rehabilitation of sport injuries. Additional controlled investigations are needed to further substantiate the role of psychological interventions in reducing injury risk and enhancing physical and psychological recovery from sport injury.

References

Andersen, M. B., & Stoove, M. A. (1998). The sanctity of p < .05 obfuscates good stuff: A comment on Kerr and Goss. *Journal of Applied Sport Psychology, 10,* 168-173.

Andersen, M. B., & Williams, J. M. (1988). A model of stress and athletic injury: Prediction and prevention. *Journal of Sport & Exercise Psychology, 10,* 294-306.

Andersen, M. B., & Williams, J. M. (1999). Athletic injury, psychosocial factors, and perceptual changes during stress. *Journal of Sports Sciences, 17,* 735-741.

Astle, S. J. (1986). The experience of loss in athletes. *Journal of Sports Medicine and Physical Fitness, 26,* 279-284.

Bianco, T., Malo, S., & Orlick, T. (1999). Sport injury and illness: Elite skiers describe their experiences. *Research Quarterly for Exercise and Sport, 70,* 157-169.

Bijur, P. E., Trumble, A., Harel, Y., Overpeck, M. D., Jones, D., & Scheidt, P. C. (1995). Sports and recreation injuries in U.S. children and adolescents. *Archives of Pediatric and Adolescent Medicine, 149,* 1009-1016.

Blackwell, B., & McCullagh, P. (1990). The relationship of athletic injury to life stress, competitive anxiety and coping resources. *Athletic Training, 25,* 23-27.

Brewer, B. W. (1991, June). *Causal attributions and adjustment to athletic injury.* Paper presented at the annual meeting of the North American Society for the Psychology of Sport and Physical Activity, Pacific Grove, CA.

Brewer, B. W. (1994). Review and critique of models of psychological adjustment to athletic injury. *Journal of Applied Sport Psychology, 6,* 87-100.

Brewer, B. W. (1999). Adherence to sport injury rehabilitation regimens. In S. J. Bull (Ed.), *Adherence issues in sport and exercise* (pp. 145-168). Chichester: Wiley.

Brewer, B. W. (2001). Psychology of sport injury rehabilitation. In R. N. Singer, H. A. Hausenblas, & C. M. Janelle (Eds.), *Handbook of sport psychology* (2nd ed., pp. 787-809). New York: Wiley.

Brewer, B. W., Andersen, M. B., & Van Raalte, J. L. (2002). Psychological aspects of sport injury rehabilitation: Toward a biopsychosocial approach. In D. I. Mostofsky & L. D. Zaichkowsky (Eds.), *Medical and psychological aspects of sport and exercise* (pp. 41-54). Morgantown, WV: Fitness Information Technology.

Brewer, B. W., Cornelius, A. E., Van Raalte, J. L., Brickner, J. C., Sklar, J. H., Corsetti, J. R., Pohlman, M. H., Ditmar, T. D., & Emery, K. (2004). Rehabilitation adherence and anterior cruciate ligament outcome. *Psychology, Health & Medicine, 9,* 163-175.

Brewer, B. W., Jeffers, K. E., Petitpas, A. J., & Van Raalte, J. L. (1994). Perceptions of psychological interventions in the context of sport injury rehabilitation. *The Sport Psychologist, 8,* 176-188.

Brewer, B. W., Van Raalte, J. L., Cornelius, A. E., Petitpas, A. J., Sklar, J. H., Pohlman, M. H., Krushell, R. J., & Ditmar, T. D. (2000). Psychological factors, rehabilitation adherence, and rehabilitation outcome following anterior cruciate ligament reconstruction. *Rehabilitation Psychology, 45,* 20-37.

Brewer, B. W., Van Raalte, J. L., & Linder, D. E. (1991). Role of the sport psychologist in treating injured athletes: A survey of sports medicine providers. *Journal of Applied Sport Psychology, 3,* 183-190.

Burt, C. W., & Overpeck, M. D. (2001). Emergency visits for sports-related injuries. *Annals of Emergency Medicine, 37,* 301-338.

Chan, C. S., & Grossman, H. Y. (1988). Psychological effects of running loss on consistent runners. *Perceptual and Motor Skills, 66,* 875-883.

Cupal, D. D. (1998). Psychological interventions in sport injury prevention and rehabilitation. *Journal of Applied Sport Psychology, 10,* 103-123.

Cupal, D. D., & Brewer, B. W. (2001). Effects of relaxation and guided imagery on knee strength, reinjury anxiety, and pain following anterior cruciate ligament reconstruction. *Rehabilitation Psychology, 46,* 28-43.

Dalhauser, M., & Thomas, M. B. (1979). Visual disembedding and locus of control as variables associated with high school football injuries. *Perceptual and Motor Skills, 49,* 254.

Davis, J. O. (1991). Sports injuries and stress management: An opportunity for research. *The Sport Psychologist, 5,* 175-182.

de Heredia, R. A. S., Munoz, A. R., & Arteza, J. L. (2004). The effect of psychological response on recovery of sport injury. *Research in Sports Medicine, 12,* 15-31.

Derscheid, G. L., & Feiring, D. C. (1987). A statistical analysis to characterize treatment adherence of the 18 most common diagnoses seen at a sports medicine clinic. *Journal of Orthopedic and Sports Physical Therapy, 9,* 40-46.

DeWitt, D. J. (1980). Cognitive and biofeedback training for stress reduction with university athletes. Journal of Sport Psychology, 2, 288-294.

Draper, V. (1990). Electromyographic biofeedback and recovery of quadriceps femoris muscle function following anterior cruciate ligament reconstruction. *Physical Therapy, 70,* 11-17.

Draper, V., & Ballard, L. (1991). Electrical stimulation versus electromyographic biofeedback in the recovery of quadriceps femoris muscle function following anterior cruciate ligament surgery. *Physical Therapy, 71,* 455-464.

Evans, L., & Hardy, L. (1995). Sport injury and grief responses: A review. *Journal of Sport & Exercise Psychology, 17,* 227-245.

Evans, L., & Hardy, L. (1999). Psychological and emotional response to athletic injury: Measurement issues. In D. Pargman (Ed.), *Psychological bases of sport injuries* (2nd ed., pp. 49-64). Morgantown, WV: Fitness Information Technology.

Evans, L., & Hardy, L. (2002a). Injury rehabilitation: A goal-setting intervention study. Research Quarterly for Exercise and Sport, 73, 310-319.

Evans, L., & Hardy, L. (2002b). Injury rehabilitation: A qualitative follow-up study. *Research Quarterly for Exercise and Sport, 73,* 320-329.

Fields, K. B., Delaney, M., & Hinkle, J. S. (1990). A prospective study of type A behavior and running injuries. *The Journal of Family Practice, 30,* 425-429.

Flint, F.A. (1998). Integrating sport psychology and sports medicine in research: The dilemmas. *Journal of Applied Sport Psychology, 10,* 83-102.

Garrick, J.G., & Requa, R.K. (1978). Injuries in high school sports. *Paediatrics, 61,* 465-473.

Gordon, S. (1986, March). Sport psychology and the injured athlete: A cognitive-behavioral approach to injury response and injury rehabilitation. *Science Periodical on Research and Technology in Sport,* 1-10.

Gordon, S., Milios, D., & Grove, J. R. (1991). Psychological aspects of the recovery process from sport injury: The perspective of sport physiotherapists. *Australian Journal of Science and Medicine in Sport, 23,* 53-60.

Gordon, S., Potter, M., & Ford, I. (1998). Toward a psychoeducational curriculum for training sport-injury rehabilitation personnel. *Journal of Applied Sport Psychology, 10,* 140-156.

Gould, D., Udry, E., Bridges, D., & Beck, L. (1997). Stress sources encountered when rehabilitating from season-ending ski injuries. *The Sport Psychologist, 11,* 361-378.

Griffin, L. Y., Agel, J., Albohm, M. J., Arendt, E. A., Dick, R. W., Garrett, W. E., Garrick, J. G., Hewett, T. E., Huston, L., Ireland, M. L., Johnson, R. J., Kibler, W. B., Lephart, S., Lewis, J. L., Lindenfeld, T. N., Mandelbaum, B. R., Marchak, P., Teitz, C. C., & Wojtys, E. M. (2000). Noncontact anterior cruciate ligament injuries: Risk factors and prevention strategies. *Journal of the American Academy of Orthopaedic Surgeons, 18,* 141-150.

Grove, J. R., & Bahnsen, A. (1997). *Personality, injury severity, and coping with rehabilitation.* Unpublished manuscript, University of Western Australia, Nedlands.

Hanson, S., McCullagh, P., & Tonymon, P. (1992). The relationship of personality characteristics, life stress, and coping resources to athletic injury. *Journal of Sport & Exercise Psychology, 14,* 262-272.

Hardy, C.J., & Crace, R.K. (1990). Dealing with injury. *Sport Psychology Training Bulletin, 1,* 1-8.

Hardy, C. J., Richman, J. M., & Rosenfeld, L. B. (1991). The role of social support in the life stress/injury relationship. *The Sport Psychologist, 5,* 128-139.

Heil, J. (1993). *Psychology of sport injury.* Champaign, IL: Human Kinetics.

Holmes, T. H. (1970). Psychological screening. In *Football injuries: Paper presented at a workshop* (pp. 211-214). Sponsored by Subcommittee on Athletic Injuries, Committee on the Skeletal System, Division of Medical Sciences, National Research Council, February 1969. Washington, DC: National Academy of Sciences.

Ievleva, L., & Orlick, T. (1991). Mental links to enhanced healing: An exploratory study. *The Sport Psychologist, 5,* 25-40.

Johnson, U. (1997). A three-year follow-up of long-term injured competitive athletes: Influence of psychological risk factors on rehabilitation. *Journal of Sport Rehabilitation, 6,* 256-271.

Johnson, U. (2000). Short-term psychological intervention: A study of long-term-injured competitive athletes. *Journal of Sport Rehabilitation, 9,* 207-218.

Johnston, L. H., & Carroll, D. (1998). The context of emotional responses to athletic injury: A qualitative analysis. *Journal of Sport Rehabilitation, 7,* 206-220.

Kerr, G., & Goss, J. (1996). The effects of a stress management program on injuries and stress levels. *Journal of Applied Sport Psychology, 8,* 109-117.

Kleiber, D. A., & Brock, S. C. (1992). The effect of career-ending injuries on the subsequent well-being of elite college athletes. *Sociology of Sport Journal, 9,* 70-75.

Kolt, G., & Kirkby, R. (1996). Injury in Australian female competitive gymnasts: A psychological perspective. *Australian Physiotherapy, 42,* 121-126.

Kraus, J. F., & Conroy, C. (1984). Mortality and morbidity from injury in sports and recreation. *Annual Review of Public Health, 5,* 163-192.

Krebs, D. E. (1981). Clinical EMG feedback following meniscectomy: A multiple regression experimental analysis. *Physical Therapy, 61,* 1017-1021.

Kubler-Ross, E. (1969). *On death and dying.* New York: Macmillan.

LaMott, E. E. (1994). *The anterior cruciate ligament injured athlete: The psychological process.* Unpublished doctoral dissertation, University of Minnesota, Minneapolis.

Larson, G. A., Starkey, C. A., & Zaichkowsky, L. D. (1996). Psychological aspects of athletic injuries as perceived by athletic trainers. *The Sport Psychologist, 10,* 37-47.

Laurence, C. (1997, September). *Attributional, affective and perceptual processes during injury and rehabilitation in active people.* Paper presented at the 14th World Congress on Psychosomatic Medicine, Cairns, Australia.

Lavallee, L., & Flint, F. (1996). The relationship of stress, competitive anxiety, mood state, and social support to athletic injury. *Journal of Athletic Training, 31,* 296-299.

Leddy, M. H., Lambert, M. J., & Ogles, B. M. (1994). Psychological consequences of athletic injury among high-level competitors. *Research Quarterly for Exercise and Sport, 65,* 347-354.

Levitt, R., Deisinger, J. A., Wall, J. R., Ford, L., & Cassisi, J. E. (1995). EMG feedback-assisted postoperative rehabilitation of minor arthroscopic knee surgeries. *The Journal of Sports Medicine and Physical Fitness, 35,* 218-223.

Little, J. C. (1969). The athlete's neurosis—A deprivation crisis. *Acta Psychiatrica Scandinavia, 45,* 187-197.

Locke, E. & Latham, G. (1990). *A theory of goal setting and task performance.* Prentice-Hall, Englewood Cliffs, NJ.

Lynch, G. P. (1988). Athletic injuries and the practicing sport psychologist: Practical guidelines for assisting athletes. *The Sport Psychologist, 2,* 161-167.

Macchi, R., & Crossman, J. (1996). After the fall: Reflections of injured classical ballet dancers. *Journal of Sport Behaviour, 19,* 221-234.

Maddison, R. (2004). *Sport-related injury: Prediction, prevention and rehabilitation—A psychological approach.* Unpublished doctoral dissertation, The University of Auckland, New Zealand.

May, J., & Brown, L. (1989). Delivery of psychological services to the U.S. Alpine ski team prior to and during the Olympics in Calgary. *The Sport Psychologist, 3,* 320-329.

McDonald, S. A., & Hardy, C. J. (1990). Affective response patterns of the injured athlete: An exploratory analysis. *The Sport Psychologist, 4,* 261-274.

McGowan, R. W., Pierce, E. F., Williams, M., & Eastman, N. W. (1994). Athletic injury and self diminution. *Journal of Sports Medicine and Physical Fitness, 34,* 299-304.

Meeuwisse, W. H., & Fowler, P. J. (1988). Frequency and predictability of sports injuries in intercollegiate athletes. *Canadian Journal of Sport Sciences, 13,* 35-42.

Meichenbaum, D. (1985). Stress inoculation training. New York: Pergamon Press.

Morrey, M. A., Stuart, M. J., Smith, A. M., & Wiese-Bjornstal, D. M. (1999). A longitudinal examination of athletes' emotional and cognitive responses to anterior cruciate ligament injury. *Clinical Journal of Sport Medicine, 9,* 63-69.

Murphy, S. M. (1988). The on-site provision of sport psychology services at the U.S. Olympic Festival. *The Sport Psychologist, 2,* 337-350.

Pargman, D., & Lunt, S. D. (1989). The relationship of self-concept and locus of control to the severity of injury in freshmen collegiate football players. *Sports Training, Medicine and Rehabilitation, 1,* 203-208.

Passer, M. W., & Seese, M. D. (1983). Life stress and athletic injury: Examination of positive versus negative life events and three moderator variables. *Journal of Human Stress, 9,* 11-16.

Patterson, E. L., Smith, R. E., Everett, J. J., & Ptacek, J. T. (1998). Psychosocial factors as predictors of ballet injuries: Interactive effects of life stress and social support. *Journal of Sport Behavior, 21,* 101-112.

Paul, G. (1967). Strategy of outcome research in psychotherapy. *Journal of Consulting Psychology, 31,* 109-118.

Penpraze, P., & Mutrie, N. (1999). Effectiveness of goal setting in an injury rehabilitation programme for increasing patient understanding and compliance [Abstract]. *British Journal of Sports Medicine, 33,* 60.

Peretz, D. (1970). Development, object-relationships, and loss. In B. Schoenberg, A. C. Carr, D. Peretz, & A. H. Kutscher (Eds.), *Loss and grief: Psychological management in medical practice* (pp. 3-19). New York: Columbia University Press.

Perna, F. M., Antoni, M. H., Baum, A., & Gordon, P. (2003). Cognitive behavioral stress management effects on injury and illness among competitive athletes. *Annals of Behavioral Medicine, 25,* 66-73.

Petrie, T. A. (1992). Psychosocial antecedents of athletic injury: The effects of life stress and social support on female collegiate gymnasts. *Behavioral Medicine, 18,* 127-138.

Petrie, T. A. (1993). Coping skills, competitive trait anxiety, and playing status: Moderating effects of the life stress-injury relationship. *Journal of Sport & Exercise Psychology, 15,* 261-274.

Quinn, A. M., & Fallon, B. J. (1999). The changes in psychological characteristics and reactions of elite athletes from injury onset until full recovery. *Journal of Applied Sport Psychology, 11,* 210-229.

Rose, J., & Jevne, R. F. J. (1993). Psychosocial processes associated with sport injuries. *The Sport Psychologist, 7,* 309-328.

Ross, M. J., & Berger, R. S. (1996). Effects of stress inoculation on athletes' postsurgical pain and rehabilitation after orthopedic injury. *Journal of Consulting and Clinical Psychology, 64,* 406-410.

Rotella, B. (1985). The psychological care of the injured athlete. In L. K. Bunker, R. J. Rotella, & A. S. Reilly (Eds.), *Sport psychology: Psychological considerations in maximizing sport performance* (pp. 273-287). Ann Arbor, MI: Mouvement.

Schomer, H. H. (1990). A cognitive strategy training programme for marathon runners. South African Journal for Research in Sport, *Physical Education and Recreation, 13,* 47-78.

Shapiro, E. T., Richmond, J. C., Rockett, S. E., McGrath, M. M., & Donaldson, W. R. (1996). The use of a generic, patient-based health assessment (SF-36) for evaluation of patients with anterior cruciate ligament injuries. *American Journal of Sports Medicine, 24,* 196-200.

Silver, R. L., & Wortman, C. B. (1980). Coping with undesirable events. In J. Garber & M. E. P. Seligman (Eds.), *Human helplessness: Theory and applications* (pp. 279-375). New York: Academic Press.

Smith, R. E., Ptacek, J. T., & Smoll, F. L. (1992). Sensation seeking, stress, and adolescent injuries: A test of stress-buffering, risk-taking, and coping skills hypotheses. *Journal of Personality and Social Psychology, 62,* 1016-1024.

Smith, R. E., Smoll, F. L., & Ptacek, J. T. (1990). Conjunctive moderator variables in vulnerability and resiliency research: Life stress, social support and coping skills, and adolescent sport injuries. *Journal of Personality and Social Psychology, 58,* 360-370.

Smith, A. M., Scott, S. G., O'Fallon, W. M., & Young, M. L. (1990). Emotional responses of athletes to injury. *Mayo Clinic Proceedings, 65,* 38-50.

Smith, A. M., Scott, S. G., & Wiese, D. M. (1990). The psychological effects of sports injuries. Coping. *Sports Medicine, 9,* 352-369.

Sparkes, A. C. (1998). An Achilles heel to the survival of self. *Qualitative Health Research, 8,* 644-664.

Taylor, J. & Taylor, S. (1998). Pain education and management in the rehabilitation from sports injury. *The Sport Psychologist, 12,* 68-88.

Tedder, S., & Biddle, S. J. H. (1998). Psychological processes involved during sports injury rehabilitation: An attribution-emotion investigation [Abstract]. *Journal of Sports Sciences, 16,* 106-107.

Theodorakis, Y., Beneca, A., Malliou, P., Antoniou, P., Goudas, M., & Laparidis, K. (1997). The effect of a self-talk technique on injury rehabilitation [Abstract]. *Journal of Applied Sport Psychology, 9* (Suppl.), S164.

Theodorakis, Y., Beneca, A., Malliou, P., & Goudas, M. (1997). Examining psychological factors during injury rehabilitation. *Journal of Sport Rehabilitation, 6,* 355-363.

Theodorakis, Y., Malliou, P., Papaioannou, A., Beneca, A., & Filactakidou, A. (1996). The effect of personal goals, self-efficacy, and self-satisfaction on injury rehabilitation. *Journal of Sport Rehabilitation, 5,* 214-223.

Thompson, N. J., & Morris, R. D. (1994). Predicting injury risk in adolescent football players: The importance of psychological variables. *Journal of Pediatric Psychology, 19,* 415-429.

Treacy, S. H., Barron, O. A., Brunet, M. E., & Barrack, R. L. (1997). Assessing the need for extensive supervised rehabilitation following arthroscopic surgery. *American Journal of Orthopedics, 26,* 25-29.

Tripp, D. A. (2000). *Pain catastrophizing in athletic individuals: Scale validation and clinical application.* Unpublished doctoral thesis, Dalhousie University, Halifax, Nova Scotia, Canada.

Tuffey, S. (1991). *The use of psychological skills to facilitate recovery from athletic injury.* Unpublished master's thesis, University of North Carolina at Greensboro.

Udry, E. (1997). Coping and social support among injured athletes following surgery. *Journal of Sport & Exercise Psychology, 19,* 71-90.

Udry, E. (1999). The paradox of injuries: Unexpected positive consequences. In D. Pargman (Ed.), *Psychological bases of sport injuries* (2nd ed., pp. 79-88). Morgantown, WV: Fitness Information Technology.

Udry, E., Gould, D., Bridges, D., & Beck, L. (1997). Down but not out: Athlete responses to season-ending injuries. *Journal of Sport & Exercise Psychology, 19,* 229-248.

Uemukai, K. (1993). Affective responses and the changes in athletes due to injury. In S. Serpa, J. Alves, V. Ferreira, & A. Paula-Brito (Eds.), *Proceedings of the 8th World Congress of Sport Psychology* (pp. 500-503). Lisbon, Portugal: International Society of Sport Psychology.

Van Mechelen, W., Twisk, J., Molendijk, A., Blom, B., Snel, J., & Kemper, H. C. G. (1996). Subject-related risk factors for sports injuries: A 1-yr prospective study in young adults. *Medicine and Science in Sports and Exercise, 18,* 1171-1179.

Weiss, M. R., & Troxel, R. K. (1986). Psychology of the injured athlete. *Athletic Training, 21,* 104-109, 154.

Wiese-Bjornstal, D. M., Smith, A. M., Shaffer, S. M., & Morrey, M. A. (1998). An integrated model of response to sport injury: Psychological and sociological dimensions. *Journal of Applied Sport Psychology, 10,* 46-69.

Williams, J. M. (2001). Psychology of injury risk and prevention. In R. N. Singer, H. A. Hausenblas, & C. M. Janelle (Eds.), *Handbook of sport psychology* (2nd ed., pp. 766-786). New York: Wiley.

Williams, J. M., & Andersen, M. B. (1997). Psychosocial influences on central and peripheral vision and reaction time during demanding tasks. *Behavioral Medicine, 23,* 160-167.

Williams, J. M., & Andersen, M. B. (1998). Psychosocial antecedents of sport injury: Review and critique of the stress and injury model. *Journal of Applied Sport Psychology, 10,* 5-25.

Williams, J. M., Hogan, T. D., & Andersen, M. B. (1993). Positive states of mind and athletic injury risk. *Psychosomatic Medicine, 55,* 468-472.

Williams, J. M., Tonymon, P., & Andersen, M. B. (1990). Effects of life-event stress on anxiety and peripheral narrowing. *Behavioral Medicine, 16,* 174-181.

Williams, J. M., Tonymon, P., & Andersen, M. B. (1991). Effects of stressors and coping resources on anxiety and peripheral narrowing in recreational athletes. *Journal of Applied Sport Psychology, 3,* 126-141.

Williams, J. M., Tonymon, P., & Wadsworth, W.A. (1986). Relationship of life stress to injury in intercollegiate volleyball. *Journal of Human Stress, 12,* 38-43.

Wise, A., Jackson, D. W., & Rocchio, P. (1979). Preoperative psychologic testing as a predictor of success in knee surgery. *American Journal of Sports Medicine, 7,* 287-292.

Wittig, A. F. & Schurr, K. T. (1994) Psychological characteristics of women volleyball players: Relationships with injuries, rehabilitation, and team success. *Personality and Social Psychology Bulletin 20,* 322-330.

Author Note

Preparation of this chapter was supported in part by grant number R29 AR44484 from the National Institute of Arthritis and Musculoskeletal and Skin Diseases. Its contents are solely the responsibility of the authors and do not represent the official views of the National Institute of Arthritis and Musculoskeletal and Skin Diseases.

6.2

The Study of Perceived and Sustained Effort: Concepts, Research Findings, and New Directions

GERSHON TENENBAUM

Introduction

The majority of studies on perceived effort have been carried out in the scientific disciplines of psychophysiology, clinical pediatrics, psychobehavioral assessment, exercise testing and prescription, and exercise physiology and psychology (see Robertson, 2001, special issue of the *International Journal of Sport Psychology*). While the study of perceived effort has not been among the mainstream topics in the sport psychology domain, a few studies in this area have been published in the sport and exercise psychology literature. This chapter reviews the dominant, traditional trends in the study of perceived ef-

fort, mainly perceived exertion and pain, and offers a new conceptual-theoretical framework that consists of recent social cognitive theories and advances in measurement concepts.

The chapter begins with the definitions of the main terms used in the research on perceived and sustained effort, namely *perceived exertion* and *pain*. It points out the conceptual and measurement limitations of these two terms in the study of perceived effort, as well as offers an alternative concept believed to provide a more adequate representation of the effort perception of people engaged in physical exercise. The new concept of effort symptomatology consists of a variety of affective, cognitive, physical, physiological, and motivational sensations that are perceived during ongoing exercise. The intensity of these symptoms alters with the degree of effort expended and environmental conditions. Familiarity and experience with such sensations mediates between the effort intensity and perceived and sustained effort. Along with the conceptualization of effort, traditional and new concepts of self-regulation and coping strategies pertaining to effort are introduced and discussed.

The social cognitive theories, primarily achievement motivation and self-efficacy, are used to establish a conceptual framework. Dispositional (perceived physical efficacy, perceived goal orientation, dispositional perceived exertion, and sustained effort) and state-related factors (task-specific determination, commitment, competence, self-efficacy, readiness to invest effort, perceived effort, and sustained effort), together with coping strategies, self-regulation, familiarity with the task, and physical conditioning, determine and mediate the effect that the physical load, task characteristics, and the environmental conditions have on the perception of effort and task endurance. Recent scientific evidence to support this concept is introduced, and new directions in the study of perceived effort are outlined.

Definition of Main Terms in the Study of Perceived and Sustained Effort

The study of effort perception is associated with many terms, which are aimed at describing the psychological state of the exerciser at various stages of effort exertion. The most studied state is perceived exertion. Noble and Robertson (1996) defined perceived exertion as a subjective intensity of effort, strain, discomfort, and/or fatigue that is experienced during exercise (i.e., detecting and interpreting sensations arising from the body). Perceptual responses represent sensory links between external stimuli, which arise from physical work, and the responses to internal functions. Borg (1962) distinguished between perceived force and perceived fatigue/exertion. The former term was associated with short-term exercise duration, while the latter was associated with aerobic and long-term exercise. Borg's (1998) "Perceived Exertion" was introduced during the late 1950s as a

holistic concept that incorporated perceived exertion, local fatigue, and breathlessness. The terms *fatigue* and *exertion,* according to Borg, have much in common, but each has its unique qualities. "Fatigue refers to a state that might be called 'drowsiness' or high level of tiredness or exhaustion. In this state an individual's performance capacity has diminished… Fatigue is, thus, often defined physiologically or in relation to decrements in performance rather than the perceptual terms" (p. 2). The perception of exertion, according to Borg, may be similar to that of fatigue at the end of the effort continuum. However, "[a]t low or moderate intensity it may be related to a state of activation, an 'arousal' that has a positive effect on performance" (p. 2).

Currently, Borg (1998) conceptualizes exertion within a *gestalt* framework, i.e., a configuration of sensations such as strain, aches, and fatigue that stem from the peripheral muscles, pulmonary system, somatosensory receptors, cardiovascular system, and other sensory organs and cues. Within the gestalt conceptualization of perceived exertion, motivation and emotions are psychological variants that are also viewed as an integral part within the experience of exertion. In this respect, Borg views the term exertion as a latent variable that incorporates many other symptoms, though he uses measures to estimate exertion level that fail to account for the many symptoms that comprise exertion.

When one reviews the dozens of published articles in the literature, it becomes clear that perceived exertion became the main concept of interest, which represents the perception of effort invested in ongoing physical activity. Earlier in the 1970s and the beginning of the 1980s, Kinsman and Weiser (1976), Weiser and Stamper (1977), and Pandolf (1982) clearly outlined the relations between physiological symptoms occurring during exercise and their related perceived symptoms. The levels of subjective-sensory link were identified as discrete, subordinate, ordinate, and superordinate. The discrete level includes sweating, perspiring, panting, heart pounding, leg aches and cramps, muscle tremors, leg twitching, heavy and shaky legs, tiredness, drive, vigorous mood, and determination. The second level, the subordinate, is associated with cardiopulmonary, leg, and general fatigue. The third level, ordinate, is linked with task aversion and the motivation to adhere in the task. The fourth level, superordinate, is associated with extreme fatigue and/or physical exhaustion. This conceptualization of the stimulus-response linkage via the sensory and interpretative systems indicates that perceived exertion may result from each of the effort stages. However, exertion is only one of many sensations that are felt and experienced during exercise engagement, which vary in duration, load, and environmental conditions. Recent research (Tenenbaum, Fogarty, Stewart, et al., 1999) shows that, in line with the above concept, recreational runners who regularly participate in races reported that the most intensive symptoms they experienced while running were mental toughness and task-completion thoughts. The least-felt symptoms were proprioceptive (physiological in nature), such as numbness, blurred vision, dizziness, pain in arms, heavy arms, loss of balance, swollen hands, burning eyes, leg pain, respiratory difficulties, and head and stomach pains. Symptoms such as disorientation, dryness, and heat were experienced moderately. These results indicate that the measurement of perceived effort through one variable viewed as a *gestalt* is insufficient to capture the whole range of sensations that people experience when exercising or being physically active. A more comprehensive concept should replace the traditional one-item perceived exertion concept in the study and measurement of effort perception.

An additional variable that has attracted much attention in both clinical and research settings is the perception of pain. It has been defined as a conscious acknowledgement of noxious stimuli affecting the body (Melzack, 1973). It is composed of complex perceptual experiences, and, therefore, is difficult to describe in terms of discrete stimulus conditions. Skevington (1995) used Merskey's (1988) definition, describing pain as "[a]n unpleasant sensation and emotional experience, which is associated with actual or potential tissue damage or is described in terms of such damage" (p. 8). It is a sensation that is unpleasant and is considered an emotional experience. Such a definition fails to capture the sensation of pain that is associated with effort expenditure, unless an injury of some type occurs. Borg (1998), however, claims that it is common that increases in physical stimulus load to very extreme intensities, while running and/or cycling, turns sensations such

as exertion, fatigue, aches in legs, and breathlessness into perceptions of pain. However, he also refers to the dictionary definitions of pain, which emphasize the suffering, distress, soreness, mental troubling, grief, and sorrow usually associated with injury, disease, and emotional disorders. This, however, is not the type of pain we refer to when discussing effort expenditure. Sensations of pain, which are transmitted to the central nerves system (CNS) from the working body's organs, are the result of physical effort. It is this type of sensation to which we refer here.

The perception of effort (i.e., exertion, pain, fatigue, and others) consists of sensations that the CNS can interpret and differentiate via unique representations and labeling. Once a person is engaged in physical activity, each of these sensations can be reported to a certain degree of intensity ranging from minimum to maximum on a well-defined continuum. Figure 1 provides a visual depiction of this concept. Various symptoms, which are experienced during effort exertion, are organized in an ascending fashion so that when effort intensifies, each symptom is experienced to some degree. At the outset of the effort expenditure, symptoms such as local pain and breathing are felt more than others, while at extreme intensities, undifferentiated pain, mental toughness, and task completion thoughts are more dominate. One should keep in mind that this refers to response conceptualization of physical effort perceptions. These responses are mediated by several internal and external factors, which are outlined in the next section.

A Conceptual Model

The perception of effort is mediated by three external factors: (a) the physical load and the duration of work (i.e., nature and extent of the activity), (b) the environmental conditions (e.g., temperature, humidity, altitude, social facilitation), and (c) task characteristics (e.g., running, cycling, walking; see Noble and Robertson, 1996). The influence of these factors on sustained effort, such as how long one can sustain and adhere in physical activity, is not clear and has attracted less attention (see Tenenbaum, 2001).

A recent study by Tenenbaum et al. (1999) demonstrated that while running road races ranging from 5 to 42 kilometers, runners reported more extensive

Figure 1: Perceived Effort Sensations (Physical, Emotional, Cognitive) as a Function of Physical Load and Environmental Conditions.

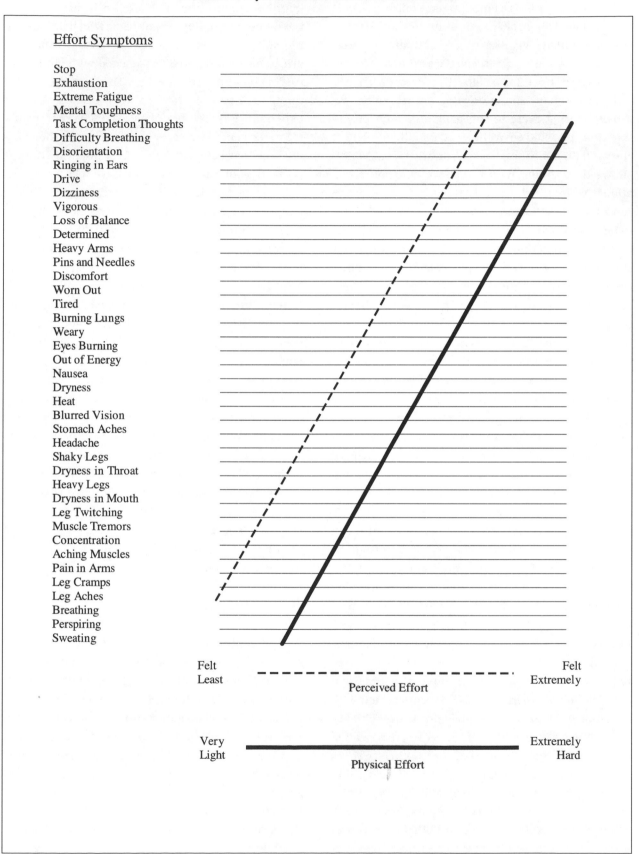

psychological sensations associated with physical effort than physiological and physical symptoms. It seems that even physical conditions that evoke local and central pain and activate *neural gating circuits* in the dorsal horns of the spinal cord, as proposed by gate control theory (GCT; Melzack and Wall, 1965), do not necessarily cause high physical and physiological sensations. Runners in distance races were more concerned with task completion thoughts and mental toughness strategies than with physical symptoms coming from their legs, respiratory system, proprioceptive system, or head and stomach. Thus, under moderate to high extreme conditions of physical effort, the self-regulated mechanisms are more likely to determine the perceptions of effort and sustained effort while facing aversive stimuli, such as physical effort. Therefore, the main mediators of perceived effort and activity adherence stem from a psychological base.

Two of the important psychological mediating components of perceived and sustained effort are the mechanism of self-regulation and the coping strategy implemented during task engagement. The other mediator involves the type and the nature of motivation one maintains during the exercise. These have recently been embedded within the social cognitive (Bandura, 1997) and achievement orientation theories (Ames, 1992; Dweck, 1999; Dweck and Leggett, 1988; Duda, 1993; Duda and Hall, 2001; Maehr and Braskamp, 1986; Nicholls, 1984a, 1989; Roberts, 1993). Task familiarity and experience, as well as the physical conditioning of the performers, are additional components that have a significant effect on the perception and persistence of physical effort. Though Noble and Robertson (1996) introduced several studies linking psychological components and mechanisms to perceived exertion, the reported findings were weak and the research designs lacked a sound theoretical and conceptual base. These studies were aimed at correlating dispositional psychological variables with perceived exertion; neither the disposition of perceived effort and effort tolerance nor the motivational states during effort expenditure were studied. The conceptual model illustrated in Figure 2 outlines the causal relations between the dispositions of perceived and sustained effort, physical self-efficacy, and achievement goal orientation and state perceived and sustained effort, mediated by

external and internal factors. Scientific evidence on the psychological factors, which mediate between the dispositional and state components of perceived and sustained effort, such as social cognitive components and self-regulations and coping strategies, are reviewed in the subsequent sections.

Research on Social Cognitive Components and Perceived and Sustained Effort

One of the features of exercising is the willingness of participants to tolerate unpleasant sensations that stem from the physical activity engagement. In sport and exercise, individuals often demonstrate high levels of effort expenditure and perseverance under conditions of extreme physical effort. Though the demands facing the exerciser may be intense, both in training and in competition, athletes, nevertheless, often persist at high levels of exertion, discomfort, and pain in order to reach their goals. The psychological factors associated with demanding endurance events such as long-distance running, swimming, cycling, and adventure sports were studied until recently by relying mainly on personality theories and measurements (see Morgan, 2001). Morgan claims that personality theorists have recognized that differences in personality structure account for outstanding performances in events that require high levels of physical and mental coping with physical effort symptoms.

Morgan and Costill (1972) used idiographic and nomothetic observations to show that high-ranking long-distance runners scored significantly higher than the population average on extroversion. They used research results to show that extroversion is also beneficial in the pain tolerance, perception of effort, and exercise load preference of these runners (Morgan, 1994). Furthermore, Morgan and Pollock (1977) and Morgan and Costill (1972) have shown that elite runners are characterized by an *iceberg profile* of mood state, scoring lower than the average population on tension, depression, anger, fatigue, and confusion, while scoring higher in vigor. Morgan (2001) claims that the "profile represents a nomothetic characterization, and there are elite marathon runners who do not posses this profile" (p. 3). The pioneering research in the field of effort perceptions

Figure 2: A Conceptual Model that Illustrates the Mediating Role that External and Internal Factors Have on the Relationship Between Dispositional and Performance Components of Perceived and Sustained Effort.

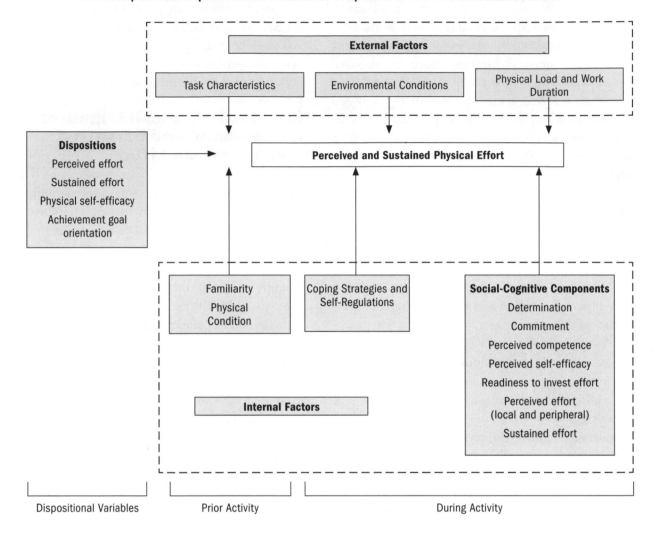

and sustained effort was influenced by stable personality traits of elite endurance performance. Presumably, the samples were limited to few experts compared to the large population, and the results could not be generalized to the broad range of active people engaged in physical effort. Also, the results were limited to the psychological components as measured by common personality inventories that were not designed for measuring perceived and sustained effort. The majority of these questionnaires were designed for clinical uses and diagnoses rather than for healthy people engaged in sport and exercise. Thus, their external validity is questionable. A more comprehensive approach to the study of perceived and sustained effort should replace an approach based solely on personality traits.

Current social cognitive perspectives on sport motivation suggest that goal orientations and self-efficacy are major determinants of both effort investment and adherence in such contexts. Moreover, these perspectives consider task-specific psychological states, such as perceived ability and confidence, as important attributes that interact with an individual's goal orientations to influence effort and persistence, while ultimately determining how a person copes with the perceived demands of an activity (see Roberts, 1992).

The importance of self-efficacy, goal-orientation, and task-specific psychological components in accounting for perceptions and sustained effort are placed within the broader context of achievement goal theory. Individuals give meaning to their investment through the achievement goals they endorse (Ames, 1992; Dweck, 1999; Dweck and Leggett, 1988; Duda, 1993; Duda and Hall, 2001; Maehr and Braskamp, 1986; Nicholls, 1984, 1989; Roberts, 1993) and it is these goals, which define integrated pattern of beliefs, attributions, and affect. The central tenet of this approach to motivation is that achievement behavior is a function of the subjective meaning that an individual assigns to perceived accomplishments (Maehr & Braskamp, 1986). The amount of effort expended, the level of persistence one commits and sustains under aversive conditions, and the cognitions and affective responses associated with performance outcomes are all underpinned by the meaning of achievement.

Nicholls (1984, 1989) suggested that individuals adopt different achievement goals as a direct consequence of the manner in which they construe ability. He identified two specific achievement goals: a *task goal,* which focuses on the development of competence, and an *ego goal,* which is ultimately concerned with the demonstration of competence or the avoidance of being judged incompetent. When endorsing a task goal, individuals believe that ability and effort are undifferentiated (Ames, 1992; Dweck, 1999; Nicholls, 1989) and that, when effort is applied, competence increases. Because their perceptions of self-accomplishments are based upon self-referenced standards, these individuals will often maintain this task focus under the most aversive conditions. Regardless of perceived competence, a task goal will foster adaptive achievement striving (Ames, 1992; Duda, 1992; Dweck, 1999; Dweck and Leggett, 1988; Nicholls, 1989; Roberts, 1992). Thus, when faced with physical effort, individuals endorsing a task goal tend to put forth effort and demonstrate persistence. Challenging, frustrating, or aversive conditions may not be enough to dissuade those endorsing task goals from expending effort, because they believe effort leads to desired accomplishments.

In contrast, people who endorse ego goals are concerned about validating their competence or, alternatively, with avoiding a judgment of comparative incompetence. However, when this goal predominates, a positive validation of competence can only be achieved if performance compares favorably with that of others. Consequently, adaptive achievement striving is conditional on an individual's holding a comparatively high perception of competence (Nicholls, 1989). Although effort is of critical importance to both the demonstration of competence and the avoidance of a judgment of incompetence, it is not always forthcoming. Individuals holding an ego goal often become threatened when they begin to question their ability. This is because they realize that expending maximal effort is likely to result in comparative failure. Under these circumstances, all that can be demonstrated is a lack of competence. Thus, when these people are faced with challenging, frustrating, or aversive conditions, such circumstances may be viewed as an opportunity to demonstrate incompetence, leading to the withdrawal of effort.

Individuals engaging in physically demanding tasks inevitably expose themselves to aversive situations. The typically aversive consequences that many experience when engaged in exercise activities are associated with physical effort. Duda, Sedlock, Noble, Cohen, and Chi (1990) examined the effects of goals on perceived exertion and affective responses of participants performing a cycle ergometer task at 70% VO2 max. Findings revealed that high task with low ego orientations led to lower perceptions of exertion and more positive affect associated with exercise than a combination of high ego and low task orientation. Stevens, Janz, and Mahoney (1996) showed that a task orientation was negatively related to perceived exertion in girls but not in boys.

Self-efficacy, conceptualized as the belief that an individual is in possession of strategies to alter the aversiveness of negative stimuli (Bandura, O'Leary, Taylor, Gauthier, and Gossard, 1987; Thompson, 1981), can be seen as both a disposition and a coping tool when tolerating physical effort. Furthermore, perceived self-efficacy, a specific form of self-confidence, has been shown to affect different forms of physical and health-related behaviors (Bandura et al., 1987). Bandura et al. (1987) have maintained that judgments of self-efficacy not only determine the course of action people choose to pursue, but also the effort they invest while performing a task and their perseverance in the face of either aversive experiences or taxing environmental demands.

Physical effort leads participants to experience severe discomfort or even pain, and this may act to discourage perseverance. Bandura et al. (1987) have suggested several ways by which perceived coping efficacy brings relief from pain. One way is through developing the belief that ability to manage pain lies within one's control. This belief mobilizes ameliorative coping skills and leads to perseverance with various coping strategies. A second way that coping efficacy is considered to operate is by reducing distressing anticipations that result in negative consequences such as elevated physiological arousal, bodily tension, exacerbated pain sensations, and discomfort. A further way of bringing pain relief is by diverting cognitive attention away from any pain sensations to an alternative focus.

Tenenbaum et al., (2001) studied the separate and additive effects of the social cognitive variables (see Figure 2) on sustained effort in 50% maximal handgrip task and 90% VO2 max treadmill run. Their results indicated that exercisers (i.e., athletes who train regularly in long distance running) endured the two tasks and sustained effort for a longer time than their untrained counterparts, though task difficulty level was standardized and kept relatively equal among all the participants. This clearly indicates that experience and familiarity with the type of physical effort perceptions enables exercisers to sustain effort for a longer period of time without ceasing effort. Though both ego and task orientation in the Tenenbaum et al. study accounted for substantial variance in the prediction of exertion, each of them separately did not correlate with the amount of time participants sustained effort. Tenenbaum et al.'s (2001) results concerning the influence of goal orientations on sustained physical effort are inconclusive, although they are not altogether inconsistent with those from previous research examining aerobic exertion (Duda et al., 1990; Stevens et al., 1996). Together, goal orientations accounted for both local muscular effort (i.e., squeezing a hand dynamometer) and running effort (i.e., 90% VO2 treadmill run). However, neither a task orientation nor an ego orientation emerged as significant predictors. It is possible, however, that the predicted positive effects of endorsing a task orientation can only be seen with further repeated exposure to similar demanding conditions.

Sustained exertion in Tenenbaum et al's (2001) study was substantially determined by perceived dispositional and task-specific self-efficacy. Several explanations have been formulated to account for the crucial role that self-efficacy plays while experiencing aversive stimuli. For example, Bandura (1997) and Bandura et al. (1987) argue that all kinds of behavioral changes are somewhat mediated by changes in self-efficacy, and McAuley and Courneya (1992) have proposed that in sporting activities self-efficacy is a significant predictor of how well individuals persist in the face of aversive conditions. Bandura et al. reported that an actual decrease in the appraisal of aversive stimuli might be responsible for the relatively high levels of pain tolerance observed in laboratory studies in individuals possessing high control-efficacy (Bandura et al., 1987). Furthermore, Bandura et al. demonstrated that the stronger the self-efficacy to reduce pain, the greater the opioid activation while tolerating a painful cold stressor. In addition, they reported that self-efficacy increased pain tolerance even when opioid mechanisms were blocked by naloxone.

Tenenbaum et al.'s (2001) study demonstrated that task-specific psychological components such as commitment, determination, perceived competence and ability, and readiness to invest and maintain effort accounted for a substantial endurance-time variance in both the strength and running tasks. It is evident that participants who commit themselves to successfully completing a physically demanding task, and who are ready to tolerate effort symptoms associated with it, regardless of their other dispositional characteristics, will sustain the effort for longer than participants who lack these motivational states.

Physical self-efficacy plays an influential role in moderating the motivational effects of painful sensations that result from physical effort. This is because it represents a critical aspect of self-worth (Harter, 1990). Self-judgments about one's physical competence on meaningful tasks can elicit affective responses that, in turn, moderate achievement behavior. Therefore, high levels of motivation are expected in individuals who judge their competence in this important domain to be high. Because the environment itself plays such an important role in influencing motivation and achievement behavior, context-specific variables such as task-specific perceived ability, perceptions of effort, determination, commitment, and readiness to invest effort and sustain it are also thought to play a decisive role in determining their sustained endurance.

Similar to the role that self-efficacy plays in physical effort tolerance, according to Bandura (1991), pain-coping efficacy can bring pain relief in three ways: (a) seeking necessary information, developing skills, and persistence, (b) reduction of distressing expectations that create aversive reactions and the physical tension that aggravates discomfort, and (c) viewing unpleasant sensations much more benignly, rather than fearfully and uncontrolled. Skevington (1995), however, argues that research shows that the implementation of self-efficacious beliefs in pain sufferers is not as simple as one may expect. Suffering pain is associated with other behavioral disorders that minimize the effect of control over matters, and in some cases may even worsen the situation by losing control over unwanted behaviors. In this respect, pain arising from physical effort should be distinguished from pain that emerges from illness or injury.

Research on the Use of Self-Regulatory Mechanisms and Coping Strategies with Aversive Stimuli

Self-regulation strategies used to cope with effort sensations are important mediators of perceived and sustained effort (see Figure 2). Research on strategies people use to cope with physical effort has been conducted in isolation from research on strategies employed to cope with pain. Therefore, they are addressed separately in this section.

Coping with Physical Effort

Earlier research by Morgan and Pollock (1977) on world-class runners and non-elite college runners, who ran at speeds of 10 to 12 miles per hour on a motorized treadmill, showed that the groups of runners did not differ in any physiological variables or rate of perceived exertion. However, heart rate, lactate production, and minute ventilatory volume were lower for the elite runners. The sense of effort for the different groups of runners did not parallel the actual physiological cost. The elite runners, however, reported using association strategies in which they concentrated on bodily sensations, race strategy, and relaxation. The non-elite runners utilized dissociation methods, such as playing mind games, to distract themselves from the stress of the task. Recently,

Morgan (2001) summarized his and his colleague's findings, stating,

> Instead of ignoring stressful sensations by dissociating sensory input, the elite runners reported that they paid close attention to multiple signals of somatic nature (e.g., muscle pain, cramps, parathesias, respiration, effort sense). It was common for these runners to make a conscious decision to slow the pace if they began to experience respiratory distress... There is a compelling theoretical rationale, along with empirical research evidence, in support of 'effort sense' to dictate the pace in a competitive run (11,15)... preferred to 'read their own bodies' and 'run their own pace.'... to stay loose,' 'relax,' 'don't get tight,' 'remember to drink,'... [T]hese runners tended to minimize the importance of 'pain zones' and 'the wall.' (p. 4)

Morgan (2001) concluded that dissociative cognitive strategies might enhance endurance performance by increasing tolerance of the distress associated with prolonged effort. He also stated that hypnotic suggestions could increase or decrease the perceptions of effort (Morgan, 1981, 1993, 1994). Recently, the use of MRI technology has shown that hypnotic perturbation of effort sense during steady-state exercise altered regional cerebral blood flow to selected brain regions (Williamson, McColl, Mathews, et al., 2001). For participants cycling under hypnotic conditions of perceived level grade, perceived downhill, and perceived uphill grades, Williamson et al. (2001) reported that downhill perceptions were associated with decreases in rate of perceived exertion (RPE) and cerebral blood flow (rCBF) in the left insular cortex, with no change in heart rate (HR) and (blood pressure) BP responses. Perceived uphill cycling increased RPE, HR, mean BP, right insular activation, and right thalamus activation. Thus, changes in effort-sense seem to affect brain activity despite imposing on the body different physical effort than that perceived through hypnotic suggestion.

In other studies with recreational exercisers in swimming (Couture, Jerome, & Tihanyi, 1999), rowing (Scott, Scott, Bedic, & Dowd, 1999), and race walking (Clingman & Hilliard, 1990), the associative strategy was the predominant strategy used to cope with perceptions of effort. In more recent studies (Acevedo, Dzewaltowski, Gill, et al., 1992; Masters & Lambert, 1989; Okwumabua & Meyers, 1987; Okwumabua, Meyers, Schlesser, & Cooke, 1983; Schomer, 1986; Silva, 1989; Stevinson & Biddle, 1998; Summers, Sargent, Levey, & Muurray, 1982; Tammen, 1996; Wrisberg & Pein, 1990; Ungerleider, Golding, Porter, & Foster, 1989), in which participants were not classified as elite runners, the association-dissociation distinction was not as clear as Morgan et al. (1983) and Morgan and Pollock (1977) have reported. Stevinson and Biddle (1998) also found that non-elite runners tend to use association strategies during runs. However, this may be a consequence of widespread reporting of these findings affecting other runners and exercisers (Raglin and Wilson, 1991). Morgan (2001) claims, however, that the subsequent research devoted to this issue "has suffered to a large degree by the operationalism of association, along with major differences in exercise mode and performance status" (p.6).

In summary, Morgan (2001) argues that dissociation of sensory input focused on distress, fatigue, and general discomfort may reduce the feelings of distress and even enhance performance (Morgan, Horstman, Cymerman, & Stokes, 1983). However, the use of such strategies may result in injuries of various severity (Morgan, 1978). It seems prudent to rely on associative cognitive strategies when engaged in prolonged physical activity, in particular when the physical effort is extremely high. The use of associative and dissociative strategies by exercisers, whether elite or recreational, can be accounted for the recent model offered by Tenenbaum (2001), as well as extensive scientific evidence (see Noble & Robertson, 1996 for review) demonstrating that, with increases in physical load, effort feelings intensify and attention narrows and shifts from an external to an internal focus. As long as the physical load and the environmental conditions are light to moderate, attention shifts from associative to dissociative voluntarily. However, under extreme environmental conditions and physical effort, one can attend only to internal sources, in which determination, commitment, mental stamina, and readiness to cope with effort play a major role. Thus, elite runners use associative strategies linked to narrow attentional resources, which pertain to their body, feelings, and thoughts, because their effort is extremely high from the outset of the race. Recreational competitors and exercisers can shift attention voluntarily from dissociative to associative modes and back as long as their physical effort is not extreme. Once the physical effort takes its toll, however, they shift attention internally and become associative, similar to their elite counterparts. It is my belief that the discrepancy of research findings on the use of association-dissociation strategies is not linked to the skill-level and the methodological flaws, as Morgan (2001) argues, but rather to the effort intensity and the environmental conditions under which the exercisers are engaged at each stage of the race or exercise. Indeed, Morgan summarizes this in similar terms when stating, "The extent to which one strategy becomes predominant at any given time should be governed by both internal (i.e., the runner's bodily responses) and external (i.e., temperature, course, opponents) factors. Put simply, one might enjoy running in a pleasurable state that accompanies dissociation, but he or she would be well advised to shift into associative mode when circumstances dictate" (p. 8).

Morgan (1980) also argued that athletes have varying training plateaus, which are the boundaries of their performance, and that these plateaus are extended through consistent activity at these levels (i.e., familiarity and experience in the model depicted in Figure 2). Performance enhancement is a direct result of applying this mechanism. Morgan also notes that an important consideration in relation to performing physical tasks is not related to the physiological demands of the nature of the task, but rather to what the performers think or feel that they are doing. This notion was supported in a study by Morgan, Raven, Drinkwater, and Horvath (1973; as cited in Morgan, 1980). Five adult male participants exercised on cycle ergometers at a constant resistance and pedal rate for 5 min. On the following three days, they cycled under the same resistance and pedal rate for 5 min but were told that the resistance was changed to light (50 Watt [W]), moderate (100W), or heavy (150W), on these occasions. Each of the five participants reported that the work actually felt light, moderate, or heavy, respectively, and four of the five believed that the time of the experiment had been reduced to about half. Thus, perception of effort on a task is partly determined by how the person feels or thinks he or she is doing on the task. If people feel that the effort required for the task is less than they had anticipated, they are able to extend their "psychological boundaries" much further.

Research on the effect of various coping strategies on effort perceptions has been conducted and reported in the published literature. This line of research stems from the conceptual framework that underlies the various cognitive, emotional, behavioral, and mixed techniques. Each of these techniques relies on the premise that effort can be perceived and individuals can cope with it effectively and efficiently. External techniques reduce perceptions of neural signals coming from the muscles, joints, and the cardiopulmonary systems. Internal strategies are aimed at directly coping with aversive feelings through fighting against them. A passive form of coping with exertion exists when the performer takes no coping initiative while perceiving aversive sensations.

External focusing techniques were employed through activating environmental street sounds, while internal techniques involved attending to one's own breathing, for participants walking on a treadmill (Pennebaker & Lightner, 1980). The external technique was found to be superior, as exercisers who utilized the internal technique experienced greater fatigue. Counting the word 'dog' and concentrating on breathing and heart rate were used as external and internal techniques, respectively, for subjects running on a treadmill (Fillingim & Fine, 1986). Again, the external technique resulted in greater reduced-effort symptoms than the internal one. Similar results were reported by Johnson and Siegel (1987), who asked the participants to solve problems while running, as opposed to focusing attention on the run.

The superiority of the external technique over the internal technique in the reduction of perceived aversive symptoms is not conclusive. Boutcher and Trenske (1990) reported that under high intensive effort, participants who were attending to music, visual, auditory, and no-stimuli did not differ in effort perceptions. However, under light and moderate

physical effort, attending to music resulted in lower perceived exertion compared to the visual, auditory, or no-stimuli conditions (Karageorghis & Terry, 1997). The results of the various studies support the claims of Tenenbaum's (2001) model, in which attentional resources can be shifted voluntarily from external to internal and from wide to narrow focus. However, under extreme effort levels, attentional resources cannot be voluntarily controlled, and thus, the effectiveness of external strategies on perceived and sustained effort are limited. At this stage, the motivational components, internal in nature, predominate in the level of sustained effort.

An additional technique for coping with aversive stimuli is imagery. The use of imagery while engaging in physical effort rests on the premise that close links exist among emotions, images, and sensations. In the same way that emotions are accompanied by physical sensations, images evoke emotions. Relaxation techniques such as meditation, rhythmic breathing, and attending to music are often used to decrease stress symptoms. Progressive relaxation is frequently used with guided imagery (Edgar & Smith-Hanrahan, 1992) to better cope with effort and pain sensations. In Coote and Tenenbaum (1998), emotive and relaxation imageries were contrasted to each other in a muscular endurance task of squeezing a 50% maximal dynamometer hand-grip until voluntary exhaustion. Rate of perceived exertion and sustained effort were also measured, as this task involved high effort sensations. The results indicated that participants who used emotive and relaxation techniques increased their sustained effort times by 31% and 28%, compared to a 4% reduction time in the control group participants. Perceived exertion, however, was similar in both the imagery and the control groups. These results indicate that the use of relaxation imagery (i.e., distracting attention of effort sensations to external relaxing stimuli) and emotive imagery (i.e., coping with effort sensations directly through emotive images) fail to alter effort sensations. Instead, these techniques enhance the internal motivational resources, which results in increased sustained effort. These findings support Tenenbaum et al.'s results (2001) and Tenenbaum's model (2001), which asserts that under high levels of effort, when one feels extreme effort sensations, mental techniques have limited influence on the perceptions of effort. In such aversive conditions, it is determination, commitment, readiness to sustain effort, and self-efficacy beliefs that play major roles. Techniques such as imagery help to set motivational self-regulations, which increases an individual's capacity to sustain aversive conditions.

Coping with Pain

Skevington (1995) summarized all the psychological treatments used to ease painful feelings of patients who suffer various medical problems. The reader is directed to this reference and others for more details on the characteristics and applications of these techniques. However, because of the close link that perceived effort has with pain feelings, especially under conditions of high exertion (Borg, 1998), a short overview of these techniques is introduced in this section.

According to the gate control theory (GCT; Melzack & Wall, 1965), somatic input is moderated by the influence of cognition, affect, and behavioral factors before evoking a perception of pain. The psychological processes, regulating pain by altering participants' appraisal of threats and their perceived capability to control noxious stimuli, are referred to as cognitive strategies (Turk, Meichenbaum, & Genest, 1983). Although pain tolerance research in the sport setting has been limited (Witmarsh & Alderman, 1993), the cognitive control of pain has received increasing attention in recent years. Several studies have shown that cognitive strategies can be very effective in the management and reduction of pain (Barber & Hanan, 1962; Hilgard, 1975; Spanos, Horton, & Chaves, 1975), even more so than several kinds of analgesic drugs (Levendusky & Pankratz, 1975). The mechanisms by which such cognitive strategies mediate pain management are not yet thoroughly understood. The nature of coping strategies, for instance, has not yet been proven to account for their generally beneficial effects (Turk, Meichenbaum, & Genest, 1983).

Behavioral medicine teaches patients to decrease or to stop visible behaviors they may enjoy and to do things that they previously considered to be unnecessary or undesirable. A major aim here is to reduce levels of addictive medications through the use of a *cocktail,* where the proportion of active analgesic ingredients is steadily reduced with the patient's consent. In this respect, pain is a learned behavior, and therefore, the tenet of this approach is to minimize social contacts with patients who take benefits from such behaviors. This operant-type treatment resulted in fewer patients' dependence on drugs, as well as changes in verbal expressions related to pain (Fordyce, Roberts, & Sternbach, 1985).

The cognitive-behavioral and the social-cognitive approaches assume that behaviors are determined by conscious appraisals and the perceived importance of the events for them, as well as by social norms and social interactions. The therapy consists of changing the faulty cognitions and attributions of pain that underpin emotional and behavioral disturbances (Turk & Rudy, 1986).

Relaxation training is one of the salient treatments of this approach. There are many variations in relaxation training. Some rely on breathing, some on muscles, others on imagery, and many on different combinations of the three. It involves the development of mental representations of reality or fantasy aimed at reducing pain and autonomic reactivity. The principle is to hold the image in a peaceful, pain-free scene during a painful experience (James, 1992). Imagery was found to help transform pain into numbness or an irrelevant sensation. Imagery may divert attention from internal to external modes so that attention shifts from the pain sensation to another external stimulus, enabling enhanced coping. Furthermore, pain can be controlled through somatization, i.e., focusing attention on the painful area but in a detached manner (Melzack, 1989).

Flor, Fydrich, and Turk (1992) reported that multidisciplinary treatments for chronic pain are superior to no-treatment waiting list, unidisciplinary treatment, or physical therapy alone. However, chronic pain, like low back pain, can be accounted for by the combinations of pain perception threshold and pain tolerance (Shcmidt & Arntz ,1987). Any treatment capable of decreasing the pain threshold and increasing pain tolerance will be beneficial for those individuals attempting to cope with pain.

Pain that is experienced from extreme physical effort, however, cannot be considered similar to chronic types of pain that result from medical causes. To better cope with physical effort pain, one should consider the associative and dissociative techniques, depending on the amount of effort and the environmental conditions under which the performer operates (see previous sections of the chapter). The concepts of *perceived effort* and *sustained effort* have been studied in the past without a foundation of motivational theories. Perceived pain and coping with pain have been studied in the context of disease, illness, and injury. Within the context of effort, pain is viewed as one of several sensations that are substantiated under extreme effort-sense and demanding environmental conditions. Under these circumstances, effort-associated pain is not identical, in many respects, to pain resulting from damaged tissue or illness. Therefore, pain should be studied within the context of effort and be treated as one symptom within the multidimensional construct of perceived effort.

Summary

The studies reviewed in this chapter indicate that psychological components, which stem from the social cognitive and the achievement goal orientation motivation theories, account for a substantial variation among individuals in both perceived and sustained effort. These findings are generalized across people and physical tasks, and are not limited to a very small sample of elite performers. Furthermore, it is believed that these components, which together define *mental toughness,* have a strong discriminatory power and determine who can sustain effort also within the elite group of performers. However, this should be further addressed in future studies.

The findings also suggest that the model presented by Tenenbaum (2001) accounts for the artificial dispute among long distance runners' use of associative or dissociative strategies during a race. It was suggested that runners of any caliber can shift attention from internal to external or from wide to narrow mode, depending on the physical load and the environmental demands imposed on the performer. When the cumulative demands are light to moderate, attention is more flexible and may shift voluntarily, or even from automatic to intentional modes. However, under extremely hard effort, where sensation symptoms are focused on extreme fatigue, pain, and 'toughness thoughts,' attention can no longer be controlled voluntarily and is focused internally. At this stage, the method one uses to regulate these symptoms and the degree of determination and motivation to sustain these extreme effort sensations determine performance quality. It is also noted that this is also true for recreational exercisers who participate for health, fun, and social reasons.

References

Acevedo, E. O., Dzewaltowski, D. A., Gill, D. L., et al. (1992). Cognitive orientations of ultramarathoners. *Sport Psychologist, 6,* 242-252.

Ames, C. (1992). Achievement goals, motivational climate, and motivational process. In G. C. Roberts (Ed.), *Motivation in sport and exercise* (pp. 161-176). Champaign, IL: Human Kinetics.

Bandura, A. (1977). Self-efficacy: Toward a unifying theory of behavioural change. *Psychological Review, 84,* 191-215.

Bandura, A. (1991). Self-efficacy mechanisms in physiological activation and health promoting behavior. In J. Madden (Ed.), *Neurobiology of learning, emotion, and affect* (pp. 229-269). New York: Raven Press.

Bandura, A. (1997). *Self-efficacy: The exercise of control.* New York: W. H. Freeman.

Bandura, A., O'Leary, A., Taylor, B., Gauthier, J., and Gossard, D. (1987). Perceived self-efficacy and pain control: Opioid and non-opioid mechanisms. *Journal of Personality and Social Psychology, 53,* 563-571.

Barber, T. X., and Hahan, K. W. (1962). Physiological and subjective responses to pain-producing stimulation under hypnotically-suggested and walking imagined "analgesia." *Journal of Abnormal and Social Psychology, 65,* 411-418.

Borg, G. (1962). Physical performance and perceived exertion. *Studia psychologia et paedagogica, 11,* 1-35.

Borg, G. (1998). *Borg's perceived exertion and pain scales.* Champaign, IL: Human Kinetics.

Boutcher, S., and Trenske. M. (1990). The effects of sensory deprivation and music on perceived exertion and affect during exercise. *Journal of Sport and Exercise Psychology, 12,* 167-176.

Clingman, J. M., and Hilliard, V. D. (1990). Race walkers quicken their step by turning in, not stepping out. *The Sport Psychologist, 4,* 25-32.

Coote, D., and Tenenbaum, G. (1998). Can emotive imagery aid in tolerating exertion efficiently? *Journal of Sports Medicine and Physical Fitness, 38,* 344-354.

Couture, R. T., Jerome, W., and Tihanyi, J. (1999). Can associative and dissociative strategies affect the swimming performance of recreational swimmers? *The Sport Psychologist, 13,* 334-343.

Duda, J. L. (1992). Motivation in sport settings: A goal perspective approach. In G. C. Roberts (Ed.), *Motivation in sport and exercise* (pp. 57-92). Champaign, IL: Human Kinetics.

Duda, J. L. (1993). Goals: A social-cognitive approach to the study of achievement motivation in sport. In R. N. Singer, M. Murphey, and L. K. Tennant (Eds.). *Handbook of research on sport psychology* (pp. 421-436). New York: Macmillan.

Duda, J. L., and Hall, H. (2001). Achievement goal theory in sport: Recent extensions and future directions. In R. N.

Singer, H. Hausenblas, and C. Janelle (Eds.). *Handbook of sport psychology* (pp. 389-416). New York, NY: Wiley and Sons.

Duda, J. L., Sedlock, D. A., Noble, B., Cohen, B., and Chi, L. (1990). *The influence of goal perspective on perceived exertion and affect ratings during sub-maximal exercise.* Paper presented at the annual meeting of the American Alliance for Health, Physical Education, Recreation and Dance. New Orleans, LA.

Dweck, C. S. (1999). *Self-Theories: Their role in motivation personality and development.* Philadelphia: Psychology Press.

Dweck, C. S., and Leggett, E. (1988). A social-cognitive approach to motivation and personality. *Psychological review, 95,* 256-273.

Edgar, L., and Smith-Hanrahan, C. M. (1992). Nonpharmacological pain management. In J. H. Watt-Watson and M. I. Donovan (Eds.). *Pain management-nursing perspective* (pp. 162-199). Sydney: Mosby Year Book.

Fillingim, R., and Fine, M. (1986). The effect of internal versus external information processing on symptom perception in an exercise setting. *Health Psychology, 5,* 115-123.

Flor, H., Fydrich, T., and Turk, D. C. (1992). Efficacy of multidisciplinary pain treatment centers: A meta-analytical review. *Pain, 49,* 221-230.

Fordyce, W. E., Roberts, A. H., and Sternback, R. A. (1985). A behavioural management of chronic pain: A response to critics. *Pain, 22,* 113-125.

Harter, S. (1990). Causes, correlates, and the functional role of global self-worth: a life span perspective. In R. J. Sternberg and J. Kolligan (Eds.). *Competence considered* (pp. 67-97). New Haven, CT: Yale University Press.

Hilgard. E. R. (1975). Hypnosis. *Annual Review of Psychology, 26,* 19-44.

James, F. R., and Large, R. G. (1992). Chronic pain relationships and illness self construct. *Pain, 50,* 263-271.

Johnson, J., and Siegel, D. (1987). Active versus passive attentional manipulation and multidimensional perceptions of exercise intensity. *Canadian Journal of Sport Sciences, 12,* 41-45.

Karageorghis, C. I., and Terry, P. C. (1997). The psychophysical effects of music on sport and exercise: A review. *Journal of Sport Behavior, 20,* 54-68.

Kinsman, R. A., and Weiser, P. C. (1976). Subjective symptomatology during work and fatigue. In E. Simonson and P. L. Weises, (Eds.) *Psychological aspects of fatigue* (pp. 336-405). Springfield, IL: Charles C. Thomas.

Levenduski, P., and Pankratz, L. (1975). Self-control techniques as an alternative to pain medication. *Journal of Abnormal Psychology, 84,* 165-168.

Maehr, M. L., and Braskamp, L. (1986). *The motivation factor: A theory of personal investment.* Lexington, MA: Lexington Books.

Masters, K. S., and Lambert, M. J. (1989). The relations between cognitive coping strategies: Reasons for running, injury, and performance of marathon runners. *Journal of Sport and Exercise Psychology, 11,* 161-170.

McAuley, E., and Courneya, K. S. (1992). Self-efficacy relationships with affective and exertion responses to exercise. *Journal of Applied Social Psychology, 22,* 312-326.

McDougal, J. D., Wenger, H. A., Green, H. J. (1989). *Testing of the elite athlete.* Ontario: Hamilton.

Melzack, R. (1989). Folk medicine and the sensory modulation of pain. In P. D. Wall, and R. Melzack (Eds.), *Textbook of pain* (2nd Edition) (pp. 897-905). Edinburgh: Churchill Livingstone.

Melzack, R. (1973). *The puzzle of pain.* New York, NY: Basic Books.

Melzack, R., and Wall, P. D. (1965). Pain mechanisms-a new theory. *Science, 150,* 971-979.

Merskey, H. (1988). Back pain and disability. *Pain, 34,* 213.

Morgan, W.P. (2001). Psychological factors associated with distance running and the marathon. In D. T. Paedoe (Ed). *Marathon medicine 2000* (pp.1-18). London, UK: Royal Society of Medicine.

Morgan, W. P. (1994). Psychological components of effort sense. *Medicine and science in sport and exercise, 26,* 1071-1077.

Morgan, W. P. (1993). Hypnosis and sport psychology. In J. Rhue, S. J. Lynn., and I. Kirsch (Eds.). *Handbook of clinical hypnosis* (pp. 649-670). Washington, DC: American Psychological Association.

Morgan, W. P. (1981). Psychophysiology of self-awareness during vigorous physical activity. *Research Quarterly for Exercise and Sport, 52,* 385-427.

Morgan, W. P. (1980). Psychophysiology of self-awareness during vigorous physical activity. *Research Quarterly for Exercise and Sport, 52,* 385-427.

Morgan, W. P. (1978). The mind of the marathoner. *Psychology Today, 11,* 38-40.

Morgan, W. P., Horstman, D. H., Cymerman, A., and Stokes, J. (1983). Facilitation of physical performance by means of a cognitive strategy. *Cognitive Therapy Research, 7,* 252-264.

Morgan, W. P., and Pollock, M. L. (1977). Psychological characteristics of the elite distance runner. In P. Milvy (Ed), *Annals of the New York Academy of Sciences, 301,* 382-403.

Morgan, W. P., and Costill, D. L. (1972). Psychological characteristics of the marathon runner. *Journal of Sport Medicine and Physical Fitness, 12,* 42-46.

Okwumabua, T. M., Meyers, A., and Santille, L. A. (1987). A demographic and cognitive profile of master runners. *Journal of Sport Behavior, 10,* 212-220.

Okwumabua, T. M., Meyers, A., Schlesser, R., and Cooke, R. (1983). Cognitive strategies and running performance: An exploratory study. *Cognitive Therapy Research, 7,* 363-369.

Pennebaker, J. W., and Lightner, J. W. (1980). Competition of internal and external information in an exercise setting. *Journal of Personal Social Psychology, 39,* 165-174.

Nicholls, J. G. (1984a). Achievement motivation: Conceptions of ability, subjective experience, task choice, and performance. *Psychological Review, 91,* 328-346.

Nicholls, J. G. (1989). *The competitive ethos and democratic education.* Cambridge, MA: Harvard University Press.

Noble, B. J., and Robertson, R. J. (1996). *Perceived exertion.* Champaign, IL: Human timelines.

Pandolf, K. B. (1982). Differentiated ratings of perceived exertion during physical exercise. *Medicine and Science in Sport and Exercise, 14,* 397-405.

Raglin, J. S., and Wilson, G. S. (1991). Psychology in endurance performance. In R. J. Shepard and P. O. Astrand (Eds.). *Endurance in sport (Encyclopedia of sport medicine)* . Oxford: Blackwell Scientific.

Roberts, G. C. (1992). Motivation in sport and exercise: Conceptual constraints and convergence. In G. C. Roberts (Ed.). *Motivation in sport and exercise: Conceptual constraints and convergence* (pp. 3-30). Champaign, IL: Human Kinetics.

Roberts, G. C. (1993). Motivation in sport: Understanding and enhancing the motivation and achievement of children. In R. N. Singer, M. Murphey, and L. K. Tennant (Eds.). *Handbook of research on sport psychology.* (pp. 405-420). New York: Macmillan.

Robertson, R. J. (2001, Ed.). Perceptual exertion. *International Journal of Sport Psychology (special issue), 32,* 109-196.

Schmidt, A. J. M., and Arntz, A. (1987). Psychological research and chronic low back pain: A standstill or breakthrough? *Social Science and Medicine, 25(10),* 1095-1104.

Schomer, H. H. (1986). Mental strategy and the perception of effort of marathon runners. *International Journal Sport Psychologist, 17,* 41-59.

Scott, L. M., Scott, D., Bedic, S. P., and Dowd, J. (1999). The effect of associative and dissociative strategies on rowing ergometer performance. *The Sport Psychologist, 13,* 57-68.

Silva, J. M., and Appelbaum, M. I. (1989). Association-dissociation patterns of United States Olympic trial contestants. *Cognitive Theoretical Research, 13,* 185-192.

Skevington, S. M. (1995). *Psychology of pain.* Chichester, UK: Wiley and Sons.

Spanos, N. P., Horton, C., and Chaves, J. F. (1975). The effects of two cognitive strategies on pain threshold. *Journal of Abnormal Psychology, 86,* 677-681.

Stevens, D., Janz, C., and Mahoney, L. (1996). Goal orientation and RPE in exercise testing of young adolescents. *Journal of Applied Sport Psychology, 8 (Supp),* S140.

Stevinson, C. D., and Biddle, S. J. H. (1998). Cognitive orientations in marathon running and "hitting the wall." *British Journal of Sports Medicine, 32,* 229-235.

Summers, J. J., Sargent, G. I., Levey, A. J., and Murray, K. D. (1982). Middle-aged, non-elite marathon runners: A profile. *Perceptual Motor Skills, 54,* 963-969.

Tammen, V. V. (1996). Elite middle and long distance runners associative/dissociative coping. *Journal of Applied Sport Psychology, 8,* 1-8.

Tenenbaum, G., Fogarty, G., Stewart, E., Calcagnini, N., Kirker, B., Thorne, G., and Christensen, S. (1999). Perceived discomfort in running: Scale development and theoretical considerations. *Journal of Sport Sciences, 17,* 183-196

Tenenbaum, G. (2001). A social-cognitive perspective of perceived exertion and exertion tolerance. In R. N. Singer, H. Hausenblas, and C. Janelle (Eds.), *Handbook of sport psychology* (pp. 810-820). New York, NY: Wiley and Sons.

Tenenbaum, G., Hall, H. K., Calcagnini, N., Lange, R., Freeman, G., and Lloyd, M. (2001). Coping with physical exertion and negative feedback under competitive and self-standard conditions. *Journal of Applied Social Psychology, 31,* 1582-1626.

Thompson, S. C. (1981). Will it hurt if I can control it? A complex answer to a simple question. *Psychological Bulletin, 90,* 89-101.

Turk, D. C., and Rudy, T. E. (1986). Assessment of cognitive factors in chronic pain: A worthwhile enterprise. *Journal of Consulting and Clinical Psychology, 54(6),* 760-768.

Turk, D. C., Michenbaum, D., and Genest, M. (1983). *Pain and medicine: A Cognitive-behavioral approach.* Hillsdale, N.J.: Earlbaum.

Ungerleider, S., Golding, J. M., Porter, K., and Foster, J. (1989). An exploratory examination of cognitive strategies used by masters track and field athletes. *The Sport Psychologist, 3,* 245-253.

Weiser, P. C., and Stamper, D. A. (1977). Psychophysiological interactions leading to increased effort, leg fatigue, and respiratory distress during prolonged strenuous bycicle riding. In G. Borg (Ed), *Physical work and effort* (pp. 401-416). New York: Pergamon Press.

Whitemarsh, B. G., and Alderman, R. B. (1993(. Role of psychological skills training in increasing athletic pain tolerance. *The Sport Psychologists, 7,* 388-399.

Williamson, J.W., McColl, R., Mathews, D., Mitchell, J. H., Raven, P. B., and Morgan, W. P. (2001). Hypnotic manipulation of effort sense during dynamic exercise: Cardiovascular responses and brain activation. *Journal of Applied Physiology, 90,* 1392-1399.

Wrisberg, C. A., and Pein, R. L. (1990). Past running experience as a mediator of the attentional focus of male and female recreational runners. *Perceptual Motor Skills, 71,* 427-432.

Courtesy of John Bright Images

6.3

An Action-Oriented Perspective on Exercise Psychology

DIETER HACKFORT AND HANS-ALBERT BIRKNER

Introduction

The recent emphasis on fitness and health in western societies has strongly influenced the development of related sciences. Sport psychology has expanded and seen a dramatic increase in related research. Sport psychology has differentiated into specialized areas with sport and exercise psychology now regarded as branches.

This chapter offers an overview of existing concepts regarding the psychological effects of exercise behavior, and presents the action-theory approach as a comprehensive conceptual framework that fits some of the conceptual gaps for which other theories have not sufficiently accounted. The first section of this paper will characterize the field. The second section provides an overview of the psychological effects of exercise behavior and offers some possi-

ble explanations concerning their origins and functional relations. The third section concentrates on understanding exercise, its initiation and adherence. Finally, practical interventions to help individuals adhere to exercise are described.

Terminology and Subject Matter

This first section concentrates on characterizing the field of exercise psychology. Definitions of exercise and exercise psychology are presented, and the field of exercise psychology is characterized in the context of other sport and health sciences.

As Rejeski and Barwley (1988) have noted, there is a definitional ambiguity in the field of exercise psychology. This section will specify what the term "exercise" denotes and offer insight into the field's main objectives and topics.

According to Bouchard, Shephard, Stephens et

al. (1990), exercise can be regarded as a special area of participation in physical activity. It is characterized by the use of skeletal muscles to move the body in ways intended to maintain or enhance physical fitness, well-being, and health. Therefore, exercise can be defined as fitness- and health-oriented motor or movement actions. Exercise and sport as special areas of movement actions refer to different kinds of physical activity organized with regard to different intentions (see Figure 1). Our focus here is on exercise, but we should mention that the scope of sport includes modern forms of adventure and fun sports (e.g., scuba diving) as well as more traditional forms of achievement-oriented and competitive sports.

Physical fitness involves a number of components, including the body's structure and skills and physiological fitness vs. the effectiveness of the biological system and psychic fitness or mental (cognitive and affective) functioning. "Fitness" is a relative concept and must take the situation into consideration. The person-environment-task constellation: P-E-T fit can be subdivided into P-E fit (see French, Rodgers & Cobb, 1974), P-T fit, and E-T fit.

Whereas overall fitness focuses on the functional aspect, exercise includes movements designed to improve the body shape with regard to appearance. This aspect has resulted in the design of special programs by exercise scientists (e.g., exercise physiologists) but has been neglected in exercise psychology.

In addition, it is important to emphasize (see Bouchard et al., 1990) that exercise is characterized as leisure-time physical activity (see also Biddle & Mutrie, 1991; Caspersen, Powell, & Christensen, 1985). Exercise should be regarded as a bio-psycho-social process which can be analyzed from three perspectives: psychological, sociological, and biological disciplines (See Figure 2).

Exercise psychology is concerned with psychological factors coupled with antecedents of participation in exercise such as adoption and maintenance, and the processes involved in organizing and regulating exercise. Also, it encompasses cognitive and emotional outcomes and their consequences. Motor or movement actions are characterized as goal-directed, intentional, and purposeful motor behavior. From an exercise psychology perspective, fitness- and health-orientated actions focus on the maintenance and enhancement of psychosomatic and psychological fitness, body shape, health, well-being, and the prevention of illness.

As the terminological network of Figure 1 shows, there are substantial differences between the disciplines of sport and exercise psychology and even within exercise psychology itself. Exercise psychologists focus upon numerous areas including the welfare of individuals, the well-being of the exercise participant, and the lifestyles of those who are not yet involved in exercise programs. The general intention of exercise psychology is to develop

Figure 1: Terminological Network

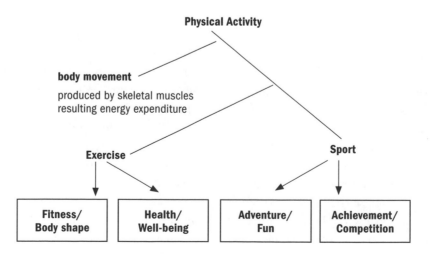

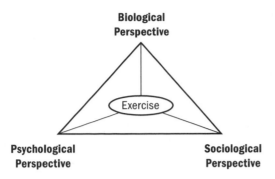

and encourage programs that will contribute to the maintenance or enhancement of fitness, body shape, health, and well-being and to prevent illness. To increase exercise participation it is necessary to research the background of physical activity. Exercise psychologists need to understand the barriers to and motives for exercise participation and how and why maintenance and attrition from exercise ensues. Therefore, a main objective of exercise psychology research is to contribute to the understanding of intentional organized fitness- and health-oriented motor actions with a view to developing educational strategies and psychological interventions designed to increase initiation, maintenance, and adherence in such programs. This information will help establish appropriate exercise behavior patterns so that programs offered can have a positive impact on participants' lifestyles and improve their quality of life. Not included within the realm of exercise psychology research are exercise programs designed to treat psychological problems, or those for rehabilitation or socialization purposes.

Exercise psychology has three main goals. They are:

(1) The development of a theoretical framework for the description, explanation, and prognosis of exercise including: (a) an analysis of exercise conditions with regard to the action situation, that is the person, the environment, and the task and its interplay (see Nitsch & Hackfort, 1981); (b) an analysis of the psychological processes involved in organizing and regulating exercise; and (c) an analysis of psychological outcomes and consequences of

exercise (short-term outcomes, e.g., mood and cognitive functioning; long-term consequences, e.g., traits such as trait anxiety, trait anger, and self concept, etc.).

(2) The development of appropriate methods and instruments for research, diagnosis, and evaluation of programs.

(3) The development of educational and interventional strategies and techniques for the initiation, adoption, maintenance, and integration of exercise into a healthy lifestyle.

Exercise psychology has its roots in both sport science and psychology, and is linked to other subdisciplines such as health psychology. It is similar to exercise physiology regarding its status within sport science.

Outcomes and Effects of Exercise Behavior and Attempted Explanations

This section provides an overview of the psychological effects of exercise behaviors. We describe some common assumptions regarding the outcomes of exercise behavior on psychological processes. We offer a few representative empirical findings, and then outline the various theoretical approaches that have been used to explain psychological outcomes.

Assumptions

There are a number of assumptions regarding the physiological and psychological outcomes of exercise behaviors.

As is shown in Table 1, some of psychological effects refer to state aspects, while others refer to more lasting trait aspects. The last two items listed refer specifically to the effects of aerobic physical activity. According to Hollmann and Hettinger (1990), this type of activity is characterized by the use of more than 1/6 of the skeletal muscular system and 60-80% of the maximum oxygen uptake, and requires that energy will be provided constantly through the circulatory system without any accumulation of anaerobic metabolism by-products such as lactate.

Table 1: Common Assumptions on Psychological Effects of Physical Exercise
· Distraction or diversion from unpleasant cognitions effect on state aspects
· Sense of mastery/self-control which is associated with a sense of well-being effect on state and trait aspects
· Ability to adapt and cope with the environment effect on trait aspects
· Synthesization of morphine-like chemicals (endorphins) in the brain resulting in a sense of euphoric well-being effect on state aspects by aerobic exercise
· Reduction in autonomic responses which reduces excitation effect on trait aspects by aerobic exercise

Empirical findings: psychological effects of exercise

An analysis of the existing empirical research reveals confusing data with few clear conclusions drawn. We will differentiate between short-term and long-term effects in our review of this material. Short-term effects relate to the actual emotional state, while long-term-consequences relate to general well-being and to personality traits.

Short-term effects of exercise

A popular assumption is that *cognitive functioning* is improved by any physical activity. A review of Tomporowski and Ellis (1986) reveals that increases in cognitive functioning seem to be highly dependent on the intensity, duration, and type of physical activity. Studies from Paas and Adam (1991) and Adam, Teeken, Ypelaar, Verstappen, and Paas (1997) found improvements in information processing during ergometer-work, revealing a better performance on attentional tasks but not on short-term retention tasks. However the small sample sizes of the studies make it difficult to issue clear statements concerning short-term changes in cognitive functioning from physical exercise.

The situation is similar regarding the short-term effects of exercise on mood. A decrease of anger, depression, and an increase in energy and calmness are frequently reported for individuals who exercise (Abele & Brehm, 1991; Berger & Owen, 1983, 1988; Morgan, 1985). Increased ability to cope with stress and anxiety has also been investigated. However, findings are still inconsistent, showing a great dependency on the intensity of the physical activity. Some authors have found reductions in state-anxiety

(Morgan, 1985; Berger & Owen, 1983) while others found an increased level of state-anxiety at high intensities (Steptoe & Cox, 1988) or no changes at all (Berger & Owen, 1986, 1988; Ewing, Scott, Mendez, & McBride, 1984).

Long-term effects of exercise

Consequences of exercise on personality traits and general well-being are even more unclear. Some studies indicate that physical activity will result in the long-term improvement of self-assurance, self-confidence, and self-concept (Plante & Rodin, 1990). However, it is not clear whether personality traits like self-concept are consequences or antecedents of physical exercise. Trait anxiety and depression are likely to be slightly influenced by physical activity (Abele & Brehm, 1991; Berger, 1989; Folkins & Sime, 1981), but the validity of the findings is unclear because the subjects studied were depressive patients. Some authors like Schwenkmezger (1985) even doubt the effectiveness of aerobic training on depressive patients.

The findings regarding long-term consequences of physical exercise on cognitive functioning are inconsistent. The positive effects on cognitive functioning, including memory, intelligence, or neuropsychological test results, have been conducted on geriatric mental patients (Folkins & Sime, 1981) reducing the external validity of these findings.

According to Steptoe (1994) many short-term physiological and psychological effects are found after intense physical exercise. Thus, it is possible that long-term changes result from the accumulation of positive after-exercise effects. Although this is still a hypothesis, a study by Steptoe (1994) considers it a reasonable explanation for the more positive mood state of people who exercise on a regular basis. In one of Steptoe's studies, competitive athletes and sedentary men were randomized to one of the three conditions: exercise at 70% of VO2max, 50% VO2max or light exercise (control group). After 20 minutes on a bicycle ergometer, followed by a 30 minute recovery period, all participants were tested on two mental stress tests (mental arithmetic and public speech). Subjects who cycled at the highest level had significantly lower systolic and diastolic blood pressure at both tasks than subjects who exercised at the intermediate intensity or were in the control group. These findings "indicate that vigorous exercise does buffer cardiovascular responses to later mental stress" (Steptoe, 1994, p. 87). However, contrary to the expectation, there was no significant difference between athletes and sedentary men.

The long-term effects of exercise on physiological responses to mental stress remain unexplained. One reason might be that the results, especially in longitudinal studies, are not as promising as the effects of exercise on physiological or other psychological factors (e.g. anxiety). Only a few cross-sectional or longitudinal studies have shown that physiological responses to stressful mental tasks are reduced following aerobic training. Blumenthal et al. (1988) measured two different groups' blood pressure at rest and in response to mental arithmetic. One group had passed a three month aerobic training program while the other group took part in a flexibility and strength training program. There was no effect for either group on systolic blood pressure at rest, but a significant smaller increase in response to mental arithmetic was found in the aerobic training group. There was no such difference in the flexibility and strength group. Steptoe (1994, p. 84) points out, "the results of this study are exceptional." Only a few of all controlled longitudinal studies show reductions in physiological responses to mental stress after aerobic training, and the rest show either no change or a change in exercise and control group. One such study was conducted by Steptoe, Moses, Edwards, and Mathews (1993). They trained sedentary adult volunteers in a randomized 10-week study with moderate aerobic exercise or attention-placebo condition. After the training both groups showed a reduction of systolic pressure and heart rate but no significant difference was found between the groups.

The discrepancies among findings of more positive effects in cross-sectional and less promising results in longitudinal studies have not been resolved. Steptoe (1994, p. 84) lists two possible reasons. First, he suggests that a change in physiological stress responsivity takes longer than changes in a subjective state of well-being. Second, different processes may underlie these effects (see the physiological and psychological processes mentioned above).

Attempted explanations

Some hypotheses have been formulated to provide explanations for exercise behaviors. These are "attempted explanations" because they lack sufficient empirical evidence to confirm them. There are three main concept groups. In the first group physiological processes are emphasized and specific intensity-dependent changes of physiological states are responsible for subsequent effects on well-being, mood enhancement, or stress-reduction. In the second group, the focus is on psychological processes and their effects on cognitive, meditative and/or attention processes, and the third group refers to the interrelationship and interaction of psychosocial and physiological processes.

Physiological based hypotheses

These hypotheses offer explanations for the so called "feeling better" phenomenon that occurs during or after physical activities. This phenomenon is apparent due to an improvement in mood factors such as a reduction in state-anxiety and depression or an increase in quietness and well-being.

The hypothesis of general physiological activation and thermoregulation

This theory directly connects a higher physiological activation level to an improvement of actual well-being (de Vries, Wiswell, Bulbulian, & Mortani, 1981; Raglin & Morgan, 1985). It has been shown that aerobic physical activity results in a certain increase in oxygen-uptake and an elevation in blood-circulation in the central nervous system as well as in the periphery organs. The latter affects thermo-regulation resulting in a higher central body-temperature and an increase in the sensitivity of sensory receptors (Hollmann & Hettinger, 1990). The reported improvement of psychological well-being immediately after aerobic physical activity could be the result of either the general positive feeling of increased body-temperature or by the extension of the sensory perception of both the body and the environment. A study by Petruzzello, Landers, Hatfield, Kobitz, and Salazar (1991) showed there was a clear relationship between body temperature and state anxiety. They determined that only 8% of the variance was explained by body temperature indicating that other variables such as blood pressure might have a greater effect. A reduction in resting muscle action potential following physical exercise or training was discussed (de Vries, 1968; Sime, 1978) as a further reason for the resulting tension relief. The thermoregulation hypothesis offers a plausible explanation but lacks empirical evidence; more research is needed on this topic.

The endorphins hypothesis

Aerobic physical activity is said to increase production and secretion (from 100 up to 130%) of natural opioides like endorphins (esp. beta-endorphin) (Harber & Sutton, 1984). The receptors for these endorphins can be found in the limbic system which is responsible for the perception of pain and closely connected to motivational and emotional processes. Higher concentrations of endorphins are thought to reduce pain-perception and improve the emotional state and general well-being.

The popularity of this theory has diminished in recent years due to methodological and medical shortcomings of the several investigations into the topic. Several studies measured endorphin concentration after an activity, which is difficult to compare to psychological effects during the activity. Factors like circadian rhythms or the menstrual cycle have largely been ignored, thus it is not clear if a concentration of beta-endorphins measured in the periphery has any relevance to the central nervous system (e.g., Feldman & Quenzer, 1984). Moreover, significant increases in beta-endorphins require intensity (over 4mmol/lactat) or duration (over 30 min) of physical activity (Schwarz, Biro, & Kindermann, 1989). Thus, the hypotheses may only provide an appropriate explanation for the results of vigorous activity.

The catecholamines hypothesis

Catecholamines are hormones of the sympathetic nervous system (e.g., adrenaline or noradrenaline and their metabolic by-products such as serotin or dopamin). These are produced or absorbed in the limbic system, where emotions are thought to be generated and regulated (LeDoux, 1996). High concentrations of catecholamines are connected to psychological well-being, while a deficiency is regarded as an origin of negative moods or depression. Aerobic exercise causes an increase in catecholamines, depending not only on the exercise intensity, but also on the state of metabolism. While earlier studies, e.g., from Christensen, Galbo, Hansen et al. (1979), found catecholamine increases only at intensity-levels higher than 50% VO2max, Rieckert (1991) stated catecholamine emission could remain high even at rest as long as a steady state of oxygen demand remains. Significant increases are found in noradrenalin and serotin during aerobic exercise (e.g., Butler, O'Brien, O'Mally, & Kelly, 1982; Hollmann, de Meirleir, & Arentz, 1989). Increases in catecholamines caused by physical activity can be interpreted as a consequence of a controlled stress-situation for the individual. However, if individuals participate in frequent aerobic exercise, they can cope more effectively with daily stressors resulting in improved general well-being.

With regard to long-term effects, two contradictory findings must be considered. Blood concentrations of catecholamines decrease more quickly with frequent aerobic exercise, but the body-tissue sensitiveness increases (Hollmann & Hettinger, 1990). The higher sensitivity of the nervous-system is realized by increasing the number of catecholamine-receptors (e.g., Lehmann et al., 1984). Both a lower resting catecholamine concentration, as well as a higher number of receptors in physically trained individuals, should influence mood or psychological well-being in the short and long term. Research on the catecholamine-hypothesis has to be regarded as a work in progress, because of limited knowledge on these complicated mechanisms.

Psychological based hypotheses

Psychological concepts attempt to explain the ongoing effects of physical activity rather than the acute effects. However, a closer look at these hypotheses reveals that the chronic effects are mainly explained by the frequent repetition of acute effects.

Distraction (time-out) hypothesis

Representatives of this idea state that physical activity distracts from stressful perceptions or situations (Bahrke & Morgan, 1978; Schwartz, Davidson, & Goleman, 1978). They propose that physical activity itself requires a certain amount of information reception and processing capacity, thus limiting stress from other external stimuli. This hypothesis is based on considerable research and a frequently cited study by Raglin and Morgan (1985) which showed similar psychological effects between exercise training and resting periods (Berger & Owen, 1992). The hypothesis is not confined to aerobic exercise, but it seems to account mainly for the acute effects of physical exercise because the distraction is only present for a short time after the exercise. Considering that regular physical training may repeatedly distract from stressful daily events, it could account for a general stress reduction. However, long lasting stress reduction from regular activity is regarded to be less probable.

Critics of the distraction-hypothesis emanate from self-attention or self-perception and from the area of coping research. When viewed from a self-attention theory perspective, distraction from external stimuli is more likely to lead to an individual placing emphasis on internal processes such as emotions and therefore reinforces stress-emotions, e.g. anxiety (Carver, Blaney, & Scheier, 1979). According to coping research, cognitive avoidance like distraction could have positive short-term effects, but holds that a vigilant strategy would offer more long-term positive effects on psychological health (Suls & Fletcher, 1985). Schwartz, Davidson, and Goleman (1978) proposed a capacity-theoretical model, arguing that in the act of a positive or neutral activity, "positive" emotions must compete with the "negative" emotions first. This idea has yet to be empirically tested.

Control-belief hypothesis

Physical activity is said to improve control-belief (belief of the individual's capability to control situations) and to improve general factors that build up the construct of self-efficacy. The latter concept refers to an individual's ability to consciously master difficult problems, and the belief of individual's power to control situations (Bandura, 1977; 1986). An improved self-assurance resulting from the perception of control and mastery in sports or an increased self-confidence resulting from better body-perception is likely to influence self-concept or control-beliefs. It is the assumption that self-efficacy, self-assurance, self-confidence, and control-beliefs (Bandura, 1977) are all a part of what can be referred to as psychological well-being and that by increasing these factors, well-being will be increased. Control-beliefs are likely to change through the mastering of problems or tasks requiring high skills being solved without external

help (Bandura, 1977). Though not specifically restricted to it, this hypothesis would include aerobic endurance training as a task capable of changing control-beliefs or self-efficacy.

The key question is whether the control-beliefs remain sport-specific or can change into generalized beliefs. This may be influenced by the importance a subject attaches to physical activity relative to other dimensions of daily life like social or professional activities. The theory seems to be empirically plausible (Berger & Owen, 1988; Crews & Landers, 1987; Dyer & Crouch, 1987). Individuals practicing physical training showed fewer stress-reactions to a stressor than physically inactive individuals and reported fewer stress-symptoms such as depression. Nevertheless, there are also studies (Dowall, Bolter, Flett, & Kammann, 1988; Hansford & Hattie, 1982; Sinyor, Golden, Steinert, & Seraganian, 1986) that indicate no or low correlations between physical fitness and stress-reactions or self-report variables of well-being. The reason for the apparent contradiction in findings may be insufficient differentiation between the short-term effects of physical exercise on mood and long-term effects of physical training on generalized control-beliefs. This hypothesis refers to chronic effects that should be analyzed by longitudinal studies, and most of the noted investigations had a cross-sectional design.

Meditative states of mind (flow) hypothesis

This hypothesis is based on the findings by Csikszentmihalyi (1975; 1982), who focused his studies on intrinsic motivated activities. When he asked mountain-climbers, surgeons, chess-players, and rock-dancers what they felt during their activities, he detected a phenomenon he called "flow." During "flow" an individual is fully involved in an activity, performing it just for itself; consciousness is well-ordered and fully functioning (Csikszentmihaly, 1982). Nevertheless, flow is quite different from artificial states of mind caused by drugs because it is strongly connected to the experience of control and self-efficacy. To reach such an experience, the task at hand must be just a little above the individual's regular abilities, but not so difficult that it cannot be solved successfully alone. A flow or flowlike meditative state of mind during physical activity has been reported frequently for both extreme physical endurance and everyday activities (Csikszentmihalyi, 1988; Massimini & Carli, 1988). It is doubted whether usual leisure activities fulfill the conditions for flow. However, the flow-conception in its basic form offers an explanation for actual effects of physical exercise. It is doubtful whether a single flow-state can change general well-being (Diener, 1984).

Changes in mastery and exercise related cognitions

Sonstroem and Morgan (1989) point out that one direct result of taking part in an exercise program may be a higher confidence in a person's (exercise) ability and a rise in one's (physical) self-efficacy. Being successful in progressive training could improve an individual's beliefs in physical competence, physical satisfaction and basic concepts about potential and abilities. The perception of these changes may positively influence self-esteem and enhance self-concept resulting in a heightened state of well-being. Findings by McDonald and Hodgdon (1991) support this hypothesis, however, Steptoe (1994, p. 87) warns, that "these responses might simply be components of the mental response to training, rather than being part of the mediating process."

Interactional hypotheses

The last two hypotheses refer to interactions between physiological and psychological processes as possible functional mechanisms.

The bidimensional activation hypothesis

Thayer (1989) proposed the existence of two dimensions of activation or arousal: energetical and tensional. Energetical arousal is based on circadian rhythm, motor or cognitive activity; tensional arousal comes from emotions or moods like anxiety, fear, anger, and by tranquility, calmness, or inner balance. On a low level, the two dimensions are positively correlated: i.e., a low energetical arousal is usually connected with moods like calmness. At high levels the two dimensions are negatively correlated: high states of tension result in a feeling of less energy and tiredness. Thayer's concept is not sport specific, but it may explain acute psychological effects of physical activity. Exercise, a form of high energetical activation, should reduce tensional arousal resulting in a reduction of negative moods and an improvement in positive mood or emotions.

Empirical evidence for the concept can be found in studies reporting a reduction in tension in people after 10 minutes of walking and arm swinging (Thayer, 1987), specifically showing a reduction of induced anxiety after moderate ergometer-training (Otto, 1984, 1990). However, there are many studies providing results that contradict those findings. Steptoe and Cox (1988) found that short (8 minutes) intensive ergometer work increased anxiety and tension. However, in the study by Steptoe and Cox (1988) as in other studies (e.g., Duda, Sedlock, Melby, & Thaman, 1988) anxiety is operationalized in anxiety scales by items that refer mainly to somatic symptoms, which reduces the generalization of the findings. Further research is needed to judge the relevance of this model.

Psychological effects by improved cardiorespiratory fitness

Increases in cardiorespiratory fitness have been associated with psychological responses associated with a range of central and peripheral neurochemical changes. However, it is unclear how these neurochemical changes from aerobic exercise affect psychological responses and whether this is unique to aerobic forms of exercise. Evidence suggests (e. g., Emery & Blumenthal, 1988; Martinsen, Hoffart, & Solberg, 1989) that both aerobic as well as anaerobic training may lead to psychological responses. Another argument against the above-mentioned mediating processes is the lack of dose-response associations, as several studies (e. g. Stevenson & Topp, 1990) of different aerobic exercise intensities (moderate or intense) showed. Furthermore, studies conducted by Hughes, Casal, and Leon (1986) and by Fremont and Craighead (1987) have found little evidence to suggest that fit people do, in fact, feel better. Similarly, Steptoe (1994, p. 86) stated that "significant correlation between changes in fitness and changes in psychological state are rarely observed."

Open questions

Physical activity occurs under varying circumstances and conditions; the circumstances under which physical exercise occurs might be more responsible for psychological benefits than is the improvement of physical processes (Jasnoski, Holmes, Salamon, &

Aguiar, 1981). Further research is needed to account for the influence of the conditions of exercise. Preconditions of physical activity include expectations concerning training effects, the presence of emotional issues, or certain personality traits. One of the most discussed circumstances of physical exercise relates to the social support found in the exercise setting, which can lead to an improved general state of well-being. This topic will be discussed in more detail later.

Theoretical Approaches on Exercise Initiation and Adherence

Beyond the explanation of the functional mechanisms leading to exercise outcomes, another necessary task in the field of exercise psychology is the development of theoretical models to analyze exercise conditions. We must learn more about the action situation with regard to the person, the environment, and the task (Nitsch & Hackfort, 1981), which lead to increased initiation and maintenance of physical activity.

In a review of the multiple narrative studies and meta-analyses on the relationship between physical exercise, fitness training, and psychological effects (Hackfort, 1994), we find that the results vary widely and are sometimes contradictory. A detailed theoretical model in which the determinants of the situation and the process of engaging in physical activity are outlined for a sophisticated analysis and explanation of exercise and exercise related effects can be found in the action-theory approach (Hackfort, 1991; Nitsch, 2000; Nitsch & Hackfort, 1981, 1984). This model is regarded as an original approach that synthesizes all of these factors; we briefly outline it here. Afterwards, we offer isolated theoretical approaches that have been used to explain exercise initiation and maintenance behaviors and compare their adequacy with the possibilities offered by the action-theory perspective.

Starting point of an action-theory perspective in exercise psychology

When discussing the action-theory perspective (see also Hackfort & Huang in this volume; Hackfort & Munzert in this volume; Hackfort & Schlattmann in

this volume), it is important to understand that an action situation is developed by the integration of three determinants: (1) the person, (2) the environment, and (3) the task—in a situation definition (definition of these components by the individual subject). Goal-directed, intentional, and purposive behavior (action) is influenced not only by the objective person-environment-task assimilation but mainly by the subjective appraisal of this system which builds up the definition of the situation.

With regard to exercise this perspective makes it necessary to consider the following factors:

(a) personal factors such as sex, age, traits (e.g. hardiness, optimism, locus of control), and the self concept;

(b) environmental factors such as ecological and social variables, and the environment concept; and

(c) task factors such as the kind of physical exercise, the intensity, duration, and frequency, and the task concept.

Furthermore, the relationships between these factors and concepts are important (see Figure 3).

This approach can be utilized to analyze and explain exercise as an intentional, organized, and mentally regulated physical activity (the action), the process of exercising is divided into three phases: (1) the anticipation phase, (2) the realization phase,

Figure 3: Components of an Action Situation.

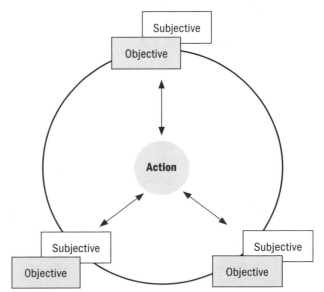

and (3) the interpretation phase (for more details see Hackfort & Munzert in this volume). In the following sections we will discuss how various theoretical approaches contribute to understanding exercise behavior and where there are gaps that have to be considered for a more comprehensive understanding.

Main aspects in previous theoretical approaches

This section provides an overview of the various theoretical approaches that have been used so far to explain the processes influencing initiation and maintenance of exercise behaviors. Additionally, these concepts are compared with the action-theory perspective.

Health belief model

This concept (Rosenstock, 1966; Becker & Maiman,1975) was developed to explain the public's poor compliance to health programs (Maddux, 1993). The fundamental idea is to predict health behavior by a value-expectation-calculation process in which individuals weigh the advantages and disadvantages of a particular behavior. This is illustrated in Figure 4.

If the advantages subjectively outweigh the disadvantages, the individual will adopt a behavior (e.g., exercise). The process of weighing the benefits and costs against each other relies on the individual's (subjectively rated) value of the potential behavior-outcome and on their expectation of their ability to reach the desired behavior-outcome. This model is mainly applicable to people anticipating or experiencing health problems. Godin and Shephard (1990) propose that individuals will decide to engage in

physical activity if a sedentary lifestyle is perceived as a threat to their health, and they believe that this threat will be reduced by engaging in a regular exercise program. These authors suggest that the health belief model is most applicable in populations already affected by disease, e.g. heart disease, however even in this context the results appear contradictory and ambiguous. The key problem with this model is that it does not encompass all the reasons that an individual may exercise as health may be just one factor (Godin, 1994).

This model relates to the anticipation phase of the action-theory model. It also accounts for the interpretation-phase as the perceptions of the benefits of and the barriers to health behavior are considered and evaluated by the individual. The health belief model also takes personal factors like age, gender, personality, and environmental factors like social class, illness of a family member, and exposure to media campaigns and newspaper articles into consideration. These factors are thought to modify the individual's evaluation process. However, task-factors seem to be less regarded in the model. It strongly emphasizes the avoidance of an illness, disregarding that there might be other motives than health to begin an exercise program and that there might be different kinds of health behavior exercises, which also might modify the health behavior orientation and practice.

Reasoned action model

The concept by Ajzen and Fishbein (1980) is based upon the intentions of individuals as a result of their attitudes towards a particular behavior and their perception of the subjective norms. Specifically it

Figure 4: Health Belief Model

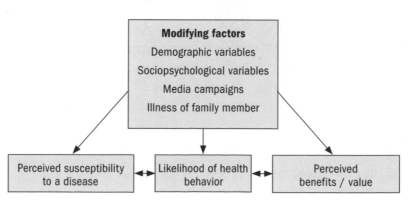

regards the belief of other's opinions about their behavior and the motivation to comply with other's opinions. Attitudes are determined by a person's beliefs about the outcome of the behavior and the value placed on that outcome. Therefore, behavior is explained through beliefs about exercise and what others believe about it, which lead to certain attitudes to exercise and perceptions of social norms. Attitude and subjective norms further influence the individual's intentions to determine actual exercise behavior. For example, if an individual has a positive attitude regarding participating in exercise, coupled with the subjective norms from others favoring the adoption of an exercise program, then the intention to exercise is likely to be high. The model is illustrated in Figure 5.

The model was especially useful in predicting volitional behavior and has been applied to exercise with some success. Godin (1993) and Godin and Shephard (1990) have reviewed the research that has been conducted using this theory in exercise contexts. From 21 studies reviewed, they concluded that the theory is useful in explaining the decision making processes that underpins exercise behavior and that in most studies approximately 30% of behavioral variance is explained by attitudes and social norms. Indeed, they confirmed that all but one study (Greenockle, Lee, & Lomax, 1990) found that attitude is the major predictor of behavioral variance in exercise. These relationships are mediated by intentions and in 12 studies the strength of the relationship between intention and behavior averaged at 0.54, all being statistically significant. In general the empirical findings support the assumption of a correlation between intention and behavior and between beliefs about the consequences of a behavior and participation in the behavior (Riddle, 1980). Nevertheless, attitudes and subjective norms only account for a small amount of the variance in exercise intention (Pender & Pender, 1986). The intention to engage in exercise behavior can be influenced by a number of other factors, e. g., past experience and real and perceived barriers to exercise influence the transition of an intention to exercise to actual exercise behavior. Consequently there must be other strong moderating variables in the process of intention-creation.

According to this approach, only mental regulation-systems, such as the emotional-regulation system, are considered to have any influence on behavior. Moreover, other factors are only recognized as important to the extent that they influence a person's beliefs, attitudes, or perceptions of normality. This is a strong emphasis on personal factors. The environmental and task factors are represented indirectly through the subjective norm based on the individual's attitudes to a particular behavior. Intentions from an action-theory perspective may be considered as conditions for planning-processes during the anticipation-phase of an action. Thus, the realization- and interpretation-phases of action are barely regarded in the reasoned action model suggesting that potential outcomes or consequences of behavior are not important.

Figure 5: Reasoned Action Model

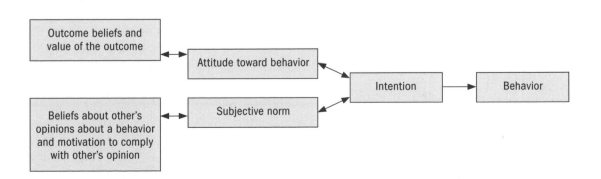

Planned behavior model

An extension to the reasoned behavior concept is the planned behavior model of Ajzen (1985). This model adds a further control variable (perceived-behavioral control) to the variables of attitude and subjective norm. Perceived behavioral control encompasses the individual's perception of his/her ability to perform the behavior and can be affected by a number of internal factors (e.g., skills and abilities) and external factors (e.g., time, opportunity, and dependence on others). The model postulates that the perceived control over external and internal factors affects exercise participation and is the most powerful determinant to certain behaviors. The belief in one's own resources to perform a behavior may influence the intention to engage in a behavior as well as the behavior itself. This is summarized in Figure 6.

Empirical findings provide more evidence to support the planned behavior model than the reasoned action concept. After reviewing exercise studies, Godin (1993) confirmed that the control variable added between 4 and 20% of variance with an average of 8% with regard to intention to exercise. Only three of the studies reviewed by Godin (1993) provided significant predictors of perceived control directly on behavior. Therefore, the empirical evidence provides only partial support for the predictive validity of the theory of planned behavior for exercise behavior.

The theory of reasoned action possesses a number of inadequacies. Maddux (1993) noted that the operational definition of perceived behavioral control is strikingly similar to that of self-efficacy expectancies. He also indicated that there are a number of ambiguities when measuring this construct as some studies did this through perceived barriers to performing the behavior. It is also unclear whether the notion of perceived control regards the measurement of control of the behavior or control over the attainment of a specific goal (Maddux, 1993). Empirical evidence concerning this question is ambiguous to date.

From an action theory point of view the perceived behavioral control variable can be considered as a variable created through processes of control and evaluation after a behavior has occurred. Thus, the planned behavior concept and the reasoned action concept both consider the interpretation phase of action. When considering the situation, analysis of an action through the planned behavior concept indirectly regards environmental and task determinants. However, they are subordinate to the perceived behavior control variable.

Self-efficacy model

The concept of self-efficacy (Bandura, 1977) is based on operant conditioning, social learning theory, and cognitive psychology. It proposes that personal, behavioral, and environmental factors operate as interacting determinants. The reciprocal understanding of interaction emphasizes that each determinant influences the other (see Figure 9).

According to Bandura (1986) the development of self-efficacy is bound to processes of attribution

Figure 6: Planned Behavior Model

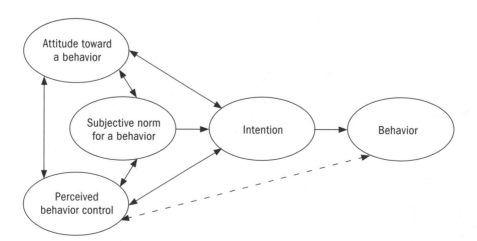

and is moderated by the perceived difficulty of the task, including the required exertion to solve the task, the amount of social support needed to solve the task, and the frequency of task solving. More difficult tasks require higher exertion and less social support. The more frequently a task is solved, the more likely that self-efficacy will occur. However, it is important to learn how self-efficacy acts as a primary variable influencing people's behavior and how this is enhanced. According to Bandura's (1986) theory of social learning, self-efficacy in individuals is a result of direct reinforcement of their own behavior (conditioning) or a result of observing the consequences of other's behavior (modeling). Furthermore, self-efficacy development is based on the repeated accomplishment of performance.

Self-efficacy was found to be behavior-specific (e.g., Barling & Abel, 1983), that is self-efficacy for exercise is different from self-efficacy for nutrition or smoking-cessation. As self-efficacy has been found to be a good predictor of a variety of behaviors like coping, stress-reaction, depression, physiological arousal, self-regulation, self-motivation, and athletic attainments (Annis & Davis, 1988; Bernier & Avard, 1986; Sallis & Owen, 1999) it may play an important role in explaining human behavior. This theory has also been applied to exercise with some success. McAuley (1992) proposed that the self-efficacy theory could be viewed as both an antecedent (IV) and as a consequence (DV) of exercise. In terms of viewing self-efficacy as an antecedent, he suggests that those individuals who are more efficacious in terms

of physical activity participation, are more likely to adopt and adhere to exercise regimens. Similarly, if an individual engages in exercise, self-efficacy can increase and is a manifestation or consequence of physical activity participation. A number of studies (Greenwood et al, 1990; McAuley & Jacobson, 1991; McAuley, 1991; Poag-DuCharme & Brawley, 1993) provide support for the mediational role of self-efficacy and subsequent exercise behavior and adherence. For example, Desharnais, Bouillon, and Godin (1986) confirmed that expectations of self-efficacy were a more central predictor of adherence to an exercise program than was the expectation of outcome.

Comparing the above scheme to situation-analyses from an action-theory perspective, it can be understood how a health behavior or exercise can be explained. Performing the behavior is dependent on two cognitive processes. First, the outcome-expectations represent the beliefs and knowledge about the effects of a behavior (e.g., improvement of health status, receiving social support, or experiencing self-satisfaction). Second, self-efficacy represents the subjective judgment of one's ability to successfully perform a behavior which is regarded as a central influential factor on behavior. In situations where an individual experiences a lack of self-efficacy it is inconsequential if the individual knew what, and how to do the activity, because they would not perform the activity, would do it ineffectively, or stop doing it at a certain degree of difficulty due to the decrease self-efficacy level. From an action-theory point of view, self-efficacy development may be regarded

Figure 7: Reciprocal Determination of Relevant Personal, Environmental, and Behavioral Factors

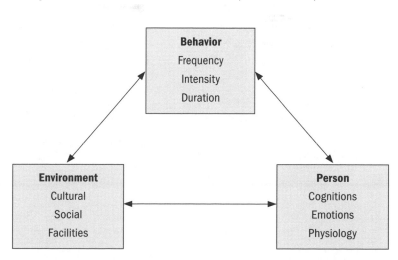

as the result of control- and evaluation-processes in the interpretation-phase of action: the goal has been reached and the causal attribution is internal.

Locus of control model

The locus of control concept by Rotter (1954) and Lefcourt (1982) states that people mainly have two different sets of control beliefs that determine their behavior: internal and external beliefs. Internal locus of control represents the view that life is dependent upon one's own behavior, while external locus of control represents the view that life is controlled by external factors such as luck, other people, or chance. Applying the concept to health behavior it is believed (Wallston, Wallston, & DeVellis, 1978) that internal locus of control raises the chance of people choosing healthy behaviors. Therefore, raising the internal locus of control is suggested as an appropriate means to initiate health behavior. Unfortunately internal locus of control is a personality trait (Dishman, 1988) and the concept does not explain how internal locus of control can be developed in individuals.

To date, only preconditions in the anticipatory phase of action have been considered with this concept, excluding any processes during realization and interpretation phases. If it is possible that the locus of control could be changed to an internal direction by the repeated perception of mastering a task or a behavior, internal, stable locus of control factors may contribute to the realization phase and especially the interpretation phase of action. The differentiation in internal and external control beliefs is known as a social-psychological concept, and takes into consideration social-environmental and psychological personal aspects. The task determinant is not exclusive to this concept; it may be a subordinate part of external control beliefs. In summary the concept of locus of control suggests some level of personal determinant to health behavior, but does not offer an explanation on how it influences health behavior.

Physical activity participation model

Like the concept of self-efficacy, the psychological concept of physical activity participation developed by Sonstroem (1974, 1976) considers the whole process of behavior. The concept emphasizes the realization phase of action, assuming that physical activity increases physical ability, which raises one's physical self-estimation and leads to higher levels of overall self-esteem. Higher self-esteem will lead people to continue to exercise in order to maintain or increase fitness. In short, a relationship between involvement in physical activity and self-esteem is assumed, whereby the relationship is reciprocally moderated through self-estimation and attraction.

An interpretation from the action-theory perspective reveals that the environmental determinant is not included, while the physical activity itself (the task) is central to the theory. The personal factors such as self-estimation and self-esteem are already regarded as more or less dependent on the activity as is the perceived physical ability as the result of the activity itself. The theory offers some explanation to the processes or factors that may initiate physical activity. There is empirical evidence that the perception of physical ability is related to self-esteem and to the actual level of performance (Sonstroem, 1976). Nevertheless, the concept still lacks power to predict exercise adherence (Sonstroem & Kamper, 1980). Sonstroem (1988) acknowledged that there are some weaknesses in the concept due to the inclusion of only two factors (attraction and self-estimation) as predictors of sustaining exercise. The construction of the scales to measure self-estimation and attraction and the power of prediction of behavior by attitudes are also questionable.

Figure 8: Physical Activity Participation Model

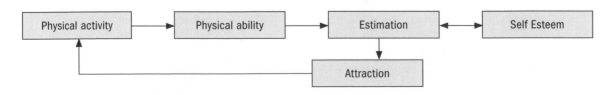

Salutogenesis model

As opposed to many risk-factor models, several protection-factor models have been developed. One which refers to exercise behavior is the salutogenesis model developed by Antonovsky (1974), which basically focuses on the question of why and how people stay healthy in a rather unhealthy environment. Antonovsky adopted many main components of the above mentioned health belief model, reasoned action model, and planned behavior model and extended them with another factor, the perception of control. Therefore, Antonovsky`s model is similar to Bandura's (1977) theory of self-efficacy and Rotter's (1954) locus of control.

In his model, Antonovsky (1974) does not strictly differentiate individuals as being in a state of being ill or healthy. Rather he sees a continuum between the two dimensions, disease and health-ease. Whether an individual is more or less healthy depends on how she or he can withstand a state of internal psychophysiological tension, which is caused by psychophysiological stressors and reduced by resilience sources (e.g., physical exercise). The sense of coherence (SOC) is, as Antonovsky (1974) points out, "a major determinant of maintaining one's position on the health-ease/dis-ease continuum and of movement toward the healthy end." SOC can be further differentiated into three factors: Consistent experiences (related to the human need for stability), load expe-

rience (Do our resources enable us to meet the demand?) and experiences of participation in shaping the outcome. Even though Antonovsky's model was not primarily developed for use in sport sciences, he postulated that exercise could improve the general ability to withstand and cope with tension and thus create a higher SOC. Figure 9 summarizes the main points of the salutogenesis-model through an action theory perspective.

Methodological Problems and Deficits

Research on the subject of psychological effects of physical activity is characterized by serious methodological deficits and problems. The critics refer to studies and to reviews of studies (see Hackfort, 1994). General methodological problems in the field of exercise psychology research include:

- Most of the studies are cross-sectional, descriptive, or correlational and therefore they are of limited value for explaining psychological processes because of potential selection bias. More longitudinal or time-series studies are needed.

- Because many researchers and subjects in this field believe that exercise does produce psychological benefits, experimental

Figure 9: Integrated Saluto-and Pathogenesis Model from an Action-Theory Perspective

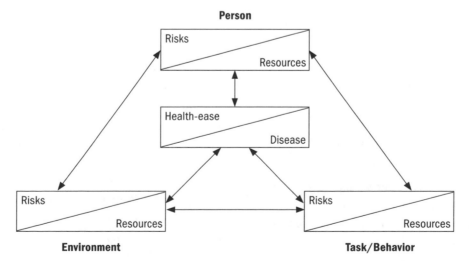

demand and subject expectancy biases are likely to occur (Hughes, 1984).

- Although self-ratings by individuals are an indispensable means to measure psychological states, the data of self-report scales are likely to be influenced by a number of effects (e.g., reactive effects, Hawthorne-effect, etc.) and therefore lack some measure of external validity.

- Experiments in general are said to deliver the most valuable data but the more closely experimental standards are met, the more artificial the situation. In such artificial situations, the subject's actions are partialized and decoupled from individual biases resulting in an increased chance of bias.

Besides these general methodological problems there are specific deficits in many of the research studies to date, e.g.:

- Lack of control-group designs with placebo conditions or double or total blind designs.

- Posttest-only designs without control of selection biases.

- One-group pretest-posttest designs that lack internal validity caused by statistical regression.

- The use of global instead of specific measurements for specific research questions.

- The lack of randomized assignment of subjects to control and experimental group increasing threats to internal validity.

- Inadequate sample size.

- Lack of description of initial data.

- Insufficient documentation and descriptions of methods and treatments.

- Poorly designed self-report measures with a lack of a theoretical basis and appropriate statistical procedures employed to validate them.

All of these problems contribute to the difficulty of making clear decisions among competing explanation and the testing of theoretical models. We need to develop a theoretical framework that provides increased integrative power to overcome this situation.

Applied Considerations Using the Action Theory Perspective

This last section offers an analysis of the factors affecting the initiation and maintenance of exercise behaviors. We will introduce motivational research and refer to personal factors affecting motivation. Later, the perspective is broadened with respect to the three components of an action situation (person, environment, and task) to consider the factors influencing exercise adherence. Finally, we will illustrate how the action-theory perspective can be used to develop comprehensive and powerful interventions to enhance exercise adherence.

Motivation and exercise adherence

The central question of motivational research is why people engage in exercise. Starting from the three components, the person, the task, and the environment, the action theory gives various reference points for motivation analysis and motivational intervention.

Participation in exercise cannot be explained by one single motive (monothematic); its initiation, adoption, maintenance, and attrition is multithematic. According to the specific and subjective interpretation of task and environment components, people show individual differences in their dynamic process of motivation and in their (multi-) motivational orientation.

"Health" is usually a predominant initiation motive for exercise, but if there are no further motive themes such as, e.g., enjoyment of motor activity, affiliation, or performance improvement, the probability of attrition is high and the probability of maintenance is low. Thus, we can not refer only to various motive themes but also to different functions of motive themes. The functional meanings of initiation, maintenance, avoidance, and withdrawal must also to be considered.

Many studies (Dishman, 1988; Sallis & Owen,

1999) have shown that it is easier to initiate an exercise program than to adhere to it. Six months after beginning an exercise program, nearly 50 percent of the participants have dropped out. Therefore, the important question to consider is what determines adherence to physical activity and exercise? Again, we will answer this question with regard to action theory categories and have a closer look at personal, environmental, and task determinants of exercise adherence.

Personal factors

Exercise history

Extensive reviews of research (e.g., Dishman, 1987) have shown that people who were active as children are more likely to be engaged in lifelong physical activity. According to Dishman (1987) the most reliable predictor of exercise adherence is past participation in an exercise program. Someone who has remained in a fitness class for more than six months is more likely to stay in the program for the next year. Gender specific differences are not found.

Knowledge of the benefits of physical activity

Unfortunately, the knowledge of and belief in the benefits of physical activity may be motivational, but they do not predict exercise adherence (Reid & Morgan, 1979). One of the crucial factors of initiating individuals into exercise regimens is knowledge of the possible health benefits of regular exercise. Therefore, scientists and physical educators are strongly encouraged to spread the news of the positive effects of engaging in regular physical activity to those who are still uninformed.

Personality

Personality traits are possible predictors of adherence to exercise activities. For example, people with a type A behavior are more likely to drop out of exercise classes than people with a type B behavior (Doan & Scherman, 1987 for an overview).

Healthy lifestyle

In general it is assumed that smokers tend to live a more sedentary life than non-smokers. Also, they are more prone to drop out of exercise programs.

Table 2: Factors Associated with Exercise Adherence	
Personal Factors	**Environmental factors**
· Exercise history	· Social support
· Knowledge of the benefits of physical activity	· Opportunities of exercise
· Personality	**Task factors**
· Healthy lifestyle	· Quality of the exercise leader
· Occupation and income	· Type of exercise
· Time	· Type of program

Referring to Weinberg and Gould (1995), smokers tend to avoid high-intensity and high-frequency exercises. They feel more fatigue and discomfort after exercise and therefore do not stick with an exercise routine. People with a high percentage of body fat are more likely to drop out than slender people. As with smokers, obese individuals feel more discomfort which deters further participation regardless of the activity.

Occupation and income

Highly educated people with a higher occupational status and with higher incomes are more likely to take part in fitness programs than less educated people with lower incomes. Also, white-collar workers lead a more active life than blue-collar workers. This may be closely connected with education and socialization. Certain patterns were also found for healthy eating, smoking, and sick leave from work. This may be as a result of 'blue collar workers' having less leisure time (Dishman, 1993). In addition, the advent of modern appliances encourage a sedentary lifestyle since these devices reduce energy expenditure, e.g., elevators and escalators. The increase of computer games, television offerings, and video equipment means that sedentary pursuits are enhanced (Report of the Surgeon General, 1996).

Time

A frequent excuse to stop exercising is the lack of time. But in most cases the participants have a lack of interest, motivation, or differing personal priorities (Oldridge et al., 1983) not a true lack of time. Two examples support this statement. Weinberg and Gould (1995) found that working women are more prone than nonworking women to exercise on a regular basis, and single parents are more physically engaged than families with two parents. There are many people with odd and long working hours for whom physical exercise programs need to be tailored. Most suitable times seem to be before and immediately following work, whereas exercise classes during lunchtime have a much higher dropout rate (Weinberg & Gould, 1995).

Environmental factors

Social support

Social support from close friends or family members is vital to maintaining a regular exercise program (e.g., Carpenter & Di-Rienzo, 1997). Especially important is encouragement from a spouse who demonstrates a positive attitude toward the initiation and maintenance of an exercise program. Oldridge, Donner, Buck et al. (1983) and Erling and Oldridge (1985) showed that the dropout rate in a cardiac rehabilitation program was much lower among people with spousal support than for those without it. One reason for staying in a program was the social reinforcement that should be a part of any physical activity. We need to examine if this is also true for leisure time physical activity (exercise).

Opportunities of exercise

A convenient or perceived convenient exercise opportunity as well as the proximity of an exercise location appears to be necessary for most people to participate in a regular fitness activity. The likelihood of starting or maintaining an exercise program is greater if the exercise area is close to home or work (Weinberg & Gould, 1995). Also the socio-economic status of an individual is important to note as those who have less disposable income may have less opportunity to exercise.

Race and ethnic group

Health behaviors vary according to race and ethnic groups. For example, the Japanese have the longest life expectancy in the world (6-7 years longer than in the UK). This has been attributed to good public health services, a less fatty diet, and an equal distribution of income over the country. Similarly within countries racial health behaviors vary dramatically. In the U.S., African Americans have higher rates for 13 of the 15 leading causes of deaths, have more psychological stress, and decreased well-being due to low socio-economic status. Duda and Allison (1990), report that African-Americans and Hispanics are less likely to engage in regular exercise than whites in the U.S.

Task factors

Type of exercise

Vigorous exercise is perceived to be more stressful than exercise at a moderate or light intensity, especially for sedentary people (e.g., Sallis, Haskell, Fortmann, et al., 1986). Another fact for choosing an average intensity is that people tend to overestimate their abilities. Many people want to get in shape quickly and do too much at the beginning of a program. Hence, they run a high risk for injury, which may be another excuse to quit exercising.

Type of program

People who exercise in groups are more likely to adhere to an exercise program than people who practice on their own. Support by others or greater enjoyment might be possible explanations for this. Also, other psychological benefits such as the fulfillment of an individual's affiliation motive or the feeling of belonging to a group are available when exercising with others. A final advantage for exercising in groups is that participants typically exhibit a stronger commitment to the program (social commitment).

Quality of the exercise leader

A good leader can motivate individuals to adhere to an exercise program. An unskilled, uncaring, or inflexible exercise leader may destroy the possible results of a solid program.

Recommendations: Enhancing Motivation and Exercise Adherence

This last section provides some ideas concerning the use of the action theory to analyze and organize the practice of exercise so that it fosters enhanced motivation and adherence. The factors used to enhance exercise adherence are classified by the components of an action situation. Table 3 provides an overview of these factors.

Table 3: Factors to Enhance Exercise Adherence

Personal factors	Environmental factors	Task factors
· Balance sheet	· Cues for exercise	· Type of activity
· Personal participation statement	· Feedback	· Rewards for attendance
· Goals		

Personal factors

Balance sheet

Before starting an exercise program everyone should complete a balance sheet. recording all of the possible negative consequences of exercising and the possible positive effects. When viewed in this way, most people realize the advantages of exercise. This procedure is fundamental in the anticipation phase of action (exercise) to determine whether an individual will exercise.

Personal participation statement

Signing a personal participation statement before starting an exercise program may increase the commitment to an exercise program.

Goals

Goals should be subdivided into short and long term goals. Main and subgoals support the basic action orientation and protect new exercisers from doubts. The fulfillment of intermediate goals serves to establish a self-reinforcing system.

Environmental factors

Cues for exercise

Verbal, physical, or symbolic prompts are helpful in the initiation of a behavioral change. A prominent study regarding the success of a visual prompt was conducted by Brownell, Stunkard, and Albaum (1980). They placed a large poster near elevators in public buildings to encourage stair climbing. After three months, the percentage of people using the stairs had increased from 6% to 14%. To avoid possible negative effects after removing the prompts, the prompts should be eliminated step by step (fading process).

Feedback

Individual social-emotional feedback given by an exercise leader will help to create a positive atmosphere. A study by Martin et al. (1984) points out that giving individual feedback during a program is more effective and leads to higher adherence than praising the whole group at the end of the session. Feedback is also available through social support networks.

Task factors

Type of activity

From a psychological perspective, moderate exercise conducted three to four times a week for 20 to 30 minutes is sufficient to heighten the probability of experiencing positive psychological changes such as a reduction in stress, fun, higher control competence, and increased self-efficacy. Therefore, it is better to practice at a reduced level of intensity and complexity of the required task. One efficient way of doing so is to structure the task and break it up into different smaller parts.

Rewards for attendance

Rewards for attendance are a way to encourage people to exercise. Epstein, Wing, Thompson, and Griffiths. (1980) paid participants in a jogging program $1 weekly for regular attendance while a control group received no incentives. After five weeks the attendance in the first group was 65 percent, whereas joggers in the control group only had an attendance of 40 percent. But, while financial or material rewards are good to initiate exercise adherence, the results in the long run are not quite as promising. Therefore, rewards should not be used as the main intervention to increase exercise adherence. The best reward may be just to have fun and to enjoy exercising.

References

Abele, A. & Brehm, W. (1991). Welcher Sport für welche Stimmung? Differentielle Effekte von Fitness—versus Spielaktivitäten auf das aktuelle Befinden. In J.R. Nitsch & R. Seiler (Eds.) *Gesundheitssport—Bewegungstherapie* (pp. 133-149). Sankt Augustin: Academia Verl.

Adam, J.J., Teeken, J.C., Ypelaar, J.C., Verstappen, F.T.J., & Paas, F.G.W. (1997). Exercise-Induced Arousal and Information Processing. *International Journal of Sport Psychology, 28* (3), 217-226.

Antonovsky, A. (1974). *Health, stress, and coping.* San Francisco: Jossey-Bass.

Ajzen, I. (1985). From intentions to actions: A theory of focus on these important subgroups. In J. Kuhl & J. Beckmann (Eds.), *Action-control: From cognition to behavior* (pp. 11-39). Heidelberg: Springer.

Ajzen, I. & Fishbein, M. (1980). *Understanding attitudes and predicting social behavior.* Englewood Cliffs, NJ: Prentice-Hall.

Annis, H.M. & Davis, C.S. (1988). Assessment of expectancies. In D.M. Donovan & G. A. Marlatt (Eds.), *Assessment of addictive behaviors* (pp. 84-111). New York: Guilford.

Bahrke, M.S. & Morgan, W.P. (1978). Anxiety reduction following exercise and meditation. *Cognitive Therapy and Research, 2,* 323-333.

Bandura, A. (1977). Self-efficacy: Toward a unifying theory of behavior change. *Psychological Reviews, 84,* 191-215.

Bandura, A. (1986). *Social foundations of thought and action. A social cognitive theory.* Englewood Cliffs, NJ: Prentice Hall.

Barling, J. & Abel, M. (1983). Self-efficacy beliefs and performance. *Cognitive Therapy and Research, 7,* 265-272.

Becker, M.H. & Maiman, L.A. (1975). Sociobehavioral determinants of compliance with health care and medical care recommendations. *Medical Care, 13,* 10-24.

Berger, B.G. (1989). The role of activity in the life of older adults. In American Academy of Physical Education (Ed.), *Physical activity and aging* (pp.42-58). Champaign: Human Kinetics.

Berger, B.G. & Owen, D.R. (1983). Mood alteration with swimming - swimmers really do "feel better". *Psychosomatic Medicine, 45* (5), 425-433.

Berger, B.G. & Owen, D.R. (1986). Mood alteration with swimming: A reexamination. In L. Van der Velden & J.H. Humphrey (Eds.), *Current selected research in psychology and sociology of sport* (pp. 97-113), New York: AMS Press.

Berger, B.G. & Owen, D.R. (1988). Stress reduction and mood enhancement in four exercise modes: swimming, body conditioning, hatha yoga, and fencing. *Research quarterly for exercise and sport, 59* (2), 148-159.

Berger, B.G. & Owen, D.R. (1992). Mood alternation with yoga and swimming: Aerobic exercise may not be necessary. *Perceptual and Motor Skills, 75,* 1331-1343.

Bernier, M. & Avard, J. (1986). Self-efficacy, outcome and attrition in a weight reduction program. *Cognitive Therapy and Research, 10,* 319-338.

Biddle, S. & Mutrie, N. (1991). *Psychology of physical activity and exercise.* London: Springer.

Blumenthal, J. A., Emery, C.F., Walsh, M.A., Cox, D.R., Kuhn, C.M., Williams, R.B., & Williams, R.S. (1988). Exercise training in health Type A middle-aged men: effects of behavioral and cardiovascular responses. *Psychosomatic medicine, 50,* 418-435.

Bouchard, C., Shephard, R.J., Stephens, T., Sutton, J.R., & Pheson, B.D. (Eds.). (1990). *Exercise, fitness and health: A consensus of current knowledge.* Champaign, IL: Human Kinetics.

Brownell, K., Stunkard, A., & Albaum, J. (1980). Evaluation and modification of exercise patterns in the natural environment. *American Journal of Psychiatry, 137,* 1540-1545.

Butler, J., O'Brien, M., O'Mally, K., & Kelly, J. (1982). Relationship of Beta-Adrenoreceptor Density to Fitness in Athletes. *Nature, 198,* 60-62.

Caspersen, C. J., Powell, K. E., & Christensen, G. M. (1985). Physical activity, exercise and physical fitness: Definitions and distinctions for health related research. *Public Health Reports, 100,* 126-131.

Carpenter, P. J., & Di-Rienzo, L. (1997). *Social physique anxiety: The role of social support.* Paper presented at the International Conference for Applied Sport Psychology.

Carver, C.S., Blaney, P.H., & Scheier, M.F. (1979). Focus of attention, chronic expectancy, and responses to a feared stimulus. *Journal of Personality and Social Psychology, 37,* 1186-1195.

Christensen, N., Galbo, H. Hansen, J., Hesse, B., Richter, E., & Trap-Jensen, J. (1979). *Catecholamines and Exercise. Diabetes, 28,* 58-62.

Crews, D.J. & Landers, D.M. (1987). A meta-analytic review of aerobic fitness and reactivity to psychosocial stressors. *Medical Science and Sports Exercise, 19,* 114-120.

Csikszentmihalyi, M. (1975). *Beyond boredom and anxiety.* San Francisco: Jossey-Basse.

Csikszentmihalyi, M. (1982). Toward a psychology of optimal experience. In L. Wheeler (Ed.), *Review of Personality and Social Psychology* (pp. 13-36). Beverly Hills: Sage.

Csikszentmihalyi, M. (1988). The future of flow. In M. Csikszentmihalyi & I.S. Csikszentmihalyi (Eds.), Optimal experience. *Psychological studies of flow in consciousness* (pp. 364-383). Cambridge: University Press.

Desharnais, R., Bouillon, J., & Godin, G. (1986). Self-efficacy and outcome expectations as determinants of exercise adherence. *Psychological Reports, 59,* 1155-1159.

de Vries, H.A. (1968). Immediate and long-term effects of exercise upon resting muscle action potential level. *Journal of Sports Medicine and Physical Fitness, 8,* 1-11.

de Vries, H.A., Wiswell, R.A., Bulbulian, R., & Mortani, T. (1981). Tranquilizer effect of exercise: Acute effects of moderate aerobic exercise on spinal reflex activation level. *American Journal of Physical Medicine, 60,* 57-66.

Diener, E. (1984). Subjective well-being. *Psychological Bulletin, 95,* 542-575.

Dishman, R.K. (1987). Exercise Adhérence. In W. P. Morgan & S. N. Goldston (Eds.), *Exercise and mental health* (pp. 57-83). New York: Hemisphere.

Dishman, R.K. (Ed.) (1988). *Exercise adherence: Its impact on public health.* Champaign, IL.: Human Kinetics.

Dishman, R.K. (1993). Exercise adherence. In R.N. Singer, M. Murphy, & L.K. Tennant (Eds.), *Handbook of research on sport psychology* (pp. 779-798). New York: MacMillan.

Doan, R.E. & Sherman, A. (1987). The therapeutic effect of physical fitness on measures of personality: A literature review. *Journal of Counseling and Development, 66,* 28-36.

Dowall, J.R., Bolter, C.P., Flett, R.A., & Kammann, R. (1988). Psychological well-being and its relationship to fitness and activity levels. *Journal of Human Movement Studies, 14,* 39-45.

Duda, J.L. & Allison, M.T. (1990). Cross-cultural analysis in exercise and sport psychology: A void in the field. *Journal of Sport and Exercise Psychology, 12,* 114-131.

Duda, J.L., Sedlock, D.A., Melby, C.L., & Thaman, C. (1988). The effects of physical activity level and acute exercise on heart rate and subjective response to psychological stressor. *International Journal of Sport psychology, 19,* 119-133.

Dyer, J.B. III. & Crouch, J.G. (1987). Effects of running moods: A time series study. *Perceptual and Motor Skills, 64,* 783-789.

Emery, C.F. & Blumenthal, J.A. (1988). Effects of exercise training on psychological functioning in healthy type A men. *Psychology and Health, 2,* 367-379.

Epstein, L.H., Wing, R.R., Thompson, J.K., & Griffiths, M. (1980). Attendance and fitness in aerobics exercise: The effects of contract and lottery procedures. *Behavior Modification, 4,* 465-479.

Erling, J. & Oldridge, N.B. (1985). Effect of spousal support program on compliance with cardiac rehabilitation. *Medicine and Science in sport and Exercise, 17,* 284.

Ewing, J.H., Scott, D.G., Mendez, A.A., & McBride, T.J. (1984). Effects of aerobic exercise on affect and cognition. *Perceptual and Motor Skills, 59,* 407-414.

Feldman, R.S. & Quenzer, L.F. (1984). *Fundamentals of neuropsychopharmacology.* Sunderland: Sinauer.

Folkins, C.H. & Sime, W.E. (1981). Physical fitness training and mental health. *American Psychologist, 36,* 373-389.

French, J. R. P., Rodgers, W., & Cobb, S. (1974). Adjustment as person-environment fit. In G. V. Coelho, D. A. Hamburg, & J. E. Adams (Eds.). *Coping and adaptation* (pp. 316-333). New York: Basic Books.

Fremont, J. & Craighead, L.W. (1987). Aerobic exercise and cognitive therapy in the treatment of dysphoric moods. Cognitive *Therapy and Research, 11,* 241-251.

Godin, G. (1993). The theories of reasoned action and planned behavior: Overview of findings emerging research problems and usefulness for exercise promotion. *Journal of applied Sport Psychology, 5,* 141-157.

Godin, G. (1994). Theories of reasoned action and planned behavior: usefulness for exercise promotion. Medicine and *Science in Sports and Exercise, 26,* 1391-1394.

Godin, G. & Shepard, R.J. (1990). Use of attitude-behavior models in exercise promotion. *Sports Medicine, 10,* 103-121.

Greenockle, K.M., Lee, A.A., & Lomax, R. (1990). The relationship between selected student characteristics and activity patterns in a required high school physical education class. *Research of Quarterly Exercise Sport, 61,* 59-69.

Greenwood, C., Dzewaltowski, D.A., & French, R. (1990). Self-efficacy and psychological well-being of wheelchair tennis participants and wheelchair nontennis participants. *Adaptive physical Activity quarterly, 7,* 12-21.

Hackfort, D. (1991). Emotion in sports: An action theoretical analyses. In C.D. Spielberger, J.G. Sarason, Z. Kulcsar, & G.L. Van Heck (Eds.). *Stress and emotion Vol. 14* (pp. 65-73). New York: Hemisphere.

Hackfort, D. (1994). Health and Wellness: A Sportpsychology Perspective. In S. Serpa, J. Alves & V. Pataco (Eds.), *International Perspectives on Sport and Exercise Psychology* (pp. 165-183). Morgantown: Fitness Information Technology.

Harber, V. & Sutton, J. (1984). Endorphins and Exercise. *Sports Medicine, 1,* 154-171.

Hansford, B.C. & Hattie, J.A. (1982). The relationship between self and achievement/performance measures. *Review of Educational Research, 52,* 123-142.

Hollmann, W. & Hettinger, Th. (1990). *Sportmedizin [Sportsmedicine].* Stuttgart: Schattauer.

Hollmann, W., de Meirleir, K., & Arentz, K. (1989). Gehirndurchblutung, Neurotransmitter, Stimmung, muskuläre Arbeit [Braincirculation, neurotransmitters, mood]. In D. Bönig, Braukmann, K. M., Busse, M. W., Maasen, N., & Schmitt, W. (Eds.), Sport: Rettung oder Risiko für die Gesundheit?[Sports: Rescue or risk for health?] (pp. 263-272). Köln.

Hughes, J.R. (1984). Psychological effects of habitual aerobic exercise: A critical review. *Preventive Medicine, 13,* 66-78.

Hughes, J.R., Casal, D.C., & Leon, A.S. (1986). Psychological effects of exercise: a randomized cross-over trial. *Journal of Psychosomatic Research, 30,* 355-360.

Jasnoski, M.L., Holmes, D.S., Salamon, S., & Aguiar, C. (1981). Exercise, changes in aerobic capacity, and changes in self-perception: An experimental investigation. *Journal of Research and Personality, 15,* 460-466.

LeDoux, J. (1996). *The emotional brain.* New York: Simon & Schuster.

Lefcourt, H.M. (1982). *Locus of control—current trends in theory and research.* Hillsdale: Lawrence Erlbaum Associates.

Lehmann, M. Dickhut, H., Schmid, P., Porzig, H., & Keul, J. (1984). Plasma catecholamines, ß-adrenergic receptors, and isoproterenol sensitivity in endurance trained and non-endurance trained volunteers. *European Journal of Applied Physiology and Occupational Physiology, 52,* 362-369.

Maddux, J.E. (1993). Social cognitive models of health and exercise behavior: An introduction and review of conceptual issues. *Journal of Applied Sport Psychology, 5,* 116-140.

Martin, J., Dubbert, P.M., Katell, A.D., Thompson, J.K., Raczynski, J.R., Lake, M., Smith, P. O., Webster, J.S., Sikora, T., & Cohen, R.E. (1984). The behavioral control of exercise in sedentary adults: Studies 1 through 6. *Journal of Consulting and Clinical Psychology, 52,* 795-811.

Martinsen, E.W., Hoffart, A., & Solberg, O.Y. (1989). Comparing aerobic and non-aerobic forms of exercise in the treatment of clinical depression: a randomized trial. *Comprehensive Psychiatry, 30,* 324-333.

Massimini, F. & Carli, M. (1988). The systematic assessment of flow in daily experience. In M. Csikszentmihalyi & I.S. Csikszentmihalyi (Eds.), *Optimal experience. Psychological studies of flow in consciousness* (pp. 364-383). Cambridge: University Press.

McAuley, E. (1991). Efficacy, attributional, and affective responses to exercise participation. Journal of Sport and Exercise Psychology, 13, 382-393.

McAuley, E. (1992). Self referent thought in sport and dgdon, J.A. (1991). *The Psychological Effects of Aerobic Fitness Training.* New York: Springer-Verlag.

Morgan, W. P. (1985). Affective benefice of vigorous physical activity. *Medicine and Science in Sports and Exercise, 17,* 94-100.

Nitsch, J.R. (2000). Handlungstheoretische Grundlagen der Sportpsychologie. In H. Gabler, J.R. Nitsch & R. Singer (Eds.) *Einführung in die Sportpsychologie,* Teil 1: Grundthemen (3. erweit. Auflage; S. 43-164). Schorndorf: Hofmann.

Nitsch, J.R. & Hackfort, D. (1981). Streß in Schule und Hochschule—eine handlungspsychologische Funktionsanalyse [Stress in school and university - an action-psychology based functional analysis]. In J.R. Nitsch (Ed.), *Streß. Theorien, Untersuchungen, Maßnahmen* [Stress. Theories, investigations, strategies] (pp. 263-311). Bern: Huber.

Nitsch, J.R. & Hackfort, D. (1984). Basisregulation interpersonalen Handelns im Sport (Tuning of interpersonal acting in sports). In E. Hahn & H. Rieder (Hrsg.), *Sensumotorisches Lernen und Sportspielforschung* (Sensori-motor learning and research in sports games; pp. 148-166). Köln: bps.

Oldridge, N.B., Donner, A.P., Buck, C.W., Jones, N.L., Andrew, G.M., Parker, J.O., Cunningham, D.A., Kavanagh, T., Rechnitzer, P.A., & Sutton, J.R. (1983). Predictors of dropouts from cardiac exercise rehabilitation: Ontario exercise-heart collaborative study. *American Journal of Cardiology, 51,* 70-74.

Otto, J. (1984). Self-awareness and coping-style: Differential effects of mild physical exercise. In R. Schwarzer (Ed.), *The self in anxiety, stress, and depression* (pp. 297-311). Amsterdam: Elsevier.

Otto, J. (1990). The effects of physical exercise on psychophysiological reactions under stress. *Cognition and Emotion, 4,* 341-357.

Paas, F.G.W.C., & Adam, J.J. (1991). Human information processing during physical exercise. *Ergonomics, 34,* 1385-1397.

Pender, N.J. & Pender, A.R. (1986). Attitudes, subjective norms, and intentions to engage in health behaviors. *Nursing Research, 35* (1), 15-18.

Petruzzello, S.J., Landers, D.M., Hatfield, B.D., Kubitz, K.A., & Salazar, A. (1991). A meta-analysis on the anxiety reducing effects of acute and chronic exercise. *Sport Medicine, 11,* 143-182.

Plante, T.G. & Rodin, J. (1990). Physical fitness and enhanced psychological health. *Current Psychology: Research and reviews, 9,* 3-24.

Poag-DuCharme, K.A. & Brawley, L.R. (1993). Self-efficacy theory: Use in the prediction of exercise behavior in the community setting. *Journal of applied Sport Psychology, 5,* 178-194.

Raglin, J.S. & Morgan, W.B. (1985). Influence of a vigorous exercise on a mood state. *The Behavior Therapist, 8,* 179-183.

Reid, E.L. & Morgan, W.P. (1979). Exercise prescription: A clinical trial. *American Journal of Public Health, 69,* 591-595.

Rejeski, W.J. & Brawley, L.R. (1988). Defining the boundaries of sport psychology. *Sport Psychologist, 3,* 231-242.

Riddle, P.K. (1980). Attitudes, beliefs, behavioral intentions, and behaviors of women and men toward regular jogging. *Research Quarterly for Exercise and Sport, 51* (4), 663-674.

Rieckert, H. (1991). *Leistungsphysiologie* [Performance physiology]. Schorndorf: Hofmann.

Rosenstock, I.M. (1966). Historical origins of the health belief model. *Health Education Monographs, 2,* 328-329.

Rotter, J.B. (1954). *Social learning and clinical psychology.* New York: Prentice Hall.

Sallis, J.F., Haskell, W.L., Fortmann, S.P., Vranizan, K.M., Taylor, C.B. & Solomon, D. S. (1986). Predictors of adoption and maintenance of physical activity in a community sample. *Preventive Medicine, 15,* 331-341.

Sallis, J.F., & Owen, N. (1999). *Physical activity and behavioral medicine.* Thousand Oaks, CA: Sage.

Schwartz, G.E., Davidson, R.J., & Goleman, D.J. (1978). Patterning of cognitive and somatic processes in the self-regulation of anxiety: Effects of Meditation versus exercise. *Psychosomatic Medicine, 40,* 321-328.

Schwarz, L, Biro, G., & Kindermann, W. (1989). Beta-Endorphin, Kortisol und Katecholamine während erschöpfender Ausdauerbelastung [Beta-endorphin, cortisol and catecholamines during exhausting endurance load]. In D. Bönig, Braukmann, K. M., Busse, M.W., Maasen, N., & Schmitt, W. (Eds.), *Sport: Rettung oder Risiko für die Gesundheit?* [Sports: Rescue or risk for health?] (pp. 273-277). Kˆln.

Schwenkmezger, P. (1985). Welche Bedeutung kommt dem Ausdauertraining in der Depressionstherapie zu? [Which meaning has an endurance-training in depression-therapy?] *Sportwissenschaft [Sportscience], 15,* 117-135.

Sime, W.E. (1978). Acute relief on emotional stress. *In Proceedings of the American Association for the Advancement of Tension Control,* Louisville, Kentucky.

Sinyor, D., Golden, M. Steinert, Y., & Seraganian, P. (1986). Experimental manipulation of aerobic fitness and the response to psychosocial stress: heart rate and self-report measures. *Psychosomatic Medicine 48* (5), 324-337.

Sonstroem, R.J. (1974). Attitude testing examining certain psychological correlates of physical activity. *Research Quarterly, 45* (2), 93-103.

Sonstroem, R.J. (1976). The validity of self-perceptions regarding physical and athletic ability. *Medicine and Science in Sports, 8* (2), 126-132.

Sonstroem, R.J. (1988). Psychological models. In R.K. Dishman (Ed.), *Exercise adherence: Its impact on public health* (pp. 125-153). Champaign, IL: Human Kinetics.

Sonstroem, R.J. & Morgan, W.P. (1989). Exercise and self-esteem: rationale and model. *Medicine and Science in Sports and Exercise, 21,* 329-337.

Sonstroem, R.J. & Kampper, K.P. (1980). Prediction of athletic participation in middle school males. *Research Quarterly for Exercise and Sport, 51* (4), 685-694.

Steptoe, A. (1994). Aerobic exercise, stress and health. In J.R. Nitsch & R. Seiler (Hrsg.), *Bewegung und Sport—Psychologische Grundlagen und Wirkungen. [Movement and Sport—Psychological Foundations and Effects.] Band/Volume 4. Gesundheitssport—Bewegungstherapie [Health Sport—Movement Therapy].* Proceedings of the VIII European Congress of Sport Psychology 1991 in Köln. Academia: Sankt Augustin.

Steptoe, A. & Cox, S. (1988). Acute effects of aerobic exercise on mood. *Health Psychology, 7,* 329-340.

Steptoe, A., Moses, J., Edwards, S., & Mathews, A. (1993). Exercise and responsivity to mental stress: discrepancies between the subjective and physiological effects of aerobic training. *International Journal of Sport Psychology, 24,* 110-129.

Stevenson, J.S. & Topp, R. (1990). Effects of moderate and low intensity long term exercise by older adults. *Research in Nursing and Health, 13,* 209-218.

Suls, J. & Fletcher, B. (1985). The relative efficacy of avoidant and nonavoidant coping strategies: A meta-analysis. *Health Psychology, 4,* 249-288.

Thayer, R.E. (1987). Energy, tiredness, and tension effects of a sugar snack versus moderate exercise. *Journal of Personality and Social Psychology, 52,* 119-125.

Tomporowski, P.D. & Ellis, N.R. (1986). Effects of exercise on cognitive processes: A review. *Psychological Bulletin, 99,* 338-346.

Wallston, K.A., Wallston, B.S., & DeVellis, R. (Eds.). (1978). Development of the multidimensional health locus of control scales (MHLC). *Health Education Monographs, 6* (2), 160-170.

Weinberg, R.S. & Gould, D. (Eds.). (1995). *Foundations of sport and exercise psychology.* Champaign, IL: Human Kinetics.

Section VII
Educational Programs and Ethical Issues in Applied Sport and Exercise Psychology

Introduction

In this final section of the book, the authors address both educational programs for sport and exercise psychology, and basic reflections on the application of sport and exercise psychology. Both issues demand perspective and input both from an international and intercultural point of view.

In the first chapter, Dorothee Alfermann and Ronnie Lidor focus on two educational programs for sport psychologists and mental coaches. The first one, the "European Masters Degree in Exercise and Sport Psychology," is realized in Europe and organized by a cooperation of some European universities. The second program, the "Denis Glencross International Course in Exercise and Sport Psychology," is organized and offered by the International Society of Sport Psychology (ISSP) and realized every four years in conjunction with the World Congress of ISSP. The program is composed of selected research and applied topics which are taught by international sport psychology experts.

The next three chapters of this section provide reports on programs and experiences from three different regions in the world: Gloria Solomon distinguishes between the two major routes of training, the sport science versus the psychology orientation, and then focuses on continuing education in applied sport psychology in the United States. Daniel Smith and Si Gangyan summarize the programs offered in different parts of Asia. Dietmar Samulski and Benno Becker summarize the various endeavors to establish sport and exercise psychology in South America.

In the final chapter of the section and closing chapter of the book, Richard Gordin and Gloria Balague address ethical aspects in applied sport psychology. They outline "The Ethical Principles of Psychologists and Code of Conduct" by the American Psychological Association (APA, 1992) and discuss how it fits to the work of sport psychologists. The fundamental mission of the contribution is that each colleague who is practicing as a sport and exercise psychologist should be prompted to assess his or her own ethics and values.

The contributions to this final section are especially intended to initiate further discussions on ethical standards (see also the position stand of the ISSP on ethical standards) and endeavors to differentiate educational programs, training programs, and clinics in sport and exercise psychology for psycholgists, sport and exercise psychologists, mental coaches, and sport scientists and to disseminate educational programs for sport and exercise psychologists from all over the world designed to follow standards and criteria accepted and agreed upon by our international scientific community. For this community, the ISSP is the umbrella organization.

Courtesy of Eyewire

7.1

Educational Programs for Sport Psychologists—An International Perspective

DOROTHEE ALFERMANN AND RONNIE LIDOR

Introduction

During the second half of the 20th century and the beginning of the 21st century, sport psychology established itself as one of the most prominent sport sciences, from both research and applied perspectives (Gill, 1997; Lidor, Morris, Bardaxoglou, & Becker, 2001; Salmela, 1981). In the third edition of *The World Sport Psychology SourceBook*, Lidor et al. (2001) made three observations with respect to the status of sport psychology at the beginning of the new millennium:

(1) There has been a dramatic increase in the number of sport psychologists around the globe during the last three decades of the 20th century. For example, the number of sport psychologists obtained from the international reports included in the third edition of the *SourceBook* (see Table 3, p. 10) is more than double the number of sport psychologists presented

in the second edition (Salmela, 1992). This trend can be seen not only in countries with large populations, such as the United States of America, Germany, and India, but also in "small" countries, such as Belgium, Denmark, and Finland.

(2) Academic programs in sport psychology exist in 44 out of the 48 (91.6%) countries that submitted a report to the *SourceBook* (Lidor et al., 2001; Table 2, p. 9). In these countries students can study sport psychology either at the undergraduate level, at the graduate level, or both.

(3) Few countries around the globe have a formal certification process. Only 12 of the 48 countries (25%) that submitted a report to the *SourceBook* (Lidor et al., 2001) have some kind of certification process (see Table 2, p. 9). In some countries the psychology departments require that the certification process be under their

academic responsibility. In others, the human movement science departments are the ones that provide the certification process.

Although undergraduate and graduate academic programs in sport and exercise psychology are available in many countries around the globe, in many other countries, particularly in Africa and Asia, students are not able to obtain a degree in this area or in related areas such as motor development, motor learning, and motor control (Lidor et al., 2001). In addition, in many countries coaches and practitioners who work with children, youth, and adults in individual and team sports do not have any opportunity to study the relevant communication and psychological skills that could be effectively used during their practical work. From another perspective, the sport psychology programs—either at the academic level or the applied level—that do exist in many countries differ in their educational guidelines and professional requirements (Lidor et al., 2001; Morris, Alfermann, Lintunen, & Hall, 2003). As Morris et al. (2003) noted: "[I]t is acknowledged that sport and exercise psychology [are] emerging in ways that are influenced by the culture and traditions of each country and region around the world" (p. 140). This diversity results in preparation and training programs for sport psychologists whose objectives, themes, and evaluation procedures vary from country to country and from continent to continent.

In this respect, students who are not able to study sport psychology in academic and professional institutes in their own countries, or students who would like to increase their theoretical and practical knowledge by participating in international clinics, seminars, and symposia, should be provided with the relevant assistance by international and worldwide educational bodies and scientific organizations. Most of these organizations have strong foundations that can assist young scholars who have the goal of becoming exercise and sport psychology professionals. Continental and international academic and educational networks already exist, such as those within the European Union and within international scientific organizations such as the International Society of Sport Psychology (ISSP), and can serve as the appropriate academic framework for disseminating sport psychology knowledge.

It is not an easy task to establish internationally oriented academic and professional sport psychology programs, or other programs in other scientific domains, for students who come from varied cultures and backgrounds. A variety of obstacles, among them economical, political, ethical, and logistical may stand in the way of establishing such an international scientific program. Thus, only active and well-established international bodies and organizations have the required capabilities and potential to take the initiative to develop such programs. It is our contention that due to the fact that many countries have not yet established undergraduate and graduate programs in exercise and sport psychology, efforts should be made by international bodies such as the European Union and ISSP to disseminate theoretical and practical knowledge to young scholars from these regions.

The purpose of this chapter is to present two international academic programs in exercise and sport psychology that were offered during the last decade of the 20th century to undergraduate and graduate students from all over the globe. These programs were established for students who had no programs in sport psychology in their native countries. The programs are also offered to students who studied sport psychology in academic or applied programs in their countries, but would like to enrich their theoretical and applied knowledge in exercise and sport psychology by participating in short-term overseas academic programs.

The first program, "European Master's Degree in Exercise and Sport Psychology," is the only international sport psychology program that provides a master's degree for students in this field. The program is a result of a combined effort made by several countries in Europe. The second program, "The Denis Glencross International Course in Exercise and Sport Psychology," is offered every four years in conjunction with the World Congress of ISSP. This program is composed of selected research and applied topics, which are taught by international sport psychology experts from all over the world who are invited by the hosting organizing and scientific committees of the ISSP World Congresses. The Denis Glencrose Course is offered for both undergraduate and graduate students as well as for coaches, physical educators, and sport administrators.

European Masters Degree in Exercise and Sport Psychology

Based on efforts within the European Union to help its member countries guarantee equal opportunity in education and to have comparable educational degrees, some European universities have joined in a program called "European Masters Degree in Exercise and Sport Psychology" (Van den Auweele, 2003). This one-year program is offered by universities from northern, southern, and western Europe who cooperate within academic and professional networks. The aim of this program is to develop in-depth understanding of exercise and sport and related skills and to create a common language among European sport scientists and psychologists in the areas of health, sport performance, youth sports, and new research methodology. Due to the different standards of the academic sport psychology programs among the European countries, this program is a unique opportunity to share the expertise and knowledge of established sport and exercise psychology departments with those individuals and departments that would like to improve their expertise, and to bring together students from a variety of European universities. As such it is a truly international endeavour.

Students who apply for the European master's degree in exercise and sport psychology must have a degree (preferably bachelor's) in sport sciences, physical education, or psychology, and have sufficient knowledge of English. The structure of the program contains four modules:

(1) a distance-learning module where students

(a) are asked to read selected theoretical and applied material, such as selected chapters from Singer, Hausenblas, and Janell's (2001) comprehensive handbook on research in sport psychology, and

(b) are required to take exams on the selected topics;

(2) a module of academic classes;

(3) a module of an intensive course;

(4) a thesis.

The program includes one semester of course work at the home university of the participating students and one semester of selected courses at one of the network universities (i.e., module 2), as well as a two-week intensive course where lecturers of the network universities teach the students (i.e., module 3). All lectures are given in English. The course is not only an intensive learning experience in exercise and sport psychology, but in cultural diversity as well, although confined to one continent. Students who have fulfilled all requirements are awarded a degree from their home university.

Whereas the program described above leads to a university master's degree in exercise and sport psychology, and is established and officially accredited by university committees, somewhat less extensive programs exist in some European countries that are developed and accredited by the various national sport science or psychology organizations, and may lead to the title of a registered sport psychologist (Biddle, Bull, & Seheult, 1992). These programs are offered to individuals who have a master's degree in sport science or psychology. They contain several modules that are taught in intensive courses, mainly during weekends, and qualify the participants for working with athletes and/or with patients in clinical rehabilitation. These courses are usually organized by national scientific organizations, and their objective is to qualify sport scientists or clinical and educational psychologists for counseling in applied exercise or sport psychology.

The Denis Glencross International Course in Exercise and Sport Psychology

The ISSP is the only international organization devoted to promoting research and development in the discipline of sport psychology throughout the world (Lidor et al., 2001). The Society exists to (a) encourage and promote the study of human behavior of individuals and groups associated with sport, exercise, and physical activity; (b) facilitate the sharing of information worldwide among its members through a newsletter, meetings, and a quadrennial congress; and (c) improve the quality of research and counseling practices in sport psychology. In its effort to fulfill these objectives, the Society is active in (a) promoting a medium for the exchange of ideas from individuals and groups representing different countries, and (b) taking the initiative in launching scientific programs and activities in every region of the world.

The principal activity of ISSP is the organization of the World Congress of Sport Psychology every four years. The truly international flavor of the ISSP is illustrated by the diverse locations of its past World Congresses, places such as Rome, Italy (1965); Ottawa, Canada (1981); Singapore (1989); and Skiathos, Greece (2001). The Congress provides an excellent opportunity for researchers and practitioners from all over the globe to interact with each other and to gain knowledge of recent scientific findings and applied intervention techniques in exercise and sport psychology.

One of the initiatives of the ISSP was to establish the Dennis Glencross International Course in Exercise and Sport Psychology in 1997. Prior to the 1997 (Wingate Institute, Israel) and 2001 (Skiathos, Greece) World Congresses, the host scientific committees were asked to organize a student workshop named in memory of Denis Glencross, the former president of ISSP, for whom student development was a priority. Denis Glencross died in 1994 at the age of 55 and is remembered as the father of sport psychology in Australia. Beyond his extensive research on various topics such as human skill and performance, alcohol and driving performance, keyboard skills training and retraining, and motor programming theory development, Glencross was active in formalizing the field of sport psychology in Australia and overseas (ISSP Newsletter, 1994).

The Denis Glencross Course is conducted two days prior to the beginning of the World Congress, and is made up of undergraduate- and graduate-levels classes, which are offered to students from all over the world who have basic knowledge in sport psychology (e.g., undergraduate studies in exercise and sport psychology). The course is composed of two days of lectures and workshops given by sport psychology experts from different countries and continents.

The academic program of the 1st Denis Glencross International Course, which was organized prior to the 1997 World Congress in Israel, included the following themes:

(1) Sport psychology as an academic and applied field: Development and current challenges;

(2) Anxiety: Diagnosis, functional, meaning, and control;

(3) Personality and sport;

(4) Motivational issues in sport and exercise;

(5) The motivational significance of goal perspectives in recreational and elite athletes;

(6) Learning motor skills;

(7) Developmental of expertise;

(8) Methodological challenges in sport psychology research;

(9) Exercise and health: Psychological aspects;

(10) Antecedents of anxiety in sport;

(11) Stress management techniques in competitive sport;

(12) Competitive sport and counseling;

(13) Applied mental skills.

The academic program of the 2nd Denis Glencross International Course, which was organized prior to 2001 World Congress in Greece, was composed of the following themes:

(1) How to implement findings from cognitive sport psychology into practice;

(2) Coaches' leadership behaviors;

(3) Coach-athlete relationship in the sport training process;

(4) Pre-performance routines in sport: Developmental, educational, and psychological considerations;

(5) Exercise activity across the life span;

(6) Motivation: Links between perfectionism and achievements goals;

(7) Understanding and enhancing motivation in sport and exercise;

(8) The concept and application of emotion modulation;

(9) Interventions for coping with stress in elite sport;

(10) Methods of teaching performance enhancement skills;

(11) Overview of self-concept research;

(12) Mentally preparing Olympic athletes;

(13) Goal setting principles for coaches, athletes, and sport psychologists: Nuts and bolts;

(14) Monetary rewards for achievements in sport.

The students who registered for the Denis Glensross Courses were invited to attend the Congress sessions as well. Not only are there substantially reduced fees for the students, but also hosts are encouraged to provide travel and accommodation support for them. The students were provided with written assignments during the Congress and a summary session on the final day of the Congress. A diploma was issued to the students who completed the course requirements. The course was considered as a 1-credit class accredited by the local universities of the hosting countries.

At the end of each course, the students were asked to complete an evaluation form. The main objective of the evaluation procedure was to examine the contribution of the course and its selected themes to the professional development of the students, from both theoretical and practical perspectives. In addition, the students were asked to outline some topics in exercise and sport psychology they thought should be included in future programs. For example, the students who participated in the 1st Denis Glencross Course requested that more applied sessions be included in the program. They wanted to see how applied sport psychologists, who have

worked for many years with elite athletes in individual and team sports, used their psychological skills with their athletes. They asked for actual demonstration of the interventions, techniques, and strategies that they read about in the literature. In addition, they thought it would benefit them as beginners in the field if they could experience these techniques in a practical training session led by an experienced applied sport psychologist. As a result of the evaluative process, the organizers of the 2nd Denis Glencross Course attempted to fulfill the students' requests by including, for example, more "how to" sessions in the program.

The national sport psychology societies in many countries and regions distribute scientific and applied knowledge in exercise and sport psychology to researchers and practitioners around the world (Lidor et al., 2001; Morris et al., 2003). The national societies, in a combined effort with academic institutions such as universities and colleges, attempt to strengthen the cooperation among researchers, counselors, coaches, students, and athletes. Electronic means of communication among members of the sport psychology community exist in most countries. In addition, national and sometimes international conferences on a variety of topics related to exercise and sport psychology are organized in many countries around the world.

Unfortunately, at the beginning of the third millennium there are still many countries around the globe for which these vehicles of scientific communications do not exist on a regular basis. For the students who would like to study and practice sport psychology in organized academic and professional programs, but are not able to do it in their native countries, international education and sport psychology organizations should provide some kind of support. The two academic projects that were described in this chapter have the potential to serve as a long-term academic framework for these students. However, these projects should be supported and promoted by national sport psychology societies, as well as national academic institutions, in countries that do have the ability to offer educational programs in sport psychology to their local students. Within-continent and worldwide scientific cooperation among continental and international bodies and organizations is the key factor in the establishment of international educational programs.

The two existing educational programs—The European Masters Degree in Exercise and Sport Psychology and The Denis Glencross International Course in Exercise and Sport Psychology—should be provided with constant support, both from academic and economical perspectives, and this may enhance the chances of many students around the globe to become acquainted with sport psychology and improve the psychological services they provide to their athletes, students, and hopefully, the sport community at large.

References

Biddle, S. J. H., Bull, S. J., & Seheult, C. L. (1992). Ethical and professional issues in contemporary British sport psychology. *The Sport Psychologist, 6,* 66-76.

Gill, D. (1997). Sport and exercise psychology. In J. D. Massengale & R. A. Swanson (Eds.), *The history of exercise and sport science* (pp. 293-320). Champaign, IL: Human Kinetics.

ISSP Newsletter (1994). Denis Glencross: In memoriam. October, 1-2.

Lidor, R., Morris, T., Bardaxoglou, N., & Becker, B. (2001). *The world sport psychology sourcebook* (3rd ed.). Morgantown, WV: Fitness Information Technology.

Morris, T., Alfermann, D., Lintunen, T., & Hall, H. (2003). Training and selection of sport psychologists: An international review. *International Journal of Sport and Exercise Psychology, 2,* 139-154.

Salmela, J. H. (1981). *The world sport psychology sourcebook.* New York: Mouvement.

Salmela, J. H. (1992). *The world sport psychology sourcebook* (2nd ed.). Champaign, IL: Human Kinetics.

Singer, R. N., Hausenblas, H. A., & Janelle, C. M. (Eds.). (2001). *Handbook of sport psychology* (2nd ed.). New York: Wiley.

Van den Auweele, Y. (2003). Sport psychology and education: The European masters in exercise and sport psychology. In E. Apitzsch & G. Schilling (Eds.), *Sport psychology in Europe: FEPSAC - An organizational platform and a scientific meeting point* (pp. 38-48). Biel, Switzerland: FEPSAC.

Courtesy of U.S. Army

7.2

Continuing Education in Applied Sport Psychology in the United States

GLORIA B. SOLOMON

Introduction

The field of sport psychology has a unique world-wide heritage. From ruminations that early forms of athletic competition, such as the ancient Olympics, included an awareness of mental dynamics to current ideas of the significance of mental training, sport psychology themes appear universal (Mahoney, 1989; Wann, 1997). While the awareness of mental components of physical activity is timeless, sport psychology began to emerge as a scientific discipline in the late 19th century. Further, while inquiry concerning sport psychology is over 100 years old, there are facets of this discipline that are still in an embryonic stage. One underdeveloped aspect relates to training and continuing education for professionals in sport psychology. The purpose of this chapter is to explore the current status of continuing education opportunities in applied sport psychology. First, I provide a brief historical overview. Second, I distinguish between the two major routes of training,

the sport science versus the psychology orientation. Third, I delineate continuing education opportunities available in the United States. Finally, I offer a forecast of the future of continuing education in applied sport psychology.

Historical Overview of Applied Sport Psychology

The evolution of the field of sport psychology would not be complete without acknowledging the influence of the mother discipline of psychology and the sister discipline of motor learning. In order to truly understand the progression of this field, one must contextualize it within the framework of concurrent developments in psychology and motor learning.

The Contributions from Psychology

While many early thinkers such as Plato and Socrates pondered psychological concepts, it was not until the late 19th century that psychology became identified as a scientific discipline. Credit for this formalization is extended to German philosopher and psychologist Wilhelm Wundt. Trained as a medical doctor at the University of Heidelberg in the mid 19th century, Wundt became a professor of "inductive philosophy" at Leipzig University where he stayed until his retirement in 1917. During his tenure at Leipzig, Wundt established the first research laboratory for the study of psychology in 1879 (Biographical Dictionary of North American and European Educationists, 1997). His contributions earned him the distinct title of "Founder of Modern Psychology." While Wundt did not perform physical activity research, his contemporaries in the United States began this quest shortly after the creation of Wundt's lab.

The psychologist identified as performing the first activity related research is Norman Triplett. A professor at Kansas State Normal University at the turn of the 20th century, Triplett is credited with conducting the first social psychology experiment (Davis, Huss, & Becker, 1995). His classic cycling and reeling studies contributed to a unique understanding of social influences in physical performance tasks and later led to the creation of social facilitation theory (Zajonc, 1965). The import of his pioneering work (Triplett, 1898) is unanimously acknowledged (Davis et al., 1995).

Another major contributor to the early machinations of sport psychology is Coleman Griffith. After earning his degrees from the University of Illinois, Griffith was hired and stayed there until his retirement. Griffith is a man of many "firsts." He created the *first* laboratory devoted to sport psychology research, taught the *first* sport psychology course, was the *first* person to be hired as an athletic team consultant, and wrote the *first* sport psychology books. His impact on the field is unquestionable. While the results of his prodigious research efforts have minimal relevance today, the serious approach he brought to the scientific study of sport is immortalized in the field (Gould & Pick, 1995).

Attention on elements of applied sport psychology emerged in the 1960s (Silva, 2002; Williams & Straub, 2001). Two psychologists from San Jose State University, Bruce Ogilvie and Thomas Tutko, awakened athletic coaches and scholars with their classic book, "Problem Athletes and How to Handle Them," published in 1966. While both controversial and in-

triguing, this book brought sport psychology to the attention of scientists and the lay public. Ogilvie and Tutko continued to impact the field by doing applied work with many athletic teams.

While there are no female contemporaries of Triplett and Griffith who conducted research in physical activity, women research psychologists existed around the turn of the century. Women such as Mary Calkins, Margaret Washburn, and Leta Hollingworth were actively researching, publishing, and participating in psychology organizations (Furumoto & Scarborough, 1985). However, it would be several years before women were having a direct impact on the evolution of applied sport psychology.

The Contributions from Motor Learning

Interest in learning about movement also has a long history. In fact, motor learning inquiry has its origins in the field of psychology (Schmidt & Lee, 1999). The learning of skilled behaviors stimulates questions that intertwine with psychological factors. Specifically, motor learning connects with the sub-disciplines of cognitive psychology and the psychology of sensation and perception. A noted motor learning expert and sport psychology professional, Dr. Linda Bunker states, "I generally describe the relationship [between motor learning and sport psychology] ... in terms of both evolving from the original sub-discipline in physical education called the Psychology of Motor Learning" (Personal communication, November 28, 2001). We will now examine the contributions of motor learning experts to the development of sport psychology.

During the 20th century, motor learning and sport psychology were closely related fields. From the 1920s into the 1970s much of the research "related to the psychology of motor learning" (Silva, 2002, p. 15). John Lawther conducted valuable research at the Motor Learning Lab at Pennsylvania State University in the 1930s where he studied various sport psychology principles such as motivation, personality, and emotions. In the Midwest, Clarence Ragsdale established the Motor Learning Lab at the University of Wisconsin, Madison, where he was also involved in studying various psychological components of motor skill development.

Later, beginning in the 1950s, Franklin Henry conducted research in motor learning and also created the first psychology of physical activity course and graduate emphasis in the psychology of movement at the University of California, Berkeley (Silva, 2002). During the middle part of the 1960s, sport psychology began to establish a unique identity. Landers (1995) labels this time of transition the "formative years" of sport psychology. By the 1960s the field of sport psychology was becoming autonomous. This is evidenced by the development of distinct sport psychology organizations such as the International Society of Sport Psychology in 1965 and the North American Society for the Psychology of Sport and Physical Activity in 1967 which served to publicly articulate a further division between sport psychology and motor learning.

North American Sport Psychology

There is general agreement that the seeds of sport psychology were laid by early psychologists and motor learning experts. Although the "formative years" lasted until the 1960s, early evidence of what we still define today as sport psychology research exists in the work of Coleman Griffith. For example, in his lab at the University of Illinois, he studied the relationship between personality and performance. Later Professor Henry studied psychological aspects involved with the acquisition of motor and sport skills. In fact, Weinberg and Gould (2003) suggest that "Franklin Henry ... was largely responsible for the field's scientific development" (p. 10).

In the 1960s women began making substantial contributions to the field. Most notably, Dorothy Harris contributed to the field through her research, publishing, and professional activities. Harris is credited with starting the first graduate specialization in sport psychology at Pennsylvania State University (Gill, 1995). Since the 1960s, many women have had an impact on the direction of applied sport psychology.

Future historians will be left to document the growth of sport psychology over the past 30 years. The list of contemporary scholars across at least three generations would include an array of committed professionals who seek to advance applied sport psychology. The backgrounds of those who identify with the field of sport psychology differ. Next, I will distinguish between the types of training currently available in the United States in preparation for a career in sport psychology.

Training for Careers in Applied Sport Psychology

There are two viable academic paths to take when committing to a career in sport psychology. Presently, one can pursue education through programs in psychology or programs in sport science or kinesiology. I will explain each of these two avenues briefly.

Psychology Orientation

Psychology programs have been in existence in North American academic institutions for over 100 years. Currently, many professionals seek to advance their knowledge of sport psychology through the study of psychology. There are undergraduate programs in psychology at virtually every accredited university in the United States. A typical program will require students to take a broad array of psychology courses as part of the major area of study. However, few psychology departments offer courses in sport psychology (McCullagh & Noble, 2002). At the graduate level, students would be expected to focus on a sub-discipline such as cognitive or social psychology. Some graduate programs housed in psychology departments are now offering an emphasis in sport psychology such as programs at the University of Washington and the University of North Texas.

Sport Science Orientation

Those students who choose to study sport psychology through a sport science or kinesiology program will undergo very different experiences from their psychology counterparts. If one is fortunate enough to identify an interest in sport psychology as an undergraduate student, there exists several programs throughout the country. See Table 1 for a sample listing of recognized programs. For most students, the major area of study will likely be a broad combination of courses in the exercise sciences including biomechanics, exercise physiology, sport sociology, and sport psychology.

Similar to the psychology route, the sport science orientation will become more focused at the graduate level. This may include more specialized courses in sport, exercise, and rehabilitation psychology. Fortunately, Sachs and his colleagues (Burke, Sachs, & Smisson, 2004) have kept a current description

Table 1: Undergraduate Programs in Sport Psychology in the United States

School	Name	Type
Empire State College	Sport Psychology	Concentration
Samford University	Sport Psychology	Minor
Texas Christian University	Psychosocial Kinesiology	Major
Towson University	Sport Psychology	Concentration
Truman State University	Psycho-Social Aspects	Concentration
University of Evansville	Sport Psychology	Minor
University of Idaho	Sport Psychology	Concentration/Minor
University of Northern Iowa	Sport Psychology	Major
University of Utah	Sport Psychology	Concentration
Western Washington University	Sport Psychology	Concentration/Minor
West Virginia University	Sport Psychology	Major

of graduate programs in applied sport psychology. In its 7th edition, this handbook describes over 100 institutions, primarily in North America, which offer programs in applied sport psychology.

Students will likely select the psychology or sport science orientation contingent upon several factors. A degree in sport science would be most appropriate if one chooses to provide educational interventions in varied physical activity settings. Those seeking to provide clinical interventions pursue a psychology degree. Refer to Taylor's (1991) detailed comparison and contrast of these two types of graduate programs. To explore the type of training and background of current sport psychology professionals and students, an overview of the member demographics of the largest sport psychology organization in North America was obtained. The most recent membership report published by the Association for the Advancement of Applied Sport Psychology (AAASP) for the year 2003 indicates that of the 1,244 members, 36% report academic training in psychology, 24% report training in kinesiology or sport science, and 26% acknowledge training in both disciplines (AAASP Newsletter, 2003). Regardless of the academic training one pursues, there are choices to be made during and after formal educational preparation. Opportunities for both formal and informal continuing education in applied sport psychology exist nationwide.

Parameters of Continuing Education in the United States

The concept of continuing one's education after various career benchmarks, such as earning an advanced degree, is decades old. The American Association for Adult and Continuing Education (AAACE), founded in 1982, posits in the mission statement that this organization seeks

to provide leadership for the field of adult and continuing education by expanding opportunities for adult growth and development; unifying adult educators; fostering the development and dissemination of theory, research, information, and best practices; promoting identity and standards for the profession; and advocating relevant public policy and social change initiatives. (American Association for Adult and Continuing Education, 2001)

This organization provides continuing education (CE) opportunities through 26 units that represent topics of interest to adult learners. Several of these units encompass continuing education via higher education avenues. There even exists an "International Adult and Continuing Education Hall of Fame." This entity was established in 1995 to honor those who have contributed to adult learning (Oklahoma College of Continuing Education, 2001).

Generally, there are three major types of

continuing education for the adult learner. One may choose to enter a continuing education program, which offers credit towards a degree at a specific academic institution. Such programs are typically targeted toward adults who are employed and wish to return to school to complete undergraduate or graduate degrees. Most of these programs offer courses in the curriculum at alternative times such as evenings and weekends.

Programs also exist which offer continuing education courses for credit but are not related to the culminating experience of earning a degree. These non-degree programs are sought by individuals who have intellectual curiosity in a given subject area but do not seek a terminal degree. Finally, there are programs that are non-credit and non-degree awarding. In the field of applied sport psychology, most individuals seeking further education pursue credit-based courses that are not directed toward completing a degree. An overview of continuing education opportunities available in applied sport psychology follows.

Role of Continuing Education in Sport Psychology Professions

Continuing education serves three primary roles in the varied sport psychology professions. Many psychologists earn advanced degrees and become licensed only to find that they become interested in sport psychology. Post-graduate training opportunities exist through several sources that will be explained shortly. Second, individuals trained in sport psychology may choose to avail themselves of continuing education courses in order to learn about new topics or keep abreast of recent developments in the field. Finally, graduate students training in either psychology or sport science may find that continuing education courses add a unique dimension to their current programming. Any or all of these professionals might find themselves participating in the same continuing education course.

Formal Continuing Education Courses for Credit—Degree

Many types of programs exist whereby one can obtain academic credit toward a degree. There are direct and distance learning approaches which can be pursued contingent on individual needs. These programs with varied missions also vary in quality. The purpose of the next section is to distinguish between these forms of continuing education opportunities.

Institutes and Conferences

Colleges and universities have sponsored institutes or conferences with sport psychology themes for more than 25 years. Currently, several sites host such events. These programs are short in length, typically from one to four days, and are usually attended by those accumulating academic credit. The oldest continuing education conference which offers academic credit is hosted by the University of Virginia. During every June since 1975, an intensive and extensive program is held centering on a relevant topic in applied sport psychology. For example, the most recent conference theme in 2004 was "Motivation in Sport: The Passion Driving Participation Excellence." Experts in sport psychology contribute to the lectures and workshops. By attending this conference, a student can earn three units of academic credit.

Another university sponsored continuing education course is offered annually by the Department of Psychology at the University of Southern Maine. The Sport Psychology Institute is a 3-day summer session with different themes every year. Academic credit is available for any student currently enrolled in an accredited university.

New conferences and institutes are being developed. For instance, the first conference sponsored by the Mendelson Center for Sport, Character & Culture at the University of Notre Dame was held in 2001. This inaugural conference focused on "Promoting Social and Moral Development Through Sport" and featured many noted professionals in sport psychology, sociology, and athletics. These types of programs offer continuing education for academic credit and require participants to attend on-site sessions. For those who cannot be in attendance, other continuing education options exist.

Distance and Online Programs

A recent mode of continuing education is via a distance or online format. One can peruse the Internet and find numerous programs being offered by

Table 2: Sample Distance and Online Continuing Education Courses in Sport Psychology

Sponsor	Course	Length
California State University Long Beach	Character Development in Sport and Physical Activity	N/A
Capella University	Sport Psychology: Performance Enhancement And Leadership Skills	5 weeks
Loyola Marymount University	The Psychology of Sport	self-paced
San Diego University for Integrative Studies	Advanced Sport Psychology Intervention Techniques	semester
University of Texas	Applied Sport Psychology	semester

various types of institutions. Through professional development and independent study formats, individuals can opt to enroll and participate in sport psychology courses. In fact, one can even pursue graduate degrees in sport psychology online. This venue for continuing education courses and degrees is relatively new and will likely undergo substantial growth over the next few years. The difficulty now for consumers is ascertaining the quality of programming. There is no central location whereby students can access information regarding program quality. A glimpse of sample online course offerings is provided in Table 2. A certificate program was recently developed for practicing psychologists, sport educators, and participants to gain competency in sport psychology.

Certificate Program

John F. Kennedy University in Pleasant Hill, California, boasts a unique certificate program. The Continuing Education Certificate in Sport Psychology, initiated in 1996, is targeted toward "counselors, coaches, educators, athletes and others in the physical or mental health fields who want to develop a specialty in the field of sport psychology" (John F. Kennedy University, 2001). The curricula involve five graduate-level courses in sport psychology. Approximately 50 people have acquired a certificate in sport psychology through this venue (T. Johnson, Personal communication, November, 26, 2001). I am not aware of any comparable program in the United States at this time. However, there are other forms of continuing education in applied sport psychology in the United States.

Formal Continuing Education Courses for Credit—Non-Degree

Many people directly and indirectly related to the field of sport psychology are required to enroll in courses and workshops to obtain a required number of continuing education units (CEUs). Athletic trainers, health professionals, psychologists, and certified consultants seek educational workshops, which satisfy prescribed criteria regarding acceptable CEU experiences. Organizations, educational institutions, and private agencies provide continuing education courses for credit. These sessions do not count toward a degree but rather fulfill the requirements mandated by licensure or certification.

Organization-sponsored Courses

Perhaps the most comprehensive systems, which offer formal continuing education for current professionals, are provided through professional organizations. Although the purposes vary, the three programs discussed here provide regular continuing education course offerings for the sport psychology professional. For many years, the American Psychological Association (APA) has been offering continuing education courses for practicing psychologists. Now through the efforts of APA Division 47, Exercise and Sport Psychology, CE courses in sport psychology are held each year prior to the annual conference in August. For example, a course, taught by Dr. Shane Murphy, was titled "Sport Psychology Interventions with Children, Adolescents, and Families" and allowed the participant to earn seven CEUs.

The largest professional sport psychology

Table 3: AAASP Continuing Education Workshops from 2000-2004

Year/Location	Workshops
2000/Nashville	Mental Skills and Drills: An Applied Teaching Experience for Sport Professionals Facilitating Life Skills and Mentoring Youth Through the First Tee Integrated Rehabilitation Model: Combining Sport Psychology And Sports Medicine in Athletic Injury Rehabilitation Effective Team Building Strategies for Sport and Non-sport Organizations Everything You Wanted to Know About Building a Successful Consulting Practice...But Were Afraid to Ask
2001/Orlando	Resonance: A Model for Performance Excellence and Meaningful Living You Make the Call: Case Studies for AAASP Certified Consultants Only Strategies for Gaining Acceptance into the Golf and Tennis Cultures On-site Interventions
2002/Tucson	Sport Psychology in Athletic Training Injury Supervision in Sport Psychology Services and Delivery: A Career-Long Process Safeguarding Young Performers: Raising Awareness and Setting Good Standards Taking it to the Court: A Hands-On Applied Sport Psychology Consulting Experience in Tennis The Climate Counts! Techniques and Strategies for Fostering a Task-Involving Motivational Climate
2003/Philadelphia	Anger Management for Athletes: The Nuts and Bolts The Nine Mental Skills of Successful Athletes: A Practical Holistic Model for Assessing and Teaching Mental Skills to Athletes Mental Skills Training for Enhanced Sport Performance Mind Grind: Inside the Mind fo Endurance Athletes Developing and Implementing a Sports Consulting Marketing Plan
2004/Minneapolis	Athletic Training Outreach Teaching Sport, Health, and Exercise Psychology Bridging the Gap between Coaches and Sport Psychology Caring for the Concussed Athlete

organization in the United States, the Association for the Advancement of Applied Sport Psychology (AAASP), also offers a pre-conference agenda with many CEU workshop choices. Prior to the annual conference held in the fall, the AAASP Continuing Education Committee offers three to six workshops selected via a formal committee review process (Solomon, 2000). While topics vary from year to year, they generally can be cataloged into three themes: performance enhancement strategies, improving teaching skills, and the business of sport psychology (Solomon & Rhea, 2000). A licensed psychologist can earn three to six CEUs depending on the length of the session; an AAASP Certified Consultant can earn CEUs applied toward recertification. The CE workshops offered during the past five years (2000-2004) are documented in Table 3.

The American College of Sports Medicine (ACSM) is an organization that brings together a broad array of sport and health professionals and provides continuing education required of their member base. The sport psychology professional might find suitable CE courses provided by the ACSM on such topics as sports nutrition, exercise adherence, and other health-related issues. One is more likely to find more specialized exercise psychology related courses through ACSM which may be more useful for the practicing professional than the developing student. Along with organization-based CE courses, one can find a unique venue for completing CEUs for licensure and certification through on-site and Web-based University courses.

University-sponsored Courses

Some universities sponsor continuing education courses which are either on-site or Web-based. The longest continuous on-site university conference offering CE credit is housed at Springfield College in Springfield, Massachusetts. The Annual Conference on Counseling Athletes changes themes yearly; the theme for the June 2003 conference was "Sport Transitions and Life Skills." Presenters submit proposals and a panel of professionals is gathered. In March 2005, a joint summit combined the conference on counseling athletes with positive youth development through sport.

A newer venue for university-sponsored CE is through Web-based programs. Two sites were identified which offer formal continuing education units. Both of these academic institutions offered Web-based CEUs. Loyola Marymount University sponsors an "enhancement courses" series for teaching professionals. A sample course in that series is "The Psychology of Sport." A larger program is offered by the United States Sports Academy (USSA). An accredited academic institution created in 1972, the USSA's Department of Continuing Education offers many online courses including Sport Psychology, Sport Coaching Methodology, and Improving Performance Through Psychological Training. A sport psychology professional can earn four CEUs for each course completed via this distance-learning option.

Private Agency-sponsored Courses

There are a significant number of continuing education opportunities afforded through private agencies. The vast majority of these courses are associated with the American Psychological Association (APA) to meet the CE requirements mandated for licensure.

Specifically, APA approves sponsoring agencies to provide CE courses. There are hundreds of courses offered nationwide and year round but only a few relate to sport psychology. A sampling of sessions presented by these approved agencies included "Masterful Coaching" sponsored by the New England Educational Institute, "Coaching Skills and Practice Development" and "Peak Performance and Coaching" both sponsored by the College of Executive Coaching, and "Developing Your Sport Psychology Practice" sponsored by the Ohio Center for Sport Psychology.

While there are still only limited offerings in applied sport psychology, approval is pending for a series of independent study CE courses offered via sport psychology videotapes and books (J. Van Raalte, personal communication, September 4, 2001). There are four professionally produced videotapes available through Virtual Brands and one can earn credits by reading and testing on the edited

Table 4: Sampling of Web Sites Containing Continuing Education Course Information

Organization	Web Site
American Alliance for Health, Physical Education, Recreation, And Dance	www.aahperd.org
American Association for Adult and Continuing Education	www.aaace.org
American College of Sports Medicine	www.acsm.org
American Psychological Association	www.apa.org
Association for the Advancement of Applied Sport Psychology	www.aaasponline.org
Capella University	www.capellauniversity.edu
John F. Kennedy University	www.jfku.edu
Learning Resource Network	www.seminarfinder.com
North American Society for the Psychology of Sport and Physical Activity	www.naspspa.org
Ohio Center for Sport Psychology	www.sportpsych.org
Online Sports and Recreation Courses	www.worldwidelearn.com
Performance Media	www.performance-media.com
Springfield College	www.springfieldcollege.edu
United States Sports Academy	www.ussa.edu
University of Southern Maine	www.usm.maine.edu
University of Virginia	www.virginia.edu
Virtual Brands – Sport Psychology videotapes	www.vbvideo.com

Table 5: Sampling of Annual Professional Conferences with Continuing Education Courses

Conference	Dates
American Alliance for Health, Physical Education, Recreation, And Dance	March-April
American College of Sports Medicine	May-June
American Psychological Association	August
Association for the Advancement of Applied Sport Psychology	September-October
North American Society for the Psychology of Sport and Physical Activity	June
Springfield College Conference on Counseling Athletes	June
University of Southern Maine Sport Psychology Institute	June
University of Virginia Sport Psychology Conference	June

book *Exploring Sport and Exercise Psychology* (Van Raalte & Brewer, 2002). To keep abreast of the status of APA approved CE courses individuals can refer to the APA Web site (See Table 4). While some professionals are motivated to seek CE experiences for licensure and certification, others might pursue CE courses solely for the knowledge expected to be gained from such an experience.

Informal Continuing Education— No Credit, Non-Degree

As professionals in any discipline, we continually search for new ideas and information. Such is the purpose of informal continuing education courses. These sessions offer no CE credit and are not targeted toward completion of an academic degree. Rather the purpose is simply to glean knowledge from experts representing the field of applied sport psychology. There are two major categories, which reflect these types of experiences: organized conferences and private sessions.

There are numerous conferences held annually that offer an informal venue for continuing one's education in applied sport psychology. One can attend hundreds of educational sessions at these conferences, which range from large-scale proceedings hosting thousands of participants, such as AAHPERD and ACSM, to smaller intensive events, such as those hosted by the University of Virginia and Springfield College. A sample listing of these annual professional conferences is posted in Table 5.

Current professionals in the field of applied sport psychology offer another avenue for those seeking to increase their knowledge base. For example, Dr.

Jim Taylor created the Teacher Apprentice Program (TAP) for young professionals and students who wish to witness live sport psychology sessions (Personal communication, September 12, 2001). Those offering sessions are encouraged to alert the sport psychology community by posting the relevant information via a public venue such as the Sportpsy Listserv. Interested individuals may contact the presenter and request admission. This informal program is free and open to those interested in continuing their training in sport psychology. Many types of informal continuing education sources exist; one must only search the available resources to find opportunities that fulfill individual needs. For instance, a posting to the Sport Psychology List sought psychologists, psychiatrists, and graduate students to work with runners preparing for the New York City Marathon (Hays, 2001). We are in a period of expanding growth and versatility relative to continuing education courses; considerable challenges and opportunities await the field of sport psychology and will likely influence the future of continuing education.

The Future of Continuing Education in Applied Sport Psychology

Many professionals in sport psychology anticipate major changes occurring in the field. Some of the central issues surrounding these changes involve pivotal programmatic and training issues, which have been discussed over the past several years (e.g., McGowan, 1996; Murphy, 1996; Silva, 1997, Silva Conroy, & Zizzi, 1999; Zizzi, Zaichkowsky & Perna, 2002). Most recently, rigorous discussion and debate has ensued regarding the accreditation of sport psychology programs and the certification of sport psychology consultants. The direction that these debates and subsequent actions take will have a direct impact on the evolution of continuing education in applied sport psychology.

Accreditation and Continuing Education

Silva (1997) and colleagues (Silva, et al., 1999) have led the call for accrediting individual programs in sport psychology. In brief, the rationale proffered suggests that at the present time programs in applied sport psychology are underdeveloped. It is argued that program accreditation will make the field of sport psychology more visible and credible. Specifically, the benefits of program accreditation include clarified program missions, improved integration of research and practice, and enhanced prestige and status (Silva, et al., 1999). Others contend that program accreditation is not the solution to perceived deficits in the training and employment issues facing applied sport psychology. In a reply to Silva and his colleagues, Hale and Danish (1999) suggested that a demand for sport psychology professionals should first be established before expecting that the financial requirements of accreditation will be seriously considered by institutions. Clearly the debate is alive and the direction that training takes will influence the quality and quantity of continuing education experiences. While the impact of accreditation on CE is a training issue, another major theme that will influence CE in the future is the certification of sport psychology professionals.

Certification and Continuing Education

As the field of sport psychology was establishing its identity, the issue of "what makes one a sport psychology consultant?" arose. After several years of lively discussion, the designation of AAASP Certified Consultant was established. AAASP approved a certification program in 1989 and identified specific criteria to be met for certification status. The criteria include completion of a doctorate degree, specified coursework and supervised practicum experiences. In order to maintain certified status, one must undergo recertification every five years. One aspect of the recertification process is completing continuing education courses or comparable experi-

ences (Solomon, 2000; Zizzi, Zaichkowsky & Perna, 2002). AAASP certification has been both praised and criticized, and the debate on certification continues. Recently, the Certification Committee has discussed adapting the certification criteria by creating a master's level certification process (Burton, 2000). The Fellows of AAASP approved master's level certification in 2002. The criteria for master's level certification is identical to those standards originally set for doctoral level applicants, with one exception. Those with terminal master's degrees must complete 700 supervised internship hours, while those applying for certification with a doctorate degree must complete 400 supervised hours. While AAASP certification undergoes revamping, the relationship between certification and continuing education remains strong. Like any professional, sport psychology professionals must keep updated on new developments. Whether CE requirements for certification and recertification become more or less stringent will be determined by the direction that emerges from the current discussions. While that chapter is yet to be written, I prophesize that formal continuing education will be a more significant feature of the certification process based on my experience as AAASP Continuing Education Chair from 1997-2000.

Needs Assessment Recommendation

As the new millennium gets underway, with the future of sport psychology being prominently debated, it is a good time to determine the needs of current and future sport psychology professionals. Due to the lack of centralization in accessing continuing education courses, it can be difficult to determine the quality and quantity of available continuing education experiences. The purpose of this chapter is to provide a context for the current status of continuing education in the field of applied sport psychology. A next logical step might be to conduct a formal needs assessment. Querying sport psychology students and professionals regarding the content and structure of CE courses might offer new insight into the possibilities that could lend direction and vision to CE participants and providers.

Conclusion

Almost every professional, from the electrician to the physician, is responsible for first obtaining the necessary knowledge and skills to practice the profession and second for remaining up-to-date on new principles and techniques. Due to the unique progression of applied sport psychology, some of its growing pains are still evident. New developments in the field and training and programmatic issues will directly influence the demand for continuing education. I predict that the need for continuing education experiences will likely swell due to the increase in number of professionals and the projected boost in service demands. As the field continues to grow, so will the need for high quality, easily accessible continuing education experiences in applied sport psychology.

References

American Association for Adult and Continuing Education. (2001). Mission statement. Retrieved November 16, 2001, from http://www.aaace.org/general.html

Association for the Advancement of Applied Sport Psychology. (2003). 2003 membership report. *AAASP Newsletter, 18*(3), 23.

Biographical Dictionary of North American and European Educationists. (1997). London: Woburn Press.

Burke, K. L., Sachs, M. L., & Smisson, C. P. (2004). *Directory of graduate programs in applied sport psychology*, 7th Ed. Morgantown, WV: Fitness Information Technology.

Burton, D. (Fall, 2000). Fellows agree: Time is right to explore major certification changes. *AAASP Newsletter, 15*(3), 11-12.

Davis, S. F., Huss, M. T., & Becker, A. H. (1995). Norman Triplett and the dawning of sport psychology. *The Sport Psychologist, 9*, 366-375.

Furumoto, L., & Scarborough, E. (1985). Placing women in the history of psychology: The first women psychologists. *American Psychologist, 41*, 35-42.

Gill, D. L. (1995). Women's place in the history of sport psychology. *The Sport Psychologist, 5*, 418-433.

Gould, D., & Pick, S. (1995). Sport psychology: The Griffith Era, 1920-1940. *The Sport Psychologist, 5*, 391-405.

Hale, B. D., & Danish, S. J. (1999). Putting the accreditation cart before the AAASP horse: A reply to Silva, Conroy, and Zizzi. *Journal of Applied Sport Psychology, 11*, 321-328.

Hays, K. (2001, September). Psyching team opportunities. Message posted to Sportpsy electronic mailing list, archived at http://listserve.listserv.edu/log0109A.

John F. Kennedy University. (2001). Graduate school of professional psychology. Retrieved November 16, 2001 from http://www.jfku.edu/psych/masp-overview.html

Landers, D. M. (1995). Sport psychology: The formative years, 1950-1980. *The Sport Psychologist, 5*, 406-417.

Mahoney, M. J. (1989). Psychological predictors of elite and non-elite performance in Olympic weightlifting. *International Journal of Sport Psychology, 20*, 1-12.

McCullagh, P., & Noble, J. M. (2002). Education and training in sport and exercise psychology. In J. L. Van Raalte & B. W. Brewer (Eds.), *Exploring sport and exercise psychology*, 2nd Ed. (pp. 439-457). Washington, DC: American Psychological Association.

McGowan, R. W. (1996). Eclecticism: An anti-egocentric model of performance. *Journal of Applied Sport Psychology, 8*, S50.

Murphy, S. (1996). Wither certification? *Journal of Applied Sport Psychology, 8*, S52.

Oklahoma College of Continuing Education, University of Oklahoma. (2001). International adult and continuing education hall of fame. Retrieved November 16, 2001, from http://www.occe.ou.edu/halloffame/hallhist.html

Schmidt, R. A., & Lee, T. D. (1999). *Motor control and learning: A behavioral emphasis.* Champaign, IL: Human Kinetics.

Silva, J. M. (2002). The evolution of sport psychology. In J. M. Silva & D. E. Stevens (Eds.), *Psychological foundations of sport* (pp. 1-26). Boston: Allyn and Bacon.

Silva, J. M. (1997). Initiation program accreditation in sport psychology. *Journal of Applied Sport Psychology, 9*, S47-S49.

Silva, J. M., Conroy, D. E., & Zizzi, S. J. (1999). Critical issues confronting the advancement of applied sport psychology. *Journal of Applied Sport Psychology, 11*, 298-320.

Solomon, G. B. (2000). *Association for the Advancement of Applied Sport Psychology Continuing Education Policy Manual.* Unpublished manual.

Solomon, G. B., & Rhea, D. J. (Fall, 2000). Continuing education. *AAASP Newsletter, 15*(3), 26-28.

Taylor, J. (1991). Career direction, development, and opportunities in applied sport psychology. *The Sport Psychologist, 5*, 266-280.

Triplett, N. L. (1898). Dynamogenic factors in pacemaking and competition. *The American Journal of Psychology, 9*, 507-533.

Van Raalte, J. L., & Brewer, B. W. (1996). *Exploring sport and exercise psychology.* Washington, DC: American Psychological Association.

Wann, D. L. (1997). *Sport psychology.* Upper Saddle River, NJ: Prentice Hall.

Weinberg, R. S., & Gould, D. (2003). *Foundations of sport and exercise psychology*, 3rd Ed. Champaign, IL: Human Kinetics.

Zajonc, R. B. (1965). Social facilitation. *Science, 149*, 269-274.

Zizzi, S., Zaichkowsky, L., & Perna, F. M. (2002). Certification in sport and exercise psychology. In J. L. Van Raalte & B. W. Brewer (Eds.), *Exploring sport and exercise Psychology* 2nd Ed. (pp. 459-477). Washington, DC: American Psychological Association.

Courtesy of Getty Images

7.3

Educational Programs for Sport Psychologists in Asia

DANIEL SMITH AND SI GANGYAN

Introduction

In order to secure information for this chapter, the authors requested a variety of information from sport psychology academics working throughout the vast Asian region. Scholars were asked to provide the following information about sport psychology in their country: first, the history of the field and a list of the academic leaders who developed the discipline; second, how applied sport psychology is utilized by athletes and coaches; third, details on certification issues in applied sport psychology; and fourth, anticipated future and needs for the development of the field. We also asked our participants to include any information that they felt was unique to their country.

It is important to recognize that not all Asian countries are represented in this chapter. A few of our requests for information were not returned despite numerous attempts. There may also be other countries in the region with an academic interest in sport psychology about which we were unaware. However, we were able to include most of the countries where students are graduating in sport psychology and where professors are publishing in the field.

Sport Psychology in P.R.China

Si Gangyan

Sport psychology existed in ancient Chinese culture, especially related to the aspects of skill formation, physical competition, competitive tactics, and mental training. These thoughts have exerted a positive effect on the emergence and development of modern sport psychology in China.

The first paper on sport psychology in modern Chinese society, titled "Transfer Value of Sports," was written by John Ma and published in 1926. In 1942, Wu Wenzhon translated "Sport Psychology" into Chinese. Beginning in 1957, some sport psychology textbooks were introduced into China from Russia, and sport psychology became a required course for students of physical education throughout the country. For political reasons, sport psychology was undeveloped in the mid-1960s. Then, in 1979, Dr.

Ma Qiwei and others organized and promoted the Chinese Association of Sport Psychology (CASP) in Tianjin. Sport psychology was developed from the field of physical education, not from psychology. The Chinese Association of Sport Psychology is a sub-organization of both the Chinese Society of Sport Science and the Chinese Society of Psychology. The CASP has a membership of more than 200 people under a managing council represented by all provinces in mainland China. The CASP holds a national conference every 2-3 years, and currently publishes the "Newsletter of Chinese Sport Psychology" twice each year. In 1999, together with Wuhan Institute of Physical Education, CASP held the 3rd ASPASP (Asian-South Pacific Association of Sport Psychology) International Congress in Wuhan. It gave an impetus to the further development of sport psychology in China and promoted more academic exchanges with international sport psychologists.

At the present time, Beijing University of PE, Shanghai Institute of PE, and Eastern China Normal University offer doctorate and master's programs in sport psychology; and Wuhan Institute of PE offers master's and bachelor programs in sport psychology. Ma Qiwei, Lian Chengmou, Liu Shuhui in Beijing, Qiu Yijun, Yao Jiaxin, Si Gangyan in Wuhan, and Zhang Jianchen, Ji Liu in Shanghai are the prominent professors of sport psychology in China.

Chinese national teams employ three full-time sport psychology staff members (headed by Dr. Zhang Zhongqiu at the National Research Institute of Sports Science) to provide consistent services to athletes. Additionally, five to ten professionals from universities and institutes of PE also work with national athletes according to various working contracts for the Olympic and Asian Games.

Elite level (national and provincial) coaches receive sport psychology training from time to time. Usually they attend training sessions in the Beijing, Wuhan and Shanghai Institutes of PE. The China National Sports General Administration requires elite level coaches to complete required courses in the sport sciences, including sport psychology.

Although there is no official certification requirement for sport psychology practitioners in China, sport psychologists who work with athletes independently must satisfy at least two conditions: a master's degree and three years interning or working in the field. There are committees in the administration centers of various sports that are responsible for selecting technical staff for all sports science consulting.

During the past 20 years, sport psychology research in China has mainly focused on three areas:

(1) The psychological selection of athletes. Psychological selection is based on the concept of heredity, superiority, and the starting point of training. The psychological selection of athletes includes the measurement and evaluation of an athlete's cognitive processes, emotional process, willpower, psychological dynamics, personality, and other similar traits. The major steps in psychological selection include choosing parameters, selecting instrumentation, working out detailed rules of measurement, pre-testing, testing, data processing, establishing models of prediction, and follow-up studies. Research methods relate to experimental psychology, psychometrics, physiopsychology, and social psychology. The process of selection is characterized by its long duration, which involves a variety of athletic levels, including primary selection, semi-selection, and precise selection.

(2) The psychological diagnosis of athletes. The psychological diagnosis of athletes is a comprehensive program. Since 1986, Chinese sport psychologists have used various methods and criteria to measure psychomotor abilities, intelligence, personality, anxiety, emotional state changes, psychological load, and so on. A psychological diagnosis system has been established and applied to sports training, sports psychological consultation, and sport talent selection. The system includes: the theories, principles, contents, procedures, indices, and methods for the psychological diagnosis of athletes; and a system of criteria for the psychological diagnosis of different sport events.

(3) <u>Psychological consultation with and mental training of top athletes</u>. At the beginning of 1980s, several sport psychologists were invited to work with some athletes of the Chinese Shooting Team and the Archery Team. After a period of systematic mental training, one shooter overcame her psychological barrier and broke a world record. After that, more Chinese sport teams asked sport psychologists for help. Thus, psychological consultation and mental training of Chinese elite athletes gradually developed. In 1987, CASP took a project from the National Sport Committee (An Investigation on Psychological Consultation and Psychological Characteristics of Chinese Top Athletes) and set up a consultation center on the site of the Sixth National Games. Sport psychology practitioners used various methods and interventions to athletes on the field, including cognitive adjustment, massage relaxation, music relaxation, imagery, etc. Coaches and athletes welcomed this service. There were 288 athletes from 15 different provinces who visited the consultation center, seeking advice during the two weeks of the Sixth National Games. From 1988 to 2000, Chinese sport psychologists, through combining applied research with practical service, provided support to many Chinese top athletes preparing for important international competitions. Among these athletes, more than 50 were gold medal winners at the Olympic Games, World Cup, and World Championships. Today, psychological consultation and mental training is recognized and accepted by many Chinese top athletes and coaches.

It is expected that both research and application of sport psychology in China will experience rapid development in the next several years. Sports for all Chinese have been encouraged, so sports psychology related to general exercise will also be stressed. However, competitive sport psychology will probably develop faster, mainly because the 2008 Summer Olympics will be held in China. Systematic training programs and the certification programs for sport psychology practitioners are needed for the development of this field.

Hong Kong

Roy Chan and Si Gangyan

The first sport psychology course in Hong Kong was offered by The Chinese University of Hong Kong in 1989. Roy Chan taught this original course and continues to teach sport psychology. This course was offered in the Department of Physical Education (later renamed the Department of Sport Sciences and Physical Education). Thus sport psychology in Hong Kong was developed from the field of physical education and not from psychology. There are currently several sport psychology courses in The Chinese University's Bachelor of Education Degree Program for physical education teachers. In addition to Roy Chan, Siu-yin Cheung teaches sport psychology at The Hong Kong Baptist University and Chou Wah teaches in this area at The Hong Kong Institute of Education. These individuals also serve as consultants to various sport teams.

Hong Kong Society of Sport and Exercise Psychology (HKSSEP) was founded in 2003. Roy Chan is currently the president and HKSSEP currently has 20 members. There is no type of certification of sport psychologists in Hong Kong. In fact, the term sport psychologist is not used much. Instead professionals in sport psychology call themselves sport psychology consultants. We are not aware of any cases of unqualified individuals attempting to practice sport psychology.

Within the Hong Kong Sports Institute (HKSI) there is a Sport Psychology Unit with three full-time consultants and one full-time research assistant. Si Gangyan heads this unit. These consultants work with about 300 elite athletes in 13 focus sports, and are funded by the government. Some academics in different universities also consult with various athletes or sport associations. Psychological assessment, specific skills training, counseling, and psychotherapy are provided by the Sport Psychology Unit of the HKSI. Assessment results are shared with the athletes and/or coaches and serve as a basis for performance enhancement training and improvement of training programs. This unit also provides workshops and seminars for the athletes and coaches both in the HKSI and in the community. In addition, research projects are conducted by Sport Psychology Unit staff throughout the year. The HKSI also offers coach certification courses. Sport psychology is included in these courses.

The future of sport psychology in Hong Kong is uncertain. Until there are enough interested practitioners and until the potential of sport psychology training becomes recognized, there will probably be little development of the field. However, since the professional degree in teaching physical education is already 12 years old, many physical education teachers have had some exposure to sport psychology which has been a part of their curriculum since the degree originated. About 10 individuals have earned higher degrees with a sport psychology emphasis.

The Olympic Games in China in 2008 may spur interest in the development of all sport sciences in China and in Hong Kong. By that time, there may be enough qualified individuals working in this area to promote more funding for sport psychology research and application.

Indonesia

Yuanita Nasution

Sport psychology in Indonesia began in 1967 when Dr. Singgih Gunarsa was assigned as the psychology consultant for the national badminton players to the Thomas Cup (world badminton team championship, similar to Davis Cup in tennis). He also worked with Indonesian athletes in their preparation for the 1968 Olympic Games in Mexico. Until the late 1970s, Gunarsa, and his colleague Saparinah Sadli, worked with national athletes, especially in preparation for the Thomas and Uber Cups.

In the 1980s, several retired national athletes from various sports (i.e., diving, softball, tennis and water polo) completed their graduate studies from the Faculty of Psychology, University of Indonesia, and began practice as general psychologists. J. A. A. Rumeser, Yuanita Nasution, the late Myrna R. Sukasah followed their professors to become sport psychology consultants. Several more young psychologists from the same university also began working with national athletes.

Some psychology scholars conducted research on sport psychology for their theses and dissertations (e.g., Dr. Nitya Wismaningsih and Dr. Enoch Markum, now the Dean of Faculty of Post-Graduate Studies, University of Indonesia). The main topic of their research was competitive anxiety in sport. In 1995, psychologist Yuanita Nasution, who worked mainly with the national badminton players, secured a scholarship from the Australian Government (AusAID) and took a master's degree in sport psychology by conducting research on coping with stress in Indonesian elite badminton players. Nasution became the first Indonesian psychologist to formally pursue education in sport psychology. Meanwhile, four dissertations related to sport psychology were also produced by physical education researchers (Sudibyo Setyobroto, Harsono, Toho Cholik Mutokhir—now the Director General of Sport—and Dr. Danu Hoedaya) when they took their doctoral degrees overseas in the U.S. and Australia.

Until the year 2000, there was no institution in Indonesia that offered academic programs to qualify sport psychologists. Yet sport psychology is one of the core subjects for post-graduate programs in physical education, coaching science, and sports medicine. Among the academic institutions that provide sport psychology subjects in their curriculum are University of Indonesia, University of Tarumanagara, and the Institutes of Teaching and Educational Science. In mid 2001, the Faculty of Post-Graduate Studies, University of Indonesia, commenced a master program on sport psychology. It started with eight students. In the year 2002 more students applied for the program.

The development of sport psychology in Indonesia is in its infancy. Formerly, the psychologists only applied their expertise to psychometrics and delivered consultation services to athletes. One major step was taken in 1990 when the Indonesian Badminton Association invited Dr. Robert Singer to conduct a one-week intensive workshop on sport psychology for their psychologists and coaches, followed by a one-day seminar for psychologists, coaches, athletes, scholars, and others who involved in sport. After his visit, the Indonesian psychologists were made aware that more than just psychological testing and personal consultations were needed when working with athletes.

The Indonesian National Sports Committee (KONI) involves psychologists in preparation for multi-event sports such as the Olympics, Asian Games, and Southeast Asian Games. There are no full time sport psychology consultants in Indonesia, so three to eight psychologists, depending on the number of athletes, usually handle this preparation. The ratio is approximately one psychologist for about 80 to 100 athletes. To maximize the consultancy and psychological training services, priorities should be established. Sixty to eighty percent of the psychologists who worked during the Asian, Southeast Asian, and Olympic Games preparations traveled with these athletic teams.

Even though the sports institutions could not provide sufficient funds to contract a full-time psychologist, some national sport associations, such as badminton, soccer, swimming/diving, archery, track & field, boxing, karate, shooting, fencing, and tennis have their own sport psychology consultants, who work voluntarily and at times receive a monthly stipend. Meanwhile, in some big events like the Asian Games, Olympics, Thomas and Uber Cups in badminton (Indonesia has many world class badminton players), psychologists sometimes receive bonuses when the athletes are successful.

The leading sport psychology consultants in the country reside in Jakarta and are mostly alumni of the Faculty of Psychology, University of Indonesia. Five among them, who have more than eight years working with Indonesian national athletes from various sports, are listed here.

1. Singgih Gunarsa Known as the "Father of Indonesian Sport Psychology," Gunarsa started his consultancy services for athletes in 1967. Since then, he has been actively involved in consulting with national athletes, especially badminton players. Gunarsa is also a productive writer. He has published many books in the field of child and developmental psychology. Together with his colleagues, who were involved in sport psychology consulting, Gunarsa has edited two books on sport psychology in the Indonesian language. His extraordinary work was recognized by the government, and at the 1995 National Sports Day, Gunarsa was awarded a National Medal (Adimanggala Krida) to honor his services in sport psychology.

2. Myrna Sukasah Formerly famous as a national diver who won a bronze medal in the 1970 Asian Games and gold medal in 1977 SEA Games, Myrna has been involved in sport psychology consultancy, especially for water sports, since she became a psychologist in 1979. As the coordinator of sport psychology consultancy services in KONI until 1998, she has worked with numerous sports groups and individuals at many international events. She was elected as a Vice Secretary of the Indonesian NOC in 1999, but passed away just one year later.

3. Jo Rumeser His involvement in sport psychology started with softball. He was the captain of the Indonesian National Team in the 1970s, and became a coach and manager for the Jakarta and Indonesian Women's National Softball Team in the '80s, and for the Indonesian junior soccer team in the '90s. Jo was the Coordinator of the former Sport Psychology Society. He was appointed to run several projects in talent identification and talent development in soccer. He also worked with world level badminton players and professional tennis players, especially during Davis Cup preparation. At the moment Jo is also a member of the Indonesian Sport Psychology Society.

4. Monty Satiadarma He received his title as a psychologist from the University of Indonesia in 1982 and also completed two master's degrees at Emporia State University, Kansas, in 1986 and at the College of

Notre Dame, Belmont, California in 1990. As a clinical psychologist, Monty is trained in intervention and assessment. He began working with Indonesian national boxers in 1991 and has also worked with national archers. Monty's involvement in boxing and archery lead him to work with other sports. He joined other psychologists at the KONI and in 1998 he was appointed as the Coordinator of sport psychology consultancy services for Indonesia's national athletes. That same year Monty was elected as the Dean of the Faculty of Psychology, Tarumanagara University. He is currently the President of the Indonesian Sport Psychology Society, and is completing his dissertation in health and sport psychology.

5. <u>Yuanita Nasution</u> Her involvement in sport psychology started when she was still active as a national softball pitcher. As a student-athlete in psychology, she learned sport psychology from textbooks and applied them to herself, guided by her coach, Jo. A. A. Rumeser. Yuanita graduated from University of Indonesia in 1986. In 1988, she managed a sport psychology program for the Jakarta elite athletes in their preparation for the National Games. In 1989 Yuanita decided not to play on the national team so as to focus on sport psychology consulting. In the same year she was chosen to work with the national badminton players. A year later, in addition to her formal job at the Center for Physical Quality Development, Ministry of National Education, Yuanita was also appointed to serve as sport psychology consultant for Ragunan High School (special school for athletes). Yuanita completed her master's degree at the Victoria University of Technology, Melbourne, with associate professor Tony Morris. Yuanita is the Vice-President of the Indonesian Sport Psychology Society.

Other psychologists who have worked with elite athletes include: Enoch Markum, Rosa Hertamina, Aryati Prawoto, Abryani, Shinta, Surya Chandra, Henry Rumeser, Adrian, Surastuti Nurdadi, R. Feizal, and Nitya Wismaningsih. Interestingly, during the preparation for the 1997 SEA Games in Jakarta, several psychologists who served the Indonesian Armed Forces, such as Col. Latief, Gunawan, Chandra, Wardani, and Ning, also supported the National Training Center by providing services to athletes. Actually, there were more psychologists who worked with athletes in provincial or district levels during the National Games preparation.

General psychologists who were athletes themselves, or those who were interested in sports and worked voluntarily with athletes are to be credited with initiating sport psychology in Indonesia. These Indonesian psychologists tried to establish a society of sport psychology (i.e., Aplikasi Psikologi Olahraga, APO) in the late 1980s. Unfortunately, the organization did not run smoothly due to the mobility of the members.

Meanwhile, more and more sport associations sought sport psychologists to work with their athletes. Realizing the demand, in March 1999 the Indonesian Sport Psychology Society was established. Monty P. Satiadarma, who was appointed as the first president of the ISPS, organized it. The ISPS is instituted under the Indonesian Society of Psychology. Members of the ISPS must have a higher education background in psychology.

Japan

Atsushi Fujita and Mikio Tokunaga

The development of sport psychology in Japan is deeply rooted in physical education. Following the end of World War II, a new education system was instituted under the administrative supervision of the U.S. in which physical education was recognized as an important component. After 1949 physical education became a compulsory subject throughout the educational system from primary school to the university level. Faculty members in physical education departments began to conduct research in this newly emphasized area. In 1950 the Japanese Society of Physical Education (JSPE) was formed to oversee the direction of research in physical education and to disseminate this information to physical educators. By 1960, 13 disciplinary divisions of physical education were differentiated in the JSPE. One of these was the Division of Psychology of Physical Education. The JSPE currently has over 6,800 members, holds an annual conference, and publishes the "Japan Journal of Physical Education (JJPE)" six times a year. The Division of Psychology of Physical Education currently has a membership of about 650 and is an influential academic group. It sponsors a symposium, workshops, and presentations at the annual JSPE conference. Its members have contributed numerous articles to the JJPE pertaining to the psychological issues in physical activity.

The first major impetus given to the development of sport psychology in Japan was the selection of Tokyo as the site of the 1964 Olympic Games. In 1960, a committee of distinguished scholars in physical education and other disciplines related to physical activity, the "Sports Science Research Committee," was formed within the Japan Amateur Sports Association (JASA) to apply sport sciences to elite athletes. A subcommittee, representing sport psychology, was formed within this organization. This was the first time that a focus was directed toward sport psychology. The Sport Psychology Subcommittee primarily conducted research on the psychological issues of athletes, including performance enhancement. Later, the Sport Science Research Committee and the Sport Psychology Subcommittee were separated into two committees. One was to be affiliated with the Japan Olympic Committee (JOC) for performance enhancement of elite athletes in competitive sport and the other was to be affiliated with the JASA for promoting recreational sport to the public.

In 1966 the JASP initiated a seminar to educate trainers in both competitive and regional sport centers. Sport psychology was taught as a compulsory subject within sport science. Although there have been some changes in this trainer education, the JASP continues to educate sport instructors. These educational seminars were patterned after the Traineracademie in Cologne, Germany, which was established in 1976, to interface sport federations with sport science, where sport psychology was also a compulsory subject.

Thus, the first demand for sport psychology in Japan was derived from sport organizations themselves. Elite sport had already blossomed since the early 1960s in Japan, and research on sport had been initiated independently of physical education. This widespread interest in sport psychology also received momentum from the first worldwide congress of sport psychology and the establishment if the ISSP in Rome in 1965. This second major impetus to the development of sport psychology in Japan led to the formation of the Japanese Society of Sport Psychology (JSSP) in April 1973. Indeed, this society was formed to oversee the direction of research in sport psychology in recognition of sport as a social and cultural phenomenon. This "Sport Culture" includes numerous psychological issues difficult to treat in the psychology of physical education. Interestingly, it was also in 1973 that the North American Society for the Psychology of Sport and Physical Activity (NASPSPA), in the U.S. held its first meeting independent of the American Alliance of Health, Physical Education and Recreation (AAHPER). The JSSP has a membership more than 400 under current President Fujita. Many of these members are also members of the Division of Psychology of Physical Education in the JSPE. The JSSP holds an annual conference and publishes the "Japanese Journal of Sport Psychology" annually. The JSSP has been actively involved in international activities for promoting sport psychology. The JSSP has also served the ISSP in that Iwao Matsuda was a Managing Council member from 1973 to 1981 and Fujita has been a Managing Council member from 1981 to 1985 and subsequently a Vice President, President, and Past President during the years of 1985 to 2001.

Some of the current problems facing applied sport psychology in Japan include the following:

1. The Japanese Olympic Committee commissions sport counselors for each sport event group. However, those cases in which a sport counselor is actively engaged as a member of the coaching staff are rare. The counselor system is far from satisfactory.

2. In recent years, the necessity of mental training has been increasing in sport settings for high school students, college

students, and non-pro sport participants. However, the current status is that sport psychology researchers lend support on a voluntary basis and have little incentive to do so.

3. A small number of sport psychology researchers and private or nongovernmental psychologists have provided mental training guidance. In the past, there has been no system to train and educate mental training instructors, and no system to certify their qualifications. The problem of training and qualifying such practitioners has been discussed in a symposium and workshop at an annual conference of the JSSP. A special committee was formed independently of the Managing Council and it recently established the accreditation system for "Certified Mental Training Consultant in Sport" (CMTCS). In the first year of this accreditation system (2000) 38 members were certified.

Some of the major issues for the future of sport psychology in Japan include:

1. The initiation, promotion and continuance of the Certified Mental Training Consultant in Sport certification program.

2. The further promotion of sport psychology among physical education teachers, competitive sport instructors, and sport promotion, sport, and recreation instructors.

3. The building of closer ties with the psychological associations in addition to the established relationships with the sport science associations.

Korea

Seong-ok Kim

It is difficult to determine exactly when the first sport psychology course was taught in Korea. There are records of a "Psychology of Physical Education" course taught at Seoul National University and at Kyo-ungbuk National University in the 1950s. However, information on the faculty and course content is not available. It is possible that the course was listed in the curriculum but never actually taught.

Research efforts began to emerge in the 1960s when the Korean Society of Physical Education (KSPE) started their academic activities and a sport psychology course entitled "Psychology of Physical Education" became popular at various universities. By the 1970s more than 20 universities had physical education departments and began to teach "Psychology of Physical Education." At this time, several sport psychology texts were translated into Korean.

In the 1980s, due to the establishment of graduate programs at several universities and the 1989 formation of the Korean Society of Sport Psychology (KSSP), the number of scientific researchers in sport psychology was dramatically increased. The KSSP paved the way for the dissemination of scientific knowledge and promotion of research endeavors in sport psychology. Today, the KSSP includes almost 300 regular members and nearly 30 universities have sport psychology graduate programs.

Many scholars have contributed to the academic development of sport psychology in Korea. Jong-sun Kim (I-wha Women's University), the first president of KSSP, played a major role in organizing KSSP and providing direction for the field. Other key individuals, who played an important role in the development of the field of sport psychology include

Chung-hee Jung (Seoul National University)— applied sport psychology,

Kui-bong Kim (Kook-min University) and Ne-suk Pyo (Busan National University)— exercise psychology,

Kee-wong Kim (I-wha Women's University)— motor learning and control, and

Seong-ok Kim (Junbuk National University)— cognitive aspects of sport psychology.

In addition to these key researchers, some young scholars have developed a deep concern for sport counseling and cross-cultural issues.

Although there have been heated discussions about certification among KSSP members, no governing body to certify practitioners has yet been established. In order to establish a governing body and to determine certification requirements, more time and trained professionals are needed. Before asserting the necessity of certification, it is important that the sport psychology professionals promote the importance of sport performance enhancement to coaches and practitioners.

In Korea, sport psychology consultants are not specifically designated as such. However, the Korean Sport Science Institute (KSSI), which has been established to assist national athletes, employs 5 to 6 individuals with PhDs in sport psychology as researchers. They work closely with university professors. They perform as sport psychology consultants by diagnosing psychological limitations and designing programs to remedy them in individual athletes as well as with sport teams. Today, some professional baseball, basketball, soccer, and golf coaches invite sport psychology consultants to improve the performance of their athletes through various psychological interventions.

Although there is no required certification for national coaches, the KSSI does sponsor short-term coaching education classes for coaches of various levels. Any coach can participate in these classes at their own expense. Provincial Sport Associations also offer various coaching education courses several times a year. There is a sport psychology component in almost every course.

The field of sport psychology is continuing to grow. Of the almost 300 members of the KSSP, more than 100 have doctorate degrees. More than 20 universities now have doctoral programs in physical education. About five PhD graduates earn a sport psychology degree every year.

The term "sport psychologist" has no legal limitations in Korea. However, it is important that the role of the sport psychology consultant be recognized in enhancing athletic performance and in facilitating the players' well being.

Since there is no quality control, the university scholars should strengthen the requirements at every degree level and constantly upgrade the quality of their teaching and research. They must teach their students to link theory with practice. The future quality of sport psychology depends on the direction of the current sport psychology university faculty, practitioners, and researchers.

Singapore

**Daniel Smith, Harry Tan,
Stevenson Lai, and Edgar Tham**

The academic and applied emphasis in sport psychology is a recent phenomenon in Singapore. The 1989 hosting of the International Society of Sport Psychology Congress increased sport psychology interest within this small Southeast Asian country.

Since its 1973 inception, the Singapore Sports Council (SSC) has always promoted performance enhancement with their various national team athletes. The first Resident Chief Sport Psychologist hired by the SSC was Peter Usher from 1992-1996. The first local Chief Sport Psychologist was Edgar Tham, who served in this capacity from 1995 to 2000. Stevenson Lai has occupied this position since 2000. The Center for Mental Training (CMT) was established within the SSC in 1998.

Today three full-time and several part-time sport psychologists are employed in the CMT. They implement various group interventions with national teams and provide counseling for individual athletes. One current project involves the use of mental training in injury rehabilitation. The CMT also has the "Performance Feedback System" and a flotation tank. Various software programs like "Think Fast," "Brain Hemisphere," and the TAIS are available to Singapore athletes at the CMT.

Numerous national teams utilize the CMT to varying amounts. No team is required to be involved with the CMT. In some cases, the team is not involved with the CMT, but individual athletes from that team come in for counseling sessions. The CMT is located in the national stadium so it is convenient to the athletes who train there. Some of the services offered by the CMT include: (1) educational seminars and workshops on applied topics (e.g., mental skills training, performance enhancement issues, study skills for student-athletes); (2) ongoing individual consultations or counseling as a follow-up to the seminars or workshops; (3) computer-based interactive multimedia training tools for mental training and biofeedback training; (4) educational materials such as pocket handbooks, CD audio books and sport-specific mental training manuals developed and published yearly for athletes' and coaches' use; (5) long-term sport psychological services in preparation for major competitions like the Southeast Asian, Asian, Commonwealth, and Olympic Games are offered, with the availability of team psychologists accompanying the Singapore Contingent; and (6) Mandarin-language and translation services catering to a large number of Mandarin-speaking athletes and foreign expert coaches from China are also available.

Being housed within the Sports Medicine & Research Center, the CMT sport psychologists complement the work of the sports medicine physicians, physiotherapists, and athletic trainers. Injured athletes are taught to use and develop psychological skills like goal setting, imagery, self-talk, and relaxation to facilitate their rehabilitation. Lastly, the latest development from the CMT includes the offering of Certificate and Diploma programs in applied sport psychology and a Graduate Diploma in Counseling (Sport Psychology) to interested coaches and practitioners.

CMT sport psychologists travel with the teams to the SEA Games and consult with coaches, individual athletes, and with teams during this competition. A CMT sport psychologist accompanies the small contingent of Singapore National Team athletes to the Olympic Games as well.

From an academic perspective, the College of Physical Education (CPE), which began in 1984, included academic courses with a sport psychology component. In 1991, CPE became the School of Physical Education (SPE). With its new alignment with both the National Institute of Education (NIE) and Nanyang Technological University, SPE began to offer upper division courses in sport psychology. In 2000 the SPE became the division of Physical Education and Sport Science (PESS). In 1997 Dan Smith, PhD, became the first full-time doctoral level professor in sport psychology. The first graduate student to complete a master's (MS) degree under the mentorship of Dr. Smith was Stevenson Lai and the first to complete a doctorate of philosophy (PhD) degree was Irwin Seet. The upper division courses and graduate student interest have flourished since that time. In the years 2000 and 2001 Bervyn Lee and John Wang returned from overseas graduate study in sport psychology as the second and third PhD trained faculty in sport psychology.

All academic sport psychology course offerings in Singapore are housed in the PESS division. Thus, since sport psychology is not taught in any psychology departments, the field is more closely aligned with physical education than in North America. Before entering the PESS, all students have completed two years of general education courses at the junior college level. Thus, when they enter PESS and NIE, they are focusing entirely on courses in their major and minor and they are preparing to be physical education teachers. Students enter PESS in one of three different programs: the two-year diploma, the four-year degree, and the two year postgraduate diploma program for those who already have a degree in another subject.

All students are introduced to the discipline by completing a course entitled "Social and Psychological Foundations of Physical Education and Sports." This course includes the topics of social psychology, group dynamics, and applied issues of motivation, arousal, personality, competition, and anxiety control. During their third year, degree students must choose either a "sport studies" or "sport science" track. Those in "sport studies" complete a course entitled "Social Psychology and the Individual in Sports." During their fourth year, all students specialize in an area. Those choosing sport psychology complete two more advanced level sport psychology courses entitled "Social Psychology of Physical Activity I and II." Thus, a degree student with an emphasis in sport psychology, completes four sport psychology related courses. Two of these courses focus on the development of a theory base in sport psychology and two courses apply the theoretical constructs to applied issues and interventions. The top 15 to 20% of these degree students are offered a one-year honors program, which includes an additional course entitled "Applied Sport Psychology." The master's program offers two additional courses entitled "Advanced Applied Sport Psychology" and "Exercise Psychology." A student who completes an honors and master's program will have taken as many as seven sport psychology courses. Master's and PhD research degrees with a sport psychology emphasis are also offered, however these programs have minimal coursework requirements. Master's and PhD students in sport psychology usually complete two counseling courses from the psychology department as well.

Dr. Smith's graduate students have completed a variety of theses and dissertations since 1997. These include:

Irwin Seet implemented an extensive season-long psychological skills training program with a secondary school rugby team. He used quantitative and qualitative measures to determine that the treatment team exhibited improvement in the five psychological skills measured and this improvement was superior to that of the control group. The participants' rugby performance improved and they felt the program should be continued.

Stevenson Lai found significant differences on six mental qualities between elite national team athletes who won medals in international competitions compared to those who did not achieve medal status.

David Shepherd implemented an imagery training program with elite netball and high school female volleyball players and compared them with control groups. The results supported the efficacy of imagery as a mediating factor in enhancing physical performance, increasing state self-confidence, and reducing state anxiety levels.

Zheng Xinyi measured six mental qualities in elite athletes from America, Singapore, and China. Results showed that there exists a significant difference among the athletes from these three countries on the six variables. Follow-up comparisons displayed that only anxiety and mental preparation scores showed significant difference between the Chinese and Singapore athletes. Significant differences existed on all mental qualities between the American and Singapore athletes. Finally, differences existed on all mental variables except competitive trait anxiety between Chinese and American athletes.

Poh Yu Khing sought to discover the differences in sources of sport-confidence across age, gender, and sport-type for Singaporean student athletes. He found that younger athletes rated mastery, mental and physical preparation, and coaches' leadership as being significantly more important sources of sport-confidence than did older athletes. Team-sport athletes rated social support as a more significantly important source of sport-confidence compared to individual-sport athletes.

Ang Yen examined the relationship between social physique anxiety and exercise adherence among aerobic dance participants in Singapore. Results showed that there was no significant relationship between the subjects' exercise adherence and their social physique anxiety levels. The study also revealed a unique demographic profile among the female aerobic participants in Singapore. They were generally younger and leaner than those subjects studied in past American research. They also appeared to be less disturbed about how others viewed their body.

Abdul Nasir Bin Abdul Razzak compared the use of selected goal-setting strategies between level 1, level 2, and level 3 umpires/referees in Singapore. He found there to be significant differences by level on 12 types of goals but no significant differences on two types of goals set.

Tirumagal d/o G.K. investigated gender motivation between male and female physical education teachers and male and female students. This study found that students taught by opposite gender teachers had superior attitudes toward physical activity to a significant extent.

Rachel Tang sought to determine if the ability to use imagery as a tool for controlling anxiety levels is evident in secondary school netball players in Singapore. No significant differences were found between the imagery variables, state anxiety variables, and win-loss records. However, there was a significant relationship between the variables of state self-confidence and all the imagery variables.

Goh Wai Leng assessed the burnout levels of secondary school physical education teachers in Singapore and tried to identify the specific work conditions of the Physical Education teachers that are related to this state. It was found that Singapore Physical Education Teachers are experiencing only moderate levels of burnout. They perceive bureaucratic, psychological, and social aspects to be the main sources of burnout. No significant relationship between teachers' burnout and demographics was found.

Taiwan

Likang Chi

The Society of Sport and Exercise Psychology of Taiwan (SSEPT) was developed in 2000 and has had a major effect on promoting sport psychology as an academic discipline in Taiwan. The first president of SSEPT was Iau-Hoei, Likang Chi was the first vice president, and the first secretary general was T.M. Hung. The field of sport psychology and the professors promoting it come from physical education.

The following professors and universities currently provide academic training in sport psychology: Iau-Hoei Chien (National Taiwan Normal University), Likang Chi (National College of Physical Education and Sports), T.M. Hung (Taipei Physical Education College), Frank Lu (National College of Physical Education and Sports), Hank Jwo (National Taiwan Normal University), and Yo-Te Liu (National Taiwan Normal University).

The government currently funds one full-time sport psychology consultant to work with athletes at the National Training Center. However, four to six part-time consultants are usually funded a year before the Asian and Olympic Games. Elite coaches also receive sport psychology training through various coaching workshops.

There is currently no certification for sport psychology practitioners and there is no type of quality control to ensure that only qualified sport psychologists are working with athletes. However, the SSEPT has discussed plans for some type of certification in the future. There is no legal reason why a person cannot call himself or herself a "sport psychologist." Most people are referred to by that term if they have a doctoral degree in the field.

As the SSEPT continues to expand, sport psychology has the potential for much growth in Taiwan. It is also anticipated that this organization will take on the issue of certification at some future time.

Thailand

Supitr Samahito

Academic sport psychology was first developed in Thailand at Chulalongkorn and Kasetsart Universities in 1985. These universities began to offer sport psychology courses in both their bachelor and master's degree programs. All sport psychology courses were offered in the physical education departments. The faculty members who taught these sport psychology courses included Vorasak Pienchob and Silpachai Suwathada from Chulalongkorn University and Supitr Samahito from Kasetsart University.

Several universities now offer bachelor, master's, and doctoral degree programs with a sport psychology emphasis. There are also two academic organizations, the Sport Psychology Association of Thailand, established in 1991, and the Applied Sport Psychology Society of Thailand, established in 2000. These two societies establish their own activities, including sport psychology conferences and workshops. Participants who complete these academic activities receive certificates of completion. Universities providing academic training in sport psychology, along with the names of key professors include the following: Chulalongkorn University (Silpachai Suwanthada and Sombat Karnjanakij), Kasetsart University (Supitr Samahito and Nattaya Kaewmookda), Srinakarin Tharaviroj University (Pichit Meungnapor, Namchai Laewan, and Supranee Kwanboonchan), and Burapa University (Nareupon Wongchaturapat and Seubsai Boonweerabutr).

Sport psychology practitioners in Thailand have no type of certification and are called "participants." However, there are plans to certify sport psychology practitioners in the near future. Certification requirements are currently being discussed. There is currently no serious problem relating to unqualified sport psychologists. Several of the key persons in the field (listed above) informally approve sport psychologists to work with athletes. This allows less experienced sport psychologists to obtain experience with athletes while being supervised by the more experienced faculty.

The government does not fund any full-time sport psychology consultants to work with national athletes. However, sport psychologists who work full-time in universities and colleges of physical education are funded by the Sports Authority of Thailand and/or the National Olympic Committee for specific international competitions such as the Southeast Asian Games, Asian Games, and Olympic Games. Recently some of the sport associations have begun to offer part-time funding to sport psychology consultants who work with national athletes and sport associations. These sport associations include soccer, sepak takraw, gymnastics, volleyball, swimming, and track and field.

Sport psychology training courses for coaches are offered by various university professors and by sport psychologists consulting with national teams. Most of the elite level coaches have participated in sport psychology training both in the country and abroad.

University and college students are becoming more interested in sport psychology and consider it a viable career. For the field to grow as an academic discipline it will be important to improve educational quality, research productivity, and international connections. It is hoped that the Sport Psychology Association of Thailand and the Applied Sport Psychology Society will lend credibility to the academic discipline and bring the coaches and sport psychologists together. As the market for sport psychologists grows, it is anticipated that more individuals will pursue graduate degrees abroad to meet the demand, especially in the private sector.

Conclusion

The study of sport psychology in Asia is a relatively recent development. China (1926) and Japan (1949) established academic interest and research in the field before other Asian nations. Interest developed in Korea in the 1960s. In every country except Indonesia the field grew out of physical education as opposed to psychology. Most of the countries have an academic organization in sport psychology. The Japanese Society of Sport Psychology (JSSP) publishes a sport psychology journal and the Chinese Association of Sport Psychology publishes a newsletter.

Most countries have addressed the issue of certification but only Japan is certifying mental trainers at this time. However, most of the countries report that the occurrence of unqualified sport psychologists is not a major problem.

The number of full-time sport psychologists employed by governmental sport programs varies from country to country. Japan has numerous practicing sport psychologists. South Korea has five or six employed by their government sport organizations, Hong Kong has four, China and Singapore three, Taiwan one, and Thailand and Indonesia have none.

However, interest in each country seems to be developing for the implementation of mental training programs with athletes, which should provide more full-time positions in the future.

Each country has similar views as to the future of sport psychology. Most want to promote the field as an academic discipline. Several also want to develop more international collaboration and contacts. The major academic professional organization in sport psychology in this region is the Asian South Pacific Association of Sport Psychology (ASPASP). Each Asian country is represented on the executive board of this organization. The growth and development of ASPASP should continue to bring these Asian Countries together and promote the field throughout the region.

Courtesy of iStockphoto Inc.

7.4

Educational Programs for Sport and Exercise Psychology in South America

DIETMAR M. SAMULSKI & BENNO BECKER JR.

Introduction to the General Background of Sport and Exercise Psychology in South America

Sport psychology in South America is a very recent scientific discipline, which has only 25 years of evolution in South America. Most of the sport psychologists in South America have graduated in physical education with a master's or doctoral degree or are clinical-oriented psychologists. Unfortunately, sport psychology in South America is not an integrated discipline in the faculties of psychology in the universities, but most of the institutes of physical education offer sport psychology as an obligatory discipline for their students. It is only recently that the aspect and field of exercise psychology is coming into consideration of either educational programs or applied work in South America. A close link exists

between the fields of physiotherapy and sport with handicapped people.

In 1979 the Brazilian Society of Sport Psychology (SOBRAPE) was founded, and in 1986 the South American Society of Sport Psychology (SOSUPE) was founded. The first international symposium of sport psychology in South America was realized in 1981 in Porto Alegre, Brazil, with more than 1,750 participants. In 1990, the SOBRAPE held the II International Symposium of Sport Psychology at the Federal University of Minas Gerais in Belo Horizonte, with 450 participants representing 25 different countries.

During the symposium a regular meeting of the managing council of the ISSP was held. In the last 20 years several national societies were founded (Becker, 1991; Becker, 1997; Becker, 2002): Association of Sport Psychology from Peru (ADPD) in 1982, Society of Applied Sport Psychology of Argentina (SAPAD) in 1987, Society of Sport Psychology of Uruguay (SUPDE) in 1989, Society of Sport Psychology of Chile (APDC) in 1997, Society of Sport Psychology of Bolivia (SOBOPAD) in 1999, and the Association of Applied Psychology of Argentina (ASAPAD) in 2002.

In the last 20 years, six South American congresses of sport psychology (Becker, 2001) were held. In Brazil alone 10 national congresses of sport psychology were organized in the last 20 years (Samulski, 2002). In the last world congress of sport psychology in Skiathos, Greece, more than 25 scientific presentations were held by sport psychologists from South America.

As John Salmela (1991) mentioned in *The World Sport Psychology Source Book*, South America has a great potential in the area of sport psychology and in recent years represents an area of major growth, along with Asia, of sport psychologists in the world. The vision of the ISSP President, Keith Henschen, is to increase membership from developing countries and to support the formation of sport psychology organizations in the countries of the continents Africa, Asia, and South America.

The national Olympic committees of Argentina, Brazil, Uruguay, and Chile contacted sport psychologists who are responsible for the psychological preparation and support of the Olympic and paralympic athletes. In the last five years the Brazilian sport ministry in cooperation with the national Olympic committee created eight centers of sport excellence, which offer psychological service and assistance for elite athletes and educational programs for coaches on different levels.

Educational Programs and Interventions in Sport Psychology in Selected Countries in South America

Argentina
Educational Programs in Sport Psychology
The department of psychology at the University of Buenos Aires offers the discipline of psychology of sport in its curriculum. The discipline is also offered at the Institute of Physical Education (INEF) in Buenos Aires. A course in applied sport psychology is offered annually in the department of psychology at the University of Buenos Aires. In addition, a postgraduate course is offered at the Catholic University of Buenos Aires (UCA). Finally, sport psychology courses are offered at Juan Agustin Maza University (Becker, 2001).

Table 1: Foundation of the National Societies of Sport Psychology in South America

Year	Foundation	
1979	Brazilian Society of Sport and Exercise Psychology (SOBRAPE) First president: Benno Becker, Jr. Current president: Dietmar Samulski	
1982	Association of Sport Psychology from Peru (APDP) President: Hugo La Torre Peña	
1986	South American Society of Sport and Exercise Psychology (SOSUPE) First president: Benno Becker, Jr. Current president: Carlos Ferres	
1987	Argentinean Society of Applied Sport Psychology (SAPAD) President: Liliana Gabrin	
1989	Uruguayan Society of Sport Psychology (SUPDE) First president: Carlos Ferrés Current president: Jesus Chalela	
1995	Paraguayan Association of Sport Psychology (APPDE) President: Edgar Galeano	
1997	Chilean Association of Sport Psychology (APDC) President: Enrique Aguayo Chaves	
1999	Bolivian Society of Sport and Exercise Psychology (SOBOPAD) President: Abdon Callejás	
2002	Argentinean Association of Applied Psychology (ASAPAD) President: Marcelo Roffé	

Intervention in Sport Psychology

Applied tasks are introduced at the initiation of participation in sport and are continued through to professional sport, for healthy athletes as well as for people with special needs (e.g., in sport therapy). The department of sport psychology within Argentine National Training Center for Elite Athletes (CENARD) officially assisted the athletes in the Pan-American games in La Habana, Cuba, for the Secretary of Sports and the Argentine Olympic committee. Since then, the sport psychology department has worked in the preparation of Olympic athletes for Barcelona (Spain), Atlanta (United States), Sydney (Australia), and Athens (Greece), as well as for the Pan-American games of 1995 in Mar del Plata and the Winnipeg Games in Canada (Becker, 2001).

Brazil

Educational Programs in Sport Psychology

Talking about sport psychology in Brazil includes discussions of motor learning, motor development, and motor control as well as—more recently—exercise psychology, which embodies fitness for everybody as well as for special groups (e.g., the elderly) and rehabilitation (e.g., injured athletes, handicapped). Sport and exercise psychology are offered in university programs on different levels:

- Master's programs in sport science with an alternative priority in sport and exercise psychology. Most master's programs include sport and exercise psychology issues and seminars. People who have successfully finished these programs will find employment in various areas in sport (organizations, sports academies, etc.).

- Post graduate "specialization courses in sports training" also focus on sport and exercise psychology; one of these courses at Federal University of Porto Allegre is primarily oriented toward sport and exercise psychology. This course offers the following disciplines: motor learning, exercise and health, exercise physiology, research methods, sports pedagogy, sport and exercise psychology, developmental psychology, intervention techniques, social psychology, and practical sessions with coaches. Most of the specialization programs for sports medicine and physiotherapy include in their curricula sport and exercise psychology and motor development.

- Doctoral programs in sport science with the possibility/option to emphasize sport and exercise psychology in the doctoral thesis. Four universities in Brazil (USP-São Paulo; UFRGS-Porto Allegre; GAMA FILHO-Rio de Janeiro; UNICAMP-Campinas) offer doctoral programs in sport and movement science.

Graduates from sport sciences or from other academic areas (e.g., sports medicine, physiotherapy, sports pedagogy) who are strongly interested in sport and exercise psychology have the opportunity to elaborate their knowledge in sport and exercise psychology at annual congresses of the national societies and special workshops or clinics organized by these organizations.

Table 2: Congresses of Sport Psychology in Brazil

Year	Place	Event	Promotion
1981	Porto Allegre, RS	I Brazilian Congress of Sport Psychology	SOBRAPE
1983	Rio de Janeiro, RJ	II Brazilian Congress of Sport Psychology	SOBRAPE
1985	Recife, PE	III Brazilian Congress of Sport Psychology	SOBRAPE
1987	Tramandaí, RS	IV Brazilian Congress of Sport Psychology	SOBRAPE
1990	Belo Horizonte, MG	V Brazilian Congress of Sport Psychology	SOBRAPE
1993	Novo Hamburgo, RS	VI Brazilian Congress of Sport Psychology	SOBRAPE
1998	Tubarão, SC	VII Brazilian Congress of Sport Psychology	SOBRAPE
2001	Belo Horizonte, MG	VIII Brazilian Congress of Sport Psychology	SOBRAPE
2002	Jundiaí, SP	IX Brazilian Congress of Sport Psychology	SOBRAPE
2003	Rio de Janeiro, RJ	X Brazilian Congress of Sport Psychology	SOBRAPE
2004	Curitiba, PR	XI Brazilian Congress of Sport Psychology	SOBRAPE

Sport and Exercise Psychology in Educational Programs for Coaches on Different Levels

The national sports federations in Brazil (volleyball, handball, tennis, soccer, and swimming) offer educational programs for coaches with a duration between 60 and 120 hours and include sport psychology topics like coaching, motivation, stress control, leadership, management, and communication.

In Brazil, a national coaching academy that offers a scientific and practical program for the coaches does not currently exist. Most of the Brazilian coaches were athletes and have no academic education or formation and consequently have only a superficial view of sport psychology. The Brazilian Federation of Volleyball (CBV) exclusively offers national and international courses for coaches on different education levels, including sport psychology issues, in its curricula.

Centers of Research and Intervention in Sport Psychology in Brazil

In the last ten years, research in applied sport psychology in Brazil has developed very quickly. The following centers of research and intervention in sport psychology (Samulski, 2002) now exist:

1. Laboratory of sport psychology in the center of sport excellence at the Federal University of Minas Gerais (UFMG) in Belo Horizonte Director: Dr. Dietmar Martin Samulski Members: Dr. Luiz Carlos Moraes, Dr. Pablo Juan Greco, Dr. Rodolfo Novellino Benda, Dr. John Salmela, Prof. Ms. Franco Noce, Prof. Varley Teoldo da Costa. Research areas: Stress, motivation, expert-performance, talent development, psychology of coaching and young athletes, motor learning, decision making in game sports, creativity, prevention of sports injuries. Services: Psychological support of athletes in soccer, handball, volleyball, swimming, tennis, and judo. Psychological evaluation, preparation, and support of the Brazilian paralympic team.

Psychological evaluation: The laboratory of sport psychology offers psychological evaluation for athletes based on computer-aided psychological diagnosis, using the modern technology of the Vienna Test System. This system provides personality tests, cognitive tests, psychophysiological tests, and a specific test system for cognitive rehabilitation (Rehacom). We use this system not only for diagnosis, but also for psychological therapy and intervention for athletes. Based on the results of the psychological diagnosis, we elaborate a report with practical recommendations for coaches, and we discuss this report with the coaches. In the field of game sports, we use the system SIMI-Scout for game, tactics, and behavioral analysis. This system enables coaches to make a more comprehensive analysis of the game by using video recording.

2. Research groups in the center of sport excellence at the Federal University of São Paulo (USP) Directors: Dr. Dante de Rose and Dr. Carlos Simões Research areas: Stress and anxiety, psychological aspects of young athletes, leadership, group dynamics, social influences. Services: Psychological preparation support of athletes in cooperation with the institute of Ayrton Senna, and the national sports federation.

3. Center of Psychological Research and Evaluation in Rio de Janeiro Director: Dr. Luiz Scipião Ribeiro. Research areas: Stress and anxiety, personality, biofeedback. Services: Psychophysiological control, psychological intervention using biofeedback.

4. Research group of sport psychology at the University of Campinas (UNICAMP) Director: Dr. Pedro Winderstein Research areas: Motivation, emotions in sport, career planning. Services: Motivational training programs for teachers of physical education. Career planning for athletes.

5. Research group of sport psychology at the University of Novo Hamburgo (FEEVALE) Director: Dr. Benno Becker, Jr. Research areas: Stress and anxiety, personality, burn out, psychological health, psychological aspects of coaches and young athletes. Services: Mental preparation and psychological support of athletes and teams of different sports.

6. Laboratory of sport psychology in the center of sport excellence at the university of Recife Director: Dr. Antonio Roberto Rocha Santos. Research areas: Analysis of cognitive processes, sport and ethics, clinical issues in sport. Services: Clinical intervention and clinical-oriented support of athletes and paraolympic athletes.

7. Institute for Mental Training (Orpus) in São Paulo Director: Dr. Regina Brandão Research areas: Stress, anxiety, personality, and career planning Services: Mental preparation of athletes and teams. This institute also offers courses and workshops in applied sport and exercise psychology for psychologists, athletes, coaches, and referees.

8. Research group in sport psychology at University of Rio Claro-São Paulo Director: Dr. Afonso Machado Research areas: Emotion, anxiety, depression, social influences Services: Mental preparation and psychological support of athletes and teams.

9. Department of Sport Psychology at the Sports University in Curitiba Director: Lic. Ruth Pauls Research areas: Detection of talents in sport, especially in gymnastics. Services: Mental preparation and psychology support of the Brazilian female gymnastic team.

Psychological Support of the Brazilian Athletes for the Paralympic Games in Sydney 2000 and Athens 2004

The Brazilian Paralympic Committee (CPB) established an interdisciplinary scientific commission aiming at evaluating the athletes and giving the coaches scientific support regarding the preparation period.

The psychological evaluation and preparation of the athletes were tasks of this interdisciplinary project. The psychological evaluation of the athletes (personality tests, stress and anxiety tests, structured interviews, cognitive tests) was the first action (Samulski, 2001; Samulski & Noce, 2002; Samulski et al., 2004). A psychological training program for the athletes was developed based on this evaluation. The program was individually applied in the different paralympic training centers (Rio de Janeiro, São Paulo, Recife), and it was composed of the following techniques: relaxation techniques, stress management, attention control, goal-setting and motivation strategies, visualization, positive self-talk, and development of psychological competition routines. During the preparation of the basketball and soccer teams, some techniques of group dynamics were also applied in order to build up group cohesion and team spirit. Dr. Samulksi accompanied the Brazilian delegation to Sydney 2000 and to Athens 2004, and was responsible for psychological support for the athletes during the games. The sport psychologist applied the following intervention techniques during the games: relaxation and concentration techniques; psychological support before, during, and after competition; and interventions to solve interpersonal conflicts. It is recommended for the future to establish a permanent psychological training system as well as educational and social support processes for the athletes with special needs. Finally, the coaches in Paralympic Sport must be educated and trained in psychological and social skills.

Chile

Educational programs in sport psychology

A majority of the psychology programs offer the discipline of sport and exercise psychology as an optional discipline after the fourth year of the program. Most of the programs in physical education also offer this discipline as part of the curriculum.

Sport Psychology Services

The sport psychologists work with clubs, federations, the Olympic committee, and athletes in general. Sport psychologists have been hired by the Olympic committee of Chile. The department of sport psychology of the Center of Elite Sport (CAR) is responsible for evaluating the athletes and for their psychological training. Some psychologists work with young athletes who practice soccer in sporting clubs. In tennis, the psychologists work on a regular basis in Santiago with high-level players. Santiago's city hall hired psychologists to assist in the amateur sport programs for the general population. Social clubs have psychologists assisting the beginners of several competitive sports. Some psychologists are psychology instructors in physical education and of psychology (Becker, 2001).

Uruguay

Educational Programs in Sport Psychology
Some courses are offered in the discipline of sport psychology in the department of psychology of the university of the republic in Montevideo, the school of medicine (in the department of sport medicine), and the superior institute of physical education.

Sport Psychology Services
There is no sport psychologist under contract by the Olympic committee. However, several sport psychologists give psychological support to the Olympic athletes and teams. In addition, there are clubs that use the assistance of psychologists in sporting initiation (with children, parents, and coaches) and in professional sport (evaluation and psychological training), in sports such as soccer, tennis, track and field, and basketball (Becker, 2001).

Perspectives

In order to more systematically develop sport, exercise, and health psychology in South America, we want to give some important suggestions:

- Integrate sport psychology as a discipline in the curricula of the faculties of psychology in the universities.

- Develop specific academic programs of sport and exercise psychology on the master's and doctorate levels.

- Introduce sport psychology as an applied discipline in the curriculum of the national coaching academies.

- Integrate to a greater degree the services of psychological preparation and support in the Olympic training centers in South America.

- Initiate more research activities in the area of prevention, health, and rehabilitation for handicapped sport.

- Offer sport psychology training programs in practical intervention techniques.

- Design specific educational programs for coaches on different levels.

- Initiate the impending publication of a South American *Journal of Sport Psychology* in order to better circulate the results of investigation in the area of applied sport psychology in South America.

- Circulate the position statements of the ISSP in South America, especially the statements on ethical principles, doping, and aggression and violence in sports to help to bring sport psychology to the awareness of responsible persons.

- Collaborate with international sport psychology societies, especially with the ISSP, in order to get international support in the education of sport psychologists and to develop psychological service programs in the Olympic centers in South America.

- Promote better cooperation between the South American Society of Sport Psychology with the ISSP in order to get international support in the education of sport psychologists and to develop psychological service-and-intervention programs in South America.

References

Becker, B. (1997). El desarrollo de la Psicologia del deporte em latino America. *Revista Sociedad Sudamericana de Psicologia del deporte 1* (1997): 3-7.

Becker, B. (2001). *Manual de Psicologia del Deporte & Ejercicio.* Novo Hamburgo: Editora Feevale.

Becker, B. (2001). Sport psychology in South America. In R. Lidor, N. Bardaxoglou, B. Becker Jr., & T. Morris (Eds.), *The World Sport Psychology Sourcebook* (pp. 213-231). Morgantown, WV: Fitness Information Technology.

Salmela, J., & Becker, B. (1991). Latin American. In J. Salmela (Ed.), *The world sport psychology sourcebook* (pp. 43-44). Illinois: Human Kinetics.

Samulski, D. (2001, July). Psychological preparation of the Brazilian athletes for the Paralympic Games in Sydney 2000. 6th Annual Congress of the European College of Sport Science in Cologne, 24-28. *Proceedings of the Congress,* page 168.

Samulski, D. (2002). *Psicologia do Esporte.* São Paulo: Editora Manole.

Samulski, D., Noce, F. (2002). Avaliação Psicológica de atletas paraolímpicos. In: Mello, M.T. (Ed.). *Paraolimpíadas Sidney 2000.* São Paulo: Atheneu, 99-133.

Samulski, D., Noce, F., Anjos, D., & Lopes, M. (2004). Psychological evaluation of paralympic athletes. In M. Mello (Ed.), *Clinical evaluation and assessment of the fitness of the Brazilian paralympic athletes* (pp.147-157). São Paulo: Atheneu.

7.5

Ethical Aspects in Applied Sport Psychology

RICHARD D. GORDIN & GLORIA BALAGUE

Introduction

In this chapter we will attempt to explore the fit between the American Psychological Association Ethical Principles and Code of Conduct (2002) and the real issues faced by applied sport psychologists. These principles are very applicable to the independent practitioner who sees mainly athletes in his or her private practice, but they may not suit the sport psychologist whose job is to provide services to a club, federation, or other organization. The task for the applied consultant is to be aware of the subtle differences and act accordingly. This chapter is an adapted version of an earlier work by the first author (Gordin, 2003).

Every legitimate sport psychology organization around the world operates by a set of ethical principles and a code of conduct. In the United States, the American Psychological Association's (APA) code titled *The Ethical Principles of Psychologists and Code of Conduct (2002)* is the appropriate standard to follow. Also, The Association for the Advancement of Applied Sport Psychology (AAASP) has adopted this set of Ethical Principles with a few modifications as advocated by the APA's code (Etzel & Whelan, 1995; Meyers, 1995).

In the United States there are two organizations that oversee the field of sport psychology: Division 47 of the APA, which represents more of the clinical side of the field, and AAASP, which is more interested in the applied aspect of sport psychology. Petitpas, Brewer, Rivera, and Van Raalte (1994) conducted a survey of AAASP members to ascertain and obtain preliminary data on ethical beliefs and behavior practices of applied sport psychologists. There were few differences noted as a function of gender, professional training, or academic discipline. However, results of open-ended questions indicated that most of the questionable ethical practices cited by respondents to the survey violated APA guidelines in some fashion. These findings provided support to the notion that the field of sport psychology must address the issue of ethics and also institute training in ethics to the applied sport psychologists. In a more recent web-based survey (Etzel, Watson, & Zizzi, 2004), the authors inquired about the ethical beliefs and behaviors of the AAASP membership. Some small to moderate effect sizes were found between men and women, professionals and students, AAASP Certified Consultants and non-Certified Consultants, and individuals from a sport science training background and psychology background. In this chapter it is our intent to cover these principles and to illustrate various case examples of how these principles work in the world of applied sport psychology.

The authors of this chapter have been practicing sport psychology consultants for more than 25 years and our unique perspective will be the primary viewpoint of this chapter. We understand that these ethical issues are seldom black and white in scope. After reading this chapter, you should be prompted to assess your own ethics and values. After all, each individual interprets and makes his/her own operational principles and ethics. In effect, we police ourselves.

Preamble

Sport psychologists fulfill many roles based upon their professional training and expertise. Professionals work diligently to develop a body of professional literature and knowledge based upon good science. Sport psychologists respect the freedom of academic inquiry and individual expression in the practice of sport psychology, whether it is in sport or exercise psychology settings. The statement adopted by the Association for the Advancement of Applied Sport Psychology (AAASP) provides a set of principles designed to protect clients and establish good practice habits. A code of conduct does not ensure competency. It is designed to provide an overview of acceptable practice procedures. AAASP members protect and respect human rights and civil rights, and do not knowingly discriminate unfairly. Members also encourage ethical behavior in the profession among members, students, and supervisees. All principles are followed with each member's personal value and culture and experience embedded in the practice and interpretation of these guidelines.

This preamble serves a purpose for all sport psychology consultants. One must be able to act proactively—not reactively—to potentially harmful situations. Our profession is comprised of individuals with a variety of training experiences. This preamble to a set of ethical guidelines is an attempt to level the field for conduct issues. In this section, a comparison will be made between the consultant trained in sport science and the consultant trained in clinical psychology.

General Principles

There are five general principles of ethics and conduct in the APA code: Beneficence and Non-maleficence, Fidelity and Responsibility, Integrity, Justice, and Respect for People's Rights and Dignity.

Principle A: Beneficence and Non-Maleficence

The first mandate that the code instills is to do good AND do no harm. This includes an obligation to be aware of the possible negative repercussions of working with someone. The timing of an intervention must also be considered: What would be appropriate during a regular session may have a very negative impact if done before a major competition. It also explicitly states that the professional must be aware of his or her own issues, so that they do not interfere or cause any harm to the athlete or team.

Psychologists strive to maintain high standards of competence in their work. They recognize the boundaries of their particular competency. They only provide services that they are qualified to provide based upon adequate training and certification. Practitioners also maintain an updated survey of the scientific evidence of information that is relevant to what they do. Ongoing education remains a must. They also are cognizant of the competencies required to serve a broad constituency of clients.

The origins of the field of sport psychology are imbedded in sport science. Many of the early practitioners were trained in this discipline. It is therefore essential for all to become familiar with ethical dilemmas within psychology. In fact, AAASP requires this area as a competency for certification. However, the diversity of training experiences is beginning to meld sport science with psychology for new sport psychology professionals. It is essential for all to be familiar with both fields. Likewise, if one has not experienced the world of sport from inside or lacks training in the main sport sciences, it is possible for some grievous errors to occur in the practice of good sport psychology. If a clinical psychologist, for instance, blindly applies techniques that have been developed primarily for the clinical setting to sport, it is possible for harm to occur. The typical solutions to clinical issues do not often fit in the sporting environment. The classical, yet absurd, example is that of a baseball player in a hitting slump. The clinical sport psychologist approaches the situation from a pathology model and hypothesizes that there is some neurosis driving the slump. Someone within the organization suggests that the hitter seek the help of an ophthalmologist and it is determined that a prescription change is all that is needed. We must be careful to ask the correct questions prior to delving into treatment. That is not to say that an athlete is immune to psychological problems. After all, athletes are ordinary people performing extraordinary physical feats. A sport psychologist trained in traditional sport science must possess the ability to distinguish true need for intervention when it concerns personal problems, and learn to refer appropriately when necessary. In fact, one of the most important skills is that of identifying the need for outside referral. If a consultant, trained in sport sciences, discovers halfway through the performance enhancement work an issue such as an eating disorder or clinical depression or anxiety, it is essential that a referral be made to a professional with the adequate training. Not to do so would be an ethical violation.

Personal bias must also be recognized and adapted to practice. If, for instance, a sport psychology consultant brings the bias of prior experience with poor coaching into the consulting relationship, then a poor initial relationship with the coach might impede progress with the athlete.

The coach/athlete relationship is sacred in sport. If the sport psychologist places himself/herself in between the coach and athlete, then failure will occur. The consultant will be dismissed and the athlete loses. Moreover, the consultant trained in sport science must recognize his/her lack of training in more clinically related procedures and refrain from experimenting with these procedures. This environment is delicate and does not lend itself to experimentation for the sake of training. We have found it invaluable over the years to have a group of colleagues with whom we can share concerns and gather a professional consultation concerning biases. We would encourage all that consult to develop a peer group that will serve this very purpose.

One of the controversial issues within sport psychology that falls inside the competence code is that of psychological assessment. First of all, let us state a personal bias concerning this issue. We have used and continue to use psychological assessment over the past 25 years. We will follow the lead of Henschen (1997), who has argued that the question should not be whether testing should be used but rather who should test and under what guidelines. The training of all future and current sport psychology consultants should include psychological assessment. In our field, this has been a bitter dispute. We also believe that all sport psychology professionals assess in one way or another (i.e., subjective or objective). Psychological testing is not a panacea or an end in itself; rather it is a skill to be utilized to help athletes. It is unfortunate that the skill of psychological testing has been mystified in our profession. If one is merely trying to obtain information that will aid in helping the athlete, then it is more than useful. One might argue that the APA's guidelines are the only appropriate guidelines to follow when administering tests. However, we believe that some additional considerations are warranted. We would advocate the following guidelines in utilizing tests in sport psychology.

1. The individual being tested has the right to know why he/she is being tested and how the information will be utilized (with whom test results will be discussed and what will be discussed).

2. The athlete has the right to know the conclusions based upon test results. The sport psychologist has the responsibility to communicate the results in a way that is appropriate and understandable to the athlete. Avoid the use of professional and clinical jargon.

3. The reports are given only to people who are able to interpret them and with the expressed permission of the test taker (athlete).

4. The tester must possess the appropriate training in administering and evaluating tests.

5. The sport psychologist should always administer the test face-to-face and explain beforehand why the tests are given and to whom the results will be shared.

6. Confidentiality must always be respected.

7. The testing results should always be triangulated and substantiated with the athlete. Observations and incongruencies should be resolved

8. The instrument should be adequate to the situation. Using a test normed in clinical settings to predict behavior in an athletic setting may not be appropriate. Validity of the test for sport psychology purposes must be established (Nideffer, 1981).

Psychological assessment is only one tool to use to gather pertinent information about athletes. Attending training sessions, observing competitive situations, and conducting personal interviews are also necessary and desirable actions before making decisions about interventions. If one follows the rudimentary professional guidelines mentioned, then one possesses a valuable tool to help the client. An illustration will perhaps demonstrate the concept of abuse of competence issues. The first author of this chapter was once working with a very prominent professional on the PGA Tour and had traveled to the U.S. Open to observe his play. At this point in the relationship, the two had been working approximately two years together. The golfer was rather distraught at the idea that he had "flunked" a psychological test. A sport psychologist had approached him to take a psychological test. The golfer showed us the test results that were scored and left in his locker by the psychologist. A "psychological profile" disclosed that he had a lower than average profile on several subscales of the test when compared with the average profile of excellent players. We had to interpret the results so that he understood the measurement error and the problems with averaging psychological data. We had to reassure him that he was ready to play. The testing procedures were unethical and potentially very harmful on the part of the sport psychologist. This psychologist either did not understand the

ethical competence issues of psychological testing or was ignorant of the existing guidelines. Information pertaining to psychological testing should always be presented face to face with the client in terms understandable to the athlete. Also, when information is shared, it should cause no harm. This is not to mention the idea of testing an athlete without asking if he/she was in an ongoing relationship with another sport psychologist.

Another area of concern is the competence issues within team sports. An applied sport psychologist usually deals in areas of team dynamics, group dynamics, conflict resolution, team motivation issues, general counseling issues, and assessment. Clinical sport psychologists generally deal with clinical issues of individual athletes that are affecting team performance and assessment for diagnostic purposes. Occasions might arise when the question is posed, how is an individual's behavior affecting the good of the team? Other issues encountered include coaching staff issues that are affecting team performance. In our work with USA Track and Field, the National Team staff is assigned based upon merit and service within the organization. Some have athletes on the team and some do not. All are usually head coaches at their respective institutions and all are used to being the boss. One of the most valuable services that can be provided to this group of dedicated coaches is to help them become a team within a team. The pressures of the Olympic Games upon these individuals are immense. Some see this assignment as the capstone of their careers. All are dedicated to doing a great job and to helping the team succeed in one of the most visible stages in sport. We have found, along with our colleagues, that if we are to be successful as a team, a considerable amount of time must be spent on this endeavor. A consultant must have sufficient training to be able to handle this group of coaches as a facilitator as well as a member of the group. Such questions will arise such as, Who is the client? Who invited me into this setting? How do I best serve them? What is the issue(s)? Where did they come from? What is the ultimate goal? To have a strong team? To win games? To win people? What price is the team willing to pay for the goals set? The consultant who accepts an assignment to work with a team during a major competition (i.e., Olympic Games) must be competent in group issues and interventions. The consultant must also be able to make decisions quickly in pressure situations. Sport does not always provide the time necessary to thoroughly discuss all options and one must act quickly and well or disaster might occur. Part of the solution comes from having a philosophy of service delivery that is set prior to the work with the team. Is your philosophy service or self-service? Are you the one on stage or are you willing to be off stage? Do you have strong foundational beliefs in the worth of each group member? Can you deal with the seduction of success and the agony of failure? Until a consultant has tested these beliefs in the heat of the battle we do not believe he/she can be as effective. Likewise, the Olympic Games are not a time to train yourself and experiment with your foundational beliefs.

This last statement has powerful practical implications: Many professionals find the field of sport psychology attractive and decide that is something they want to do. Students close to graduation have clear ideas about their ideal professional position. In many cases they all want to work with elite level or professional athletes, despite the fact that they do not have experience in this environment. Many of the interventions and textbooks are based on studies conducted with college athletes and the issues; pressures and needs of the elite/professional world are different. It is not ethical to want to start at the top if the expertise and training are not there. Working one's way up the ladder of sport performance is a good way to gain understanding about the complexity of issues. Professionals would be well trained if they have worked with communities, colleges, elite junior athletes, etc., in a regular progression. It is also possible to bring experience from other fields, such as expertise working with executives, which could transfer to understanding of some of the issues elite coaches face. We do not believe that ours is the only path, but we strongly believe that there must be a learning path before one works with elite athletes. As Vernacchia (1990) puts it, "the stakes are much higher at this level."

In summary, it is important to meet the competency issue by knowing what you know, as well as what you don't know. We should strive to maintain high standards of competence while recognizing our limitations and setting boundaries upon our use of techniques and intervention methods. We should continually seek opportunity for continuing education and take all appropriate precautions to protect the welfare of those with whom we work, whether it is with individual or team sport athletes. Practicing beyond one's expertise is a serious breach of ethical boundaries.

Principle B: Fidelity and Responsibility

Psychologists establish relationships of trust with those with whom they work. They are aware of their professional and scientific responsibilities to society and to the specific communities in which they work. Psychologists uphold professional standards of conduct, clarify their professional roles and obligations, accept appropriate responsibility for their behavior, and seek to manage conflicts of interest that could lead to exploitation or harm. Psychologists consult with, refer to, or cooperate with other professionals and institutions to the extent needed to serve the best interests of those with whom they work. They are concerned about the ethical compliance of their colleagues' scientific and professional conduct. Psychologists strive to contribute a portion of their professional time for little or no compensation or personal advantage.

Sport psychology consultants are responsible for safeguarding the public from members who are deficient in ethical conduct. They uphold professional standards of conduct and accept appropriate responsibility for their behavior. We consult with, refer to, or cooperate with other professionals and institutions to the extent needed to serve the best interests of the recipients of their services. We must safeguard the public's trust in our profession. When appropriate, we consult with colleagues in order to prevent, avoid, or terminate unethical conduct. In essence, this is a personal as well as professional obligation for our field to survive with credibility. Some professional organizations such as the AAASP and the APA Division 47 have taken the leadership role in establishing this trust. Very simply, we must conduct ourselves in such a way that brings credit to the field. We do not exploit relationships with athletes for personal gain thorough media or publicity. We do not exploit relationships for personal gratification or jeopardize the safety and well-being of our clients. Nor do we discriminate in any way.

It is our intent to put ourselves out of a job with a client. That is, a goal of ours is to make them self-sufficient and independent. Once these athletes have achieved independence, then the relationship is appropriately terminated or changed. Coaches with whom we are consulting are the real sport psychologists. We are consultants. Therefore, it seems logical that the role of mental consultant be turned over to the coaches and the athletes. We are truly a resource and therefore try very diligently not to establish a dependency model in the relationship. We do not terminate service prematurely; rather we wean the coach and athlete to perform independently. We often joke that our eligibility has expired anyway. In our 25 years of consulting, one of the biggest errors we see in consultants is trying too hard to do too much. It is not done in a premeditated fashion but out of the need to help. It seems plausible that this could happen. This is where a well-placed consultation with a colleague can contain the problem rather than let it fester and explode.

A related issue, but in the opposite direction, is that of professional relationships abruptly terminated with the athletes because a change in management terminates the consultant's involvement with the team. It is the ethical responsibility of the psychologist to provide alternatives for continuity of care and, again, this is an issue best addressed at the very beginning of the relationship.

Always seek to be honest, fair, and respectful of all people with whom you work. Clarify your roles as well as define the obligations you accept. Finally, avoid improper and potentially harmful dual relationships and conflicts of interest (Moore, 2003). In appearance, the issue of dual relationships seems like an easy one to avoid, but in reality it presents many opportunities for conflict, specifically for sport psychology consultants. A large number of consultants are employed in college or university settings and divide their time between teaching and providing services to athletes. It is highly likely that at some point a consultant will have, as a student in class, one or several athletes with whom he or she is working or has been working. The athlete may feel like he or she deserves special treatment because the consultant

knows his or her difficulties and stressors. The consultant may feel some pressure to make sure that the athlete's grade in the class does not render him or her ineligible or that the working relationship is not damaged by the academic demands. In either case, it is a situation that merits forethought and clarification. In some schools there is no alternative, as there is only one instructor for sport psychology and applied work. In this case the issue must be addressed beforehand and the rules clarified in advance. The situation is similar to that experienced by psychologists practicing in rural areas, where it is very likely, for example, that one's client is also one's banker. In those cases it is important that both parties agree to how roles are going to be separated. For example, the consultant may agree that in class she or he will address the athlete more formally, by last name, if that is how the other students are addressed. The consultant will refrain from asking about class assignments during sessions and the athlete will agree to similar rules.

In the field of sport psychology boundaries are more fluid than in the field of clinical or counseling psychology. The strict application of APA rules may not suit the field, but that just makes it more important for us to think about the topic and come up with our own set of ethical guidelines.

Psychologists in private practice have very clear boundaries and in most cases do not need to socialize with their clients; but that is not the case for psychologists who travel with a team. Sport psychologists often are expected or even required to attend technical meetings, social situations such as awards banquets or team dinners, and not doing so would likely damage the working relationship.

Another of the dual relationships that must be avoided is the establishment of a sexual relationship with the client. This question is not specific to the sports domain, but there are several elements in sport psychology that make this issue even more relevant. The boundaries in sport psychology work are different than those in clinical practice: We often travel with our clients, spend a lot of time together when not directly working, and social interactions are unavoidable. By definition, consultants working in sport psychology will be working with a population that expresses itself physically, a population of young, often physically fit, and beautiful clients.

Attraction, even sexual attraction, is a normal consequence, as is the desire to be associated with someone famous or rich (record holder, gold medalist, professional athlete, etc.). The ethical question is then to ensure that professionals in our field have the necessary tools in their training and professional development to handle such feelings appropriately.

Principle C: Integrity

One should seek to promote integrity in science, teaching, and practice of one's profession. Sport psychology consultants should be honest and fair in describing qualifications, services, products, fees, and one should refrain from making statements that are false, misleading, or deceptive. To the extent feasible, one should clarify to all parties the roles they are performing and the obligations adopted. Especially, potentially harmful dual relationships should be avoided.

The player-coach-sport psychologist relationship can be a very fruitful one. The key to making this work is to clarify from the onset the various roles. That is, who is the client? Who is paying the consulting fee? How do these activities interact and mesh? In the field of clinical or counseling psychology, these roles are usually identified and very few questions arise. In the field of sport, however, these roles can sometimes conflict. If one has been hired by a sports franchise, is one part of management or an independent contractor? How does information get transferred within the organization? When establishing our relationships within team sports, we operate on the premise that the athlete is our client. This is true even if they do not pay our consultation fees directly. If management does not like this arrangement, then a referral is made to a colleague. This is the only ethical way for us to be effective. We do not consider ourselves part of management; rather our relationship to them is as independent contractors.

However, in sports a consultant cannot alienate oneself from management. Bruce Ogilvie (1977) has referred to this situation as walking the razor's edge. There is some art to walking this razor that does not fit cleanly into the established ethical principles. For instance, if management's goals start to interfere with the athlete's goals you have a decision to make that is crucial to the success of the relationship. We always go back to the first author's rule that the athlete is the client. We can use him/her as a clearinghouse for information without breaking coaching confidentiality. We have found that if an athlete trusts you and believes that you can help, then cooperation in easily conferred upon the consultant. However, our caution remains. Do not cross the coach in the role as coach without examining the consequences. Once again, this is an art more than a science. One must operate in an ethical framework while still realizing that the sporting orientation and obligations are different than many other settings. A clear mission in sport, for instance, is winning. How does one cope with this? Philosophically a consultant must make clear her/his way of viewing the world of sport before he/she enters the arena. If a consultant does not fully understand the consequences of viewing the sports world as it exists, then conflicts can arise constantly.

The field of psychology considers the role of providing psychological services to a third party and requires that issues of goals and professional responsibilities be shared at the onset of the consulting relationship. It is possible that the organization itself is the client, and not the athletes, and a conflict may arise when their goals diverge, but ethical difficulties will be avoided if this information is clear to all parties from the beginning (APA, 2002).

With the emergence of our field has come a competitive marketplace. Within this marketplace, there have emerged consultants who have misrepresented their qualifications and expertise. It is essential that we protect the integrity of our domain of practice. We often tell our classes, our audiences at national training camps, and anyone anytime we get the chance that if you meet a sport psychology consultant that promises you miracles, then you must run as fast as you can in the other direction. This is where the referral process is important in our field. It is also extremely important to represent our services well and educate the various consumers. We do not promise them anything except that together we will help them perform nearer their potential.

In this world of marketing and public relations, advertisement is seen as an important piece of the "business plan." A consultant in private practice may need to advertise in order to have a successful practice. Ethical issues may arise, as stated earlier, if the person makes false claims, but there are other specific concerns in our field, which make other practices, acceptable in business, questionable in psychology. Specifically the use of "testimonials," which is a common marketing practice, may pose problems in sport psychology. First of all, it requires giving up the confidentiality of the relationship; second, asking someone who has been a client may put the person in a position where they feel they cannot decline, thus creating an ethical dilemma. The athlete who felt his or her work with the consultant was helpful is likely to feel thankful and be willing to do something that is clearly good for the consultant, when it may not be good for the athlete. Again, we do not think that testimonials are always bad, but we feel that this is an area where caution must be exercised.

Principle D: Justice

Sport psychology consultants accord appropriate respect to the fundamental rights, dignity, and worth of all people. They respect the rights to individual privacy, confidentiality, self-determination, and autonomy. Consultants also are aware of cultural, individual, and role differences with respect to age, ethnicity, race, gender, national origin, religion, sexual orientation, disability, language, and socioeconomic status. Consultants do not condone discrimination in any form. Also, consultants seek to contribute to the welfare of those with whom they interact in a professional way in situations of power relationships and are accountable to the community in which they work. Once again, these principles lead to an awareness of exploitative relationships, misleading the public, and complying with the law. Many ethical principles seem self-evident. However, unless one is cognizant and observant of one's behavior, then ethics can be overlooked. Our credo over the years has been athletes first, winning second. Each one of us needs to have these credos to live by. Sport ethics is an interesting area of study. Vernacchia (1990) has alluded to false sport ethics in his writings. Several of these are worth noting. The "I agree with you in principle, but..." sport ethic is of special note. As in any counseling relationship, what follows the "but" is usually the most interesting part

of the statement. "The loophole ethic" is evident in the world of sport where the end justifies the means. The use of ergogenic aids supports the "high tech/low conscience" ethic. All of us in the profession must operationalize our ethics and explore our own biases. If we do, we stand a very good chance of "being ethical."

Principle E: Respect for People's Rights and Dignity

One of the greatest challenges is to mold a collection of individuals into a group without sacrificing all individuality within the group. One of the tasks faced by all coaches of team sports and sport psychologists working with team sports is to accomplish group synergy without sacrificing individual rights. One must be concerned with team goals and dreams as well as individual accomplishments and individual success within group success. We believe this is important in youth team sports as well as professional team sports. In youth sports, these emerging athletes are primarily involved to have fun. Yet, leaders are also concerned with group progress toward team goals. How does one balance the two ideals? In professional team sports, winning is the franchise goal. What are the goals of the members of the group? All of these concerns fall under respect for people's dignity and rights. In the field of sport, there is a saying "There is no I in Team." However, we must remember there is an "I" in Win. We must nourish the individual as well as the team.

The right to privacy, confidentiality, self-determination, and autonomy are specifically listed by the APA Ethical Principles of Psychologists. In the field of sport psychology, there are several situations that may challenge some of these rights. **Confidentiality:** The consultant working with a team or organization may find him/herself in situations where an athlete reveals information that would greatly impact the performance of the team or club, such as existence of an injury, a very low level of motivation, or great levels of stress. If the consultant has a good working relationship with the coach, as is to be expected, he/she is likely to feel increased pressure to disclose such information to the coach or to managers. Sometimes, just in the day-to-day contact, innocent questions from the coach—such as "how is XYZ doing?"—may put the consultant in a difficult position: On the one hand, he or she wants to be of help to the coach, on the other hand the athlete's confidentiality must be respected. Being aware of these issues and clarifying the central nature of trust in the consultant-athlete relationship *in the very beginning* is essential to prevent difficult situations later on. If the athlete discloses information such as awareness of a new injury or extreme anxiety, and the consultant feels that the athlete's performance is likely to be detrimental to the team, the best course of action is to encourage the athlete to share this with the coach and problem solve together. An elite level athlete at the Olympic Games revealed that he had hurt himself in the qualifying rounds but did not want anyone to know. He was scheduled to be a relay member. If he competed poorly he was likely to hurt the national team's chances of a medal. At the same time the athlete felt that being part of the Olympic relay was a great financial asset to himself. The discussion centered on helping the athlete understand the consequences for himself and for others, including the negative label it may generate if word got around that he knew he was hurt and did not disclose it. Eventually the athlete had a meeting with the coach and the physician and was taken out of the relay. If he had refused to share that information with the coach, the consultant ethically could not have shared it. For licensed psychologists the issue of confidentiality is not just an ethical one, but a legal one as well.

In sports, as indicated earlier, it is possible that the organization itself is the client. This must be made explicit to the individual athletes from the beginning because then the information has to be shared with the client, the club. Individual athletes need to make an informed decision about the information they share, and that requires they know who will have access to that information.

Confidentiality When Working with Minors

This is a special case with the issue of confidentiality. As consultants, we often work with young athletes, most often referred by the coach or parents. Do young athletes have the same right to confidentiality? According to the law they do, and the APA recommended age limit is 12 and above, even though some state laws have different cut-off points. Still, the age limit does not entirely resolve the issue.

Parents bring the child in and pay for the sessions. They want to know what is going on. How much to share? Gustafson and McNamara (1995) provided the following guidelines. The therapist should consider several points when deciding the degree of confidentiality afforded a minor: (1) the age of the child, (2) the needs and desires of the child, (3) the concerns of the parents, (4) the particular presenting problem, and (5) specific state laws regulating confidentiality with minors. Since age is only a rough indicator of a child's cognitive abilities, an assessment of the child's comprehension level should be carried out. In many cases, periodic family sessions may be appropriate due to the nature of the problem. In those cases the consultant should decide jointly with the young client the specific information to be shared, the purpose, etc. Again, clarifying confidentiality and its limits should always be done in the very first meeting for all parties concerned: parents, coaches, athletes, etc.

Mandated Visit to the Consultant

A specific issue that emerges occasionally, related to respecting the rights and dignity of people, is the issue of athletes, young and old, who are "sent" to the consultant by the coach. It is important to clarify that working with the consultant must be a personal decision and the athlete must be given the freedom to make the decision for him or herself as to whether to talk or not. The consultant must recognize that the coach has the power to "send" athletes to the consultant, but the coach has to be informed that the consultant cannot make anyone talk or disclose information against his or her will.

The first author was once sent an athlete who acted out in practice. He was thrown out of practice because he had shouted at the coach and thrown a water cooler across the floor. The coach called and asked if I would see the athlete about his anger problem. I refused because I did not think the athlete would see me as part of the solution at that time, but as part of the problem. I stated I would see him at a later date if he felt inclined to seek help.

Informed Consent

Traditionally, sport psychology has not addressed the issue of "informed consent." It is important to clarify at the onset of services all the specifics involved, such as financial issues, specific descriptions of length and place of services, confidentiality rules, and any specific responsibilities of both the client and the professional. Only when all this information is available can the client make an informed decision about consenting to treatment or not. If any research may be conducted with the client's data, even if it is reported anonymously, the client has to specifically consent to it. If psychological tests will be administered, the issue of who has access to the test results should also be covered (Zuckerman, 1997). Informed consent allows for a chance to clarify possible issues before they become a problem and protects both the client and the practitioner.

Special Interest Topics

Internet Consulting

The use of the Internet and computer technology in the field of applied sport psychology is becoming more prevalent. With this added dimension to consulting comes concerns about the ethical usage of this medium for consulting purposes. This Internet usage can have both positive and negative effects upon the field and upon the clients served. It is the intent of this section to draw attention to both benefits and potential dangers with the increased usage of this technology. The International Society of Sport Psychology (ISSP) has published a position statement regarding Internet usage. It is the intent of this section of the chapter to use this statement as guideline for discussion of the issue. (ISSP Position Stand on The Use of the Internet in Sport Psychology, 2002). The authors rightfully point out that not much empirical evidence has been collected in the field of applied sport psychology as to the efficacy of this medium for performance enhancement purposes. That is, does this service provision method equate to face-to-face quality? Do clients benefit more from this medium presentation than from more traditional methods of delivery? How can we, as practitioners, be assured that the clients are actually receiving and benefiting from this method of service delivery? Some limited research is cited in the field of clinical psychology in the position statement but, to date, no definitive studies have been conducted in applied sport psychology. The position statement also mentions several potential uses of the Internet, such as

marketing, distance learning and supervision opportunities, counseling and performance enhancement advice, locating practitioners and referrals, and serving as a medium for discussion.

Marketing

The use of marketing of services on the Internet has experienced significant growth within the past 10 years. There are numerous sites devoted exclusively to service provision and advertisement utilizing the Internet. Dissemination of information has also experienced growth because of technological advances. This growth was facilitated, especially to disadvantaged groups, clients, and consumers who would otherwise be unable to partake of new information in the field. The plethora of home pages, web sites, bulletin boards, and search engines has made the field more visible to the general public at large. Also, more outlets for book purchases have been created.

Distance Learning Opportunities

More and more opportunities for the study of applied sport psychology have emerged due to Internet access. Several universities and colleges, as well as independent providers, have established degree programs via the Internet. These websites have emerged within the different medium opportunities, including interactive groups and email chat rooms, and access to professionals has experienced an increase. Supervision opportunities have increased as well. These advances have aided AAASP, which requires a supervised practicum for certification purposes.

Performance Enhancement

The ability to work with clients over the World Wide Web has reached a heightened usage. The sport psychology professional can do intake interviews, psychometric assessment, and other preparatory work prior to ever meeting the athlete. Also, correspondence with athletes has been facilitated by the use of electronic media.

Referral and Discussion Groups

A number of websites and discussion groups in sport psychology have emerged within the past 10 years. The various National Governing Bodies (NGBs) within the spectrum of the United States Olympic Committee (USOC) have utilized the Internet for referral bases, and online discussion groups are utilized to provide a forum for dialogue and information dissemination as well. The number of list-serves and collaborations among professionals has increased.

Potential Problems Associated with Internet Consulting

The main problem with Internet consulting appears to be confidentiality. Any information transmitted over the Internet should not be considered confidential. There is no way to ensure the confidentiality of personal communications at this time. All assessment procedures utilized should be accompanied with valid disclaimers and the accompanying manual should always be distributed on the website. Currently, the transmission of service provision across state boundaries leaves the profession in a quandary about appropriate regulations pertaining to licensure and state regulations. What are the effects of the client/practitioner relationship when given via the medium of the Internet? At this time, no valid and reliable empirical evidence has been produced to answer this question. Are text-based interactions more effective than face-to-face interactions via electronic media? How can empathy be expressed via the written word as compared to facial expression and body language? The research is well developed in the counseling literature regarding proxemics. How does this translate via the electronic medium? Can clients become addicted to the Internet? Is the information that is available on the Internet receiving any kind of peer review? All of these questions have yet to be answered in a fashion that leaves us in a foolproof world.

The athletes and coaches that we serve at the present time cannot be assured protection under the present system in place. The ethical considerations at a minimum would include a proposed set of guidelines. The ISSP has developed such a set of guidelines to be considered. These guidelines include at a minimum privacy of information as provided by secured sites. That is, the providers should ensure that they use the latest encryption devices for any online service provision. The use of general online information should only be used with the disclaimer of the limited use of such information. The providers should

use steps to ensure client confidentiality and also include client waiver agreements within the sites themselves (Watson et al., 2002). It is also important that appropriate liability insurance be obtained for Internet service delivery and that any state statutes are followed implicitly. If you are maintaining a website, it is your responsibility to maintain and ensure the accuracy of all published materials. It is also the responsibility of the consultant to notify the potential consumers of the limits of the site, such as security, information concerning credentials, waivers, client identification risks, and any other concerns regarding service delivery and access to the website. The consumer should also be properly informed of the length of any saved materials and accurately represent the security of this information and how it will be safeguarded, including the transfer of confidential information to third parties.

When an applied sport psychologist decides to initiate an online consulting relationship, several boundaries must be established. The appropriateness of the relationship should be considered. Also, a counseling plan should be developed, including scheduled contact times, alternative communication plans, alternative counselors, and local backup. It is also of utmost importance to establish the credibility of the client. That is, how will the consultant verify that it is truly the client who is receiving the information (Watson et al., 2002)?

Packaged Programs

The field of applied sport psychology is filled with packaged programs that were developed for intervention. The advantages of these programs are that they are available without much consultation with the practitioner and require little face-to-face consultation. The athlete has the freedom to proceed at his/her own speed and the mental training can be learned in a more efficient manner. Most of these programs are available on audio or videotape. The athlete can carry the program on trips and work out of the comfort of his or her own home. These programs develop independence from the applied sport psychologist and teach the athletes responsibility for their own care. The disadvantages include the impersonal nature of the contact, the "one size fits all" syndrome, and the probability that procrastination and boredom might develop in the athlete's mental training. We have seen some success with these types of programs for the stated reasons that were given. However, without adequate follow-up with the applied sport psychologist, these types of programs do not work well.

This chapter will conclude with some practical suggestions for selecting a sport psychology consultant. These suggestions were developed by the AAASP (1998). Athletes in team sports as well as coaches of team sports often are interested in contacting someone to help them with ethical decisions within the team sport context. Such issues as dealing with problematic athletes within team sport organizations, enhancing the moral and ethical orientation of youth sport athletes, and helping athletes make decisions related to life challenges are only a few reasons for contacting a sport psychology consultant regarding team sport issues. Consultants can provide information regarding communication issues, team building, cohesion factors, and motivation factors within groups among other services. One of the best ways to select a qualified consultant is by word of mouth. If you talk to athletes and coaches who have worked with a sport psychology professional, you have an opportunity to hear about the qualifications of the ones who are good. Sport psychology professionals are somewhat like coaches in this regard. If you are asked back or if you have a lot of work, this is an excellent indicator of your effectiveness. Another way to obtain information is to consult your local university or athletic department, as well as consulting with the major sport psychology organizations in your country. In North America, three excellent sources are the AAASP, APA Division 47, and the USOC Sport Psychology Registry.

In conclusion, each individual is responsible for his or her ethical behavior. We, in the field of sport psychology, are held to a higher standard. This chapter has been an attempt to highlight these principles and to provide food for thought concerning this topic. It is our wish that all of you enjoy your experience in the field of sport. The opportunity for growth is tremendous.

References

Association for the Advancement of Applied Sport Psychology (1998). *Sport psychology: A guide to choosing a sport psychology professional.* Brochure. Washington, D.C.

Ethical principles of psychologists and code of conduct. (2002). *The American Psychological Association.*

Etzel, E., & Whelan, J. (1995, Summer). Considering ethics. *Association for the Advancement of Applied Sport Psychology, 10,* 25-26.

Etzel, E., Watson, J., & Zizzi, S. (2004). A web-based survey of AAASP members' ethical beliefs and behaviors in the new millennium. *Journal of Applied Sport Psychology, 16*(3), 236-250.

Gordin, R. D. (2003). *Ethical issues in team sports.* In R. Lidor & K. Henschen (Eds.). The psychology of team sports (pp. 57-68). Morgantown, WV. Fitness Information Technology.

Gustafson, K., & McNamara, R. (1995). Confidentiality with minor clients: Issues and guidelines for therapists. In D. Bersoff (Ed) *Ethical conflicts in psychology.* American Psychological Association, Washington, DC.

Henschen, K. (1997, Winter). Point-counterpoint: Using psychological assessment tools. *Association for the Advancement of Applied Sport Psychology, 12,* 15-16.

Meyers, A. (1995). Ethical principles of AAASP. Association for the *Advancement of Applied Sport Psychology, 10,* 15.

Moore, Z. E. (2003) Ethical dilemmas in sport psychology: Discussion and recommendations for practice. *Professional Psychology: Research and Practice, 34*(6), 601-610.

Nideffer, R. M. (1981). *The ethics and practice of applied sport psychology.* Ithaca, New York: Mouvement Publications.

Ogilvie, B. (1977). Walking the perilous path of team psychologist. *The Physician and Sports Medicine, 5,* 62-68.

Petitpas, A. J., Brewer, B., Rivera, P., & Van Raalte, J. (1994). Ethical beliefs and behaviors in applied sport psychology: The AAASP ethics survey. *Journal of Applied Sport Psychology, 6,* 135-151.

Vernacchia, R. A. (1990, April). *The death of sport: Ethical concerns of drugs and performance.* A paper presented at the American Alliance for Health, Physical Education, Recreation and Dance National Convention, New Orleans, LA.

Watson, J. C., Tenebaum, G., Lidor, R., & Alfermann, D. (2002). *ISSP position statement on the use of the Internet in sport psychology.* Retrieved May 8, 2002, from http://www.issponline.org

Zuckerman, E. L. (1997). *The paper office: Forms, guidelines and resources* (2nd. Ed.) New York: Guilford Press

Closing Remarks

This volume represents an initial attempt to address the current status of and perspectives taken in applied sport and exercise psychology research. Another major aspiration of the *Handbook* was to provide ideas for future work and, perhaps more importantly, propose additional ways in which research and practice could be further joined as we move the field forward. With respect to such broad purposes, the reader should consider this volume to be just "the tip of the iceberg" in terms of a much larger and divergent discipline. We attempted to do justice to the depth and diversity of work conducted regarding the targeted topics, knowing it would be difficult to accomplish such a monumental task in the pages allotted. Moreover, we acknowledge that there are areas of study and application within the field that did not receive attention here. Finally, it should be stated that the chapters within this *Handbook* are primarily oriented to applied work in competitive sport in contrast to unstructured exercise. Indeed, it could be argued that enough work has been done recently that a handbook focused on sport and a second compilation on exercise are warranted.

As reflected in the endorsement of the International Society of Sport Psychology (ISSP), cultural diversity of the editors, and inclusion of work from colleagues from around the world, there was a strong effort to make this volume international in perspective. With respect to the latter feature, the chapters contained within represent contributions from authors from four continents. Thus, it was our hope that the overview of research in applied sport and exercise psychology afforded does reflect, to some degree, national and cultural differences in approaches to applied sport and exercise psychology research. It is important to note, however, that the perspectives of colleagues in the field from Africa are unfortunately missing in this volume. In 2004, the first International Congress of Sport Psychology in Africa was organized in Marrakech. The title of this Congress was "Introducing Sport Psychology to Africa" and a broad range of topics that focused on the science and application of sport and exercise psy-

chology were presented by numerous African colleagues. It was clear from this Congress that sport psychology researchers and practitioners in Africa have a lot to offer to the international literature and their ever-growing efforts should be considered in the next edition of the *Handbook*.

The various contributions contained in this volume give some insight into what is meant when we refer to "applied" research in sport and exercise psychology. In some cases, we see the progression from highly controlled laboratory studies, to field research, to work that is truly applied-oriented. Overall, the chapters centered on applied techniques and programs demonstrate how theory and empirical research lay the bases for intervention efforts in sport and exercise psychology. It is also evident, from the *Handbook's* contributions, that applied research does not only involve testing hypotheses but also generating hypotheses for subsequent research and potential theory development or modification. Taken in their totality, the applied research work described in this volume allows insight into areas where we have more or less evidence regarding sound and accountable practice.

Regarding the future of professional practice in applied sport and exercise psychology, the last chapters in this volume particularly point to the importance of developing internationally accepted standards for the education and certification of sport and exercise psychologists. This is a mission of the ISSP and there is a hope that one day the ISSP can serve as an umbrella forum for regional, national, and continental organizations, provide coordination across these various programs, and foster cooperation in the offering of continuing education in the field. In this way, the integrity and visibility of applied sport and exercise psychology may prosper worldwide.

Index

About the Editors

Dr. Dieter Hackfort

Dr. Dieter Hackfort is a professor of sport and exercise psychology and is currently serving as the dean of the Department for Quality Management, Education, and Social Affairs (QESA) in ASPIRE Academy for Sports Excellence in Doha, Qatar. He received his doctoral degree in 1983 from the German Sports University. In 1986, he was a visiting professor at the Center for Behavioral Medicine and Health Psychology at the University of South Florida in Tampa, Florida, and received tenure at the University of Heidelberg. From 1991 to 2004, Dr. Hackfort was the head of the Institute for Sport Science at the University AF of Munich. Since 1986, he has served as a counselor for professional performers and athletes of various sports at the Olympic Centers in Germany. Dr. Hackfort is the editor of several national (Germany) and international book series in sport science and sport and exercise psychology. Since 1996, he has served as the editor of the *International Journal of Sport and Exercise Psychology* (IJSEP). His research has been published in 25 books and edited volumes, and

in more than 150 contributions in national and international journals. His main research interests are in (1) stress, emotions, and anxiety with respect to its functional meaning for action regulation in sports with an emphasis on elite sports, (2) self presentation with a focus on emotion presentation, (3) career management in elite sports, and (4) the development of a mental test and training program. These special issues are connected with the development of an action theory approach in sport and exercise psychology and the development of psycho-diagnostic measurements based on this conceptual framework. In 1984, Dr. Hackfort received an award from the German Sports Federation for the best research in the social sciences 1983-84 (Carl-Diem-Plaque). In 2001, he received the Honor Award of the International Society of Sport Psychology (ISSP) in recognition of significant contributions to national and international sport psychology through leadership, research, and personal service. In 1999, he was appointed Honor Professor of Wuhan Institute of Physical Education, China.

Dr. Joan L. Duda

Dr. Joan L. Duda is a professor of sport psychology in the School of Sport and Exercise Sciences at the University of Birmingham, United Kingdom. She is past-president of the Association for the Advancement of Applied Sport Psychology (AAASP), has been a member of the executive boards of the North American Society for the Psychology of Sport and Physical Activity, the Sport Psychology Academy, Division 47 of the American Psychological Association, and the International Society for Sport Psychology. She is currently on the Scientific Committee of the European Congress of Sport Science. Dr. Duda has previously served as the editor of the Journal of Applied Sport Psychology and is on the editorial board of several other leading journals in the field. A Fellow of the Association for the Advancement of Applied Sport Psychology and the American Academy of Kinesiology and Physical Education, Dr. Duda has edited one book (Advances in Sport and Exercise Psychology Measurement in 1998) and has authored more than 170 publications focused on motivation in the physical domain and the psychological aspects of sport and exercise performance and participation. She is certified as a mental skills consultant by AAASP and is listed on the U.S. Olympic Registry. At the University of Birmingham, she works with sport scholars and other elite athletes, and also offers consultation with respect to performance excellence and motivational issues among professional ballet dancers.

Dr. Ronnie Lidor

Dr. Ronnie Lidor is a senior lecturer at both the Zinman College of Physical Education and Sport Sciences at the Wingate Institute and at the Faculty of Education at the University of Haifa (Israel). Since 1997, he has served as the head of the Motor Behavior Laboratory at the Zinman College of Physical Education and Sport Sciences at the Wingate Institute. His main areas of research are (1) learning strategies and skilled performance, (2) cognitive processes in motor skill acquisition, and (3) talent detection and early development in sport. Dr. Lidor has published approximately 90 articles, book chapters, and proceedings chapters in English and Hebrew. His articles have been published in *The Sport Psychologist, Human Performance, Journal of Sports Sciences, International Journal of Sport Psychology, Inter-national Journal of Sport and Exercise Psychology, Psychology of Sport and Exercise, Journal of Aging and Physical Activity, Pediatric Exercise Science,* and *Physical Education and Sport Pedagogy.* He is the senior editor of the books *Sport Psychology: Linking Theory and Practice* (1999), *The World Sport Psychology SourceBook* (3rd ed., 2001), and *The Psychology of Team Sports* (2003) published by Fitness Information Technology (USA). From 1997 to 2001, Dr. Lidor served as president of the Israeli Society for Sport Psychology and Sociology (ISSPS). Since 1997, he has been a member of the Managing Council of the International Society of Sport Psychology (ISSP). In 2001, he was elected as the secretary general of ISSP. He has been the editor of *Movement—Journal of Physical Education and Sport Sciences* (Hebrew) since 1999.

About the Authors

Dorothee Alfermann

Dorothee Alfermann is a professor of sport psychology at the University of Leipzig, Germany. She is co-editor-in-chief of *Psychology of Sport and Exercise*. Her research interests are exercise and health, structure and development of physical self-concept over the life-span, sport career development and career transitions, and gender identity and its relation to social attitudes and behaviours. She published several monographs on sport psychology and gender issues and approximately 100 journal articles and book chapters in English and German.

Mark Anshel

Mark Anshel is a professor of sport and exercise psychology in the Department of Health, Physical Education, and Recreation at Middle Tennessee State University in Murfreesboro, Tennessee. His degrees are from Illinois State University (BS) in physical education, and psychology of human performance from McGill University in Montreal (MA) and Florida State University (PhD). He has authored several books including *Sport Psychology: From Theory to Practice* (2003, 4th ed.), *Concepts in Fitness: A Balanced Approach to Good Health* (2003), and *Aerobics For Fitness* (4th ed., 1998). His primary research interest, on which he has published numerous research articles, concerns coping with acute stress in sport. He is an AAASP certified sport psychology consultant.

Gloria Balague

Gloria Balague started her professional career in her native Barcelona, Spain, at the National Sports Research Center. She obtained her doctorate in clinical and social psychology at the University of Illinois at Chicago, where she is currently a clinical assistant professor. She has worked extensively with athletes and teams, including USA Track & Field, USA Gymnastics, and USA Field Hockey. She served as a sport psychologist at the 1992 and 1996 Olympics. She has presented extensively at international conferences and was Keynote Speaker at the Olympic Conference held in Brisbane in 2000 and also at the European Conference of Sport Psychology in Copenhagen, Denmark, in 2003.

Isabel Balaguer

Isabel Balaguer is an associate professor in the Faculty of Psychology at the University of Valencia, Spain. She teaches graduate and undergraduate courses in social psychology and the social psychological aspects of sport and exercise. In terms of research interests, Isabel has focused on the antecedents and consequences of coach behaviors and the psychosocial predictors of positive youth development and lifestyles in teenagers. She has worked as a mental skills consultant for several years with the Spanish Tennis Federation.

Michael Bar-Eli

Michael Bar-Eli is a professor in the Department of Business Administration, Ben-Gurion University of the Negev, and senior researcher at the Wingate Institute. He studied psychology and sociology in Israel and Germany. Bar-Eli has published more than 100 international refereed journal articles and book chapters, and numerous publications in Hebrew. He has been the associate editor and section editor of two leading sport psychology journals. He served in senior psychology positions of the Israel Defense Forces and has often acted as psychological consultant to elite athletes. Bar-Eli is current senior vice president of ASPASP (Asian South-Pacific Association of Sport Psychology).

Benno Becker Jr.

Benno Becker Jr. is a professor of sport psychology at the Federal University in Porto Alegre, Brazil, and in the Faculty of Sports Medicine at the University of Cordoba, Spain. He has a PhD in psychology from the University of Barcelona, Spain, and a post-graduate degree in sport psychology. He is honorary president of the Brazilian Society of Sport psychology and has published many books in the area of mental training, coaching, and children in sport.

Hans-Albert Birkner

Hans-Albert Birkner holds diplomas in sport science and psychology. He received his PhD in sport science in 2001 from the University AF Munich, Germany. He has been working as a senior lecturer for sport psychology and sport pedagogy and also as a research associate in the field of adventurous, health oriented and high performance sports. He currently is working as the chief officer for Research and Social Affairs at ASPIRE Academy for Sports Excellence in Doha, Qatar.

Bryan Blissmer

Bryan Blissmer is currently an assistant professor in the Department of Kinesiology and a research faculty member at the Cancer Prevention Research Center at the Univertsity of Rhode Island. He received his BS in kinesiology (1996) from the University of Illinois, his MS in health appraisal and enhancement from Miami (Ohio) University (1997), and his PhD in kinesiology, focusing on exercise psychology, from the University of Illinois (2000). His research interests are centered around exercise psychology, focusing on both the determinants and consequences of engaging in regular physical activity. He has been involved in a number of NIH funded research projects to promote physical activity and is currently funded by the American Cancer Society to study multiple behavior change within individuals.

Boris Blumenstein

Boris Blumenstein, PhD, is the head of the Sport Psychology Section and Biofeedback Laboratory of the Ribstein Center for Sport Medicine Sciences at the Wingate Institute, Israel. His current research interests include mental skills training for performance enhancement, the relationship between stress and performance, and the effectiveness of different mental interventions in athletic competition readiness. He has been the sport psychology consultant and advisor to the Soviet and Israeli Olympic teams, including the delegations to Atlanta, Georgia, in 1996; Sydney, Australia, in 2000; and Athens, Greece, in 2004. He is the author of more than 80 referenced journal articles and book chapters, and has presented more than 40 scientific keynote lectures and workshops in international conferences.

Brenda Light Bredemeier

Brenda Light Bredemeier is an associate professor at the University of Missouri at St. Louis. She served as a professor and administrator at the University of California at Berkeley for 20 years, and then moved to the University of Notre Dame, where she founded and co-directed, with David Shields, a center for sports, character, and community. At the University of Missouri at St. Louis, Bredemeier teaches and is helping launch a new center for character development and citizenship education. Her interests involve moral behavior, ethical development, and character education, especially as these relate to women's experiences, responsible citizenship, and social justice.

Britton W. Brewer

Britton W. Brewer, PhD, is a professor of psychology at Springfield College in Springfield, Massachusetts, where he teaches undergraduate and graduate psychology courses and conducts research on psychological aspects of sport injury. He is listed in the United States Olympic Committee Sport Psychology Registry, 2004-2008, and is a certified consultant, Association for the Advancement of Applied Sport Psychology.

Joanne Butt

Joanne Butt is a PhD student at Miami (Ohio) University. Joanne received a BA honors degree in sport and human movement studies at the University of Wales Institute Cardiff before pursuing graduate work at Miami. Her research interests include competitive anxiety and psychological skills training.

Nichola Callow

Nichola Callow is a lecturer at the University of Wales, Bangor. She is a chartered psychologist with the British Psychological Society and an accredited sport psychologist with the British Association of Sport and Exercise Sciences. The main focus of her research is on the cognitive and motivational effects of imagery, but other areas of research include group dynamics in sport and interventions for patient populations.

Albert V. Carron

Albert V. Carron is a professor in the School of Kinesiology at the University of Western Ontario in London, Ontario. His teaching and research focus on group dynamics in sport and exercise groups. Carron has published extensively on such topics as group cohesion, role ambiguity, the home advantage, and exercise adherence.

Jennifer Cumming

Jennifer Cumming is a lecturer in sport and exercise psychology at the University of Birmingham. She received her PhD from the University of Western Ontario, Canada, in 2002. Her research interests are primarily focused in the area of imagery use in sport, exercise, and dance.

Mark A. Eys

Mark A. Eys is an assistant professor in the sport psychology program at Laurentian University in Sudbury, Ontario, Canada. He teaches courses in sport and exercise psychology. His research program focuses on group dynamics in sport and exercise environments, and he has published peer-reviewed articles related to role ambiguity and cohesion in sport as well as social influences related to exercise adherence.

Si Gangyan

Si Gangyan, PhD, is the head sport psychologist at Hong Kong Sports Institute, and also a professor in the Department of Sport Psychology at Wuhan Institute of Physical Education, P. R. China. His current work is primarily with mental training and consultation for elite athletes in Hong Kong, as well as mainland China. He travels with athletes for major international competitions, such as Asian Games, World Championships, and Olympic Games. His research interests include competitive sport psychology and social psychology in sport.

Richard D. Gordin

Richard Gordin is a professor in the Department of Health, Physical Education and Recreation and an adjunct professor in the Department of Psychology at Utah State University. Dr. Gordin has published more than 80 articles and book chapters and has made 300

professional presentations at regional, national, and international conferences. He has been a sport psychology consultant for numerous sports teams, including teams at his university, USA Gymnastics, USA Track and Field, and numerous professionals on the PGA Tour. He recently was a sport psychology consultant for USA Track and Field for the 2004 Olympic Games in Athens, Greece.

Sandy Gordon

Sandy Gordon is a professor of exercise, health, and sport psychology within the School of Human Movement and Exercise Science at the University of Western Australia. In addition to career transitions, his applied research interests include the psychology of sport injuries, emotional labor, mental toughness, and resilience. He is a fellow member of the Australian Psychological Society (APS) and past national chair of the APS College of Sport Psychologists. He currently serves on the national committee of the APS Interest Group on Coaching Psychology.

J. Robert Grove

J. Robert Grove is a professor of exercise, health, and sport psychology within the School of Human Movement and Exercise Science at the University of Western Australia. His academic qualifications include a master's degree in social and organizational psychology from Southern Methodist University and a PhD in movement science from Florida State University. Specific areas of current interest include career transitions, coping processes, psychological aspects of exercise, and physical self-concept.

Lew Hardy

Lew Hardy is a professor at the University of Wales, Bangor. He is a chartered psychologist and a fellow of both the British Association of Sport and Exercise Sciences, and the European College of Sports Scientists. Additionally, he served as the chairperson of the British Olympic Association's Psychology Steering Group for three four-year cycles from 1989 to 2000. He has written more than 100 full-length research publications and co-authored two books.

Keith Henschen

Keith Henschen is a professor at the University of Utah in the Exercise and Sport Science Department.

He has published more than 200 articles and five books. He has served as a sport psychology consultant for many Olympic and professional teams. He is currently president of the International Society of Sport Psychology (ISSP).

Zhijian Huang

Zhijian Huang is an associate professor of sport psychology, as well as the vice-director of the Department of Sport Kinetics and Sport Psychology at the Wuhan Institute of Physical Education (WIPE). From 2000 to 2002, he completed his doctoral project at the UniBw, in Munich, Germany. His dissertation focuses on the career transition process of elite athletes with a cross-cultural perspective. He is a member of the International Society of Sport Psychology (ISSP) and the China Society of Sport Science (CSSS) and presently serves as general secretary of the sport psychology branch of the CSSS.

Gerald J. Jerome

Gerald Jerome received his PhD in kinesiology from the University of Illinois and held a NIA post-doctoral fellow position in the Center of Aging and Health at Johns Hopkins University. His interests center on translational research and theory driven health behavior change programs. Specifically, he is interested in the use of communication technology in multiple health behavior change programs that address chronic disease and other conditions related to aging.

Jay C. Kimiecik

Jay Kimiecik is a professor at Miami (Ohio) University and an author, consultant, and motivational speaker on the topics of self-development, well-being, and physical activity. He is the author of *The Intrinsic Exerciser: Discovering the Joy of Exercise* (Houghton Mifflin, 2002). For the YMCA of the USA, he developed and authored *The YPersonal Fitness Program* (YPF), an exercise behavior change program for the beginning exerciser that is used in more than 500 YMCAs in North America.

David Lavallee

David Lavallee is a reader in sport and exercise psychology in the School of Sport and Exercise Sciences at Loughborough University. His educational qualifications include a master's degree in psychology from Harvard University and a PhD in sport and exercise psychology from the University of Western Australia. He is also a chartered psychologist of the British Psychological Society and is a co-editor of *Career Transitions in Sport: International Perspectives* (Fitness Information Technology, 2000).

Todd M. Loughead

Todd Loughead is an assistant professor in the Department of Kinesiology and Physical Education at McGill University in Montreal, Quebec, Canada. He teaches courses in the area of exercise and sport psychology. He has published numerous peer reviewed journal articles focusing on the social psychology of physical activity, exercise, and sport with an emphasis on group cohesion, adherence behavior, leadership, and aggression.

David X. Marquez

David X. Marquez earned his BS degree in psychology from Loyola University Chicago and his master's and doctoral degrees in kinesiology from the University of Illinois. His area of specialization is exercise psychology, and his primary interests are twofold. His research agenda utilizes a social cognitive framework and includes study of the physical activity levels of Latinos and the physical, cultural, and psychological determinants and outcomes of physical activity of Latinos. His research agenda also includes research with older adults. Specifically, he conducts studies with caregivers examining the psychological, physical, and functional changes as a result of physical activity.

Aidan Moran

Aidan P. Moran is a professor of psychology at the University College, Dublin, Ireland. A Fulbright Scholar, he has published extensively in cognitive and sport psychology on imagery and concentration. His most recent book is *Sport and Exercise Psychology: A Critical Introduction* (2004, Psychology Press). He is a consultant to many of Ireland's elite athletes and teams and is a former official psychologist to the Irish Olympic squad.

Jörn Munzert

Jörn Munzert's general research interests include the study of motor control and learning. Special interests lie in imagery and mental training, verbomotor training, and observational training. He received a degree in psychology and in 1987 his PhD from the Technical University of Berlin, Germany. In 1996, he was appointed associate professor of sport psychology at the University of Giessen. Since 2000, he has served as the chair of Sport Psychology and Movement Science. He presently is president of the German Sport Psychology Association. He is editor of the journal *Zeitschrift fuer Sportpsychologie* and a member of the editorial board of the *International Journal of Sport and Exercise Psychology*. He has authored two books and more than 50 papers and book chapters.

Glenn Newbery

Glenn Newbery is a lecturer in sport psychology at the University of Western Sydney, Australia. Prior to taking this position, he worked as a tennis professional. He has recently completed his doctoral thesis on the topic of motivation in sport. While the topic of motivation is his primary research interest, he is currently involved in projects concerning motor learning, the history and philosophy of psychology, and psychoanalytic psychology.

Michelle M. Patterson

Michelle M. Patterson completed her PhD in the School of Kinesiology, University of Western Ontario, Canada, and her master's degree at the University of Ottawa, Canada. Her general area of interest is sport psychology, with a focus on group dynamics. Specifically, her research involves investigating norms in sport teams and their relationships to other variables within sport teams.

Dietmar M. Samulski

Dietmar Martin Samulski is a professor of sport psychology at the Federal University of Minas Gerais, Brazil. He is the current president of the Brazilian Society of Sport Psychology and a member of the managing council of ISSP. He is also a member of the Brazilian Olympic and Paralympic Committee. He published several books in the area of motivation, mental training, stress control, and paralympic issues.

Andreas Schlattmann

Andreas Schlattmann currently is a senior lecturer and head of the sport psychology laboratory in the Institute for Sport and Exercise Psychology, University FD Munich, Germany. He received his doctoral degree in 1991 from the University of Heidelberg. Since 1986, he has served as a counselor for professional performers and athletes of various sports at the Olympic Centers in Germany (especially in Heidelberg and Munich). His primary research interests center on the development of action theory based empirical methods. His research on emotion, emotion presentation, self-concept, self-presentation, images, and career counseling has been published in 15 books and edited volumes, and in more than 50 contributions in national and international journals.

David Light Shields

David Light Shields, PhD, is an affiliate associate professor in the Division of Teaching and Learning in the College of Education at the University of Missouri at St. Louis. His research has focused on social and moral development, and he also has expertise in citizenship education. He is the author, co-author, or editor of three books and has authored or co-authored more than 30 research articles or book chapters. Previously, he was the co-director of the University of Notre Dame's Mendelson Center for Sports, Character and Community. While in Indiana, he was appointed by Governor Frank O'Bannon to the Governor's Task Force on Character Education.

Robert N. Singer

Robert Singer is a professor emeritus in the Department of Applied Physiology and Kinesiology at the University of Florida.

Daniel Smith

Daniel Smith, PhD, is the Instructional Dean of Health, Physical Education and Athletics at Cerritos College in Norwalk, California. From 1997 to 2002, he was a senior lecturer and master's program coordinator at the National Institute of Education at Nanyang Technological University in Singapore. In addition to instructional responsibilities, he mentored master's and PhD students and consulted with Singapore Sports Council teams. His consulting also includes several professional and university sports teams in the United States. He has numerous academic publications and presentations in various parts of the world.

Ronald E. Smith

Ronald E. Smith is a professor of psychology and the director of Clinical Psychology Training at the University of Washington. He has published widely in the areas of anxiety, stress, and coping. His sport psychology work focuses on coaching behavior research and intervention and on performance enhancement. He is a past president of the Association for the Advancement of Applied Sport Psychology.

Frank L. Smoll

Frank L. Smoll is a professor of psychology at the University of Washington. His research focuses on coaching behaviors in youth sports and on the effects of competition on children and adolescents. He is a fellow of APA, AAKPE, and AAASP, and was the recipient of AAASP's 2002 Distinguished Professional Practice Award.

Gloria B. Solomon

Gloria B. Solomon, PhD, is a faculty member in the Department of Kinesiology and Health Science at California State University, Sacramento, where she serves as director of the Sport Performance Lab, conducting research on coach development and teaching graduate and undergraduate courses in sport and exercise psychology. She also serves the Department of Athletics, providing mental training for coaches and athletes in several sports including basketball, football, softball, tennis, track and field, and volleyball.

Gershon Tenenbaum

Gershon Tenenbaum is a professor and coordinator of sport and exercise psychology at Florida State University. He was the presidents of the International Society of Sport Psychology (ISSP) from 1997 to 2001, and since 1996 has served as the co-editor of the *International Journal of Sport and Exercise Psychology*. He received his PhD in measurement and statistics from the University of Chicago, and was the director of the Center for Research and Sport Medicine at the Wingate Institute, Israel, from 1982 to 1994. He has published extensively in refereed

journals and books on topics such as cognition and decision-making, expertise, psychometrics and measurement, linking emotions-cognition-performance, and effort perceptions.

Patsy Tremayne

Patsy Tremayne is an associate professor of psychology at the University of Western Sydney. She has been head of the only master's program in sport psychology in the State of New South Wales since 1998. She has had a broad experience with sport psychology since the early 1980s, working not only with Olympic athletes, but also with children in sport and professional people to enhance their performance in a variety of fields. She is an executive member of the Australian College of Sport Psychologists and has a continuing interest and involvement in the development of quality training programs for sport psychologists.

Dean A. Tripp

Dean A. Tripp, PhD, is an assistant professor of psychology, anesthesiology & urology at Queen's University, Kingston, Ontario, Canada. He teaches in undergraduate and graduate programs in both psychology and medical programs and conducts research focused on pain perception and clinical outcome in athletes and other medical populations.

Robert Weinberg

Robert Weinberg is a professor in the Physical Education, Health and Sport Studies Department at Miami (Ohio) University. He was editor of the Journal of Applied Sport Psychology and past president of AAASP and NASPSPA. He is co-author of the popular textbook, *Foundations of Sport and Exercise Psychology*, as well as more than 130 refereed scholarly publications. He is a certified consultant for AAASP.